EMPIRICAL FOUNDATIONS
OF MARKETING

EMPIRICAL FOUNDATIONS OF MARKETING:

Research Findings
in the Behavioral and Management Sciences

Edited by

Marcus Alexis
University of Rochester

Robert J. Holloway
University of Minnesota

Robert S. Hancock
Southern Illinois University

MARKHAM PUBLISHING COMPANY • CHICAGO

MARKHAM SERIES IN MARKETING

Preface

The idea for a volume of readings based on empirical research in the social and applied sciences, which makes a basic contribution to the understanding of marketing processes, was originally conceived in the summer of 1962, when the compilers were all in residence at the University of Minnesota. There are several reasons why we decided that such a volume should be made available to our colleagues and to students of marketing.

First, our experiences, based on use of such empirical research findings, clearly demonstrate the value of such materials in developing and applying concepts. The readings give meaning to otherwise abstract generalizations and theories.

Second, teaching with research articles is a challenging and stimulating experience for teacher and student. Experience with similar books in social psychology has been most successful in providing teachers with studies to illuminate theoretical constructs and in stimulating student interest and involvement in the discipline.

Third, marketing scholars and practitioners have, over many years, reported a large number of studies which are difficult to utilize because of crowded library conditions, multiple journal use, and the like. By assembling a selection of these articles in one volume, the student has research findings which supplement his basic and advanced work in marketing.

Finally, we believe this volume will make a positive contribution to efforts to increase the level of sophistication in marketing courses.

On the whole, the articles in this volume assume no prior instruction in any of the contributing disciplines. The spirit of this undertaking is that significant efforts in disciplines related to marketing should be made available to as large an audience as possible. That same spirit resulted in a selection of readings whose only prerequisites are intellectual curiosity and maturity.

The readings follow a traditional approach to marketing. The selections may be used at most any level, but it would be expected that they would be most appropriate for work beyond the basic course. At the graduate level, they may even supplement the basic course. Conceivably, they could be used in conjunction with a research course, since examples of experiments, surveys, motivational research and other techniques are included in the readings. The primary purpose, however, is to improve on the substance of marketing topics that are covered in other than research courses.

Rochester, New York
Minneapolis, Minnesota
Carbondale, Illinois

December, 1968

Marcus Alexis
Robert J. Holloway
Robert S. Hancock

v

Contents

Part I

The Field of Marketing

Several alternative approaches to the study of marketing have been suggested as vantage points from which to observe and understand the process which results in the exchange of goods and services. They include the commodity approach; the functional approach; and the institutional or structural approach.

In the first named approach, marketing is studied in terms of the market arrangements which are present and serve to facilitate the movement of commodities from producer to final owner. The student learns of the great variety in market elements which are present in the marketing of, for example, an agricultural commodity such as wheat and a consumer convenience good such as cigarettes and of the similarities and differences in distribution channels, financing, pricing, and other conditions surrounding their purchase and sale.

The functional approach is concerned with the functions or tasks required in moving goods from producer to final owner. Many enumerations of these tasks have been made. Listings of tasks to be performed are reducible to three general groupings: those required for exchange; those related to physical supply; and those facilitating exchange. Buying and selling are tasks required for exchange. Physical supply requires storing and transporting. The facilitating functions include financing, risk bearing, standardization and grading, and market information.

Institutions of marketing refer to those configurations of producers, distributors, transporters, and financers of marketing activity who occupy a prominent position in the elaborate system which makes possible the orderly flow of goods and services from producing to consuming units.

Another approach to the study of marketing is to concern oneself with the reasons of forces motivating individuals to exchange valuable resources. In some

From *Survey of Current Business*, Vol. 41, No. 5 (May, 1961), pp. 25-28.

cases the buyer is purchasing for personal consumption. In others, he is an intermediate owner who further fabricates or converts the product before passing it on to others further down in the channel of distribution. Or, he may accept the risks of ownership and merchandising without physically changing the product. These different motives for purchasing goods identify distinct groups of buyers. Those who buy for personal or household consumption are said to be members of the consumer market; the others are said to belong to the industrial market.

The division of markets into consuming units and industrial buying units is a useful dichotomy but it does not contribute much by itself to an understanding of the process by which the persons involved in the exchange are influenced by considerations of income, wealth, social class membership, ethnic or religious affiliation, or their needs, aspirations, perceptions, and adaptation mechanisms. To understand the role these influences play, we must turn to economics, sociology, anthropology, and psychology. For here we are raising

questions about human behavior, some of which is individual in nature and some of which is group behavior. Recent research evidence supports the long-held view that the complex of personal experiences and group identifications interacts with economic variables to determine market behavior.

In Part I we introduce the consumer and industrial goods markets. Factors underlying the demand for consumer goods (section A) and services (section B) and for industrial goods (section C) are presented first. This is followed by overviews of consumers and their market behavior and by a discussion of motives in industrial buying (section D). These latter studies are microscopic in contrast with the paper in sections A, B, and C which survey the entire consumer or industrial market for some good service.

Finally, we consider the environment in which marketing agents act out their roles (section E). Factors internal and external to those engaged in exchange are shown to contribute to the market choices made. The section is completed with a reference to the impact of spatial conditions on marketing.

A. MARKET FOR CONSUMER GOODS

1. Determinants of Consumer Demand for House Furnishings and Equipment

VERNON G. LIPPITT

PURPOSE OF INVESTIGATION

The purpose of this study was to extract from the BLS Survey of Consumer Expenditures in 1950 information which would be useful in forecasting consumer expenditures for house furnishings and equipment.

METHOD OF ANALYSIS

Working first with the published tabulations and then with punched cards supplied by the Wharton School, I employed analysis of variance calculations to detect the influence of various family characteristics on the percentage of family income devoted to house furnishings and equipment in 1950. This paper reports primarily on the findings derived from the punched cards for some 5700 city families in the North region of the country. Families with negative income (taxes in excess of gross income) were excluded from the analysis.

The dependent variable used in the analysis was the percentage of family income spent for house furnishings and equipment. This variable was chosen rather than dollar expenditures for two reasons: (1) There was evidence of interaction between income and other variables, e.g., family type, in their influence on dollar expenditures. This interaction was greatly reduced by using the expenditure percentage as the variable to be explained. This seems eminently reasonable. A family event

such as the purchase of a new home may well boost dollar expenditures on household durables more for a high income than a low income family, but the increase in percentage of income spent for household durables might well be about the same at all income levels. (2) Dollar expenditures show greatly increased variance (or standard deviation) at higher income levels. The expenditure percentage variable does not show such extreme changes in variance with income level; hence it more nearly satisfies the assumptions underlying variance analysis.

Analysis of variance calculations were used to determine simultaneously the influence of several family characteristics on the percentage of income spent for house furnishings and equipment. Survey data, after all, are quite similar to the data from agricultural experiments. Dollar expenditures or the percentage of income allocated for house furnishings and equipment are analogous to crop yield. The classes of various family characteristics are analogous to various dosages of fertilizer, temperature, moisture, sunlight, and soil types. Analysis of variance calculations permit determination of the separate net effect of each family characteristic on spending behavior. Usually we think of analysis of

From *A Study of Consumer Expenditures, Income, and Savings: Proceedings of the Conference on Consumption and Savings*, Vol. 1, edited by Irwin Friend and Robert Jones (Philadelphia: University of Pennsylvania, 1960), pp. 225-46.

3

variance as leading to tests of significance for main effects and interaction.
However it is also, like multiple correlation, a least-squares method of estimating the influence of the explanatory
variables included in the analysis. This
is the aspect of variance analysis which
is emphasized in this report because it
is most relevant to the purpose of this
study—obtaining information useful for
forecasting.

Five family characteristics were used
in the variance analysis of the punched
cards: family income (9 classes), home
tenure (5 classes), age of head (7
classes), family type (8 classes), and
family size (5 classes). The effects of
these family characteristics on percentage of income spent for house furnishings and equipment were computed by
an IBM 650 machine program which
solves simultaneously for the influence
of the 34 classes of the five family characteristics. The computation allows for
the differing cell frequencies also.
(Actually the same results could be obtained by a multiple correlation calculation utilizing, I believe, $34 - 5 = 29$ explanatory variables.)

It seems to me that analysis of variance computations should be much
more widely used in multivariate analysis of survey data. Analysis of variance is
more general than ordinary multiple
correlation in that it can handle variables expressible only as classes without quantitative measures and also in
that it does not require the assumption
of a linear or other specified form of
functional relation between independent and dependent variables. The computed effects, class by class for each
family characteristic, trace out the form
of the relationship, as will be shown in
the charted results of the computations.
The assumption of additivity of the effects of the independent variables is
maintained, as in correlation analysis,
but the magnitude of interaction effects
can be tested for significance.

In a second stage of the analysis a residual was computed for each family,
i.e., the difference between its actual
expenditure percentage and the value
predicted from knowledge of the family's classification by the five characteristics used in the analysis of variance
computations. The residuals of the family expenditure percentages were averaged for families classified by other
characteristics than those used in the
variance analysis. An attempt was made
to find out what variables other than the
initial five might be significantly related
to family buying of house furnishings
and equipment.

SUMMARY OF FINDINGS

MAIN FAMILY CHARACTERISTICS

As indicated above, families were
described by five characteristics believed to be related to their spending
on house furnishings and equipment.
There were five to nine classes in each
characteristic, and the analysis of variance computations led to values for the
effect of each class of each characteristic
on the expenditure percentage. If we
call the average expenditure percentage
of all families $\bar{R}$, then the effect of a
given family characteristic is the deviation from $\bar{R}$ associated with possession
of that family characteristic. *Gross effects* are calculated before allowing for
the effects of other characteristics and
are obtainable from row or column averages in tabulated data. *Net effects* are
the deviations attributable to a given
family characteristic after allowing for
the influence of other characteristics,
and these net effects are the important
output of the analysis of variance
calculations.

Table A and Charts 1 through 5 at
the end of this report summarize the
gross and net effects on expenditure
percentage for house furnishings and
equipment of the following family characteristics: family income, home tenure,
age of head, family type, and family size.
As was mentioned above, the effects of
the various characteristics are assumed

additive. Thus the predicted expenditure percentage for a given family equals R̄ plus the sum of the effects estimated for families in its classification on each of the five main characteristics used. Thus for a husband-wife family with one child under six, head aged 25-34, rented dwelling, and income of $6000 to $7500, the calculated expenditure percentage, based on data in Table A, would be:

R̄	=	6.5%
Income effect	=	− 0.6
Home tenure effect	=	− 0.5
Age of head effect	=	+ 1.0
Family type effect	=	+ 0.4
Family size effect	=	+ 1.0
Calculated percentage	=	7.8%

The results obtained would seem to justify the following conclusions regarding the influence of the five main characteristics on purchases of house furnishings and equipment by city families in the North *during 1950*. The unusual nature of the year 1950, when the Korean War started and "scare-buying" occurred, must be kept in mind in interpreting and using the findings.

1. *Income effect*. The expenditure percentage tended to be above average at incomes (after tax) below $1000, held nearly constant for incomes between $1000 and $6000, and then declined steadily at higher incomes. See Chart 1. (The difference between estimates of gross and net effects shows the value of eliminating the effects of other family characteristics to obtain a truer picture of the variation dependent on income. Note also that the assumption of linearity in a multiple correlation analysis with income as an explanatory variable would have failed to show the detailed pattern of relationship between expenditure percentage and income.)

2. *Home tenure effect*. Families who bought homes during the survey year tended to spend 2 to 2½ times the average percentage of income on house furnishings and equipment.

3. *Age of head effect*. The expenditure percentage declined steadily with age of head, from about 50 percent above average for the "Under 25" group to 50 percent below average for the "75 and over" group.

4. *Family type effect*. Husband-wife families with no children tended to be the highest spenders on house furnishings and equipment. The expenditure percentage declined with increasing age of children. (Note that the gross effects would have given a misleading impression of the variation of expenditure percentage with family type.)

5. *Family size effect*. Unattached individuals were apt to spend well below the average on house furnishings and equipment; families of two persons were near average spenders; and larger size families tended to fall somewhat above the average.

ADDITIONAL FAMILY CHARACTERISTICS

As was noted above, an attempt was made to determine whether other family characteristics might have significant influence on the percent of family income allocated to house furnishings and equipment. The residuals of the expenditure percentage, after allowing for the effects of the five main characteristics, were averaged for families classified by 12 other family characteristics. It should be realized that this procedure is apt to understate the influence of these additional characteristics. One or more of the main variables may be correlated with one of the additional characteristics. If so, it would have incorporated some of the influence of the additional variable into the original predictor, thus excluding it from the residual. If an additional characteristic seems promising, its true effect should be obtained by including it in an extended analysis of variance calculation, but this was not done in the present study.

The findings obtained by averaging residuals are presented in Table B and may be summarized briefly as follows.

1. *Automobile purchase.* There was a fairly clear inverse relation between expenditures for automobile purchase and the residual expenditure percentage for house furnishings and equipment. That is, families which bought an automobile in 1950 tended to show expenditure percentages for house furnishings and equipment which were below the level expended on the basis of each family's five main characteristics.

2. *Installment debt.* There seemed to be no clear relation between the residual expenditure percentage for 1950 and the family's installment debt outstanding at the beginning of the year, though several debt classes show average expenditures between 1 percent and 2 percent. It might have been preferable to express installment debt as a percentage of income in setting up classes. Also the scare buying of consumer durables in 1950 may have upset normal relationships between installment debt and spending on house furnishings and equipment.

3. *Education of head.* The residual expenditure percentage was not related to the educational level of the head of the family.

4. *Type of city.* The percentage of income spent for house furnishings and equipment tended to be slightly below average in large cities, slightly above average in suburbs, and a little further above average in small cities. The effects are reliable but less than ½ percent, probably negligible for most purposes.

5. *Number of earners.* Families with no earners, presumably retired persons or families with head unemployed, tended to display a negative residual of about 1 percent. Spending was a little above expected where there was more than one earner in the family, but the effect was less than ½ percent.

6. *Level of housing expenditures.* The residual expenditure percentage seemed to be positively associated with the level of housing expenditure, both for home owners and for renters. The effect was clearest for families with high levels of home valuation and high rent. Here again the level of housing expenditure might better have been measured as a percentage of income, but the effect seems to be unmistakable even with classes in dollar terms.

7. *Income change.* Families with about the same income in 1950 as in 1949 tended to spend somewhat below the expected percentage of income for house furnishings and equipment. Families with income changes, either up or down, tended to spend above the calculated level. The effects were ½ percent or less.

8. *Expected income change.* Again in the case of expected 1951 income relative to 1950 income, families expecting unchanged income spent a little less than normal, and those expecting an income change, either up or down, spent a little above normal in 1950. The effects were ½ percent or less.

9. *Level of saving.* An inverse relation between saving and the residual expenditure percentage was clear-cut and significant, when saving was expressed as a percentage of income. For families who dissaved 25 percent or more of income, spending for house furnishings and equipment tended to be nearly 4 percentage points above normal. Families with savings between −5 percent and +5 percent of income and families with positive saving tended to spend from 1 percent to 1½ percent below the level expected on the basis of the five main family characteristics. Apparently in 1950 there was a tendency for families to use savings to buy house furnishings and equipment.

10. *Change in net worth.* The dependence of the residual on changes in net worth (without regard to income) exhibited a curious nonlinear relation. For decreases in net worth of $1000 or more, spending for house furnishings and equipment was below the calculated percentage. For changes in net worth between − $1000 and zero, the residual was positive and increasing. The high value for families with zero to

$100 decrease in net worth may be spurious because of the small number of families in that class, but the classes with decreases of net worth from $100 to $1000 contained large numbers of families and exhibited significantly large positive residuals (1.4 to 3.6 percent). Families with increases in net worth showed negative residuals ranging between 1.3 percent and 1.8 percent of income and substantially independent of the magnitude of the rise in net worth. Perhaps the data indicate that large declines in net worth inhibited buying of household durables but that small declines were correlated with such purchases because financial assets were run down to buy the furnishings and equipment. The latter items are not counted among assets. Similarly, increases in financial assets may be characteristic of families which spent little on household durables during 1950.

11. *Occupation of head.* Occupation seems to account for very little of the residual expenditure percentage. Perhaps families of private household workers and laborers spend less than expected, and conversely for a miscellaneous group of families with head self-employed, not gainfully employed, or occupation unreported.

12. *Other money receipts.* The receipt of inheritances, gifts, insurance payments, etc., does seem to increase spending on house furnishings and equipment above the calculated percentage of income. The effect seems to be greatest (+ 2 to + 3 percent) when the "Other money receipts" fall in the range between $200 and $1000.

USEFULNESS OF BUDGET-STUDY DATA FOR FORECASTING

Given the results uncovered in the analysis of cross-section data (as described above), the question arises: What good are they for forecasting consumer expenditures for house furnishings and equipment? Should we blow them up to national totals, or should we just blow them up?

Considerations relative to this question may be summarized by four matched hopes and doubts.

HOPES

1. If we know how families with given characteristics allocate their incomes, perhaps we can predict the future distributions of families by these characteristics and then aggregate the spending of all groups to predict total national spending or saving.

2. Though observable family characteristics explain little of the variance in family expenditures in cross-section study, they may account for a higher proportion of the changes in aggregate spending through time, if the factors which account for the unexplained variance do not change much or largely cancel out from one time period to another. Also the cross-section analysis may help to suggest variables which it is important to include in the time series analysis.

3. Repeated budget surveys may permit us to detect trends in relations and to pick up dynamic influences, especially if reinterviews are involved. Also, it may be impossible to evaluate correctly the influence of dynamic factors in time series analysis unless the influence of the cross-section variables is allowed for simultaneously.

4. Perhaps repeated surveys of attitudes and expectations could supplement the usual budget surveys for short-term forecasting, and effects of dynamic variables could be worked in too. For long-term forecasting it may be admitted that cross-section variables do not tell the whole story, but they are a vital part of it. If their effects are not allowed for, the influence of the dynamic variables could not be correctly estimated.

DOUBTS

1. Even if we can predict future distributions (perhaps joint distributions)

of families by various characteristics, it is questionable whether the relation between given characteristics and spending remains constant. Recall that the budget study information on the relation between saving and income level was an insufficient guide for forecasting changes over time in aggregate saving ratios. Note also that blow-ups of budget-study expenditure data often miss time series aggregates for the same year by wide margins.

2. Correlations or analyses of variance relating spending to family characteristics explain only a small share of the total variance in spending among families. In the present analysis the five family characteristics involved in the analysis of variance computations explained only 6.2 percent of the variance of family expenditure percentages. When the predicted percentages were converted into predicted dollar expenditures, however, it was found that 26 percent of the variance of family dollar expenditures was explained.

3. We are interested in forecasting a time series, but cross-section data represent a snapshot and can give us little or no information about the effects of dynamic variables such as changes in relative prices, income changes, changes in tastes, new products and advertising, consumer attitudes and expectations.

4. The distributions of family characteristics usually recorded in surveys change slowly in the short-run; in the long-run changes in tastes and in standards of living may overwhelm the influence of cross-section variables.

In summary, it seems clear that cross-section data have important limitations for forecasting purposes. So do time series data. Best results can probably be achieved by combining information from the two sources. Important contributions from the budget-study data might well include the following.

1. The cross-section analysis may point to important explanatory variables which should be included in time series analysis, e.g., the number of families

buying homes or the number of recent marriages or spending for automobiles. It may also suggest the approximate magnitude of their influence.

2. The cross-section data may permit direct estimation of the influence on aggregate expenditures of changing distributions of families on various family characteristics. Such influence may be an important element in forecasts and may need to be allowed for in historical data to permit correct evaluation of the influence of time series variables. This direct use of cross-section data for forecasting requires the assumption of stability over time in the effects of the family characteristics, and it involves the forecasting of future distributions of families by the relevant characteristics.

3. The wealth of detail in cross-section data permits a much more complete analysis of the simultaneous influence of many variables, their net effects and their interactions.

4. Repeated surveys, including reinterviews, may permit determination of the effects of both cross-section and time-series variables in joint relationships which it would be impossible to detect from either type of data alone, e.g., how price or income changes affect the buying of different types of families. Trends in demand relations, i.e., change in tastes, might also be detected and measured in data from repeated interviews.

NEEDED IMPROVEMENTS IN COLLECTION AND ANALYSIS OF SURVEY DATA

Optimum methods for combining the data from consumer surveys with that from time series remain to be worked out. Consideration of this subject would carry us off the main track at this time. Let me conclude by suggesting some improvements in the collection and analysis of survey data which seem needed from the point of view of a forecaster of consumer expenditures for house furnishings and equipment.

1. Marriage is the birth of a new family. Interval since marriage appears to be related to expenditure patterns. So information on date of marriage should be gathered in consumer surveys.

2. Move to a new residence may influence spending patterns, as well as home purchase. It would be desirable to have information on dates of occupancy for surveyed families, in order to test the effect of a move on spending patterns.

3. It would be very desirable to have information on stock of durables owned by families. Among other gains, this would permit separate analysis of families who are new buyers of specific items of equipment and those who are buying for replacement.

4. Additional information would be useful regarding purchases and receipts of items as gifts, and also on acquisition of house furnishings and equipment by inheritance or by inclusion in the dwelling unit, rented or purchased.

5. Much more effort needs to be devoted to competent analysis of the survey data that has been collected.

Multivariate analyses are needed rather than one-way tabulations, and the analysis of variance computations described in this paper could contribute to the effort. In addition, coded data cards embodying survey findings in anonymous forms need to be made readily available to competent research workers.

6. More survey data are needed covering family expenditures by major categories, especially repeated or reinterview surveys. Then it would become possible to test the stability of spending patterns in relation to family characteristics, and to choose between dollar expenditures or expenditure percentage and between absolute or relative income as the better variables for yielding stable relationships.

7. More investigations of consumer behavior should be pushed through to the point where forecasts of aggregate spending can be made. This will necessitate combining cross-section and time-series data. To me it seems that ability to forecast is the ultimate test of the usefulness of our knowledge.

TABLE A

EFFECTS OF FAMILY CHARACTERISTICS ON PERCENT OF FAMILY INCOME SPENT
FOR HOUSE FURNISHINGS AND EQUIPMENT, CITY FAMILIES IN THE NORTH, 1950

$\bar{R} = 6.48\%$; the average percentage of family income spent for house furnishings and equipment.

Effects of various family characteristics are expressed as deviations from $\bar{R}$ which are associated with possession of a given family characteristic. The effects of various characteristics are additive, interaction being ignored in the analysis of variance computations.

Gross effects are the deviations from $\bar{R}$ of the average expenditure percentage for all families possessing one given characteristic.

Net effects are the deviations from $\bar{R}$ attributable to the given characteristic after the effect of the other four family characteristics included in the variance analysis have been allowed for.

INCOME EFFECT (CHART 1)			
Family Income	Number of Families	Gross Effect	Net Effect
Under $1,000	279	+ 1.3%	+ 5.0%
$1,000 to 2,000	615	− 1.4	+ 0.4
$2,000 to 3,000	1,035	− 0.2	− 0.0
$3,000 to 4,000	1,416	− 0.1	− 0.7
$4,000 to 5,000	1,023	+ 1.0	+ 0.2
$5,000 to 6,000	550	+ 0.6	+ 0.0

INCOME EFFECT (CHART 1)

Family Income	Number of Families	Gross Effect	Net Effect
$6,000 to 7,500	390	− 0.1%	− 0.6%
$7,500 to 10,000	222	− 1.1	− 1.4
$10,000 and over	156	− 1.5	− 1.8

HOME TENURE EFFECT (CHART 2)

Home Tenure	Number of Families	Gross Effect	Net Effect
Owner all year, bought 1950-51	55	+ 11.3%	+ 11.2%
Owner all year, bought 1946-49	805	− 0.0	− 0.4
Owner all year, bought before 1946 or year not reported	1,594	− 0.3	+ 0.2
Owner end-year, renter earlier	150	+ 7.9	+ 6.9
Renters and others	3,082	− 0.4	− 0.5

AGE OF HEAD EFFECT (CHART 3)

Age of Head	Number of Families	Gross Effect	Net Effect
Under 25	164	+ 3.4%	+ 3.5%
25-34	1,225	+ 1.3	+ 1.0
35-44	1,330	+ 0.2	+ 0.2
45-54	1,190	− 0.7	− 0.4
55-64	978	− 0.6	− 0.4
65-74	577	− 0.7	− 0.9
75 and over	222	− 2.5	− 3.3

FAMILY TYPE EFFECT (CHART 4)

Type of Family	Number of Families	Gross Effect	Net Effect
Husband and wife only	1,276	+ 1.1%	+ 1.9%
H & W, oldest child under 6	775	+ 2.0	+ 0.4
H & W, oldest child 6-15	975	+ 0.6	− 0.4
H & W, oldest child 16-17	175	+ 0.4	− 0.3
H & W, oldest child 18 or over	655	− 0.8	− 0.9
One parent, oldest child under 18	104	+ 0.0	− 0.7
Other adults only, no children	1,264	− 2.3	− 0.9
All other	462	− 0.4	− 1.1

FAMILY SIZE EFFECT (CHART 5)

Family Size	Number of Families	Gross Effect	Net Effect
0-1.0	718	− 3.1%	− 2.8%
1.1-2.0	1,599	+ 0.5	− 0.6
2.1-3.0	1,380	+ 0.7	+ 1.0
3.1-4.0	1,105	+ 0.4	+ 0.7
4.1 and over	884	+ 0.1	+ 0.9

TABLE B
EFFECTS OF ADDITIONAL FAMILY CHARACTERISTICS AS MEASURED BY AVERAGE RESIDUALS FOR EXPENDITURE PERCENTAGES

Residual for each family is the difference between the percent of its income spent for house furnishings and equipment and the percent calculated by adding to $\bar{R}$ the predicted effects (or deviations) attributable to the five family characteristics used in the analysis of variance.

For example, for a husband-wife family with one child under 6, head aged 25-34, rented dwelling, and income of $6,000 to $7,500, the calculated expenditure percentage, based on data in Table A, would be:

$$\bar{R} \qquad\qquad\qquad\qquad = \quad 6.5\%$$
$$\text{Income effect} \qquad\quad = \quad -0.6$$
$$\text{Home tenure effect} \quad = \quad -0.5$$
$$\text{Age of head effect} \quad\; = \quad +1.0$$
$$\text{Family type effect} \quad\;\; = \quad +0.4$$
$$\text{Family size effect} \quad\;\; = \quad +1.0$$
$$\text{Calculated percentage} = \quad 7.8\%$$

	Number of Families	Average Residual
(1) Net Expenditures for Automobile Purchase		
None	4,393	+ 1.3%
$0-999	648	− 0.4
$1000-1499	246	− 0.4
$1500-1999	212	− 0.9
$2000-2499	133	+ 0.5
$2500-2999	34	− 1.6
$3000-3499	11	− 1.2
$3500-3999	0	−
$4000 and over	5	− 0.4
(2) Installment Debt on January 1, 1950		
None	4,968	− 0.0%
$1-99	226	+ 0.7
$100-199	188	− 0.4
$200-299	126	+ 1.2

	Number of Families	Average Residual
$300-399	77	− 0.4%
$400-499	33	− 2.1
$500-999	51	+ 0.2
$1,000 and over	7	+ 1.8
Not known	6	− 1.5

(3) *Education of Head of Family*

0-8 years	2,328	+ 0.0%
9-12 years	2,429	− 0.0
13-16 years	787	+ 0.1
17 years and over	138	− 0.4

(4) *Type of City*

Large cities	3,817	− 0.1%
Suburbs of large cities	1,241	+ 0.2
Small cities	624	+ 0.4

(5) *Total Number of Earners in Family*

None	423	− 1.0%
1	3,128	+ 0.0
2	1,606	+ 0.2
3	379	+ 0.1
4 or more	146	+ 0.3

(6) *Level of Housing Expenditures*

    A. *Homeowners — market value of home*

$1-4999	280	+ 1.0%
$5000-7499	503	− 0.7
$7500-9999	475	− 0.4
$10,000-12,499	514	+ 0.0
$12,500-14,999	212	+ 0.3
$15,000-17,499	208	− 0.4
$17,500-19,999	74	+ 0.5
$20,000-24,999	98	+ 1.0
$25,000 and over	90	+ 1.6

    B. *Renters — level of rent*

$0-249	430	− 0.6%
$250-499	1,067	− 0.3
$500-749	1,189	− 0.2

	Number of Families	Average Residual
$750-999	377	+0.7%
$1,000-1,249	92	+0.7
$1,250-1,499	43	+2.5
$1,500-1,999	19	+17.9
$2,000-2,999	9	−2.1
$3,000 and over	2	+6.9

(7) *1950 Income Relative to 1949 Income*

Higher	2,243	+0.2%
About the same	2,316	−0.4
Lower	983	+0.5
Don't know	140	+0.3

(8) *1950 Income Relative to Expected 1951 Income*

Higher	676	+0.5%
About the same	2,557	−0.3
Lower	1,933	+0.3
Don't know	516	−0.1

(9) *Saving as Percentage of Income*

Deficit of 25% or more	866	+3.9%
Deficit of 5% to 25%	1,271	+1.3
Deficit or surplus of less than 5%	1,849	−1.3%
Surplus of 5% to 25%	1,384	−1.5
Surplus of 25% or more	312	−1.6

(10) *Increase in Net Worth*

Decrease: $5000 and over	414	−1.3%
$1000-4999	320	−0.6
$500-999	780	+1.4
Decrease: $200-499	548	+1.7
$100-199	694	+3.6
$0-99	32	+24.9
Increase: $0-99	147	−1.7
$100-199	342	−1.3
$200-499	298	−1.3

	Number of Families	Average Residual
Increase: $500-999	705	− 1.4%
$1000-4999	502	− 1.8
$5000 and over	395	− 1.5
No indication	505	− 2.4

(11) *Occupation of Head*

Salaried professional, technical	414	− 0.3%
Salaried officials, managers	340	− 0.2
Clerical workers	456	+ 0.4
Sales workers	280	− 0.2
Craftsmen	1,042	− 0.2
Operatives	1,095	+ 0.3
Private household workers	78	− 0.8
Service workers, other	407	+ 0.1
Laborers	299	− 0.8
Self-employed, not gainfully employed, and occupation not reported	1,271	+ 1.8

(12) *Other Money Receipts*

$0-99	5,540	− 0.0%
$100-199	18	+ 0.2
$200-299	18	+ 2.0
$300-499	19	+ 2.7
$500-999	26	+ 1.0
$1000-1999	25	− 0.0
$2000-2999	10	− 0.7
$3000-4999	12	+ 0.6
$5000-9999	9	+ 0.5
$10,000 and over	5	+23.9

CHART 1

INCOME EFFECT ON PERCENT OF FAMILY INCOME
SPENT FOR HOUSE FURNISHINGS AND EQUIPMENT,
CITY FAMILIES IN THE NORTH, 1950

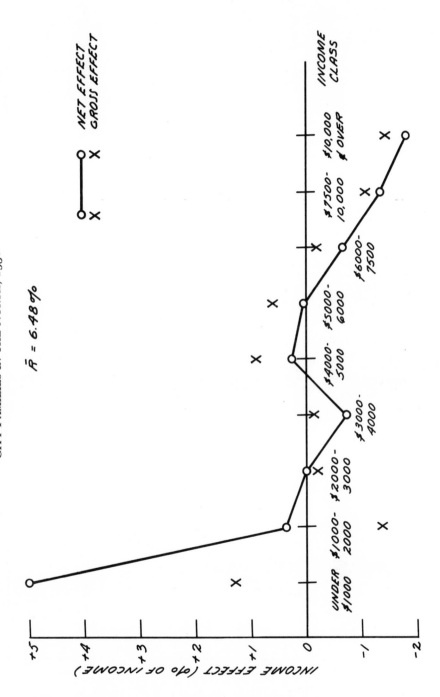

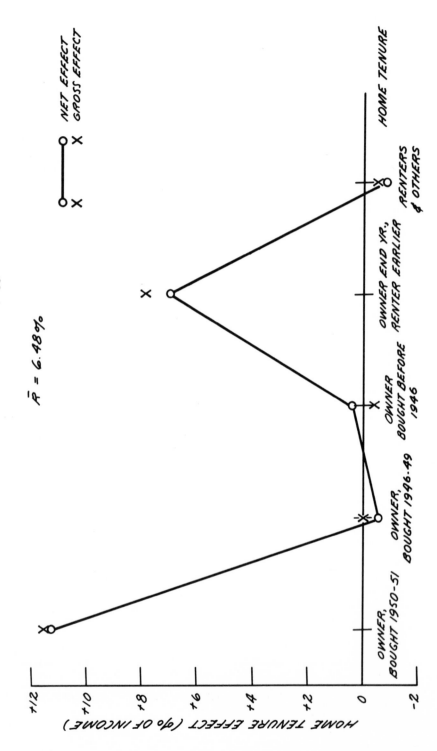

CHART 2

HOME TENURE EFFECT ON PERCENT OF FAMILY INCOME
SPENT FOR HOUSE FURNISHINGS AND EQUIPMENT,
CITY FAMILIES IN THE NORTH, 1950

CHART 3

AGE OF HEAD EFFECT ON PERCENT OF FAMILY INCOME
SPENT FOR HOUSE FURNISHINGS AND EQUIPMENT,
CITY FAMILIES IN THE NORTH, 1950

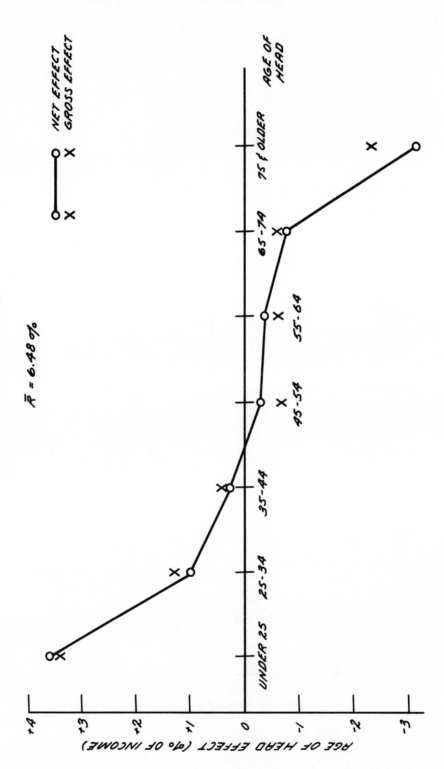

VERNON G. LIPPITT

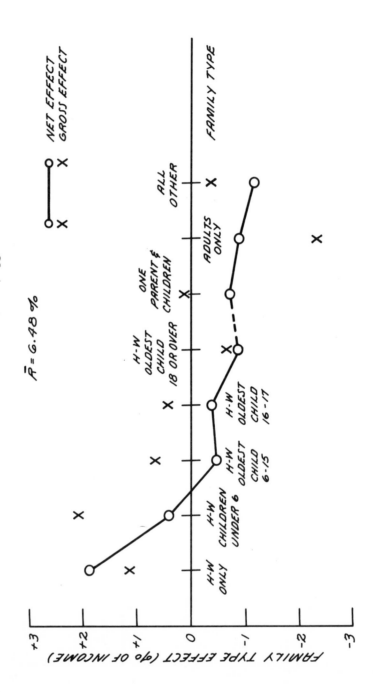

CHART 4

FAMILY TYPE EFFECT ON PERCENT OF FAMILY INCOME
SPENT FOR HOUSE FURNISHINGS AND EQUIPMENT,
CITY FAMILIES IN THE NORTH, 1950

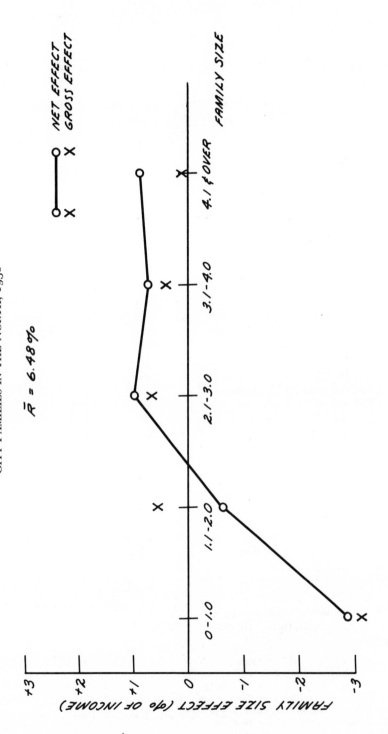

CHART 5

FAMILY SIZE EFFECT ON PERCENT OF FAMILY INCOME
SPENT FOR HOUSE FURNISHINGS AND EQUIPMENT,
CITY FAMILIES IN THE NORTH, 1950

2. Some Determinants of Food Buying Behavior*

MARCUS ALEXIS, LEONARD S. SIMON,
AND KENNETH M. SMITH

OBJECTIVES

Food and housing expenditures comprise approximately 50 per cent of all consumption expenditures. Any index of consumer well-being must necessarily focus on these items. Variations in quality of housing, however, are extremely difficult to measure. On the other hand, information about food purchases lends itself to quantification more readily because (1) food is purchased more frequently than any other consumption item; and (2) comparability among food items is facilitated by the widespread use of standards, grades and branding. For these reasons, we have chosen food expenditures as a vehicle by which to measure the influence of socioeconomic class and demography upon consumption patterns.

The purpose of this research effort is to examine empirically the means by which the desired food mixes for each socioeconomic group are obtained. The variables of primary interest are: income; weekly family expenditures for food; occupation, age and education of household head; family size; sex and race of respondent; quantity of food purchased; automobile ownership and distance of retail units from consumer residences.

* This research was supported by research funds of the College of Business Administration, University of Rochester. We gratefully acknowledge this support. The views expressed are those of the authors. An earlier version of this paper was presented at the Eastern Meeting of the Institute of Management Sciences, Rochester, New York, October 15, 1965.

Two areas of particular interest to the authors are expressed in the following hypotheses:

Hypothesis: 1. Consumers in the lower income classes ($5,000 or less) are more likely to patronize small neighborhood stores than consumers in the middle and upper income groups.

Hypothesis: 2. There exists a negative correlation between the physical mobility of the consumer and the number of services offered by the retail units at which they shop, irrespective of economic class.

The analysis is broken into three categories: stores shopped; socioeconomic variables; and food commodities purchased. Relationships resulting from correlation analysis are reported only if the coefficient of correlation was greater than .4 and significant at the 5% level. Although there are statistically significant coefficients of lesser value, they are not reported because they do not appear to have any practical significance. Results of correlation analyses in each of the income and demographic subgroups in the income and stores shopped variables are reported only if they differ significantly from other subgroups within the same variable.

SAMPLE SELECTION

Respondents were selected from the Rochester, New York, Metropolitan area. The 130 census tracts comprising this area were classified into high-, middle-, and low-income groups based upon median income. Low tracts were defined as those with median family incomes of $4,999 or less, middle as $5,000 to $9,499, and high as $9,500 and over. This resulted in 18 low-income tracts, all contained within the City of Rochester; 102 middle-income tracts; and 10 high-income tracts all contained within the suburban areas. The low-income group represented 7.3 per cent of the population, middle 83.3 per cent, and high 9.3 per cent. As the principal objective of the study was to compare income groups, the census tracts were stratified to obtain a random sample of ten tracts from each stratum. Ten interviews were taken in each tract, two interviews from each of 150 predesignated locations.

Respondents were also asked to report their family income in the course of the questioning. Table 1 compares published census tract median income data with the income reported on the questionnaires for those tracts. It should be noted that census tract designations as high, middle, or low income are based on the median income in the tract and that all tracts contain some high-, low-, and middle-income families. Therefore, it was not expected that low-income tracts, for example, would yield only low-income families. One test of the sampling procedure is the extent to which a tract designated as low, middle,

or high produced actual respondents with corresponding incomes. An inspection of Table 1 reveals that 204 of the 300 respondents, or better than 2 out of 3, had incomes corresponding to the designation of their tract. Of the remaining respondents, 90 or exactly 30% were one income group higher or lower and only 6 or 3% were two income designations away from their tract designation. Considering the fact that the census data are four years old and the heterogenity of the tracts, the sampling results seem quite reasonable.[1]

RELATIONSHIPS AMONG VARIABLES

Analysis of the relationships between income, occupation, age, and education for the respondents showed that the sample group conformed to known interrelations among the variables. For example, it was then found that, as income increased, both the level of occupational skill and education increased. Similarly, the low-income groups contained proportionally more older people than either the middle or high groups. One other interesting, but not unexpected, observation was that over 50 per cent of the low-income group were unem-

---

[1] All analysis that follows is in terms of reported income.

TABLE 1

CENSUS TRACT INCOME DATA VS. REPORTED INCOME DATA

Census Tract Income (Medians)	Low ($0-$4,999)	Questionnaire Income—Middle ($5,000-$9,999)	High ($10,000 and over)	Totals
Low $0-$4,999	74	21	5	100
Middle $5,000-$9,499	21	71	8	100
High $9,500 and above	1	40	59	100
	96	132	72	300

ployed, on relief, retired, or widowed.

Families with annual income of $3,000 or less were separated out and scrutinized to determine what, if any, differences exist between this potential "poverty group" and the other low-income groups as defined herein. Significant differences are reported as each subject area is discussed rather than devoting a whole section of the $3,000 and below group.

STORES SHOPPED

MAJOR STORES

Respondents reported the name and location of the store that was used most often in doing major shopping for food and groceries. Table 2 shows a breakdown of these replies by income. Analysis of the replies showed that about 70 per cent of all families made the bulk of their purchases at the outlets of one of four food chains located in Rochester. Another 6 per cent bought from large food discount centers and the remaining 24 per cent from one type of independent grocer or another. The χ^2 of this distribution is significant at the .01 level clearly indicating a difference in store patronage by income group.

There are no major differences in the shopping patterns of high- and middle-income groups. However, a substantially different pattern exists for the low-income group where 35 per cent of the shopping is not done in chain or discount stores compared to about 14 per cent for the middle- and high-income groups.

Lack of physical mobility may be a major reason for the lower frequency of food chain patronage by low-income families. Car ownership is presented in Table 3. The middle- and high-income car ownership rates are respectively about 94 per cent and 99 per cent. On the other hand, low-income family car ownership is evidenced in only 43 per cent of the cases. An examination of families in the less than $3,000 income and those in the $3,001-$5,000 income groups reveals that auto ownership in the latter is more than three times the rate of the former, but shopping patterns are nearly identical.[2] This suggests that factors other than mobility are also operating.[3]

---

[2] The rates are respectively: 72.5% in the $3,001-$5,000 income group and 22% in the less-than-$3,000 income group.

[3] Unfortunately, we did not uncover these other factors though a method to detect them was built into the design of the research. The income elas-

TABLE 2

MAJOR STORE SHOPPING PATTERNS BY INCOME LEVEL

Income Level	Independents (%)	Discount Stores (%)	Chains (%)	No Major Store (%)
Low ($0-$4,999)	33 (34.4)	2 (2.1)	57 (59.3)	4 (4.2)
Middle ($5,000-$10,000)	18 (13.6)	9 (6.8)	102 (77.3)	3 (2.3)
High ($10,000 and above)	10 (13.9)	6 (8.4)	56 (77.7)	0
Totals	61 (20.3)	17 (5.7)	215 (71.7)	7 (2.3)

$$\chi^2 = 23.2$$

$$\chi^2_{.01} = 16.8$$

TABLE 3

CAR OWNERSHIP BY INCOME LEVELS

	Low Income ($0-$4,999)	Middle Income ($5,000-$9,999)	High Income ($10,000 and above)	Total
Owner	46	124	71	241
Nonowner	50	8	1	59

When distances to major stores are considered (by income level), further support is given to the mobility hypothesis. A breakdown of distances traveled is contained in Table 4. The low-income family median distance traveled is less than the other income groups. The medians are respectively ½ to ¾ mile for the low-income group, ¾ to 1 mile for middle-income families, and more than 1 mile for the highest income group. For the under $3,000 income class, the median distance to major stores is 3-5 blocks—this is also the modal class.

Correlation analysis yielded a relationship showing that the greater the distance to the major store shopped, the greater also the distance to the fill-in store. The total pattern indicates that wealthier people are less constrained by distance and may be able to select from a wider array of major stores.

Additional findings relating to mobility and major store shopped were: the more school years completed, the greater the likelihood of car ownership; the higher the income; and finally, the lower the level of occupational skill, the less the likelihood of car ownership. Combining these factors with those above, it becomes apparent that many poor persons are quite immobile and, therefore, constrained in their choices of store to an area within walking distance or possibly within a very short public bus ride.

The next categorization considered was the number of major stores shopped by the respondents. Eighty-nine per cent of the shoppers interviewed reported making the major amount of their food purchases at only one store. The results of this investigation clearly indicate that most shoppers have a major store they consider to be "their major store," indicating an extremely high level of store loyalty for the purchase of foodstuffs.

Only 9 per cent of the respondents shopped at *two major stores*, but some of the findings for this group were quite interesting: the greater the distance to the major stores, the greater the likelihood that the shopper is white; the higher the level of occupational skill, the less the likelihood of the spouse accompanying the shopper; a larger number of adult equivalents[4] are associated more with Negro than with white shoppers; the greater the age, the more likely the shopper is white—that is, Negroes shopping in two major stores tend to be younger. The two major store shopper is the principal case in which consumption differences between Negro and white appeared so decisively with Negro consumers reporting a much high proportion of multistore usage. But the size of the Negro cell is quite small,

ticity of services (as defined in the last paragraph before the section headed Fill-In Stores) was not significantly different from zero. To what extent this is due to the configuration of food stores in Rochester, New York, is unknown. Useful research might well be directed toward testing the generality of the results in this paper.

[4] A standardization of family size based on caloric intake of children and adults to permit comparison of families of different sizes and age structures. For a more detailed explanation, see first paragraph under Commodities Purchased.

TABLE 4
DISTANCES TRAVELED TO MAJOR STORES BY INCOME LEVELS

	Low Income ($0-$4,999)	Middle Income ($5,000-$9,999)	High Income ($10,000 and above)	Totals
1 block or less	13	6	1	20
1-2 blocks	11	9	1	21
3-5 blocks	21	22	7	50
½ to ¾ mile	22	15	9	46
¾ to 1 mile	3	16	14	33
More than 1 mile	24	64	39	127
Totals	94	132	71	297

and the results are not statistically significant, but potentially important.[5]

In no more than 10 per cent of the cases did major stores offer services other than check cashing and the giving of trading stamps[6] (other possibilities were payment of utility bills, delivery, credit and telephone ordering), as reported by the respondents. The importance of trading stamps and check cashing services is revealed by the fact that 66 per cent of the respondents shopped at stores offering trading stamps and 78 per cent at stores providing check cashing. Check cashing service in major stores was much more common as income increased; this

seemed to be the only income sensitive service. Finally, over 50 per cent of the people who shopped major stores with delivery service or telephone ordering also used fill-in stores providing these same services.

A weak verification of the higher credit use by low-income families hypothesis is contained in the observation that, for major stores, low-income families reported the greatest number of stores offering credit. Also, these families were heavier users of stores providing telephone and delivery service than were either middle- or high-income families. These observations, taken together, tend to indicate that low-income families are more likely to patronize service oriented stores. However, high-income families do not exhibit this tendency to any greater extent than middle-income families, leading to only partial confirmation of the high-low income service store orientation thesis which argues that high-income families, because of their financial ability, are willing and able to pay a higher premium for such services. The argument further states that low-income families

[5] Alexis has commented elsewhere on Negro-white consumption differences and has given a rationale for differential shopping behavior; cf. "Racial Differences in Consumption Patterns," *Business News Notes*, Minneapolis: School of Business Administration, University of Minnesota, No. 49, 1960, and "Some Negro-White Differences in Consumption," *American Journal of Economics & Sociology*, Vol. 2, No. 1 (January 1962), pp. 11-28.

[6] It is recognized that trading stamps are not a service, but the goal of this section was to establish "extras" which stores utilized to attract patrons.

TABLE 5
"FILL-IN" STORE USERS BY INCOME LEVEL

	Low Income ($0-$4,999)	Middle Income ($5,000-$9,999)	High Income ($10,000 and over)
User	72%	80%	81%
Nonuser	28%	20%	19%

will be inclined towards service-oriented stores because of their need for credit and, in the case of the aged poor, telephone and delivery as well.

FILL-IN STORES

Almost 80 per cent of the respondents indicated that they used a "fill-in store." "Fill-in" shopping was defined as shopping for items you either forgot to buy at your regular store or that you unexpectedly needed more of. The percentage of "fill-in" store users is given by income level in Table 5. Surprisingly, the differences among the groups are not significant at the .05 level when subjected to a χ^2 test.

A significantly lower figure was expected for the low-income group since somewhat more of the low-income families shop in neighborhood independent grocers for *all* their purchases (if a store was mentioned by a respondent as his major store, the same response was not permitted for his fill-in store). In addition, the under $3,000 income class does not have a significantly greater percentage of nonusers than the $3,000-$5,000 income class. Table 6 shows the distances traveled to fill-in stores by those indicating use. As in the case of distances to major stores, the medians progress upward one distance category at a time as income increases, but all income levels utilize fill-in stores substantially nearer to their home than the major stores patronized.

As in the case of major store, the majority of respondents, 76 per cent, had only one fill-in store; thus, it would seem that people are store loyal for both major and fill-in stores, and clearly, the bulk of the respondents are one major and one fill-in store shoppers. Two findings concerning fill-in store users uncovered by the correlation analysis were: as income increased, the distance

TABLE 6
DISTANCE TRAVELED TO "FILL-IN" STORE BY INCOME LEVELS

	Low Income ($0-$4,999)	Middle Income ($5,000-$9,999)	High Income ($10,000 and over)	Total
1 block or less	30	21	5	56
1-2 blocks	17	20	4	41
3-5 blocks	16	23	7	46
½ to ¾ mile	3	13	17	33
¾ to 1 mile	2	14	10	26
More than 1 mile	3	15	15	33
Total	69	106	58	233

traveled to the fill-in store became greater; and whites tended to travel further to fill-in stores than did Negroes. It would appear that poorer people, especially Negroes, patronize fill-in stores nearer their homes. Since a similar finding was uncovered for major stores, it would be reasonable to believe that the low-income family's shopping pattern is decidedly more constrained by the distance of store units from the home.

A sizeable group of the respondents, about 22 per cent, however, have no fill-in store. Some interesting findings were uncovered specifically within this group: shoppers who own automobiles are more likely to have freezing capacity; the higher the level of occupational skill and the greater the distance to the major store, the higher is the likelihood of auto ownership, and the greater the number of adult equivalents; also, the higher the level of occupational skill, the larger the (unadjusted) family size and the higher the amount spent weekly on food; as the number of children under fourteen increases, weekly food expenditures also increase.

In contrast to the major stores, the distribution of services (stamps, payment of bills, etc.) reported for fill-in stores was much more evenly spread among the potential services including the offering of no services, with the following exceptions: check cashing was reported for 48 per cent of the cases (which was approximately three times more frequently used than any other service) and utility payments were not reported at all. It is worth noting that, although a wider variety of services was available across the fill-in stores, not a very large number of the stores were reported to offer these services; and for both the major and fill-in stores, the highest incidence of services being offered occurred in the middle-income groups. Cell frequencies in the fill-in store data are so small that they preclude drawing inferences.

INCOME

INCOME — ALL CASES

The only two remaining correlational findings for the sample as a whole which centered on reported family income were that, as the level of occupational skill increased and the greater the number of school years completed, the greater the family income.[7] The percentage of families in which both spouses did the shopping had an inverted, U-shaped distribution when plotted against family income. Joint shopping occurred most frequently, about 55% of the cases, in families having incomes between $3,000 and $10,000; that is, in both the very low-income groups and the high-income groups, spouse-accompanied shopping occurs in only 25% of the cases. The total sample was divided into three subsets by low, middle, and high income and correlation analysis was conducted within each subset.[8] The results are reported below.

LOW INCOME

In this class, there was a stronger relationship than in the all cases classification showing that, as age increased, the level of occupational skill decreased — this relationship was even more marked for those with income of $3,000 or less. This is to be expected because the unskilled older persons are very likely to be poor. A finding, which did not exist in the all groups class, was that as age increased weekly food expenditures decreased. Other results that did not appear in the all cases category were: as age increased, the race of the respondent tended to be white; as total family size and the number of adult equivalents increased, the likelihood of

---

[7]Other correlational relationships including income are reported under the major and fill-in store analyses.
[8]Findings in subsets are reported only if they differ significantly from the all cases group.

shopping accompanied by one's spouse decreased; and, as total family size or the number of children under fourteen increased, race tended to be Negro. The low-income families might then be characterized as older whites with lesser occupational skills and young Negroes with large families. Most of the Negro families in the sample fall in this latter class, but there are not significantly more of them in the under $3,000 group as compared to the $3,000-$5,000 income group.

Among the very low-income families ($3,000 and under annual income), a rather interesting result was obtained: the greater the number of school years completed, the greater the distance to the major store. Perhaps, in low-income families, additional years of schooling lend a type of sophistication to purchasing habits that causes the purchaser to search further from his home to maximize his shopping objectives or utility.

MIDDLE INCOME AND HIGH INCOME

There were no significantly new or different findings in these categories. One hypothesis which might explain this lack of particular results, at least the middle-income group, may be that the middle-income group exhibits the normative behavior towards which the higher and lower income respondents tend.

FAMILY SIZE

Table 7 presents the mean family size and the mean number of children fourteen years old or less according to reported income. The largest families are in the two middle-income groups which are very homogeneous in character. The two high-income groups also show considerable homogeneity. These four groups might all be approximately equal in family size if their age composition was the same. The high-income shopper was, on average, ten years older than the middle-income shopper which might account for the fewer number of children under fourteen. In the low-income classifications, family size and small children increase with increasing income level. This is explained by observing that the oldest members of the low income are the poorest and that the younger families in the low-income group increase the sizes of their families as incomes rise. The highest income category within the low-income classification exhibits characteristics more

TABLE 7
MEAN FAMILY SIZE ACCORDING TO INCOME GROUP

	Mean Family Size	Mean Number of Children 14 Years Old or Less
Incomes		
Low		
Up to $2,000	1.92	0.52
$2,001 to $3,000	3.10	1.07
$3,001 to $5,000	4.07	1.29
Middle		
$5,001 to $7,000	4.83	2.15
$7,001 to $10,000	4.91	2.03
High		
$10,001 to $15,000	4.21	1.00
$15,001 and above	4.48	1.48

closely associated with the middle- and upper-income levels.

COMMODITIES PURCHASED— ANALYSIS BY INCOME LEVELS

This set of findings has primarily to do with family purchases of food commodities by income levels. Since varying sizes of families can influence the results, a means was developed for standardizing family size. Children were defined as those under fourteen years of age. This basis was selected for two reasons: first, the daily food intake of a child over fourteen probably is roughly equal to that of an adult; second, a child over fourteen may be capable of contributing to household income, and this income might be used for expenditures upon food. A conversion factor relating the food consumption of children under fourteen to that of an adult was developed. Through use of the conversion factor, the number of adult equivalents in each family was determined. All of the analysis for specific commodities is based upon mean consumption per family in each income class—where family size was defined in terms of adult equivalents. There were two findings from the correlation analysis that should be reported here: as total family size increased, the number of children under fourteen increased; and, as either total family size, or the number of adult equivalents, increased, the amount spent weekly for food increased.

This study is only concerned with actual food purchases from grocery stores and not with other food purchases made by consumers such as meals purchased away from home. The figures reported here are, therefore, an understatement of the total food bill. This difference between grocery purchases and total cost increases as income rises.

There is an important limitation in the analysis of commodities purchased. It is extremely difficult to take into account differences in the quality of similar items purchased at various income levels; for example, the mean amount of ground beef purchased is about the same in the high- and low-income classes, but it is readily conceivable that the quality, in terms of the type of beef used, may vary considerably. The authors recognize that this drawback clouds the results, but have been unable to devise an economic and feasible means of accounting for quality differences.[9]

If it is true that quality improves with income although the mean amounts purchased remain constant, then the effect would be to magnify any differences found in this study. Higher-income families do not only buy more of goods with positive income elasticities, but, in many cases, also buy better quality in that good. This is almost certainly the case with the fruit and vegetables in Column 1 of Table 8.

The sensitivity of various commodities to income effects is given in Table 8. This information is based solely upon the quantities purchased, standardized for variations in the size of the unit of purchase, and does not reflect differences in quality.

In addition to the items already mentioned, information was collected on three other commodities, but these exhibited quite different patterns: ground beef and canned fruit exhibited a U-shaped pattern, being purchased in about equal amounts by the high- and low-income groups and in substantially smaller amounts by the middle-income group; chili had an inverted U-shape, being purchased mostly by the middle-income group.

---

[9] The Consumer Price Indices of the Bureau of Labor Statistics do not take account of quality differences adequately, probably because of the not insignificant difficulties involved; cf. William H. Kruskal and Lester G. Telser, "Food Prices and the Bureau of Labor Statistics," *Journal of Business of the University of Chicago*, Vol. 33, No. 3 (July 1960), pp. 258-279.

TABLE 8

The Effect of Income Upon Family Purchases of Foodstuffs

As Income Rises, the Mean Amount Purchased Per Family° of These Commodities

Increases	Remains the Same	Decreases
Frozen Orange Juice	Onions	Bread
Frozen Vegetables	Fresh Milk	Pork Chops
Fresh Tomatoes	Margarine	Pork & Beans
Fresh Fruit	Ketchup	Canned Soup
Cartoned Orange Juice	Peanut Butter	Canned Orange Juice
Regular Coffee	Laundry Soap	Canned Milk
Butter		Spam
		Chicken
		Canned Vegetables
		Potatoes
		Instant Coffee
		Tea
		Powdered Milk
		Jelly
		Rice
		Sugar

° Standardized, as explained earlier, in terms of adult equivalents.

The appropriate way to view Table 8 would be in terms of the shifts in behavior patterns that occur as income for the family unit changes. This table also has important implications for the product assortment a grocery store should offer, dependent upon the types of clientele it serves. There are only three items which fall into classifications that seem surprising on an *a priori* basis. They are regular coffee, instant coffee, and tea. It was thought these results might be due to the correlation of age and income. The authors hypothesized that convenience was a factor in both instant coffee and tea consumption. Older people were hypothesized to be both more convenience conscious and poor. Regression analysis of coffee—regular and instant—and tea sales with age and income as independent variables failed to uncover any such effect. Whether the results in Table 8 are general can only be determined by observing a sample from a wider geographical area.

An interesting future comparison will be the costs of the various amounts purchased by the income classes when the price study (referred to earlier in this section) is completed. The authors suspect that consumers in the lowest economic groups pay higher prices for comparable food items than do consumers in the middle economic groups. This stems from two hypotheses: (1) that the price level in small neighborhood stores is higher than in large-scale food retailers; and (2) that with the exception of the highest income group ($15,000 and over), there is a negative correlation between physical mobility and prices paid.[10]

FAMILY FOOD EXPENDITURES

One of the objectives of this study was to determine total family expenditures for food and to relate those expenditures to a set of economic and demographic variables. The expenditures were

[10] Since the completion of this paper, the study of prices in stores has been concluded. It confirms the hypothesis above. Further confirmation is contained in a study by the Bureau of Labor Statistics reported in the July 12, 1966, *New York Times*, "The Poor Unable to Buy in Volume, Found to Pay Higher Prices for Food," p. 56.

treated as the dependent variable in a regression analysis in which the independent variables were:

(1) freezing capacity
(2) distance to major store
(3) distance to fill-in store
(4) spouse accompanied on shopping trips
(5) car ownership
(6) total family size
(7) number of children under 14
(8) number of adult equivalents
(9) school years completed
(10) age
(11) income
(12) race
(13) sex
(14) occupation

Variables (1), (4), (5), (12), and (13) are "dummy variables" in the sense that they are discrete and can have only one of two states. In the case of (1), (4) and (5), it is "yes" or "no." Variable (12) is either "white" or "nonwhite" and (13) "male" or "female."

Four of the variables—car ownership, number of adult equivalents, income, race—explained almost one-third of the total variance. Equation (1) below is the final regression with b weights. Equation (2) contains the same four variables and gives their β (Beta) weights where

E_F = total food expenditures

X_1 = car ownership

X_2 = number of adult equivalents

X_3 = family income

X_4 = race of respondent

$$(1) \ E_F = -4.5956X_1 + 3.1169X_2$$
$$(1.8619) \quad (0.3947)$$

$$+ 0.0311X_3 - 5.0871X_4$$
$$(0.0132) \quad (1.8704)$$

$R^2 = .3169$ Multiple $R = 0.5630$

$$(2) \ E_F = -0.1418X_1 + 0.4201X_2$$
$$(0.0575) \quad (0.0532)$$

$$+ 0.1295X_3 - 0.1472X_4$$
$$(0.0548) \quad (0.0541)$$

the quantities in parentheses are the standard errors of estimate.

Considering the inherent variability in consumer behavior, the results reported in this section indicate that the four predictor variables in equations (1) and (2) do a very good job of accounting for total family food expenditures. Of particular interest are the significance— in both a statistical and practical sense— of car ownership and race.[11]

SUMMARY

Many of the findings of this study reinforced already existing knowledge; for instance, the fact that low-income families in the $5,000 and under class are made up, in large part, of retired, white persons or young Negro families is not new. Nor are the foodstuff profiles and their implications for grocery store product assortment based upon type of clientele a marked departure from what would have been expected. There are, however, several findings which are new in that they offer evidence of ideas that have heretofore been discussed primarily on a theoretical basis and several findings which are quite unexpected.

Consumers in the lowest economic group are more likely to patronize independent neighborhood stores than consumers in the middle- and upper-income groups. This tendency is primarily a function of the lack of mobility due to a lower level of automobile ownership; but, a lesser amount of schooling may also be an important influence in

---

[11] The negative effect of the dummy variable

$\left. \begin{array}{l} 0 \text{ white} \\ 1 \text{ nonwhite} \end{array} \right\}$

is consistent with the earlier findings of Alexis, *op. cit.*, relating race and food expenditures.

reducing purchasing sophistication and causing consumers to remain closer to home in the $3,000 and under income group. Generally, wealthier people are less constrained by geographical considerations in their choice of stores. Also, low-income families have a higher relative frequency of patronizing service-oriented major stores — those offering delivery, credit, and telephone service. Delivery and telephone are mobility related services; credit reflects the financial constraints. If the same phenomena were observed in the high-income class, the explanations would be a positive income elasticity for these services since neither poor mobility nor stringent financial limitations would be operative.

Store loyalty is extremely strong. Most families use only one store each for their major and fill-in shopping. In addition, with the exception of check cashing and the offering of trading stamps, the array of services offered as patronage inducements to either low- or high-income shoppers is quite limited at both major and fill-in stores, but less so for middle-income shoppers.

An unexpected finding was that families with incomes of $3,000 and under do not differ significantly in terms of their shopping patterns from families earning $3,001 to $5,000 annually. The significance of this is that it is the families with $3,000 or less who are frequently considered part of a "poverty class." This paper suggests that their shopping behavior is very much like those in the $3,001-$5,000 income class so that their situation is not relatively more worsened by the way in which they purchase their foodstuffs. This statement does not apply to particular commodities purchased, inasmuch as the $3,000 and under groups purchase either greater or lesser amounts per family of certain foods depending upon whether the commodity has a positive or negative income elasticity. One explanation for the observed similarity in shopping patterns may be that it results

from the transition of families who retain their prior shopping patterns as they move out of the $3,000 and under class into the next higher class. Implicit in this statement are two additional hypotheses: (1) the $3,001-$5,000 income class is a "trapping state" (in an ergodic process) for certain family types (with given education, skills, etc.); (2) a behavioral change takes place as families move from the $3,001-$5,000 income level to higher plateaus. In essence, people of very low income exhibit shopping behavior that is consistent with the hypothesis that their objectives are to emulate upper-lower or lower-middle class standards.

LIMITATIONS

The findings of this study are limited by several considerations. First, the sample is comprised entirely of families living in the Rochester, New York, Metropolitan area. Rochester is, on the average, a well-to-do area, having, for example, the third highest country income level in New York State, and one of the lowest unemployment rates in the nation. On the other hand, it can be argued that this prosperity should only serve to heighten the differences between the low-income groups and the other groups.

Second, some of the methodology employed, although statistically significant, has practical limitations in terms of application, for example, the use of $r = .4$ or greater as a basis for determining whether or not to report correlation analysis results. Third, the inability to account for quality variations in the commodities purchased may cloud the results, although the authors, as explained earlier, would expect determination of quality differences to reinforce the present findings. In spite of the preceding reservations, the authors believe that many of the behavior patterns uncovered herein are probably appropriate descriptions of many of the urbanized areas of the country.

REFERENCES

Alexis, Marcus, "Racial Differences in Consumption," *Business News Notes*, No. 149, Minneapolis: School of Business Administration, University of Minnesota, 1960.

_____, "Some Negro-White Differences in Consumption," *American Journal of Economics and Sociology*, Vol. 21, No. 1, January 1962, pp. 11-28.

Burk, Marguerite C., *Influences of Economic and Social Factors on U.S. Food Consumption*, Minneapolis: Burgess Publishing Company, 1961.

_____, "Ramifications of the Relationship Between Income and Food," *Journal of Farm Economics*, Vol. XLIV, No. 1, February 1962.

_____, "The Study of Regional Food Consumption," *Journal of Farm Economics*, Vol. XLI, No. 5, December 1959.

Caplovitz, David, *The Poor Pay More*, New York: The Free Press of Glencoe, 1963.

Food and Nutrition Board, Recommended Dietary Allowances, Washington, D.C., National Academy of Sciences—National Research Council, 1958.

Holdren, Bob R., *The Structure of a Retail Market and the Market Behavior of Retail Units*, Englewood Cliffs, N.J.: Prentice-Hall, Inc., 1960.

Reese, Robert T., *Family Purchases of Selected Frozen Fruits and Vegetables*, Marketing Research Report No. 314, U.S. Department of Agriculture, April 1959.

U.S. Bureau of Labor Statistics, *Study of Consumer Expenditure Incomes Savings*, Vol. III, Summary of Family Expenditures for Food, Beverages, and Tobacco, Philadelphia: University of Pennsylvania, 1956.

U.S. Department of Agriculture, *Consumption of Food in the United States 1909-52* with supplements through 1960, Handbook No. 62, Washington, D.C., 1953.

U.S. Department of Agriculture, *Household Food Consumption Survey*, 1955, Washington, D.C., 1956:
  Report #1, "Food Consumption of Households in the United States," 1956.
  Report #17, "Food Consumption and Dietary Levels of Households of Different Sizes: United States—by Region," 1963.

U.S. Department of Agriculture, *Income and Household Size: Their Effects on Food Consumption*, Marketing Research Report No. 340, Washington, D.C., 1959.

B. MARKET FOR CONSUMER SERVICES

3. Trade and Services Outlays Related to Income

CLEMENT WINSTON

The close relationship between consumer purchasing and income may be observed more directly in graphic form by comparing for a given year the pattern of purchasing and income by States. Such a cross-sectional approach serves to bring out the similarities and differences among the States, relative to expenditures and income at one point in time.

The accompanying scatter diagram, in the upper section of the chart, presents the relationship between State sales and personal income in 1958 and, the one in the lower section, the relation between service receipts and income. The States generally cluster along a line with New York at the upper end and Vermont, Wyoming, and Nevada at the lower end; a similar pattern has been found to exist for each of the Census years.

The close correspondence between State sales and income in a given year (r = .995 in the year 1958 and is not much different in other years) is in part a function of the population of each State. However, the relation between State sales and income on a per capita basis shows a lesser but still very significant correspondence.

The slope of the line is very near unity indicating that within the cross-section of States, with time held constant, the difference in sales among the States is directly proportional to income differentials.

Although the States are generally close to the average line of relationship there are several outstanding exceptions. For example, Delaware with a total personal income of $1.2 billion reported retail sales of $580 million while New Hampshire and South Dakota with income not too different from Delaware had sales of $700 and $780 million, respectively. Also Connecticut with $6.6 billion of personal income had sales of $3.0 billion while Virginia and North Carolina had substantially higher sales with about the same income. On the high side, that is, with higher-than-average sales relative to income, were Florida and Texas.

There are a number of factors other than the level of income itself that tend to influence the sales-income position of a State compared to the others. Where a large metropolitan area spills over into two or more States there will be tendencies for people living in one State which is credited with their income to make substantial purchases in the State in which the center of the metropolitan area is located. This is true, for example, for Connecticut and Maryland as well as for Delaware and New Jersey which are on the low side in sales relative to income.

Mail-order sales also play an important role especially in certain States which are not close enough to extensive shopping areas. The effect of mail-order purchases is to lower sales within the given State relative to its income potential and to raise that of the State

From *Survey of Current Business*, Vol. 41, No. 5 (May, 1961), pp. 25-28.

34

RETAIL BUSINESS AND SERVICE RECEIPTS ARE DIRECTLY
PROPORTIONAL—WITH SOME EXCEPTIONS—TO THE SIZE OF TOTAL INCOME

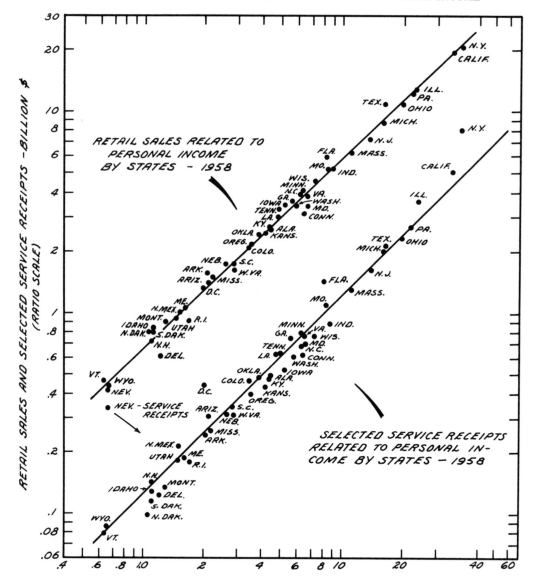

NOTE - SELECTED SERVICE RECEIPTS INCLUDE PERSONAL, DOMESTIC, AND
BUSINESS SERVICES, AUTO AND OTHER REPAIRS, AMUSEMENTS,
GAS, ELECTRICITY, LIFE INSURANCE, AND HOTELS AND MOTELS.

DATA - CENSUS, OBE, AND PRIVATE AGENCIES.   61-5-12

U.S. DEPARTMENT OF COMMERCE, OFFICE OF BUSINESS ECONOMICS.

in which the mail-order firms operate.

In States such as Minnesota, Iowa, the Dakotas, Nebraska, and Kansas sales of lumber, building-hardware stores (including farm equipment dealers) form an unusually large proportion of their total sales. The average proportion for these States is about twice that shown for the Nation. The ratio of gasoline service station sales to total sales in these States also exceeds the overall ratio but not to the same extent. The differences largely reflect purchases for farm use. In the case of Florida and Texas the kind of business groups in which sales are high relative to the national average are the automotive group and gasoline service stations.

SERVICES SHOW SIMILAR PATTERN

The data on service receipts for the various States are shown plotted against income in those States on the upper portion of the charts. The close relationship between service receipts and income by States is immediately evident although it is not so close as in the case of retail sales in which the store receipts represent a much greater proportion of consumer items.

The measure of the closeness of the relationship r = .97 compares with r = .99 for retail sales. The points representing the States fall generally along a line almost parallel to the regression line between sales and income but they are seen to be more dispersed about their average line.

It is of interest to compare the deviations of States from their respective lines of relationship in the two cases. Retail sales expenditures in Nevada appear somewhat below the line reflecting in part purchases of goods outside the State because of the lack of distributive facilities within the State. In the case of service receipts, Nevada is far above the average. Personal income in Nevada is not too different from that in Vermont or Wyoming but the service

receipts in Nevada are nearly double the combined figure for both of these States. The high level of the service receipts for Nevada is related to tourist activities for which the State is noted.

Florida is found to be above the line of relationship for both sales as well as services. The high level of purchases relative to income reflects mostly the influence of the extensive tourist trade.

For Illinois, California, and New York service receipts are high relative to the average line although these States are generally in line relative to sales. In Illinois and New York business service expenditures are important factors in the high service figures while in California heavy tourist traffic is probably most influential.

On the low side for services relative to income were found many of the less industrialized areas, such as the Dakotas, Kansas, and Iowa. Delaware and Connecticut are found on the low side relative to income for service receipts as well as sales. Expenditures in both of these States are influenced by their close proximity to big metropolitan areas in adjoining States.

REGIONAL DIFFERENCES BY KINDS OF BUSINESS

Variations in climate, in natural resources, in geographical features, in industrial structure and other factors tend to lead to considerable variation in the patterns of spending from region to region and from State to State. In Table 3 there is presented a percentage distribution of State and regional sales by kind of business for the year 1958. It is noted that the relative distribution of retail sales among the States varies considerably from State to State. The proportion of a State's sales accounted for by the lumber, building-hardware group (including farm equipment dealers) ranges from 4 percent for the lowest to 23 percent for the highest. For furniture and appliance stores, the range is

TABLE 3

PERCENTAGE DISTRIBUTION OF RETAIL STORE SALES BY KIND OF BUSINESS WITHIN EACH STATE, 1958

	Retail trade, total	Auto-motive dealers	Furni-ture home fur-nish-ings equip-ment stores	Lumber, building materials, hard-ware, farm equip-ment dealers	Ap-parel, acces-sory stores	Drug stores, propri-etory stores	Eating, drink-ing places	Food stores	Gaso-line service sta-tions	Gen-eral mer-chan-dise stores	All other retail-ers[1]
United States	100.0	15.9	5.0	7.2	6.3	3.4	7.6	24.5	7.1	11.0	12.0
New England	100.0	14.3	4.5	5.5	6.9	3.3	7.3	26.3	5.9	10.1	15.9
Maine	100.0	16.7	3.3	5.8	5.7	2.6	4.4	28.0	7.1	10.4	16.0
New Hampshire	100.0	16.5	3.8	6.0	6.4	2.7	5.4	28.6	6.9	7.6	16.1
Vermont	100.0	17.3	3.7	7.0	4.5	2.2	4.4	26.1	6.8	10.1	17.9
Massachusetts	100.0	13.2	4.5	5.0	7.2	3.3	8.3	25.8	5.4	10.6	16.7
Rhode Island	100.0	14.1	4.6	5.8	7.8	3.7	7.5	25.5	6.1	10.8	14.1
Connecticut	100.0	14.7	5.4	6.0	6.9	3.5	7.1	26.4	6.2	9.4	14.4
Middle Atlantic	100.0	13.1	5.4	4.9	8.3	2.9	9.5	26.2	5.3	10.7	13.7
New York	100.0	11.5	5.4	4.3	9.5	2.9	10.7	26.5	4.5	10.7	14.0
New Jersey	100.0	13.9	6.0	5.5	7.8	2.6	9.2	26.4	6.1	8.4	14.1
Pennsylvania	100.0	15.4	5.0	5.3	6.6	3.0	7.8	25.7	6.0	12.2	13.0
East North Central	100.0	15.8	4.9	7.6	5.7	3.5	8.1	24.4	7.3	11.2	11.5
Ohio	100.0	16.0	4.9	7.2	5.1	3.3	8.0	25.8	7.5	12.7	9.5
Indiana	100.0	16.7	4.8	8.6	5.1	3.6	7.2	23.5	8.2	10.9	11.4
Illinois	100.0	14.1	4.8	7.0	6.6	3.4	8.6	22.9	6.5	10.2	15.9
Michigan	100.0	17.7	5.1	7.5	5.6	4.0	7.1	26.1	7.9	11.0	8.0
Wisconsin	100.0	15.7	4.7	9.6	5.4	2.9	9.6	23.5	6.9	11.0	10.7
West North Central	100.0	16.6	4.4	12.6	5.1	3.4	6.5	21.5	7.9	10.2	11.8
Minnesota	100.0	15.4	4.2	12.3	5.0	3.2	7.3	21.4	7.2	10.9	13.1
Iowa	100.0	16.2	4.5	15.1	5.1	3.0	6.0	21.0	8.1	8.7	12.3
Missouri	100.0	15.7	4.5	8.0	5.7	3.8	6.6	22.4	7.6	12.0	13.7
North Dakota	100.0	18.7	4.0	22.8	5.3	2.9	7.0	17.1	7.5	8.3	6.4
South Dakota	100.0	17.6	3.7	19.1	4.6	3.3	6.3	19.9	8.6	8.6	8.3
Nebraska	100.0	17.2	4.6	15.0	4.7	3.1	6.8	20.1	8.5	10.1	9.9
Kansas	100.0	19.4	4.7	12.3	4.7	3.6	5.2	23.2	9.1	8.4	9.4
South Atlantic	100.0	17.0	5.1	6.4	6.1	3.6	6.4	24.0	7.6	11.9	11.9
Delaware	100.0	15.7	5.3	6.0	5.8	3.0	6.0	22.4	7.1	10.9	17.8
Maryland	100.0	14.6	4.2	5.4	5.5	4.2	8.4	26.9	6.8	11.0	13.0
District of Columbia	100.0	14.1	6.8	2.5	9.1	4.7	9.6	18.1	4.8	14.2	16.1
Virginia	100.0	16.9	4.8	5.8	5.6	3.8	6.0	24.8	8.2	12.7	11.4
West Virginia	100.0	16.7	5.2	5.6	6.1	3.2	5.6	26.5	7.7	15.3	8.1
North Carolina	100.0	17.4	5.1	7.6	6.1	3.2	4.3	22.8	8.1	12.7	12.7
South Carolina	100.0	17.8	5.1	7.5	5.8	3.4	4.4	25.4	8.8	11.8	10.0
Georgia	100.0	17.3	4.8	7.2	6.0	3.3	4.6	23.1	8.2	12.5	13.0
Florida	100.0	18.7	5.6	7.0	6.3	3.8	7.9	22.4	7.3	9.6	10.4
East South Central	100.0	17.8	4.9	7.6	5.9	3.5	5.1	24.9	8.0	12.1	10.2
Kentucky	100.0	17.3	4.8	8.0	5.7	3.6	6.6	25.6	7.6	11.1	9.7
Tennessee	100.0	18.0	4.9	7.1	5.3	3.4	4.8	24.7	8.2	12.6	11.0
Alabama	100.0	17.6	5.4	7.1	6.6	3.5	4.6	24.7	7.7	12.8	10.0
Mississippi	100.0	18.8	4.4	8.7	6.5	3.6	4.1	24.2	8.7	11.6	9.5
West South Central	100.0	18.8	4.7	8.1	5.9	3.5	5.8	24.2	8.1	11.0	9.9
Arkansas	100.0	19.1	4.3	9.8	5.2	3.2	4.5	23.4	8.0	10.3	12.2
Louisiana	100.0	16.7	5.2	7.5	6.8	3.6	7.2	24.6	7.5	11.8	9.1
Oklahoma	100.0	19.0	4.8	9.3	5.5	3.8	6.0	24.4	8.8	10.8	7.6
Texas	100.0	19.3	4.6	7.8	5.8	3.5	5.5	24.1	8.1	10.9	10.4
Mountain	100.0	18.8	4.8	9.2	4.8	4.0	7.7	22.2	8.9	10.4	9.2
Montana	100.0	18.9	3.8	12.9	5.0	3.2	9.4	22.2	8.0	8.6	8.0
Idaho	100.0	19.9	4.5	12.8	3.5	3.6	6.7	21.2	8.1	10.3	9.4
Wyoming	100.0	18.7	4.5	11.0	4.8	3.9	8.3	21.2	11.1	8.0	8.5
Colorado	100.0	18.3	4.8	9.3	4.4	4.4	7.2	21.6	7.8	11.9	10.3
New Mexico	100.0	20.2	4.7	7.8	5.3	3.4	7.4	21.9	9.9	9.6	9.8
Arizona	100.0	18.6	5.5	7.5	5.5	4.1	8.5	23.4	9.3	9.4	8.2
Utah	100.0	18.3	5.1	8.0	4.4	4.4	6.0	22.5	9.1	13.1	9.1
Nevada	100.0	16.7	4.3	4.7	6.5	5.5	9.8	23.2	11.5	8.9	8.9
Pacific	100.0	16.2	5.8	6.2	5.5	3.6	8.3	24.9	7.6	10.7	11.2
Washington	100.0	14.5	4.8	7.0	4.3	3.6	7.3	25.3	7.1	12.3	13.8
Oregon	100.0	18.3	4.3	7.1	4.3	3.1	7.0	25.1	7.9	10.6	12.3
California	100.0	16.2	6.1	6.0	5.9	3.6	8.7	24.8	7.7	10.4	10.6
Addenda[2]											
Alaska	100.0	12.5	4.4	4.9	4.8	4.4	14.0	23.4	5.8	14.3	11.5
Hawaii	100.0	13.7	5.1	1.3	6.5	3.0	12.6	29.8	7.3	12.0	8.7

[1] Includes nonstore retailers.
[2] Not included in total.
Source: U.S. Department of Commerce, Bureau of the Census and Office of Business Economics.

from 3 percent to 7 percent, in drug stores 2 percent to 6 percent.

BUILDING MATERIALS
AND AUTOMOTIVE GROUPS

States in which agriculture was an important source of income showed a high proportion of their sales in the lumber, building, hardware group (including farm equipment) — North Dakota 23 percent, South Dakota 19 percent. In New York State such stores accounted for only 4 percent of sales. In the automotive group also, the proportion of sales was high in the farm States with New York again lowest. A somewhat similar pattern was exhibited for sales of gasoline service stations, with Nevada and Wyoming showing the largest proportions of their sales at such stores.

FOOD STORES AND EATING
AND DRINKING PLACES

Large cities and density of population are dominant factors in such sales. In most of the agricultural States less than 30 percent of sales went to food stores and eating and drinking places, while a third or more of all sales was expended in these outlets in New York, New Jersey, Pennsylvania, and other more urbanized areas.

Differences in State and local liquor laws influence spending at eating and drinking places. All the States in the southeast and south where "on premise" consumption of alcoholic beverages is limited entirely or in part show a lower-than-average proportion of sales going to eating and drinking places.

APPAREL AND OTHER RETAIL STORES

New York recorded the highest share in the apparel group, 9½ percent of total sales. Massachusetts, Rhode Island, and New Jersey had proportions of 7 percent to 8 percent while Idaho had the lowest proportion of its sales in this group, 3½ percent. New York as the style and apparel manufacturing center tends to attract a large number of purchases from outside the State as well as within it.

The general merchandise group comprising department, variety, general stores and dry goods, and other general merchandise stores forms a rather heterogeneous group and the distribution of the State ratios is rather mixed. The State with the lowest proportion of its sales in this group is Vermont, 7 percent, and the highest is West Virginia, 15 percent.

To some extent stores in the less urbanized States are more likely to sell a variety of products than to specialize as in the high population States. For this reason a larger proportion of stores in the less populous States is likely to be classified as general merchandise stores rather than in the more specialized categories.

Since demand for gasoline in a State is related in large part to the number of cars on the road and to the agricultural use of gasoline it is found that State patterns in gasoline service station sales resemble those of the automotive group. The smallest share of sales going to this group, 4½ percent, was recorded in New York and the highest, over 11 percent, in Wyoming and Nevada.

REGIONAL DISTRIBUTION OF SERVICE TRADE

The percent distribution of service receipts by selected services shows considerable variation among the regions. The largest variation in the percentage of specific services to total service receipts within a given region was the miscellaneous business services and life insurance group. Here the proportions ranged from 34 and 38 percent for the East North Central and Middle Atlantic region to 17 percent for the Mountain region. This reflects the heavy expenditures for advertising, news syndicates and employment agencies which are more important in heavily industrialized areas with very large cities.

TABLE 4
PERCENTAGE DISTRIBUTION OF SELECTED SERVICE RECEIPTS BY REGIONS, 1958

	Total[1]	Hotels, motels, etc.	Personal services	Insurance and business services	Repairs	Amusement	Utilities	Domestic service
United States	100.0	8.4	16.0	29.5	13.2	11.0	14.5	7.4
New England	100.0	9.2	18.4	24.4	13.7	9.2	16.2	8.9
Middle Atlantic	100.0	7.1	14.0	38.0	10.1	12.9	11.1	6.8
East North Central	100.0	6.5	16.6	34.2	12.2	8.9	16.7	4.9
West North Central	100.0	8.7	16.8	24.7	15.8	8.7	19.8	5.5
South Atlantic	100.0	11.4	17.2	20.5	14.2	9.5	14.7	12.5
East South Central	100.0	7.2	19.1	19.9	15.0	7.7	18.6	12.5
Mountain	100.0	18.6	13.9	17.2	14.7	16.7	14.1	4.8
Pacific	100.0	8.6	15.5	27.9	15.3	14.7	11.8	6.2

[1] This total excludes many important categories of services purchased by consumers. Principal exclusions are services connected with medical care, foreign travel, housing, communications, purchased transportation, and religious and welfare activities.
Sources: U.S. Department of Commerce, Bureau of the Census and Office of Business Economics, Edison Electric Institute and American Gas Association.

Insurance expenses, personal services, and auto and other repair services are relatively stable as a percentage of total service receipts among the regions.

The largest proportion of expenditures for hotels, motels and related services is in the Mountain region where tourist activities are high. The South Atlantic region also shows a higher-than-average proportion in this category.

Outlays for motion pictures and other amusements are relatively high in the Mountain States and in Pacific States reflecting conditions similar to those which tend to raise expenditures in hotels and motels. The State data indicate that motion picture expenditures are especially important in California, and expenditures for motion pictures and for theatres are relatively high in New York with its large transient population.

For domestic services the South Atlantic and East South Central regions stand out with a proportion considerably greater than the United States total. This may reflect, in large part, the greater availability of labor for this type of work in these States.

Demand for gas and electric utilities depends to a large extent on the availability and cost of these products as against other fuels, as well as on climatic factors. The West North Central farm areas and the East South Central Tennessee Valley area utilize electricity to an especially large extent, while in the Middle Atlantic and Pacific States which showed the lowest ratio in this field, the use of a great deal of fuel oil reduces demand for gas and electricity.

C. PURCHASE BEHAVIOR — CONSUMERS

4. Customer Loyalty to Store and Brand

ROSS M. CUNNINGHAM

Confronted with rising operating costs, many food store managements have decided to expand private brands offerings in order to increase gross margins. Most of this expansion has taken place in products where management believes that manufacturer brands do not yield sufficient margins to cover the costs of doing business, but it is evident in other product classes as well.

As for manufacturers, they are increasingly concerned with this trend. They are experiencing the keen competition of private brands for shelf space and share of market, and are finding that their bargaining power is reduced as retailers become larger. Many of them are countering with increased promotion in behalf of their own brands.

ROLE OF LOYALTY

The key assumption behind all this activity is customer loyalty. To the retailer this means loyalty to his store. To

From *Harvard Business Review*, Vol. 39, No. 6 (November/December, 1961), pp. 127-37. © 1961 by the President and Fellows of Harvard College; all rights reserved.

AUTHOR'S NOTE: This study was financed by the Sloan Research Fund of the School of Industrial Management at Massachusetts Institute of Technology.

Mrs. Elaine B. Andrews served as Technical Assistant and provided invaluable help in processing and analyzing the detailed purchase data derived from weekly diaries. Pierre Martineau, Director of Research and Marketing at the Chicago *Tribune*, cooperated by permitting use of data on 50 families from the *Tribune* consumer purchase panel.

the manufacturer this means loyalty to his brand. Both parties have a big stake in the strengths of these loyalties. Will store loyalty sell the private brand (and in turn reinforce store loyalty), or will brand loyalty keep the manufacturer brands on top?

For food retailers, in particular, store loyalty could be of vital help in meeting the problem of overstored areas. If some families are more loyal than others, a retailer might be able to secure a larger share of these more profitable customers. Or perhaps the loyalty of present customers could be upgraded. Either or both would help to improve market position, whereas the usual competitive efforts to build volume through higher traffic may only speed up the circulation of low-loyalty customers among all of the food stores in that market.

NEW MEASURES

A few years ago I reported to HBR readers on new measures of brand loyalty for certain frequently purchased consumer products — toilet soap, scouring cleansers, regular coffee, canned peas, margarine, frozen orange juice, and headache tablets.[1] This report

[1] Ross M. Cunningham, "Brand Loyalty — What, Where, How Much?" HBR January-February 1956, p. 116; see also "Measurement of Brand Loyalty," *Proceedings of the 37th National Conference*, American Marketing Association, December 1955, p. 39.

brought out a number of findings of import to management.

● For *particular products* families varied widely in their *per cent* of concentration of total purchases on a "favorite" brand—from the high 80's to 90's to the 20's.

● There were #2 brands with concentrations from 30% down to 10%.

● Loyalty-proneness tendencies *across product groups* were not strong enough to be an important factor in planning marketing strategy.

● Purchases on deals tended to be concentrated among low brand-loyal buyers.

● Consumption rates and socioeconomic characteristics had little relation to brand loyalty.

There was also evidence that store loyalty and brand loyalty were in some fashion interrelated, so I decided to undertake a detailed study of these two aspects of consumer buying behavior. Since the issue of store loyalty has now become even more important to both retailers and manufacturers, this article will report some of the major findings from my analysis of the food store buying patterns of 50 Chicago families over the 12 months of 1956.

RETAILER'S QUESTIONS

This study has implications for manufacturers of branded and advertised products sold through food stores, and there is an interpretation of the data for their consideration toward the end of the article. But, even for them, much of the import lies in what retailers are doing about brands; and the retailers obviously have an immediate stake. So, for the sake of vividness, I shall present the general findings as answers to a number of questions that a food retailing executive might wish to put to me.

What do you mean by store loyalty; how do you measure it?

A family can make most of its purchases of food and household supplies in only one store and just a few in some others, or it can spread its purchases more evenly over a number of stores. Store loyalty is not measured by the *number* of stores in which a family shops. What is important is the *proportion* of a family's total food purchases that are made in any one particular store. It is this proportion of total purchases for each family that describes that family's loyalty to any given store or combination of stores.

For example, the single store which obtains the highest proportion of a given family's total food purchases is called that family's first or "favorite" store, and its loyalty to that store is designated as 1SL-T (or 1 for first, SL for store loyalty, and T for total purchases). One can then rank the other major stores in which that family shops, identifying the #2 proportion of total purchases at a store as (2SL-T), the #3 proportion (3SL-T), and so forth—until most of the food purchases made by the family are covered. Using the volume of purchases at different stores and relating it to the sum total of a family's food purchases provides a realistic means of describing family buying behavior.

You may be wondering whether this measurement of store loyalty could be distorted by differences in the availability of stores to individual families. For example, if a family had only one store reasonably accessible to it, then a high store-loyalty ranking would simply reflect that situation. However, as will be apparent presently, all of the 50 families shopped in many stores during the year studied; also, an examination of the family locations indicated that there were multiple stores available in each neighborhood.

Although family requirements in food stores include a vast range of foods and household supplies, you are primarily interested in the *total* amount purchased in your store by the family rather than the assortment of individual products which it comprises. However, there may be times when a knowledge of store loyalty for *particular product* groups would be helpful in merchandising decisions. This measurement can be made in much the same way by calculating the proportions of product purchases a family made in its favorite store (1SL-P). This has been done for 18 food products, in most of which there was active private branding by Chicago food retailers during the period of the study.

As for what can be considered to be high or low store-loyalty behavior, this question should be postponed until there has been an opportunity to discuss the findings. What you yourself might want to consider to be highly loyal behavior depends on which of the two descriptive measures of store-loyalty behavior you are looking at, and what point on the range from top to bottom you would want to pick up as a dividing line.

What families did you study; and are they "typical"?

I selected a probability sample of 50 families from the 700 families in the Chicago *Tribune* consumer purchase panel located in metropolitan Chicago. The purchasing of this group was similar to that of the total panel in terms of brand shares and store shares. The correlation coefficients for seven different products ran as follows:

	Brand shares	Store shares
Canned corn	.91	.96
Canned fruit cocktail	.91	.88
Vegetable shortening	.91	.90
Canned peaches	.90	.84
Regular coffee	.89	.94
White bread	.79	.93
Margarine	.68	.90

The Chicago *Tribune* consumer panel has been able to provide a good reflec-

tion of store and brand purchasing patterns in the Chicago metropolitan area, and this subsample of 50 families can therefore be considered reasonably representative of the area. It cannot, of course, predict whether similar buying behavior patterns prevail in other areas. However, some data published by the Market Research Corporation of America suggest that multiple store shopping with many of the characteristics of the Chicago pattern is widespread throughout this country.[2]

The basic purchase information for this study was taken from 2,600 weekly purchase diaries kept by the families throughout 1956. These diaries contained detailed information concerning each product, including the store where it was bought. Three families moved to new locations within the area during 1956, but a careful review of the effects of these moves on store loyalty indicated that they did not distort the study.

Fortunately, trading stamps were not introduced to the Chicago market until after 1956, and thus any shift in buying patterns during their introduction was not a complicating factor. There is a positive advantage here too, in the fact that retailers can figure the strategy of trading stamps from the viewpoint of what the *basic* loyalty pattern is that stamps can take advantage of and/or reinforce.

What are the most important things you discovered about store loyalty?

EXHIBIT I shows the 50 families ranked from high to low by first store loyalty, based on total food purchases (ISL-T). This exhibit also includes the additional purchase proportions contributed by the #2 through the #6 stores, as well as the cumulations of these proportions. Finally, EXHIBIT I lists the number of stores in which each family made one or more purchases during the year.

In EXHIBIT II, the families as ranked

[2] "How People Shop for Food," *MRCA Reports* (undated).

EXHIBIT I

FIFTY FAMILIES VARY WIDELY IN INDIVIDUAL AND CUMULATED
LOYALTIES TO THEIR FIRST SIX STORES

(Families ranked by favorite-store loyalty for total food purchases — 1SL-T)

	(1)	(2) #2	(3)	(4) #3	(5)	(6) #4	(7)	(8) #5	(9)	(10) #6	(11)	(12) No. stores
Family number	1SL-T	store	2SL-T	store	3SL-T	Store	4SL-T	store	5SL-T	store	6SL-T	shopped
1695	91.7% +	3.5% =	95.2% +	1.6% =	96.8% +.	1.1% =	97.9% +	0.6% =	98.5% +	0.5% =	99.0%	14
1767	80.5	4.9	85.4	3.8	89.2	2.6	91.8	1.9	93.7	1.2	94.9	20
1311	79.7	12.7	92.4	4.3	96.7	1.0	97.7	0.6	98.3	0.4	98.7	17
1301	78.2	4.8	83.0	4.4	87.4	3.1	90.5	2.0	92.5	1.4	93.9	17
1713	77.7	4.7	82.4	3.6	86.0	2.5	88.5	1.9	90.4	1.1	91.5	45
1571	77.6	10.0	87.6	3.6	91.2	1.5	92.7	1.1	93.8	1.1	94.9	34
1572	76.8	11.4	88.2	4.5	92.7	3.9	96.6	2.8	99.4	0.2	99.6	17
0071	69.5	17.0	86.5	10.1	96.6	1.9	98.5	0.5	99.0	0.4	99.4	14
0937	64.6	13.0	77.6	5.7	83.3	4.6	87.9	2.3	90.2	1.8	92.0	31
0199	63.6	16.2	79.8	16.1	95.9	0.8	96.7	0.8	97.5	0.5	98.0	22
0711	61.8	26.6	88.4	5.3	93.7	2.3	96.0	1.1	97.1	0.7	97.8	13
1539	60.1	31.1	91.2	5.4	96.6	2.4	99.0	0.9	99.9	0.1	100.0	7
0678	58.8	8.9	67.7	5.1	72.8	3.1	75.9	4.4	80.3	4.4	84.7	28
1034	58.0	26.8	84.8	6.5	91.3	5.4	96.7	2.0	98.7	0.3	99.0	14
1289	54.9	14.1	69.0	9.4	78.4	7.6	86.0	5.9	91.9	5.4	97.3	16
1415	54.9	25.9	80.8	14.0	94.8	2.3	97.1	1.3	98.4	0.5	98.9	12
1108	53.5	16.0	69.5	6.3	75.8	5.5	81.3	3.1	84.4	1.9	86.3	51
1594	52.8	11.5	64.3	9.7	74.0	9.1	83.1	6.4	89.5	1.6	91.1	29
1652	52.4	11.4	63.8	4.9	68.7	2.9	71.6	3.6	75.2	3.3	78.5	54
1609	51.5	43.6	95.1	2.2	97.3	1.0	98.3	0.9	99.2	0.8	100.0	8
1241	50.1	31.4	81.5	8.4	89.9	1.9	91.8	1.3	93.1	1.2	94.3	40
0588	49.1	25.3	74.4	22.6	97.0	1.0	98.0	0.8	98.8	0.7	99.5	12
1591	48.1	22.7	70.8	10.2	81.0	4.9	85.9	3.7	89.6	3.7	93.3	38
0276	47.1	25.2	72.3	9.0	81.3	4.0	85.3	2.5	87.8	1.9	89.7	35
1452	45.7	26.4	72.1	5.4	77.5	4.3	81.8	2.7	84.5	2.6	87.1	26
1329	44.6	12.6	57.2	8.1	65.3	5.9	71.2	4.9	76.1	4.5	80.6	50
1129	43.7	26.4	70.1	12.1	82.2	8.1	90.3	7.8	98.1	0.6	98.7	19
1295	42.7	34.0	76.7	15.2	91.9	2.2	94.1	1.7	95.8	1.3	97.1	31
1626	41.4	20.7	62.1	14.4	76.5	9.9	86.4	3.7	90.1	3.5	93.6	24
1636	40.9	35.6	76.5	8.8	85.3	1.8	87.1	1.8	88.9	1.8	90.7	26
1770	40.7	20.5	61.2	11.9	73.1	9.7	82.8	6.7	89.5	3.7	93.2	40
0308	39.4	26.8	66.2	18.8	85.0	10.2	95.2	2.3	97.5	0.6	98.1	26
0210	38.9	30.9	69.8	6.8	76.6	3.4	80.0	3.4	83.4	2.6	86.0	39
0505	38.4	32.5	70.9	7.8	78.7	6.0	84.7	5.7	90.4	3.3	93.7	17
0291	38.2	35.6	73.8	6.3	80.1	6.3	86.4	2.7	89.1	2.7	91.8	23
0595	38.1	28.0	66.1	11.7	77.8	10.5	88.3	4.0	92.3	2.4	94.7	16
1432	37.3	33.6	70.9	14.3	85.2	6.9	92.1	2.7	94.8	2.6	97.4	22
1794	37.2	14.3	51.5	12.0	63.5	9.5	73.0	4.7	77.7	3.6	81.3	37
0356	35.8	19.4	55.2	10.0	65.2	9.9	75.1	5.4	80.5	5.1	85.6	44
1641	35.2	34.6	69.8	10.4	80.2	4.2	84.4	2.8	87.2	2.6	89.8	24
1363	34.4	16.7	51.1	15.5	66.6	10.5	77.1	6.7	83.8	3.8	87.6	29
0888	32.4	23.0	55.4	17.4	72.8	10.4	83.2	2.7	85.9	2.0	87.9	36
1668	32.0	28.0	60.0	10.1	70.1	8.6	78.7	8.1	86.8	6.1	92.9	16
0371	30.3	23.1	53.4	16.3	69.7	13.3	83.0	4.0	87.0	3.1	90.1	28
0218	29.8	23.3	53.1	15.1	68.2	8.0	76.2	6.9	83.1	4.3	87.4	22
0923	27.2	19.8	47.0	13.2	60.2	6.9	67.1	6.8	73.9	4.0	77.9	47
1577	24.3	19.7	44.0	17.3	61.3	17.0	78.3	10.3	88.6	4.3	92.9	28
1532	23.8	16.9	40.7	15.7	56.4	8.5	64.9	6.9	71.8	4.8	76.6	56
1276	23.5	16.4	39.9	13.9	53.8	11.0	64.8	6.2	71.0	5.2	76.2	45
0590	19.3	9.2	28.5	8.7	37.2	8.9	46.1	8.4	54.5	7.7	62.2	68
Average family	48.6	20.9	69.5	9.9	79.4	5.7	85.1	3.6	88.7	2.5	91.2	29

in the first column of EXHIBIT I have been divided into ten groups or deciles of five families each, and the averages for each of these deciles for all of the store-loyalty combinations are shown graphically.

Let me point out some of the highlights from these two exhibits:

Families vary widely in their first

store loyalty. The average family in the whole group of 50 makes 48.6% of its food purchases in its favorite store. But as you run your eye down Column I, you can see that single store-loyalty for individual families ranges from 91.7% of total food purchases for Family 1695 to 19.3% of total food purchases for Family 0590. In fact, one of the reasons for including all the detail of EXHIBIT I is to

EXHIBIT II
SUMMARY BY DECILES OF CUMULATED LOYALTIES TO FIRST SIX STORES
(AVERAGES OF DECILES RANKED BY 1SL-T)

EXHIBIT II
SUMMARY BY DECILES OF CUMULATED LOYALTIES TO FIRST SIX STORES
(AVERAGES OF DECILES RANKED BY 1SL-T)

PER CENT SINGLE-STORE LOYALTY TO:

| 1ST STORE | 2ND STORE | 3RD STORE | 4TH STORE | 5TH STORE | 6TH STORE | ALL OTHERS |

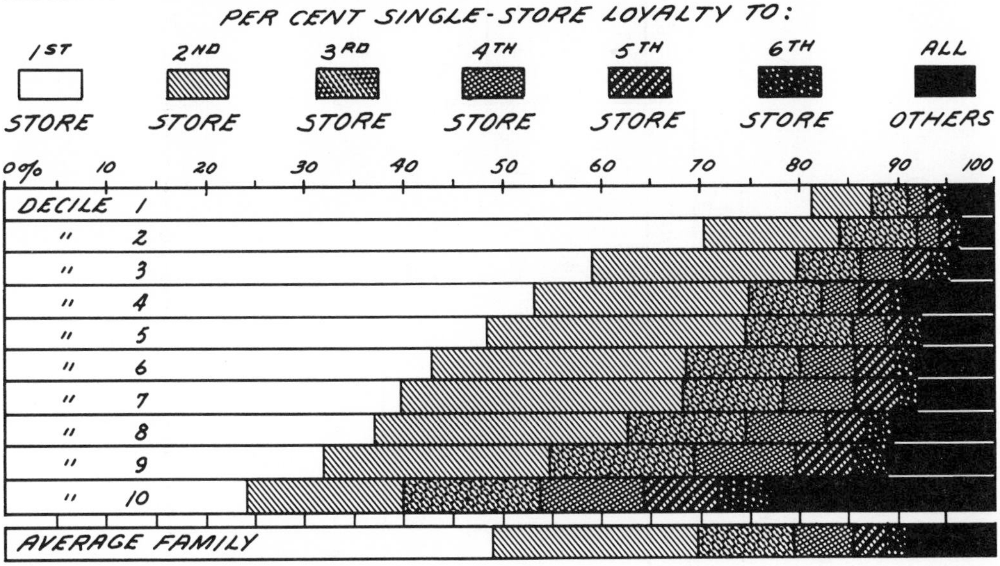

emphasize the panoramic range of the individual loyalty patterns.

Families with high first store loyalty do not necessarily shop in fewer stores. Looking at Column 12, one can see that there is no clear-cut pattern as to the total number of stores shopped by high or low store-loyal families. For example, Family 1713, with the fifth highest first store loyalty of 77.7%, shopped in 45 stores, while Family 1577, fourth from the bottom with a favorite store loyalty of 24.3%, shopped in 28 stores.

Decile averages were calculated but showed little dispersion from the figure of 29 for the entire group, except for the bottom five families, whose average was 49. The surprisingly large numbers of stores shopped by the fifty families are due in part to the inclusion in this count of *any* store at which one or more purchases were made during the year. Other contributing factors are the number of stores readily accessible to the family, the normal travel patterns of family members, the number of fill-in purchases, and the housewife's prefer-

ences for many or for few suppliers.

There is a heavy concentration of purchases in the first few stores. As noted above, the average family makes 48.6% of its total food purchases at its favorite store. Add to this the 20.9% made in the second store, and you have accounted for 69.5% of the average family's total food purchases. The third store takes an average of 9.9% of total purchases, making almost 80% for only the first *three* stores. The fourth, fifth, and sixth ranking stores add 5.7%, 3.6%, and 2.5%, respectively, raising the cumulated figure to 91.2% of total food purchases. Yet remember that this average family shopped for food items in a total of 29 stores!

Even low store-loyalty families make the bulk of their purchases in only three stores. For example, EXHIBIT II shows that families in Decile 8 made about three quarters of their purchases in the first three stores, while those in Decile 9 made nearly 70%. It is only in Decile 10, which contains the five most disloyal families, that the first three stores ac-

EXHIBIT III
Concentration of Total Food Purchases by 50 Families
For Store-Loyalty Measures of 1SL-T Through 6SL-T

Per cent of total Purchases	1SL-T		2SL-T		3SL-T		4SL-T		5SL-T		6SL-T	
	Families	%	Families	%	Families	%	Families	%	Families	%	Families	%
Buying 90% +	1	2	4	8	13	26	19	38	25	50	33	66
Buying 80% +	2	4	14	28	26	52	37	74	43	86	45	90
Buying 70% +	7	14	26	52	38	76	46	92	49	98	49	98
Buying 60% +	12	24	38	76	47	94	49	98	49	98	50	100
Buying 50% +	21	42	45	90	49	98	49	98	50	100	50	100
Buying 40% +	31	62	48	96	49	98	50	100	50	100	50	100
Buying 30% +	44	88	49	98	50	100	50	100	50	100	50	100
Buying 20% +	49	98	50	100	50	100	50	100	50	100	50	100
Buying 10% +	50	100	50	100	50	100	50	100	50	100	50	100

count for as low as barely half of total food purchases. In these very low store-loyal families, even with six stores, the accumulated total comes to less than 80%.

This pattern of purchasing the vast majority of family food needs in six or fewer stores can be seen even more clearly when the data are analyzed as in EXHIBIT III. All the families studied buy more than 60% of their total food purchases in six stores; 45 families buy 80%+ in six stores; and 33 families buy 90%+ in six stores.

How stable is this behavior; do families switch favorite stores?

The behavior patterns reported here are reasonably consistent over time, and not a chance result of when a particular family happened to be studied. This became evident from an analysis of quarterly store-loyalty data for the entire 50 families during 1956 and for 25 of them over a three-year period.[3] For the 50 families that could be studied over four consecutive quarters in 1956, 28 out of 50 were loyal throughout this period to the same favorite store. Also, 15 more families were loyal to the same store for three out of the four quarters. *In effect, 86% of the group studied can be said to have been essentially loyal to a specific store during the year.*

Naturally, more switching would be expected over three years than over one year, and the study of the 25 families for twelve quarters confirms this. EXHIBIT IV presents an assessment of store switching for these 25 families. Eight families (about one-third) had the same store as their favorite for all twelve quarters. The remaining families distributed their loyalty from a total of ten quarters with the same store on down to only

---

[3]Quarterly first store loyalty measurements for the two preceding years have been secured from Thomas F. McCabe, "Changes in Store Loyalty," B.S. Thesis, School of Industrial Management, Massachusetts Institute of Technology, 1959 (unpublished).

four quarters with the same store. As for loyalty to a second store, one fifth of the families stayed with the same second

EXHIBIT IV

TWENTY-FIVE FAMILIES SHOW VARYING
SWITCHING RATES IN THEIR 1SL-T
AND 2SL-T STORES
OVER TWELVE QUARTERS

Number of quarters	1SL-T store		2SL-T store	
	Number of families	Per-cent	Number of families	Per-cent
12	8	32%	5	20%
11	–	–	1	4
10	2	8	1	4
9	3	12	–	–
8	2	8	3	12
7	3	12	7	28
6	3	12	4	16
5	3	12	–	–
4	1	4	4	16
3	–	–	–	–
2	–	–	–	–
1	–	–	–	–
Total	25	100%	25	100%

store for twelve quarters, while one family remained loyal to the same store for eleven quarters, and another family to its store for ten quarters. Better than one half of the 25 families had the same second store for six, seven, or eight quarters.

As might be expected, as many as six of the eight families who had not switched their favorite store over 12 quarters placed in the upper half of the 1SL-T ranking. It would take a drastic change in buying behavior for a family with high loyalty to one store to transfer that same loyalty to another store.

Conversely, those families with low first store loyalty tended to switch their top store more frequently; often only a few percentage points separated the #1 and #2 stores. In effect, this means that, here too, most families maintained about the same loyalty to their favorite store during the three years of the study, although the favorite store was less frequently the same store over the entire period.

In fact, using the basic measure of level of loyalty over time, a special tabulation reveals that during the twelve quarters studied only 4 families out of the 25 deviated as much as 15% or more from their average level for the entire period. (An analysis of variance run on the quarterly effects confirms this conclusion.)

Does store loyalty vary with the total amount of food a family buys?

While it would seem plausible that families with high volumes of total food purchases might have low 1SL-T ratings as a result of extensive shopping to secure lowest possible prices, an analysis of the relationship between the volume of expenditures and first store loyalty proportions for each of the 50 families yields a correlation coefficient of −.23. Since any correlation supporting this hypothesis would be inverse, the minus sign is on the corroborative side. On the other hand, a correlation of this low magnitude, in conjunction with the size of the sample, does not test as statistically significant (at the .05 level). Even if the results *were* statistically significant, a correlation of −.23 on a scale of from 0 (no correlation) to − 1.00 (perfect correlation) would indicate a very low order of association between loyalty and total food expenditures.

In short, store loyalty appears to be independent of the total amount spent for food purchases by the family. Families with a high volume of food purchases are just about as likely to have high 1SL-T ratings as they are to have low ratings — and the same goes for their compatriots who purchase considerably less.

Are families more loyal to chains than to independent stores?

In order to answer this question, I divided the top six stores for each family into three categories:

Chain Stores — This category includes both the corporate chains (such as Kroger, Jewel Tea, A & P, and National Tea) and groups of retailers affiliated in various types of contractual relationships with supplying organizations (like I.G.A. or Certified).

Specialty Stores — These are stores which concentrate on a particular product mix such as dairy products, bakery products, or meat. Home deliveries of dairy, bakery, or other food products are treated here as specialty stores.

Independents — These, of course, are full-line food stores not affiliated with a central group of any type.

The results of the analysis in Table 1 indicate that the answer is a strong YES, families *are* more loyal to chains.

Note how, taking the six-store spectrum, the chain stores have neatly "divided the field," accounting for exactly half of the 300 possible choices, with independent and specialty stores *combined* taking the other half. But for the favorite or first store choice the score is 3-to-1 in favor of chains, and for the #2 store it is 3-to-2; not until the #3 store does the opposition catch up.

Actually, the chains do even better than this indicates, for the indepen-

TABLE 1

	Chain	Independent	Specialty	Total
First store	38	11	1	50
Second store	29	11	10	50
Third store	17	11	22	50
Fourth store	26	15	9	50
Fifth store	19	18	13	50
Sixth store	21	12	17	50
Total	150	78	72	300

dents are their direct competitors, and they are behind chains the whole way down to the #6 choice. It is only the patronage of specialty stores, for the special-purpose buying they are intended for in the first place, that keeps the chains from walking away with the field.

Of the 10 specialty stores cited as #2 choices, 7 were dairy operators, usually with home delivery routes, while 14 of the 22 specialty stores in the #3 position were dairy outlets. A different way of stating these findings might be: many people (from half to three quarters) make their large purchases at a few stores (twice as often in chain stores as in independents), yet consistently buy enough products from a specialty store (quite often a dairy route) to make that the #2 or #3 store; and then fill in-between or special needs at independent or chain stores without very much distinction.

Have some corporate chains achieved higher store loyalty than others?

The answer is again, YES. For the 30 units of *corporate* chains (out of the 38 chain stores ranked as the favorite store, the other 8 being from affiliated retailer groups), the distribution of #1, #2, and #3 stores for each chain is shown in Table 2.

Despite the small numbers involved, the differences are large enough in the first two instances to suggest that Chain A has achieved higher store loyalty than Chain B. The pattern for the others is less clear.

TABLE 2

	First store	Second store	Third store	Total
Chain A	14	4	4	22
Chain B	7	10	3	20
Chain C	5	4	4	13
Chain D	3	1	1	5
Chain E	1	2	–	3
Total	30	21	12	63

Do families with high 1SL-T prefer one type of store over another?

Grouping the 25 most loyal and the 25 least loyal families, in order to give their store preference between chains, independents, and specialty stores, reveals the data in Table 3.

Though one cannot draw specific conclusions because of the small sample size, it would appear that for the favorite store position chain stores seem to draw more from the families with high store loyalty than from those with low store loyalty, while the reverse seems to be the case for the second store position. In interpreting these findings it is important to keep in mind that the data do not differentiate between the reasons for store loyalty. For example, high store loyalty can reflect such diverse patterns as (a) buying from independents for the sake of charge account and delivery service, and (b) planning purchases ahead and then traveling several miles once a week to make them.

Do families with high store loyalties have high brand loyalties?

To answer this question accurately,

TABLE 3

	First store			Second store			Third store		
	C	I	S	C	I	S	C	I	S
25 most loyal families	22	3	–	10	6	9	10	5	10
25 least loyal families	16	8	1	19	5	1	7	6	12
Total	38	11	1	29	11	10	17	11	22

I first have to get into the problem of brand loyalty and its relationship to loyalty in terms of individual product classes. Thus:

Brand Loyalty. For each family, brand loyalty can be measured in the same manner as store loyalty, by using the "share-of-market" concept. (See my previous article, described earlier.) That is, we can describe a family's brand loyalty as the proportion of total purchases in a given product class represented by the largest single brand. This is called "single brand loyalty" (SBL) and is similar in concept to first store loyalty.

For the 50 families in this study, 18 products were covered, most of which had substantial numbers of private as well as manufacturer brands. For the products as a group, the average family concentrated 65% of its product class purchases on a favorite brand. The range of loyalties among the 18 product classes as shown in Part A of EXHIBIT V indicates that this average family had an SBL rating from 83.5% for all-purpose flour, down to 54.6% for canned peaches at the low end.

Store Loyalty by Product Class. This same average family, if you recall, is loyal to its favorite store to the extent of making 48.6% of its total food purchases there. However, it may very well concentrate an even higher proportion of its purchases in a given product class in one store. This store may or may not be the same store to which it is most loyal — but more about this later.

The range of concentration of purchases of a given product class in one store can be seen in Part B of EXHIBIT V. As you will note, these concentrations run from 57.5% of all white bread bought by the average family in the same store to 80.7% of all canned peaches bought by this family in the same store.

Now it is evident why this question really has to be answered in two ways; it depends on whether store loyalty is measured by concentration of total food purchases or on a product-by-product basis. In any event we are ready to answer now:

● The answer is NO when measured

EXHIBIT V

VARIOUS STORE-LOYALTY AND BRAND-LOYALTY INTERRELATIONSHIPS

Product class	No. of families buying*	Part A Average SBL	Part B Average 1SL-P	Part C Correlations between 1SL-T and SBL Correlation coefficients	Significance†	Part D Correlations between 1SL-P and SBL Correlation coefficients	Significance†
White bread	48	61.2	57.5	.03	No	.71	Yes
Regular coffee	41	67.6	73.6	.19	No	− .03	No
Instant coffee	20	59.5	60.8	.42	No	.61	Yes
Tea	36	82.8	77.6	.04	No	.20	No
All-purpose flour	37	83.5	74.7	.06	No	.18	No
Butter	41	65.9	69.3	.53	Yes	.64	Yes
Margarine	37	71.1	75.0	.41	Yes	.41	Yes
Vegetable shortening	24	68.1	78.3	− .15	No	− .01	No
Salad dressing	45	59.1	72.1	.01	No	.04	No
Canned spaghetti	26	68.5	73.9	− .05	No	.24	No
Canned peaches	41	54.6	80.7	.15	No	.52	Yes
Canned pineapple	37	65.8	71.2	.29	No	.45	Yes
Canned fruit cocktail	36	66.8	79.4	− .11	No	.45	Yes
Frozen juices	37	55.7	73.3	.29	No	.60	Yes
Canned peas	40	57.2	74.1	.29	No	.22	No
Canned corn	45	59.0	75.8	.09	No	.45	Yes
Frozen vegetables	44	59.3	75.2	.64	Yes	.55	Yes
Canned tuna & bonita	32	63.7	78.3	− .20	No	.05	No

* Families making three or more purchases during 1956.
† At .05 level.

by ISL-T. Part C of EXHIBIT V lists the correlations found for 18 product classes studied. Only three product classes: butter (.53); margarine (.41); and frozen vegetables (.64) show statistically significant correlation coefficients. In other words, high store loyalty *does not* go hand in hand with high brand loyalty; families with high brand loyalty do not necessarily concentrate their total purchases in one store more than do other families with lower brand loyalties.

● On the other hand, the answer is a qualified YES when measured on a product-by-product basis, but not nearly so definite as was the negative answer when measured the other way. As can be seen in Part D of EXHIBIT V, for 10 of the 18 product classes studied, there is a significant association of high brand-loyal families concentrating their purchases in that product class in one store.

What is the explanation of this difference? It could be that, if any substantial proportion of these purchases is in private brands, then the high correlation for certain products could merely be the result of measuring store loyalty on a product basis. That is, with private brands available only in the sponsoring store, a high brand-loyalty rating would *necessarily* result in a high store-loyalty rating for that product. At the same time, for manufacturer brands — which are available in many different stores — it is perfectly possible, in the case of a given product, for high store loyalty to be associated with low brand loyalty or for high brand loyalty to be associated with low store loyalty. This leads us directly to the next question.

Do families with a high loyalty to their favorite store (measured by total purchases) have higher brand loyalty to private brands than families with a low level of loyalty to their favorite store?

EXHIBIT VI contains a comparison of the private brand (and manufacturer brand) purchasing and loyalty patterns of the 25 families having the highest loyalty to their favorite store with the purchasing and loyalty patterns of the 25 families with the lowest loyalty to their favorite store. For all families as a group there were 217 cases of single-brand loyalty to private brands as compared with 540 cases for manufacturer brands. Taking the high store-loyal families from within this group, we find these two facts:

● Families with high store loyalty are somewhat *more* loyal to the *particular* private brands they purchase then are families with low store loyalty. This can be seen by comparing the average single-brand loyalties as shown in Column 4 of EXHIBIT VI. The ratings for the high store-loyal families were higher in 13 out of the 16 product classes in which data were available with an average spread of about 14 percentage points. As a contrast, manufacturer brands were split down the middle with one-half of the products showing higher ratings for high store-loyal families, and one-half showing lower ratings. In sum, *once a high store-loyal family decides to buy a private brand, it is more loyal to that brand than a family with low store loyalty.*

● But high store-loyal families are *not* more likely to purchase *all* private brands. Column 2 of EXHIBIT VI shows the numbers of private brand-loyal families for each product in the most loyal and least loyal store groups. For the 16 products in which there were private-brand ratings, there were 103 in the high store-loyal group, and 114 in the bottom group. Although the number is fewer in the upper group, the difference is small; and it may be concluded that high store-loyal families have about an equal chance of having their favorite brand a private brand as do low store-loyal families. Manufacturer brands as shown in Column 3 are split completely evenly, with 270 SBL ratings in both of the groups.

EXHIBIT VI

DISTRIBUTION OF SBL PURCHASES FOR 18 SELECTED PRODUCTS BETWEEN PRIVATE BRANDS AND MANUFACTURER BRANDS FOR 25 MOST STORE-LOYAL FAMILIES AND 25 LEAST STORE-LOYAL FAMILIES MEASURED BY TOTAL FOOD PURCHASES (ISL-T)

	(1)		(2) Number with single-brand loyalty to private brands		(3) Number with single-brand loyalty to manufacturer brands		(4) Average single-brand loyalty to private brands	(5) Average single-brand loyalty to manufacturer brands
Product class	Total families purchasing							
	No.	%	No.	%	No.	%		
White bread								
Most store-loyal	25	100.0%	10	40.0%	15	60.0%	65.8%	64.3%
Least store-loyal	25	100.0	5	20.0	20	80.0	50.8	63.1
Regular coffee								
Most store-loyal	23	100.0	7	30.4	16	69.6	76.7	70.8
Least store-loyal	22	100.0	12	54.5	10	45.5	68.9	67.5
Instant coffee								
Most store-loyal	12	100.0	–	–	12	100.0	–	76.1
Least store-loyal	15	100.0	1	6.7	14	93.3	42.9	66.8
Tea								
Most store-loyal	20	100.0	8	40.0	12	60.0	85.7	88.4
Least store-loyal	20	100.0	5	25.0	15	75.0	77.6	83.0
All-purpose flour								
Most store-loyal	21	100.0	2	9.5	19	90.5	100.0	83.1
Least store-loyal	24	100.0	2	8.3	22	91.7	66.7	89.8
Butter								
Most store-loyal	22	100.0	14	63.6	8	36.4	· 75.4	77.2
Least store-loyal	23	100.0	14	60.9	9	39.1	55.1	68.7
Margarine								
Most store-loyal	20	100.0	6	30.0	14	70.0	73.2	84.9
Least store-loyal	20	100.0	5	25.0	15	75.0	64.2	65.5
Vegetable shortening								
Most store-loyal	21·	100.0	2	9.5	19	90.5	71.0	78.7
Least store-loyal	13	100.0	3	23.1	10	76.9	82.2	78.2
Salad dressing								
Most store-loyal	24	100.0	7	29.2	17	70.8	53.3	73.5
Least store-loyal	24	100.0	4	16.7	20	83.3	46.7	57.7
Canned spaghetti								
Most store-loyal	15	100.0	2	13.3	13	86.7	86.3	70.5
Least store-loyal	18	100.0	–	–	18	100.0	–	–
Canned peaches								
Most store-loyal	20	100.0	5	25.0	15	75.0	56.9	58.6
Least store-loyal	24	100.0	11	45.8	13	54.2	55.2	59.0
Canned pineapple								
Most store-loyal	20	100.0	1	5.0	19	95.0	100.0	72.5
Least store-loyal	21	100.0	7	33.3	14	66.7	59.4	67.3
Canned fruit cocktail								
Most store-loyal	17	100.0	6	35.3	11	64.7	63.5	67.5
Least store-loyal	22	100.0	9	40.9	13	59.1	77.4	68.4
Frozen juices								
Most store-loyal	23	100.0	4	17.4	19	82.6	58.0	66.2
Least store-loyal	23	100.0	9	39.2	14	60.8	45.1	76.1
Canned peas								
Most store-loyal	24	100.0	9	37.5	15	62.5	70.0	73.5
Least store-loyal	23	100.0	8	34.8	15	65.2	44.2	60.3
Canned corn								
Most store-loyal	24	100.0	9	37.5	15	62.5	64.3	58.8
Least store-loyal	24	100.0	4	16.7	20	83.3	52.1	62.8
Frozen vegetables								
Most store-loyal	22	100.0	7	31.8	15	68.2	52.4	73.0
Least store-loyal	24	100.0	13	54.2	11	45.8	43.3	62.3
Tuna & bonita								
Most store-loyal	20	100.0	4	20.0	16	80.0	71.3	66.9
Least store-loyal	19	100.0	2	10.5	17	89.5	100.0	69.6
Total single-brand loyalties			217		540			

Is private-brand loyalty more likely to lead to store loyalty, or is store loyalty more likely to lead to private-brand loyalty? The data do not answer the question, but in this connection it is interesting to note that the private brands favored by families with high store loyalty usually were sponsored by their favorite store to a greater extent than in the case of families with low store loyalty. To be precise, 93% of the private brands purchased by the 25 high store-loyal families were sponsored by the favorite store, while only 32% of the private brands purchased by the 25 low store-loyal families were sponsored by the favorite store.

In part this sharply contrasting behavior of the lower store-loyal group undoubtedly reflects the greater degree to which they do multiple store shopping—but, then, this still means that, as far as they are concerned, there apparently is less to hold them to fewer stores.

What do your findings mean to me in dollars and cents?

First of all, it ought to be clear that, when a family in the upper half of the store-loyalty range has your store as its favorite, most of its private-brand purchases will be made in your store. This is especially significant in view of the fact that this same family will also give you more than 48.6% of its total food business.

In effect, because families differ in their store-loyalty behavior, there are a number of opportunities that are available to you for increasing your dollar volume. Let me discuss this using an example.

As you will remember, most families purchase the bulk of their food in a few stores. For the average family—adding to the 48.6% of all food purchased in its favorite store, the 20.9% in its #2 store, the 9.9% in its #3 store, and 5.8% in its #4 store—we get a total of 85.2% purchased in four stores. Imagine, for the moment, that there are 8,000 families in your shopping area, that you have three major competitors, and that there is no important competition on the perimeter of your market area. Assume also that family loyalties to the #1, #2, #3, and #4 stores are evenly distributed over the four competitors. Thus, each store would have 2,000 families for whom it was their favorite store, a different 2,000 families for whom it was their #2 store, and so on. For easy figuring, say that these families spend $1,000 per year in food stores.

Now under these circumstances you could attempt—using trading stamps, advertising, store improvements, and other promotional devices at your command—to increase your volume in either of the following ways:

● You could try to capture a group of first store families over and above the 2,000 who already consider your store their favorite. Such families on the average would add $486 in sales annually (48.6% × $1,000). To refine the point, make the arbitrary assumption that your store is limited to 8,000 customers, so that every customer added must be offset by a customer lost. Then the addition of a family who considers you their favorite store is still desirable, provided the family you lose views you as the #2, #3, or #4 store. For example, you gain $486 and lose $209 (20.9% × $1,000) on a #2 store customer, or a net increase of $275. Thus, it is very worthwhile to secure a larger fraction of 1SL-T buyers than would be your expectation under random distribution conditions.

● The other opportunity is to concentrate on attracting *only* those families who have high store loyalty. For every one of these families you can attract, you will get on the average 62.3% of its total food purchases (half again as much as the average family). In your #1 store group, if you can exchange 1,000 average families for 1,000 high-loyalty families, your sales will rise to $623,000 as compared with $486,000. This represents an increase in dollar volume of 27% *without any increase in store traffic.*

In sum, your greatest opportunities lie in getting the best possible mix of customer loyalties for the traffic that your store will carry. In a shopping area with many competitors, in fact, your best bet for holding and increasing sales volume is to improve the quality of your customer loyalty mix.

What steps can I take to do this?

First of all, learn more about the store-loyalty patterns of your customers and your competitors' customers. Such a study will require direct interviewing, in person or by telephone, of a carefully selected cross section of families in your trading area. Even though most housewives will not have any detailed records of their purchases at different stores, they can estimate their distribution of purchases among the first three stores with usable accuracy. This will reveal the distribution of loyalty patterns within each of the several stores in that market and thus indicate where you stand as compared with competition.

Secondly, learn as much as possible about *why* these people buy where they do. These are the clues that you need in order to determine how to make yours their favorite store. Part of your study should measure your store image in relation to the images of your competitors — in terms of what the customers in your area are looking for in a place to shop. This information, plus information about the kinds of store loyalty behavior and other data, will suggest the directions for constructive action.

FOR MANUFACTURERS

Since shopping for food is a major operation requiring substantial time and effort on the part of the housewife, it is entirely plausible that store loyalty, especially for a favorite store, will at times override brand loyalty. The

housewife may very well be willing to put up with a considerable amount of brand annoyance if she considers a total store satisfactory in terms of convenience, range of products, price, personnel, layout, and the whole complex of factors which are involved.

However, private brands make up a significant share of the over-all purchases of most families. And a substantial fraction of these families are quite loyal to a private brand as their favorite in a given product class. Furthermore, the more store loyal a housewife is (in terms of concentrating a large proportion of her total purchases in one store), the more likely she is to be brand loyal to the private brands of that store *if* she decides to buy a private brand.

For the manufacturer, this means that the housewife is essentially the captive of the stores in which she concentrates the #1, #2, and #3 proportions of her total purchases. She will be exposed to his brand only if he can persuade these three retailers to stock and display it. This requires a good and preferably outstanding product, consumer demand stimulated by advertising, reasonable retailer margins, and an aggressive sales force. While many of these points are not new, what they do indicate is the degree to which the manufacturer is dependent on continuing such policies. Similarly, his share-of-market in a given area will be of vital importance in persuading retailers to carry his brand on their crowded shelves.

Consumer loyalty to store units certainly indicates the bargaining power of the retail unit. As retail stores continue to grow, the bargaining power of the manufacturer will be increasingly threatened. The battle will become more and more difficult as the improved images of the retail units lend more and more credence to the quality image of private brands, for everything the retailer does to improve his store loyalty will increase the chances that customers who are brand loyal to private brands of particular products will buy those which he sponsors.

Further, as my previous study shows, even people with high loyalty to a particular product brand, including, of course, a manufacturer brand, also have a strong second choice, they *will* take another brand *upon occasion*. The question is, who will shape the occasion, the retailer or the manufacturer?

5. Brand Loyalty Revisited:

A Twenty-Year Report[1]

LESTER GUEST

During the spring of 1953, a follow-up study of brand preference and use for 15 products was conducted (Guest, 1955). Twelve years before, 813 public school students distributed across Grades 3-11 (last year of high school) had given evidences of brand awarenesses and preferences (Guest, 1942, 1944). In spite of obvious inadequacies, it was necessary to collect subsequent data by mail questionnaire. Usable responses in 1953 were returned from 165 respondents, and in 1961 from 162 respondents.

Although the term loyalty seems in disrepute in some quarters because of known brand switching, possibly resulting from the many variables operating on purchasers, it is nevertheless important to determine the *degree* of consistency of preferences and the *degree* of relationship between preferences and purchasing behavior. Cunningham (1956) presents some evidence on these questions obtained using other techniques and time intervals.

The present report relates results of a 20-year follow-up of the 1941 universe to determine the degree of correspondence of previous preferences with present preferences and with brand usage.

METHOD

As in 1953, questionnaires eliciting brand preference, brand use, and reasons for discrepancies when they existed, were sent to all persons for whom any reasonable addresses could be determined. The questions concerning preference were in multiple-choice form with opportunity to indicate preference for one of five brands listed for each product or to indicate that none of those listed was preferred. If "None" was chosen, respondents were asked to indicate also which of those listed would be preferred. Each respondent was also asked which brand was owned or used most frequently. Finally, reasons for preference-use discrepancies were ascertained by means of a check list. Although there was reason to consider some changes in format in 1961, for consistency it was thought wiser to retain the same format that was previously used as nearly as possible.

Of the 424 questionnaires mailed (52% of the 1941 universe), 149 (35%) were returned for want of a better address (none was available), 104 (25%) apparently were received by a responsible person but were never returned, 9 (2%) were found to be addressed to deceased persons, and 162 (38%) were returned completed. This compares favorably with the 1953 results although it is far from satisfactory. It is interesting to note that of the 162 usable returns, 75 (46%) had *not* returned a questionnaire

From *Journal of Applied Psychology*, Vol. 48, No. 2 (1964), pp. 93-97.
[1] Funds for this research were made available by the Central Fund for Research of the Pennsylvania State University.

TABLE 1
SAMPLE DATA

Variable	1941	1953	1961
Sex			
Males	52	46	55
Females	48	54	45
N	813	165	162
Age			
7	0	1	1
8	8	9	15
9	10	10	12
10	10	9	12
11	9	11	7
12	9	7	7
13	10	7	7
14	11	9	9
15	13	19	14
16	11	12	10
17	5	4	6
18	3	2	1
N	813	165	162
Socioeconomic status			
A	5	8	12
B	38	45	49
C	44	39	30
D	9	4	5
?	4	4	4
N	813	165	162
IQ			
79 down	1	1	1
80-89	5	1	2
90-99	15	10	7
100-109	22	24	26
110-119	20	25	22
120-129	11	16	17
130 up	4	8	7
?	21	15	18
N	813	165	162
Family status			
Married (no children)	—	12	6
Married (1 child)	—	9	13
Married (2 children)	—	7	38
Married (3 children)	—	3	20
Married (4 children)	—	1	13
Unmarried	100	19	10
?	—	49	1
N	813	165	162

Note. — All data are given in percentages with the exception of Ns.

in 1953. Hence, comparisons between years should take into account that precisely the same subjects were not involved both times and that 1953-61 comparisons are based on a very small number of cases.

Table 1 presents the sample data from the present study with comparison data from the original sample and the 1953 sample of that sample. One should note the tendency (apparent in 1953) for distortion of mail returns compared with the original sample. Except for the variable of sex, the 1961 sample continues the trend noted in 1953 for the higher socioeconomic groups and the higher IQ groups to respond at a statistically significant (.01) higher rate than others. Except for family status, the classifications are those imposed in 1941 and so represent a status of 20 years previous. Some of these clearly would not change, some might show minimal change, and some, for example, socioeconomic status, might be radically different in 1961. Clearly caution should be exercised in generalizing from this small sample which also might be biased for the major factors under study. The data that follow should be of some value when considered with appropriate reservations.

RESULTS

The responses permitted the assembling of the data in Table 2. The left half of the table is concerned with comparisons of brand preferences for various years. Columns 5, 6, 11, and 12 are similar to the others except that whenever a respondent indicated that the 1941 preference was for a brand not listed, his responses for that product category were excluded. The latter procedure was followed because lumping many unlisted brands together might lead to artificially high correspondences. As the results show, this did not seem to be important in most instances.

Although there are individual differences in amount of preference agreement among the 15 brand categories,

TABLE 2

PERCENTAGES OF AGREEMENT BETWEEN VARIOUS YEARS

	Preferences with preferences						Preferences with use					
	Total sample				Minus "none listed"		Total sample				Minus "none listed"	
Category	1941-53	1941-61	1953-61	Diff. (3-2)	1941-53	1941-61	1941-53	1941-61	1961-61	Diff. (9-8)	1941-53	1941-61
	(1)	(2)	(3)	(4)	(5)	(6)	(7)	(8)	(9)	(10)	(11)	(12)
Coffee	35	31	37	6	33	26	33	35	73	38	27	29
Typewriter	36	26	54	28	38	28	25	23	41	18	25	21
Dept. store	38	33	62	29	38	33	36	26	49	23	36	27
Automobile	24	19	47	23	23	18	20	19	58	39	18	18
Gasoline	33	22	45	23	33	24	29	21	76	55	30	22
Razor	38	39	61	22	51	49	36	38	90	52	50	46
Magazine	36	24	41	17	35	24	32	21	70	49	32	21
Watch	35	29	50	21	35	30	26	27	61	34	22	21
Tooth paste	27	18	44	26	25	16	29	16	85	69	28	14
Soap	31	20	41	21	31	20	30	20	85	65	31	21
Cereal	23	26	46	20	21	25	25	23	80	57	22	22
Bread	31	20	30	10	30	18	23	14	73	59	22	13
Tire	34	29	24	-5	36	32	25	20	59	39	24	18
Gum	29	24	52	28	28	24	28	24	83	59	27	24
Radio	31	24	32	18	38	25	22	23	54	31	22	22
Average	32	26	44	18	32	26	28	23	69	46	27	23

ranges are generally not great. Considering average percentages, 1961 results provide a third point for a trend line. For example, degree of agreement with 1941 data gets smaller the farther one gets from the preferences made as a child. There was 32% agreement between 1941 and 1953 preferences, a drop to 26% between 1941 and 1961, but 44% agreement between 1953 and 1961 (note Columns 4 and 10). The shorter time interval plus the fact that most subjects had reached adult status and possibly answered somewhat more realistically in 1953 than in 1941 might explain the results. Almost the same results were obtained when the "none of those" category was omitted. After 20 years, about one quarter of the subjects who responded prefer the same brands of products preferred as school-age young people.

Even more important is the relationship between preference and use, and as the data in the right half of the table show, nearly the same results as above were obtained. On the average, a little less than one fourth of the subjects say they use the brands in 1961 that they said they preferred in 1941, which is only slightly less than the percentage obtained for 1941-53 time period. These data seem unaffected by eliminating the "none-of-these" category. The data in Column 9 show that there is a very high correspondence between stated preferences and use when both sets of data refer to 1961, although there is variation from 41% to 90% for individual products.

It is thought that these results indicate a substantial amount of agreement and loyalty toward brands of products, especially when, as mentioned below, there are "legitimate" reasons for many lacks of correspondence. Consideration of what degree of agreement is high is partly judgmental. For instance, it might be argued that heavy concentrations of preferences or usages artificially increase degrees of agreement. It is true that these are not spread equally across brands or across products. However, there is nothing to prohibit changes in preference (and often, use). Furthermore, in the case of use, if one brand has a high share of the market so that shifts in and out of the market are *minimal*, this is only supporting evidence of strong loyalty obtained from data external to the present study. At any rate, inspection of the data indicates that in only four cases was either preference or use for any yearly comparisons concentrated in one category more than 50% of the time, and there were relatively few cases where the concentration exceeded 40%.

Whenever there was a discrepancy between 1961 preference and use, the subjects were asked to indicate the reason on a prepared check list. Such a procedure can result in rationalized and perfunctory answers, and even carefully probed personal interviewing realizes difficulties isolating "real" motivations. However, the data presented in Table 3 do permit some tentative conclusions.

TABLE 3

REASONS FOR DISCREPANCIES BETWEEN
1961 PREFERENCE AND 1961 USE

Someone else decided on brand used; got as a gift	23.60%
Difference in price overrides preference	16.13
Don't use, don't own, don't buy	14.87
Not sold around here, no such store, just can't get	7.47
Inconvenience in getting brand or to place where available	7.00
Have no real preference, just don't care	3.47
Bought to please someone else, husband, wife, etc.	3.33
Haven't yet had chance to change to preferred brand	2.53
Difference in quality	2.33
Others (less than 2% each): dealer relationships (likes or dislikes, personal friend or relative), get more prestige where friends buy or go, special premiums, just likes variety, has charge account, don't know	4.87
Confused answers and reasons	6.73
No answer-omission	7.07
Total	99.40

The data presented are averaged percentages using small and variable Ns (those where there is disagreement between 1961 preference and use; Ns

between 16 and 96). The primary reasons for discrepancies vary a great deal among some product categories. The fourth and fifth reasons listed seem especially legitimate because some of the brands listed in 1941 no longer exist (Packard, Collier's) or are local brand names that subjects, distant from their original homes, cannot buy. Most discrepancies are for "good" reasons, at least half of them being "unavoidable." Therefore, in the absence of special limiting conditions, stated preferences provide pretty fair indications of likely purchasing behavior.

A number of variables often related to attitudes that are routinely checked were analyzed in relation to preferences given in 1941 and 1961. Again, average percentages were computed with no attempt to alter the automatic weights from obtained numbers of cases.

The data in Table 4 vary to some degree with those found in 1953. Here, the differences between the obtained percentages and the expected percentages in terms of size of the group are negligible with one or two exceptions. It does appear that more of the high economic group than the low have loyalty in terms of expectation, and that slightly more of the older subjects have loyalty. In both cases the differences are small, even though the former is significant at the 5% level and the latter significant at the 1% level. Some of the comparisons by individual products result in differences, but they are not large as a rule, nor do they seem to be consistent with expectations (e.g., higher socioeconomic group more likely to have higher agreements for expensive products such as automobiles or watches). In the light of these data, it would not seem as if degree of loyalty is a function of these variables.

Finally, it was thought important to ascertain the degree of loyalty within subjects across brands to determine whether there might be some persons who were generally loyal, and others for whom there was little or no loyalty. For

TABLE 4

AVERAGE PERCENTAGE AGREEMENT
BETWEEN 1941-61 PREFERENCES BY
STANDARD VARIABLES

Variable	Obtained	Expected
Sex		
Males	55	55
Females	45	45
Socioeconomic status		
High	68	64
Low	32	36
Age		
Young	33	40
Middle	32	30
Old	34	31
Intelligence		
High	30	30
Middle	58	58
Low	12	12
Marital status (1952)		
Married (few children)	54	55
Married (many children)	10	7
Unmarried	36	37
Marital status (1961)		
Married (few children)	57	57
Married (many children)	32	33
Unmarried	10	11

each subject, there were 15 opportunities to display loyalty, both for 1941-61 preferences, and for 1941-61 preferences and use. The results indicate that loyalty is not a general characteristic of persons but rather of brands and products, and these are different for different persons. Not many subjects have few or no agreements for the 15 categories, and few have loyalties for brands for over half the products. For the 1941-61 preference comparison, the median number of agreements is 3.53 (mode = 3, range from 0 − 9), and for the 1941 preference and 1961 use comparison,

the median number of agreements is 3.13 (mode = 3, range from 0 − 8). In spite of the inability to be consistent in some cases because of the demise or unavailability of some brands, the number of agreements per person is relatively high, especially with use. It should be remembered that these subjects could hardly have inflated their agreements purposely since they would not likely have remembered what they said in 1941 in response to the questions.

CONCLUSIONS

It is surprising how much correspondence exists between the results of the 1953 study and the present follow-up. Hence, these conclusions are almost replications of those reached earlier.

This 20-year follow-up presents suggestive evidence that there is a rather high degree of loyalty toward brand names, especially where special considerations such as unavailability, price considerations, and the respondent not being the primary purchaser, do not play a major part in brand selection. After a lapse of 20 years, with preferences originally being verbally expressed during the ages of 7 through 18, there is an average amount of agreement between early and current preferences of 26%. The average degree of agreement between 1941 preferences and 1961 use is slightly less, 23%.

In the present study there is little indication that sex, intelligence, or marital status is related to preference agreements, and only slight indication that a few more subjects in the higher socioeconomic status groups have greater preference agreements. Opposed to the 1953 results, it does appear that the older subjects have more agreements than the younger ones, perhaps because original preferences might have been more rational. There still is no indication that there is a general loyalty factor in people. Rather it appears that it is related to specific products and brands, as well as to special pressures impinging upon people. Although most people can be changed and do change over a long period of time, the results of this study show that even early childhood experiences exert considerable influence upon later brand purchasing behavior. The implications for other preference areas should be clear.

REFERENCES

Cunningham, R. Brand loyalty: What, where, how much? *Harv. Bus. Rev.*, 1956, **34**, 116-128.

Guest, L. The genesis of brand awareness. *J. appl. Psychol.*, 1942, **26**, 800-808.

Guest, L. A study of brand loyalty. *J. appl. Psychol.*, 1944, **28**, 16-27.

Guest, L. Brand loyalty: Twelve years later. *J. appl. Psychol.*, 1955, **39**, 405-408.

6. Prepurchase Behavior of Buyers of Small Electrical Appliances

JON G. UDELL

This article summarizes the results of a study of shopping behavior in the selection of small electrical appliances during December, 1964.

The primary objective was to gather data on the *types of information* and *sources of information* that consumers use in shopping for small appliances.

A second objective was to determine the extent and significance of *out-of-store shopping* and *in-store shopping* leading to the purchase. Out-of-store shopping includes all searching and information gathering which occurs outside the retail store, such as reading or listening to advertisements and discussing with other people the merits of various product and patronage alternatives. In-store shopping is the gathering of information by visiting a store or number of stores.

THE SURVEY

The two principal difficulties were to identify a representative sample of persons who had purchased a small electrical appliance, and to secure personal interviews with the selected respondents shortly after the date of purchase.

Because many small appliances are purchased as gifts, personal interviews could not be conducted within the purchasers' homes prior to Christmas. Rather than wait until after Christmas or

From *Journal of Marketing,* Vol. 30, No. 4 (October, 1966), pp. 50-52, by permission of The American Marketing Association.

use a mail questionnaire, personal interviews were conducted in retail stores immediately following the purchase of an appliance.

Interviewers were stationed in the small electrical-appliance departments of four Madison, Wisconsin, stores — including downtown, west-side, and east-side shopping center stores, that is, the major geographical areas. The areas north and south of the downtown area are comprised mainly of lakes. The stores included in the study represented the major types of retailers handling small appliances.

In the three weeks preceding Christmas, 770 shoppers were asked to be interviewed, with 705 (90%) cooperating.

Small electrical appliances up to $75 in price were included in the sample. Six products — radios, hair dryers, toasters, coffee makers, electric can openers, and irons — accounted for almost one-half the appliances bought; and 65% of the purchased appliances were priced from $7.51 to $22.51.

As for the respondents: 95% were from 19 to 65 years of age; 75% were married; 60% were males and 40% were females.

OUT-OF-STORE SHOPPING

Out-of-store sources of information are *controllable* or *noncontrollable*. Controllable sources are those that manufacturers and retailers can influence or control to a substantial degree, such as advertising. Noncontrollable sources are those over which manufacturers and retailers usually have little or no control, such as discussions about products with friends and relatives.

Direct questions were used to secure data on sources of information, on the assumption that the information requested was not strongly associated with social-psychological factors that might induce biased responses. Although this could be a limitation of the study, the apparent frankness and excellent cooperation of the respondents indicated that the direct-questioning approach was appropriate.

An inability to remember may have resulted in a considerable understatement of shopping activity, especially activity related to out-of-store influences and sources of information. However, respondents clearly indicated that advertising and other out-of-store sources of information played a very important role in their shopping behavior.

The respondents were asked if they remembered getting *helpful* information from any sources of information in shopping for the appliance bought. They were also asked which of the sources (that they had mentioned) was *most useful* in providing shopping information.

Advertising in printed media was the most frequently mentioned *controllable source* in shopping for the appliances. As shown in the table, the most frequently mentioned advertising medium was the newspaper. Mail-order catalogs and circulars were mentioned second most frequently. A majority of the consumers indicated that some type of advertising was helpful in shopping for the purchased appliance.

The *most useful controllable sources* of information were mail-order catalogs and newspaper advertising. Respondents who had purchased at Sears selected mail-order catalogs as most useful more frequently than those purchasing elsewhere; the latter indicated

OUT-OF-STORE SOURCES OF INFORMATION

Sources of information	% finding helpful[a]	% finding most useful[b]
Controllable:		
Newspaper advertising	25.0	9.6
Mail-order catalogs and circulars	20.7	10.2
Magazine advertising	15.0	2.4
Television advertising	14.2	3.7
Radio advertising	7.0	0.4
Noncontrollable:		
Past experience with the product brand	50.2	33.2
Discussions with friends, relatives, neighbors	33.9	18.7
Consumer rating magazines (e.g., *Consumer Reports*)	9.1	3.0
Telephone calls to stores	3.5	1.0

[a] Percentages do not total 100% because many respondents mentioned more than one source of information; in addition, the less frequently mentioned sources are not shown in the table.
[b] There were 10% who could not recall obtaining helpful information from any source of information other than visiting a store.

that newspaper advertising was the most useful controllable source.

The most frequently mentioned and *most useful noncontrollable source* of information was past experience with product or brand. One-half found it to be helpful, and one-third said it was most useful. In addition, a substantial number of the respondents indicated that discussions with friends and relatives were helpful in shopping for their purchased appliance.

The role of out-of-store sources of information varied considerably with the demographic characteristics of the respondents. Married persons, particularly married women, mentioned newspaper advertising more frequently than single persons. Single persons, especially single women, mentioned television advertising and magazine advertising more frequently than the married respondents. In fact, television advertising was the most frequently mentioned advertising medium by single women.

Single persons mentioned discussions with friends and relatives more frequently than married persons; for example, 44% of the single men as compared with 28% of the married men mentioned discussions. Past experience with products and brands was mentioned most frequently by the single women and married men.

Families with incomes ranging from $7,500 to $10,000 mentioned newspaper advertising most frequently, and families with incomes below $3,000 mentioned this medium least frequently.

THE DECISION TO BUY

Respondents were asked *when they had tentatively decided to buy* the product which they bought, even though they might not have been sure of such things as the model, brand, and price. There were 83% who bought within one month, 50% within one week, and 22% on the same day they made their tentative purchase decision.

The men respondents indicated that they carried out their decision to purchase an appliance earlier than the women. For example, one-fourth of the male respondents purchased on the day of the decision to buy, in contrast to less than one-fifth of the women.

Respondents also were asked whether their purchase decision was made before, during, or after visiting any stores to look at the product bought. *Most of the purchases (73%) were planned prior to shopping in a store* — with 13% making their decision during their first store visit, and 13% after visiting a retail store (1% could not recall).

High-income purchasers were more likely to make their purchase decisions prior to visiting the retail store — 85% of those with annual family incomes over $15,000 made prior decisions to buy. Also, more women (79%) than men (69%), and more married (74%) than single respondents (69%), tentatively had decided to buy prior to visiting a store.

Planning to purchase prior to visiting a store was most prevalent among consumers who purchased items priced from $27.51 to $32.51.

READINESS TO PURCHASE

The respondents who indicated that they had made a tentative decision to buy before shopping in a store were asked, "When you went to a store for the first time, did you feel that you were ready to buy on the basis of information which you already had?" *Almost two-thirds (65%) of the purchasers believed that they had sufficient information and were ready to buy when they made their first visit to a retail store.*

Readiness to purchase during the first store visit was more prevalent among respondents earning $15,000 or more than any other income group.

IN-STORE SHOPPING

Nearly 60% of the respondents had shopped for the small appliance only in the store where the purchase was made. There were 16% who said they had shopped in the store of purchase and one additional store, and 22% in three or more stores. The remaining 2% could not recall how many stores they had visited.

There was a direct relationship between the price of the item purchased and number of stores visited. Only 28% of the purchasers of inexpensive small appliances ($7.50 or less) shopped in two or more stores, whereas 63% of the purchasers of appliances costing over $50.00 shopped in two or more stores.

There was no difference in the number of stores visited by men and women shoppers. However, more single respondents (48%) than married respondents (38%) shopped in more than one store; and those with higher levels of education tended to shop in more stores than those with less education.

The number of stores visited was negatively correlated with age. Of 173 purchasers less than 25 years of age, 52% shopped in two or more stores, whereas 37% of those over 25 years shopped in more than one store.

NUMBER OF VISITS

The majority of respondents (77%) had visited the store of purchase only once, 19% made two visits, and 4% made three or more trips. *Apparently a shopper is not likely to examine a small appliance, leave the store without buying it, and return at a later time to make the purchase.* Using the statistics of this study, there is only a 23% probability that this will occur.

The probability of occurrence is even lower if the shopper's family income is below $5,000 or above $10,000, or if the shopper is over 50 years of age. If the commodity involved is priced at less than $7.50, there is only a 3% probability that the potential purchaser will not buy during an initial visit but will return to purchase at a later date.

However, the probability of this occurring increases progressively as the value of the item increases. In fact, 57% of those buying an appliance costing over $50.00 made more than one visit to the store of purchase.

OBTAINING INFORMATION

Interviewers stated to respondents: "There are two major methods of getting information on stores, products, and prices. The first is to visit a store or stores. The second includes discussions with friends, the use of advertised information, the use of catalogs, and all additional sources other than visiting stores."

Respondents were then asked to indicate which general method was most helpful in shopping for the purchased appliance. "Visiting stores" was most helpful for 57% of the respondents, and "sources other than visiting stores" for 30%. There were 8% who stated that the two methods were equally helpful, and 5% of the respondents did not know which method of shopping was most helpful.

IMPLICATIONS

Both availability of shopping information and desire for convenience probably account for many of the shopping patterns revealed in this study.

In any event, it appears that the typical consumer does *not* go from store to store to gather information and to compare products and prices when shopping for small electrical appliances. He or she prefers to do much of this searching and shopping in the comfort of the home by using out-of-store sources of information, especially past experience with products and brands, discussions with friends, and printed media advertising.

This was especially true of those purchasers with higher levels of education and income. Perhaps out-of-store shopping with only one visit to the retail store is likely to become more prevalent as levels of education and income rise.

D. INDUSTRIAL BUYERS

7. Motives in Industrial Buying

GEORGE M. ROBERTSON

At the request of its subscribers, the Industrial Advertising Research Institute undertook a study of "Motives in Industrial Buying." This was an experimental project applying some techniques of motivation research to industrial purchasing. I served as chairman of the Project Council.

Our objectives were:

1. To determine whether the techniques of motivation research can be used effectively in the industrial field. And the findings indicate that the newer indirect techniques studied can be used as effectively as conventional direct questioning. Respondents were equally cooperative and complete in their answers to the two types of questions.

2. To determine the extent to which the newer indirect methods of motivation research improve upon conventional methods in obtaining industrial marketing information.

3. To determine some of the underlying or hidden reasons for making industrial buying decisions.

I would like to share with you the studies which we did on behalf of our second and third objectives. This material will, I believe, enable you to make some interesting comparisons between conventional direct questioning and the newer indirect techniques usually asso-

From *Dynamic Marketing for a Changing World*, edited by Robert S. Hancock (Chicago: American Marketing Association, 1959), pp. 26-76.

ciated with motivation research. The findings may give you:

1. Some insights as to whether the newer techniques are actually an improvement upon traditional questioning; and

2. Whether the indirect methods really disclose any hidden motives — any additional information about the buyers' motives, ideas, and attitudes, and their images of suppliers' products and their companies.

In selecting the techniques to be tested by this study, we chose those that might be generally used by industrial marketers who might want to undertake their own surveys from time to time. Depth interviewing, of course, had been proved practical over a number of years; so had some of the other so-called motivation methods. It was agreed at the outset that such devices as thematic apperception tests, Rorschach ink-blot tests, or strictly clinical methods requiring advanced psychological treatment and administration would not be used. Such techniques would be impractical in most surveys which industrial advertisers might conduct.

With these things in mind, we selected the following motivation research techniques for testing:

1. *Balloons* — as in comic strips. The respondent projects himself into one of the characters and either agrees with

what is said, or fills in an empty balloon with what he would say.

2. *Projections to Other Persons* — as a sales executive evaluating salesmen's excuses.

3. *Agree-Disagree Attitudes* — expressions of attitudes through the medium of agreement or lack of agreement with individual statements.

4. *Adjective Choice* — expression of attitude toward a person or company through the medium of selection of applicable adjectives from a long list.

5. *Depth Probing* — questions in series to discover underlying attitudes.

Our approach was to parallel indirect questioning with direct questioning. In other words, each indirect question would have a parallel direct question. Thus, the two techniques could be compared.

Our sample was 58 key buying influences — purchasing agents, engineers, production men, and executives — in 24 companies. They represented four industries and eight classes of products. Those interviewed were divided into two groups. Half of the questions asked of each person were direct questions, and the other half, indirect. However, the questions which were asked directly of one person were asked indirectly of the second. As a result of this approach, we could compare direct and indirect questioning without having to ask each person the same question twice — once as a direct question and again as an indirect question. The interviews were conducted by trained industrial interviewers from the staff of Stewart, Dougall & Associates.

Before we review some of the major findings of this study, let me remind you of two things. First, this was an experimental study — a pilot study employing certain techniques relatively new to industrial buying studies. Secondly, this was a qualitative — not a quantitative — study. Moreover, unresolved problems of interpretation do exist. These factors in no way detract from the value or use-fulness of this study. They simply put the findings into proper perspective so that they can be used with telling effectiveness.

To provide comparative testing of indirect versus direct interviewing techniques, we decided to operate both approaches within a group of eight factors which would be illustrative of the type of resistances or aids met in typical selling conditions and fairly common to different products and different kinds of customers. These were:

Attitudes toward suppliers
Fixed loyalty to certain suppliers
Specific factors in buying decisions
Effect of supplier size
Effect of supplier location
Effect of private versus public ownership
Attitudes about sales and service
Attitudes toward salesmen

Since there isn't space to report our findings on all of the newer indirect questioning techniques and the underlying or hidden reasons behind buying decisions which they revealed, I'll just cover four situations in some detail.

Using the balloon technique, we wanted to see what clues or insights motivations research might give us about the loyalty of buyers to certain suppliers. How many times have you heard a buyer say something like this: "We've been buying motors from Smith for ten years, and we aren't about to change." Here, we wanted to see if motivation research could tell us if buyers like this really meant what they said — that there wasn't a Chinaman's chance of getting their business because of such fixed loyalties. Therefore, a direct question was asked of one-half of the respondents.

Question: As far as you personally are concerned, do you feel it's better to stay with the old suppliers or to make changes from time to time?
Answer: Eighteen said stay with old

suppliers; nine said change from time to time.

On the other half of the respondents, we used a motivational question of the projective type. Respondents were shown a cartoon as the interviewer said:

This shows a conference that's in progress. The purpose of the meeting is the periodic review of suppliers.

As we look in on the conference, Pete is saying:

Now this is our present supplier list. We've been with them for quite a while and they've been doing a good job. I see no reason for making any changes. The next subject is . . .

While Tom interrupts to say:

Hold on Pete . . . Loyalty is fine, but there are a lot of other considerations. I think we're due for a change.

And the interviewer said:

In this case, with which man would you be in most agreement? Why is that?

Answer: Ten said, "I see no reason for making any changes." Thirteen said, "I think we're due for a change." Eight said, "Neither." 2 didn't answer.

Here, we see a reversal. By indirect questioning, more people agreed with the idea of change than held for no change. In other words, 13 versus 10, and of the total, less than one-third indicated a strong supplier loyalty. The atmosphere, then, would be one of open-mindedness, of willingness to listen to change. Therefore, in only one case out of three would the salesman encounter serious entrenched loyalty. And the conclusion would seem to be that the indirect approach provides a better measure of this resistance than the factual, direct method.

Another of the newer techniques selected for testing was adjective choice — expression of attitude towards a person or company through the medium of selection of applicable adjectives from a long list. For this test, we chose the selling situation involving positive and negative attitudes towards suppliers. These are the prejudgment factors which the salesman meets upon arrival and which may be a barrier to overcome or a wave of good will on which to ride. We wanted to know the extent to which such prejudgments exist pro or con and something of their nature.

To obtain an insight as to the positive attitudes towards suppliers, we asked half of the respondents this direct question: "Are there any suppliers about whom you have a more favorable attitude than others, in any respect? Why?"

In reply to this direct question, these buying influences indicated that suppliers about whom they had favorable attitudes provided in this order:

1. Superior engineering and research
2. High quality products
3. Superior service

Good delivery, good cooperation, and superior salesmen were next in order, and each received the same rating. Other responses ranged all the way from superior personnel to good management.

On the other half of the respondents, we used the indirect approach. They were handed a card containing this list of 45 adjectives, and the interviewer said:

Now think of a supplier toward which you have a naturally favorable reaction. Got one? Now would you go over this list quickly, giving me the numbers of the words that best describe your feelings toward this company?

The largest number of respondents said that "competent" best described their feelings toward the supplier. Next in order of rank were dependable, aggressive, alert, flexible, and intelligent.

To summarize, we find that direct questioning concerning positive and negative attitudes brings out specific factors such as price, quality, and delivery. However, indirect techniques appear to indicate that there are other images of selling companies in the mind of the buyer. The indirect techniques also seem to indicate that the buyer is concerned as to whether the seller is genuinely interested in the buyer's problems. Additionally, there are many more favorable attitudes towards sellers than unfavorable. In effect, then, the seller is mainly working in a market which is favorable to him rather than one which is unfavorable.

Of course, there is the problem of secondary interpretation. Just what does this list of adjectives mean? One interpretation might be that the buyer thinks favorably of the seller on whom he can depend for help in solving his problems. The buyer wants a competent, dependable, reliable product, but he also wants a seller that can keep up with the ever-changing needs and market—an alert, flexible, intelligent supplier who is aggressive.

The third of the newer interviewing techniques that we wanted to take a reading on was "projection to other persons." Here, a series of actions or things to be done by a person are listed and the respondent is asked to describe the kind of person who did do such things or act in such a way. The basic assumption is that the respondent reveals something of his own personality, his own ideas, motives, wishes, and attitudes by "projecting" himself into the test situation. This technique was tested in another typical sales situation; namely, the key or catalyzing factors which produce the ultimate decision to buy. In other words, what is it that finally determines where to place the order?

In this test, the direct question asked of one-half of the buying influences studied was as follows:

When you're making decisions as to what suppliers will get the business and so forth, what would you generally consider to be the deciding factors that tipped the scales in the final analysis?

For the indirect approach, the interviewer said this to the other half of the buying influences:

I'd like also to discuss supplier sales representation. Here's a short list of excuses a salesman might use on his boss in explaining why he's not making quota. If you were a sales manager, how would you consider these excuses? That is, would you generally say that they were acceptable or unacceptable?

The list included six excuses of which I'll read just the first. "It's not me—it's the factory. If those people would just keep delivery promises, it would help out a lot." The deciding factor here, of course, is "delivery."

The important difference between the two methods is the ranking of price in the purchase decision. Based on direct questioning, price ranked 2nd, while as a result of indirect questioning, it ranked 7th. It may be that because of methodology, the relative rankings of price by the two methods are not quite accurate. Regardless of this, however, it is abundantly clear in both instances that price is *not* the most important final factor and that the final decision may arise from one of several factors. Certainly, quality and performance rank high in both techniques, as does delivery, which ranked first in indirect and 3rd on direct.

As every sales manager knows, a major factor in the purchase of an industrial product is the personalities of the people involved in the purchase decision. For this reason, our Council decided to explore the personality traits of individuals to see what we could learn through the use of direct and indirect methods to discover the existence or absence of six personality traits which might be factors. The six traits chosen for study were:

Superior phobia — a fear of the boss.

Preconceptions — a lack of open-mindedness.

Inertia — a lack of agressiveness and cooperation.

Undue influence of associates — a similar hesitancy to express opinions in disagreement with associates, coupled with a tendency to accept their opinions without question.

Shoulder-chips — a semi-belligerent attitude at the start.

Inadequate knowledge — a tendency to prejudge due to lack of information or to misunderstanding.

Two techniques were used to rate each of the 58 buying influences interviewed. In the direct approach, professional interviewers, trained in executive and management interviewing, had to decide whether or not each of the six traits was present in the respondent's personality. For the indirect technique, executives accepted or rejected each of five representative excuses a salesman might give to explain to his sales manager why he did not make a sale. This is typical of the excuses. "I feel with this company that their minds are made up in advance before I go in there." The personality trait involved here is, of course, preconceptions — a lack of open-mindedness. Our approach was this: If a buyer being interviewed agreed with a salesman's explanation, it was assumed that, to some degree, his personality included the trait implicit in the so-called excuse.

In the direct approach, then, the interviewers rated each respondent; while in the indirect approach, respondents, in effect, rated themselves by agreeing or disagreeing with the salesmen's excuses.

The frequency of the traits based on respondents' answers can be contrasted to the interviewers' observations. Respondents disclosed a much higher frequency than do interviewers' observations. Only 14 per cent of the respondents disclosed no bad traits while the interviewers judged that 42 per cent had no bad traits. This would appear to indicate that direct observation is not too good a measure of the extent or frequency of personality factors entering into the purchase decision.

Now let's look at the findings concerning specific personality traits. The percentage of respondents who appear to have each of the personality traits under study may be indicated — superior phobia, 52 per cent; preconceptions, 50 per cent, etc. This percentage is based on combining the objective rating of the interviewer with the number of respondents revealing the trait through the indirect test. In summary then, more than half, or 52 per cent, of the buyers interviewed tended toward "superior phobia." These particular respondents showed, in effect, some degree of fear of having superiors disagree with their actions or opinions. They're afraid of displeasing the boss. This suggests that many buyers are apt to stick to what they think management wants rather than to recommend what, in their judgment, is best. The significance of this trait is further emphasized when you note that 39 per cent of the respondents had a similar hesitancy to express opinions in disagreement with their associates.

Another observation is that in selling an industrial product, the seller must keep in mind the personality factors of those having buying influence. It would appear that providing product information is not sufficient in all cases to make a sale. A seller must advertise and sell "up and down the line" in a buying company's hierarchy. He must reassure the decision-maker that the choice is right, and he must, through personal and mass selling, overcome some of the resistance factors in the personalities of the buyers.

This experimental study of "Motives in Industrial Buying" raised a number of questions for industrial marketers; gave clues or answers to some of them; left other questions unresolved. It has been suggested that I comment on "Where do we go from here?" I believe these questions chart the course for us.

1. Does your marketing "sell" your company as well as its products?

— The report indicates that the image of the company may be intermixed with the image of the product and its features. To be more specific, let me ask the question this way: Does your *advertising* sell your company as well as its products? The significance of this question was underscored in the findings of a corporate image study in which my own company participated recently. Witness this excerpt:

> The communications challenge coming out of this study is to provide buying influences with information that ranges beyond the product area. One implication, it appears, would be for General Electric to seek out opportunities to convey more than a product image through its advertising.

I'm sure that you see the challenge which this has for marketing people — to suggest in specific terms various ways of depicting a broader image of our company through its product advertising and in this way to make our advertising work harder — make it more productive.

2. Do you emphasize a variety of reasons for buying the product?

— The report indicates that no one reason for buying is a major appeal to more than a third of its buyers.

3. Does your marketing, including advertising, communicate with *all* of the people who influence purchasing in their companies?

— The findings show that, on the average, six persons are concerned with an industrial purchase. Does your marketing effort reach all of them, one way or another?

In this area, however, there are several unresolved questions. For example, shouldn't we, as individual marketers, know something about the relative importance of each of the six people that are involved in an industrial purchase? And, in each of these six minds, what is the relative importance of the rational and irrational factors which we know enter into the decision? For instance, is the rank order of these factors the same for a purchasing agent as for an engineer?

4. Does your marketing reassure the final decision-maker that he has made the right purchase?

— The findings indicate that the final decision-maker in a purchase is influenced by his superiors and his associates. He "wants" to be reassured that he has made the right decision.

5. Is your marketing "product-oriented" or "customer-oriented?"

— This report indicates that "price," "quality," "product features," and "delivery" are not the only factors entering into a purchase decision. Buyers are individuals with underlying attitudes, images, prejudices, etc.

While we're exploring this area, let me remind you that our study of positive and negative attitudes towards suppliers indicated that the buyers want to do business with suppliers who can keep up with the ever-changing needs of the market — alert, flexible, intelligent suppliers who are aggressive. Our unresolved problem here would be how do we communicate to buyers that we are alert, or flexible, or intelligent?

6. Does your marketing, and particularly your direct selling, take into account the fact that buyers are *people* —

that they have many different types of personalities—that they have the same biological needs, and psychological drives, urges, and desires as you and I? Some of us are inclined to forget that buyers are human beings. At least, a recent issue of *Grey Matter* seemed to think so, for it said, and I quote:

Even many decision-makers in marketing and advertising have become so engrossed with mechanical thinking that their primary interest—people—has receded into the background.

They talk of 'mass markets and mass minds.' They focus on statistics, 'mechanical brains,' charts, graphs.

The findings of our study indicate that there are various personality factors which must be considered and, perhaps, overcome before a sale can be made. In our study of personality traits, you'll recall that superior phobia—fear of the boss—bobbed up most frequently—52 per cent. And preconceptions was second in order of frequency. The question is how do we overcome these and other bad personality traits? Perhaps our sales training should include some instruction in basic personality characteristics and how to deal with them. At General Electric, we have developed a Sales Situation Analysis Course for this express purpose—and our sales engineers think it's wonderful.

8. Marketing Organizations in the Defense/Space Industry

HEROLD A. SHERMAN

INTRODUCTION

The purpose of analyzing marketing functions within the Defense/space industry is to compare these functions to industrial marketing practices. Are the marketing capabilities similar? What are the essential differences, if any? What are the implications of converting Defense/space industries to industrial pursuits? What are the organizational problems facing a Defense/space marketing organization? Answers to these questions will be developed in this paper.

RESEARCH – SAMPLE AND METHOD

The sample for the research was 20 major prime contractors. Of the 20, fifteen were in the top 25 firms contracting to DOD and NASA. The total annual sales of these firms was over $31 billion in 1964. The 20 firms are arbitrarily divided into three groups – aerospace, electronics, and diversified. The criterion is simply to group, as "aerospace," the old airframe companies; as "electronics," firms producing primarily electronic components and electronic systems; the "diversified" group is identified as corporations whose Defense/space business accounts for less than 25 per cent of the firm's total re-

venue, but still is substantial enough to place them on the list of 100 top prime contractors.[1]

Over 100 clinical interviews were held at various corporate, group, and division headquarters throughout this country. In addition, interviews were held at SUD in France, British Aircraft Corporation in England, Fiat in Italy, and SABCA and M.B.L.E. in Belgium.

CONCEPTUAL FRAMEWORK

To provide a conceptual framework for a comparative evaluation of marketing capabilities, let us use the managerial functions of marketing.[2] These functions are shown in Figure 1. The right side of this figure shows comparable functions as performed by Defense/space marketing organizations. These are:

- *Market delineation* – executed in the market planning and research department.
- *Purchase motivation* – not formally the responsibility of any department.
- *Product adjustment* – performed primarily in an advanced engineering or development group.
- *Physical distribution* or channels

From Proceedings of the American Marketing Association, *New Directions in Marketing*, edited by Frederick E. Webster, Jr. (Chicago: American Marketing Assn., 1965), pp. S-23 – S-37. Footnotes have been renumbered.

[1]"Top 100 Defense Contractors FY 1964," *Defense Industry Bulletin*, Vol. I, No. 4 (Washington, D.C.: Department of Defense, April, 1965), p. 8.
[2]Thomas A. Staudt and Donald A. Taylor, *A Managerial Introduction to Marketing* (Englewood Cliffs, New Jersey: Prentice-Hall, Inc., 1965), pp. 17-25.

FIGURE 1

THE MANAGERIAL FUNCTIONS OF MARKETING RELATED
TO THE DEFENSE/SPACE MARKETING ORGANIZATION

Managerial Functions of Marketing   *Defense/Space Marketing Organizations*

- Market Delineation   ⇒   Market Planning and Research
- Purchase Motivation   ⇒   Not Formally Performed
- Product Adjustment   ⇒   Advanced Engineering (or Development)
                                     RFP Sets Product Parameters
                                     Meet Teaming Requirements

- Physical Distribution   ⇒   Performed Only by Component Manufacturers
- Communications   ⇒   Performed Many Places Using Varied
    Advertising   Techniques
    Sales
    Public Relations
- Transaction   ⇒   Contract Administration
- Post Transaction   ⇒   Product Support

of distribution—maintained only by some of the component manufacturers.

- *Communications*—in most cases total effort is a "fuzzy" function in the Defense/space industry.

- *Transaction function*—negotiating the sale; called Contract Administration in the Defense/space industry.

- *Post transaction function*—servicing of the product, system, and customer after the sale (usually referred to as product support).

Three of these managerial functions of marketing need a brief explanation.

Purchase motivation (or why the customer selects a particular firm): This function frequently is unappraisable. A post-mortem of bids lost usually discloses opinions for every possible variable. Who really knows? Even when one gets a jump on preparing a proposal, he may get a curve. The recent Request for Proposal (RFP) for the Voyager spacecraft is an example. Many firms had prepared detailed technical data and designs. Then came the RFP, which said, "Answer the following 28 questions in 100,000 words." This leads one to the next function.

Product adjustment: The product or

system parameters are usually established by the RFP or the team leader under current procurement approaches. Matching the product to the market (*product adjustment*) can be achieved conceptually, however, by making a thorough analysis of the "threat." This develops potential "needs" for study and Independent Research and Development (IR&D). When this approach is used, the function is generally a part of the responsibility of market planning and research and/or advanced engineering and development.

Communications: This function in a Defense/space organization presents analytical problems. Analysis reveals that a variety of techniques are utilized. Responsibility is frequently centered in "strange places" as organizational practices oftentimes attempt to hide the communications effort.

RELEVANT FUNCTIONS

Four relevant functions will be discussed: market delineation, communications, transaction, and post transaction. The substance of these functions is shown in Figure 2. This functional analysis of tasks performed in the

FIGURE 2

THE MANAGERIAL FUNCTIONS OF MARKETING RELATED
TO THE DEFENSE/SPACE MARKETING ORGANIZATION

Function

● MARKET DELINEATION   ⇒   MARKET PLANNING AND RESEARCH
   Advertising Research   Market Planning
   Business Economics and   Product Development
      Research
   Product Research   IR and D Marketing
   Sales and Market Research   Systems Analysis

● COMMUNICATIONS   ⇒   COMMUNICATIONS
   Sales Organizations   Field Offices
      Branch Offices   Sales Organization
   Advertising   Advertising
   Public Relations   Public Relations
                                            Capability Brochure
                                            House Organ
                                         Employee Newspaper
                                            Scientific and Technical Journal
                                            Publicity
                                         Proposals
                                         Engineers
                                         Top Level Contacts

● TRANSACTION   ⇒   CONTRACT ADMINISTRATION
   Contract Negotiation Pricing

● POST TRANSACTION   ⇒   PRODUCT SUPPORT
   Product Service   Parts and Spares
   Information Feedback   Modifications
                                         Logistics Management
                                         Field Maintenance and Engineering
                                         Technical Manuals and Training

Defense/space industry indicates some
initial differences.

MARKET PLANNING AND RESEARCH

First, the market planning and research department performs planning,
market development, and, in many
cases, systems analysis using operations
research techniques. In industrial marketing, the delineation function emphasizes advertising research, business
economics, product research, and sales
and market research.[3]

---

[3]Dik Warren Twedt (ed.), *A Survey of Marketing
Research* (Chicago: American Marketing Association, November, 1963), p. 40.

COMMUNICATIONS

In the functional area of communications, the Defense/space industry has
extensive *field office* organizations for
firms marketing to the government.
Sales organizations utilizing a branch
office approach exist only for the component manufacturers. *Advertising* is employed as an effective component in the
communications mix in a limited number of firms. *Public relations* usually
includes the preparation of capability
brochures, house organs, employee
newspapers, possibly a scientific or
technical journal, and publicity. *Proposals* are the major effort to communicate
with the customer organization (pros-

FIGURE 3
TYPICAL ORGANIZATION CHART
MARKET PLANNING AND RESEARCH DEPARTMENT

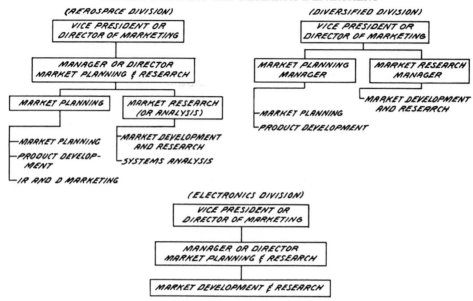

FIGURE 4
MARKET PLANNING AND RESEARCH DEPARTMENTS
(AVERAGE SIZE STAFF)

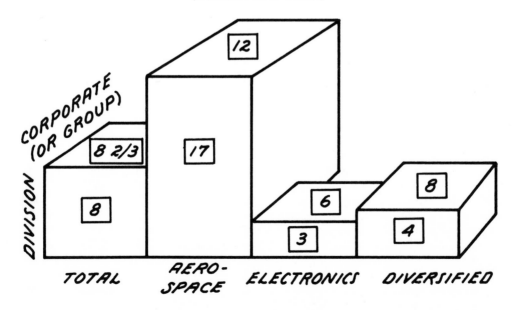

pects) in printed form. The Defense/space industry also practices frequent personal contacts by engineers and top level executives with the customer's organization.

CONTRACT ADMINISTRATION

A contract administration department usually has the responsibility for negotiating the final contract with the customer in the Defense/space industry.

PRODUCT SUPPORT

Product support in the Defense/space industry may include the sale of parts and spares, modifications, logistics management, field maintenance, and engineering, preparation of technical manuals, and the supervision of training for the customer's personnel.

FINDINGS AND GENERALIZATIONS

The empirical research compared marketing functions in the Defense/space industry to industrial marketing practices. It is possible to state several generalizations from this study.

MARKET PLANNING AND RESEARCH

● Aerospace—Larger market planning and research staff. More sophisticated in applying quantitative techniques and operations research.
● Aerospace and Diversified—Marketing responsibility for long-range planning.
Marketing responsibility for unit's total resource allocation plan.
● Electronics—Smaller market planning and research staff. Few sophisticated techniques used (systems divisions excepted).

A composite organization chart (for a division of a company) of the market planning and research department in each of the three groups studied is shown in Figure 3. In the *aerospace* division the manager or director of market planning and research reports to the chief marketing executive. In the *diversified* division there is usually a larger span of control for the chief marketing executive, and one supervisory level is frequently eliminated.

In the *electronics* division the functions of the market planning and research department are primarily market development and research. There is generally little effort expended on planning, product development, IR&D marketing, or systems analysis by the marketing organization. (The systems divisions of electronics firms are sometimes exceptions).

Relative staff sizes in the three groups are summarized in Figure 4. In this summary the corporate or group staffs are shown separately because, in many cases, a large planning staff is retained at corporate or group offices with a small staff at the division level, or vice versa. Looking at the data in this manner, we see that the aerospace group at both the division and corporate levels has a considerably larger average staff size than either of the other groups.

COMMUNICATION

The function of communication (Figure 5 and 6) was the most difficult function to analyze because of the wide variety of practices and the number of components in the "communications mix." The generalizations regarding the components of communications follow.

Field office: A subjective tentative summary shows field offices, which are usually the key to the intelligence network and the bid-pipe of the firm, are more developed in the aerospace group. In electronics firms, field offices are found only in the systems divisions. In these cases the field offices report directly to the division. In the aerospace

FIGURE 5

MARKETING COMMUNICATIONS – GENERALIZATIONS

	Aerospace	Electronic	Diversified
Field Offices	Excellent	Systems Only	Good
Sales Organization	Small	Varies	Good (well-trained)
Advertising	PR Department	Some Marketing Department	Marketing
Proposals	Usually in Engineering	Some in Engineering	Most in Marketing

FIGURE 6

MARKETING COMMUNICATION – GENERALIZATIONS

	Aerospace	Electronic	Diversified
Public Relations	Not Marketing Responsibility	Some Marketing Responsibility	Most Marketing Responsibility
Capability Brochures	Excellent PR and Engineering	Good – Some Marketing Coordination	Excellent Marketing
House Organs	Good PR Department	Good – Some Marketing Coordination	Excellent – PR and Marketing Coordination
Employee Newspapers	Good Personnel Department	Good – Some Marketing Coordination	Varies PR and Personnel
Scientific and Technical Journals	None	Some – With Marketing Coordination	Excellent – PR and Some Marketing
Publicity	PR Department	PR and Marketing	Excellent Marketing

and diversified groups, the field office organization reports to the corporate or group office.

Sales organization: Typically, sales organizations are small in the aerospace group. The staff size of the sales organization varies considerably in the electronics group, depending on systems or component orientation. A significant difference was noted in the diversified group where (in all cases but one) sales personnel were given formal training after the application of standard personnel selection procedures. No formal training for marketing or sales existed in the aerospace or electronic groups.

Advertising: Advertising in the aerospace group is a function of the public relations department. This practice varies in the electronics group. Advertising in the diversified group is a different story. It is usually the responsibility of the marketing organization. One has only to view "Disneyland" on TV to be reminded that "RCA is the greatest name in electronics." Similar campaigns are run by Westinghouse and G.E. In fact, the total advertising expenditures of only six diversified firms – RCA, Westinghouse, G.E., Ford, G.M., and Chrysler – average over $100,000,000 annually per firm. Naturally it is easy to allocate a portion of this to a government-oriented division. The diversified group is certainly using more advertising than the pure aerospace or electronics firms.

Public relations: Public relations is not a marketing responsibility in the aerospace industry. In the electronics group occasionally it is. However, in the diversified group public relations is generally a marketing responsibility.

1. *Capability brochures:* These are usually not prepared by the marketing organization in the aerospace industry, although they may be consulted about them. There is some coordination in electronics, but again in the diversified group this is primarily a function of the marketing organization.

2. *House organs:* House organs are published for external distribution to the customer organization, financial community, stockholders, and the general public. The house organ is coordinated by the marketing organization only in the diversified group.

3. *Employee newspapers:* These publications manage to get wide distribution in the customer's organization because of photographs, articles, and stories. These newspapers are normally the responsibility of the personnel department. However, in the electronics and diversified groups the marketing organization exercises greater coordination than in the aerospace group.

4. *Scientific and technical journals:* The scientific and technical journals published by the firm do not exist in the aerospace group. Some electronics companies have used this technique

most effectively as a communications and promotional device. One firm, for example, receives an average of 2,000 inquiries per issue from the technical journal. An average of 500 sales are made from inquiry follow-ups.

In the diversified group, several firms published technical journals but with little promotional orientation. In both the electronics and diversified groups the scientific journal provides an outlet for publications by scientific personnel. In three companies, articles were solicited by the marketing organization and were keyed specifically to pending sales campaigns or programs.

5. *Publicity:* This is handled by the marketing organization in few of the electronics firms, but is a marketing responsibility in most of the diversified group.

PROPOSALS

The proposal effort is the major technique used to communicate with the customer. Although proposal production costs may account for two to six per cent of annual sales, the aerospace group usually prepares its proposals in the engineering organization. Frequently this communications effort is disguised, or "buried," under "advanced systems" or "advanced development" departments.

In the electronics groups, proposal preparation is the responsibility of marketing in about 50 per cent of the firms. In the diversified group, most proposal efforts are the responsibility of the marketing organization.

FIGURE 7
MARKETING RESPONSIBILITY
(NO. OF FIRMS)

	Aerospace	Electronics	Diversified
Function			
Transaction			
Contract Administration	2	5	5
Post Transaction			
Product Support	1	4	5

FIGURE 8
SUMMARY
WEIGHTED RESPONSIBILITY OF MARKETING ORGANIZATIONS

Function	Aerospace	Electronics	Diversified	Industrial Marketing
Market Delineation (Market Planning and Research)	4*	1	3*	3
Communications Field Office Sales Organization Advertising Public Relations Proposals	(2)	3*	4*	4
Transaction Contract Administration	(1)	3*	3*	4
Post Transaction Follow—On Sales and Service	(1)	3*	3*	4
Total Points	8	10	14	15

*Strengths (3 and 4).
()Weaknesses (1 and 2).

TRANSACTION AND POST TRANSACTION

Marketing's responsibility for the transaction and post transaction functions (Figure 7) is shown by a simple listing of the number of firms where the marketing organization has this responsibility. In the aerospace industry, this is generally not a marketing function. However, in the diversified and electronics groups it usually is.

MARKETING CAPABILITY GROUP ANALYSIS

A comparison of the marketing capability among the three groups for the four relevant functions of the marketing organization discussed are presented in Figure 8. The functions have been assigned an arbitrary weighting. A well-developed marketing organization for a specific function would have a weight of

4. Little or no marketing responsibility for the function would have the weight of 1.

No attempt has been made to weigh the importance of the separate functions, although intuitively the market delineation and communications functions are probably much more important than the latter two. The point totals by group are: aerospace group—8, electronics group—10, diversified group—14.

In summary it appears that marketing organizations in the aerospace group have strength only in the area of market planning and research. The same area is a weakness in the electronics group. The diversified group, possibly because of the influence of the marketing organization in the parent firm, has a more developed marketing organization and has strength in all areas, particularly communications.

FIGURE 9
INDUSTRIAL MARKETING CAPABILITY

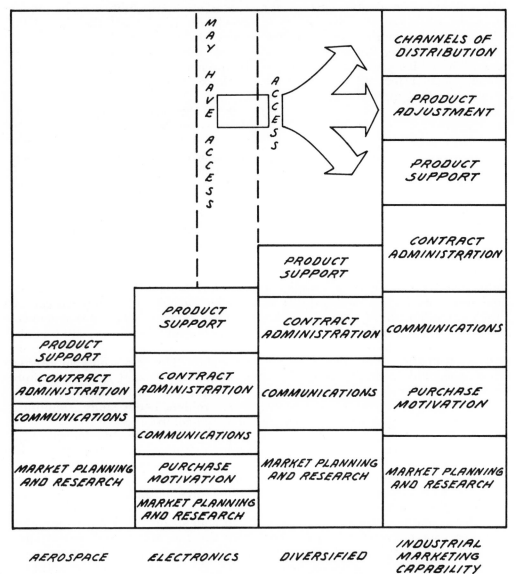

The data may also be viewed by listing the managerial marketing functions performed by each industry group and comparing this to industrial marketing capability. The results are shown in Figure 9.

The aerospace group doesn't have it! The electronics group has industrial marketing capability only if they are strongly diversified in their component or production areas.

The diversified group is not only stronger by itself, but, having direct access to channels of distribution and the ability to adjust the product to the market (using the parent firm), has a total industrial marketing capability.

Again, it is important to recognize that

these functions are not weighted according to their importance as components of the marketing organization. For example, while the aerospace group is efficient in developing capability brochures and turning out excellent proposals, it is highly unlikely that these communications techniques would have much industrial application.

CONCLUSION

Marketing capabilities of Defense/space firms, then, are *not equal* to industry if analyzed functionally. Essential differences exist.

CONVERSION

The aerospace group can't convert to industrial markets because sufficient and necessary marketing capability is lacking. Incidentally, *all* the aerospace firms in the study indicated they aren't interested in industrial markets anyway.

The electronics group has been the most successful in diversifying. Many firms have corporate staffs to make acquisitions: however, most acquisitions have been Defense/space oriented firms.

As far as the diversified group's converting, there is a definite potential for application of technology and fall-out to the parent organization. However, the findings in the diversified group indicate that marketing executives in these firms are not conversion-inclined because the sole purpose of their charter by group or division is to penetrate and diversify *into* the government market. Their performance as a group is evaluated partially on the success of this penetration.

PROBLEMS

Marketing capability can be developed. As first steps, the "problem" areas characteristic of many Defense/space marketing organizations should be improved.

These problem areas are:

● *Communications*—too infrequently there is no "mix concept," or little or no coordination between public relations, advertising, and the marketing organization.

● *Selection*—usually there is no rhyme or reason to the selection of marketing or sales personnel.

● *Training*—there is little or no training given new employees or engineering personnel transferred to the marketing organization.

● *Interfacing*—the typical individual in a Defense/space marketing organization has so many "faces" that a sociometric map would have to be computerized to permit analysis of the marketing organization. This is not only an internal problem, but in many instances a problem with the customer organization. This problem needs study, simplification, and control.

● *Evaluation*—finally, for the marketing organization to attain status and stature, techniques—effective techniques—must be developed for evaluating individual and group performance.

In conclusion, all of these problems, plus the functional weaknesses noted earlier, require correction or improvement. When a marketing organization has a total capability, it can become both effective and efficient—requisites to implementation of a "marketing concept."

E. THE MARKET ENVIRONMENT

(1) Economic

9. Long-Run Automobile Demand

HANS BREMS[1]

SHORT-RUN VERSUS LONG-RUN DEMAND

In the past, the theory and measurement of automobile demand have been subjected to econometric scrutiny in the pioneering work by Roos and Szeliski.[2] Their purpose was to estimate the demand for cars *year by year*, as indicated by the word "changes" in the title of their paper. But suppose one is merely interested in the long-run *trend* of automobile output because one wants to know whether current levels are above or below normal. This would be a relevant question to ask if one is concerned with long-run investment decisions. If trend rather than year-to-year changes is the information we seek, a very simple tool — much simpler than the Roos-Szeliski tools — can be applied. Admittedly, the tool will do only as a first, very rough approximation. But refinements and qualifications can always be added.

THE TOOL

Suppose we have a perfectly smoothly growing stock S of automobiles. Suppose, furthermore, that the useful life of an automobile has some distinct value, L years. Let the proportionate rate of growth of our automobile stock be g per annum. Then the demand x for new automobiles will consist of two components, that is, one which replaces the automobiles retired and one which makes the stock of automobiles grow.[3] Now, at any particular time in our perfectly smoothly growing automobile market, there exists an extremely simple value of the ratio between automobile demand and automobile stock, namely,

$$(1) \qquad \frac{x(t)}{S(t-1)} = \frac{g}{1-(1+g)^{-L}}$$

where $x(t)$ is automobile demand in period t, and $S(t-1)$ is automobile stock at time $t-1$. Period t is the period ending at time t. Formula (1) has been

From *Journal of Marketing*, Vol. 20, No. 4 (April, 1956), pp. 379-84, by permission of the American Marketing Association.
[1] The author is grateful to his colleague Robert Ferber for criticism and suggestions.
[2] C. F. Roos and Victor von Szeliski, "Factors Governing Changes in Domestic Automobile Demand," *The Dynamics of Automobile Demand* (New York: General Motors Corporation, 1939).

[3] The reader may at first sight question the realism of the notion that retired automobiles are replaced by new ones. But, ignoring the length of time that a used car spends on the dealer's used-car lot, we can say that when a new-car buyer trades in his used car, the latter will replace somebody else's still older car which in turn will replace someone's still older car until finally a jalopy is junked.

rigourously derived in the appendix at the end of the present paper. The value of the ratio

$$\frac{x(t)}{S(t-1)}$$

as determined by (1) is called the *equilibrium* value of that ratio. It will exist only in a smoothly growing automobile market, and it is expressed in terms of two structural parameters, rate of growth g and useful life L. Table I tabulates the ratio (1) for alternative values of the structural parameters g and L.

TABLE I

VALUES OF RATIO $\dfrac{g}{1-(1+g)^{-L}}$ FOR

ALTERNATIVE VALUES OF g AND L

L/g	.03	.04	.05	.06
7	.161	.167	.173	.179
8	.142	.149	.155	.161
9	.128	.134	.141	.147
10	.117	.123	.130	.136
11	.108	.114	.120	.127
12	.100	.107	.113	.119

The application of our tool to any particular situation proceeds as follows. Suppose we want to know whether the volume of new passenger-car sales in 1955 is above or below equilibrium. The latest available figure for S is 44 million passenger cars in operation on July 1, 1954. All we have to do, then, is to multiply this figure by our equilibrium ratio as determined by formula (1). We shall then obtain the equilibrium value of x(t), which can be confronted with the actual value of x(t), which was close to 8 million cars. Table II tabulates the equilibrium value of x(t) for 1955 as determined by (1) the given value of S(t−1), that is, 44 million, the total number of passenger cars in operation on July 1, 1954; (2) values of the proportionate rate of growth g ranging from .03 to .06; and (3) values of the useful life L ranging from 7 to 12 years. For example, if the stock of automobiles at time t − 1 is 44 million, if stock is grow-

ing at 5 per cent per annum, and if useful life is 11 years, then the equilibrium value of the demand for cars during period t is 5.3 million units. It should again be emphasized that this is a hypothetical figure showing what under the circumstances demand would be in a *smoothly* growing automobile stock. Actual demand may differ very much from this equilibrium value, but the sign and size of the difference is an important clue to the future.

EMPIRICALLY PLAUSIBLE VALUES OF THE STRUCTURAL PARAMETERS L AND g

The useful life L of an automobile is an average covering a wide range of values. Some cars are wrecked during the first weeks of their lives, and well-maintained prewar models may give excellent service for many years to come. The only available clue to an empirically plausible value of L is the estimate by the Automobile Manufacturers Association of average age of cars when retired. It should be realized that useful life and average retirement age would coincide only if automobile stock remained stationary. If the stock is growing, cars retired while still young represent a more numerous generation than cars retired at a very old age. Consequently, excessive weight is given to the former at the expense of the latter,

TABLE II

SALES OF NEW PASSENGER CARS IN MILLIONS OF UNITS IN PERIOD t AS A FUNCTION OF RATE OF GROWTH g OR PASSENGER CAR STOCK AND USEFUL LIFE L PER CAR WHEN STOCK IN PERIOD t − 1 IS 44 MILLION

L/g	.03	.04	.05	.06
7	7.06	7.33	7.60	7.88
8	6.27	6.54	6.81	7.09
9	5.65	5.92	6.19	6.47
10	5.16	5.42	5.70	5.98
11	4.76	5.02	5.30	5.58
12	4.42	4.69	4.96	5.25

and the general statement can be made that useful life exceeds average retirement age in a growing stock. With this qualification in mind, we can use the Automobile Manufacturers Association data on average retirement age, reproduced in Table III. The general impres-

TABLE III
AVERAGE RETIREMENT AGE, YEARS*

1925	6.5
1930	7.0
1935	8.3
1941	10.2
1952	14.3
1953	13.8

*Source: Automobile Manufacturers Association, *Automobile Facts and Figures 1955* (Detroit, Michigan), p. 8.

sion is that retirement age has been growing rather smoothly from 6.5 years in 1925 to 14.3 years in 1952. However, wartime restrictions upon motor travel caused many cars to be placed in storage for the duration of the war, and the absence or scarcity of new cars in the market gave an inducement to maintain and service cars much better than was usually done. Generally speaking, then, late prewar cars played the role that would otherwise have been assumed by 1943 through 1945 models, had these existed. When the last prewar models are being scrapped, early postwar models will play the role previously played by the late prewar models, and a reduction of average retirement age no doubt will occur. The long-run trend toward longer lives will then be temporarily reversed. The 1953 figure, 13.8, actually indicates that this is already happening, so the 1952 figure, 14.3, is not likely to prevail. All in all, the useful life to be expected for the longer run would appear to be somewhat lower than 14 years. A figure between 10 and 12 years would not seem implausible, but this is probably the lowest the industry can possibly hope for.

Our second structural parameter is g, the proportionate rate of growth of automobile stock. As for an empirically plau-

TABLE IV
PASSENGER CARS IN OPERATION IN THE UNITED STATES AS OF JULY 1, 1950-1954

Year	Millions*	Proportionate rate of growth
1950	35.9	.072
1951	38.5	.034
1952	39.8	.069
1953	42.2	.052
1954	44.4	

*Source: *Automotive News Almanac*, 1951 through 1955.

sible value of g, the best we can do is to examine automobile stock statistics since 1950. Growth of automobile stock was abnormally low during the war and abnormally high between 1945 and 1950. Since 1950, growth has settled at around 5½ per cent per annum. Table IV reproduces available figures on passenger cars in operation as of July 1 for the years 1950 through 1954. The entire growth from 35.9 million in 1950 to 44.4 million in 1954 corresponds to an overall proportionate rate of growth of slightly below .055 per annum. It might be added that the U.S. Bureau of Public Roads has estimated the proportionate rate of growth of passenger-car stock from 1954 to 1955 at .051, corresponding well to the over-all average for the early 1950's.[4] *Fortune*, on the other hand, has estimated the proportionate rate of growth from 1954 to 1959 at a conservative 4 per cent per annum.[5]

Our conclusion, then, is that for L an empirically plausible value would be between 10 and 12, and for g it would be between .04 and .06.

CHANGING VALUES OF THE STRUCTURAL PARAMETERS L AND g

So far, we have studied the equilibrium value of the ratio $\frac{x(t)}{S(t-1)}$ as deter-

---

[4] *Automotive News*, August 29, 1955, p. 6.
[5] "A New Kind of Car Market," *Fortune*, September 1953, p. 100.

mined by equation (1) and as tabulated in Table I. If our estimates of the structural prarmeter L and g are sound, the equilibrium value will be between .136 and .107 corresponding to equilibrium new-car sales between 5.98 million and 4.69 million, which is considerably below actual 1955 output. But what if the structural parameters are themselves subject to change over time? In fact, they are; we have already seen that over the decades, passenger cars seem to have increasing longevity. If such changes are slow and numerically small, our equilibrium analysis is still a good, first approximation. But if the changes are abrupt and large — as they may well be in the short run — our equilibrium analysis will merely indicate a normal level from which we are moving away and another normal level toward which we are moving, but it will tell us nothing about the path to be followed between the two.

Suppose, for example, that the useful life L for one reason or another drops from, say, 12 to 11 years but that desired automobile stock still grows at the same proportionate rate of growth g. In that case, *two* generations — that is, the cars eleven years old along with those twelve years old — will be scrapped at the same time. Added to the normal growth demand, this double scrappage will greatly expand new-car demand. Next year, only one generation will be scrapped, but after eleven years there will be the familiar "echo effect." Since not all cars have the same useful life, the echo effect will eventually die out, and we are left with a permanent increase in new-car demand relative to automobile stock (cf. Table I). Shortening car life at unchanged growth rate means that motorists want *better* (newer) but not *more* cars in their garages. Such is likely to be the case when (1) employment and real income levels are rising; (2) new-model stimuli are becoming more powerful; (3) finance terms become easier; (4) used-car prices are dropping, so used-car owners will be stimulated to buy a

newer used car and scrap the old one; and (5) the cost of repairing wrecks is rising significantly. All five things are, in fact, happening in the mid-1950's, and they could conceivably explain the fact that actual new-car sales are now much higher than our equilibrium analysis would make us believe. If so, the important conclusion can be drawn that the present state of affairs is not going to last.

Or suppose that the industry suddenly faces a switch in growth of automobile stock from 4 per cent per annum to 5 per cent per annum but that useful life L remains constant. Under such circumstances, the entire increase in stock must be brought about by output of new cars. This will give us the familiar accelerator effect with its violent changes in output. Let automobile stock at time $t-2$ be 42.31 million. A 4 per cent annual growth then means that during period $t-1$, stock will grow by 1.69 million in order to reach 44.00 million at time $t-1$. Now, let the growth rate rise suddenly from 4 to 5 per cent per annum. During period t, stock will then grow by 2.20 million and will reach 46.20 million at time t. Continuing to grow at 5 per cent per annum, it will grow by 2.31 million during period $t+1$ and will reach 48.51 million at time $t+1$. Thus, we find the growth component of new-car demand to be

Period $t-1$	1.69 million
Period t	2.20 million
Period $t+1$	2.31 million

Here, we can clearly see the once-and-for-all effect of the change in the growth rate. First, the growth component rises from 1.69 to 2.20 or by .51 million; then it rises merely from 2.20 to 2.31 or by .11 million. Thus the rise itself is reduced to one-fifth once the market has settled down at the new, higher rate of growth. Again, of course, there will be an echo effect that will die out eventually. Rising growth rate at unchanged useful life means that motorists want *more* but not necessarily *better* cars in their garages. This is likely to happen at rising employment and real income levels and when households move to the suburbs. Suburbanization no doubt is a factor in the 1950's, but the industry's optimism about the rising number of two-car families may be exaggerated. In our hypothetical case, we assumed that there was a rising growth rate at *unchanged* useful life. However, many a second car may be a jalopy whose market value in a declining used-car market was too low for trade-in on a new car, the "first" car. Or it may be a jalopy which was purchased at a nominal sum from a used-car dealer who would otherwise have junked it. (Factories allow new-car dealers $25 to $50 for junking trade-ins.) Thus, conceivably, two-car ownership may be accompanied by a tendency toward longer useful life. To the extent that this is the case, the stimulus to new-car demand may fail to materialize.

Whether we imagine changes in the useful life or changes in the growth rate, lasting marks will have been left on the market in the form of an uneven age distribution, that is, a distribution which differs from the one that would exist in a smoothly growing stock. This is a third reason, besides the possible initial changes in *L* and *g*, why our equilibrium analysis will not give us a good forecast for any particular year, except by pure accident.

CONCLUSION

From what we know about empirically plausible values of the two structural parameters, useful life *L* and rate of growth *g*, we conclude that the current level of automobile output in the United States, close to 8 million cars for 1955, is considerably higher than the level that would materialize in equilibrium, that is, somewhere between 6 and 4½ million. Deviations within any one year of such magnitude are, of course, perfectly possible. We have already mentioned three possible reasons why such devia-

tions may arise in any particular year: (a) changing *L*; (b) changing *g*; and (c) uneven age distribution of cars partly resulting from such changes in the past. Our equilibrium analysis should not be interpreted in any mechanistic way. Ours is a free economy, at least outside the agricultural sector. The price mechanism is constantly at work—even in an industry as frequently blamed for "administered" pricing as the automobile industry. And the price mechanism is itself a factor in reasons (a) and (b) above. Pushing new-car sales as vigorously as has been done by the factories in 1955 will, first, depress new-car prices as paid by the consumers. Dealer's profit takes the first beating.[6] Second, however, dealers' attempts to dispose of all the trade-ins will depress the used-car market, and the second beating is therefore taken by the consumer who suffers a faster depreciation of the car he owns, new or used. The depressed used-car prices constitute a powerful stimulus to one out of two things. One is earlier retirement of used cars: the used-car owner can buy a better used car at very little and will retire the old car himself or let the dealer do it for him. The other is that low used-car prices constitute a stimulus to two-car ownership: rather than trade it in on a new car, the owner will keep his jalopy, buy the new car for cash, and end up with two cars. Thus the price mechanism will stimulate shorter life *or* multi-car ownership so the market can absorb all the new cars, if not without pains.

There is some evidence of a short-run reduction of useful life *L* temporarily reversing the long-run trend toward increased longevity; but there is no evidence of an abnormally high growth rate of automobile stock. In fact, the growth rate for 1954-1955 is practically identical with the 1950-1954 overall average. Abnormally high sales but

---

[6]*Automotive News*, September 12, 1955, carries a typical indignant letter from a Minnesota dealer blaming the current Ford-Chevrolet race for the low or negative levels of dealers' profit.

normally growing stock means abnormally high retirement, brought about by the short-run reduction of useful life combined with uneven age distribution. There is as yet no indication that the structural parameter L will permanently have a *low* enough value or that the structural parameter g will permanently have a *high* enough value to sustain permanently the current high ratio of output to stock. It would be unwise to base long-run investment in plant upon such a ratio.

APPENDIX

Let the number of new automobiles sold during period t be $x(t)$, the stock of automobiles in operation at time t be $S(t)$, and the number of used automobiles retired during period t be $r(t)$. The change in stock from $t-1$ to time t will then be the difference between the number of new automobiles sold and the number of used automobiles retired, or

$$(2) \qquad S(t) - S(t-1) = x(t) - r(t)$$

But, in a perfectly smoothly growing stock, growing at the proportionate rate of growth g, we have

$$(3) \qquad S(t) = (1+g)S(t-1)$$

And, if the useful life of an automobile is L periods, then the number of used automobiles retired during period t equals the number of new automobiles sold during period $t-L$, or

$$(4) \qquad r(t) = x(t-L)$$

Taking (2), (3), and (4) together, we have

$$(5) \qquad x(t) = gS(t-1) + x(t-L)$$

and replacing t by $t-L$ in (5) gives us

$$(5a) \qquad x(t-L) = gS(t-L-1) + x(t-2L)$$

Inserting (5a) into (5) gives us

$$x(t) = gS(t-1) + gS(t-L-1) + x(t-2L)$$
$$= gS(t-1)\left[1 + (1+g)^{-L}\right] + x(t-2L)$$

In this way, we can keep on going back L periods at a time n times. Then, we get

$$x(t) =$$
$$gS(t-1)\left[1 + (1+g)^{-L} + \ldots + (1+g)^{-nL}\right]$$
$$+ r(t-nL)$$

For n approaching infinity, we have, therefore,

$$(1) \qquad x(t) = \frac{gS(t-1)}{1-(1+g)^{-L}}$$

which is our formula used in the second paragraph of this paper.

10. A Note on Long-Run Automobile Demand[1]

MARC NERLOVE

In a recent article in this *Journal*, Professor Brems has developed a long-run relationship between the demand for new automobiles and the total number of automobiles.[2] On the basis of this relationship, he concludes: (1) ". . . that the current level of automobile output in the United States, close to 8 million cars for 1955, is considerably higher than the level that would materialize in equilibrium, that is, somewhere between 6 and 4½ million;" and (2) that "it would be unwise to base long-run investment in plant upon [the current ratio of new car purchases to the total number of cars]."

Brems claims simplicity for his approach as contrasted with previous work on the problem of the long-run demand for new automobiles. His approach may be, however, too simple; it does not appear to permit an adequate understanding of the forces which govern the long-run equilibrium of new car purchases, nor does it appear to be an approach upon which automobile manufacturers can base investment decisions. The purpose of this note is to suggest why Brems' approach may be inadequate. Time available to the writer does not permit a full-scale statistical analysis of long-run automobile de-

From *Journal of Marketing*, Vol. 22, No. 1 (July, 1957), pp. 57-64, by permission of the American Marketing Association.
[1] The author is indebted to J. P. Cavin, R. J. Foote, and F. V. Waugh of the U. S. Agricultural Marketing Service for helpful comments and suggestions.
[2] Hans Brems, "Long-Run Automobile Demand," *The Journal of Marketing*, April 1956, pp. 379-84.

mand; consequently, this note deals chiefly with a theoretical formulation of what is believed to be a better approach.

SUMMARY OF BREMS' FORMULATION

In his article Brems develops a relation between the long-run equilibrium purchases of new cars and the total stock of automobiles using two factors: (1) the rate of growth in the total number of automobiles and (2) the average length of life of an automobile.

The main objection to Brems' formulation is that the relationship between the ratio of new car purchases to the total number of automobiles and (1) the rate of growth in the total number of automobiles and (2) the average length of life is not a stable one. Brems himself notes that changes may take place in both the average length of life of an automobile and in the rate of growth of the stock of automobiles, and ". . . if the changes are abrupt and large—as they may well be in the short run—our equilibrium analysis will merely indicate a normal level from which we are moving away and another normal level toward which we are moving, but it will tell us nothing about the path to be followed between the two."

The rate of growth in the number of automobiles people own is determined by both the long-run equilibrium level and the current level from which they are moving: if the former exceeds the latter, the more widely separated they

FIGURE 1

THE EFFECT OF CHANGES IN THE LONG-RUN EQUILIBRIUM DEMAND FOR AUTOMOBILES
ON THE RATE OF GROWTH OF THE NUMBER OF AUTOMOBILES IN USE

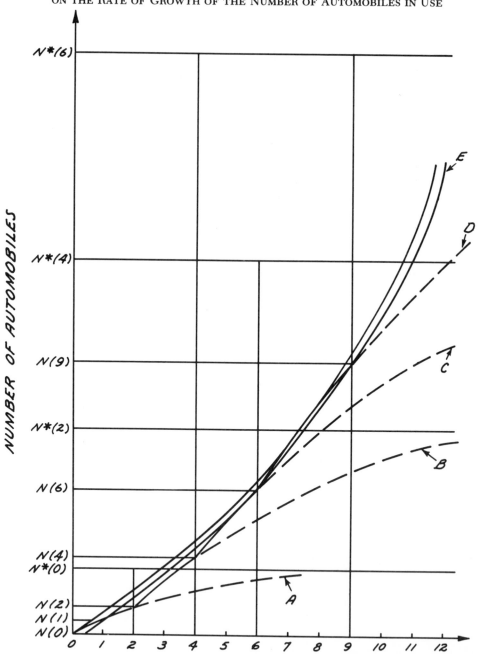

are and the more rapid is the rate of growth. Knowledge of the rate of growth would, other things remaining the same, enable us to determine the long-run equilibrium position. But the long-run equilibrium position is continually changing over time in response to economic forces; consequently, the observed rate of growth at a point in time is continually changing in response to these factors. The average rate of growth which Brems takes as given tells us little about the long-run equilibrium position toward which people are now moving; if anything, it tells us something about positions toward which they were moving *in the past*. This point is illustrated by Figure 1.

Let us neglect, for the moment, the problem of the average length of life of an automobile. Let $N(t)$ equal the number of automobiles at time t, and let $N^*(t)$ equal the long-run equilibrium number of automobiles also *at time t*. We assume, for reasons outlined below, that consumers adjust the number of cars[3] they own in proportion to the difference between the long-run equilibrium number of cars demanded and the current number of cars owned. Thus, in Figure 1, if, at $t=0$, the current number is $N(0)$ and the long-run equilibrium level is $N^*(0)$, we assume that consumers will adjust the number of cars they own along a curve labeled A which asymptotically approaches the horizontal line through $N^*(0)$ as the period of time allowed for adjustment increases. If the long-run equilibrium level remained at $N^*(0)$, consumers would own $N(1)$ cars at $t=1$, $N(2)$ cars at $t=2$, and so on. Suppose, however, that at $t=2$ the long-run equilibrium level shifts to $N^*(2)$: Starting from the level they have now achieved, $N(2)$, consumers will adjust toward $N^*(2)$ along the curve labeled B.

Again suppose, at $t=4$, that the long-run equilibrium level shifts to $N^*(4)$: consumers now adjust along C. Finally, suppose that, at $t=6$, the long-run equilibrium level shifts to $N^*(6)$: consumers now adjust along D. Such changes as shown in Figure 1 may lead us mistak-

enly to believe that there is a constant proportionate rate of growth in the total number of cars if we do not take into account relevant economic variables. This is shown in Figure 1 by the double-line curve, E, fitted to the observed total number of cars owned for periods 1 through 9.[4] If we think of the long-run equilibrium number of cars shifting in the manner shown in Figure 1, but more rapidly and over a longer period of time, it is clear that a curve such as E will be approximated closely. It would be wrong, however, to extrapolate such a curve in the way Brems does, for we have no guarantee that the economic forces which cause shifts in the long-run equilibrium level will cause such shifts in exactly the same way as they did in the past.

We may also question Brems' use of the average length of life of an automobile as a constant in his analysis. Brems' figures show that the average length of life has been increasing, perhaps as a result of technological improvements, but it has not been increasing steadily. This suggests that economic forces are at work; for example, it is reasonable that old cars will be scrapped earlier the cheaper are newer cars.

AN ALTERNATIVE FORMULATION

Like Brems, we consider a total stock of automobiles. Brems, however, identifies this total stock with the total number of automobiles in existence; he thus counts a 1937 Plymouth, say, and a 1955 Cadillac with equal weight. It is clear that cars of different makes or of different ages are not equivalent. If we follow Brems' formulation, we compute the total stock of automobiles by adding together all purchases for past years back to some year, depending on the average length of life of an automobile. This implies that automobiles do not

---

[3] We use *number* here rather than *stock adjusted for age composition*, as we do below, in order to maintain a correspondence with Brems' formulation.

[4] Brems assumes such a constant percentage rate of growth on the basis of data on the number of cars in use.

depreciate at all up to a certain point and then become valueless just like the celebrated one-horse shay. It is common knowledge, however, that cars depreciate rapidly the first few years and more slowly thereafter. Constant *percentage* depreciation would thus seem more nearly to approximate the situation than the type of depreciation implied by Brems' formulation.[5]

If we assume a constant percentage rate of depreciation over time, we may derive the total stock of automobiles, *adjusted for the age composition of the stock*, from an index of past purchases of new cars derived in a way to adjust for differences in make and model. Let s(t) be the stock of automobiles during period t, d be the percentage rate of depreciation, x(t) be new car purchases during period t, x(t-1) be new car purchases during period t-1, and so on. Then we may write:

(1) $s(t) = x(t) + (1-d) x(t-1) + (1-d)^2 x(t-2) + \ldots$

From (1) it is clear that the stock of automobiles during t, adjusted for age composition, is just new purchases during t plus (1-d) times the stock in the previous period, t-1, or:

(2) $s(t) = x(t) + (1-d) s(t-1).$

The demand for automobiles may be considered as the demand for a stock of automobiles adjusted for both age and make, that is, s(t).[6]

This demand may depend on a variety of factors: (1) the price of automobiles relative to other commodities, (2) real disposable income, (3) population, (4) the extent and quality of the highway network, (5) the degree of urbanization and /or suburbanization, etc.[7]

In his article Brems assumes that the long-run demand for a stock of automobiles grows at some constant percentage rate. Clearly, however, the rate of growth in the long-run equilibrium demand for automobiles depends upon the factors we have mentioned. The pattern of change in these factors will shape the rate of growth of long-run demand, as illustrated by Figure 1. Unless we know how changes in these variables determine the rate of growth, we have little basis on which to forecast long-run automobile demand.

---

[5] Chow's findings, based on an analysis of the prices of used cars of various ages reported in newspaper advertisements, tend to support the hypothesis of constant percentage depreciation. See Gregory Chow, *Demand for Automobiles in the United States: A Case Study in Consumer Durables*, forthcoming volume in the series Contributions to Economic Analysis (Amsterdam: North-Holland Publishing Co.), especially Table 4.

[6] *Ibid.* Chow develops an index of the stock of automobiles based on their total value. This procedure may not be entirely appropriate if the second-hand market is imperfect. It is, perhaps, a fair approximation in the case of automobiles, but we would not expect it to apply to most other durables.

[7] Atkinson found a significant effect of relative price on the purchases of new automobiles (see L. Jay Atkinson, "Consumer Markets for Durable Goods," *Survey of Current Business*, April 1952, pp. 19-24). Atkinson writes, on page 20: "Aside from the influence of other factors, each 1 percent increase in the ratio of the price of cars to the Consumers' Price Index was associated with an average decrease of one and one-third percent in new car sales in the base period [1925-40]." Atkinson's result refers to *new* car purchases and not to the total stock adjusted for age composition. Chow, *op. cit.*, found that—for the period 1920-1953, other things being the same—each 1-percent *increase* in the average price of the stock of automobiles relative to the Gross National Product deflator was associated with an average *decrease* in the per-capita stock of automobiles of 1 and 1.5 percent. Atkinson, *op. cit.*, p. 20, also found: "The most important factor affecting new automobile sales is the real purchasing power of individuals. This is measured by real disposable income. Excluding the influence of other factors, each change of 1 percent in the level of real disposable income was associated with a change of 2.5 percent in the same direction in new automobile sales during the base period [1925-40]." Atkinson goes on to add that ". . . each change of 1 percent in the ratio of the current to the preceding year's income was associated with a change of 2.3 percent in the same direction in sales." Chow, *op. cit.*, found that, other things being the same, an increase of 1 percent in real disposable income per capita was associated, on the average, with a 2-percent increase in the per-capita stock of automobiles.

LONG-RUN EQUILIBRIUM ADJUSTMENTS

As Brems rightly implies, the observed stock of automobiles at a given time may differ substantially from the long-run equilibrium stock. It does not, however, seem reasonable to identify the long-run equilibrium stock with that stock which would have existed had a constant percentage rate of growth been maintained. Because consumers may be unable or unwilling to adjust immediately to a long-run equilibrium position, net additions to stock, that is, new purchases, may not bring the levels of stock into line with the long-run equilibrium stock. This lag in adjustment may result from a variety of causes: (1) The used-car market is imperfect so that consumers may not be able, individually or as a group, to distribute a given number of cars with a given age and make distribution among themselves in such a way as to achieve an optimum. (2) Various items in the consumer's budget may be of a contractual nature, for example, life insurance premiums or installment payments, so that it may be costly or difficult for him to make funds available for an increased stock of automobiles. (3) The consumer may be unwilling to change his stock of automobiles now because he believes the current levels of the economic variables which determine his equilibrium stock may change at some future date.[8]

The variables mentioned above determine the long-run equilibrium demand for automobiles. For the reasons mentioned, consumers may not react fully to changes in these variables during any one period of time; consequently, there may be a difference between the stock of automobiles they hold now and the

[8] These points are discussed in more detail in the author's *Distributed Lags and Demand Analysis*, unpublished manuscript (March 1957). Point (3) is closely related to Friedman's "permanent income hypothesis" (see Milton Friedman, *A Theory of the Consumption Function*, to be published by Princeton University Press for the National Bureau of Economic Research).

stock they would eventually hold if the variables mentioned changed and then remained constant over time. In such a situation, consumers would gradually adjust the stock they hold to an equilibrium position. Since the variables which determine long-run demand are constantly changing over time, consumers continually move toward, but never actually reach, the equilibrium position. It follows that consumers' reactions to changes in price, income, population, etc., depend on what changes have occurred in these variables in the past. Consequently, the current stock of automobiles is not related to the current values of these variables, but the long-run equilibrium stock is.

We never observe consumers at long-run equilibrium positions but only at short-run equilibrium positions. This is because the economic factors such as price, income, and the like, which determine the long-run equilibrium position of the consumer, are continually changing; thus, the long-run equilibrium positions toward which consumers are moving are changing. The alternative formulation suggested here enables one to *deduce* the relation of the long-run demand for automobiles to price, income, and other variables from observed short-run changes in new purchases, price, income, and other variables.

If we let $s^*(t)$ be the long-run equilibrium stock, $p(t)$ be the relative price of automobiles, $y(t)$ be real disposable income, and $z(t)$ be other variables (such as population, degree of urbanization and/or suburbanization, extent and quality of the road and highway network, etc.) — each during time-period t — we may write the long-run demand for automobiles as:

$$(3)\ s^*(t) = a_0 + a_1 p(t) + a_2 y(t) + a_3 z(t).$$

The long-run equilibrium stock of automobiles demanded by consumers, $s^*(t)$, cannot be observed; hence, equation (3) cannot be estimated statistically. In order to derive a relationship that can be estimated statistically, we must say something about the *way* in which consumers adjust the stocks they actually hold to the equilibrium stock, $s^*(t)$. It seems reasonable to suppose that the rate of growth of actual stocks toward a new equilibrium position depends on the difference between the equilibrium stock and the actual stock; that is, the closer consumers are to a long-run equilibrium position, the less incentive they have as a group to overcome the costs and frictions of adjustment and, hence, the less will be the extent of their adjustment; whereas the farther out of line actual and equilibrium stocks are, the more rapidly will consumers try to adjust their holdings. If we assume, as an approximation, that the rate of adjustment of the actual stock is *proportional* to the difference between the equilibrium stock and the actual stock, we may write this dynamic adjustment relation as:

$$(4) \quad s(t) - s(t\text{-}1) = b[s^*(t) - s(t\text{-}1)],$$

where $s(t)$ is the actual stock during period t, $s(t\text{-}1)$ is the actual stock during t-1, and b is the constant of proportionality.[9]

STATISTICAL DERIVATION OF THE COEFFICIENTS

Equations (2)−(4) permit us to derive a relationship between actual new car purchases, relative price, real income, and other variables which are summarized in $z(t)$. This relationship is:[10]

---

[9] This same model was suggested by Chow, *op. cit.*, in his discussion of a dynamic theory of the demand for automobiles. The model is similar to that suggested by Roos and von Szeliski, provided we interpret their "variable maximum ownership level" as our $s^*(t)$. See C. F. Roos and Victor von Szeliski, "Factors Governing Changes in Domestic Automobile Demand," in *The Dynamics of Automobile Demand* (New York: General Motors Corp., 1939), especially pp. 32-35. This and several other models are discussed more fully in the author's paper on distributed lags.
[10] The derivation of equation (5) is as follows—
From equation (4) we have:
(i) $s(t) = bs^*(t) + (1\text{-}b)s(t\text{-}1)$.

$$(5) \quad x(t) = a_0bd + a_1bp(t) - a_1b(1\text{-}d)\,p(t\text{-}1)$$
$$+ a_2by(t) - a_2b(1\text{-}d)\,y(t\text{-}1)$$
$$+ a_3bz(t) - a_3b(1\text{-}d)\,a(t\text{-}1)$$
$$+ (1\text{-}b)x(t\text{-}1)$$
$$= A_0 + A_1p(t) + A_2p(t\text{-}1) +$$
$$A_3y(t) + A_4y(t\text{-}1)$$
$$+ A_5z(t) + A_6z(t\text{-}1) + A_7x(t\text{-}1)$$

If equation (5) is fitted statistically, estimates of the coefficients permit us to estimate the appropriate rate of depreciation, d, and the constant of proportionality, b. We can also estimate the parameters a_0, a_1, a_2, and a_3 which enter equation (3), the long-run demand for automobiles.

A full-scale statistical study is beyond the scope of this note. Nevertheless, the presentation of a few tentative statistical results may clarify the discussion above. In the statistical analyis presented below, new car purchases and real disposable income are taken in per capita terms and variables such as the extent and quality of the highway network, the degree of urbanization and/or suburbanization, and the operating cost of running an automobile are neglected.

The variables of equation (5), except for $z(t)$, were measured for statistical purposes as follows:

$p(t)=$ an index of new car prices deflated by the deflator used to obtain Gross National Product in constant dollars (1937 = 100)

$y(t)=$ total disposable income divided by an estimate of the population of the United States and deflated by the deflator used to obtain GNP in constant dollars (1937 = 100)

$x(t)=$ an index of new car purchases,

Lagging (i) one period, multiplying through by (1-d) and subtracting the result from (i), we have:
(ii) $s(t) - (1\text{-}d)s(t\text{-}1) = b[s^*(t) - (1\text{-}d)s^*(t\text{-}1)]$
$$+ (1\text{-}b)[s(t\text{-}1) - (1\text{-}d)s(t\text{-}2)].$$
By equation (2) of the text, we may therefore write:
(iii) $x(t) = b[s^*(t) - (1\text{-}d)s^*(t\text{-}1)] - (1\text{-}b)x(t\text{-}1)$.
Substituting in equation (iii) for $s^*(t)$ and $s^*(t\text{-}1)$ from equation (3) of the text and equation (3) lagged one period, we obtain equation (5) of the text.

based on retail sales figures, divided by population.[11] Equation (5), excluding the variables $z(t)$ and $z(t\text{-}1)$, was fitted by least squares to the data for the periods 1922-1941 and 1948-1953. The result was as follows:

$$(6)\; x(t) = 0.0046 - 0.018\; p(t) + 0.006\; p(t\text{-}1)$$
$$(\pm.006)\qquad (\pm.006)$$
$$+ 0.013y(t) - 0.007y(t\text{-}1)$$
$$(\pm.002)\qquad (\pm.003)$$
$$+ 0.268x(t\text{-}1),$$
$$(\pm.211)$$

where the figures in parentheses below the coefficients are their respective standard errors. Approximately 91 per cent of the variance of new car purchases during the periods 1922-1941 and 1948-1953 is explained by the regression, that is, $R^2 = 0.91$. The meaning of (6) may be best explained by stating the effects in terms of percentages of the mean price, income, and new car purchases for the periods under consideration (1922-1941 and 1948-1953). It is then found that equation (6) implies that, at the average levels of the respective variables for the period (1) a 1-per cent increase in current price is associated with a 0.9-per cent decline in new car purchases, that is, the elasticity of new purchases with respect to current price is approximately -0.9; and (2) a 1-per cent increase in real disposable income is associated with a 2.8-per cent increase in new car purchases, that is, the elasticity of new car purchases with respect to current real disposable income is approximately $+2.8$. The coefficients of lagged price, lagged income, and lagged new car purchases in equation (6) have meaning only in terms of the long-run demand for automobiles, a subject to which we now turn.

THE LONG-RUN DEMAND FOR AUTOMOBILES

As indicated above, the estimates obtained enable us to estimate the ap-

[11] All data were obtained from Tables 1 and 2, Chow, *op. cit.*

propriate rate of depreciation, d, and the constant, b, of equation (4); these, in turn, enable us to estimate the effects of price and income on the long-run demand for automobiles. Thus, although equation (6) explains the year-to-year, or short-run changes in new car purchases, it is set up in such a way that we can see beyond it to equation (3), which represents the long-run demand for automobiles to price, income, and other variables from observed short-run changes in new purchases, prices, income, and other variables.

Comparison of equations (5) and (6) suggests that the appropriate rate of depreciation, d, may be derived in two different ways: (1) by dividing the coefficient of $p(t\text{-}1)$ by the coefficient of $p(t)$ and subtracting the result from one; or (2) by dividing the coefficient of $y(t\text{-}1)$ by the coefficient of $y(t)$ and subtracting the result from one. Due to sampling fluctuations and errors in the data, the two estimates are not, of course, the same. Since we have reason to expect greater errors in the series of prices of new cars than in the income series, the latter method of deriving d is to be preferred. We find that the appropriate rate of depreciation is approximately 45 per cent. While this may seem rather high, we should remember that it does not represent an accountant's measure of depreciation; rather, it represents that rate of depreciation implicit in the behavior of consumers, and it reflects their tastes and preferences as well as the technology of automobile manufacture. Furthermore, the statistical results are illustrative only. Many important variables have been omitted from equation (6); their inclusion could well change the estimates of the coefficients of $y(t)$ and $y(t\text{-}1)$. Since d depends on the ratio of these two coefficients, it could change greatly even if they only changed slightly.

Comparison of equations (5) and (6) suggests that the constant of proportionality, b, in equation (4) may be derived by subtracting the coefficient of $x(t\text{-}1)$

from one; thus, b is approximately 0.73. Consequently, equation (4) may be written:

(7) $s(t)-s(t-1)=0.73[s^*(t)-s(t-1)]$.

We may interpret (7) as implying, for example, that a 10-per cent discrepancy between the long-run equilibrium stock of automobiles and the actual stock would be associated with a 7-per cent rate of growth in the actual stock. Conversely, an observed average rate of growth of, say, 3½ per cent would imply that the equilibrium stock and the actual stock differed continuously from one another by about 5 per cent.

If the relationship between the rate of growth of the total stock of automobiles and the discrepancy between the equilibrium stock and the actual stock is known, we can derive estimates of the long-run effects of price and income on the stock of automobiles which consumers own. The effect of price and income upon the long-run equilibrium stock is obtained by dividing the coefficient of $p(t)$ and $y(t)$, respectively, in equation (6) by our estimate of b. The constant term in equation (3) may be obtained by dividing the constant term in equation (6) by the product of our estimates of b and d. Thus, the long-run demand for automobiles may be written:

(8) $s^*(t)=0.014-0.025p(t)+0.018y(t)$,

where $s^*(t)$ should be interpreted as the per-capita stock of cars adjusted for age

and make. Equation (8) may be interpreted as follows: a 1-per cent increase in the relative price of automobiles — from the average price for the periods 1922-1941 and 1948-1953 — was associated with a 1.2-per cent decrease in the equilibrium stock, that is, the long-run elasticity of demand for automobiles with respect to the relative price of automobiles is about −1.2. Similarly, the long-run elasticity of demand for automobiles with respect to real income per capita is about +3.8.

CONCLUSIONS

The purpose of this note has been to clarify certain difficulties in Brems' formulation of the long-run demand for automobiles. In the process of clarification, some illustrative statistical results are presented; however, they should be regarded merely as illustrative. A detailed statistical analysis of the demand for automobiles would carry us far beyond mere criticism and thus beyond the scope of this note.

It is hoped that the model developed here may prove useful in statistical analyses not only for automobiles but also for other consumer durables or near-durables such as refrigerators, household appliances, textiles, and the like. Such statistical analyses would prove useful to producers as a basis for their investment decisions.

11. The Application of Engel's Laws of Personal Consumption (1857) to the European Common Market (1957—1961)

J. ALLISON BARNHILL

INTRODUCTION

More than twenty-one centuries ago, Plato suspected that as wealth increased, "many will not be satisfied with the simple way of life. They will be for adding sofas, and tables, and other furniture; also dainties and perfumes, and incense, and courtesans, and cakes, all these not of one sort only, but in every variety."[1]

In 1857, Ernst Engel, after a study of the budgets of low income families[2] laid down four generalizations or "laws." Despite the uncertainty as to where the study took place, there is a consensus as to what Engel's study concluded. The four laws held that, as family income increases:

1. a smaller percentage is spent for food,
2. the percentage spent on clothing remains approximately the same,
3. the percentage spent for rent, fuel and light remains invariably the same, and
4. the percentage spent for miscella-

neous items (such as recreation, amusements, education and religion) increases.[3]

Ninety-nine years later, the *Life Study of Consumer Expenditures* reached basically the same conclusions with the exception of the expenditure for clothing which was found to increase marginally.

From the point of view of economic theory, Richard H. Leftwich states that

> When circumstances are held constant in defining a given state of demand change, the demand curve itself will change. Thus, an increase in consumer incomes will shift the demand curve to the right. With higher incomes, consumers will usually be willing to increase their rate of purchase at each alternative price.[4]

The relation between income and consumer expenditures with the European Economic Community is referred to frequently. For example, the *Quarterly Survey on Economic Situation in the Community* states,

From *The Marketer*, Vol. II, No. 2 (Spring, 1967), pp. 17-22.

[1] "The Republic" Book II, *The Dialogues of Plato*, translated by B. Jowett, (New York: Random House, 1937). Volume X, p. 636.

[2] A lack of agreement is present among marketing people as to where Engel's study was conducted. Converse, Huegy and Mitchell state the "study considered Belgian workers" and Mathews, Buz-zell, Levitt and Frank claim Engel conducted his study in Germany.

[3] Paul D. Converse, Harvey W. Huegy and Robert V. Mitchell, *Elements of Marketing*, (Englewood Cliffs: Prentice-Hall, Inc., 1958), p. 47.

[4] Richard H. Leftwich, *The Price System and Resource Allocation*, (New York: Holt, Rinehart and Winston, 1961), p. 29.

	Exhibit I															

PERSONAL CONSUMER EXPENDITURES IN THE EUROPEAN COMMON MARKET

1955 - 57 - 59 - 61

	Percentage Distribution															
Country	Food				Clothing				Housing				Miscellaneous			
	1955	1957	1959	1961	1955	1957	1959	1961	1955	1957	1959	1961	1955	1957	1959	1961
Belgium	36.2	35.5	36.0	34.0	10.8	10.9	9.6	10.0	29.4	29.6	28.9	31.0	23.3	23.9	25.0	25.0
France	43.7	40.8	41.4	39.5	13.1	13.3	11.7	12.0	18.4	19.8	19.7	19.7	24.0	24.2	26.0	27.7
Germany[1]	44.6	42.4	42.5	40.7	13.4	14.2	13.1	12.9	22.1	22.4	22.5	22.7	19.9	21.0	21.9	23.7
Italy	58.8	55.9	55.5	52.2	11.2	11.7	11.2	11.1	12.7	16.1	17.5	18.4	17.3	16.3	15.8	18.3
Luxembourg	43.7	44.0	44.3	43.0	13.2	13.4	12.9	12.0	23.8	23.5	23.4	24.0	20.4	19.5	19.8	21.0
Netherlands	39.2	38.7	38.6	37.5	17.1	16.2	15.4	16.1	24.5	25.5	25.7	26.3	20.5	20.4	21.1	20.8

	Percentage Distribution of Miscellaneous															
	Health				Transportation				Recreation				Others			
	1955	1957	1959	1961	1955	1957	1959	1961	1955	1957	1959	1961	1955	1957	1959	1961
Belgium	23.3	23.2	25.3	26.9	29.6	30.0	29.2	28.8	31.8	31.2	30.6	29.2	15.3	15.7	14.8	15.1
France	28.5	30.0	30.9	32.0	29.6	28.5	27.7	27.7	32.1	31.2	30.6	29.7	9.9	10.3	10.7	10.7
Germany[1]	22.4	23.3	24.1	25.7	20.4	19.3	18.1	18.9	43.8	44.6	45.5	42.6	13.2	12.6	12.2	12.7
Italy	16.4	17.1	17.6	19.7	36.5	37.2	37.4	37.6	39.0	38.0	37.4	35.3	8.1	7.7	7.6	7.5
Luxembourg	26.9	27.6	28.7	30.2	42.2	41.2	40.8	40.2	26.9	27.3	26.3	25.7	3.9	3.9	4.2	4.0
Netherlands	25.3	28.0	29.1	29.3	22.4	20.4	20.1	21.2	35.3	33.9	31.7	30.8	17.1	17.7	19.1	18.6

Source: United Nations, Yearbook of National Accounts-Statistics, New York, 1963.
[1] Federal Republic of Germany, Handbook of Statistics, 1961, p. 173.

In particular, the growth of private consumption was again considerable, rising in step with the practically unabated expansion of income from wages and salaries.

In general, household consumption increased a little more than it did in 1961, reflecting the rapid increase of income from wages in most of the member nations and also the even more noticeable expansion of the other categories of income. (See Exhibit I.)

More specifically, economic expansion in France was quite clearly accelerated during 1962. Consumption increased more rapidly than it did in 1961. As a matter of fact, consumption increased by more than 6.5% for the entire year 1962, due to a combination of the return of more than 700,000 French from Algeria and the growth

amounted to 12 percent in the overall income from wages and salaries.[5]

A similar condition existed in Italy. The increase in Gross National Product with set prices was approximately 6 percent in 1962. The increase in private consumption, which reflects the considerable wage increases, was the main factor in the 1962 expansion.[6]

It should be emphasized at this point that this paper does not ignore the prices of goods, consumer tastes and preferences, the number of consumers under consideration, and the range of goods available to consumers. Rather

[5] Common Market Reporter, Quarterly Survey on Economic Situation in the Community, "Europe Today", (New York: Commerce Clearing House, Inc., 1963), No. 24, p. 9056.
[6] Common Market Reporter, 5th Annual Report of the Monetary Committee, (New York: Commerce Clearing House, Inc., 1963), No. 25, p. 2712.

and due to obvious restrictions, this paper will concentrate predominantly on consumers' incomes and their resultant patterns of consumption.

Choosing the European Economic Community as a unit of analysis was based on several considerations. First, since the inception of the Common Market in 1957, there has been a continued growth of income and significant changes in consumer demand. The nations of the European Common Market have ever-expanding consumer needs to be satisfied, some of which can be provided for by Canadian marketers, especially items on List B (raw materials). Second, the economic growth has occurred within a relatively short span of time thus enabling this study to present a fairly complete perspective of the changing patterns of consumption from the near-subsistence level to the affluent stage. Third, the countries of the E.C.M. have experienced a general, aggregate change in consumer expenditures. The pattern changes encompass all income and social classes. Finally, it was within the region of the member countries of the Common Market that Engel originally conducted his study of consumer patterns.

PRICES

Inflationary tendencies present serious problems for the Common Market. In 1963 alone, consumer prices increased more than 6.5 percent in Italy and France, and more than 3.5 percent in Belgium, the Netherlands and Germany.[7] Since 1958, the European Common Market has been enjoying a business boom with generally tight labor markets and long delivery time for many products.

Several factors contributed to the growth of income in the E.C.M. As a consequence of the preferential and reciprocal trade agreements among the six member nations, international competition for the market diminished significantly. Increased certainty of demand increased production and distribution of all the member nations to the point of speculation and, conceivably, undue risk.

In order to meet demand, automation, as well as the labor force, was increased greatly. Thus conditions are approaching full employment in the E.C.M. even though large numbers of women have joined the labor force. Consequently, the increased income expands the family's consumption capabilities, thus influencing consumption patterns. The strong demand for labor has also resulted in two other important conditions. One condition is that labor wages have soared. Secondly, labor mobility has increased significantly. Germany alone has added 300,000 immigrants in the past 5 years to its labor force, most of them coming from Italy, Spain, and Greece.[8]

ENGEL'S LAWS AND E.C.M. PATTERNS OF CONSUMPTION

FOOD

"As family income increases, the percentage spent for food decreases."

From a survey of the findings of this study, several conclusions can be reached. (See Exhibit II.) The first premise in that Engel's Law regarding food consumption is validated. Every country showed a decreased percentage expenditure for food. As a percentage of total consumer expenditures, food accounted for between 34 and 56 percent of per capita consumption. True to Engel's postulate, as income increased, the percentage spent for food decreased. More explicitly, although the total number of dollars expended increased, the increase was smaller than the increase in income.

Consumers in the poor countries spend much larger proportions of their

---

[7] The Chase Manhattan Bank, *Report on Western Europe,* (New York: April/May, 1964), No. 29.

[8] ("How Labor Fares Under E.C.C.") *Business Week,* (December 20, 1961), p. 76.

	Country					
"As income increases,	*Belgium*	*France*	*Germany*	*Italy*	*Luxem-bourg*	*Nether-lands*
1. the percentage spent on food decreases,	decreased	decreased	decreased	decreased	decreased	decreased
2. the percentage spent on clothing remains constant,	decreased	decreased	decreased	decreased	decreased	constant
3. the percentage spent for housing remains the same,	increased	constant	constant	increased	increased	increased
4. the percentage spent for miscellaneous items increases."	increased	increased	increased	increased	increased	constant

EXHIBIT II
PATTERNS OF CONSUMPTION MATRIX
MEMBER COUNTRIES OF THE EUROPEAN COMMON MARKET

Note: a deviation of ± ½ of 1 percent is the standard used to determine changes between the years 1957 and 1961.

smaller incomes for food than the consumers in the rich countries spend of their larger incomes, while the "middle class" countries are also in the middle range relative to food expenditures. France, which traditionally attaches a high value to the pleasures of the table, and Luxembourg, another high-income country, has an above-average and disproportionate share of its income being allocated to food.[9]

Within the European Common Market there is one principal dietary pattern which includes all the member nations except Italy. Essentially, the diet is composed of potatoes and vegetables with a moderate amount of livestock products being consumed. Protective tariffs keep the domestic price of sugar high in these countries, except in the Netherlands; consequently sugar consumption is low. The calorie value ranges from 2870 to 3000 calories per person per day.

Within the group of five nations making up the similar dietary pattern there are various individual country characteristics. The Belgians are big potato eaters and low milk consumers. The French have the highest consumption of meat, vegetables and wine. Consumption of meat in France has expanded very rapidly since the inception of the E.C.M., because livestock import duties have been eliminated on member nations. It is difficult to believe that the French eat twice as many vegetables as the Belgians, whose dietary habits are generally similar. The Germans are great potato eaters. However, their diet is short in protein since they eat only moderate amounts of cereals, milk, and meat. The Dutch eat not much more than one-half as much meat per capita as the French, but consume large quantities of milk and record the highest fats consumption in the E.C.M.[10]

Italy is identified as having a southern diet and it differs greatly from the other member nations. The diet averages only

[9] Twentieth Century Fund, *Europe's Needs and Resources*, (New York: MacMillan and Company, Ltd., 1961), p. 152.

[10] Same reference as footnote 9 at page 182.

2500 to 2600 calories daily, is deficient in energy value and is very low in animal protein. Per capita consumption of cereals is the highest amount in the E.C.M. and the consumption of fruits and vegetables is also very high.[11] Italy's meat consumption is less than one-third of the French, while her use of milk and fats is extremely small.

Historically, geography and income have been major determinants of food consumption habits. Geography has set the basic pattern by influencing what can be grown locally, (i.e. hard wheats for spaghetti and macaroni in Italy; rye and oat crops in Germany for rye bread and oatmeal).

But during the past century, the influence of climate has weakened and the influence of income has increased. The countries most affected by the revolutions in manufacturing and farming techniques forged ahead rapidly to relatively high levels of prosperity. At no time in European history have the member nations of the E.C.M. prospered simultaneously, as they have since 1957. As a result, the people have become increasingly able to afford dietary diversifications, not merely of the regionalized foodstuffs such as meat, milk and eggs, but also with the products of tropical countries (for example, tea, coffee, citrus fruits, bananas and vegetable oils). These propensities have been facilitated by increasing levels of income.

CLOTHING

"As family income increases, the percentage spent for clothing remains approximately the same."

Undoubtedly, the most significant finding in this study was the pattern of consumption for clothing. In five of the countries, the percentage spent on clothing decreased. In the Netherlands, it fluctuated a little but tended to remain constant.

The explanation of this behavior is not clear but appears to be based on the Europeans' relative view of the unimportance of clothing. Within the hierarchy of personal psychological needs, clothing rates very low. Social mores do not command conspicuous consumption of clothing. Although there is some amount of emphasis placed upon expensive and large wardrobes in the high income class, in general, most Europeans attach little importance to clothing. Generally, the percentage appears to rise with rising income where the outlay on clothing at lower income levels is relatively low; conversely, the percentage tends to fall where the initial percentage is high. The expenditures made are for well-made, durable articles. Little attention is directed to clothing styles and color schemes in dressing within the masses. There is also a tendency to purchase "year-round weight" clothing with little concern for seasonal changes. At the most, only two seasonal distinctions, spring and fall, are made for the mass consumer public in the E.C.M.

For the most part, clothing expenditures among 5 of the 6 members (except the Netherlands) do not vary significantly as a percentage of family consumption expenditures. Belgians expend 10 percent, the low, and Germans spend 12.9 percent, the high. One situation exists that lacks any conclusive explanation; consumers in the Netherlands allocated roughly 6 percent more of their expenditures to clothing than do consumers in neighboring Belgium.

Apparently consumers within the E.C.M. are satisfied, for the time being, with a subsistence level of clothing, and are more intent upon increasing their expenditures for other goods, notably housing.

HOUSING

"As family income increases, the percentage spent on rent, fuel and light remains invariably the same."

---

[11] Same reference as footnote 10.

Housing rates is the second largest average class of expenditure in this study of the E.C.M. Except for France and Germany where different, but effective constraints were imposed, the patterns of consumer expenditure for housing is contrary to Engel's law. Expenditures for housing increased in Belgium, Italy, Luxembourg, and the Netherlands. These countries increased even though in most of the countries demand for housing was brought under control at an early stage of the boom. In Germany, the government revoked the tax-free status of bonds newly issued by mortgage societies. Building permits were limited in the Netherlands and in Belgium applications for building permits were checked for a time by a tightening in facilities for credits and subsidies.[12] In France, building resources have been under severe strain and this, rather than scarcity of finances or government restrictions, has been responsible for the limited amounts of housing completions even though the demand is very strong.[13]

In face of these restrictions it is clear as to the amount of importance placed upon the need for housing in Europe. Both in quality and quantity, the housing in much of Western Europe presently falls below the standards that might be expected to correspond to the income levels of the region. Many of the dwellings, having been built a century or more ago, do not conform to modern ideas of hygiene. The need for housing in the E.C.M. can be attributed, also, to the physical shortage engendered by wars and depression and in part by rent control, where this was not compensated by subsidies or other stimulating measures.

Most countries adopt two or more persons per room as their definition of overcrowding. More than 20 percent of the dwellings are overcrowded in Germany (24.1 percent) and Italy (21.6 percent). France has significant overcrowding with 16.8 percent having two or more persons per room and Belgium (5.9 percent) and the Netherlands (4.3 percent) have moderate overcrowding.[14]

The average percentage devoted to housing is about twice as large in the high income group as in either of the other groups. Because of climatic differences, lower proportions of expenditures are required to provide fuel and light in the southern countries, Italy and, to a lesser degree, France. The contrast between the relative expenditures for housing in Belgium and France is principally a reflection of different rent control policies while the contrast between Italy and Germany reflects differences in these policies as well as in the quality of housing provided.

The level of a nation's housing is not reflected solely by the quantity of housing and climatological conditions. Much also depends upon the type and quality of the construction and on the interior equipment.

Houses in Europe are built to last for a long period. The normal life of a brick or a stone building is at least 100 years and often much more, while wooden houses are expected to last for 75 years. In a century when opinions as to what is acceptable housing have undergone major changes, this great durability might be considered as socially disadvantageous.

Other criteria of sub-standard housing conditions include the absence of running water inside the home. 64.1 percent of Italy's dwellings did not have such facilities in 1961. Belgium with 51.5 percent and France with 41.6 percent also were conspicuous by their lack of housing which was equipped

---

[12] United Nations, *Economic Bulletin for Europe*, New York: Volume 15, footnote 130.
[13] Organization for European Economic Cooperation, *Policies for Sound Economic Growth*, No. 10, 1959, p. 19.
[14] Economic Commission for Europe, *Annual Bulletin of Housing and Building Statistics for Europe, 1957*, (Geneva: 1958), Table 4, p. 12.

with inside running water. In the same three countries, less than 11 percent had baths.[15]

It becomes readily apparent what reasons stimulate the members of the E.C.M. in their consumption of housing. The fact that the standard of housing is extremely low generally in these countries, to a major degree, identifies the reasons why the pattern of consumption of these countries does not comply with Engel's third law.

MISCELLANEOUS EXPENDITURES

"As family income increases, the percentage spent for miscellaneous items (such as recreation, amusements, education and religion) increases."

Miscellaneous expenses in general rise with rising incomes in every country and an analysis of the items included in this large group shows that health and personal care is the one expenditure classification that rises most sharply. Although Engel did not break down his miscellaneous classification very precisely, such a breakdown merits consideration in that a clearer picture is obtained of consumer expenditure patterns.

HEALTH

Since the beginning of the E.C.M., there has been a steady increase in health expenditures in each of the member nations. Italy, as a whole, prefers to allocate income to transportation and recreation rather than health care. At the other end of the spectrum is France which has nearly twice as large a health expenditure. A paradox is seen in the mortality rates of these two countries. Italy's mortality rate was 9.1 per 1,000 inhabitants and France's was 11.2 per 1,000 inhabitants in 1958.[16]

Health care is purchased indirectly in a variety of different ways. The most common of these in Western Europe is through health insurance, which has long been compulsory for the majority of the working population. Approximately four-fifths of all medical goods and services are bought through health insurance funds,[17] in which are included the numerous voluntary funds, which cater to particular occupations or income groups.

Although health conditions have generally improved due to the medical advances made, various diseases still take a drastic toll of lives each year. As a consequence, until these conditions are improved to a satisfactory degree, consumer expenditures will continue to be directed toward treatment and medicines. Although the health of the E.C.M. populus has improved, there is no sign that the progress has come to an end. Each year continues to show a better health record than the previous one, and the only question is at what rate this can be expected to continue. Similarly, although health expenditures have expanded quite rapidly for many years, they are still rising in most countries and seem likely to continue to do so. The European peoples show a clear propensity, as they grow richer, to devote a rising proportion of their incomes to the purchase of good health.

TRANSPORTATION

With the exception of Italy and the Netherlands, the expenditures for transportation as a percentage of consumer spending in the E.C.M. have shown a steady decrease. This trend should not be interpreted as meaning that absolute expenditures for transportation have decreased. It only indicates that transportation consumption has increased at a decreasing rate relative to the increase in income.

---

[15] Same reference as footnote 14, at p. 9-11.

[16] United Nations, *Monthly Bulletin of Statistics*, (New York: April 1959), p. 8.

[17] Same reference as footnote 9 at p. 334.

In actuality, Europe's automobile industry has become a close rival to that of the United States. The five-year period 1950-1955 saw a rapid increase, but the succeeding two years exceeded that by thirty-three percent. In 1958 there were more than five million trucks, buses and passenger cars in France and more than four million in Germany. Adding two-wheeled motor vehicles (the single largest class of vehicle) the total number of vehicles was highest in France, where ten million units were in operation. There were nearly nine million motor vehicles in Germany and 4.7 million vehicles registered in Italy.[18]

The growth in motor transportation reflects not only the increase prosperity but the deferred demand of the economic depression of the 1930's, the war years, and the post-war reconstruction period. By 1957, the largest number of passenger cars in relation to population were found in France, Luxembourg and Belgium, in that order, with 90.1, 87.9 and 65.5 vehicles per thousand inhabitants.[19]

Motor vehicle registrations indicate that the trend in motor vehicle purchases has increased sharply. Automobile ownership has been promoted by rising personal incomes, extensive road improvement programs and better automobiles. Many people who owned motor scooters or motorcycles have found it financially possible to shift to four-wheeled vehicles. In the past several years, the number of new car registrations has exceeded the number of newly registered "two-wheelers" everywhere. Expenditures for automobiles have risen faster than outlays for any other consumer durables.[20]

The growing use of consumer credit for automobile purchases supports the sustained growth in car ownership. In 1957, Belgians purchased only 47 percent of their cars on credit, Germans 26 percent.[21]

The needs of a growing and more affluent population have also indirectly increased the demands for transportation. Higher incomes have meant changes in how people spend their money, where they live and work, how much time they will have for leisure and where and how they will use it. These conditions are reflected in larger transportation expenditures.

EDUCATION

Historically, the educational process of the six countries in the Common Market has been that of family education at the lower levels and then into public schools (which to the North American actually means private schools) for higher education. This private education has been, for the most part, restricted to only the economically and socially privileged classes. There has been a strong education reform movement under way since the inception of the E.C.M. which is reflected in the Reform Plan of 1959 in Germany and the Reform Bill of 1960 in France. The objective of the French reform was to make education compulsory for children who entered primary school in the fall of 1959 until they were sixteen years old.[22] The German bill had broader goals. It was aimed at the neglect of elementary schools, the lack of student opportunities for education, and the inadequacy of programs preparatory to higher education.[23] "Altogether it is probably true that education is the weakest spot in the present West Germany."[24] Because of these conditions and the aspirations to remedy them, it has been apparent that the Common

[18] Same reference as footnote 9 at p. 294.

[19] European Commission of Economics, *Annual Bulletin of Transport Statistics for Europe,* (Geneva, 1959), p. 47.

[20] Same reference as footnote 9 at p. 302.

[21] *Economic Survey of Europe in 1958,* Chapter V, p. 25.

[22] Cultural Services of the French Embassy, *Education in France,* (Paris, 1961), No. 4, p. 9.

[23] Walter Stahl, *Education for Democracy in West Germany,* (New York: Frederick A. Praeger, Inc., 1961), p. 218.

[24] Same reference as footnote 23 at p. 218.

Market family has been devoting more attention and income to the area of education.

RECREATION

As unanimously indicated in Exhibit I every country in the E.C.M. had a decreasing percentage of its consumption being allocated to recreation. However, just as in the cases of food and clothing, the absolute number of dollars spent for this class of consumer goods and service is very significant. Recreation, although it decreased as family income increased, was the largest consumer expenditure in the miscellaneous classification in four of the six countries.

Much of the recreational endeavors of the European are family affairs which do not entail much expense. In addition, such expenses are difficult to measure on an aggregate basis. The European has not had the income to devote to spectator entertainment. Rather, the emphasis has been on participation sports.

FUTURE CONSUMPTION PATTERNS

From the patterns that have been established within the past seven years within the E.C.M. it is possible to make some rather well calculated generalizations.

The basic necessities, food, clothing and shelter, continue to absorb the major share of the household budget, although with rising incomes more money is available for luxuries and discretionary purchases but a smaller percentage of total per capita consumption is directed to miscellaneous goods and services.[25]

The increases in average incomes of the poorer countries is accompanied by less than proportional increases in expenditures for food, while in the countries at the highest income levels, percentage gains in food expenditures parallel the increases in per capita consumption expenditures.[26] Against a background of rising real incomes the trend toward increasing diversification of the diet continues because people are able to spend more for food than they did in the past. It is anticipated that there will be a significant increased demand for more processed foods as well as more elaborate packaging and distribution services.

Clothing expenditures continue to decrease as a proportion of the total family expenditure and will do so until such time as the more pressing needs of housing, medical care, education and transportation are met.

Although there is an expressed demand to increase the standards of housing within the E.C.M. countries, the consumer faces continued restraints in his spending for housing. It is anticipated, however, that this classification of expenditure will continue to absorb an increased percentage of the increasing family income.

As suggested previously, major emphasis is placed on health and education. Consequently, it is expected that these classes of consumer expenditure will continue to require an increasing percentage of the increasing family income. Such is not the case with recreation. Recreation will continue to demand a decreasing percentage of the family income until such time as the more essential needs are taken care of, and European patterns of recreation become more commercially developed.

CONCLUSION

This study of the consumer expenditures of the family within the European Common Market countries has brought to focus some important discrepancies in Engel's Laws and the findings of the *Life Study of Consumer Expenditures.* The most noteworthy derivation was with clothing expenditures where with-

---

[25] Same reference as footnote 9 at p. 162.

[26] Same reference as footnote 9 at p. 163.

out exception clothing took a smaller percentage of the family income as it increased. Almost as significant was the pattern of consumer spending for housing. Clearly, there is a definite tendency for an increased percentage of family income to be allocated to housing.

Should the governmental restrictions be removed, the increase will be of even greater proportions.

Food and miscellaneous classifications of expenditures both conformed to Engel's Laws with the exception of recreation spending.

(2) Psychological

12. Postdecision Exposure To Relevant Information[1]

DANUTA EHRLICH, ISAIAH GUTTMAN,
PETER SCHÖNBACH, AND JUDSON MILLS

Under what conditions will persons voluntarily expose themselves to information? This is an important theoretical and practical question for those interested in social influence processes. It is widely accepted that the audiences of mass media are to a large extent self-selected. However, there has been little rigorous specification or systematic research concerning the variables related to seeking out or avoidance of new information. Festinger has recently proposed a theory (2) which makes some definite predictions about selective exposure to information following decisions, and it is the purpose of this study to test several of them. Before the specific predictions from the theory are stated the relevant parts of Festinger's theory will be summarized briefly.

The theory is concerned with relations among cognitive elements, that is, things which a person knows about himself or his environment. For example, knowing that one is on a picnic is a cognition about one's behavior; knowing that it is raining, a cognition about the environment. Cognitive elements may be either consonant, dissonant, or irrelevant to one another. A behavioral element is consonant with an environmental element if, considering these elements in isolation, the behavioral would follow from the environmental element; dissonant if, considering them alone, it would *not* follow. Thus knowing that it is raining is ordinarily dissonant with going on a picnic; consonant with staying home.

According to the theory, the presence of dissonance gives rise to pressure to reduce or eliminate it. The strength of these pressures is a function of the magnitude of the dissonance. The theory also states that the greater the importance or the value of the elements involved, the greater is the magnitude of the dissonance and hence the greater the pressure to reduce it.

The total magnitude of the dissonance between a behavioral element and the cluster of relevant environmental elements, assuming they are all equally important, is equal to the proportion of dissonant elements in this cluster. Therefore, one way that a person can reduce dissonance is to add new environmental elements that are consonant with his behavior. Thus the theory predicts that persons with dissonance in general seek out consonant information and avoid information that would introduce new dissonant elements.

When a person makes a decision, a corresponding behavioral element is established and his cognitions about the alternatives among which he has chosen are then consonant or dissonant with

From *The Journal of Abnormal and Social Psychology*, Vol. 54, No. 1 (January, 1957), pp. 98-102.

[1]This research was carried out under the direction of Dr. Leon Festinger while the authors were members of his graduate seminar at the University of Minnesota. They would like to thank him for his generous advice and constructive criticism. This study was also part of the research program of the Laboratory for Research in Social Relations.

this element. All the favorable aspects of the unchosen alternatives and unfavorable aspects of the one chosen are dissonant with the choice. Consequently, the creation of dissonance is a common result of decisions. After the choice has been made, the person therefore tends, according to the theory, to expose himself to information that he perceives as likely to support the decision and to avoid information that is likely to favor the unchosen alternatives.

The purchase of a new automobile, for example, is usually a rather important decision for a person. Considerable dissonance should exist for a new car owner immediately after he has bought his car, all "good" features of the makes he considered, but did not buy, and "bad" features of the one he bought are now dissonant with his ownership of the car. He should also attempt to reduce this dissonance. In this instance of postdecision dissonance, sources of information in support of the decision are readily available. Since automobile advertising contains only material favoring the particular car advertised, reading advertisements of his own make is one way a new car owner can get information supporting his choice and thereby reduce his dissonance. On the other hand, reading advertisements of other cars may increase his dissonance.

The specific hypotheses of the study were as follows:

1. After a decision persons tend to seek out dissonance-reducing information. Thus new car owners will read advertisements of their own cars more often than those of (a) cars which they considered but did not buy and (b) other cars not involved in the choice.

2. After a decision persons tend to avoid dissonance-increasing information. Thus new car owners will read advertisements of considered cars less often than of other cars.

3. Postdecision dissonance is, in general, reduced over a period of time. Thus these selective tendencies in read-

ership of advertising will not exist for owners of old cars.

The theory predicts other consequences of postdecision dissonance, for example, changes in desirability ratings of chosen and unchosen alternatives as investigated by Brehm (1). Our present concern is limited to the effect of decision making on exposure to information.

METHOD

One hundred and twenty-five male residents of Minneapolis and its suburbs, who owned one of eight popular automobile makes, were interviewed[2] in an "advertising survey," after an appointment had been made by telephone. Sixty-five of the respondents were new car owners chosen randomly from a list of recent auto registrations, dated four to six weeks before the time of the interview. The other 60 respondents owned cars manufactured in 1952 (three years before the study was done) or before, and were selected from the Minneapolis telephone directory. (Actually about a third of the old car owners bought their cars after 1952; however, none of the purchases were made during the year in which the study was done.) The number of owners in different makes of cars was approximately equal in both groups.

During the course of the interview:

1. Each respondent was asked to recall recent automobile advertisements which had impressed him particularly and to say where and when he had seen the advertisement, whether or not his impression was favorable, and how much he had read (Recall Data).

2. Each was shown issues of popular magazines which appeared four weeks or less before the interview (after the new car owners had made their decisions) and copies of one of the two Minneapolis newspapers for seven days

[2] We would like to thank Craig Erickson and Peter Liebes for their assistance in conducting the interviews.

prior to the interview. Only those publications were included which the respondent previously indicated as having read regularly. For each issue the respondent was asked if he had seen it, and if so, he was shown each car advertisement it contained, and asked whether he had noticed the advertisement, and, if he had, whether he had "read all," "read some," or "just glanced at it" (Recognition Data).

3. Each was presented with eight large plain envelopes bearing the names of the eight popular makes. The respondent was told that his reactions to some "new automobile advertising" were desired and asked to choose two of the envelopes in order to read and comment upon the material they contained (Envelope Data).

At the conclusion of the interview the respondent was asked to name other makes which he "seriously considered" before he decided to buy his present car.

RESULTS

As a prerequisite for the predicted selectivity in a person's exposure to information, he must have some expectation about the likelihood that a given item will reduce or increase dissonance for him. Thus the new car owners must first recognize that a particular make is being advertised, i.e., they must at least notice the advertisement. For each respondent the percentage of advertisements which he read, of those which he noticed, was therefore calculated separately for his own car, the cars he considered, other cars not involved in the choice, and also for those considered and other cars combined. (The categories "read all" and "read some" were combined because there were too few advertisements reported as read completely to make a separate analysis feasible; results are essentially the same for these categories.) The means of these percentages for the two groups and the corresponding N's are reported in Table 1,

which also contains means for the percentage of advertisements noticed of those which were shown.

TABLE 1
MEAN PERCENTAGES OF ADVERTISEMENTS NOTICED AND OF
ADVERTISEMENTS READ OF THOSE NOTICED
(Corresponding N's appear in parentheses)

| Car Owners | Make Advertised | | | |
	Own	Considered	Other	Considered Plus Other
	Percentage Noticed			
New	70 (52)	66 (50)	46 (64)	48 (64)
Old	66 (51)	52 (31)	40 (60)	41 (60)
	Percentage Read of Those Noticed			
New	67 (47)	39 (46)	34 (64)	35 (64)
Old	41 (44)	45 (20)	27 (57)	30 (57)

Note.—The N's are reduced because in some cases no advertisements of a particular kind appeared in the issues shown or none of those which appeared were noticed. They are further reduced because not all respondents named cars as "seriously considered."

It can be seen from Table 1 that new car owners read advertisements of their own make more often than advertisements of both considered and other cars. These differences do not appear among old car owners; in fact the difference between reading of own and considered car advertisements is in the opposite direction. However, it is obvious from Table 1 that new car owners do not read advertisements of considered cars less often than of other cars. Finally, it is apparent that readership of advertisements, in general, is greater among new car owners.

The significance of these differences was determined by means of the sign test. For each respondent the sign of the comparison between the percentage of advertisements read of the different categories was found and this distribution of signs was tested using the critical values given in Mosteller and Bush (3). Results of these comparisons appear in Table 2 which shows that the differences apparent from Table 1 are significant. New car owners read significantly more advertisements of their own car than of both considered and other cars;

TABLE 2
SIGN TEST COMPARISONS BETWEEN PERCENTAGE OF ADVERTISEMENTS READ
OF DIFFERENT CATEGORIES

Comparison	Car Owners		Comparison	Car Owners	
	New	Old		New	Old
% Own Minus % Con-sidered	+21	5	% Own Minus % (Con-sidered Plus Other)	+32	20
	−4	6		−7	17
	$p < .01$	n.s.		$p < .01$	n.s.
Between Groups $p < .05$ ($\chi^2 = 3.90$)[*]			Between Groups $p < .01$ ($\chi^2 = 6.89$)		
% Own Minus % Other	+31	20	% Considered Minus % Other	+19	10
	−8	16		−15	7
	$p < .01$	n.s.		n.s.	n.s.
Between Groups $p < .03$ ($\chi^2 = 4.93$)			Between Groups, n.s.		

[*]Corrected for continuity.

none of the other comparisons yield significant differences. It can be seen that the N's have been further reduced because these comparisons were not possible for all respondents.

The significance of the differences between new car and old car owners was tested by means of chi square. Results of these tests are also given in Table 2. The comparison *own vs. considered* is in the predicted direction with $p < .05$. The comparison *own vs. other* is significant at the .03 level, and the comparison *own vs. considered plus other* is significant at the .01 level; there is no significant difference for the comparison *considered vs. other*.

One other comparison in the recognition data is worth noting.[3] New car owners were divided into two groups; those who named less than two cars as "seriously considered" and those who named two or more. The difference in reading *own vs. considered plus other* was examined separately for these two groups and was found to be greater for those who considered more than two cars. That is, new car owners who named more than one considered car

---
[3]See the discussion section for the theoretical relevance of this comparison.

read relatively more advertisements of their own car. For this group the mean difference of the percentages was 37; that of the other group was 26. The difference between the two groups was tested by a median test and the resulting (two-sided) $p = .19$ (12 of the 19 who considered two or more were above the median; only 12 of the 28 who considered less than two were above it).

For the Envelope Data the difference between groups is in the predicted direction but not significant. Fifty-one of 60 (85%) new car owners chose an envelope of their own car, 45 of 59 (76%) old car owners chose one of their own car. Respondents in both groups obviously chose to read and comment upon "new advertising" of their own makes far more often than would be expected by chance.

The number of impressive advertisements (Recall Data) which the respondents read is too small to make analysis of these data possible. (Of course no advertisements were included which appeared before the new car owners made their decisions or before a comparable length of time for old car owners.)

The data from the recognition of advertisements which appeared in recent publications (after the new car owners made their decisions) strongly support the prediction of Festinger's theory that, after an important decision, persons seek out consonant information. New car owners were found to read advertisements of their own car more often than those of cars they considered but did not buy, and of other cars not involved in the choice. That this selective tendency in exposure to information is not simply a result of car ownership but is related to decision making is demonstrated by its failure to occur among old car owners. The Envelope Data also indicate that new car owners prefer to read advertisements of their own car although the difference between new and old car owners is not significant.

An alternative explanation of the results might be offered. If people do not remember accurately when they read an advertisement, and if shortly *before* buying a car, persons are more likely to read advertisements of *that* car than of others, then the advertisements of their own make may have actually been read before the decision and the obtained differences may be a result of the new car owners' inability to remember the issue in which they read them. This interpretation seems unlikely since it is plausible to suppose that, *before* their purchase, the new car owners attempted to learn as much as possible about all the different makes involved in their choice and therefore read advertisements of the makes that they considered as often as those of the make that they finally chose. Nevertheless, the possibility that it could account for the data was checked by determining whether the advertisements of the make actually chosen by the new car owners which they said they read also appeared during the month prior to their purchases. Only four of 54 such advertisements also appeared in this period. When these few instances in which the alternate explanation might apply are elimi-

nated from the analysis the results are essentially unchanged.[4]

The prediction that new car owners would read fewer advertisements of considered cars than other cars was not substantiated. However, the data are not sufficient to reject conclusively the hypothesis that dissonance-increasing information is avoided after a decision. It is possible that some of the new car owners expected advertisements of considered cars to decrease — not increase — their dissonance. They may have read the advertisements of the rejected cars not with the intention of getting further information about their advantages but for the purpose of finding fault with them, comparing them unfavorably with the chosen car. For example, an owner of a make with high horsepower who regards horsepower as an important feature of automobiles may read advertisements of considered cars of lesser horsepower to remind himself of their inferiority in this respect. We would not expect this to occur frequently but it might happen often enough to account for the failure of the prediction. The data do not provide any test of this interpretation.

The indication that new car owners who named more than one considered car tend to read relatively more advertisments of their own car than do those who named one or none is additional, suggestive evidence for Festinger's theory. Since the total magnitude of dissonance is a function of the proportion of dissonant elements, we would expect that these persons would in general have greater dissonance, for as the number of unchosen alternatives increases the proportion of dissonant elements increases. Therefore the theory predicts that they should show a greater

---

[4] There are only two small changes in the significance tests reported in Table 2. When the four ads are eliminated the χ^2s for the comparisons between groups for *own minus considered* and for *own minus considered plus other* are reduced to 3.61 and 5.90 respectively.

tendency to seek out consonant information.

SUMMARY

Readership of auto advertising by new and old car owners was investigated in order to test some predictions of Festinger's theory of dissonance concerning selective exposure to information following decisions. It was found that new car owners read advertisements of their own car more often than of cars they considered but did not buy and other cars not involved in the choice. These selective tendencies in readership were much less pronounced among old car owners. This finding supports the theoretical derivation that persons in general seek out consonant or supporting information after an important decision in an attempt to reduce dissonance resulting from it.

From the derivation that persons tend to avoid dissonance-increasing information it was predicted that new car owners would read advertisements of considered cars less often than of other cars. The data do not confirm this prediction. It was suggested that some of the new car owners may have expected the considered car advertisements to decrease — not increase — their dissonance.

REFERENCES

1. Brehm, J. W. Postdecision changes in the desirability of alternatives. *J. abnorm. soc. Psychol.*, 1956, **52** 384-389.
2. Festinger, L. The relation between cognition and action. Paper read at Symposium on Cognition, Boulder, Colo., May, 1955.
3. Mosteller, F., & Bush, R. R. Selected quantitative techniques. In G. Lindzey (Ed.), *Handbook of social psychology*. Vol. I. Cambridge: Addison Wesley, 1954.

13. Psychological and Objective Factors in the Prediction of Brand Choice — Ford Versus Chevrolet*

FRANKLIN B. EVANS

I. INTRODUCTION

In recent years a number of non-quantitative studies in marketing have found substantial differences in the personalities of owners of different automobile makes. Buyers of one brand are described as differing sharply, personality-wise, from those of another. Also, the brands themselves are thought to have images or personalities extending beyond their physical characteristics. These images are expected to draw buyers, often in terms of personality need satisfaction.

This study was undertaken to test the ability of psychological and objective methods to discriminate between owners of the two largest-selling automobiles, Ford and Chevrolet. The cars are objectively almost perfect substitutes; their prices, models, and other features are almost identical. However, previous research has indicated that these makes represent different psychological images to the public and that the purchas-

ers of one make are sharply different, psychologically speaking, from purchasers of the other, at least on the average.

A simple random sample of Ford and Chevrolet owners provided the basic data for the test. The owners' scores on a standard test of manifest psychological needs were used as a basis for judging the ability of psychological factors to predict the brand of car owned. Demographic and other objective factors were also obtained, and thus predictive power was measured. These variables represent two widely different approaches to market research. Manifest psychological needs may be said to represent the motivations research approach, while the objective factors typify a more traditional approach which emphasizes the economic and demographic variables influencing the demand curve.

In each class of variables some small and only barely statistically significant differences were found between Ford and Chevrolet owners. These differences, however, are too minor to use effectively in predicting the brand of car owned. Taken singly or in a linear combination, neither personality needs nor demographic variables assigned brand ownership with any considerable degree of certainty. Even the advantage of selecting the most predictive variables from each class and combining them into a single linear discriminant function did little to improve the predictive efficacy.

Reprinted from *Journal of Business*, Vol. 32, No. 4 (October, 1959), pp. 340-69, by permission of the University of Chicago Press. Copyright © 1959 by the University of Chicago Press.

* The study resulting in this publication was in part made under a fellowship granted by the Ford Foundation. This financial aid is gratefully acknowledged. However, the conclusions, opinions, and other statements in this article are those of the author and are not necessarily those of the Ford Foundation. The writer also wishes to express his appreciation to Drs. Harry V. Roberts, Morris I. Stein, and James S. Coleman for their counsel and criticisms throughout the preparation of this paper.

The bulk of the literature ascribing differences to Ford and Chevrolet owners comes from the motivation researchers. When a linear relationship of the personality variables failed to produce the desired discrimination, psychologists suggested that perhaps some other model would fit better. However, no nonlinear relationship of the personality needs could be discovered. In addition, a select group of psychologists was unable to assign the brand correctly on the basis of the need scores. Also, neither grouping the needs according to type of basic satisfaction involved nor examination of the ranges of their scores showed any important difference between Ford and Chevrolet owners.

Two subsidiary analyses of other aspects of brand choice proved no more fruitful. Brand images were found, but they were much more diffuse than others have indicated. In only five out of twenty-one cases did they show images in a rigorous sense. The loyal and non-loyal owners of each brand are much alike with respect to the most predictive of the independent variables.

MARKET RESEARCH METHODS

Traditional research. — Traditional market researchers have stressed the importance of objective variables. Implicit in the use of these objective and demographic variables is their importance as demand determinants. These researchers have also relied upon consumers' opinions and motives that can be verbalized in response to direct questions. They believe that consumers both can and will disclose the reasons for, and thus predict, their behavior. Sample sizes tend to be large, sometimes running to thousands. Traditional researchers have used, or at least advocated, standard statistical techniques.

Variables such as age, income, race, sex, or geographic location are used to describe consumers. The narrower the ranges of these variables, the better a particular market can be distinguished from other competing products. Besides describing the limits of a market, these variables can often be used to explain and predict purchase behavior.[1]

Motivation research. — Whereas most traditional researchers have had business, economic, or statistical training, motivation researchers have entered the field with behavioral science backgrounds. Most have training in psychology or social psychology, but anthropology, psychiatry, psychometrics, and sociology are also represented.

Much of the work of motivation researchers has contained the tacit assumption that common motivations exist for large segments of the population. Standard statistical techniques are seldom employed; samples are usually small, rarely exceeding a few hundred or even a few score. Survey respondents are picked either to fit a predetermined quota or to be representative of a particular social class, and the actual selection of the individual to be interviewed is often left completely to the field worker's discretion.

Drawing heavily upon the Freudian schools of psychology, motivation researchers have maintained that many purchase reasons are deeply rooted in personality. These motives are either unknown to the conscious self or too ego-threatening to be revealed by direct questioning. To uncover these motives, depth interviews are used. In addition to depth interviewing, most motivation researchers use some kinds of psychological testing.

Although the value of motivation research has been questioned for some years now, the dispute has seldom been more than polemic. Few actual experiments have been made to compare the recommendations of the different

[1] Mordechai E. Kreinen, John B. Lansing, and James N. Morgan, "Analyses of Life Insurance Premiums," *Review of Economics and Statistics*, XXXIX (1957), 46-54.

schools.[2] An indirect measure of the predictive value of motivation research was tested by the writer. It was found that the recommendations of at least one study were predictive of advertising readership at a significant level.[3] This is an over-all lack of evidence comparing the two research modes.

PSYCHOLOGICAL TESTING

Almost all motivation researchers use some kinds of psychological tests, ranging from sentence completions and adjective checklists to completely unstructured projectives like the Rorschach ink blots. As there is very little standardization in this area or agreement about the instrument used, a group of experts were questioned.[4] These experts are either well-known practitioners in the field or academic people who have studied and written on the subject.

Eleven out of the sixteen experts believe psychological tests to be valuable

and necessary adjuncts to motivation research. Of the five who did not approve their use, only one is actively engaged in the field. The five dissenters questioned the over-all value of psychological tests, not only their marketing uses.

Of the eleven experts favoring psychological tests, eight stated that the tests could be used in their clinical form. Others suggested that the tests should be modified to relate directly to product attitudes. Thus a test's basic form and presentation are maintained, but the context is modified to relate views focused upon a particular product or brand.

Seven of the experts believed that motivation research techniques are standardized enough for others to replicate them. The question is of importance because, unless replication is possible the results of a particular study hinge entirely upon the skill and intuitiveness of the analyst. Many of the critics of motivation research have stressed this point. Some also mentioned that even the psychological tests like the Rorschach and Szondi are not very well standardized in clinical use.[5]

RESEARCH ON AUTOMOBILES

Discrimination of brand purchasers. —Referring to automobiles, Pierre Martineau, director of research and marketing of the *Chicago Tribune*, recently wrote: "The buyers and non-buyers were undistinguishable except on a personality basis."[6] The same general view is often publicly expressed by executives of these companies. Henry G. Baker of the Ford Motor Company has said: "A make thus becomes a very real extension of the

---

[2] See, however, John Masek, "A Study of the Usefulness of Motivation Research in Improving the Efficiency of Direct-Mail Selling Efforts" (unpublished Ph.D. dissertation, School of Business, University of Chicago, 1957).

[3] Franklin B. Evans, "Motivation Research and Advertising Readership," *Journal of Business,* XXX (1957), 141-46.

[4] Those replying were: Wroe Alderson (Alderson and Sessions, Inc.), Seymour Banks (Leo Burnett, Inc.), George H. Brown (Ford Motor Company), Louis Cheskin (Color Research Institute), Ernest Dichter (Institute for Motivational Research), Robert Ferber (University of Illinois), Burleigh B. Gardner (Social Research, Inc.), Mason Haire (University of California), William E. Henry (University of Chicago), Herta Herzog (McCann-Erickson, Inc.), Darrell B. Lucas (New York University), Joseph W. Newman (Harvard University), Fred T. Schreier (A. J. Wood and Company), George Horsley Smith (Rutgers University), W. Lloyd Warner (University of Chicago), and Hans Zeisel (University of Chicago). Also, although they did not answer the specific questions asked (and hence are not included in the survey results), replies of a general nature were received from Steuart H. Britt (Northwestern University), Paul F. Lazarsfeld (Columbia University), and James M. Vicary (James M. Vicary Corp.).

[5] Mason Haire, personal correspondence, February 14, 1958.

[6] Pierre Martineau, *Motivation in Advertising* (New York: McGraw-Hill Book Co., Inc., 1957), p. 67. Martineau's observations were based upon a study made in 1954 by Social Research, Inc., for the *Chicago Tribune*.

owner's DESIRED personality."[7] And, referring to the symbolic aspects of automobiles, David Wallace of the same company said: "On this dimension Ford is perceived as being the most masculine of the low-priced makes. Chevrolet and Plymouth are more feminine."[8]

Although Ford and Chevrolet purchasers have comprised about half the automobile market in the last twenty-five years, they are commonly portrayed as being entirely different personality-wise. A composite of these descriptions pictures Ford owners to be independent, impulsive, masculine, alert to change, and self-confident, while Chevrolet owners are described as conservative, thrifty, prestige-conscious, less masculine, and seeking to avoid extremes.

Criticisms. — During the recession of 1958 the sales of most domestic automobiles fell sharply, while the sales of small imported cars increased. The American manufacturers were blamed for producing cars which the public did not want. One of the most vituperative criticisms came from semanticist S. I. Hayakawa. He stated: "The trouble with car manufacturers (who, like other isolated people in undeveloped areas, are devout believers in voodoo) is that they have been listening too long to the motivation research people."[9] A similar, if less caustic, view of research on automobiles was expressed by Harold E. Churchill, president of the Studebaker-Packard Corporation. Referring to Studebaker's forthcoming small car, he

said: "It is not a car based on a small sample survey of the social significance of the automobile today."[10]

STUDY DESIGN AND IMPLEMENTATION

Research strategy. — With limited financial resources it was not possible to study all the various kinds of people who own Fords and Chevrolets. Therefore, a restricted and relatively homogeneous group — residents of Park Forest, Illinois — was selected for study.[11] The purpose of this limited study is to (1) demonstrate an improved methodology and, more important, (2) give limited but well-founded results that are a challenge to others.

The universe was further restricted to Ford and Chevrolet owners of 1955-58 models. This was done to minimize the effects of style cycles of these brands and includes model years in which each was the top seller nationally. In addition, all owners are white males and have only one car. From this restricted universe a simple random sample was drawn.

By confining the sample to this limited universe, it is believed that more sensitive discrimination will be possible, especially in terms of the personality variables analyzed. Gross differences such as sex or social class could confound the results in a sample of limited size.

The findings of this study cannot be generalized statistically to populations other than Park Forest, Illinois. However, it is believed that this test of the discriminatory efficacy of psychological and demographic variables will provide knowledge germane to the larger problems of prediction of brand choice which have seldom been solved. To say it differently, the inferences that can and should be made to populations broader than Park Forest must be based

---

[7] Henry G. Baker, "Sales and Marketing Planning of the Edsel," in *Marketing's Role in Scientific Management,* ed. Robert L. Clewett (Chicago: American Marketing Association, 1957), p. 130.

[8] David Wallace, "An Adventure in People's Minds: Finding a Personality for the E-Car," in *Conference on Sales Management,* ed. Stewart H. Rewoldt ("Michigan Business Papers," No. 14 [Ann Arbor: University of Michigan, 1957]), p. 6.

[9] S. I. Hayakawa, "Irrational Dreams, but Rational Behavior," *Advertising Age,* May 12, 1958, p. 111; reprinted from the Spring, 1958, issue of *ETC: A Review of General Semantics.*

[10] *Road and Track,* July, 1958, p. 2.
[11] See Appendix, "The Park Forest Universe," for the rationale for this choice.

on marketing judgment rather than on conventional statistical inference.

Test instrument. — The questionnaire was designed to collect three specific kinds of data — demographic and factual data related to automobile ownership, role-playing questions designed to measure perceived differences of Ford and Chevrolet owners, and psychological needs reflecting the respondents' basic personalities. Data for the first two categories were taken in personal interview. Personality needs were measured by a paper-and-pencil test filled out by the respondent in the interviewer's presence.

The collection of data in Park Forest took place in June and July, 1958. One hundred and forty-six substantially completed interviews were secured; 140 on the psychological test.[12]

Analysis of the data. — The major purpose of the analysis is to discover which variables best predict brand ownership. Several methods are presented, but primary reliance is placed upon the linear discriminant function.[13] Statistically, this function reduces the multivariate problem to a univariate one. A linear equation is derived which maximizes the separation between the two groups by optimum weighting of the independent variables. This equation is of the following form:

$$Y = aX_1 + bX_2 \ldots kX_k.$$

The X_1, X_2, etc., represent the independent variables, and a, b, etc., their weights. Conventionally the first weight (a) is made unity, and the others are expressed in proportionate terms. Substitution of the group means for each variable in the equation and solving it (summation) yields a numerical index $(\bar{Y}_i)$, where $i = 1$ or 2, which describes the group. Substitution of an individual's scores gives an index (Y)

for him. Any new individual may then be assigned to the group $(\bar{Y}_1$ or $\bar{Y}_2)$ whose score is closest to his.

II. PERSONALITY FACTORS

THE PSYCHOLOGICAL TEST

Instrument. — The analysis of personality variables presented in this study is based upon the results of a psychological schedule filled out by seventy-one Ford owners and sixty-nine Chevrolet owners. The test was constructed from items in the Edwards Personal Preference Schedule.[14] This test purports to measure manifest personality needs as described by Murray.[15] This is a simple paper-and-pencil test consisting of sets of paired statements in which each sentence in a pair describes a personality need. From each pair the respondent selects the statement he feels best portrays himself. One hundred and ten sets of paired comparisons were used, somewhat fewer than the full test because of interviewing problems encountered in pretesting. These paired comparisons yielded scores for each of eleven personality needs.

As previously indicated, most of the emphasis in motivation research has been upon projective tests — tests in which the respondent is presented with an ambiguous picture or situation and an answer in this situation reveals something about the personality. A simple paper-and-pencil test was used in this study in preference to a projective test for several practical reasons.

Projective tests are time-consuming and costly to administer. They require interviewers specifically trained in their use. To secure the response necessary for this study would have increased the project's cost several fold or diminished

---

[12] See Appensix, "Data Collection," for further information on response factors.

[13] R. A. Fisher, "The Use of Multiple Measurements in Taxonomic Problems," *Annals of Eugenics,* VII (1936-37), 179-88.

[14] Allen L. Edwards, *Edwards Personal Preference Schedule Manual* (New York: Psychological Corp., 1957).

[15] Henry A. Murray *et al., Explorations in Personality* (New York: Oxford University Press, 1938), pp. 142-242.

the sample size to the point where only the grossest differences could be demonstrated. Besides cost factors, the scoring and interpretation of projective tests are both difficult and unstandardized. Their use would have entailed securing several judges to rate (and agree upon) each respondent's personality pattern.

The Edwards Personal Preference Schedule was chosen for the following reasons: (1) scoring is simple, mechanical, and unambiguous; (2) it is gaining wide use among psychologists, and published results are available for comparison purposes; (3) it is based upon Murray's system of personality needs. The same needs are used in the Thematic Apperception Test (TAT), the most popular of the projective tests. For these reasons the Edwards was chosen for this analysis, although two other personality tests were briefly tried in the pretest stage of the project.

Personality needs measured. — Psychologists believe that to a considerable extent a person is known by his needs.[16] The pattern of needs in a personality defines the individual and allows something meaningful about him to be communicated to others. To say that a person is exceptionally aggressive, for example, characterizes him in a very general way. The needs treated as psychological variables in this paper are as follows:[17]

1. *Achievement:* To do one's best, to accomplish something of great significance;
2. *Deference:* To find out what others think, to accept the leadership of others;
3. *Exhibition:* To say witty and clever things, to talk about personal achievements;
4. *Autonomy:* To be able to come and go as desired, to say what one thinks about things;

5. *Affiliation:* To be loyal to friends, to make as many friends as possible;
6. *Intraception:* To analyze one's motives and feelings, to analyze the behavior of others;
7. *Dominance:* To be a leader in the groups to which one belongs, to tell others how to do their jobs;
8. *Abasement:* To feel guilty when one does something wrong, to feel inferior to others in most respects;
9. *Change:* To do new and different things, to participate in new fads and fashions;
10. *Aggression:* To attack contrary points of view, to get revenge for insults;
11. *Heterosexuality:* To become sexually excited, to be in love with someone of the opposite sex.

Independence of needs. — In order to use these need scores as independent measures of personality, examination was made of their intercorrelations. High intercorrelations among them would indicate that the items do not measure independent personality dimensions. For his normative group of 1,509 college men and women, Edwards found relatively low intercorrelations.[18] For the sample of 140 Ford and Chevrolet owners, intercorrelations of the need scores ranged from + .255 to − .364.[19]

TEST SCORES OF FORD AND CHEVROLET OWNERS

Group means. — The average score for each of the personality needs for Ford and Chevrolet owners is shown in Table 1. For seven of the needs (achievement, deference, intraception, abasement, change, aggression, and heterosexuality) the scores show no statistically significant difference. Three other needs (exhibition, autonomy, and affiliation) are significantly different at about the 10

---

[16] Harold J. Leavitt, *Managerial Psychology* (Chicago: University of Chicago Press, 1958), p. 98.
[17] Edwards, *op. cit.,* p. 14.

[18] *Ibid.,* p. 17.
[19] For further discussion of the test's reliability see Appendix, "The Psychological Test."

TABLE 1
AVERAGE PERSONALITY NEED SCORES OF FORD AND
CHEVROLET OWNERS

	Ford (N = 71)	Chevrolet (N = 69)	Difference
Achievement	12.80	12.87	−0.07
Deference	9.47	9.77	−0.30
Exhibition	10.06	9.30	+0.76°
Autonomy	7.86	8.80	−0.94°
Affiliation	10.14	11.09	−0.95°
Intraception	11.17	11.32	−0.15
Dominance	13.69	12.41	+1.28†
Abasement	7.20	7.28	−0.08
Change	11.39	11.06	+0.33
Aggression	9.59	9.52	+0.07
Heterosexuality	6.63	6.59	+0.04

°Significant at 10 per cent level (two-tailed test).
†Significant at 5 per cent level (two-tailed test).

per cent level. Only for dominance do the groups differ beyond the 5 per cent level of significance. A two-tailed test was used to test for differences between means because, from the orientation of this study, there were no specific hypotheses indicating the direction of the differences. However, all the differences except achievement and autonomy are in the direction commonly indicated by motivation researchers. Ford and Chevrolet owners as groups agree closely in the rank order they place the needs.[20] To put it differently, the differences between mean scores for different needs are much larger than the differences between Ford and Chevrolet means for the same need. Moreover, the differences between Ford and Chevrolet means, even on dominance, which showed the greatest separation, are of slight value for predicting a person's brand selection. The distributions of scores for all needs overlap to such an extent that discrimination is virtually impossible.

Graphic analysis.—Affiliation and dominance are the two needs which showed the greatest differences in

[20] Rank-order correlation = .903. Reject the null hypothesis at .01 level of significance.

group means. Figure 1 shows a cross-classification of these needs. The overlap of the distributions and their lack of discriminatory ability is apparent. Examination shows little clustering by brand, and there are no visible patterns that would indicate any simple way for predicting the brand owned. Similarly, Figure 2 shows abasement and aggression—needs whose group means were almost identical. As in Figure 1, the lack of discrimination by these needs is obvious. Although fifty-five such graphic cross-classifications could be made of the eleven needs, it is believed that these two (Figs. 1 and 2) demonstrate the problem. They support the earlier analysis of individual need scores; considering needs in pairs seems to add little or nothing to predictive ability.

LINEAR DISCRIMINANT FUNCTION

Statistical analysis.—To test for discrimination between Ford and Chevrolet owners using ten need scores (ten independent variables) at one time, a linear discriminant function was computed. The purpose is to weight the need scores of the two contrasted

FIGURE 1. Personality Needs.
Cross-Classification of the Needs
for Affiliation and Dominance for Ford and Chevrolet Owners

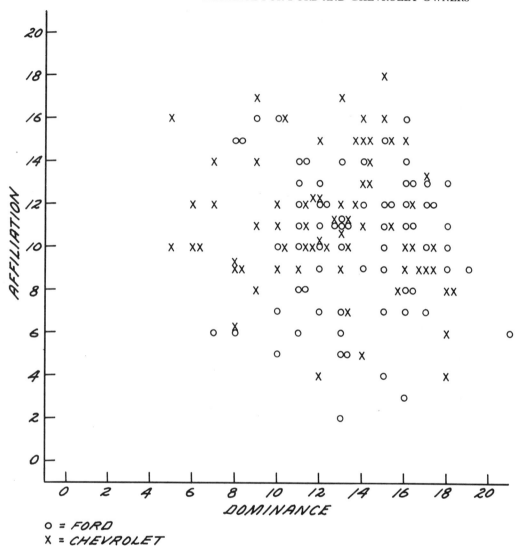

o = FORD
X = CHEVROLET

groups to provide maximum linear separation between them. That is, we restrict ourselves to a model that computes predicted scores by linear equations and finds the "best" coefficients for these equations in achieving discrimination.[21]

---

[21] Fisher, op. cit., pp. 179-88. See Appendix, "Linear Discriminant Function," for more detailed treatment and further references.

Only ten needs are used in this analysis, to avoid the statistical restrictions of a singular matrix. Sex, the need with the lowest score, was not used explicitly. The score of any individual need could vary from 0 to 20. For the ten needs used, a respondent's score could range from 90 to 110; for all eleven needs his score is necessarily 110.

Weights of the variables. – The weights of the ten psychological vari-

FIGURE 2. PERSONALITY NEEDS.
CROSS-CLASSIFICATION OF THE NEEDS
FOR ABASEMENT AND AGGRESSION FOR FORD AND CHEVROLET OWNERS

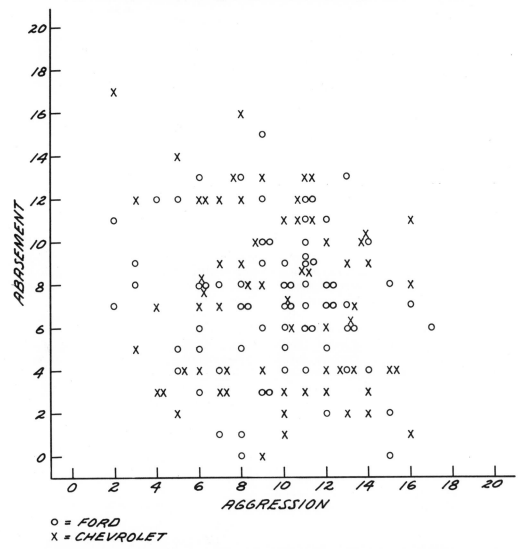

O = FORD
X = CHEVROLET

ables for the discriminant function are shown in Table 2. Group means and the mean of the Y for each group are also shown.

To test whether this function really discriminates between Ford and Chevrolet owners, an analysis of variance was performed. This is shown in Table 3. The multiple correlation coefficient (R) is .3353, and its square (R^2) is .1124. The resulting F ratio with 10 and 129 de-

grees of freedom is 1.634. This is just barely significant at the 10 per cent level, indicating that the linear discriminant function of personality needs is of doubtful statistical significance in this case.

Applying this discriminant function to the data from which it was developed, it misclassifies fifty-two individuals, or 37.1 per cent of the sample. A completely random basis of classification

TABLE 2
LINEAR DISCRIMINANT FUNCTION OF PERSONALITY NEEDS
FOR FORD AND CHEVROLET OWNERS

| | | Group Means | |
| | | Ford | Chevrolet |
Variable	Weight	(N = 71)	(N = 69)
Achievement	+1.0000 X_1	12.80	12.87
Deference	−0.0481 X_2	9.47	9.77
Exhibition	−1.4058 X_3	10.06	9.30
Autonomy	+2.0505 X_4	7.86	8.80
Affiliation	+2.0944 X_5	10.14	11.09
Intraception	−0.2356 X_6	11.17	11.32
Dominance	−2.1090 X_7	13.69	12.41
Abasement	−0.5269 X_8	7.20	7.28
Change	−1.6005 X_9	11.39	11.06
Aggression	+0.2561 X_{10}	9.59	9.52
$\bar{Y}_i = \Sigma$ weights *times* group means. . . .		−15.5150	− 7.3416

such as flipping a coin, would have misclassified approximately 50 per cent of the sample. Table 4 shows the classifications by brand. Also one would not expect the equation to predict even this accurately for new observations.[22]

Similarity of correctly and incorrectly classified cases.—Comparison was made of those classified correctly and those owners misclassified to see whether other factors could be responsible for the lack of predictive efficacy of the function. Three characteristics other than personality needs were selected for this analysis. Age of owner is a demographic factor, intention to purchase the same brand again indicates brand satisfaction, and smokers versus non-

smokers may reflect some deeper personality differences than those expressed by the need scores. Table 5 shows these comparisons both for the combined group and for Ford and Chevrolet owners separately.

Examination of these characteristics shows that those classified correctly and those misclassified are very similar, both for the combined sample and for each make separately. Tests of the largest differences for each characteristic show no significant difference for either make, even at the 10 per cent level. Also the direction of the differences within brands is often inconsistent when both

---

[22]The probability of misclassification for this discriminant function was computed by dividing half the difference between $\bar{Y}_1$ and $\bar{Y}_2$ by the within-sample standard deviation of individual Y's and finding the probability that a standard normal variable would exceed that number (see Fisher, *op. cit.*, pp. 182-83). For this function, the probability of misclassification is .366. For future samples this would be an understatement, since this procedure is a large sample approximation that assumes the sample quantities equal corresponding parameters. The true proportion of error would be higher, but exactly how much is not known.

TABLE 3
ANALYSIS OF VARIANCE OF LINEAR
DISCRIMINANT FUNCTION OF
PERSONALITY NEED VARIABLES

Source of Variation	Degrees of Freedom	Sum of Squares	Mean Square
Discriminant function	10	.1124(R^2)	.01124
Remainder	129	.8876(1−R^2)	.00688
Total	139	1.0000	
		F=1.634	

TABLE 4

CLASSIFICATION OF FORD AND CHEVROLET OWNERS BY LINEAR
DISCRIMINANT FUNCTION OF PERSONALITY AND NEED VARIABLES

	Classified Correctly	Misclassified	Total
Ford	41	30	71
Chevrolet	47	22	69
	88 (62.9%)	52 (37.1%)	140 (100%)

brands are examined. For example, mis-classified Ford owners are more satisfied with their cars than are correctly classified Ford owners; the reverse is true for Chevrolet owners.

This analysis shows that there is no readily apparent explanation for the lack of "fit" of the linear discriminant function. The incorrect classification of almost two-fifths of the sample from which the function was derived shows that the variables are of low predictive value in this case and that a linear combination of ten personality needs is not sufficient to achieve much discrimination between owners of Fords and

Chevrolets. Certainly, gross differences are simply not to be found.

NON-LINEAR RELATIONSHIPS

Psychologists, when assessing personality, attempt to look at the total or whole person as well as the individual components. From this vantage point one would expect psychologists to judge inadequate an analysis of personality in which a simple linear equation is used to express the relationships. The psychologist's assessment of personality is often a subjective process of weighting and weighing all the factors or reactions

TABLE 5

COMPARISON OF FORD AND CHEVROLET OWNERS CLASSIFIED CORRECTLY
AND MISCLASSIFIED BY LINEAR DISCRIMINANT FUNCTION OF PERSONALITY NEEDS

	Combined Sample		Ford		Chevrolet	
	Classified Correctly	Misclassified	Classified Correctly	Misclassified	Classified Correctly	Misclassified
Characteristic	(N = 88)	(N = 52)	(N = 41)	(N = 30)	(N = 47)	(N = 22)
Age of owners:						
39 years and over	20	12	9 (22.0)*	8 (26.7)*	11 (23.4)*	4 (18.2)*
31-38 years	46	28	22 (53.6)	15 (50.0)	24 (51.0)	13 (59.1)
Under 31 years	22	12	10 (24.4)	7 (23.3)	12 (25.6)	5 (22.7)
Buy same brand again	48	29	18 (43.9)	17 (56.7)	30 (63.8)	12 (54.6)
Not buy same brand again	40	23	23 (56.1)	13 (43.3)	17 (36.2)	10 (45.4)
Owner smokes	61	36	33 (80.5)	22 (73.3)	28 (59.6)	14 (63.6)
Does not smoke	27	16	8 (19.5)	8 (26.7)	19 (40.4)	8 (36.4)

* Within-subgroup percentages.

he has available. Thus, through their own intuitive processes, they may be able to discriminate between personalities in a way that reflects non-linear configurations.

Although the ten needs measured in this study cannot be considered as "the whole man" if the needs are positively or negatively cathected to automobile ownership, one would expect psychologists to be able to distinguish between two differing groups.

The psychologists discriminate.—To see whether psychologists using their own particular methods and judgments could distinguish between Ford and Chevrolet owners, a selected group of psychologists was asked to examine the need scores of ten individuals.[23] These eighteen psychologists were given the need scores of five Ford and five Chevrolet owners randomly selected from the Park Forest respondents. The judges were told that there were five Ford and five Chevrolet owners in this group.

Along with the test scores of the ten individuals, these judges were given the following protocol:

> In recent years many marketing research studies have either attributed definite personality characteristics to specific kinds of automobiles or categorized brand owners by personality. These are derived from depth-interviewing (unstructured) techniques and psychological testing. Although different methods are employed, results are often surprisingly similar. For example:
> Ford owners are said to be more independent, alert to change and experiment, more tolerant, self-confident, impulsive, interested in people and more masculine. They *drive* a Ford, and are younger people with above average incomes.

On the other hand:
> Chevrolet owners are more feminine, more cautious, suspicious, conservative, thrifty, prestige conscious, less independent, and hold their cars longer. They *own* a Chevrolet and consider it a stable and dependable car. They want to be up-to-date but to avoid being too extreme. They are interested in things more than people.

As a group, these judges picked only 70 cases correctly out of 180 possible choices, for a percentage of 39.9. The maximum number of correct choices made by anyone was 6 and the minimum was 2.[24]

Although they did not correctly assign the owners to their proper groups, these judges did exhibit a high consensus. Sixteen, seventeen, and eighteen judges, respectively, agreed that, of the five Chevrolet cases, three were Fords. Fourteen, fourteen, and fifteen of the judges, respectively, assigned three of the five Ford cases to the Chevrolet group. The three Chevrolet cases judged incorrectly consisted of individuals with high scores for achievement, aggression, and dominance and low scores for abasement. The three Ford cases most misclassified had low scores for achievement, autonomy, and exhibition and a high score for abasement. These six cases accounted for the bulk of the incorrect placements.

When apprised of their results, the psychologists themselves suggested several possible reasons for this outcome. The most common explanation offered was that the description of Ford and Chevrolet owners taken from motivation research studies was wrong or misleading. Two pointed out that these descriptions as given are internally inconsistent. The masculine attributes assigned to Ford owners are more in keeping with people interested in

---

[23] Eighteen psychologists participated; four are in the academic profession, nine in advertising or marketing research, three in psychological testing and guidance, and two are practicing analysts.

[24] The actual distribution of choices and the statistical probability of these occurring owing to chance alone are shown in the Appendix, "Psychologists' Judging by Personality Needs."

things, not in *other people* as stated, and the opposite for Chevrolet owners. However, five of the eighteen psychologists acting as judges claimed that they did not follow these protocols; of these five, one made six correct choices and the others four.

The second reason offered was that the test instrument used did not really measure the needs as described. Several of the psychologists said when taking the test that they did not expect to score very well as the data were limited, and one suggested that the psychologists themselves would probably take the test in a very defensive way, thereby distorting results. Still another reason could be that the ten randomly chosen car owners happened to be atypical of their respective groups.

The high consensus of the psychologists on the six cases previously mentioned shows that they were discriminating but apparently not by any subtle process. If a curvilinear relationship of the ten personality needs could do better than the linear discriminant function in classifying the Ford and Chevrolet owners, the psychologists did not discover it either consciously or unconsciously.

Some further investigations.—The ten needs from the test can be grouped into three general classes.[25] Affiliation, abasement, aggression, autonomy, deference, and dominance express interpersonal relations. Exhibition and achievements are inner-state needs, and intraception and change are goal-oriented needs. When aggregated into these three classes, the needs show even smaller differences than when treated separately, as several of the individual differences cancel each other. This again points to the similarity of personality factors of the two brand owners.

Differences in dispersion of the indi-

vidual need scores between the two groups would also indicate non-linear relationships. A wide range of scores for owners of one brand as opposed to a narrow range for the other would denote different personality types, even though the over-all group means are the same. However, examination of the ranges of the ten needs does not suggest that this exists. For five of the needs the range is the same, and for four more the differences in range are one, one, two, and three, respectively. Only one need — achievement — shows considerable difference in range between the two brands.

CONCLUSION

All the evidence points to the conclusion that personality needs, as measured in this study, are of little value in predicting whether an individual owns a Ford or Chevrolet automobile. Although people within a common social class have different personalities, their personalities do not appear to be systematically related to selection of the two most popular brands of cars. This result is, however, based upon the specific test instrument used, and no doubt criticism can be raised on this point. In its defense it can be said that this test is commonly accepted by many psychologists for many different uses.[26] Other reasons for its applicability in this particular study have been given previously.

The more important question is beyond the scope of this paper. This is, "Can any test really measure personality?" Psychologists themselves are deeply concerned with this problem and do not hesitate to question the entire area of personality theory.[27]

---

[25] G. G. Stern, M. I. Stein, and B. S. Bloom, *Methods in Personality Assessment* (Glencoe, Ill.: Free Press, 1956), pp. 69-73.

[26] Robert R. Blake and Jane S. Mouton, "Personality," *Annual Review of Psychology,* ed. Paul R. Farnsworth (Palo Alto, Calif.: Annual Review, Inc., 1959), p. 207.
[27] *Ibid.,* p. 226.

III. DEMOGRAPHIC AND OBJECTIVE FACTORS

THE VARIABLES

The selection of Park Forest as the area of study restricted the ranges of the demographic variables. In this study the psychological variables showed wide variation, as wide as for other groups to whom this test has been administered. However, in terms of the demographic variables, Park Forest is much more limited. The ages and incomes of the survey respondents, for example, were of much narrower range than would be found in sampling larger and less homogeneous areas. Therefore, the linear discriminant function of demographic variables is under a handicap when compared to the one based upon the psychological needs.

The variables selected. – Twelve objective variables were chosen from the interview data to represent factors commonly used by traditional market researchers. With the exception of income, all were easily collected. Nine and sixth-tenths per cent of the total sample refused to divulge their yearly family income. The twelve variables selected were as follows: (1) age of automobile presently owned; (2) use of automobile more or less than 10,000 miles per year; (3) buyer "shopped" more than one dealer before purchase; (4) smokers versus non-smokers; (5) homeowners versus renters; (6) three or more children living at home; (7) religious preference; (8) church attendance more or less than once a month; (9) political party preference; (10) age of owner; (11) owner has worked for present firm more or less than five years; and (12) family yearly income.

These twelve variables describe several different aspects of the respondents' lives. Model year and usage of the car may reflect the car's importance to the family. Smoking, shopping for new cars, and tenure with a firm may reflect personality measures possibly even more basic than those measured by the psychological needs test. And age, income, family size, politics, and religion are typical demographic variables not necessarily associated with any specific behavior patterns.

Another group of objective factors that might be predictive of brand was purposely omitted. These are details of the car, such as size, color, horsepower. The obvious reason for deleting these variables is that, if they were known, the brand would be too. To use these would be to mix "dependent" and "independent" variables. Prediction would then be little more than a mathematical exercise. In this study, for example, the number of cylinders would have been an excellent, but trivial, discriminator between Ford and Chevrolet. Over twice as many six-cylinder Chevrolets as Fords occurred in the sample.

Many of the demographic variables are qualitative, and scaling them raises important problems. These problems were mainly bypassed by treating the qualitative variables in dichotomous fashion: respondents were placed in one class or another.

Religion and politics presented special problems because there is no obvious ordering of the categories. The method of dummy variables was used.[28] Religion was treated as two variables: Protestant or not, Catholic or not. Each of these variables is dichotomous. The remaining dummy variable, non-Christian or not, was not included explicitly; this avoids the statistical problem arising from a singular matrix.[29] The number of cases involved in the omitted

---

[28] Daniel B. Suits, "Use of Dummy Variables in Regression Equations," *Journal of the American Statistical Association*, LII (1957), 548-51.

[29] In regression or linear discriminant function solutions the normal equations can be solved by placing restrictions upon the equations – setting the constant term of the equation equal to zero. The common solution, however, is simply to drop one of the dummy variables (*ibid.*).

TABLE 6

AVERAGE SCORES OF DEMOGRAPHIC VARIABLES FOR FORD AND CHEVROLET OWNERS

Variable	Scoring Range		Ford (N = 72)	Chevrolet (N = 74)	Difference
Age of car	1 (1958)	−4 (1955)	2.625	3.014	− 0.389°
Over 10,000 miles per year	1 (over)	−0 (under)	0.722	0.622	+ .100
Shopped more than one dealer	1 (yes)	−0 (no)	0.750	0.716	+ .034
Owner smokes	1 (yes)	−0 (no)	0.778	0.608	+ .170†
Own − rent	1 (Rent)	−0 (Own)	0.417	0.554	− .137‡
Three or more children at home	1 (yes)	−0 (no)	0.444	0.311	+ .133‡
Catholic or not	1 (yes)	−0 (no)	0.319	0.230	+ .089
Protestant or not	1 (yes)	−0 (no)	0.639	0.662	− .023
Attend church more than once a month	1 (no)	−0 (yes)	0.375	0.460	− .085
Republican or not	1 (yes)	−0 (no)	0.444	0.378	+ .066
Democrat or not	1 (yes)	−0 (no)	0.181	0.284	− .103
Age	1 (19)	−9 (54)	5.333	5.351	− .018
Five or more years with same firm	1 (yes)	−0 (no)	0.625	0.473	+ .152‡
Income (mid-points)	1 ($3,750)	−6 ($16,250)	3.194	3.068	+ 0.126

° Significant at 2 per cent level (two-tailed test).
† Significant at 5 per cent level (two-tailed test).
‡ Significant at 10 per cent level (two-tailed test).

dummy variable was small, less than 8 per cent of the sample. Implicitly, of course, the variable is included: "non-Protestant and "non-Catholic" jointly define "non-Christian."

In like fashion, politics was split into two variables. Republican or not and Democrat or not. The third dummy variable, Republican or Democrat versus all others, was deleted as before. The use of these dummy variables increased the total objective variables to fourteen.

The intercorrelations of these variables were examined. For the fourteen variables, including the dummy variables, ninety-one comparisons are necessary. With the exception of the dummy variables, most of these intercorrelations are low. With the dummy variables high, negative intercorrelations were found, as expected. Catholic or not and Protestant or not have an intercorrelation of − .838; Republican or not and Democrat or not, − .460.

Outside of these, the highest intercorrelation is between age and more than five years with the same firm. The relationship is + .401. The second highest non-dummy variable correlation is the relationship between Catholicism and having three or more children. The correlation coefficient is + .378. Catholicism is also highly correlated with frequent church attendance (+ .334).

GROUP SCORES OF THE OBJECTIVE VARIABLES

The average scores of Ford and Chevrolet owners are shown in Table 6. Also the scoring range and the differences between group means are given. There were no hypotheses concerning the direction of the differences, and a two-tailed test was used to compare group means.

Nine of the variables show no significant differences between means. Age, income, religion, and politics are among these. These are among the variables most commonly used in marketing research to describe specific brand markets. In addition to these, usage over 10,000 miles per year and "shopping" showed no differences between the two groups.

The most significant difference between the groups was shown in the age of the car owned. Fords were newer. Thirty-five of the seventy-two Fords were of 1957 or 1958 model compared to twenty-one out of seventy-four Chevrolets. This reflects the different popularity of the brands in different years.

In the universe sampled, Ford accounted for 53 per cent of the owners, Chevrolet for 47 per cent. The difference cannot be accounted for by the popularity of various body styles al-

TABLE 7

LINEAR DISCRIMINANT FUNCTION OF DEMOGRAPHIC VARIABLES FOR FORD AND CHEVROLET OWNERS

Variable	Discriminant Function Weight	Group Means Ford ($N = 72$)	Chevrolet ($N = 74$)
Age of car	$+1.0000\ X_1$	2.6250	3.0140
Used over 10,000 miles per year	$-1.0480\ X_2$	0.7222	0.6216
Shopped before buying	$-0.1204\ X_3$	0.7500	0.7162
Owner smokes	$-2.1629\ X_4$	0.7778	0.6081
Home owner−renter	$+1.0189\ X_5$	0.4167	0.5541
Three or more children at home	$-0.8388\ X_6$	0.4444	0.3108
Catholic or not	$-3.4376\ X_7$	0.3194	0.2297
Protestant or not	$-2.8371\ X_8$	0.6389	0.6622
Attend church more than once a month	$+0.2189\ X_9$	0.3750	0.4595
Republican or not	$+0.3198\ X_{10}$	0.4444	0.3784
Democrat or not	$+1.7266\ X_{11}$	0.1806	0.2838
Age	$-0.1304\ X_{12}$	5.3330	5.3510
Five or more years with same firm	$-1.0576\ X_{13}$	0.6250	0.4730
Income	$+0.2482\ X_{14}$	3.1940	3.0680
$\bar{Y}_i = \Sigma$ weights *times* group means		−2.7909	−1.1283

TABLE 8

CLASSIFICATION OF FORD AND CHEVROLET OWNERS BY LINEAR DISCRIMINANT FUNCTION OF DEMOGRAPHIC VARIABLES

Brand	Classified Correctly	Misclassified	Total
Ford	52	20	72
Chevrolet	50	24	74
Total	102 (69.9%)	44 (30.1%)	146 (100%)

TABLE 9

ANALYSIS OF VARIANCE OF LINEAR DISCRIMINANT FUNCTION OF DEMOGRAPHIC VARIABLES

Source of Variation	Degrees of Freedom	Sum of Squares	Mean Square
Discriminant function	14	$.1458(R^2)$	.010414
Remainder	131	$.8542(1 - R^2)$	.006521
Total	145	1.000	

$$F = 1.597$$

ledged to be popular in suburbia. For some years Ford has claimed sales superiority in convertibles and station wagons, yet in the sample there were nineteen Fords of these models and sixteen for Chevrolet; in other models the distributions were also similar.

The two next largest differences were smoking and working for the same firm for five or more years. The Ford group contains more men who smoke and more men who have stayed with the same company for five or more years. Although these variables are objective in nature, they suggest differences in personality possibly more basic than those discussed earlier.

The two other variables showing significant differences between Ford and Chevrolet owners are home ownership and three or more children living at home. In each of these cases Ford owners show a higher percentage than Chevrolet owners. The intercorrelation of these two variables is only +.219. Both of these suggest strong family life and are not exactly what one would picture a Ford owner to be from the motivation research findings previously mentioned.

For all fourteen of these demographic variables the distributions of both groups overlap substantially. Although five of the fourteen group means are significantly different, this overlap reduces the chance for successful discrimination by any one variable.

LINEAR DISCRIMINANT FUNCTION

Weights of the variables.—The weights of the fourteen variables for the linear discriminant function are shown in Table 7. The group's means and the mean of the $\bar{Y}$ for each group are also given.

Predictive ability.— In terms of the number of cases classified correctly, this discriminant function is slightly better than the one using the psychological need variables. It misclassified only 30.1 per cent of the cases, compared to

37.1 per cent for the latter. This still leaves much to be desired in terms of predictive ability.[30] The number of cases classified by brand are shown in Table 8.

The multiple correlation coefficient (R) of this discriminant function is .3819, and its square (R^2) is .1458. Analysis of variance shows this equation to be statistically significant between the 10 and 5 per cent levels, the same as the psychological need equation. This analysis of variance is shown in Table 9.

OTHER OBJECTIVE FACTORS

In addition to the demographic variables used in the linear discriminant function, several other factors were investigated. In terms of education the two groups were very similar. The distributions by brand of highest grade level completed are almost identical.

Stock ownership in the automobile companies was very rare and not associated with the brand owned. Two Ford owners held Ford Motor Company stock and one owned General Motors stock. One Chevrolet owner had Ford stock; none had General Motors.

Twenty-four Ford owners and twenty-six Chevrolet owners had high fidelity (HiFi) phonographs in their homes. None owned color television sets.

Newspaper reading habits of the two groups were also extremely similar. Sixty to 65 per cent of each group of owners read the *Chicago Tribune* and/or *Daily News*. About 30 per cent read the *Sun-Times* and 10 per cent the *American*.

CONCLUSION

The linear discriminant function of demographic variables is not a sufficiently powerful predictor to be of much practical use. It does a somewhat better

---

[30] The expected proportion of misclassification for this discriminant function is .355. For future samples this would be an understatement (see n. 22).

TABLE 10

LINEAR DISCRIMINANT FUNCTION COMBINING OBJECTIVE AND PSYCHOLOGICAL
NEED VARIABLES FOR FORD AND CHEVROLET OWNERS

Variable	Discriminant Function Weight	Group Means[*] Ford (N=71)	Chevrolet (N=69)
Owner smokes	$-1.0000\ X_1$	0.778	0.608
Homeownership	$+0.6631\ X_2$	0.417	0.554
Three or more children at home	$-0.4919\ X_3$	0.444	0.311
Catholic or not	$-1.1735\ X_4$	0.319	0.230
Protestant or not	$-0.8286\ X_5$	0.639	0.662
Republican or not	$+0.1019\ X_6$	0.444	0.378
Democrat or not	$+0.7282\ X_7$	0.181	0.284
Five or more years with same firm	$-0.1884\ X_8$	0.625	0.473
Deference	$+0.0137\ X_9$	9.470	9.770
Exhibition	$-0.0634\ X_{10}$	10.060	9.300
Autonomy	$+0.1376\ X_{11}$	7.860	8.800
Affiliation	$+0.1616\ X_{12}$	10.140	11.090
Dominance	$-0.1151\ X_{13}$	13.690	12.410
$\bar{Y}=\Sigma$ weights *times* group means		-0.9280	$+0.0630$

[*] See Table 1 for personality need scores; Table 6 for objective variable scores.

job of classification than the function based upon psychological need scores. Its results, however, are not enough better to favor strongly the traditional research mode over motivation research. Both point more to the similarity of Ford and Chevrolet owners than to any means of discrimination between them. Analysis of several other objective factors also leads to the same conclusion.

IV. COMBINED ANALYSIS: PSYCHOLOGICAL AND OBJECTIVE FACTORS

AN ECLECTIC APPROACH

The central problem of this paper dictated that the predictive abilities of the two kinds of data be treated separately. However, with the data available one would not normally restrict the analysis to these separate and distinct comparisons. It is highly possible that some combination of demographic and psychological variables would be better than either alone. To test this, a linear discriminant function was computed using as independent variables those of each kind which showed the greatest differences between Ford and Chevrolet owners.

Selecting the independent variables for this analysis upon the basis of the earlier investigations should increase the probability that prediction will improve. Statisticians know well that in correlation and regression problems any competent statistician can produce highly significant results, given enough time and data to pick and choose, rejecting what does not work and retaining what seems promising. Testing hypotheses upon the data from which they were derived is statistically unsound.[31] Therefore, the following analysis should be viewed with these limitations in mind.

Selection of variables.—The variables were selected upon the basis of their comparative significance in the previous discriminant functions.[32] Six

[31] W. A. Wallis and H. V. Roberts, *Statistics: A New Approach* (Glencoe, Ill.: Free Press, 1956), p. 405

[32] The variables selected for each type of data are

TABLE 11

CLASSIFICATION OF FORD AND CHEVROLET OWNERS BY
LINEAR DISCRIMINANT FUNCTION USING BOTH PSY-
CHOLOGICAL AND DEMOGRAPHIC VARIABLES

Brand	Classified Correctly	Misclassified	Total
Ford	46	25	71
Chevrolet	43	26	69
Total	89 (63.6%)	51 (36.4%)	140 (100%)

demographic variables and five psychological needs were chosen. The demographic variables are as follows: X_1, smoking; X_2, homownership; X_3, three or more children at home; X_4, X_5, religion; X_6, X_7, politics; and X_8, five or more years with the same company. As before, religion and politics were each split into two through the use of dummy variables. Thus in the discriminant function these six actually became eight. The five psychological needs that looked most promising are the following: X_9, deference; X_{10}, exhibition; X_{11}, autonomy; X_{12}, affiliation and X_{13}, dominance.

LINEAR DISCRIMINANT FUNCTION

Weights of the variables.—Table 10 gives the weights for each of these thirteen variables in the combined analysis. Group means and the $\bar{Y}$ for each group are also shown.

Predictive ability.—Although "loaded" to produce favorable results, this discriminant function does not show better predictive ability than the one based on demographic factors alone. It is only slightly better than the one based upon psychological needs. It misclassified 51 out of the 140 cases from which it was developed; 36.4 per cent were assigned to the wrong brand.[33] By

those with the highest F ratios of their partial regression coefficients. This was possible because the original discriminant function was computed from the multiple regression model.

[33] The expected proportion of misclassified cases for this combined discriminant function is .340. As before, this understates the real problem (see n. 22).

comparison, the demographic factor discriminant function misclassified 30.1 per cent of the cases and the psychological need discriminant function, 37.1 per cent. Classification by brand by the combined factor discriminant function is shown in Table 11.

This apparent lack of improvement of the combined variable discriminant function over the demographic factor function may be due to not including the age of automobile owned as a variable in the combined analysis. This variable showed the greatest separation on group means among demographic variables. Ideally, comparisons would be made only for specific years, and this kind of "semidependent" variable would not enter in. Sample size prohibited this, however, in this study.

The multiple correlation coefficient of the combined variable discriminant function is .3991, the highest of the three functions computed. Analysis of variance shows the equation to be statistically significant at the 5 per cent level. This is shown in Table 12.

TABLE 12

ANALYSIS OF VARIANCE OF LINEAR DISCRIMINANT FUNCTION USING DEMOGRAPHIC AND PSYCHOLOGICAL NEED VARIABLES

Source of Variation	Degrees of Freedom	Sum of Squares	Mean Square
Discriminant function	13	$.1593(R^2)$	.012254
Remainder	126	$.8407(1-R^2)$	.006672
Total	139	1.0000	
		$F=1.837$	

CONCLUSION

The combination of the most predictive variables from the two earlier analyses did not produce an effective method for distinguishing between Ford and Chevrolet owners. The linear discriminant function combining these variables is statistically significant at a higher level than the previous two, but its discriminatory ability is still low. This combined analysis does not show any significant superiority over the earlier ones, nor does it point toward some combination of the variables as explaining the choice between Ford and Chevrolet.

V. OTHER ASPECTS OF PURCHASE BEHAVIOR

Although subsidiary to the main investigation, interview data were collected specifically for analysis of other areas of behavior commonly associated with consumer products. These areas are (1) the image or stereotype that a particular brand may have in people's minds and (2) differences between owners who are loyal to one brand as opposed to those who switch brands. Each of these areas was examined for differences between Ford and Chevrolet owners and for clues to their purchase motives.

BRAND STEREOTYPES

Brand images. – A brand's image consists of all the things associated with the product or perceived about it. It is a total personality extending beyond its physical qualities. And it is this image that people are thought to purchase rather than any reality. Also an image is consistent among both users and non-users; it is commonly held views of brands that attract some customers and repel others. The image specifies what kinds of people or for what uses the particular brand is best suited.

A brand image is the result of three distinct forces. First, the product itself by nature of its physical makeup and design may be better for some uses or kinds of people than other competing products. Second, the manufacturer through his advertising tries to create the impression that his brand is best for certain people or uses. For example, a certain automobile has recently been advertised as being particularly appropriate for doctors, as it is a very dependable car. And, third, people associate a brand with the type or classes of people they observe using it. In some undefined and unspecified pattern, these elements contribute to the brand's personality. Advertising stresses the importance of the second of these factors. Current market research activities are often oriented toward the third.

Research on automobiles. – A study by Munn indicated that consumers perceive significant quality differences between brands of automobiles.[34] He also found these images to be independent of age, education, or income of the consumer. More specifically, a study by the Bureau of Applied Social Research indicated that among the low-priced automobiles the Ford owner was perceived as being more youthful, more masculine, and of lower social class than owners of Chevrolets or Plymouths.[35]

Assessment of brand images. – To measure the brand images of Ford and Chevrolet respondents were given the following instructions and twenty-one brief descriptions of people:

We often think of cars especially suitable or unsuitable for different kinds of people, the way it seems odd for a very big man to drive around in a very small car. I'll describe some people for you and I'd like you to tell me if a Ford or Chevrolet would be a

---

[34] Henry L. Munn, "An Exploratory Investigation of Brand Perceptions by Specified Classes of Consumers for Specified Classes of Consumer Goods" (unpublished Ph.D. dissertation, School of Business, University of Chicago, 1957), p. 37.
[35] Bernard Levenson *et al.*, "Social Stereotypes of Automobile Makes" (unpublished research report, Bureau of Applied Social Research, Columbia University, June, 1956), pp. 5-30.

better car for each of them. Even if you think any car will do, name the one that comes closest, in your opinion, in any way.

1. He likes to solve difficult problems, always does his best.
2. He always gets advice from others before buying anything.
3. He's always telling jokes and using big words.
4. He does whatever he pleases, doesn't like to conform.
5. He is really loyal to his friends.
6. He likes to observe others and understand how they feel.
7. He wants to be the boss, to supervise others.
8. He likes to be punished when he's wrong.
9. He likes to travel, meet new people; enjoys change.
10. He thinks he is physically attractive to women.
11. An aggressive driver, always first away from the light.
12. He's an athlete—very masculine type.
13. In picking a job, he looks for security.
14. You can tell he's a college boy.
15. A person who is very self-confident.
16. He's a very cautious driver, never had a ticket.
17. The best car for a woman.
18. You can tell he's a successful man.
19. Loves his car, tinkers with it all the time.
20. A very dignified and reserved gentleman.
21. Everything he owns is the latest style.

Seventy Ford and seventy-four Chevrolet owners completed this portion of the interview.

The images of Ford and Chevrolet.— For the combined sample of Ford and Chevrolet owners there is agreement on fourteen of the twenty-one descriptions. That is, the combined group gave a majority for the same car on fourteen items of the twenty-one. The percentage of respondents agreeing that either a Ford or a Chevrolet was the more appropriate car ranged from a low of 59.03 per cent to a high of 77.78 per cent. All are statistically significant at the 5 per cent level or beyond.

However, looking at Ford and Chevrolet owners as separate groups rather than combined shows that in nine of the fourteen images there is not true consensus independent of the brand owned, that is, while each group gave a majority to the same car, the extent of the majority was statistically significant only five times. These nine are not true images by rigorous definition.

In only five of the images is there agreement statistically significant at the 5 per cent level for each group separately as well as combined. In four of these five, the Ford owner is pictured as one who does not like to conform, is an aggressive driver, loves his automobile, or is a college boy. In the fifth, the Chevrolet owner is pictured as a very cautious driver. These five instances present the only clear-cut brand images discovered in this study. The percentages of consensus are shown in Table 13.

The other nine images which showed agreement for the combined group of owners presents two distinct pictures of the automobiles. Ford owners have views on Fords and Chevrolets that Chevrolet owners believe are unimportant. The reverse is also true.

Ford owners see their brand as best for an athlete and for someone always up to date. They picture the Chevrolet owner as always seeking advice from others. Chevrolet owners do not assign these images to either brand at a significant level. The percentage of Ford owners holding these views is shown in Table 14.

Similarly, Chevrolet owners see the Chevrolet as best for a woman, for a dignified gentleman, or a person desiring job security. They see the Ford owner as always telling jokes, wanting

TABLE 13
BRAND IMAGES OF FORD AND CHEVROLET REPRESENTING
COMPLETE CONSENSUS

Social Image	Percentage of Combined Sample (N=144)	Percentage of Ford Owners (N=70)	Percentage of Chrevrolet Owners (N=74)
Ford owner:			
Does whatever he pleases	66.0°	68.6°	63.5°
An aggressive driver	77.8°	72.9°	82.4°
A college boy	67.4°	65.7°	68.9°
Loves his car	64.6°	61.4°	67.6°
Chevrolet owner:			
Very cautious driver	77.8°	64.3°	90.5°

° Reject null hypothesis at 5 per cent level of significance (test figures carried to four decimal places).

to be boss, and thinking of himself as physically attractive. Ford owners see no differences between the brands with respect to these six images. The percentage of Chevrolet owners holding these images is shown in Table 15.

Brand images projected into own car by both groups. — The other seven brand images presented were attributed by each group to their own brand. They represent positive values to both groups. Both Ford and Chevrolet owners believe their brand is best for the person who:

1. Likes to solve difficult problems.
2. Is loyal to his friends.
3. Likes to observe and understand other people.
4. Likes to be punished when wrong.
5. Likes to travel and enjoys change.
6. Is very self-confident.
7. Is a successful man.

With the exception of the wish to be punished, these are socially desirable traits. The percentages assigning this latter image to their own brand are not sig-

TABLE 14
PERCENTAGE OF FORD OWNERS HAVING
IMAGES OF FORDS AND CHEVROLETS
WHICH CHEVROLET OWNERS
DO NOT HAVE

Social Imagery	Percentage of Ford Owners (N = 70)
Ford owners:	
An athlete	84.3°
Everything owned is latest style	68.6°
Chevrolet owners:	
Seeks advice from others	62.9°

° Reject null hypothesis of 5 per cent level of significance (test figures carried to four decimals).

TABLE 15
PERCENTAGE OF CHEVROLET OWNERS
HAVING IMAGES OF FORDS AND
CHEVROLETS WHICH FORD
OWNERS DO NOT HAVE

Social Imagery	Percentage of Chevrolet Owners (N=74)
Chevrolet owners:	
Desires job security	86.5°
Dignified gentleman	83.8°
Best for a woman	87.8°
Ford owners:	
Always telling jokes	71.6°
Wants to be boss	63.5°
Physically attractive	73.0°

° Reject null hypothesis at 5 per cent level of significance (test figures carried to four decimals).

TABLE 16
PERCENTAGE OF FORD AND CHEVROLET
OWNERS ATTRIBUTING BRAND IMAGE
TO THEIR OWN CAR

Social Imagery	Percentage of Ford Owners Answering Ford (N=70)	Percentage of Chevrolet Owners Answering Chevrolet (N=74)
Likes to solve difficult problems	65.7°	60.8°
Loyal to friends	74.3°	82.4°
Likes to observe others	60.0°	78.4°
Likes to be punished	58.6	58.1
Likes to travel	70.0°	67.6°
Self-confident	75.7°	66.2°
A successful man	62.9°	59.5

° Reject null hypothesis at 5 per cent level of significance (test based on figures carried to four decimals).

nificantly different from chance at the 5 per cent level. The percentages of owners assigning the seven images to their own brand are shown in Table 16.

Brand images and personality needs. —This weakness of brand images for Ford and Chevrolet suggests that what is commonly thought of as a brand image is somehow a function of the individual's particular personality. The first eleven brand-image descriptions used in this study were taken directly from the explanation of the personality needs measured by the Personal Preference Schedule.[36] The Brand-image descriptions were made parallel to the personality needs, so that the relationship between image and personality could be analyzed. The need-image pairings are as follows:

1. Achievement—He likes to solve difficult problems, always does his best.
2. Deference—He always gets advice from others before buying anything.
3. Exhibition—He's always telling jokes and using big words.
4. Autonomy—He does whatever he pleases, doesn't like to conform.
5. Affiliation—He is really loyal to his friends.
6. Intraception—He likes to observe others and understand how they feel.
7. Dominance—He wants to be the boss, to supervise others.
8. Abasement—He likes to be punished when he's wrong.
9. Change—He likes to travel, meet new people; enjoys change.
10. Sex—He thinks he is physically attractive to women.
11. Aggression—An aggressive driver, always first away from the light.

Analysis of these pairs shows that whatever need an individual indicated was most important to himself the corresponding image description was assigned to the car he owned far oftener than one would expect from chance alone—65.1 per cent of the time for the total sample. Thus, in almost two-thirds of the cases, the individual projects his greatest need into the brand he happens to have. In this sense, then, automobiles are extensions of the owner's personality. That is, owners use their automobiles to satisfy certain personality needs that are important to them. They believe

36 Edwards, *op. cit.*, p. 14.

the car fits their personality and ascribe it to people of similar needs. However, the lack of brand discrimination by the personality need variables also precludes discrimination on the basis of these brand-image projections. While individuals tend to project their own needs into their cars, the distribution of needs is similar for owners of each make.

Considering all the needs ranked in the top half of each individual's scale, 61.2 per cent of these are attributed to the brand owned. Slightly more Chevrolet owners than Ford owners project their top need into their car, but for the top five needs the pattern is reversed. Table 17 shows the percentages for each brand as well as the total sample.

Conclusion. — In view of all the marketing literature of recent years, the brand images found were much less focused than one would expect. For Chevrolet, only one strong image appeared, and for Ford, only four. This suggests that the exploitation of these images will be difficult. These are the two most popular and best-advertised automobiles. This finding could be due to the choice of image questions used in this study, but the factors selected were chosen after a thorough study of the current literature. Open-ended question techniques might have found more.

The relationship between the owner's personality needs and the brand images, however, suggests that brand images are not the independent phenomenon they are usually thought to be. The needs a person values greatest he tends to assign to whatever brand he happens to have.

BRAND LOYALTY

Stability of brand preference. — Customers who purchase the same brand repeatedly are often thought to be different from those who switch brands. For purposes of this study, owners whose previous car was the same as their present one were classified as brand-loyal. Thirty Ford owners and forty-three Chevrolet owners fitted this category. The percentages of loyal owners are 41.81 for Ford and 58.11 for Chevrolet. This reflects, again, increasing popularity for Ford, at least in part. Non-loyal segments include only one Ford and one Chevrolet owner whose present car was their first.

The differences between loyal and non-loyal owners are apparent in both their shopping habits and their future automobile plans. Less than two-fifths of the loyal owners shopped other brands before buying, compared to three-fifths of the non-loyal owners. Also over two-thirds of the loyal owners plan to remain loyal compared to a little over two-fifths of the non-loyal owners. By brand, the percentages vary somewhat, but the trend is constant. Table 18

TABLE 17

PERCENTAGES OF INDIVIDUALS PROJECTING
PERSONALITY NEEDS INTO CAR THEY OWN

	Ford Owners (Per Cent)	Chevrolet Owners (Per Cent)	Both Combined (Per Cent)
Single greatest need projected into own car	62.1	68.2	65.1
Five greatest needs projected into own car	64.2	58.0	61.2

TABLE 18

PERCENTAGE OF LOYAL AND NON-LOYAL FORD AND CHEVROLET OWNERS WHO
SHOPPED OTHER MAKES AND WHO PLAN TO BUY SAME CAR AGAIN

	Ford		Chevrolet		Combined	
	Loyal (N = 30)	Non-loyal (N = 42)	Loyal (N = 43)	Non-loyal (N = 31)	Loyal (N = 73)	Non-loyal (N = 73)
Percentage who shopped other makes before buying	46.7	54.8	32.6	67.7	38.4	60.3
Percentage planning to buy same brand again	60.0	40.5	72.1	41.9	67.1	42.5

shows these percentages by brand and for the combined group.

Not only were there more loyal Chevrolet owners in the sample, but also the evidence in Table 18 points to stronger loyalty. Fewer loyal Chevrolet owners shop other makes than do Ford owners, and more loyal Chevrolet owners plan to stick to Chevrolet in the future.

However, in this study the reason for classifying owners as loyal or non-loyal is not to try to explain this particular kind of behavior. Rather, it is to see whether, within a brand, the loyal and non-loyal owners represent two distinct types of people. If this is the case, lumping all Ford owners into one group and all Chevrolet owners into the other could have caused confounding of the previous results, i.e., discrimination

might have been possible, had loyal and non-loyal owners of each brand been treated separately. For each brand the loyal and non-loyal owners were compared with respect to the personality needs and the demographic variables which showed the greatest separation of the brands.

Personality needs. — The four personality needs which showed greatest differences between the Ford and Chevrolet owners are affiliation, autonomy, dominance, and exhibition. Comparison of the rank-order scores for these needs out of the eleven measured by loyal and non-loyal owners, shows very little difference. For Ford, the two groups — loyal and non-loyal — rank the four needs almost identically. Loyal Chevrolet owners ranked dominance,

TABLE 19

RANK-ORDER SCORES OF SELECTED PERSONALITY
NEEDS FOR LOYAL AND NON-LOYAL FORD
AND CHEVROLET OWNERS

Personality Need	Ford		Chevrolet	
	Loyal (N = 29)	Non-loyal (N = 42)	Loyal (N = 39)	Non-loyal (N = 30)
Dominance	3.2	3.1	4.7	3.5
Affiliation	5.7	5.5	4.7	5.6
Exhibition	6.2	6.1	6.8	6.5
Autonomy	7.9	7.7	7.4	6.9

TABLE 20
COMPARISON OF LOYAL AND NON-LOYAL FORD AND CHEVROLET OWNERS BY SELECTED DEMOGRAPHIC VARIABLES

Demographic Variables	Ford		Chevrolet	
	Loyal (N = 30)	Non-loyal (N = 42)	Loyal (N = 43)	Non-loyal (N = 31)
Percentage homeowners	53.3	59.5	39.5	51.6
Percentage families with three or more children	46.7	42.8	30.2	32.3
Percentage smokers	76.7	78.6	58.1	64.5
Percentage working for same firm for five or more years	60.0	59.5	41.9	54.8

exhibition, and autonomy slightly lower than non-loyal owners and placed affiliation higher on this scale.

If the loyal and non-loyal owners of each brand have widely differing personality need structures there is no indication of it here. The rankings by brand are shown in Table 19.

Demographic variables.—Similarly, the loyal and non-loyal owners of each brand were compared with respect to the four demographic variables that showed the greatest separation of the brands. The variables are homeownership, three or more children at home, smoking, and working for the same company for five or more years. Table 20 shows the percentages by brand for loyal and non-loyal owners.

On six of the eight comparisons, loyal and non-loyal owners are most similar. As before, loyal and non-loyal Ford owners are more alike than the comparable Chevrolet owners. Non-loyal Chevrolet owners own homes more frequently than do their loyal counterparts, and more of them have worked for the same company for five or more years. However, even the largest difference shown is not significant at a 5 per cent level.

The loyal and non-loyal owners of each brand appear to be essentially the same with respect to the variables used in this study. Pooling loyal and non-loyal owners into the same group does not wash out differences that might otherwise be important.

VI. SUMMARY AND CONCLUSIONS

Although respondents in this survey spanned wide ranges for most of the psychological and objective variables measured, none of these variables was systematically related to the brand of car owned for the two brands which constitute almost half the automobile market. The variables used here do not allow for further segmentation of this market.[37]

Two major limitations are recognized. The success of Ford and Chevrolet over the years attests to their appeal to many kinds of people. A comparison of owners of similarly priced but less popular automobiles, like the Rambler, with owners of either Ford or Chevrolet might show greater discrimination with the variables used. The writer's experiences with this study, however, cause him to be skeptical.

Second, the Park Forest universe from which the sample was drawn is in

[37] See also Gladstone Bonnick, "The Condition of Chevrolet and Ford Cars Owned by Negroes in Chicago" (unpublished term paper, Graduate School of Business. University of Chicago, June, 1959). Bonnick found no significant differences between Fords and Chevrolets of 1956 through 1959 models in need of obvious repairs. Neither group seemed to keep their cars in better condition.

no way to be construed as representative of the entire automobile market. On the other hand, restricting this study to a relatively homogeneous group in certain respects, such as age and income, makes it possible to examine other variables, especially psychological ones, with greater precision. The problem of distinguishing between owners (and prospective owners) of highly competitive brands in a homogeneous market area closely parallels problems facing the manufacturer and his advertising agency, unless it can be shown that Park Forest is wholly atypical, *in respects here studied,* of the rest of the country.

If an individual's personality and/or his demographic characteristics can be used to predict the choice between a Ford and Chevrolet, different measures and techniques must be found. The variables included in this study do not explain brand choice, and their discriminatory ability is much less than previous research has indicated. It seems to make little difference to a large percentage of car owners with widely varying psychological and other characteristics whether they own a Ford or a Chevrolet. These makes appear substitutable in many areas besides price.

This study does not point to the clearcut superiority of either research mode. Over-all, the objective factors did a somewhat better job of discrimination but still an unsatisfactory one. Table 21 compares the three discriminant

functions computed in this study. The design of the study placed some broad limitations upon the objective factors that would not be expected to apply to the psychological needs. Many motivation researchers have claimed that it is the lack of discrimination by objective variables that produces the need for their wares. This study does not bear them out.

From the standpoint of marketing strategy, this study highlights the difficulties involved in segregating the customer of one brand from those of a similar and competing one. Popular brands appeal to different kinds of people for many different reasons. What motivates these customers is not readily apparent.

By definition, a brand image cannot attract opposite kinds of people, i.e., an image must be consistent. Even with some product variation, it may be impossible for a manufacturer to create several distinct images. Within a brand family there are carry-overs from their common heritage. Also to try to create several images rather than a single one may cause a "scattering" of promotional effort and leave one open to the inroads of competitors.

This study suggests that many of the commonly held assumptions in marketing about brand images are either wrong or misleading. The evidence points neither to strong images attracting definite kinds of people nor to the use of auto-

TABLE 21

COMPARISON OF LINEAR DISCRIMINANT FUNCTIONS DESCRIBING FORD
AND CHEVROLET OWNERS

Class of Independent Variables	No. Variables Employed	Multiple Correlation Coefficient of Discriminant Function	F Ratio of Discriminant Function	Percentage Sample Misclassified by This Equation
Psychological needs	10	.3353	1.634	37.1
Demographic factors	14	.3819	1.597	30.1
Selected combination of both	13	.3991	1.837*	36.4

*Significant at the 5 per cent level.

mobiles for satisfying deep inner needs in symbolic terms.

In promoting a brand it would appear safest to be somewhat ambiguous for both personality and objective variables. People of all kinds are customers, and creation of too strong an image in certain personality terms may narrow one's market unnecessarily. If the image is ambiguous, there is a tendency for customers to read into it what they want. The things they value highly they attribute to their brand.

The implications of purchase motivations in this research may be viewed in two ways, not necessarily mutually exclusive. One is that people choose automobiles on the basis of obvious "rational" factors: lowest price, comparison of mechanical features, operating performance, etc. Second, brand choice may depend upon small things, peculiar to the individual, not usually measured in marketing research. These latter motivations can be characterized as idiosyncratic.

TECHNICAL APPENDIX

The purpose of this appendix is to give details and methodology that were a necessary part of this study, although not essential to the text or the results as presented.

THE PARK FOREST UNIVERSE

Park Forest is a post-World War II suburban community approximately thirty miles south of the Chicago Loop. It was developed by one builder from previous farm lands. It has received wide attention from sociologists.

A suburban community rather than part of Chicago proper was selected for this study for three major reasons:

1. Sociologists continually point to the suburbs as the pace-setters for American life. David Riesman, for example, recently said, "Suburbs in the last dozen years have be-

come a symbol of the American way of life."[38] If trends exist in these areas, then they are of greater importance.

2. Population in the suburban areas has grown much faster than the rest of the country. The Census Bureau reports that from 1950 to 1956 the outlying parts of standard metropolitan areas grew about six times as rapidly as did the central cities.[39]

3. It was previously known that results of the psychological test used are influenced by demographic variables.[40] The selection of a homogeneous suburb reduces the ranges (and effects) of these variables.

The universe was restricted to owners of 1955 or later models and to males with only one car registered in their names. The universe list consisted of 869 Ford owners and 770 Chevrolet owners who had purchased a $5.00 local vehicle-tax stamp. As local enforcement of this tax was alleged to be vigorous, it was believed that the listing would be accurate. However, when it came actually to interviewing those selected from this list, it was found to be almost 20 per cent in error. Of the first two hundred names randomly selected from the list, thirty-eight were in error. Eighteen had moved since purchasing the tax stamp, and twenty owned a different make of car. In the sampling, these thirty-eight cases were treated as if they were not on the list to begin with, i.e., they were ignored, and the next name selected was used.

---

[38] David Riesman, "The American Future," speech given at the University of Chicago, February 3, 1958; reported in the *Chicago Maroon*, February 7, 1958, p. 3

[39] U.S. Bureau of the Census, *Current Population Reports* (Ser. P-20, No. 71 [December 7, 1956]), p. 1.

[40] Arthur Koponen, "The Influence of Demographic Factors on Responses to the Edwards Personal Preference Scale" (unpublished Ph. D. dissertation, Columbia University, 1957).

A simple random sample was selected by assigning each person in the universe a four-digit random number. The numbers were taken from the RAND Corporation. *A Million Random Digits with 100,000 Normal Deviates* (Glencoe, Ill.: Free Press, 1955). The names were then arrayed by these random numbers and the first one hundred of each brand chosen as the sample. The errors in the universe list required more than two hundred names to be drawn before the sample was completed.

DATA COLLECTION

Interviewing. — Thirteen different women were employed as interviewers. All were married women with previous interviewing experience, and all worked only part-time. They were regular employees of an interviewing service. As the respondents were all employed men, the interviewing was restricted to Saturdays, Sundays, and the early evening hours on other days. Interviewing time ranged from forty to one hundred minutes, with the average being about sixty-five minutes.

A careful verification was made of each interviewer's work by both telephone and postal card. Although personal interview with the male members of the family was specified, the verification form asked who in the family was interviewed, how they were interviewed, if they personally filled out a long list of paired statements (the psychological schedule), and if the interviewer was courteous. In addition, the telephone verifications repeated several items from the questionnaire to check upon the accuracy of the reporting. This verification uncovered a substantial amount of cheating by the interviewers. Four of the thirteen women employed were found to have cheated on parts of a total of thirty-five interviews. These thirty-five contaminated interviews were discarded, and no other work was accepted from these women.

Other response factors. — Before the

field work was completed, a total of two hundred and sixty-five names was used in the sample. Besides the thirty-eight errors on the universe list and the thirty-five partially faked interviews, an additional forty-six could not be reached after at least four follow-ups. There were twenty-one refusals, and an additional twenty-five respondents could not be located. All of these missing cases are shown in Table 22.

TABLE 22

UNOBTAINABLE AND UNUSABLE
INTERVIEWS WITH FORD AND
CHEVROLET OWNERS IN
PARK FOREST

Source of Difficulty	To-tal	Ford	Chev-rolet
Errors in universe listing	38	22	16
Interviewer cheating	35	20	15
Respondent refused to be interviewed	21	7	14
Respondent not at home	25	14	11
Total	119	63	56

Thus, to secure 146 useful interviews, 265 randomly selected names were taken from the universe. This is a completion percentage of 55.1. Even eliminating those interviews unsecured because of errors in universe listing and those lost by cheating, only 76.0 per cent of the selected names could be interviewed.

THE PSYCHOLOGICAL TEST

Question of normalizing the test scores. — Often psychological test scores are normalized around a common mean. In his manual, Edwards gives normalized "scores with a mean" of 50 and a standard deviation of 10 for each of the needs.[41] In this study only the raw need scores from the psychological schedule were used. Normalizing each of the groups with a common mean and standard deviation performs no obviously

---

[41] Edwards, *op. cit.*, pp. 12-13.

useful function other than helping to achieve one of the assumptions of the discriminant function model. But, even here, normalizing each needs distribution separately is no guaranty that the joint distribution would be multivariate normal.

Almost half a century ago, statisticians debated the merits of assuming that observations arise from underlying normal continua. Karl Pearson and David Heron on one side claimed that the assumption is very often justified.[42] G. Udny Yule vigorously and acrimoniously opposed them, arguing that the assumption is often artificial.[43] Today Yule's position is more generally accepted among statisticians, though Pearson has won the field in psychology. The writer, being more statistician than psychologist, chose to follow Yule's reasoning and hence did not normalize the test scores.

Test reliability.—With the sample of Ford and Chevrolet owners it was not possible to make direct tests for reliability of the measures. However, with his normative group, Edwards was satisfied that answering patterns were not random or haphazard.[44] Also, for a group of eighty-nine students, he found that test-retest correlations after a one-week period ranged from $+.74$ to $+.88$.[45]

To see whether the test as taken by the Ford and Chevrolet owners was operating in its usual way, simple rank-order correlations of scores on ten needs (those used in the discriminant function) were made, comparing the combined sample in this study with other published groups. With Edwards'

normative group of 760 college men the rank correlation of needs is .903.[46] Similar comparison with 953 males living in market areas of over two million people and belonging to the J. Walter Thompson Company Consumer Panel showed a rank correlation of .806.[47] The rank correlation of nine of the needs with a group of forty hospitalized paranoid males was only .383.[48] Thus there is reason to believe that the test was functioning normally and that shortening it did not seriously affect the results, and even possibly that Park Foresters are not paranoic.

LINEAR DISCRIMINANT FUNCTION

The linear discriminant function was introduced by R. S. Fisher in the mid-1930's.[49] The statistical purpose of the function is to provide the maximum separation of two groups by maximizing the ratio of the difference between the specific means to the standard deviations within the groups. Fisher does not give any rationale for restricting his solution of this problem to linear equations, but Hodges shows that when the observations arise from normal populations and have the same covariance matrix, the function has certain optimum properties.[50]

Fisher shows that the solution of the linear discriminant function is essentially the same as that for multiple regression when the dependent variable is dichotomous and can be as-

[42] Karl Pearson and David Heron, "On Theories of Association," *Biometrika*, IX (1913), 159-315.

[43] G. Udny Yule, "On the Methods of Measuring Association between Two Attributes," *Journal of the Royal Statistical Society*, LXXV (1912), 579-642; see also Leo. A. Goodman and William H. Kruskal, "Measures of Association for Cross Classification," *Journal of the American Statistical Association*, XLIX (1954), 735-36.

[44] Edwards, *op. cit.*, pp. 10-11.

[45] *Ibid.*, pp. 16-17.

[46] *Ibid.*, p. 10. Reject the null hypothesis at better than the .01 level.

[47] Koponen, *op. cit.*, p. 27. Reject the null hypothesis at better than the .01 level.

[48] Mack Knutsen, "An Empirical Comparison of the Linear Discriminant Function and Multiple Regression Techniques in the Classifying Subjects into Three Categories" (unpublished Ph.D. dissertation, University of Washington, 1955), p. 26b. The null hypothesis would not be rejected at a 10 per cent level of significance.

[49] Fisher, *op. cit.*

[50] Joseph L. Hodges, Jr., *Discriminatory Analysis* (Randolph AFB, Texas: School of Aviation Medicine, USAF, 1955), chap. viii.

signed values separated by unity.[51] The equations for the discriminant function and those for multiple regression differ only by a constant factor on the right-hand side. Also, Garrett has shown that the coefficient weights of multiple regression and the discriminant function are exactly proportional in the dichotomous case.[52] Although in existence for over twenty years, the discriminant function has had little application to business problems. In a bibliography of over 250 uses of it listed by Hodges, only four are concerned with problems of the business world.[53] Although typically limited to comparison of two groups, the function has been expanded for use with three or more groups under certain conditions.[54]   The computations for the linear discriminant functions used in this study were done on the UNIVAC I belonging to the University of Chicago Operations Analyses Laboratory. A multiple regression program was employed. Solution of the regression equation with 146 observations for each of fifteen independent variables took less than eight minutes computer running time. The savings of both time and money, to say nothing of the error possibilities, over hand computation were almost unbelievable. The increasing availability of electronic computers should make for greater use of discriminatory analyses in the future.

PSYCHOLOGISTS JUDGING BY PERSONALITY NEEDS

The eighteen psychologists picked only 70 correct out of 180 possible choices when asked to match the car brands with randomly selected personality need profiles. The distribution of correct choices and the statistical probabilities of these occurring by chance alone are shown in Table 23. The chi-

TABLE 23
PROBABILITY OF OUTCOMES FOR CLASSIFICATION OF FIVE FORD AND FIVE CHEVROLET OWNERS

No. Correctly Placed in Own Group	Probability of each Outcome under Null Hypothesis	Outcomes of Judging by 18 Psychologists
10	1/252	
8	25/252	
6	100/252	1/18 (14/252)
4	100/252	15/18 (210/252)
2	25/252	2/18 (28/252)
0	1/252	

square goodness-of-fit test for Table 23 shows non-random discrimination by the judges significant at the 1 per cent level. But their selections were not positively correlated with the facts of brand ownership.

[51] Fisher, op. cit., pp. 184-85.
[52] Henry E. Garrett, "The Discriminant Function and Its Uses in Psychology," Psychometrika, VIII (1943), 65-79.
[53] Hodges, op. cit., pp. 47-52.
[54] C. R. Rao, Advanced Statistical Methods in Biometric Research (New York: John Wiley & Sons, Inc., 1952) pp. 307-29.

(3) Sociological

14. Some Differences in Household Consumption — Negroes and Whites

MARCUS ALEXIS

INTRODUCTION

The post-World-War-II return of the buyers' market brought with it a renewed interest in the consumer as the center around which marketing activity revolves. Marketing management became, more than ever before, consumer oriented. New and refined tools of analysis developed in the 1930s and 1940s were engaged to help marketing executives unscramble the puzzle which was the "new consumer market."

By any measure, the consumer market of the 1950s was radically different from its predecessors. It was both more prosperous and more populous. In addition there was the emergence of a new important consumer group — the American Negro.

PART I
THE NEGRO AND HIS ENVIRONMENT

It is argued that social and economic discrimination have resulted in Negroes having patterns of market behavior different from the whites with equal incomes. Some writers argue that the differences persist even after adjustments have been made for differences in assets, occupation, and family responsibilities.

EMPLOYMENT

The history of Negro employment in the United States is one of limited job opportunities and low pay. Even government agencies have been guilty of systematic job discrimination and of fostering segregation of Negro and white workers.

Historically, Negro employment has been concentrated in the service, unskilled and semi-skilled labor categories. Opportunities in clerical, managerial, skilled labor and professional occupations have been very limited. World War II did much to improve the situation. But there is evidence of continuing job discrimination based on race in defense industries, retail outlets and unionized trades. The trade union movement itself has not been free from charges of tacitly supporting such discrimination.

A University of Michigan research team using data compiled for the Federal Reserve Board's *Survey of Consumer Finances* series found several variables related to job security to have a statistically significant effect on the expenditures of Negro and white consumers (1). These findings have been corroborated in an extensive depth study by Henry Allen Bullock, who found Negroes to exhibit more employment security anxiety than whites (2) exhibit.

When one adds to these observations the fact that unemployment rates among Negroes average twice the national level in good times and bad and the greater sensitivity of Negro employment to economic downturns and more lagged response to expansion, there is good reason to expect differences in consumption behavior.

HOUSING

There are many goods purchased by Negroes which are sold in an unrestricted market. On the other hand, some commodities like housing are known to be limited in number and location. These limitations are in addition to those created by income, wealth, and economic responsibilities. The restricted boundaries on Negro communities coupled with the income and occupational patterns have exerted influences not known in the economy as a whole (3).

It is commonly argued that if Negroes are likely to have expenditure patterns different than whites, housing is likely to be a very powerful influence. Not only is the housing market of Negroes restricted, but there is evidence that Negroes pay disproportionately high prices for equal quarters (4).

The best available evidence indicates that Negroes spend more than whites for equal quality housing. However Negroes do not spend a greater proportion of their income for housing than whites in the same income class. This results from the greater frequency of "roomers" living with lower income Negroes and by the upper limit placed on the quality of housing high income Negroes can buy.

RECREATION

It is only within the past two decades that Negroes have been able to participate in, let alone enjoy, many forms of public recreation. Negro athletes were barred from major league competition in every major sport except boxing until the end of World War II. Private clubs and places of public accommodation are still closed to them in many areas of the country. A currently popular Negro comedian has quipped that Negroes can

afford to buy expensive automobiles because of all the money they "save" by not having to spend on high rent apartments, club fees and eating out. The fact that this has been regarded as clever satire is sufficient testimony to the recognition of the restrictions on the forms of recreation Negroes may consume.

PART II
HISTORICAL INTEREST IN THE NEGRO MARKET

Prior to World War II, few firms were interested in Negro consumers as a separate market. In 1932, Paul K. Edwards, a pioneer in Negro market studies observed:

It is an exceptional thing to find a manufacturer or national distributor who has given any special considerations to the market possibilities of the 12,000,000 Negroes in this country. The great majority appear to be of the opinion that the purchasing power of the Negro is practically nil; that he consumes only the very cheapest sorts of merchandise; that at all events whatever his needs may be they are adequately catered to by the sales and advertising programs utilized in reaching the domestic market in general (5).

In addition to the poverty attributed to the Negro population, there were several other reasons why firms hesitated to make any special efforts to attract them as consumers. Negroes were not only held to be so poor that they could only buy the cheapest quality merchandise; it was also said that they did not have sufficient resources to buy in large quantities. To a national distributor of even economy-appeal merchandise, this latter attribute would be enough to discourage appeals directed to Negroes. The ability of Negroes to judge quality was also questioned. This was expressed in several ways. Negroes were said to: lack discriminating taste for quality products; be ignorant as to a sense of value; be easily satisfied with any kind of merchandise.

Other factors contributing to the lack of interest in Negroes as a separate market were: the belief that they bought national brands anyway because of long domestic association with whites whom they emulate, and fear on the part of advertisers and agencies that catering to Negroes would adversely affect sales to whites. Important causes of resistance were disapproval of the high preparation costs of Negro oriented media, and dissatisfaction with the performance of some advertisements which had been placed in Negro media by venturesome advertisers.

POST-WORLD-WAR-II ATTITUDES

The lack of interest in the Negro market did not change with the end of World War II. Immediately following the war there was still a great reluctance to approach Negro consumers. But by 1951, much of this had changed. Marketing executives were very much more familiar with the Negro market. An impressive number of top American corporations were appealing to Negroes in one way or another.

Firms making direct overtures to Negroes included: Colgate-Palmolive-Peet, Pepsi-Cola, Hiram Walker, Seagrams, Crosse and Blackwell, Pillsbury Mills, Ward Baking Company, Gerbers Products Company, Phillip Morris, Liggett & Meyers (Chesterfield), P. Lorillard and Company (Old Gold), Kruger Brewing Company, Lever Brothers, Calvert Distillers, Ford Motor Company, Continental Oil Company, Pet Milk, and International Cellucotton (absorbed into Kimberly-Clark).

By the late 1950s there was widespread interest in a rather undefined "Negro market." The task still remained to find more about the characteristics of the market. Because so much of the data from Negro media and their representatives was promotional in nature, firms and advertising agencies commenced more serious inquiries to determine market characteristics.

PART III
CONSUMPTION PATTERNS

SAVING BEHAVIOR

The first category to be studied is household saving. This represents the difference between total income and expenditures. Thus savings may be positive, zero, or negative. Comparisons of Negro and white households include those in which negative saving has taken place. If two families report net savings (receipts − expenditures) of − $100 and − $200 respectively; the first family is said to have $100 more "savings." Economists often say that the second family dissaved more. In either case, the meaning of the terms will be clear by the context.

Since the *Consumer Purchases Study of 1935-36*, many studies of Negro and white saving behavior have been completed. Without exception, they have yielded evidence of higher savings (or lower dissavings) by Negro than by comparable income white families.

One recent explanation of the observed differences in Negro-white saving behavior has been called the "relative income" hypothesis. According to this hypothesis, people's savings are related to their relative position in the income distribution. That is, the amount saved depends on the decile or percentile rank of the saver in his income distribution. The higher the decile or percentile ranking, the greater the savings. If Negroes are grouped into one distribution and whites into another, Negroes with a given income will occupy a higher ranking in their distribution than will whites with the same income in their distribution. This is so because of the lower income level of Negroes as a whole when compared with whites as a whole.

Differences of the type found in

Negro and white savings have also been found in the savings behavior of urban and rural families. In comparing the incomes of families at the same relative income position, it has been found that there are larger absolute income differences between Negro and white than between rural and urban families. The relative income hypothesis gives a better explanation of urban-rural than of Negro-white differences in saving.

A competing theory to explain the observed differences in the savings of comparable income Negro and white families at the same income levels takes into account the total amount of assets owned by families. For families earning less than is required for current consumption purposes, asset holdings are an especially important factor. Holding assets makes it possible for such families either to use these assets for consumption or to borrow against them. Families without assets have less of a borrowing potential and no private means of financing deficits. Because white families generally own more assets than Negroes in the same income class, one would expect that their deficits would be larger. This has been found to be the case.

Statistical data also show regional differences in saving. Northern Negroes save a larger proportion of their incomes than northern whites with the same incomes. At the lower ranges of disposable incomes in the south, Negroes save a greater proportion of their incomes than do comparable southern whites, northern whites or northern Negroes. For higher income southern Negroes, however, the relationships are reversed. They save less than southern whites, northern whites or northern Negroes. The statistics may be misleading, however, since they do not include increases in cash on hand as part of saving. It is possible that southern Negroes in the higher income brackets save by increasing their holdings of pocket cash rather than by increasing deposit balances in savings accounts or increasing

their holdings of financial assets. It may be that prominent southern Negroes choose to keep much of their savings in cash form in order to conceal their economic well-being. A second possible explanation is that upper income Negroes in the south have social responsibilities which are much greater than those of comparable income whites. Having to serve as social leaders, Negroes with incomes which would be considered modest in the white community attempt to emulate the consumption standards of the much higher income white leaders. Because of the much lower incomes, Negro leaders do not actually maintain the same standards as their white counterparts. However, their consumption expenditures are greater than those of comparable income whites. The observation that this saving behavior is found in the south only may be attributed to the fact that in the north, the Negro community is not as completely separated from the white. Southern parallelism requires attempted duplication of all elements of the white society. Since northern communities are not so completely separate, the higher income northern Negroes are freed from many of the "social responsibilities" of comparable income southern Negroes.

It is interesting to note that the higher savings of Negroes at comparable income levels persist when purchases of consumer durables are included in the definition of saving.

At the lower income levels, non-farm, non-business Negroes are more often than comparable whites employed in occupations in which they receive non-money income. Inclusion of the dollar value of this non-money income in the income data would show the saving of low income Negroes to be closer to that of comparable whites.

Two final hypotheses to explain the greater savings of Negroes assert that they have greater difficulty obtaining credit, and have less income mobility. The credit hypothesis is sometimes

rejected on the basis of the higher proportion of credit sales to Negroes than to
white, although this test is by no means
conclusive. A better measure of Negro
credit availability would be the acceptance rate of equally risky Negro and
white applicants. Though credit may be
more strictly rationed to Negroes because of lower incomes, only a test of
the type suggested would provide the
information needed for a more definitive answer.

All available evidence consistently
points to a higher propensity to save for
Negroes than for whites at comparable
income levels. It follows, that if Negroes
save more than whites at each income
level, Negroes and whites must differ in
the way they allocate their incomes to
some classes of consumer goods. More
specifically, there must be at least one
class of consumer goods for which
Negroes and whites in the same class
spend different amounts.

In the presentation below, attention
will be focused on differences in the
expenditure patterns of Negro and
white consumers for such goods as food,
housing, clothing, house furnishings,
recreation, medical care, transportation
(automobile and non-automobile).

EXPENDITURES FOR FOOD

One of the difficulties involved in discussion of ethnic or cultural differences
in expenditures for food is the extent to
which such differences represent group
preferences for certain classes of foods.
Such preferences can affect the expenditure level although there are no differences in quantity of food consumed.

Comparisons of the food expenditures
of comparable income Negro and white
families in Nashville, Atlanta, Washington, D.C., New York, Detroit, Houston,
Memphis and several southern villages
reveal that, with few exceptions, food
expenditures of white families were
higher than the food expenditures of
Negro families. This is in spite of the
fact that Negro families were generally

larger than the white families with
whom they were compared. One explanation of this observed pattern is the
high percentage of low income Negro
families historically engaged in domestic services. It is common for domestics
to receive some meals on the job and
also to receive some free food to take
home to the family.

EXPENDITURES FOR HOUSING

A 1947 budget study of the Bureau of
Labor Statistics revealed that Washington, D.C. Negroes spent more for housing than did comparable income whites
at all income levels except the $2,000-
$3,000 level.

Bureau of Labor Statistics studies for
1948 and 1949 yielded data producing
completely different results than the
1947 study. At every income level in
Detroit, Houston and Memphis, Negro
families spent a smaller proportion of
their incomes for housing than did similarly situated whites. Data for 1950-51
from the Bureau of Labor Statistics for
small southern cities produced similar
results.

The 1948, 1949, 1950-51 Bureau of
Labor Statistics data have wider coverage than the 1947 data. The 1947 data
also stand alone in holding that Negro
families spend more for housing than
comparable income whites. Because of
these two facts, it is reasonable to conclude that Negroes generally spend less
for housing than comparable whites. In
making this observation, one must
recognize the limitations placed on
Negro housing opportunities and the
resulting impact on expenditures.

EXPENDITURES FOR CLOTHING

It is commonly argued that Negroes
spend more for clothing than do whites.
Furthermore, it is said that Negroes are
not as price conscious as white buyers.
The greater emphasis of Negroes on
clothing is "explained" by the inability
of Negroes to purchase some forms of

recreation and shelter. Thus clothing becomes a substitute for inaccessible alternatives. The price behavior proposition is more difficult to understand because of the generally lower incomes of the Negro population.

Extensive investigations carried out in Nashville, Birmingham (Alabama), Richmond (Virginia), Atlanta, New York and several other locations, and Bureau of Labor Statistics data all support the general view that Negroes spend more for clothing than comparable income whites. In Nashville, Birmingham and Richmond, it was found that Negro common laborers were paying as much for their clothing as were white semi-skilled workers and Negro professionals were paying as much, and in some cases more for their clothing, than white teachers, trained nurses, clergymen, and merchants. The interesting fact here is that the Negro professional group sampled consists largely of teachers. They do not have high incomes when contrasted with white businessmen who constitute a significant proportion of the white sample.

According to the Bureau of Labor Statistics, Detroit Negroes spent more for clothing at all income levels than did whites. In Memphis and Washington, D.C., Negroes spent more for clothing than did whites at all but one income level (the Memphis and Washington, D.C., income levels referred to were not the same). In Houston, whites spent more at all income levels except one than did Negroes.

As incomes rise, both races increase their consumption of clothing at a faster rate than they increase total consumption. It is also found that wives, without regard to race, increase their expenditures for clothing more rapidly than their husbands when incomes rise.

On the subject of price-consciousness, there is substantial evidence that the alleged lack of concern of Negro shoppers for price line merchandise is not representative of their actual behavior.

In fact, the desire of Negroes to dress well and their low incomes act as powerful forces to make Negroes price-conscious. In a study of Negro newspapers, it was found that Negro readers were unhappy not to find price-line advertising. Furthermore, it was pointed out that Negro readers consulted their local newspapers for such price information. Even more important, a majority of the Negro consumers in Birmingham, Atlanta and Richmond questioned about their buying habits cited price as the most important determinant of the vendor from whom they buy.

One researcher discovered that whites have more favorable attitudes towards brand buying than do Negroes. While whites justify brand buying as being sophisticated and associate brand with quality, Negroes think of it as habitually naive and uneconomical(6).

Some observers seem to be confused by the difference between buyers interested in high quality or prestige merchandise, and those who do not pay attention to the price of the merchandise they purchase regardless of the quality. Negro buyers certainly do not fall into the latter category. There are some very good nonprice reasons why Negroes should be particular about the merchandise they purchase. Several investigators have certified that in the Negro community there is a strong desire to wear fashionable clothes, drive expensive automobiles, and generally engage in conspicuous consumption because this is the means by which one gains status. There are also alternative explanations of any observed tendencies on the part of Negroes to shop at the better stores.

The purchases of clothing in the better stores by Negroes may be explained on the basis of the protection such stores offer and for which Negro consumers are willing to pay. The availability of credit is another inducement. A history of having shoddy merchandise passed off on them has made Negroes skeptical of unbranded merchandise. Also,

Negroes may have been able to afford higher priced garments because they did not have to purchase as many units as comparable income whites. This was due to the relatively large Negro employment in domestic services. The receipt of second-hand clothing by domestics releases some income to pay higher prices for the units purchased.

EXPENDITURES FOR RECREATION AND LEISURE

It has been said that the consumption standards of upper-class Negroes are set by the wealthiest members of the group and that as Negroes become integrated into the life of the community, the clerical worker or professional man or woman escapes from the social obligations of his upper-class role in the Negro community. This observation may shed some light on the seemingly contradictory results obtained in several studies of Negro and white expenditures for recreation and leisure.

In a Bureau of Labor Statistics study, Negro families in Detroit were found to spend more for recreation at all income levels than comparable income white families. In Houston, Negro families spent more for recreation than did comparable white families at all but one income level. Memphis Negroes, on the other hand, spent less on recreation at all but two income levels than did comparable whites and Washington, D.C., Negroes spent less than did their white counterparts at all income levels. In the 1950-51 Bureau of Labor Statistics data, one finds that Negro expenditures for recreation are less than they are for comparable whites. In the large cities of the north, however, expenditures of Negroes more closely approximated the level of whites. Even here, however, Negro consumers spent at least 12.7 per cent less than did their white counterparts.

The apparent inconsistency in the findings reported is very likely a matter of definition of terms. The 1950-51 data is based on a catch-all definition of "recreation, etc." which includes recreation, education, and reading. The 1947, 1948, and 1949 studies separate recreation from reading and education. Negro families usually spend less for reading and education than comparable income white families. Thus if the "recreation, etc." measure is employed, it could very easily result in a smaller expenditure for "social responsibilities" for Negro families than it does for comparable income whites. While this may serve to explain differences in the 1950-51 Bureau of Labor Statistics data and the earlier data for Detroit and Houston, it does not reconcile differences between the 1947, 1948, and 1949 data which are not due to differences in definition. It is also possible that the differences observed within the earlier Bureau of Labor Statistics data are due to basic differences in the social structure of the cities of Detroit and Houston on the one hand and Memphis and Washington, D.C., on the other.

EXPENDITURES FOR HOUSEHOLD FURNISHINGS AND EQUIPMENT

The 1947 Bureau of Labor Statistics study found that Negro families in Washington, D.C., spent less for furniture and equipment than did comparable whites at all income levels. However, Detroit Negro families spent more for furniture and equipment than did comparable white families at all income levels. Houston Negro families, for whom less information is available, spent less than did white families at the $1,000-$2,000 income level, but spent more at the $2,000-$3,000 income level, and as much at the $3,000-$4,000 income level; Memphis Negroes spent more at two income levels and less at three. As in the case of recreation, Detroit Negroes spent more than comparable income whites.

The 1950-51 Bureau of Labor Statistics data revealed that average expenditures for furniture and equipment of Negro families at the $2,000-$3,000 income level in large cities in the north, and in large and small cities in the south, were larger than for white families with equal incomes. The same holds for the $3,000-$4,000 income level in large northern and southern cities.

Much of the net emigration from southern rural communities is accounted for by the movement of Negroes. Negro families are more apt to be in the process of making the transition from rural to urban life. Consequently the need for household equipment and furniture is likely to be greatest in those communities in which there are relatively more Negroes making the transition. It would be interesting and valuable to have a measure of the relative number of Negroes in Washington, D.C., Detroit, and Houston who are newcomers to urban living. Estimates of the absolute and relative growth of the Negro urban populations are available, but they do not reveal points of origin of the migrants.

Another possible determinant of expenditures for household equipment and furniture could be the average annual income of the respondents over a period of five or ten years prior to the survey. A plausible hypothesis is that families which had low average annual incomes prior to the period studied, and whose incomes have increased by more than the increase in the cost of living will probably be the families making the largest outlays for furniture and equipment within the various income groups. Relatively more Negroes have been making the transition from low income rural employment to higher income urban employment since 1940. Thus, outlays for furniture and equipment by Negro families in the post-1940 studies are inclined to be greater than for comparable income whites. Before any more satisfactory explanations can be given, more research would be needed.

EXPENDITURES FOR MEDICAL CARE

The earliest studies of Negro-white consumption relations, dating back to the early 1930s, reveal lower expenditures for medical care by Negroes than by comparable income whites. Also, in each of the Bureau of Labor Statistics postwar studies, including the 1950-51 data, Negro families have been found to spend less for medical care at all income levels than comparable income white families.

An interesting explanation of the medical care practices of Negroes dating back to the late 1920s is based on the high laxative sales in Harlem and the relation of these sales to the pork vending establishments in the area. According to the explanation, the restaurants and delicatessens in Harlem are responsible for the creation of intestinal difficulties for which laxatives are helpful. An alternative explanation makes at least as much sense. This area is the home of a large number of Negroes who have migrated from the southern part of the United States and from the Caribbean. They are not in the habit of seeking medical counsel for what they believe to be minor maladies. Laxatives have been used for these maladies in their rural homes for decades. Thus the phenomenon observed in the 1920s may be only partially related to the eating establishments in the Harlem area. No quantitative evidence is presented to support the pork-laxative thesis; nevertheless, the analysis is interesting. It presents a rather unique interpretation of market behavior and it also provides a connecting link between the market for pork products and the market for laxatives.

EXPENDITURES FOR NON-AUTOMOBILE TRANSPORTATION

The relationship of non-automobile transportation expenditures and occupation is an excellent example of the effect of social conditions on market behavior. Because so many Negroes have been employed in domestic service and domestics have traditionally received part of their wages as carfare, early studies show the per cent of incomes paid by low income Negroes for non-automobile transportation to be much more than for low income whites.

Since 1940, Negro employment in the service industries has experienced a secular decline. Consequently, carfare as a part of total compensation has declined in importance. At the same time, there is evidence that the frequency of automobile ownership among Negro families is lower than among comparable income white families. Thus one would expect that non-automobile transportation expenditures would be higher for the Negro than white families in the same income grouping. An investigation of the Bureau of Labor Statistics studies of 1947, 1948, 1949 and 1950-51 indicates that this is true for the cities of Washington, D.C., (except at the $1,000-$2,000 income level), and for Detroit, Houston and Memphis at all income levels. It is also generally the case in 1950-51 for comparable income groups. Thus, one can state that in general Negroes now spend more for non-automobile transportation than comparable income whites.

EXPENDITURES FOR AUTOMOBILE TRANSPORTATION

The only data available on a racial basis giving total outlays for automobile expenditures are to be found in the 1947, 1948, 1949 and 1950-51 Bureau of Labor Statistics studies. These surveys indicate a consistent tendency for white consumers to spend more for automobile expenses at comparable income levels than Negro consumers. Whites at all income levels in Washington, D.C., and Houston spent more for automobile services than did Negroes with equal incomes. Detroit whites spent more

than Negroes at all income levels except the $4,000-$5,000. In Memphis, whites spent more for automobile expenses than did their Negro counterparts at all income levels below $5,000; Memphis data for incomes above $5,000 are not truly comparable. But Memphis Negroes in the $5,000-$7,000 income bracket spent more for automobile expenses than did whites in either the $5,000-$6,000 or the $6,000-$7,000 income brackets.

The 1950-51 data and the earlier Bureau of Labor Statistics data also support the view that Negroes spend less for automobile transportation than do whites at comparable income levels. Thus, with the exception of Memphis, all available data consistently point to lower expenditures for Negroes than comparable whites.

Independent investigations in Milwaukee and Houston have also failed to demonstrate any significant differences in racial ownership by price class. There is no available study known to this writer which supports the stereotype of large scale ownership of Cadillac-class automobiles by Negroes. Income and possibly restrictive credit practices act as a powerful deterrent to automobile ownership among Negroes. As recently as 1956, the ownership rate among Negroes was only 40 per cent of the ownership rate of whites. The relative figures were 28 per cent for Negroes and 70 for whites. Most of this is an income effect.

SUMMARY OF CONSUMPTION FINDINGS

A wealth of data has been summarized in the hope of shedding some light on potential differences which might exist in the consumption propensities of Negroes and whites for a host of commodities. When all the data have been digested, the following major findings emerge:

1. Total consumption expenditures of Negroes are less than for comparable

TABLE I

SUMMARY STATEMENT OF FINDINGS FOR STUDIES COVERED BY WHETHER
NEGROES SPENT MORE OR LESS THAN COMPARABLE WHITES

Study	Food	Housing	Clothing	Recreation and Leisure	Home Furnishings and Equipment	Medical Care	Auto Transportation	Non-auto Transportation
Edwards	less	less	more	more	less	...	...	...
Sterner	less	more[a]	more	less	less	less	...	...
B.L.S. Detroit	less	less	more	more	more	less	less	more
B.L.S. Houston	less	less	less	more	less	less	less	more
B.L.S. Washington	more	more	more	less	less	less	less	more
B.L.S. Memphis	less	less	more	less	mixed	less	less	more
Friend and Kravis	less	less	more	less	more	less	less	more
Fact Finders	less	...	...	...	...	...	...	...

[a] In the southern villages there was no difference.
Note: Edwards and Sterner discuss transporation, but do not make a breakdown by auto and nonauto.

income whites, or Negroes save more out of a given income than do whites with the same incomes.

2. Negro consumers spend more for clothing and non-automobile transportation and less for food, housing, medical care and automobile transportation than do comparable income whites.

3. There is no consistent racial difference in expenditures for either recreation and leisure or home furnishings and equipment at comparable income levels.

PART IV
PROMOTIONAL ACTIVITIES IN THE NEGRO MARKET

With the heightened interest in Negro consumers following World War II, many advertisers felt it necessary to reappraise their Negro market appeals. It was recognized that long term success would require careful analysis of consumer attitudes and motivations. The strategy to adopt would be one with the greatest likelihood of success.

Despite the rising incomes and growing Negro population, high rates and preparation costs continued to discourage many advertisers from using Negro appeal media. Some sellers such as Alagu Syrup and Connelly Shoe Company (a Minnesota manufacturer of footwear) reasoned that their Negro market volume justified the use of Negro appeal media.

Decisions on whether one should allocate any portion of his promotion budget to Negro-appeal media were not easily made. Some firms recognizing peculiarities in the market of particular interest to them did quite well in mapping campaigns and selecting media.

GENERALIZED VERSUS SPECIALIZED MEDIA

In two *Harvard Business Review* articles, Henry Allen Bullock has created something of a controversy regarding the appropriate advertising strategy for a firm to follow. He argues that it is illusory to assume that separate media are required to reach Negro and white customers effectively. If he is right, advertisers can save on their advertising or obtain larger benefits by advertising in publications with large segments of both races included in their readership.

It is not clear what Bullock means by reaching Negro and white consumers in common effectively. It has long been known that Negroes read *Life, Reader's Digest* and the other leading periodicals. It is certainly true that there is duplication of readership involved in promoting in Negro-appeal media. The real question for advertisers is not the aggregate readership alone but the probability that exposure in a particular medium will produce an attitude favorable to the purchase of the advertiser's product(s).

There is something in Bullock's data which may be a subtle indication that equal access and possibly exposure to media by Negroes and whites do not create equal interest in services and products offered. Radio was more than 250 per cent as popular among Negroes as whites with equal access to all media; 39 per cent for Negroes, 15 for whites. The pattern would have been even more pronounced if those with unequal access to all media were included. This represents a preference made on a free choice basis. It suggests a stronger identity between radio stations and personalities within the Negro group. The absence of a single major Negro television personality might well be one reason. Indeed, until Jack Paar's introduction of Dick Gregory and Nipsy Russell to national audiences, the image of the Negro comic was that of the slapstick clown.

The different attention patterns of Negroes and whites seems to argue against rather than for common media appeal. This is not to say that the pattern will necessarily persist. Rather, it says that there are reasons to suspect that the Negro's environment may necessitate special appeal. There are products used by Negroes such as skin bleachers which could not be successfully advertised in general media. For such products "in-group" media may be the only answer.

NEGRO VERSUS WHITE MODELS

Advertisers have been asking themselves whether tinting the faces of their models is helpful when using Negro media or should they use Negro models? The additional cost of Negro models has had a negative effect on willingness to use Negro-appeal media.

At first it seemed that tinted mats or colored models were considered desirable. Some Negro media offered to absorb the additional cost in order to receive the advertising. The pendulum then swung in the direction that colored models (tinted mats or use of Negro models) had little or no effect on recall and buyer response. The pendulum has swung again and we seem to be in the era of dark models.

The use of racially neutral or mixed symbols may have genuine merit in those cases in which general media is used with the intent of appealing to Negro and white consumers. Bullock comments on this subject at great length: e.g., the effective use of Harry Belafonte by Revlon in a highly successful spectacular and Gillette's use of Yankee star Elston Howard. An article in the September 24, 1961, *New York Times* cites the use of Negro models in the *Boston Herald* by Lang and Taylor, a Boston manufacturer of stereophonic equipment. The response to the advertisement was favorable.

These successes, and one might add a Bell Telephone Hour appearance by Belafonte, are sure signs that racially mixed appeals in general media can be effective. On the other hand, the Bell-&-Howell-Company-sponsored "Walk in My Shoes," a program over which the company had no editorial control, brought loud protests from some Southerners who accused the company of pushing integration. Some ABC network affiliates went so far as to refuse to show the documentary. Another doubt arises over the reported reluctance of advertisers to sponsor as popular an entertainer as the late Nat "King" Cole because of the race issue. At this writing, Negro comic Bill Cosby has already secured a co-star position on NBC's, "I Spy."

The picture is not as hopelessly confused as might appear at first glance. In viewing the acceptability of Negro sales personnel on television it is worth noting that the role expectation of the viewer is critical. White viewers might accept and applaud an hour with Belafonte. But it must be remembered that although he is a matinee idol, his role is still acceptable to white audiences for he is above all an entertainer. Negroes have long been accepted as entertainers. True he is a higher caliber performer than the dull, comical performers or dancers of yesteryear. As one sociologist has put it "He dances with his mouth." The same analysis applies to Elston Howard of the New York Yankees and many of the other Negro personalities. They are acceptable because they are entertainers in an acceptable tradition.

There are taboos which no advertiser is likely to challenge in the near future. Interracial love is not likely to be welcomed in any part of the country, not even in film form. The obvious restraint of the interracial lovers in the film, "Island in the Sun," is a case in point.

CONCLUSIONS

There are still many unresolved questions regarding the most effective way to promote to Negro consumers. The answers to the questions of general versus special media and Negro, tinted or white models require a good deal of empirical research under the strictest control conditions possible. Advertisers can help by supporting such research within their own companies, by their agencies and marketing research consultants or university people.

The changing American attitudes in the area of race relations provide a rich opportunity for marketers to augment their appeals to Negro consumers within the framework of their present promotional programs, while not risking loss of white support. With greater freedom in the civil rights arena may also come greater promotional freedom for marketing to racial minorities.

REFERENCES

1. Klein, Lawrence R., and H. W. Mooney, "Negro-White Savings Differentials and the Consumption Function Problem," *Econometrics*, Vol. 21, July, 1953, pp. 425-46.
2. Bullock, Henry Allen, "Consumer Motivations in Black and White," Parts I and II, *Harvard Business Review*, Vol. 39, May-June, 1961, pp. 89-104 and July-August, 1961, pp. 110-124.
3. Hirschom, Adrian, "Pepsi-Cola's Campaign to the Negro Market," *Printers Ink*, Vol. 228, September 9, 1949, pp. 38-39. "Negroes Get More Brand Conscious as Incomes Rise," *Advertising Age*, Vol. 17, March 18, 1948, pp. 30-31. "Negroes Favor Independent Grocers," *Advertising Age*, Vol. 23, September 1, 1952, p. 36.
4. Weaver, Robert C., "The Relative Status of the Housing of Negroes in the United States," *Journal of Negro Education*, Vol. 20, Summer, 1953, p. 350.
5. Paul Kenneth Edwards, "The Negro Commodity Market," *Harvard Business School Alumni Association Bulletin*, (May 1932), p. 242.
6. Young, Consuello C., "Reader Attitudes Towards the Negro Press," *Journalism Quarterly*, Vol. 21, June 1944, pp. 148-152, especially p. 149.

15. The Diffusion of an Innovation among Physicians[1]

JAMES COLEMAN, ELIHU KATZ,
AND HERBERT MENZEL

Anthropologists and sociologists have long been concerned with the processes through which customs, practices, attitudes, or messages spread. Traditionally, these processes have been studied by examining the ecological distribution of the trait at successive points in time. In a few cases, the actual transmission of messages from person to person has been traced out (e.g., 1, 3, 4, 5, 10). A still different approach to the study of this problem is reported in this paper. The population is physicians in four cities; the item whose use was spreading was a new drug; and the study focused on the ongoing social processes which finally led to widespread adoption of the drug by these physicians.

Data were collected 15 months after a new drug with wide potential use, here called "gammanym," had been placed on the market. By this time almost all the doctors in relevant specialties in the four cities studied had used the drug,

some almost immediately, others only after a considerable interval of time. The research problem, stated most concretely, is this: What were the social processes which intervened between the initial trials of the drug by a few local innovators and its final use by virtually the whole medical community? The results reported below concern the effectiveness of networks of interpersonal relations at each stage of the diffusion process. The study is to be reported in full elsewhere (2); a pilot study has already been reported upon (9). A separate article by one of us describes the cumulative research experiences which led to the decision to focus explicitly upon interpersonal relations, using sociometric techniques. (6)

METHODS – I

The method of survey research, involving structured interviews with a sample of physicians, was used. But since the problem as defined concerned the social structure which linked these doctors together, it was necessary to deviate in two important ways from the customary survey design which, in effect, treats individuals as so many independent units of observation. (a) Each doctor interviewed was asked three sociometric questions: To whom did he most often turn for advice and information? With whom did he most often discuss his cases in the course of an ordinary week? Who were the friends, among his colleagues, whom he

From *Sociometry*, Vol. 20, No. 4 (December, 1967), pp. 253-270, by permission of the American Sociological Association.

[1] This article may be identified as Publication No. A 239 of the Bureau of Applied Social Research, Columbia University. An earlier version was read at the annual meeting of the American Sociological Society, Detroit, Michigan, September 8, 1956. We are indebted to Helmut Guttenberg for creative assistance throughout the project. Philip Ennis, Marjorie Fiske, Rolf Meyersohn, and Joseph A. Precker participated in the design of this study. The preparation of this paper was facilitated by funds obtained from a grant made to the Bureau of Applied Social Research by the Eda K. Loeb Fund.

saw most often socially? In response to each of these questions, the names of three doctors were requested. This made it possible to trace out the links by which each doctor was connected with the rest of the medical community. (b) It was decided to include in the sample, as nearly as possible, *all* the local doctors in whose specialties the new drug was of major potential significance. This assured that the "others" named by each doctor in answer to the sociometric questions were included in the sample, so that it became possible to characterize pairs or chains of socially connected doctors. Accordingly, 125 general practitioners, internists, and pediatricians were interviewed; they constituted 85 per cent of the doctors practicing in these fields in four Midwestern cities, ranging in population from 30,000 to 110,000.[2]

The dependent variable of the analysis which follows is the month during which each doctor first used the drug. This information was *not* obtained in the interviews; it was obtained through a search of the prescription records of the local pharmacies for three-day sampling periods at approximately monthly intervals over the 15 months following the release date of gammanym. In this way, the month during which each doctor first used the drug was ascertained.[3] The research is thus based on three kinds of data: the month of each doctor's first prescription for the new drug, obtained through a search of pharmacists' files; data about the informal social structure of the medical community, derived from doctors' replies to sociometric questions in an interview; and many individual attributes of each doctor, likewise obtained by interview.

RESULTS – I

Before presenting the results concerning interpersonal relations, the results concerning other ("individual") determinants will be briefly characterized. As expected, the date on which a doctor first prescribed the new drug was related to a large number of his *individual* attributes, e.g., his age, the number of medical journals he subscribed to, his attachments to medical institutions outside his community, and certain attitudinal characteristics. To illustrate the relationship of drug introduction date to such individual attributes, one of the latter will be singled out: the doctor's relative orientation to his professional colleagues and to patients, inferred from his answer to the following question:

How would you rank the importance of these characteristics in recognizing a good doctor in a town like this?

    a. The respect in which he is held by his own patients

    b. His general standing in the community

    c. The recognition given him by his local colleagues

    d. The research and publications he has to his credit

The following rankings were classified as "profession-oriented": cdab, cadb, cbda, cabd; the following rankings were classified as "patient-oriented": abcd, acbd, acdb, bacd. The 14 doctors who gave other rankings were assigned to one group or another by a rank-order scaling procedure which will be described in detail elsewhere. (2)

---

[2] In addition, 103 doctors in other specialties were also interviewed, thus making a total sample of 228, or 64 per cent of all doctors in active private practice in these cities. The analysis presented here is based only on the 125 general practitioners, internists, and pediatricians, except that sociometric designations accorded them by the remaining 103 doctors were included when measuring the sociometric status of the 125.

[3] The date so ascertained will tend to be slightly later than the doctor's actual introduction date, due to the sampling of days. The interval between sampling periods was made to alternate between 32 and 25 days, so that each two successive sampling periods included all 6 days of the working week. Records were obtained from 64 of the 84 drug stores in the four cities. Of the remaining 20, only two had any significant pharmaceutical business.

FIGURE 1.

CUMULATIVE PROPORTION OF DOCTORS INTRODUCING
GAMMANYM: PROFESSION-ORIENTED *vs* PATIENT-ORIENTED

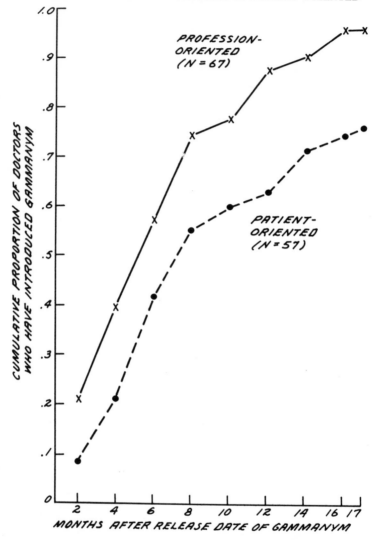

Figure 1 shows the relationship of the resulting classification to the date of introduction of the new drug. The solid curve represents those doctors who were classified as profession-oriented, and shows the cumulative proportion of gammanym users among them for each month. Thus, for example, by the fourth month 40 per cent of these doctors had used gammanym; by the sixth month over 50 per cent. The lower curve similarly represents the doctors who were classified as patient-oriented; by the

sixth month only 42 per cent had used the drug. Thus the more profession-oriented doctors in these cities generally used the drug earlier than the less profession-oriented ones.[4] Similar results were obtained for many other individ-

[4] The difference between the mean adoption dates of the two groups in Fig. 1 is 2.8 months, which is significant at the .01 level, using a standard two-tailed test of difference between means of normally distributed variables. It should be pointed out, however, that the argument of this report does not rest on the statistical significance of

FIGURE 2.

CUMULATIVE PROPORTION OF DOCTORS INTRODUCING
GAMMANYM: DIFFERENCES IN INTEGRATION ON FRIENDSHIP CRITERION

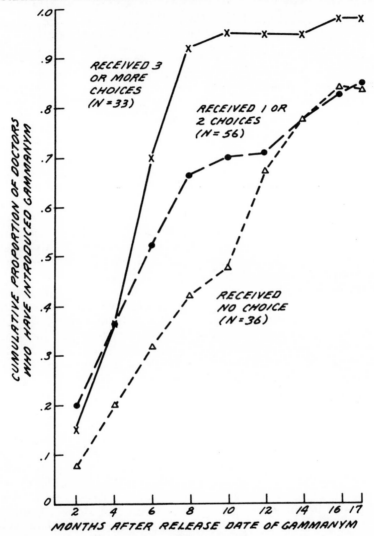

ual attributes – i.e., attributes describing individuals without reference to
their social relations with one another.

But even stronger relations were
found when we turned to *social*
attributes – those characterizing a doc-

tor's ties to his local colleagues. Doctors
who were mentioned by many of their
colleagues in answer to any of the three
sociometric questions used the drug, on
the average, earlier than those who
were named by few or none of their colleagues. More generally speaking, the
degree of a doctor's integration among
his local colleagues was strongly and
positively related to the date of his first
use of the new drug. Figure 2 shows, for
example, the results with regard to the
network of friendships. The "inte-

isolated findings so much as on the consistency
of the results of several diverse approaches with
one another and with prior theoretical notions.
It is doubtful that significance tests in the usual
sense are meaningful in situations like the
present. For a detailed statement of our position
in this matter, see (8, p. 427).

TABLE 1

The Average Relation of Twelve "Individual" Variables and of Three
Measures of Social Integration to the Rate of Gammanym Introduction at
Two Points in Time

	Average Difference in Per Cent of Gammanym Users between High and Low Groups		Ratio of Differences
	After 1 Month	After 7 Months	
Individual variables	9.2	27.4	2.98
Social integration	8.7	40.3	4.64

grated" doctors — those named as "friends" by three or more of their colleagues — were much faster to introduce gammanym into their practices than the rest. The networks of discussion and of advisorship yielded similar findings.

Two important contrasts differentiate Figure 2 from Figure 1, and, more generally, social attributes from individual ones, in their relation to gammanym introduction. First, the relationship in Figure 2 (as measured, for example, by the difference between the mean drug introduction dates of the extreme groups) is greater than that in Figure 1; greater, in fact, than the relationship of the introduction date of gammanym to all but one of the many individual characteristics which were examined. (The single exception is the doctor's total prescription volume for the general class of drugs which includes gammanym: the greater his use of drugs of this type, the earlier did he introduce gammanym.)[5] This emphasizes the importance of social contacts among doctors as a crucial determinant of their early use of the new drug.

But it may reasonably be questioned

whether the relationship shown in Figure 2 may not arise merely because the measures of social integration are themselves associated with some personality or other individual differences which predispose a doctor to early introduction. It is in answer to this question that a second contrast between Figures 1 and 2 is relevant.

Notice that the two curves in Figure 1 are roughly parallel, differing from one another only in vertical displacement. This is true as well in most of the remaining charts (not shown) which relate individual characteristics to gammanym introduction. The curves in Figure 2, by contrast, differ from each other in shape as well as location: the curve for the more integrated doctors, although not starting out much higher than the other curves, rises steeply upward with a slight gain in slope at the fourth month, while the curve for the more isolated doctors rises at a moderate and almost constant slope. To put it differently, the integrated doctors were little different from their isolated colleagues at the very beginning; but then their rate accelerated to produce an increasing gap between the curves. In contrast, the profession-oriented doctors in Figure 1 differed from the patient-oriented from the very start almost as much as later on.

The constant difference between the profession-oriented and and patient-oriented doctors suggests that they differ individually in their receptivity to new developments in medicine. On the

---

[5] The difference between the mean drug introduction dates of those high and low on integration according to the 3 sociometric questions used is 3.1, 4.1, and 4.3 months. The difference between those with high and low total prescription volume for this general class of drugs is 5.0 months. Only one other individual characteristic (number of journals read) produced a mean difference of as much as 4.0 months.

FIGURE 3

MODEL OF INDIVIDUAL INNOVATIONS, SHOWING EFFECTS
OF DIFFERENCES IN INDIVIDUAL RECEPTIVITY, k

$$\frac{dy}{dt} = k(1-y)t.$$

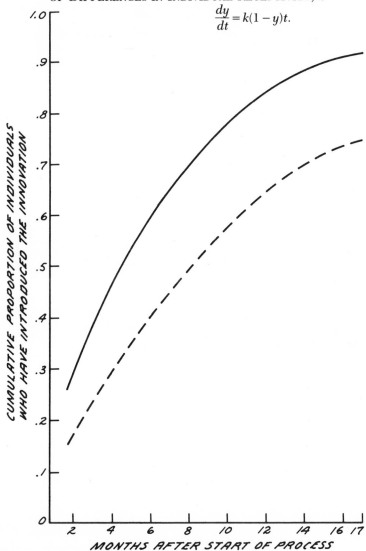

other hand, the accelerating difference between the integrated and isolated doctors suggests a kind of "snowball" or "chain-reaction" process for the integrated: They are individually little different in receptivity from their more isolated colleagues, but as their fellows come to use the drug, they pick it up from these doctors themselves; and as more of their fellows come to use it,

their chances of picking it up are greater.

The difference between the two kinds of relationship to drug introduction is also shown by Table 1, which compares the individual variables and the social variables in their relation to gammanym introduction at two points in time: 1 month and 7 months after the drug was introduced. For each of these dates, the

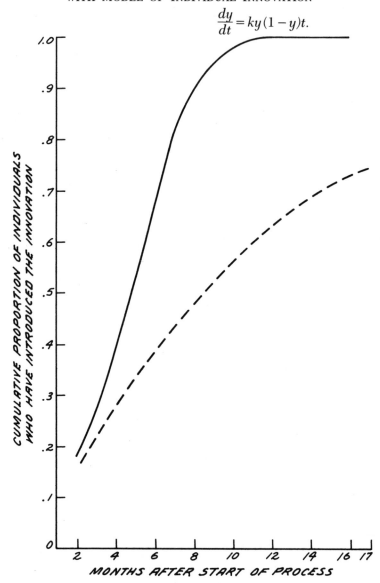

FIGURE 4

COMPARISON OF MODEL OF "CHAIN-REACTION INNOVATION
WITH MODEL OF INDIVIDUAL INNOVATION

$$\frac{dy}{dt} = ky(1-y)t.$$

table shows the average difference in per cent of gammanym users (a) between those measuring "high" and "low" on each of twelve individual variables and (b) between those measuring "high" and "low" on three measures of social integration. The latter are based on choices received in response to the three sociometric questions mentioned earlier. The twelve individual variables include all those examined which showed a difference of two or more months in mean date of introduction between the high and the low groups.

The size of these differences measures the size of the relationship at the two times. As is evident, the social integration measures show a slightly *smaller* relationship than do the individual variables after 1 month, but a much *larger* relationship after 7 months. Thus, as exemplified by the comparison between Figures 1 and 2, the socially integrated doctors "pull away" from their isolated colleagues, while the doctors differing in some individual attributes simply maintain their intrinsically different receptivity as time goes on.

Figures 3 and 4 show the difference between two corresponding theoretical "models" of the introduction process. In Figure 3, the upper and lower curves both express a model of "individual innovation"; the difference between the two is simply that the receptivity is greater for the upper. This difference in individual innovation rate or receptivity corresponds, we suggest, to the difference between profession-oriented and patient-oriented doctors (and between doctors who differ in other individual attributes as well). In contrast, in Figure 4 the upper curve (which is roughly similar in shape to the curve for the integrated doctors) represents a snowball process in which those who have introduced pass on the innovation to their colleagues. (This curve is described by an equation which has been used to characterize rates of population growth, certain chemical reactions, and other phenomena which obey a chain-reaction process). The lower curve in Figure 4 is still the individual innovation process. (Technically, the individual and snowball processes are described by equations on the graphs which can be paraphrased as follows: *Individual process* — the number of doctors introducing the new drug each month would remain a constant percentage of those who have not already adopted the drug. *Snowball process* — the number of doctors introducing the new drug each month would increase in proportion to those who have already been converted.)

In short, these comparisons suggest that the process of introduction for those doctors who were deeply embedded in their professional community was in fact different from the process for those who were relatively isolated from it. The highly integrated doctors seem to have learned from *one another*, while the less integrated ones, it seems, had each to learn afresh from the journals, the detail man (drug salesman), and other media of information.

METHODS–II

This result called for a more detailed investigation into the ways in which the networks of relations among the doctors affected their introduction of the new drug. Such an investigation required a shift of focus from the doctors to relationships among doctors or to the networks themselves as the units of analysis. Various methods could have been devised to do this. We chose to record the behavior of *pairs* of doctors who were sociometrically related to one another, reasoning that if the networks of relations were effective, then pairs of doctors who were in contact must have been more *alike* in their behavior than pairs assorted at random. That is, if there was a snowball or chain-reaction process of drug introduction from one doctor to another, then adjacent links in the chain — pairs of socially related doctors — should have introduced the drug about the same time.

In order to test this hypothesis for the discussion network, Figure 5 was constructed. (Similar figures were constructed for the networks of friendship and advisorship.) Each sociometric pair was assigned to a column of this matrix according to the gammanym introduction date of the chooser, and to a row according to the gammanym introduction date of the doctor chosen. (A mutual choice constitutes two pairs in this tabulation, since any chooser and his choice constitute a pair.) Pairs of doctors who introduced the drug during the same month (interval zero) fall in the main diagonal; pairs of doctors who differed in introducing the drug by an interval of

FIGURE 5

CHART SHOWING DATES OF ADOPTION
OF EACH MEMBER OF DISCUSSION PAIRS

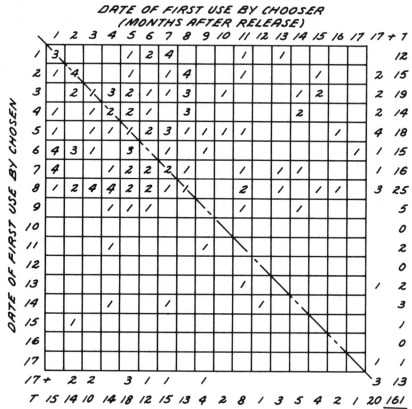

one month fall into cells adjoining the diagonal; and so on.

The resulting distribution of these intervals for the sociometric pairs was then compared to the corresponding distribution of intervals for a set of "random pairs" which has the following characteristics. If a pair is selected at random: (a) the probability that the chooser-member of the pair introduced gammanym during a particular month is the same as in the actual sample but is independent of the introduction date of the doctor chosen; (b) the probability that the chosen member introduced gammanym during a particular month is the same as in the actual sample but is independent of the introduction date of the doctor making the choice. Thus, for example, among the random pairs, those

who introduced gammanym in the first month and those who did so in the seventh gave equal portions of their choices to other first-month introducers. Similarly, those who introduced gammanym in the first month and those who introduced it in the seventh *received* equal portions of their choices from first-month introducers. Operationally, a set of "chance" frequencies satisfying these criteria can easily be obtained by computing for each cell of Figure 5 the product of the associated marginal totals, divided, for convenience, by the grand total.[6]

---

[6] A complication arose from the fact that the study was carried on in four different cities, with sociometric choices between cities excluded. This could spuriously raise any measure of pair-wise similarity of behavior, if there are large differ-

Contrary to expectations, the proportion of pairs whose members had introduced gammanym during the same month, one month apart, two months apart, and so on, according to the chance model proved to be almost identical to the proportion of actual discussion pairs who had introduced gammanym simultaneously or with varying intervals. The results for pairs of friends and for advisor-advisee pairs were similarly disappointing. This meant the rejection of our original hypothesis that pairs of doctors in contact would introduce the drug more nearly simultaneously than pairs of doctors assorted at random.

There was, on the other hand, the earlier evidence that the doctor's integration was important to his introduction of gammanym. This dictated a more intensive look at the behavior of pairs of doctors. Accordingly, we raised the question whether the networks, though ineffective for the *whole* period studied, may have been effective for the *early* period, immediately after the drug was marketed. An inspection of Figure 5 suggests that this could easily be the case. If only the upper left-hand portion of the matrix, representing the first two, three, or four months, is considered, then there appears to be a tendency for both members of a pair to introduce the drug in the same month.

In order to describe this tendency more precisely, it was decided to eliminate from consideration those associates of each doctor who used the drug only after *he* did. That is to say, the following question was now asked of the data: How closely did the drug introduction of each doctor follow upon the drug introductions of those of his associates who had introduced the drug before him? The answer is: very closely, for early introducers of the drug; not at all

closely, for late introducers of the drug.

This result is based on a measure for each month, obtained by dividing up the total matrix of pairs of doctors as shown in Figure 6. The single cell in

FIGURE 6

EXPLODED VIEW OF PORTION
OF FIGURE 5,
SHOWING MONTHLY SEGMENTS

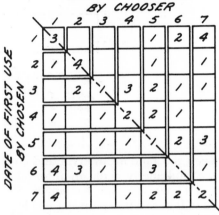

the upper left-hand corner represents those pairs both of whose members introduced the drug in the first month. The L-shaped section next to it contains the pairs which consist of one doctor who introduced the drug in the second month and one who introduced it in the first *or* second. The next L-shaped section contains all pairs which consist of one third-month adopter and one third-month-or-earlier adopter, and so on. It was now possible to determine the average interval for the sociometric pairs in each L-shaped section; likewise the average interval for the corresponding random pairs. On this basis, a measure of simultaneity was computed for each section, according to the formula:

Measure of Simultaneity (positive) =

$$\frac{\text{(avge. interval for random pairs)} - \text{(avge. interval for sociometric pairs)}}{\text{avge. interval for random pairs}}$$

This measure expresses the difference between the random and actual intervals as a fraction of the difference

---

ences in behavior between the cities. (This fact was called to our attention by Jack Feldman of NORC). In order to avoid such a spurious relation, "chance" frequencies, as above described, were calculated separately from the marginal totals for each city, and only then summed over the cities.

FIGURE 7

INDEX OF PAIR-SIMULTANEITY FOR THREE NETWORKS
AT DIFFERENT TIMES

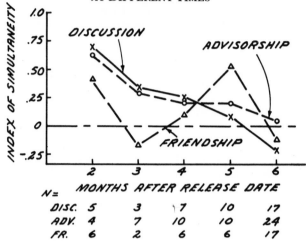

between the random interval and complete simultaneity (i.e., an interval of zero). The measure thus has a maximum of 1, and is zero when pairs are no closer than chance. In those cases where the actual interval exceeded the random interval, a different donominator was used.[7]

RESULTS–II

The values of the index are plotted in Figure 7 for the second through the sixth months. Separate curves are plotted for pairs of friends, discussion pairs, and advisor-advisee pairs. The interpretation of these results must be tentative because of the small numbers of cases;

---

[7] Measure of simultaneity (negative) =

$$\frac{\text{(avge. interval for random pairs)} - \text{(avge. interval for sociometric pairs)}}{(s-1) - \text{(avge. interval for random pairs)}}$$

s being defined as the number of the latest month included in the particular L-shaped section. (E.g., $s = 4$ in the case of pairs consisting of one fourth-month adopter and one fourth-month-or-earlier adopter.) When the index has a negative value, it therefore expresses the difference between the random and actual intervals as a fraction of the difference between the random interval and the maximum interval that is possible.

on the other hand, the patterns which emerge are rather consistent.

Figure 7 suggests, first of all, that the networks of doctor-to-doctor contacts operated most powerfully during the first 5 months after the release of the new drug: such influence as any doctor's drug introduction had upon his immediate associates evidently occurred soon after the drug became available. (Figure 7 omits the later months during which the index is negative or very small.) Second, the three networks did not behave identically.[8] The discussion network and the advisor network showed most pair-simultaneity at the very beginning and then progressively declined. The friendship network shows initially less pair-simultaneity than the other two, but—with some instability—appears to reach its maximum effectiveness later. Finally, after the fifth or sixth month following the

---

[8] Many of the sociometric ties reappear in two or three of the networks. The three sociometric questions yielded a total of 958 "pairs" within the sample of 125 doctors; but since some of these pairs were identical in answer to two or all three of the questions, there were only 704 *different* pairs. This overlap is still small enough to allow differences in patterns to emerge, as shown in the text.

FIGURE 8

INDEX OF PAIR-SIMULTANEITY AT DIFFERENT TIMES
FOR DOCTORS DIFFERING IN INTEGRATION

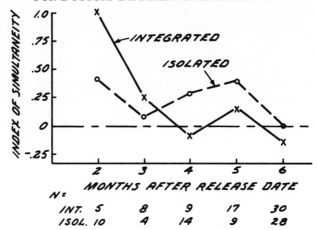

release of the new drug, none of the networks any longer showed pair-simultaneity beyond chance.

These results, however tentative, suggest that there may be successive stages in the diffusion of this innovation through the community of doctors. The first networks to be operative as chains of influence appear to be those which connect the doctors in the professional relationships of advisors and discussion partners. Only then, it seems, does the friendship network become operative — among those doctors who are influenced in their decisions more by the colleagues they meet as friends than by those whom they look to as advisors or engage in discussion during working hours. Finally, for those doctors who have not yet introduced the drug by about 6 months after the drug's release these networks seem completely *inoperative* as chains of influence. The social structure seems to have exhausted its effect; those doctors who have not responded to its influence by this time are apparently unresponsive to it. When they finally use gammanym, they presumably do so in response to influences outside the social network, such as detail men, ads, journal articles, and so on, and not in response to their relations with other doctors.

But one further phase in the social diffusion of gammanym can be discerned by examining separately the sociometrically integrated and the relatively isolated doctors. One would expect the networks of doctor-to-doctor contact to show their effectiveness first among the more integrated doctors and only then among those who are less integrated in their medical community. It has already been seen (Fig. 2 and text) that the more isolated doctors, on the average, introduced gammanym considerably later than the socially more integrated doctors. We now propose, however, that when more isolated doctors *did* introduce the drug early, it was not with the help of the social networks. While the networks were operative as channels of influence *early* for the integrated doctors, they were operative only later for the more isolated ones. This is what seems to have occurred. Figure 8 plots the index of simultaneity separately for more and less integrated doctors. (The graphs show weighted averages for all three networks; separately the numbers of cases would be so small as to produce erratic trends.)

The peak of effectiveness of doctor-to-doctor contacts for the well-integrated doctors appeared in the earliest month for which it can be plotted—the second month—after which effectiveness sharply declined. For the relatively isolated doctors, by contrast, the networks were not so effective at first as were those for the integrated doctors, but they maintained their effectiveness longer. Thus it appears that the networks of relations were effective not only for the more integrated doctors but also for the relatively isolated doctors who introduced the drug during the first 5 months of the drug's availability.

CONCLUSION

The above results, taken together, suggest a process which may be summarized as follows: At first the influence of these social networks operated only among the doctors who were integrated into the community of their colleagues through ties of a professional nature—as advisors or as discussion partners. Then it spread through the friendship network to doctors who were closely tied to the medical community through their friendship relations. By this time, social influence had also become operative in the more "open" parts of the social structure—i.e., among the relatively isolated doctors. Finally, there came a phase during which most of the remaining doctors introduced gammanym but did so in complete independence of the time at which their associates had introduced it: the networks now showed no effect. For the integrated doctors, this phase began about 4 months after the drug's release; for the isolated doctors, it began about 6 months after the drug's release. This picture is of course a tentative one, for the small size of the sample introduces variability, and there may be factors which produce spurious results.

There remains the question: Why should these sociometric ties to colleagues who have used the drug be influential during the first months of the drug's availability, but not later? One possible answer lies in the greater uncertainty about the drug that must have prevailed when it was new. (Data not reported here show that those doctors who introduced gammanym early did so far more tentatively than those who introduced it later.) We know from work in the tradition of Sherif that it is precisely in situations which are objectively unclear that social validation of judgments becomes most important.

More generally, this explanation implies that a doctor will be influenced more by what his colleagues say and do in uncertain situations, whenever and wherever they may occur, than in clear-cut situations. This explanation was confirmed by further data from the study which show that doctors influence each other more in treatments whose effects are unclear than in treatments whose effects are clear-cut. This topic will be dealt with in detail elsewhere. (7)

CONCLUDING METHODOLOGICAL NOTE

A word should be added about the significance of research of this kind, aside from the possible interest in its specific substantive findings. It exemplifies a methodological approach which will, we feel, assume a larger role in the social research of the next decade: namely, making social relationships and social structures the units of statistical analysis. To be sure, the analysis of social relations has always been the sociologist's business. Nevertheless, most empirical studies have either treated and described a community, a factory, a hospital ward, or any other large grouping of people as a single unit, or else they have statistically analyzed data collected on hundreds or thousands of single individuals, as in the typical "survey" study. What has been missing until recently is study designs which would explicitly take into account the structuring of single persons into larger units, and yet allow sophisticated quantitative treatment. The techniques of sociometry can meet this purpose, but have, with some notable exceptions (e.g., 4, 11), been applied chiefly to small closed groups and primarily for descriptive purposes.

The attempt reported here has been to carry out a design and analysis which would effect a marriage between sociometric techniques and survey research, in order to investigate quantitatively problems of the sort which community studies have ordinarily investigated by qualitative means. The attempt, of course, points up many more problems than it even partially solves: e.g., how to integrate an analysis of formal social structures with an analysis of informal ones; how to proceed from pair-analysis to the analysis of longer chains and complex networks; and so on. A set of methodological and substantive problems awaits the researcher. It is suggested that the solution will give sociologists important new tools with which to investigate social dynamics.

REFERENCES

1. Back, K., *et al.*, "A Method of Studying Rumor Transmission," in L. Festinger *et al.*, *Theory and Experiment in Social Communication*, Ann Arbor, Michigan: Research Center for Group Dynamics, University of Michigan, 1950, 307-312.

2. Coleman, J. S., E. Katz, and H. Menzel, "The Diffusion of a Medical Innovation" (tentative title), Glencoe, Illinois: The Free Press (in preparation).

3. Dodd, S. C., "Diffusion is Predictable," *American Sociological Review*, 1955, 20, 392-401.

4. Festinger, L., S. Schachter, and K. Back, *Social Pressures in Informal Groups*, New York: Harper, 1950, Chap. 7.

5. Jennings, H. H., "Leadership and Isolation," in G. E. Swanson, T. M. Newcomb, and E. L. Hartley, eds., *Readings in Social Psychology*, New York: Holt, 1952.

6. Katz, E., "The Two-Step Flow of Communication: An Up-to-Date Report on an Hypothesis," *Public Opinion Quarterly*, 1957, 21, 61-78.

7. Katz, E., J. S. Coleman, and H. Menzel, "Social Influence on Decision-Making in Ambiguous Situations—Some Data from a Survey among Physicians" (unpublished).

8. Lipset, S. M., M. A. Trow, and J. S. Coleman, *Union Democracy*, Glencoe, Illinois: The Free Press, 1956.

9. Menzel, H., and E. Katz, "Social Relations and Innovation in the Medical Profession: The Epidemiology of a New Drug," *Public Opinion Quarterly*, 1956, 19, 337-352.

10. Moreno, J. L., *Who Shall Survive?*, Beacon, New York: Beacon House, 1953, 440-450.

11. Riley, M. W., J. W. Riley, Jr., and J. Toby, *Sociological Studies in Scale Analysis*, New Brunswick, New Jersey: Rutgers University Press, 1954.

Part II

Marketing Systems

A marketing system may be defined as the set of institutions and individuals which together constitute the essential members of a network through which goods, services, messages and money flow to effect the exchange of rights to benefits derived from such goods and services. There are roles to be played by each member of the system. Failure of part of the system to behave in some expected manner causes other parts of the system either to malfunction or to modify their behavior. When the modification results in a set of operations which permit tasks to be performed, the adjustment may be said to be successful. The requirements placed on the rest of the system might, however, impair efficiency. In such a case, we would expect further adjustment, including the possibility of the introduction of new system members to restore the previously attained level of efficiency. New members of the system might also be admitted when conditions in the operating environment change. In either case, we

would expect continued modification and entrance into and exit from the system until opportunities for further improvement under the operating conditions no longer exist.

The American marketing system has indeed been characterized by an evolutionary process whereby malperformance by some constituent member(s) or change in the operating condition(s) has led to the exit of some member(s) and the entry of others. The Yankee peddler and the country store, mainstays of a pioneer nation, have been replaced by suburban shopping plazas, discount houses and many specialty vendors who cater to the indivualistic tastes of an affluent society. Even though some of the titles of system members remain the same, the jobs they do often undergo radical change. Thus, for example, the rise of the supermarket has forced the wholesale grocer to substantially modify his operational mode.

Part II presents research contributions designed to illuminate the relationships which exist at the many levels of the marketing system. The complex and sensitive relationships which exist between manufacturers and the several levels of buyers below are considered first. The functioning of middlemen is considered in the sections on wholesaling and retailing. In channels of distribution the entire network is connected for purposes of observing flow patterns. Because marketing is conventionally understood to concern itself with relationships inherent in the exchange of physical goods, usually in the domestic economy, the sections on marketing in foreign lands and the marketing of agricultural goods are individually considered.

A. PRODUCER–MANUFACTURER

16. Interfirm Relations in Oil Products Markets[1]

MARSHALL C. HOWARD

Congressional investigations, oil industry trade association meetings, and oil marketing trade journals attest to disagreement about the operations of oil products markets. The competitive struggle engenders charges and countercharges of unfairness, restrictive action, and/or monopoly. At the same time, recent studies indicate that competition is vigorous and intense.[2] It is the purpose here to help clarify this apparent contradiction.

The markets are not pure. Products are not homogeneous and competitors do not behave as though they were unaware of their rivals. Actions of firms are conditioned by interdependence. The word *control*, rather than monopoly, provides a basis for consistent recognition of impure markets and active competition. Intense competition and control can and do exist simultaneously.

Pure markets are no more obtainable here than elsewhere. The public policy maker must therefore rest content with the least impure. His judgment must consider the impact of market structure and behavior on the small and the large firms and on consumers. No one solution is completely satisfactory to all sectors.

RELATIVE POSITIONS OF THE MARKETING UNITS

Vertical integration predominates. The large firms integrate from the refining process forward into marketing and backward into crude oil production. Full vertical integration is never entirely balanced and always involves outside purchase or sale at one or more stages. Integration may not include refining. For example, the independent petroleum wholesaler may integrate forward only into retailing. Smaller firms may not be integrated at all. Further, the twenty to thirty companies which are largest in assets and are integrated (the majors) control a dominant portion of the industry's product.[3]

Two principal categories of small independent marketing units handle refined products and must deal with the large vertically integrated units or with each other. The jobber is one category. Independent bulk stations sell gasoline and/or fuel oil to their own or other service stations and farm, industrial,

From *Journal of Marketing*, Vol. 20, No. 4 (April, 1956), pp. 356-66, by permission of the American Marketing Association.

[1] The author is indebted to Professor Alfred E. Kahn for helpful comments on an earlier draft of this article.

[2] See, especially, R. Cassady, Jr., *Price Making and Price Behavior in the Petroleum Industry* (New Haven: Yale University Press, 1954), and J. G. McLean and R. W. Haigh, *The Growth of Integrated Oil Companies* (Boston: Harvard University, 1954).

[3] In 1952 the twenty leading companies accounted for 84 per cent of the total refinery runs. Joel Dirlam, "The Petroleum Industry," *The Structure of American Industry*, W. Adams, ed. (New York: The Macmillan Co., 1954), p. 238.

commercial, and residential accounts.[4] There are also peddlers or under-the-rack buyers who usually own only their own tank truck and sell either on their own account or on a commission basis.[5] Refiners' own bulk distribution is through salaried stations or through commission agents using storage facilities owned or leased by the refiner suppliers.[6]

The second category is the retail service station.[7] In 1950 refiner marketers operated only somewhat more than three thousand; but they owned or leased about 52 per cent which handled 58 per cent of service station sales of gasoline.[8] This analysis deals with the relations of these two categories to their suppliers and each other.

THE SUPPLY PROBLEM

Open market supplies have not always been available in all markets.[9] A large part of sales by majors to independents is on a contractual rather than a spot basis. In many areas, there are either no independent refineries or they are unreliable supply sources. They may operate sporadically, sell heavily to integrated units, or themselves be integrated forward.[10]

Thus, the large integrated oil companies are the principal sources of supply for the independent in a given market.[11] In 1939 there were from five to sixteen major oil companies operating in any one state, with eleven as the model number.[12]

SHORTAGE AND SUPPLY DEPENDENCE

With shortages, as from war or other emergency, the nonintegrated seller depends especially on his supplier. Much of the petroleum supply is also subject to public regulation at the well-head under state conservation laws, which gear allowable output to demand and counter the tendency to run all crude oil produced to continuously operating stills.[13] Such regulation is not

[4] J. Cross has calculated that 7,417 independent bulk stations (Census of Wholesale Trade) accounted for 15.5 per cent of the total wholesale petroleum sales in 1948. "Vertical Integration in the Oil Industry," *Harvard Business Review,* July-August 1953, p. 74.

[5] The total number of all independent jobber units has been estimated at 14,000. H. Fleming, *Oil Prices and Competition* (American Petroleum Institute, 1953), p. 44.

[6] Since bulk stations of refiners are product sources for independent distributors, the amount sold to consumers and dealers by the latter must be considerably higher than the 15.5 per cent cited in footnote 4.

[7] The 1948 Census of Retail Trade enumerated 188,000 service stations (U.S. Department of Commerce, 1951).

[8] McLean and Haigh, *op. cit.,* pp. 32-33, 35.

[9] Cassady comments that while it may ordinarily be easy to obtain small quantities of gasoline for rebrand from several alternative sources, large quantities are available, if at all, from very few firms (*op. cit.,* p. 191). Also see John Harper, *The Importance of Independent Marketers to the Oil Industry,* paper before American Petroleum Institute Annual Meeting (1951), p. 16. In the Los Angeles area of California, alternative sources of supply appear to be readily available. R. Cassady,

Jr., and W. L. Jones, *The Nature of Competition in Gasoline at the Retail Level* (Berkeley: University of California Press, 1951), pp. 39-40.

[10] Small refineries often operate on an intermittent basis in accordance with the movement in the refinery gross margin. McLean and Haigh, *op. cit.,* p. 656; Joe S. Bain, *The Pacific Coast Petroleum Industry* (Berkeley: University of California Press, 1945), vol. II, p. 194. See also Senate Report No. 25, *Oil Supply and Distribution Problems* (81st Cong., 1st sess., 1949), p. 8; McLean and Haigh, *op. cit.,* pp. 425-34, 658-59.

[11] According to the Federal Trade Commission, "Independent distributors need a source of refined products and the major oil companies are their best suppliers." Staff Report for the Senate Sub-committee on Monopoly of the Select Committee on Small Business, *Monopolistic Practices and Small Business* (1952), p. 40.

[12] Temporary National Economic Committee, *Investigation of Concentration of Economic Power* (Hearings, 76th Cong., 2nd sess., 1939), part 15, p. 8714. These numbers are undoubtedly higher today, for invasion of markets — rather than market division — has characterized the industry since the breakup of the Standard Oil monopoly in 1911.

[13] See Blakely M. Murphy, ed., *Conservation of Oil and Gas* (Chicago: American Bar Association,

aimed to create continuing shortages but to conserve through coordinating crude oil output with the volatile demands for fuel oil and gasoline. Since these demands cannot be projected perfectly, crude oil quotas based on estimates thereof may lead to shortages.

Crude oil production allowables in 1947 fell 2 per cent below demand at prevailing prices. Some suppliers rationed the short supply to their customary buyers. However, major company refiners increased distribution through their own bulk stations. Some marketers, especially peddlers without fixed sources of supply, were unable to obtain adequate supplies.[14] Thus, the need to maintain in "normal" times a "historical position" against the possibility of a shortage tends to prevent jobbers from "shopping around" on the spot market (if there is one) or even regularly shifting among suppliers (if that happens to be possible).

SALES POLICIES AND ALTERNATIVE SOURCES OF SUPPLY

Entry into business and the number of alternative suppliers available are somewhat limited by the sales policies of the refiner sellers. Exclusive dealing of differentiated oil products is common trade practice even though coercion of buyers thereto is unlawful.[15] First, the

supplier is assured of product flow. Second, differentiated oil products are most economically handled on an exclusive basis. Differentiation is accomplished by advertising, different refining processes, differently constituted crudes, and various additives. Different brands must be stored, handled, transported, and advertised separately. Major suppliers also often grant an exclusive wholesale sales franchise for a given market area. Moreover, a supplier can always sell through his own facilities. A new wholesaler must therefore usually find a major supplier seeking a new distribution outlet or one willing to distribute both through jobbers and his own bulk plants.[16]

BARGAINING POWER AND GROWTH OF THE JOBBER

The supplier will encourage existence of the jobber if he believes this to be the most efficient means of distribution in terms of unit costs and if it provides a secure and adequate flow of gallonage. But if there are alternative sources of supply, the supplier risks sudden and serious loss of volume at the end of the contract period with a high-gallonage jobber. In fact, high gallonage facilitates obtaining alternative sources of supply. With intense competition, the supplier may absorb the jobber (at a good price) rather than risk losing him.[17]

Both jobbers and suppliers may be induced to merge. The jobber may feel that his capital investment is insecure in a highly competitive market. He may prefer the greater security of a salaried employee or rentier status. He may sense that the time is simply "ripe" for the sale of his business, especially since

---

1949). The only important producing state without a conservation or prorationing law is California, where a voluntary system of control is used.

[14] Senate Report No. 25, op. cit., pp. 2-9.

[15] The Supreme Court has ruled out requirements contracts in the oil business at the retail level in two instances: Standard Oil Company of California and Standard Stations, Inc., v. U.S., 337 U.S. 293 (1949); U.S. v. Richfield Oil Corp., 99 F. Supp. 280 (1951), sustained per curiam, 343 U.S. 922 (1952). A similar case is now pending in U.S. v. Sun Oil Company, Civil No. 10483 (E.D. Pa. 1950). At the wholesale level, Shell Oil approved of a consent settlement (6051) under which it agreed not to sell or make contracts for the sales of its kerosene and fuel oil upon any condition, agreement, or understanding requiring the purchaser to handle these exclusively. Federal Trade Commission, Clip Sheet, April 6, 1953.

[16] Many oil companies are now giving up the practice of dual distribution. See footnote 36 below.

[17] J. Cross indicates that relatively few jobbers (compared with all lines of business) have been forced into bankruptcy, whereas many have sold out to their suppliers. He points out that some have built up jobbing businesses, sold out, rebuilt, sold out again, and so on (op. cit., p. 74).

it is not integrated and is dependent on limited supply sources. Or, as in the past, over-extension of credit to the jobber, perhaps deliberate, may have hastened the disappearance of the jobber.[18]

THE JOBBER MARGIN

Within limits encompassed by alternative sources, the supplier may control the jobber through the supply price, usually quoted as a cents-per-gallon margin below the "going" resale price. This latter price may be the supplier's own tank-wagon price to the service station or that of the leading marketer in the area. The supplier can squeeze out a jobber by holding a fixed margin when costs are rising. However, purchase of the jobber's facilities avoids poor public relations.

Jobbers claim that margins have not permitted them to expand with growing markets and to compete with large integrated competitors who control large-scale retail outlets or provide free equipment and property improvements to customers, allegedly subsidized by profits in other segments of the suppliers' business. Counterargument holds this is not good business sense, since every investment denies an alternative and must yield a return of its own. For the integrated oil companies, however, marketing investment may enhance stability of other operations and reduce average costs by fuller use of refinery capacity. Large oil companies may disclaim premeditation but they can and sometimes do "subsidize" marketing outlets.[19]

But, as his gallonage increases, the jobber develops greater bargaining power and more sources of supply. He can then demand a larger margin, with which he can "subsidize" the marketing operations. Further "expansion" may then occur through merger with the larger integrated unit which now may be threatened with serious loss of gallonage.

BYPASS OF THE JOBBER

Jobber growth may be restricted through direct sale by the supplier to large-volume accounts at the same price or lower than that accorded the jobber himself. This large-quantity, sealed-bid, and order-by-specification business is intensely competitive. The jobber protests, but the immediate purchaser benefits either from a cost saving in the bypass or a marginal-cost price.

JOBBER SURVIVAL

Generalization here is dangerous. However, the jobber is apparently strongest and expanding in the home fuel oil business where personal contact and service flexibility are so important and, second, in nonmetropolitan areas where volume is relatively small. The total number of independent jobbers and their average annual sales have increased.[20]

Growth and equal bargaining power depend on assuring readily available supplies to all buyers. Elimination of the product differentiation which is conducive to exclusive dealing is hostile to freedom of enterprise and innovation. And the need to maintain "historical position" would still remain. Within limits, crude oil production on

---

[18] For an excellent summary of the motives of jobbers and suppliers for merging, see *Final Report of the Marketing Division*, Petroleum Administrative Board (Washington: U.S. Department of the Interior, 1936), pp. 21-22.

[19] See, especially, Myron Watkins, *Oil: Stabilization or Conservation?* (New York: Harper & Bro., 1937), pp. 176, 187. Also see A. E. Kahn, "Standards for Antitrust Policy," *Harvard Law Review*, November, 1953, p. 46.

[20] The 1948 Census of Wholesale Distribution indicates that the number of independent bulk stations has increased from 6,357 in 1939 to 7,417 in 1948, with annual sales increasing from $627,674,000 to $1,814,677,000. The number of fuel oil dealers (retail distribution) increased from 2,843 to 4,525 — with sales increasing from $125,925,000 to $732,119,000. Although the Census did not distinguish ownership of these retail stores, over 85 per cent were unincorporated.

the "over" side would assure readily available supplies, but it would also lead to offsetting disadvantages discussed below.

CONTRACTUAL INTEGRATION AND THE RETAILER

The dependence of the independent gasoline retailer upon his supplier varies with the prevailing contractual relationship between them. There are three principal types of gasoline service stations. First, the supplier may operate his own or leased stations. The few major company-operated stations move a very small percentage of the total service station sales.[21] Second, dealers may operate stations controlled by the supplier.[22] The usual dealer lease is for one year with a cancellation clause. The third or contractor type of service station is operated by a dealer who controls a unit through ownership or lease from a third party. He contracts with the supplier for supplies only.

CONTROL OVER RETAIL OUTLETS

To maintain stable sales volume, refiner suppliers have attempted to control retail outlets. Control over 58 per cent of service station sales does not indicate a failure to reach a target of 100 per cent. Shifting location of demand requires extreme caution in investments by suppliers. The contractor station may thus serve to extend sales into riskier areas.

[21] There are exceptions, but the typical major oil company operates 1 per cent or less of the service stations through which its oil products are sold. See 1948 data in Progress Report of the Committee on Interstate and Foreign Commerce, *Fuel Investigation—Petroleum Prices and Profits* (House Report 2342, 80th Cong., 2nd sess., 1948), answers to question 13; and data in McLean and Haigh, *op. cit.*, pp. 486-87.

[22] The supplier may own or lease the station from the operator or others. One form of aid sometimes made available to a dealer in building a service station is endorsement of the dealer's mortgage note. The return favor is a long-term lease to the endorser.

Even with control over an outlet, the supplier can avoid certain responsibilities of retailing by short-term leasing to dealers on the so-called "Iowa Plan." These responsibilities include state chain-store taxes, blame for retail price making, employer's social security tax contributions, labor union troubles, and managerial inspection. And the small businessman may have more incentive than a company employee to operate efficiently and increase gallonage.

SUPPLIER-RETAILER RELATIONS

There is friction between supplier and retailer on issues ranging from hours of operation to maintenance of rest rooms to price and dealer's margin. Dealer complaints of interference are minimized where the supplier provides entry into business and suggestions and training in sales technique and accounting.[23] The contractor who controls is truly independent of his supplier, although he may accept such gifts as free station painting or signs, a compressor, or a hardtop driveway.

Here exclusive dealing thrives. An ethical obligation is implied on the part of the party assisted to sell the supplier's TBA (tires, batteries, accessories) as well as his oil products. Single-brand selling is also fostered by the economies of handling only one brand of liquid bulk oils, the believed advantages of "pushing" one line of products, avoidance of costs of "shopping around," and desire for secure supply.

Congressional hearings disclose complaints that the lessee-dealer's operations are controlled by failure to renew the lease, through the cancellation clause, raising the rent, threats to remove or charge for the "free" equip-

[23] The U.S. Department of Commerce has advised prospective retailers that there are certain advantages in entering the business by leasing a station from one of the oil companies or jobbers. *Establishing and Operating a Service Station*, Industrial (Small Business) Series No. 22 (Washington, 1945), pp. 21-22.

ment supplied the contractor dealer, or threats to erect competitive service stations. There is full independence of lessee-dealer action only for the length of the lease. The owner-operator, too, is subject to "persuasion," since sales drives are directed toward all outlets.

Freedom of dealer action is achieved by removing coercive elements, but, with assistance from or supply dependence upon any supplier, exclusive dealing at retail is not likely to diminish perceptibly. With longer dealer leases, entry by the retailer might become more difficult as the supplier appraises more fully the "reliability" or "responsibility" of the prospective dealer.[24] Greater difficulty of entry may be accompanied by acceleration of the trend to fewer and larger stations rather than by more company-operated stations.[25] But the security of longer leases might also attract better dealers.

THE FORCES FOR PRICE COMPETITION

The greatest source of interfirm friction and competition is price policy of both suppliers and their market outlets

---

[24] The pending case against Sun Oil Co. prays for leases of terms of not less than five years, the right of a lessee to freely assign or transfer the lease to an independent service station operator of his own choosing, a limitation of the right to cancel "to breach of reasonable covenants," and cancellation notice of at least 90 days. (*op. cit.*, Complaint, prayer, par. 6). A few of the major oil companies have recently initiated three-year leases without 30-day cancellation clauses for the ostensible purpose of attracting well-qualified dealers by offering greater security. The House Select Committee on Small Business has recommended that lessee dealers receive probationary periods of from six months to a year with certain dealer investment guarantees and that leases be of a minimum term of three years thereafter. House Report No. 1423 (84th Cong., 1st sess., 1955), p. 3.

[25] The trend is to the large-gallonage service station and away from the small marginal ones. Willard Wright, Sun Oil Co., reported in *The Gasoline Retailer*, May 19, 1954, p. 1. Justice Douglas in a dissenting opinion in the *Standard of California* case feared that the elimination of require-

when product is in ample supply. Recurrent periods of unstable prices, regarded now as more or less normal, are due either to the fact that the many independent units sometimes become "the tail which wags the dog" or that suppliers seek to compete in price through these small business units.

SOURCES OF PRICE WARS

The actual source of violent price competition is not easily identifiable.[26] Price competition for gallonage may break out because a dealer may think that by cutting his retail price he may greatly increase sales in spite of product differentiation.[27] Reaction by competitors depends on their number, organizational strength, degree of their business diversification, particular location, and the price policy of their suppliers. An independent jobber may cause a price war by shrinking his own margin and, through a lower tank-wagon price, inducing the retailer to cut his price. Or the integrated jobber may cut the retail price himself. Or "pressure" from a supplier may induce a retailer to cut his price.

When the supplier sees gallonage fall at his retail outlets because they are being undercut in price, the "order" may go down "to meet the competition." Compliance may be encouraged by guaranteeing openly or otherwise a minimum cents-per-gallon margin to the dealers. Such guarantees may induce further price cutting if the fixed

---

ments contracts would turn the oil suppliers to company operation of stations. 337 U.S. 293, 320 (1949). This has not occurred.

[26] Violent price competition is limited usually to the gasoline market. Fuel oil is usually routinely brought to the domestic consumer according to some schedule of consumption, is inconspicuously tucked away in the basement, and its price is not as a rule openly advertised.

[27] Unbranded gasoline, and minor brands in some cases, may achieve equal consumer acceptance only with a differential in price of between two and four cents per gallon. See V. T. Clover, "Price Influence of Unbranded Gasoline," *The Journal of Marketing*, April 1953, pp. 388-93.

margin is offered regardless of the retail price level.

Refiners may enter a new market through a price-cutting distributorship (jobber). Or "surplus" product of a major may be available to some "opportunist"—wholesaler or wholesaler retailer—or to someone offering a new method of distribution like the large-scale, large-volume, multipump service stations receiving discounts from the tank-wagon price. Sometimes even a company-operated station may initiate a retail price cut.

PRICING AND SMALL SELLER DEPENDENCE

Petroleum product prices are administered in the sense that technically defined pure competition does not exist. The tank-wagon price is the most administered, the "stickiest," and usually the last to move. Announced reductions of this price are frequently preceded by subsidies, rebates, or discounts. Announced price increases may occur in the face of rising stocks, in planning for anticipated seasonal changes in demand, or attempts to get a more "reasonable" return on investment.[28] The leading marketer in a region is frequently, but not always, used as the "reference" seller. But the many places at which price cutting may break out limits the oligopolistic "leadership."[29]

Allowing for lags and isolated markets, price appears to reflect market conditions with acceptable promptness.[30]

Periods of stable retail prices followed by violent price cutting vary among localities. Price wars seem to be chronic in some areas and absent in others and more frequent in heavily populated areas than country communities. Gasoline market areas overlap. Price wars, therefore, have a tendency to spread rapidly. When "too many" small outlets are "injured," large suppliers grant subsidies or rebates or lower the tank-wagon price. Regardless of who starts the price war, rescue is up to the large unit. But dealers' margins are reduced and the small business unit may be forced out.[31]

In this context, dealers claim that large suppliers favor some marketers with discriminatory discounts or initiate price cuts at company-operated stations in order to start price wars and thus con-

---

[28] See, for example, Hearings before the House Committee on Interstate and Foreign Commerce, *Petroleum Study (Gasoline and Oil Price Increases)* (83rd Cong., 1st sess., 1953), pp. 390-91, 427-29.

[29] See, especially, J. B. Dirlam and A. E. Kahn, "Leadership and Conflict in the Pricing of Gasoline," *Yale Law Journal*, June-July 1952, pp. 818-55. See, also, J. Markham, "The Nature and Significance of Price Leadership," *American Economic Review*, December 1951, pp. 891-905. Implementing devices necessary for effective price leadership have been sought out as conspiracies in *U.S. v. Socony-Vacuum Oil Co.,* 310 U.S. 150 (1940); *Ethyl Gasoline Corp. v. U.S.,* 309 U.S. 436 (1940); *U.S. v. General Petroleum Corp. of California,* Crim. 14149M (1939) *Nolo contendere; U.S. v. American Petroleum*

Institute, et al., Civil 8524 (D.C. 1940) dismissed 1951 by U. S. Department of Justice as being too complex and involved; *U.S. v. Standard Oil Company of California, et al.,* Civil 11584-C (S.D. Cal. 1950) pending; *The State of Texas v. Arkansas Fuel Oil Company, et al.,* 82980 (Texas 98th Jud. 1950), dismissed by the Texas Supreme Court, June 1955, for inadequate proof.

[30] According to Dirlam, the price leader in the oil industry may have a substantial range of discretion but cannot ignore basic market forces. He states that in recent years there has been no underutilization of refinery capacity, with the exception of a short period in 1949, and that refinery margins have not been unreasonably high (*op. cit.,* pp. 256-58). For studies in the behavior of petroleum markets, see E. Learned, "Pricing of Gasoline: A Case Study" (Standard of Ohio), *Harvard Business Review,* November 1948, pp. 723-56; Hansen and Niland, "Esso Standard: A Case Study in Pricing," *Harvard Business Review,* May-June 1952, pp. 114-32; Cassady. *op. cit.,* Chapter 6; A. R. Burns, *The Decline of Competition* (New York: McGraw-Hill Book Company, 1936), pp. 93-109.

[31] The annual turnover of dealers in the United States is 33 per cent, as reported by Gulf Oil Corp. *The Gasoline Retailer,* May 19, 1954, p. 1. A part of this figure is undoubtedly due to inefficiency, as case of entry may attract marginal workers. Turnover may also be attributed to the appearance of more attractive opportunities for dealers elsewhere.

trol the dealers' margin. Jobbers charge
that the large suppliers precipitate price
wars and then guarantee the jobber a
margin below that of the normal contract magnitude. Suppliers charge that
the jobbers give away part of their margin and thus start price wars. Both suppliers and their jobbers charge that the
dealers start the wars.

Should the supplier be denounced
when he does not relieve the service
station dealers or jobbers quickly
enough or does not offer a bigger guarantee, regardless of who started the
war? If so, even if not a dominant force
in the market, he can never be anything
but wrong. The supplier must avoid
giving discriminatory subsidies. It is
difficult, however, to define the market
to be subsidized. Or can rentals, especially if based on gallonage, be reduced
without discrimination?[32]

PRICE DIFFERENTIAL — THE ALTERNA-
TIVE SOLUTIONS

Retailers complain chiefly of volume
differentials. Regardless of any possible
cost basis for such price differences,
lower resulting retail prices often lead
retailers to charge intent "to injure
competition."[33] There are several alter-

native ways to eliminate the problems
of differential pricing.

The supplier could be ordered to
cease all discount sales, whether to jobbers or retailers, which result in retail
prices lower than "going" levels.[34] This
remedy either requires policing by
the supplier of resale price maintenance or it results in the elimination
of the jobber or the large-volume retailer as customers.

With jobbers only, the supplier could
be compelled to price its own service
station customers at a tank-wagon price
no higher than that charged by its jobbers to their service station customers [35]

price differential, although a low for the time,
triggered off price competition. As a result,
"large amounts of business" were diverted from
other retailers, including Standard's own service
stations, with resultant injury to them and to their
ability to continue in business and successfully
compete with said dealers in the retailing of
gasoline." (41 F.T.C. 263, 274-75) The dealers'
margin fell. Relief was first "administered" by
Sun Oil Co., not the traditional price leader, when
the retail margin fell to a very low point.

The Federal Trade Commission's case against
Standard was originally based on the contention
that the "good faith" meeting of competition
provision of Sec. 2(b) could be used only as a
procedural and not as a substantive defense to
a charge of price discrimination. The Commission,
therefore, had made no finding on "good faith"
itself. The Circuit Court upheld the Commission.
The Supreme Court, however, ruled that "good
faith" was a substantive defense and remanded
the case back to the Circuit Court with instructions to remand to the Commission for a finding.
The Commission found (3-2) that there was not
"good faith" on the grounds that the discount in
question represented a continuous rather than a
sporadic price policy (Modified Order to Cease
and Desist, Docket 4389, January 16, 1953, p. 18).
The Commission denied a petition of Standard
Oil to reopen the case. Appeal to the Court to
dismiss the Commission order was made in March
1955.

[34] The Federal Trade Commission in its first
(modified) order in the Standard of Indiana
case ordered Standard to stop all sales to jobbers
who undercut Standard's tank-wagon price in
their resale to service stations (43 F.T.C. 56,
58).

[35] This is the substance of the second (modified)
order of the Federal Trade Commission in the
Standard of Indiana case (Modified Order to
Cease and Desist, Docket 4389, January 16,
1953, p. 2).

[32] Some stations are leased on a flat rental basis;
others on the basis of so many cents per gallon of
gasoline or on gallonage with fixed minimum or
with fixed minimum and maximum.

[33] The price discrimination case under Section 2
of the amended Clayton Act against Standard Oil
Co. (Indiana) is illustrative of circumstances
when suppliers engage in differential pricing.
In the Matter of Standard Oil Company, Docket
4389, 41 F.T.C. 263 (1945), 43 F.T.C. 56 (1946),
Standard Oil Company v. F.T.C., 173 F.2d 210
(7th C.C.A., 1949), 340 U.S. 231 (1951). Standard
was selling in the Detroit gasoline market area
under dual operation. It provided direct tank-
wagon service to service stations and from 1936
to 1940 was selling the same branded gasoline in
tank-car quantities at a tank-car price, 1 1/2 cents
less than the tank-wagon price to its service
station customers, to four marketers who either
resold to retail service stations or sold through
their own retail outlets. Supplies of gasoline
in the area were abundant and the 1 1/2-cents

It is hardly likely that any supplier would sell to jobbers who could set a tank-wagon price undesirable to the supplier but binding on him and thereby eliminating any opportunity for even limited price administration. The jobber would thus endanger his source of supply unless he followed the supplier's tank-wagon price.[36] He, therefore, would fear to initiate price competition.

A third alternative would be simply to prohibit any discounts among supplier's customers who are in direct competition.[37] This would discourage integration of wholesale and retail functions. Yet, such combination of functions is often the first step in the growth of a small unit.[38]

A fourth alternative would be to use the cost-saving proviso of the Robinson-Patman Act permitting price differentials. Difficulties inherent in the allocation of the seller's costs are heightened by the discounts required to cover the functions provided by the buyer re-

seller. The Federal Trade Commission would likely become involved in continuous price fixing.[39]

Competition can be workable and equitable only if there be freedom of access to the function favored by a discount.[40] But lessee dealers lease given facilities. Actual competitive practice in gasoline has established that the *flow of gallonage* provides basis for a discount. Just as a jobber can demand a larger margin from his supplier on the basis of his gallonage, so also can a nonlease dealer gradually absorb the functions and thus obtain the discounts of the jobber.

A final alternative is the divorcement of the refiner suppliers from the marketing units. A clearly delineated selling front by refiner suppliers is implied here.[41] Those channels in which "stickiness" of the tank-wagon price is lessened would be altered. Oligopoly would be more evident, for direct price action by refiners would be felt not as a delayed reaction but immediately. Direct pressure on jobber and retailer margins would be blocked. Price would likely therefore be higher.

Such divorcement would deny dealers assistance in entering business and in sales, accounting, and other business operations. The alleged economies from vertical integration — such as planning of capital investments and inventories and avoidance of interstitial

---

[36] It may well be that the extended litigation and the orders in the *Standard of Indiana* case have been contributing factors in a declining use of dual distribution. Fleming gives the reported explanations of this trend as an inability to plan adequately a company's own sales program or the conclusion by a company that it is competing with itself (*op. cit.*, p. 15).

[37] The Federal Trade Commission prohibited the sale to a jobber at a discount of that gasoline which is sold by the jobber at retail in both of the modified orders in the *Standard of Indiana* case.

[38] "Most petroleum jobbers start out as retailers. After building up one profitable station, an enterprising dealer may acquire a second station, then a third and even a fourth. Then the efficient operator may acquire one or more large consumers, such as trucking concerns, for customers. Later he may find a few smaller retailers who agree to purchase gasoline from him. His total volume may now be sufficient to make it feasible for him to invest in a bulk storage plant and truck distribution facilities. *This is the traditional manner in which small retailers have grown to substantial distributors.* It is the general pattern of expansion in the jobbing industry." Memorandum of Empire State Petroleum Association before the Federal Trade Commission in opposition to the Commission's Proposed Modified Findings, Conclusion and Order, Docket 4389, 1953, p. 12.

[39] J. B. Dirlam and A. E. Kahn, *Fair Competition: The Law and Economics of Antitrust Policy* (Ithaca: Cornell University Press, 1954), p. 251.

[40] *Ibid.*, pp. 246-251. In the *Standard of Indiana* case, dealers — in attempts to absorb the wholesaling functions, in varying degrees — were refused the discounted (tank-car) price by Standard. F.T.C. Brief, *Standard Oil Co. v. F.T.C.*, Supreme Court, 1949, p. 8.

[41] The Gillette divorcement bill of 1949, S. 572, for example, read: "It shall be unlawful for any person directly *or indirectly* to be engaged in commerce in the marketing of refined products while such person or affiliate of such person is also engaged in one or more of the other three branches of the petroleum industry, namely, production, refining, and transporation" (emphasis added) 81st Cong., 1st sess.).

blocks to reduction of market costs and flow of market knowledge—would be eliminated.[42]

SUMMARY AND CONCLUSION

The relatively small nonintegrated marketer is insecure unless he has sound supply relations with a single supplier as protection from possible shortages. He thus tends to attach himself to one supplier and is thereby subject to his "influence." Product differentiation also tends to tie resellers to one supplier; but its elimination would be at the cost of freedom of enterprise and innovation. Legal attacks on coercive exclusive dealing in oils cannot alter those economies derived from handling a single line or brand of oils. Therefore, the basic solution to this problem of insecurity and dependence on one supplier is continuously ample market supplies. Appropriate crude oil production quotas, where they apply, and no rigid limitations on imports should insure this. Yet, abundant market supplies usually lead to price cutting. The consuming purchasers would benefit from lower prices, but the jobber and the retailer are likely to be "hurt" somewhat more than the refiner. Even assuming almost complete regulatory controls over crude oil production and imports, it would still be impossible to find the perfect balance between market demand and supply because of unpredictable needs of emergencies and because fuel oil and gasoline—whose seasonal demands are themselves somewhat unpredictable—are produced as joint products.

When supplies are abundant, major interfirm problems arise when any firm, large or small, becomes highly aggressive. Bigness itself is not the cause, for no one seller can hope to drive out all his competitors. The aggressiveness of *any* marketer, coupled with control,

striking first and hardest at the retail level leads to the charges of unfairness.

In the face of this market structure, to seek to remedy through regulation one case of believed unfairness almost inevitably leads to another or to some price-raising rigidity injurious to consumers. It is largely a matter of "whose ox is gored." To compel suppliers to sell through jobbers may freeze cases of inefficiency into distribution. To prevent suppliers from selling direct to large commercial or industrial accounts at the same prices at which they sell to jobbers would often compel use of an unnecessary middleman. Prices by suppliers to such large accounts at prices lower than those accorded to jobbers benefit even further the immediate purchaser. To require proof through accounting records that marketing operations are not subsidized is well-nigh impossible, for when is a profit or loss too high or too low? To extend or outlaw service station leases may impair market entry and exclude some dealers. To prohibit full integration, even though contractual, would remove a channel which heightens competition at both wholesale and retail. Insistence on resale price maintenance would force rigidity and restrict independence in price making. It could exclude some marketers from sources of supply.

Interested groups have sought their own solutions to these problems. To prevent active price competition, retailers have sought legislation prohibiting sales-below-cost or other price-control laws. Some organizations of retailers have engaged in collusive price fixing.

Unless competition itself is to be impaired, its undesirable effects must be borne by the individual participants, even though they are subject to certain elements of extrafirm control and in spite of the fact that the severity of the competition may differ among various parts of the market structure. The participants need to recognize the particular risks inherent in the industry.

---

[42] See McLean and Haigh, *op. cit.*, Chapter 11.

But with control, there also lies responsibility. Independent wholesalers and retailers should be able to act as independent businessmen and have reasonable access to supply and favored functions. Inequalities in bargaining power, a mark of an impure economy, require fair dealing. The dynamic competitive framework makes interfirm understanding and the avoidance of inequities difficult, especially where unfairness cannot be easily defined, but they should not be impossible to achieve.

17. Problems of Franchised Dealers

EDWIN H. LEWIS AND ROBERT S. HANCOCK

This report represents a portion of the results of a more comprehensive study of the franchise system of distribution. The research project encompassed a broad group of commodity lines, operating practices, and problems.

Any system of distribution has its share of operating problems, and the franchise system is no exception. The problems in a franchise system are, however, different from those usually found in other distribution systems. For the most part, this is explained by the relationship which exists between a franchise company and its dealers. No other system of distribution relies so heavily upon a *voluntary community of interest* to accomplish the marketing task. It is important to observe that neither the franchisor nor franchisee can survive without each other. The franchise company is entirely dependent upon the successful performance of its franchised but independent dealers. In turn the dealers expect the operating practices and policies, set forth by franchisors to be the devices which help to fulfill their business expectations. Whether or not these practices and policies do in fact contribute heavily to a dealer's success is based on how soundly they are conceived, how well they are administered, and the alertness with which policies are adjusted to meet

Abstracted from Edwin H. Lewis and Robert S. Hancock, *The Franchise System of Distribution* (Minneapolis: Small Business Administration, Research Division, School of Business Administration, University of Minnesota, 1963), pp. 67–95.

changing market conditions. It is to this issue that this summary of the research findings is directed.

One of the major research phases of this study involved personal interviews with selected franchisees, mail questionnaires directed to franchise companies and in depth studies of three newly formulated franchise dealers. In addition, the findings were strengthened by historical analyses of three mature and experienced franchised dealerships.

REASONS FOR SEEKING FRANCHISE

People from all walks of life have invested money and time in franchise businesses. The typical franchisee has had some kind of work experience in one or more of the many fields of endeavor. Many franchise owners formerly were engineers, civil-service workers, mechanics, salesmen, clerical workers, industrial workers of all kinds, retail owners or employees, skilled workers, and professional people. Some franchise offers require little or no previous work experience, whereas others are open only to those who possess a technical or professional skill.

Regardless of the past work experience and education of the franchisee the principal reasons given for seeking a franchise are: (1) the desire for independence (i.e., "to be my own boss"), and (2) the opportunity to increase one's income. These reasons are perhaps the same for all who have their own business, but they do little to explain *why* a franchise opportunity was selected. To gain an insight into *why* a franchised dealership was preferred the following responses to: "Why did you decide on this particular franchise" are helpful:

This was the best known and most progressive water conditioning service. Its promotional package and service were considered the best available.

I wanted to run a gasoline station so I could work on automobiles, but I knew a major brand of gasoline would be necessary for my success. A major brand name, a station located near my home, and the national advertising program were things I needed.

I wanted my own business, but did not have sufficient capital of my own. The franchisor helped me establish this business.

I bought some land in 1955 with the idea of putting up my own drive-in. I heard about the great success and high reputation of this franchised drive-in operation. After investigation I soon learned that their "franchise package" was much better than I could have done on my own, so I bought the franchise.

After many years as a retailer of men's and boys' wearing apparel, I learned of the centralized purchasing, merchandising aids, accounting helps, etc. offered by the wholesale company that franchises these stores. I never could have equalized these services in my old business.

Several years ago I worked for a franchised hearing-aid dealer. I had a good opportunity to observe the relationship between the dealer and the manufacturer. From this I gained a lot of respect for this business. I knew the manufacturer had a high-caliber management, was a leader in research, and had a top-flight advertising program. When a dealership became available I jumped at the chance to have my own business.

The above statements characterize the responses made by franchised dealers. It is apparent that dealers are attracted to franchised businesses because the "franchise package" is recognized as superior to the "package" that an individual could create through his singular efforts. The most difficult, and oftentimes the most challenging, business ingredients for an individual business to develop are the very components of the "franchise package": namely, an established name and reputation, widely advertised brands, objectively located outlets, merchandising and operating aids, and sources of financial help. These components also are recognized as primary to the financial success of most retail business ventures. As a consequence, the prospective franchisee visualizes the "franchise package" as a group of devices which contribute to reducing his risk of failure. While all prospective dealers harbor fond thoughts of financial success, they also registered strong fears of failure. Rather intensive fears of failure were evident among franchisees who had seriously considered an independent business venture versus a franchised business. This became apparent during the interviewing by the frequent direct and indirect expressions on the matter of financial success and/or failure.

FRANCHISEE EXPECTATIONS AND RESULTS

All franchised dealers initially enter into business with some rather definite expectations. A dealer's expectations are substantially influenced by the sales and profit potentials estimated for a business at a specific location, by the territorial protection included in the contract, and by the array of business aids included in the franchise package. The established franchisor is usually in a good position to gather typical operating results by virtue of the number of existing dealers from which he can gather data. In turn, typical operating results for the representative businesses can be supplied to the prospective dealer. Figure 1 shows representative

FIGURE 1

SALES AND PROFIT FIGURES FROM REPRESENTATIVE BEN FRANKLIN STORES

Location	Retail Sales	Total Income & Percent of Sales	Investment Required	Percent Return On Investment
Southeast	$144,815	$18,590 – 12.8%	$53,500	34.7%
Mid-South	88,007	13,259 – 15.1	40,000	33.2
Southwest	91,803	9,794 – 10.7	41,500	23.6
Mid-Central	165,210	25,600 – 15.5	57,800	44.3
East	333,206	41,036 – 12.3	86,000	47.7
Midwest	151,498	17,720 – 11.7	59,800	29.6
Mid-South	88,773	12,843 – 14.5	40,000	32.1
Mid-Central	91,520	13,055 – 14.3	41,500	31.5
West	150,799	20,711 – 13.7	59,800	34.6
Midwest	241,461	35,900 – 14.9	66,800	53.7
East	140,248	22,621 – 16.1	53,400	42.4
East	127,031	13,887 – 10.9	51,200	27.1
North Central	121,658	13,701 – 11.3	47,000	29.2
Mid-Central	126,999	20,598 – 16.2	51,200	40.2
West	196,555	25,890 – 13.2	56,500	45.8
Northwest	155,030	18,889 – 12.2	59,800	31.6
Southwest	93,167	12,192 – 13.1	41,500	29.4
Mid-South	121,629	13,063 – 10.7	47,000	27.8
West	129,256	13,028 – 10.1	51,200	25.4
East	284,142	33,061 – 11.6	75,200	44.0

operating results for Ben Franklin Stores. This particular illustration is well regarded because it shows not only what income a franchisee can expect at various sales levels, but also recognizes income variations by geographical location.

The obvious expectation which is closely watched by the dealer is his profit, whereas franchisor aid and promises of help are secondary considerations. Of the franchised dealers interviewed, three out of four felt they had realized their profit expectations, and in several instances the franchisees' expectations had been greatly exceeded. On the other hand, the remaining dealers were disappointed. Since limited-sample data of this kind cannot

be regarded as representative of the franchise field, no specific pattern of profit expectations can be presented. It is interesting to observe, however, that those dealers who had realized or exceeded their profit expectations possessed certain characteristics. Some observable characteristics among those registering results equal to or in excess of their expectations were:

(1) The franchisee's business required more than a casual knowledge about operating and managing a business. In other words, the franchisee possessed some competence in a technical or professional area. One franchisee who lacked these skills had a substantial amount of business

experience in a related field. The few exceptions to this were highly specialized dealerships in fields such as soft ice cream and soft drink drive-ins.

(2) The initial investment, with a few exceptions, was sizeable, i.e., $9,000 was the minimum invested, and $125,000 was the maximum invested by the group.

(3) Franchisor claims, promises, and dealer aids had materialized as expected and satisfaction in this regard was expressed by the franchisee.

(4) The franchise offer was one with a proven past. The most frequent successes were found among the well-established franchise companies and among those with a brand name which was either widely known or had great potential to become widely known.

(5) The franchisee, or dealer, devoted a very large amount of his time and energy to build the business to its present level. Many of the most successful learned early that a sixty or even an eighty hour week was needed to guide the business to a financial success. The successful were enthusiastic, energetic, and prudently attentive to business details.

PROBLEMS INFLUENCING THE EFFECTIVENESS OF THE FRANCHISE SYSTEM

In uncovering and isolating the problems of the franchise field, two discernible kinds of problems were observed. First, there are those which have a general impact upon the entire system, and second, there are specific problems attributable to and exerting an influence upon the franchisor/franchisee relationship.

Among the several problems detected as having a general influence on the franchise field, the following are regarded as the three most significant:

1. The legal status of franchising.
2. The difficulty of administering a franchise system as a whole rather than administering the separate units within the system.
3. The lack of adjustment of some franchise systems to changing market phenomena.

The legal status of franchising is the dominant problem affecting the future of this method of distribution. The question of legality derives from the contractual agreement between franchisor and franchisee and the use of the agreement by the franchisor as a device to restrain trade. Rufus E. Wilson, Chief of the General Trade Restraints Division of the Federal Trade Commission recently said before a conference on antitrust regulations sponsored by the Federal Bar Association that ". . . the very nature of a franchise agreement suggests restraint of trade and that although the franchise system is legal, it may be abused when either the suppliers or distributors become dominant and exert coercion."[1]

Over the years, a series of FTC decisions have been made against suppliers who became dominant in the franchise relationship and exerted coercive pressure against dealers. Wilson cites three areas in which franchise agreements are likely to run into trouble. These are "refusal to deal, restrictive territorial agreements, and customer allocation and exclusive dealing."[2] With specific reference to territorial exclusives, legal counsel for the International Franchise Association rendered the following opinion after researching a number of precedent-setting decisions.

The conclusion to be drawn from the cases is that a franchisor is free to select his franchisees and to allocate geographical areas to them in accord with the Philco opinion [reference here is to *U.S. v. Philco.*] However,

---

[1] "Legal Pitfalls of Franchising Eyed," *Automotive News*, January 15, 1962, p. 2.
[2] *Ibid.*

once he grows to a size of dominance in his industry the allocation of territorial exclusives may be risky, since, if questioned, it will probably be found illegal.

The normal franchisor may employ territorial exclusives as a legal means of expanding his business by encouraging franchisees. Certainly, territorial exclusives are justified under a "rule of reason" examination, since they assure a franchisee that he will reap the benefit of his efforts within an area and will not lose out to a new franchise outlet after developing the market.

It should, however, be remembered that for a franchise contract to be legal, the franchisor cannot exact a promise from the franchisee not to sell outside his allotted territory.[3]

An individual franchisee may not regard himself as a party to the doubtful legal status of certain aspects of franchising. The fact of the matter is that in some cases franchisees find the legal problems unavoidable because of certain provisions found in their franchise agreements. The franchise agreement is the instrument which specifies the kind and amount of control which a supplier can exert over a franchised dealer.

Antitrust problems may arise because the agreement gives the franchisor control over a businessman who by law is an independent businessman. For instance, certain franchise agreements are a type of lease that must be retained to stay in business (e.g., the automobile dealer franchise and the gasoline station lease).[4] When this is the case, and if the dealer's alternative supply sources are limited or nonexistent, the supplier (or manufacturer as

the case may be) has a captive market. Such a situation increases the supplier's temptation to abuse the rights of the dealer. Threats of franchise cancellation, coercive practices, and intimidation of franchisees by suppliers to accomplish illegal ends have been used and are documented by Federal Trade Commission investigations.[5]

Despite the legal uncertainty surrounding some aspects of franchise agreements, a businessman should not permit this to play a dominant role in his decision to enter a franchise business or adopt this method of distribution. The antitrust laws are very complex, and their interpretation should be left to the courts and expert legal counsel. The economic advantages of this system of distribution to both franchisor and franchisee can still materialize within the constraints of the law. Ample evidence to support this contention exists by virtue of the large number of franchise firms who have accomplished their financial and marketing ends without resorting to illegal means.

The very nature of a franchise business implies that the franchisee must cooperate with the franchisor to build and maintain a successful system of distribution. As a consequence, good salesmanship, aggressive marketing practices, and effective competitive strategy, as distinguished from illegal practices, are expected of franchisors if their distribution systems are to survive. Few, if any, marketing authorities would support dealers who are content with low volume, poorly conceived operating practices and high margins, all of which can jeopardize a supplier's market position. Inasmuch as close cooperation between franchisor and franchisee is essential to the success of the system, the franchisee should perhaps consider himself at best as quasi-independent.

The administration of a franchise system as a whole rather than adminis-

---

[3] Unpublished and undated opinion rendered to the International Franchise Association titled "Legality of Territorial Exclusives in Franchise Contracts" by William L. Stein, Rudnick & Wolfe, Chicago, Illinois. Brackets are those of the authors.

[4] Charles M. Hewitt, "The Furor Over Dealer Franchises," *Business Horizons*, Vol. 1, No. 1 (Winter, 1958), p. 82.

---

[5] *Ibid.*, 86

tration of the separate units within that system is a most difficult problem to overcome.[6] The significance of this problem arises because of the unique nature of a franchise business. A franchise business is one where:

> . . . There is a community of interest and interdependence such that unless the manufacturer survives and is successful the welfare of the dealer or supplier is in jeopardy. Simultaneously, the manufacturer is so dependent upon the successful performance of the group of small suppliers and dealers that he cannot afford to let them sink or swim on their own merits. The manufacturer has a vital interest in how effectively and efficiently these groups perform their particular functions. Hence we find in such situations that the manufacturer takes the initiative in providing these subordinate groups with some amount of supervision, guidance, assistance, and control so that they will be able to continue to operate in such fashion as to contribute to the welfare of the manufacturer.
>
> Together the manufacturer with his suppliers and/or dealers comprise a system in which the manufacturer may be designated the primary organization and the dealers and suppliers designated as secondary organizations. This system is in competition with similar systems in the economy, and in order for the system to operate effectively as an integrated whole there must be some administration of the system as a whole, not merely administration of the separate organizations within that system.[7]

The above quotation visualizes a manufacturer as the franchisor, but the need to administer the system as an integral unit is imperative whether the franchisor is a manufacturer or any other type of market supplier. Most of the franchisors interviewed recognized their weaknesses in this regard and sought some means to develop the degree of control implied above. Furthermore, franchisors recognize full well the advantage that corporate chains have in this regard and the competitive advantage these institutions have in presenting a uniform image to the consuming public. Retail chain operations have few problems in creating a uniform and highly standardized image because their store managers are permitted little leeway from the centrally administered policies, standards, and practices. In turn, when consumers patronize corporate chains, they are assured of a consistent and stable standard of performance. Most corporate chains have been so effective in giving a standardized character to their outlets that consumers know what to expect regardless of geographical location. As a result, their centrally administered and highly standardized sales, service, and management policies have enhanced the chains' success and efficiency.

Conflict can and does arise between franchisors and franchisees because one or both parties fail to appreciate that they are in business for a common end. All too frequently, franchisors as well as franchisees regard their roles as separate. It was shown earlier that franchisees engage in business because they want to make a profit and "be their own boss." Their status, legally and in their own minds, is that of an independent businessman. On the other hand, many franchise systems depend upon a uniform image and a highly standardized character of operation to assure success and efficiency of the system.

Franchisors, in their efforts to promote the success of their systems, see the need to exert some control over the sales, service, and management areas. Each of these areas requires a great deal of skill, and seldom is a franchisee qualified in all three. Hence, the franchisor regards any assistance and guidance in

---

[6] For a most illuminating and complete discussion of this problem, see Valentine P. Ridgeway, "Administration of Manufacturer-Dealer Systems," *Administrative Science Quarterly*, Vol. 1 (March, 1957), pp. 464–483.

[7] *Ibid.*, 466

these areas as promoting the success of the *entire system.* A dealer, on the other hand, may regard it as an attempt to stifle his own initiative and judgment. As a consequence, the dealer may reject assistance and in turn upset the uniformity and routinized functioning of the system. What franchisees often fail to comprehend is that the success and efficiency of the *system* depends upon the franchisor's ability to create a uniform image for all outlets before the general public.

It is quite conceivable that a franchisee may profit with little effort, and with little or no adherence to the established standards, by virtue of the reputation and good will generated by the franchisor and the other dealers. Such a franchisee is making no contribution to the entire system, but instead he is helping to destroy the network from which he derives benefit. If franchisees of this kind are numerous in the system, the sales and profits of all franchisees, and the franchisor, will ultimately be affected. Certainly, an apparent need exists for administration which would avoid occurrences of this sort.

Most franchisors who distribute over a wide geographical area, and through many outlets, do perceive the complexity of this problem. For most of them, it is not enough to have central administration of only those activities which contribute to the joint effort. It becomes essential to have close coordination and some degree of control over those activities delegated to the dealers as well. Without this, the dealers, by virtue of their independent status, are likely to exert their individual prerogatives to the detriment of the joint effort. Additionally, the concept and need for administration of the system as a whole dictates that the franchisor have some equitable method for the elimination of undesirable dealers.

The problem of adjustment of franchise systems to changing market phenomena is not necessarily of universal concern. This problem has direct mean-ing to those franchisors who have been on the competitive scene for an extended time, and who since their systems' inception, have undergone little or no adjustment in the products, the locations, the operating practices, and the physical style of their businesses. It has indirect meaning to the more-recently-established franchise systems insofar as they may fail to adjust to future marketing conditions.

The real significance of this problem rests in the fact that change is the normal course of events for the American economy. One of the most striking and most dynamic segments of our economy is marketing (distribution), which is carried on in a growing and ever-changing environment. Populations move, family incomes change, tastes and preferences change, and traditional habits and customs are uprooted. All of this combines to change and adjust consumer demand. Changes in consumer demand are further intensified by technological developments. Changes and adjustments in consumer demand can and often do affect existing ways of doing business. In such a dynamic environment, no brand or product, no institution, and no particular system is free from its impact.

To lend support to only one facet of this contention, Booz, Allen and Hamilton in a recent study concluded that:

> It is now commonplace for major companies to have 50% or more of current sales in products new in the past 10 years. In the next three years alone, about 75% of the nation's growth in sales volume can be expected to come from new products, including new brands.[8]

The consequence of this research finding is not only that the economy will support more new products, but also that many existing products will be displaced by new ones. Similarly, franchisors' products, their outlets, and the

---

[8] *Management of New Products,* (New York: Booz, Allen & Hamilton, Management Consultants, 1960), p. 3.

physical aspects of their systems have been and will continue to be vulnerable to the pressures of a dynamic economy.

Market research is the best way for franchisors to keep abreast of changing market conditions. Properly undertaken by qualified personnel, market research can minimize the subjectivism of business decisions. The various techniques of market research can quantify a large number of distribution problems. The location of franchise outlets, market potentials, the most effective sales appeals, price strategies, and cost problems are a few of the many problems to which market research techniques can be applied. Research does not relieve franchisors of their responsibility for making decisions, but it creates an objective base upon which sounder decisions could be made. The widespread use of this business tool by franchisors appears almost indispensable in view of the uncertainty which will continue to pervade the distribution scene.

SPECIFIC PROBLEMS INFLUENCING THE FRANCHISOR/FRANCHISEE RELATIONSHIP

The group of problems and franchisee criticisms discussed in this section can be informative to both franchisors and franchisees. For the former, some of these suggest ways in which their systems might be improved or cite practices which should be avoided. For the latter, these problems suggest a number of points which are worthy of investigation before investing in a franchise business. The problems which appear to be of greatest concern to both franchisors and franchisees are:

(1) The shortage of capital
(2) The franchisee selection process
(3) The problem of inadequate profits

Several dealer criticisms about specific operating practices of franchisors will also be discussed briefly.

The shortage of capital was the most frequently encountered problem among both franchisors and franchisees. This problem is very different in scope and complexity for a franchisor than for a franchisee. Several well-known franchisors, who have since solved this problem and are now distributing on a national scale, reported that during their formative years, they were under-capitalized relative to their expenses and expansion plans. This problem was further intensified by the reluctance of commercial banks and other conventional money sources to lend working capital to businesses without proven operating experience.

Not only was it difficult to find sources of working capital, it was also impossible to anticipate capital needs when growth got out of control. For example, a brief mention of a business proposition in a national publication and a statement that franchises were available brought hundreds upon hundreds of inquiries from people interested in a franchised dealership. Each new franchisee taxed the franchisors' working capital, inventory, and credit position, and increased his personnel problems. As a result, additional capital had to be supplied either from the franchisor's personal funds or from outside sources. With more conventional capital sources closed to them, private stock issues, other businesses, loan companies, extended credit terms on inventory and equipment from suppliers, and other miscellaneous sources were helpful in temporarily relieving the financial pressures caused by expansion. For some franchisors, the credit and capital position became so critical that they were forced to halt expansion for an interval, or they found it necessary to secure partners who would assume the responsibility for the expansion of entire geographical areas. This latter measure had to be administered carefully in order not to disrupt the standardized operating procedures and the price structure. A partnership arrangement, on an area basis, assured the franchise business of some of the profits from sales of installations, equipment, and supplies which otherwise it would not have been able to earn.

Stop-gap financial measures were no longer necessary when the franchise companies grew to a respectable size and had earnings in keeping with conservative lending practices. Then, the availability of funds and/or lines of credit permitted them almost unlimited expansion and assured financial help to their prospective dealers.

Even with the financial help given by a franchisor to his newly-established franchisees, a considerable portion of the working capital and other financial needs should be provided by the franchisee. Further, it is essential that the franchisee provide for unforeseen business and personal contingencies. Such a recommendation appears desirable, since some franchisees complained that they too were under-capitalized. Those who were, felt that the over-optimistic claims of the franchisor encouraged them to invest in the system even though they had no reserves. Most well-managed franchisors make a conscientious effort to avoid applicants who do not have sufficient funds of their own. Credit information and financial statements from prospective franchisees are often requested and analyzed by franchisors. Indirectly, franchisors establish financial eligibility by clear-cut statements of the amount of capital needed in their promotional brochures. The Chicken Delight brochure contains the following statement:

A capital outlay of only approximately $12,000 will put you in business (this figure is exclusive of vehicles and signs which may be leased) and Chicken Delight will assist in financing arrangements if you wish. Actually, you can finance your Chicken Delight operation for as little as $6,000 down.

The above statement not only shows the financial requirements for a prospective franchisee, it clearly implies the minimum amount of capital a person needs to consider this franchise. Financial prudence dictates that reserve funds over and above the minimum investment should be readily available to the franchisee. A franchisor is usually in a good position to estimate the franchisee's reserve requirements by virtue of past experience with other dealers. Some franchise companies have detailed "set-up statements" which are used to estimate objectively *all* financial needs relative to the size and physical properties of the dealership. Set-up statements include operating data, investment data, and a financial statement of the prospective franchisee. An instrument of this sort clearly shows the financial feasibility of the proposed dealership relative to the prospective franchisee's financial resources. Its use avoids attracting those persons who often are guilty of "trying to do too much with too little."

The *franchisee selection process* was another problem cited by dealers. Franchisees who have lived up to their contractual agreements and built profitable outlets are critical of the selection processes used by some franchise companies. If ineffective and uncooperative dealers are brought into the system, the more qualified and efficient dealers visualize them as a threat to the system. This problem is similar in impact to the more general administrative problem discussed earlier. It has a much different emphasis, however, because it represents a criticism of the franchisor's dealer-selection process rather than a criticism of the franchisor's administration of the system. The view held by franchisees is that the system can be as seriously weakened by a poor selection process as by poor administration of standards and activities. Most franchisees interviewed felt no special qualifications or experience was necessary to acquire an outlet so long as a person had adequate capital. As a suggested solution, the well informed and successful franchisees felt it was necessary for franchisors to adopt selection methods which would be in close correspondence with the quality of the system. It goes without saying that the ideal in building and maintaining a high quality network of dealers is a selection method which would *qualify* and *classify* prospective franchisees as carefully as the physical properties of the business are specified.

In view of the understanding that franchisors have of this problem, the above criticism may or may not be valid. During the course of the interviews with franchisors, and the written correspondence carried on with them, the authors learned that this was their single most pervasive operating problem. No franchisor failed to mention that human frailties and their inability to detect them was of deep concern. Franchisors reported that despite psychological tests, extensive interviews with prospective dealers, and the strict requirements for demonstrated competence and business ability, a number of dealers always failed to live up to expectations. Having learned that it was most difficult to predict actual performance, the franchisors sometimes became more selective in the kinds of media in which they placed advertisements to publicize their franchise opportunity. This move seemed to change only slightly the quality of prospective franchisees.

This problem is not peculiar to the franchise field, but is one with which most American businesses have been wrestling for a long time. Unfortunately, the knowledge and state of the arts concerned with this problem is not sufficiently developed to promise either an early or an easy solution. At best, well-formulated selection procedures can minimize, but not eliminate the acceptance of unqualified dealers into the system.

Inadequate profits was a problem among one-fourth of the franchisees interviewed. This group regarded their profits as unsatisfactory for a number of reasons: (1) profits were too low if they did not equal or exceed the figures set by the franchisor at the outset of the franchise sale; (2) they were inadequate because the business had not yet matured and reached its full potential; and, (3) they were too small because the dealer saw no way to develop his small-scale business into a larger-scale operation. Only a few franchisees felt they had been "oversold" on the business by a glowing profit picture painted by the franchisor. Another few were too new to have reached their full profit potential. The majority who felt that profits were too low were operating small-scale enterprises which had at one time fulfilled their expectations, but now did not provide the desired income.

Many franchise businesses are quite modest, and small-scale businesses seldom produce profits which are out of proportion to their size. Anyone anticipating starting a franchise business would do well to understand that it is indeed rare when a small investment and a small-scale business produce large dollar amounts of profit. In general, the profits of any business endeavor are relative to the scope and size of the business itself. The obvious exception to this generality is the franchise which can be purchased for a few hundred dollars and requires the holder to sell a service or product which has a reasonably good markup. In this instance, an energetic, intelligent, and creative salesman can earn a generous return if he is closing numerous sales.

The fact that many franchise businesses are modest from both the profit and personal challenge standpoint creates a unique problem. A small franchise business which at one time satisfied the aspirations of the owner can become the victim of the owner's changing aspirations. Dealers operating successful, but small, businesses will become discontent if the business does not satisfy their new levels of aspiration.

Is it not conceivable that most people's aspirations heighten with each ensuing business success? If this is so, franchisees who forsee little chance for growing profits commensurate with their aspirations will seek more profitable opportunities in other businesses. This need not be the case if the franchisor provides the leadership in developing ways in which his franchisees can profitably grow.

Growth, however, cannot always be realized within the framework of an existing franchise outlet, and this would mean the franchisee would do one of two things. First, he might relinquish the small franchise and seek another business more in keeping with his newly acquired aspirations; or, second, he might consider complementary franchise businesses which could be operated within the framework of his present business. This latter opportunity holds considerable promise and generally lessens the franchisor's chance of losing a qualified dealer. For example, a gasoline station lessee converted his small-scale operation to one of considerable size by adding, first, cross-country trailer rental, second, tool and equipment rental, and third, auto leasing. By virtue of the location of this franchisee, in a small western town, any one of the four franchises would have been a limited operation, but when all four were acquired by one well-qualified person, they combined to give him a handsome income. Franchisors may not be agreeable to the idea of a franchisee adding complementary franchises to form one sizeable concern, but it is worthy of consideration by those who are concerned with their rate of franchisee turnover to find it difficult to attract qualified dealers.

In addition to the above problems, franchisees were critical of certain operating practices of franchisors. Even though most franchisees recognized the distinct advantage of operating a franchised business, a minority disliked specific practices. The following criticisms are not regarded as problems of the franchise system of distribution because they are limited in both scope and applicability. The expressed criticisms were:

1. Franchisor fees, prices for supplies, and other charges are too high after numerous franchise outlets have been added to the chain. A few were particularly critical of the fact that advertising and promotion costs remained the same even after many new units were franchised and in operation. The thinking among franchisees is that some economies of scale ought to materialize, and hence costs should be reduced as the franchisor's volume increases.

2. Operational and financial guides appear to be based on limited experience over a short period of time and for a selected geographical region. Franchisees complain that guideposts developed in this manner are not realistic and have little applicability to their business. Standard operating ratios and monthly financial guideposts which are objectively determined are regarded as necessary by some franchisees.

3. When an outlet is the first, or one of the early few, to be opened in a particular region, the distribution lines of the system are likely to be too long. This means that inventory and supply orders must be submitted well in advance of requirements so as to have the material when needed. The long time-gap between the order for inventory and its delivery makes it almost impossible for the dealer to approximate his requirements closely.

4. The franchisors' field men, merchandising experts, and others who visit the dealer are only of moderate help. The advice they give is sometimes poorly conceived, and they do not have an awareness of local characteristics. Franchisees feel that these representatives could be of much help, but sometimes their ideas are not really constructive.

FACTORS TO WEIGH IN CONSIDERING A FRANCHISE BUSINESS[9]

There is little doubt that many Americans have successfully operated franchise businesses and in turn earned large financial rewards. On the other hand, there are many more who are continually seeking out business propositions through which they can better their lot. In their searches, many people will come into contact with and seriously consider the franchise way of doing business. The less impetuous of this group will want to weigh carefully a number of factors before accepting a franchise offer. What should the prospective investor who is considering a franchise business examine? In answering this question, the following points suggest the scope of the investigation which prospective franchisees should undertake.

1. What are your own special qualifications? Do you have the necessary educational background, experience, and know-how to operate the business successfully? Have you the personality and character necessary to operate a business? Many people fail to inventory themselves when entering a business, and yet this can well be the difference between success and failure. Business life is very demanding, and good management qualities are indispensable to soundly-operated businesses. There is no such thing in business as "no special qualifications necessary!" Finally, do you have the physical stamina and the will to work long hours?

2. Have you sufficient capital to buy the franchise under consideration? After

you have purchased the franchise and provided the needed working capital, how much do you need for unforeseen contingencies? This problem was discussed in detail earlier in this study.

3. What is the reputation of the franchise company and its principals? How long has it been in business? Are there successful dealers now in the system who can help furnish information? How is the franchisor financed? Your bank or credit agency may be able to supply a credit report.

4. What are the contractual terms and your rights under the franchise agreement? Is an exact territory covered by the contract? What obligations do you accept when you sign? Are you agreeing to unattainable quotas? Can you sell the franchise? What are the cancellation provisions? What is the period of the franchise, and is it renewable? The prospective franchisee is well-advised to examine the typical aspects of an agreement such as that presented in Section III of this study.

5. What is the purpose of the franchise fee? Franchise fees and franchise royalties are perfectly legitimate and oftentimes necessary. A prudent person, however, should determine the purpose of the payment.

6. Is there a market for the product or the service? Is the field badly overcrowded? Do you expect to have an advantage over competition?

7. Finally, don't be in a hurry to snap up the franchise. A good proposition is not usually sold by high-pressure tactics. The typical, reliable franchisor will want time to evaluate your qualifications, and by the same token will want the prospect to thoroughly investigate the opportunity.

The most difficult and time-consuming job for the prospective investor is finding the right opportunity. The majority of franchisees interviewed in this study spend considerable time in finding their opportunity. In many cases, they had a prior connection with a simi-

[9] This section is developed from the following three sources of information: (1) Franchisee interviews, (2) National Better Business Bureau, Inc., *Some Facts to Consider About Franchise Offers*, (New York, N.Y., September, 1959). (3) *The Franchise Annual*, (Chicago, Illinois: National Franchise Reports, Rogers Sherwood, Publisher, 1963), pp. 10-11.

lar business activity or they had a close associate who was helpful in guiding their decision. The obvious fact that not everyone is suited for the same kind of business suggests that it is necessary for the individual investor to weigh carefully his qualities against those of the franchise opportunity.

B. WHOLESALING

18. Distributing Electrical Products in a Dynamic Economy

EDWIN H. LEWIS

For some time, *Electrical Whole-saling* has felt that the distribution of electric apparatus and supplies badly needed some across-the-board research and expert evaluation. Actually, much of the research job has been done by various organizations over the years. But the bits and pieces have never been collected in one place and—more important—analyzed and appraised. In the absence of such a body of facts and expert opinion, marketing efficiency in the industry has suffered. Armed with such information, electrical distributing stood to be strengthened.

Dr. Lewis has spent almost two years researching and writing the study. Much of it is based on personal interviews he has had with executives of approximately 150 manufacturing, distributing and user companies. Dr. Lewis has also drawn on available data. It should be emphasized that the analysis of this information is entirely his own and arrived at independently.

Here is how Dr. Lewis sums up what he attempted to accomplish: "I have tried to create a broad-gauge picture in order to put the industry in perspective and to show the basic forces responsible for the movement of goods from the point of production to the user. I gave particular attention to the specific marketing jobs which have to be done and the alternative methods of accomplishing them."

Adapted from Edwin H. Lewis, "Electrical Distributing—An Over-all Appraisal," *Electrical Wholesaling* (June, 1958).

The last 20 years have seen a tremendous growth in the electrical apparatus and supplies industry. The number of plants devoted to the manufacture of these lines has more than doubled, and dollar sales volume—now running about $10 billion—is at least 8 times the prewar level. In physical terms, current output is roughly 5½ times the output two decades ago.

Significance of Expansion.—The marketing significance of this expansion of production, both in terms of the increased quantity of material and the many new lines, is very great. Several things have happened:

1. More middlemen, both wholesale distributors and manufacturers' representatives or agents, have entered the market to participate in the distribution of these lines.

2. Even with a larger number of middlemen, newly established manufacturers have had increasing difficulty securing distribution for their lines.

3. Service has become the watchword in many lines, particularly in relation to delivery. Consequently, an increasing number of manufacturers have established local stocks at strategic points across the country.

4. Price competition has become a more dominant factor. This has been apparent in many lines and in virtually all markets, but it has been especially severe in construction materials.

5. The emphasis on price has resulted in the growth of "brokerage" operations. This limited-service activity

has been adopted both by established, full-service wholesalers and by newer firms which do the bulk of their business on this basis.

6. The pressure for markets has thrust the manufacturers' representative into a more dominant position in some lines — especially wiring devices and fixtures sold to contractors. In many areas, the representative is performing functions historically performed by distributors.

7. Better sales promotion has been required of both manufacturers and wholesalers. Many manufacturers, therefore, have found it necessary to aid distributors in their promotional activities.

8. The need for greater marketing efficiency has had a double-barreled effect on the distribution of individual lines: (a) Some manufacturers have reduced the number of wholesalers which they will recognize as "authorized distributors," and (b) Wholesale distributors have, in many cases, reduced the number of competing lines which they will carry.

9. Faced with a complex market of many different requirements, some wholesalers have found it profitable to specialize in certain types of business. Conversely, however, other distributors have seen opportunities to go into new fields and have developed the organization necessary to sell in these new markets successfully.

10. As a result of the competitive situation in major appliances, electrical distributors are dropping their major appliance lines and are getting out of this business.

11. Distributors are serving smaller geographical markets. This development has resulted from the growth of independent houses and branches in smaller cities which were formerly served by distributors located in metropolitan areas. Since these newer establishments have a cost and service advantage in their own trading areas, outside distributors are at a disadvantage and generally find it necessary either to withdraw or to reduce their efforts in these areas.

CREDIT RISKS

Distributors who sell primarily to utilities, institutions, and large industrials have no serious credit problems in the normal course of events. When sales are made to contractors, however, the credit risk increases substantially unless the distributor is very careful with whom he deals.

About 95 per cent of the sales of electrical apparatus and supplies distributors are on credit. Only 43 of the 3159 establishments reported for 1954 sold exclusively for cash. On the average, receivables in that year were 10 to 12 per cent of sales and bad debt losses were about .2 per cent. During the postwar years the average collection period has ranged from 35 to 45 days.

These averages, however, hide a type of situation which is all too prevalent: the contractor who is operating with insufficient capital and who is always deeply in debt to someone. His income from one job is used to pay the suppliers of another. Oddly enough, regardless of how bad a contractor's credit may be, some distributor is always willing to sell to him on the assumption that *he* will be paid.

Some electrical distributors feel that they are justified in extending liberal credit to contractors if they are not forced to cut prices. However, this is a rather dangerous policy. The added risk and expense may more than offset the larger income. Most wholesalers try to hold their collection period to 30 or 40 days with a maximum of about 60 days, after which they may stop selling to the contractor.

Credit terms which are too liberal create a vicious cycle. Contractors whose credit is over-extended become desperate to get new business. In the process, they bid low to get additional jobs. This forces market prices down, with resulting pressure on other contractors and on distributors. Meanwhile, the marginal contractor robs one job to pay for another and seldom comes out even.

The only remedy for this unhealthy situation is to force out unethical contractors or induce them to improve their practices. A tight credit policy on the part of distributors would help materially in this respect. Some builders and architects also have been able to stabilize the situation by not giving jobs to low bidders unless they are financially responsible.

FUTURE OF THE WHOLESALER

The position of the electrical wholesaler will not be in jeopardy provided he adopts a philosophy which will permit him to operate effectively as a wholesaler. There are several aspects of such a philosophy. In the first instance, it is quite essential that the wholesaler decide which type of market he wishes to serve. He must make some choices. The range of both products and types of buyers is too broad to enable the wholesaler to be all things to all people.

If a wholesaler wishes to cater to the contractor market, it is unlikely that he can also do a job with specialized industrial lines, and he should not try to. Furthermore, whatever market the wholesaler chooses to serve, he needs to perform the necessary functions as efficiently as possible.

It would appear that many electrical wholesalers are not able to differentiate profitable from unprofitable operations. They attempt to secure unprofitable types of business and to give unprofitable services. There is no necessary relationship between sales volume and net profit, and being volume conscious is not the same as being profit conscious.

The wholesaler needs to be keenly aware of unprofitable business and either discourage it or find ways to make it profitable. Every wholesale establishment is faced with various alternatives with respect to product lines, geographical markets, types of customers, etc. The choices among these alternatives spell the difference between profit or loss in the wholesale operation.

The wholesaler must develop the necessary cost and control records which will permit him to make the most profitable choices. Only then can he become aware of the losses resulting from price cutting, for example, or from giving services which are not justified by the returns.

The days of easy wholesale profits are over, but profitable wholesaling is a basic and continuing need in the electrical industry. Further effort and inquiry are necessary to develop ways by which the wholesaler can adapt his operations to the changes constantly occurring in the market.

This is the challenge facing the electrical distributor. It can be met only by improving wholesale management practices and by each wholesaler finding the niche where he can operate best. There is no magic formula by which either of these objectives can be accomplished.

THE MANUFACTURERS' AGENT

Agents contend, and their contention is probably sound, that man for man they can do a better sales job than an average manufacturer's salesman. There are several reasons for this:

1. Agents are paid on commission. This is a stronger incentive than the typical salesman's compensation which is seldom straight commission.

2. The agent is more likely to have a "customer-point-of-view." All of his activities are customer-oriented. He isn't hampered by a sales organization with its organizational rivalries, conflicting personalities, etc. The agent's welfare is more closely tied to his customer's welfare. He can't be promoted or transferred. He is in the same territory serving the same customers for his working lifetime.

3. The agent fully appreciates the value of service and he can perform

many small services for his customers.

4. The agent is intimately familiar with his customers and their needs.

These points would not always stand up against a well-trained, well-operated manufacturer's sales organization, but there is a basic validity to them none-the-less. It should be made clear that the comparison is between a *good* agent and a *typical* manufacturer's salesman, especially one employed by the smaller companies. This is not too unrealistic, however, since only the better agents survive.

During the past few years, manufacturers have attempted to reduce commission schedules and some reductions have been made. Perhaps some of these have been necessary. It is a truism, however, that the manufacturer will get the service for which he pays. If it is necessary for the representative to do an aggressive selling job, this effort must be reflected in his commissions. Perhaps commision schedules need to be revised to eliminate the possibility of windfalls, but windfalls must not be confused with the results of long and intensive effort over a period of years.

The wire and cable industry is in need of a housecleaning. An attempt to produce and sell an unnecessary variety of products increases marketing costs and is an economic waste. Manufacturers in other fields with the aid of the Commodity Standards Division of the U. S. Department of Commerce have curtailed their lines under the Department's Simplified Practice procedure. It would be beneficial to all concerned in the manufacture and distribution of wire and cable to take similar steps at once.

It is quite apparent that the maintenance of field stocks either in manufacturers' warehouses or in the hands of agents has become a factor of considerable competitive importance to fittings manufacturers. In key markets, such as Chicago, which have come to be major warehousing centers it probably is necessary for manufacturers to have regional stocks. Also, where long distances are involved, as to the West Coast, and where large shipments can be made by boat, it may be efficient to carry stocks.

Wiring devices and supplies manufacturers seem to feel that distributors' salesmen are not sufficiently informed to do a good job of selling their lines but do not do very much about it. Manufacturers that conduct training programs for distributors and their salesmen are in the minority. Some companies publish sales training literature for the use of distributors and also conduct short training sessions at the distributors' place of business. One company operates a two-day training school at the plant conducted by its sales engineers. One day is spent in the classroom and the second day in the factory.

DISCOUNT STRUCTURE FOR DISTRIBUTION AND CONTROL APPARATUS

The discount structure used in the industry recognizes the positions of the distributor, the contractor, the utility, and the industrial user. A manufacturer of distribution equipment may have a discount schedule such as shown in the Table, which would cover most lines.

The distributor discounts on lighting and distribution panels, and trolley and bus ducts may be cut to 50 and 10 per cent. On enclosed aircircuit breakers, distributors may receive a 15 per cent discount, and other buyers will be quoted net.

A manufacturer of power fuses and load interrupters quotes net prices to ultimate users such as utilities, R.E.As., railroads, industrials, and contractors. Shipments to OEMs carry a 10 per cent discount, and shipments to jobbers have a discount of 5 per cent or 10 per cent on items stocked and 5 per cent on items which are drop-shipped.

Distributor discounts for motor controls are generally about 43 per cent, but

	Less than $100 list	$100 list and over	$2500 list and over
Distributors	50 and 18%	50 and 18%	50 and 18%
Contractors	45%	50%	
Central stations	45%	50%	50 and 8%
Users	35%	40%	

discounts may vary widely by type of use. Thus, refrigeration controls and valve controls may be quoted net to distributors, and other controls may carry varying discounts below 43 per cent.

A manufacturer of time switches and timers has jobber discounts which range from 30 per cent to 55 per cent, depending on the type of product and quantity, and contractor discounts which range from 20 per cent to 48 per cent. Industrial users are quoted net. OEM buyers receive jobber prices with higher discounts for larger quantities. Terms are 1 per cent 10 days, net 30, and prices are quoted f.o.b. factory.

Another manufacturer of time controls has distributor discounts which increase from 50 per cent to 50 and 10 per cent as quantities increase from 1 unit to 60 or more. Terms are 2 per cent 10th proximo. This firm allows freight on 26 units or more to any one distributor in the U.S.

For distribution equipment, terms of payment vary from ½ of 1 per cent 10 days, net 30 from date of invoice to 2 per cent 10th proximo, net 30. Other terms between these two are also quoted, such as 2 per cent 10, net 30 from date of invoice; and 2 per cent 25th of the month, net 30 for invoices dated the first half of the month, and 2 per cent 10th proximo, net 30 for invoices dated the last half of the month.

Most distribution equipment is sold f.o.b. point of shipment with freight prepaid to the nearest common carrier delivery point. Some manufacturers require minimum quantities, typically 200 pounds, before freight is prepaid. Others specify a lower minimum, sometimes 100 pounds, on selected items.

Industrial and household fuses are sold f.o.b. factory with freight allowed, cheapest way, to any common carrier point in the United States and on shipments of any quantity. Terms are 2 per cent 10th proximo, net 25th proximo. It is quite probable that the terms of payment and freight allowances for this line of products are governed by the practices of the industry price leader. This, therefore, becomes an extension of a basic price-leadership situation.

Price quotations are usually firm for a 30-day period. This is true for written quotations only, however. Verbal quotations generally expire in 24 hours. Prices charged are typically those in effect at the time of shipment. If price increases go into effect prior to shipment, some companies will protect the buyer by an escalation clause. A typical clause states that price increases are limited to 10 per cent and may further state that this escalation will not be applied if the manufacturer is allowed to ship at his earliest convenience. If prices fall prior to shipment, manufacturers will generally charge reduced prices on shipments made after the change occurs.

Minimum billings are a customary practice in the distribution equipment field. Orders amounting to less than $5 net usually are billed at $5 plus transportation cost. Fuse manufacturers may have a minimum charge of $1 per delivery.

Some wholesalers feel that manufacturers are producing too many types and colors of lamps and in too many sizes. There appears to be some reluctance among lamp manufacturers to drop lines. The prestige of a wide line and the desire to meet almost every type of demand seems to lie back of this situation. As is true in other electrical lines, however, this can be carried too far.

Manufacturers have been overly cautious in scrapping obsolete lines. If product cost analyses were made, certainly many of these lines would be in the loss column.

At times, manufacturers knowingly carry certain items at a loss because they bring in other business or help to retain major accounts which otherwise might be lost. The results of carrying such lines need to be constantly watched, however, and steps taken to remedy the situation of the first opportunity.

Over the years, a division of labor has been worked out in this industry which has increased the efficiency with which transformers are marketed. OEM accounts, at least those requiring large quantities of customer-designed equipment, require services which can best be obtained by direct contact with the manufacturer. Not only are special designs frequently necessary, but negotiations must be undertaken to settle such matters as price, terms of sale, and delivery dates. The distributor is most valuable when the products are standard items which do not require selling and engineering know-how beyond the competence of the distributor and which can be carried in stock by the distributor.

The market structure for motors may seem unnecessarily complex, but this complexity is the result of the many kinds of markets, the varied requirements of buyers, and the various uses of the product. The need to maintain adequate repair service is another charac-teristic of the field. Consequently, more types of middlemen are engaged in the distribution of this product than some other electrical lines, and they each play a necessary role.

Frequently the discounts offered to distributors by manufacturers have not been very attractive. As a result, some distributors do not carry integral motors. On one line of integral motors, for example, the distributor's margin ranges from 13.1 per cent to 23.5 per cent for h.p. motors and below (depending on the type of customer and whether the motor is shipped direct or from stock) down to 4½ per cent for motors of 125 h.p. and over. Some of this business may not be very attractive to the distributor.

A manufacturer of fractional h.p. motors who wishes to build up his distributor business provides a margin of about 17.5 percent when 10 or more motors are purchased and 23.1 per cent when 100 or more are purchased. This is a more satisfactory margin for the distributor.

If manufacturers wish to get distributor support for motors or even interest distributors in carrying motors, some analysis of the distributor margins which they are providing would be in order. Distributors indicate that their sales of motor controls have grown substantially since these manufacturers increased the distributor's margin. If this can be done for motor controls, there seems to be no good reason why the same results cannot be accomplished for motors.

C. RETAILING

19. The Supermarket — A Study of Size, Profits, and Concentration

ROM J. MARKIN

Is the farmer's status being reduced to that of a hired hand for food processors and large chain stores? And are the large supermarket chains now so powerful that they can arbitrarily determine what prices housewives will pay for foodstuffs? These and other questions relating to the apparent increase in economic power of large integrated supermarket chains are being raised in the press and the trade literature.

This article is an effort to report and analyze several relative facets of the increasing size and complexity of supermarkets especially during the time period 1948-1958. Attention will be focused on three major areas of supermarket operations: the overall increase in size of units and some economic consequences thereof; trends in supermarket profit figures; and recent tendencies toward widespread horizontal integration and its consequent implications.[1]

Many of today's supermarkets are prime examples of large-scale business. Retail grocery stores sales were $52 billion in 1960. A single new unit of one of today's glamorous super stores may require an investment of upwards of $1 million.

Retail grocery stores fall into three size categories; the small store — with annual sales volume under $75,000; the superette — with annual volume of $75,000 to $375,000; and the supermarket — with annual volume over $375,000. This classification is adequate for giving us a "broad brush" view of the retail food store field as it is composed of the various size stores.

In many respects there is little difference between a supermarket operation doing $400,000 annual volume and one whose annual volume is twice that, or $800,000. The essential elements of supermarketing, *i.e.*, cash and carry, departmentalization, and self-service are evident in many retail food stores even though there is a wide range in volume.

There is no "typical" supermarket nor is there a typical or average size supermarket about which one can generalize. Conditions, sizes, and operations vary from one area to another; no reporting agency or trade association has yet to

From *Journal of Retailing* (Winter, 1964-1965), pp. 22-36.

[1] A thoroughgoing discussion of vertical integration is beyond the scope of this treatment. Horizontal integration for food chains is, however, the *sine qua non* of those chains that have vertical integration ambitions. The reason for this lies largely in a so-called theorem of Adam Smith's, *i.e.*, that "Division of labor (specialization) is limited by the extent of the market." The implication is that before vertical integration becomes feasible for a food chain the chain must be of such a size in terms of units and volume that real economies of scale will result from integrating backward toward sources of supply. Without sufficient econ-

omies (reduced acquisition costs, captive suppliers, savings in physical handling, and other costs), the undertaking is not warranted.

provide the typical store or a typical operating statement. Students of super-marketing are left to their own designs, ingenuities, and trade literature articles to decide for themselves what constitutes large supermarkets and how prevalent they are today.

The Super Market Institute has established that a supermarket must do an annual volume of over $1 million to qualify for membership. Consequently, the annual report of this association includes only stores doing $1 million or more annually in its sample.

That many supermarkets exceed $1 million annual sales volume and that these supermarkets comprise a significant proportion of all supermarkets in general can be shown in a rather elementary way.

Progressive Grocer reports in 1960 that supermarkets with annual volumes exceeding $375,000 per year account for 69 percent or 36.17 billion dollars of all retail food store sales. Super Market Institute, in its annual reports, bases statistics on 355 companies operating a total of 5,222 stores with combined sales of $7.4 billion. This figure then represents supermarket sales for those markets with $1 million or more in annual volume. These stores ($1 million or more in annual volume) account for 20.4 percent of all supermarkets.

The Super Market Institute reports that the average sales of supermarkets (doing $1 million or more per year in annual volume) were $1,840,000 for 1959.[2]

One other interesting statistic appears to support the argument of the trend to bigness in supermarket operations. Super Market Institute reports that of their membership, sales ranged from $1 million to many millions for individual stores. In fact, 14 percent of these supermarkets did $3 million or more annual volume, 25 percent between $2 and $3

million, and 61 percent between $1 and $2 million annually.[3]

CHANGES IN SIZE OF STORES IN THE POSTWAR PERIOD

In addition to growth of volume and expansion in number of units, supermarkets have been increasing the size of their individual stores and widening the variety of products sold. (See Federal Trade Commission study compiled from data supplied by corporate food chains operating 11 or more stores as of December 31, 1958.[4]) The total number of reporting retail food store corporations was 142. Inasmuch as chains do something over 50 percent of the total volume of retail supermarkets, the Federal Trade Commission study would appear highly relevant as an indicator of changes in store size not only for chains, but for independent food operators also. Table 1 will show visually this trend to larger units from smaller units in all sales size categories.

The 142 companies with 11 or more stores at the end of 1958 that had been in operation throughout the 1948-1958 period reported that they had closed 2,830 stores on net balance between 1948 and 1954, and opened 1,069 on net balance between 1954 and 1958.[5]

Sales per store had been approximately $425,000 in 1948, $814,000 in 1954, and $1,097,000 in 1958 (see Table 1).

Perhaps one tenth of this increase in sales per store was the result of the rise in food prices, amounting to 15.6 percent (Bureau of Labor Statistics Consumer Price Index) between 1948 and 1958. A $425,000 store in 1948 would have sold about $490,000 in 1958 if

---

[2]Super Market Institute, "The Super Market Industry Speaks," Twelfth Annual Report, 1960, p. 9.

[3]*Ibid.*, p. 9.
[4]Federal Trade Commission "Economic Inquiry Into Food Marketing," Part I, Concentration and Integration Into Food Marketing (Washington, D.C.: United States Government Printing Office, January 1960).
[5]*Ibid.*, p. 110.

TABLE 1

AVERAGE ANNUAL SALES PER STORE OF 142 FOOD CHAINS:
1948, 1954, 1958[*]

	1948		1954		1958	
Average Sales Per Store	Number of Companies	Number of Stores Operated	Number of Companies	Number of Stores Operated	Number of Companies	Number of Stores Operated
3,000,000 and over	1	7	5	82	6	124
2,000,000-3,000,000	2	16	6	135	9	373
1,500,000-1,000,000	3	66	7	350	13	742
1,000,000-1,500,000	9	216	26	1,060	38	10,788
800,000-1,000,000	4	53	17	6,402	21	2,571
600,000- 800,000	16	418	21	4,197	15	443
400,000- 600,000	28	8,673	22	1,720	12	478
200,000- 400,000	44	7,403	21	878	14	388
Under 200,000	35	1,454	17	652	14	631
Total	142	18,306	142	15,476	142	16,545
Average Sales Per Store	$425,407		$813,537		$1,097,147	

[*] *Source:* United States, Federal Trade Commission, *Economic Inquiry Into Food Marketing*, Part I (Washington, D.C.: United States Government Printing Office, 1960).

physical volume had not changed. Thus, price inflation is not a noticeable cause for the increase.

The increase in size is to be reckoned by two factors: expanding the size of existing stores and especially by building new and larger stores.

The Federal Trade Commission study reveals that in 1948 one company had average sales per store of over $3 million (this is certainly a large store doing about $10,000 per day in volume); 5 companies, however, reached this volume in 1954, and 6 in 1958. The number of companies in the next four size groups (sales running between $800,000 and $3,000,000) also increased in both 1954 and 1958.

The 16 companies whose sales averaged $1 million or more per store in 1948 operated only 305 stores. Ninety-six percent of all chain store units were operated by the 107 companies that averaged less than $600,000 per store. By 1954, however, average sales had moved higher, and a little over 68 per-cent of the stores were operated by the 38 companies, with average sales between $600,000 and $1 million per store. In 1958 the highest concentration had moved to the class selling between $1 million and $1.5 million, and 73 percent of the stores belonged to the 66 companies selling over $1 million per store.[6] In 1958 the average size of the chain supermarket, as reported in the Federal Trade Commission study, was 12,000 square feet.[7] Many new markets were running around 20,000 square feet, truly colossal stores. The age of the "super" supermarket had arrived.

CHANGES IN NUMBER OF FOOD STORES IN THE POSTWAR ERA

A more comprehensive look at the changes in number of retail food stores as it reflects on the trend to bigness can be had by examining Table 2.

[6] *Ibid.*, p. 111.
[7] *Ibid.*, p. 115.

TABLE 2

NUMBER OF FOOD STORES IN THE UNITED STATES BY
KIND OF STORES FOR THE YEARS 1948, 1954, AND 1958

Kind	1948 Stores[a]	1954 Stores[b]	1958 Stores[c]
Grocery stores (without meats)	152,185	N.A.[d]	72,300
Combination markets	218,840	279,440	188,700
Meat and seafood markets	29,341	27,354	22,500
Fruit and vegetable markets	15,669	13,136	12,000
Confectionery stores	32,063	20,507	20,000
Bakery product stores	19,985	19,034	18,500
Delicatessen stores	8,633	8,132	8,000
Other food stores	16,824	13,777	15,000
Country general stores	18,500	17,701	16,000
Total	512,040	399,081	373,000

[a]United States Bureau of the Census, *Retail Trade—General Statistics*, Vol. II (Washington, D.C., United States Government Printing Office, 1952), p. 16.
[b]United States Bureau of the Census, *Retail Trade Summary Statistics*, Vol. I (Washington, D.C., United States Government Printing Office, 1957), pp. 2-3.
[c]*Facts in Grocery Distribution* (New York: *Progressive Grocer*, 1959), p. F-5.
[d]Grocery stores without meat were not classified separately in the 1954 census and are contained in the combination market classification.

Several interesting points can be obtained by observing Table 2:

1. Total retail food stores declined from 512,040 units in 1948 to 373,000 in 1958 or 27 percent. This occurred in a period of increasing population, rising incomes, and increasing expenditures. Why then did the total number of retail food stores decline? The answer obviously is that as smaller stores went out of business they were replaced by fewer but larger establishments.

2. The replacement of many small units of all kinds with larger units (or having their merhandise lines taken on by other establishments) again can be seen. From 1948 to 1958 the number of retail food stores declined in all food store categories. This trend has occurred particularly in grocery stores (without meats), small combination markets, and country general stores. The small specialty food stores (bakery, fruit and vegetable markets, and delicatessen stores) have generally held their own.

3. The major retail food store has continued to be the combination market—composed mainly of supermarkets and superettes. In 1958, it was estimated that there were 20,413 supermarkets, or 5.5 percent for all the food stores and 10.8 percent of the combination stores.

This small percentage (5.5) of the total number of food stores and of combination markets is not necessarily, however, an impressive statistic. The percentage of total sales volume is more indicative of the supermarket's strategic position, as will be revealed in the subsequent section and Table 3.

The period 1948 to 1958 for retail food stores was characterized by change—in terms of consolidation, adaptation, growth, and development. The emphasis in many respects was on increasing numbers of larger stores, and as will be further investigated in the following section, increasing sales volume performance by the retail grocery stores.

CHANGES IN SALES BY KIND OF RETAIL FOOD STORE

Just as the number of the various retail food stores changed downward

TABLE 3
FOOD STORE SALES IN THE UNITED STATES BY KIND OF STORE
FOR THE YEARS 1948, 1954, AND 1958 (IN MILLIONS)

Kind	1948 Sales[a]	1954 Sales[b]	1958 Sales[c]
Grocery stores (without meat)	$ 4,008	N.A.[d]	N.A.[e]
Combination markets	20,642	$34,421	$44,547
Meat and seafood markets	1,778	2,128	
Fruit and vegetable markets	397	485	
Confectionery stores	649	568	
Bakery product stores	743	862	
Delicatessen stores	310	480	
Country general stores	N.A.	707	
Other food stores	2,125	818	5,716
Total	$12,589	$40,469	$50,263

[a] United States Bureau of the Census, *Retail Trade—General Statistics*, Vol. II. (Washington, D.C., United States Government Printing Office, 1952), p. 16.
[b] United States Bureau of the Census, *Retail Trade Summary Statistics*, Vol. I (Washington, D.C., United States Government Printing Office, 1957), pp. 2-3.
[c] *Ibid.*, p. 833.
[d] Grocery stores without meat were not classified separately in the 1954 census or in the 1958 estimates. Statistics for this group are contained in combination markets.
[e] For 1958 the other food stores classification contains all food stores with the exception of combination markets. The data were not reported separately and are grouped as specialty food stores.

rather remarkably during the 1948 to 1958 period, so too, have rather remarkable upward changes occurred in the sales volumes of these different kinds of retail food store institutions. Table III visually dramatizes some of these changes.

Some analysis of Table 3 would appear in order:

1. While the number of retail food stores of all kinds declined by over 20 percent in the 1948 to 1958 period, the sales of all kinds of retail food stores witnessed a fourfold increase in this same period. As discussed earlier, only a small percentage of this sales increase is attributable to price inflation.
2. The combination market is the mainstay of today's retail food industry. Its sales, which include those of both supermarkets and superettes, are by far the largest of any of the food retailers.
3. Perhaps one of the greatest factors leading to the healthy growth and

position of the combination market, especially the supermarket and the superette, has been their tendency toward scrambled merchandising.

The age of product sales specialization began to decline early, in the late 1920s and early 1930s. One authority made the following comment:

It is an era of scrambled merchandising. Grocery stores sell cigarettes; drug-stores sell grocery products; and tobacco stores sell razor blades. Grocery stores are on the way to becoming food department stores.[8]

POSTWAR BEHAVIOR OF SUPERMARKET PROFITS

Measure of profit can be made as a percentage of sales, as a percentage of total assets, or as percentage of net worth, or as owner's investment. These

[8] Malcolm P. McNair, "Trends in Large Scale Retailing," *Harvard Business Review*, X, No. 1 (Fall 1932), p. 31.

measures, in turn, can be made on a before- or after-tax basis. Utilizing material from the study *Economic Inquiry Into Food Marketing* conducted by the Federal Trade Commission, we will now examine profit trends for large supermarket chains.[9]

Table 4 shows the profit trend of 33 large chains for the 1948-1958 period.

Profits as a percentage of sales on a before-tax basis have fared rather well in the 1948 to 1958 period. The behavior of profits on this basis will appear differently for individual companies, due of course to internal company practices and policies, geographic considerations, and other factors. However, the weighted average of profits as a percentage of sales on a before-tax basis shows that in all three size groups, profits on this basis have either improved during this period or remained relatively constant. One important point does appear evident. Rising costs of the early 1950s appear to have stimulated managements to a new awareness of expense and profit responsibilities. Since early 1953 and 1954 most companies have been able to report steady or increasing profits as a percentage of sales on a before-tax basis. Profits as a percentage of sales on a before-tax basis are considered by many to be a preferred measure of a company's health and soundness because the changing income tax structure is no longer a variable.

Profits as a percentage of sales on an after-tax basis report much the same trend as the before-tax statistics. Note, however, that no one group reports a higher profit ratio on an after-tax basis for 1958 over 1948. Group 1 and Group 3 stores report the same weighted average profit as a percentage of sales on an after-tax basis for 1948 as for 1958. Group 2 stores show a rather marked decline from the 1948 weighted average of 1.6 percent to the 1958 figure of 1.3

percent. Remember when discussing profit percentages on either a before- or after-tax basis, that the relative percentage change, though quite small, can be quite large when interpreted in dollar figures for the large supermarket operations.

One other observation should perhaps be made at this point. Profits as a percentage of sales, either on a before- or after-tax basis, for supermarkets may appear quite low when compared to other retail industries such as drugstores, department stores, variety stores, and hardware stores. Yet, again, when this modest 2 or 3 percent profit of the supermarket is viewed against its very large volume, it becomes highly significant.

The comparison of net profits (before and after income taxes) with total assets of the companies shows Group 1 and 2 ratios rather close to each other through 1955. Group 1 appears to have improved materially after 1956, as Safeway — and to some extent A&P — raised their earnings markedly. Prior to 1956, Group 3 showed the best earnings each year, but the profit resurgence of the two largest companies since 1956 has put Group 1 ahead of Group 3.

Observe that the rapid turnover of inventory is reflected in the much greater return on assets over return on sales. Observe also that the 33 leading food chain stores as a group had a pretax profit margin in the most recent years of 15 to 16 percent on total assets.

RETURN ON STOCKHOLDER INVESTMENT

The much larger after-tax return on total assets, as opposed to return on sales, is further magnified when the rate of return is measured against the book value of stockholders' investment. The after-tax basis is perhaps the best measure, not only because of the reasons previously mentioned, but also because it offers a better measure of what the stockholder actually earns.

[9]United States Federal Trade Commission, "Economic Inquiry Into Food Marketing" (Washington, D.C.: United States Government Printing Office, January 1960), pp. 83-93.

TABLE 4

WEIGHTED AVERAGE RATIO OF NET PROFITS TO NET SALES, TOTAL ASSETS,
STOCKHOLDERS INVESTMENT BEFORE AND AFTER TAXES FOR LEADING FOOD CHAINS
1948 TO 1958°

Ratio and 1958 Sales Size (Ratios in Percentages)	1948	1949	1950	1951	1952	1953	1954	1955	1956	1957	1958
GROUP 1: $500 million and over:											
Net profit before income taxes to net sales:	2.2	2.3	2.4	1.9	2.0	2.2	2.1	2.2	2.5	2.7	2.8
Net profit after income taxes to net sales:	1.3	1.4	1.3	0.9	0.9	1.0	1.0	1.0	1.2	1.3	1.3
Net profit before income taxes to total assets:	15.8	15.9	14.6	11.2	12.4	13.8	13.2	13.0	15.3	16.7	16.3
Net profit after income taxes to total assets:	9.4	9.4	7.6	5.4	5.5	6.2	6.4	6.3	7.3	8.0	7.8
Net profit to stockholders investment before taxes:	26.2	25.5	25.8	20.9	22.5	25.0	23.4	23.9	27.2	29.5	29.1
Net profit to stockholders investment after taxes:	15.5	15.1	13.4	10.2	9.9	11.3	11.4	11.5	13.0	14.0	13.8
GROUP 2: $110 to $500 million:											
Net profit before income taxes to net sales:	2.6	2.9	3.2	2.5	2.4	2.5	2.7	2.9	2.8	2.8	2.6
Net profit after income taxes to net sales:	1.6	1.7	1.7	1.2	1.1	1.1	1.3	1.4	1.4	1.4	1.3
Net profit before income taxes to total assets:	14.5	15.6	16.0	12.5	12.7	12.6	13.8	13.9	13.7	13.4	11.9
Net profit after income taxes to total assets:	8.8	9.2	8.3	6.2	5.8	5.6	6.7	6.8	6.9	6.7	5.9
Net profit to stockholders investment before taxes:	24.9	26.3	28.5	23.4	23.9	24.8	26.2	26.7	28.3	28.2	25.0
Net profit to stockholders investment after taxes:	15.1	15.6	14.9	11.5	10.9	11.0	12.7	13.1	14.1	14.1	12.3
GROUP 3: $50 to $110 million:											
Net profit before income taxes to net sales:	3.1	3.1	3.3	2.8	2.6	3.0	3.1	3.1	3.1	3.2	2.9
Net profit after income taxes to net sales:	1.9	1.9	1.7	1.2	1.1	1.2	1.5	1.6	1.5	1.6	1.4
Net profit before income taxes to total assets:	19.3	18.9	16.9	15.9	14.2	16.6	16.9	15.8	15.1	16.9	15.1
Net profit after income taxes to total assets:	11.9	11.7	9.6	7.2	6.3	6.7	8.1	7.9	7.4	8.5	7.4
Net profit to stockholders investment before taxes:	31.3	31.6	31.4	29.0	27.3	33.2	33.9	32.7	29.2	29.8	26.2
Net profit to stockholders investment after taxes:	19.4	19.6	17.6	13.0	11.7	12.9	16.3	16.4	14.2	19.9	12.9

° *Source:* United States, Federal Trade Commission, *Economic Inquiry Into Food Marketing*, Part I (Washington, D.C.: United States Government Printing Office, 1960), pp. 84-91.

The after-tax profit rate on stockholders' investment ranged from 2.1 percent for Mayfair Markets in 1949 to 28.8 percent for Big Bear stores in 1948; and in 1958 ranged from 4.7 percent for Purity Stores to 23.2 percent for Winn-Dixie.

For all stores the annual averages were a little over 15 percent in 1948 and 1949, fell to a little over 10 percent in 1951 and 1952, and were running at something around 13 or 14 percent in 1958. Group 3 stores reported higher earnings that the average in every year except 1958. Group 1 stores have appeared to make the best percentage recovering after 1952, and in 1958 had the highest reported profit ratio.

The return on sales on large supermarkets on an after-tax basis is a very modest 1.3 percent. Yet the return on stockholders' investment on an after-tax basis is a rather sizable 13.5 percent.

The low return on sales is explained partly by the operating philosophy of most supermarket groups, *i.e.*, low prices equal high volume. The large volume of sales generated by many supermarket operations makes this philosophy meaningful.

The much larger profits on stockholders' investment is enhanced to a large extent by the high degree of leverage in the supermarket field and by the policy of leasing fixed assets. Here are perhaps the two essential ingredients of the supermarket success story.

INTEGRATION AS A MEANS OF GROWTH

The rapid growth of supermarkets in the 1948-1958 period can be attributed primarily to three factors: (1) increased sales of supermarkets, (2) new stores opened by both chains and independents, and (3) stores acquired from other companies by both chains and independents. The chain stores have, however, far outdistanced the independents in terms of growth via acquisitions.

Progressive Grocer estimated that retail food store sales in 1960 amounted to 52.61 billion dollars. Of this amount, 69 percent was attributed to supermarkets and 37 percent to chain operated supermarkets. Truly this bespeaks a significant role for the chain operated supermarket in retail food store distribution.

By successfully emulating and adapting the supermarket practices of the early independents, the chains soon became the nation's major distributors of retail foodstuffs. Table 5 reports the relative position of chain and independent ownership controlled supermarkets.

The table shows that in 1958, of the total supermarkets numbering 20,413, no less than 13,590 of these stores were operated by a chain organization (operating 11 or more stores). This amounted to 66.6 percent of the total supermarkets and accounted for 69.1 percent of total supermarket sales.

When an organization of retail stores, or simply a single store, acquires a unit of the same type from another company or individual, then the firm is said to have grown through integration. Integration can take several forms. The two most prevalent types of integration are horizontal, as in the example just presented, and vertical. Vertical integration occurs when a retailer acquires wholesaling or manufacturing facilities.

Integration of both types has played a major role in the growth and development of large supermarket operations, especially those owned by chains. Many chains and independent supermarkets have integrated to some extent vertically, and for several chain supermarkets the extent of vertical integration (including manufacturing) is nearly complete. The remarks here will be limited to a discussion of horizontal integration and its effect on supermarket

TABLE 5

OWNERSHIP OF SUPERMARKETS CLASSIFIED BY SIZE OF ORGANIZATION FOR THE YEAR 1958[°]

Size of Organization	Number of Stores	Percent of Stores	Sales (millions)	Percent of Sales
1 store	4,236	20.7	$ 5,224	18.2
2-3 stores	1,343	6.6	1,813	6.3
4-10 stores	1,244	6.1	1,835	6.4
11 or more stores	13,590	66.6	19,792	69.1
Totals	20,413	100.0	$28,664	100.0

[°] *Source:* "True Look at the Super Market Industry," *Super Market Merchandising*, XXIV No. 4 (April 1959), p. 102.

TABLE 6
FOOD STORE ACQUISITIONS BY FOOD CHAINS, BY YEAR, 1949 TO 1958[a]

Year of Acquisition	Acquiring Companies	Acquisitions	Stores Acquired	Annual Sales When Acquired
1949	6	6	72	$ 66,180
1950	5	5	5	3,889
1951	10	12	69	27,829
1952	5	10	273	70,800
1953	11	12	71	86,617
1954	17	20	70	60,580
1955	23	48	455	434,166
1956	36	70	439	397,325
1957	34	54	363	322,520
1958	38	78	421	450,003
Total	83[b]	315	2,238	$1,919,909

[a] *Source:* United States, Federal Trade Commission, *Economic Inquiry Into Food Marketing*, Part I (Washington, D.C.: United States Government Printing Office, 1960), p. 128.
[b] (Column does not add as some companies made acquisitions in more than one year.

size and growth. Again, much insight into this problem can be had by analyzing the findings of the Federal Trade Commission.[10]

Table 6 shows that the acquisition of food stores by corporate chains operating 11 or more stores has increased sharply in the postwar period, with the year 1955 marking a substantial increase. From 1949 through 1954, the annual averages were: 9 acquiring chains, 11 acquisitions, 93 stores, and $52.6 million current sales; from 1955 through 1958 they were 22 chains, 63 acquisitions, 420 stores, and $401 million sales.

A few of the large chains were especially active in making food store acquisitions in the years studied by the Federal Trade Commission, 1949 to 1958. The ten chains that acquired the largest number of stores and the largest volume of retail sales are shown in Table 7. Only one of these ten companies acquired food stores in 1949, 1950, or 1952. Two to five made acquisitions in 1951, 1953, and 1954. In 1955, seven made acquisitions, followed by nine in 1956, five in 1957, and nine in 1958.

The 1958 sales of food stores acquired by the ten chains over the entire period amounted to $996 million, or 61 percent of the $1,639 million in sales of all stores acquired by corporate chains. The $996 million was 11.9 percent of the 1958 sales of the ten chains.

The immediate question becomes, "Why all the merger activity?" What are the forces and factors behind this merger movement? Several reasons for this have been advanced.[11]

1. The nature and spirit of the supermarket industry has been one of growth and change. Managers are willing to experiment with new methods and are anxious to see store operations and size increase.

2. Profits, as witnessed in the previous section, have been good and reasonably steady. The seeming invulnerability of the food industry to economic recession builds in a somewhat safe growth factor. New merchandising activities for earnings are constantly being sought.

3. Larger concerns have more and more begun to realize the economies of scale that come from increased size.

[10] Federal Trade Commission, *op. cit.*, pp. 127-156.

[11] Frank J. Charvat, *Supermarketing* (New York: The MacMillan Company, 1961), pp. 182-183.

TABLE 7
FOOD STORE ACQUISITIONS BY TEN LARGE FOOD CHAINS: 1949 TO 1958°

Company	Acquisitions	Stores Acquired	Annual Sales When Acquired
American Stores Company	5	93	$ 34,442
Colonial Stores, Inc.	10	99	121,906
Food Fair Stores, Inc.	6	67	107,731
The Grand Union Company	15	128	128,417
Jewel Tea Company, Inc.	2	43	56,234
The Kroger Company	5	130	174,064
Lucky Stores, Inc.	4	56	72,612
National Tea Company	24	485	251,612
Safeway Stores, Inc.	25	67	33,016
Winn-Dixie Stores, Inc.	11	306	221,070
Total ten chains	107	1,474	$1,201,104

° *Source:* United States, Federal Trade Commission, *Economic Inquiry Into Food Marketing*, Part I (Washington, D.C.: United States Government Printing Office, 1960), p. 138.

Operators are able to spread costs and risks over a larger number of operations.

4. It is becoming increasingly difficult to find satisfactory locations. As new locations become more expensive, firms seek new outlets via merger or acquisition of stores already built.

5. The larger firms are stronger in terms of the marketable securities they have to exchange for the shares of the smaller companies than are the firms under $100 million annual volume. This gives the larger firms an advantage in acquisition through stock exchange.

6. The smaller organizations were started and operated for a long time by owner-managers. As these men became older and faced the need of retirement, many sold out to larger chains.

7. Finding suitable and available sources of outside capital has also been a serious problem impeding expansion by smaller sized organizations. Failing to obtain borrowed or debt capital and lacking the means of facilities to sell equities, the smaller concerns could expand only through retained earnings. Frequently, the threat of stronger competition and the inadequacy of the smaller concerns to grow, forced them or resigned them to sell out.

Thus, through aggressive merchandising strategies, sound financial backing, and a strong willingness and desire to grow, the large supermarkets (especially those operated by corporate chains) have come to command a significant role in retail food store distribution.

The independents have not "withered on the vine," however. They continue to supply much of the nation's retail food store needs. Nor have the independents taken an indifferent and apathetic view of the corporate chains' growth. They have fought back in many instances with vigor. A discussion of their efforts at fighting back is examined in the subsequent section.

GROWTH OF VOLUNTARY AND COOPERATIVE ORGANIZATIONS

Upon threat of extinction by the large chains, the independent retail food merchants (especially those with supermarket and superette operations) soon realized that to survive they must adapt. And survival meant buying at low cost so that they, too, could pass on their economies in lowered prices to the consumer.

Two rather unique methods were hit upon by the independent food retailers and also by the whosesalers who serviced them and depended upon them.[12] The first of these two methods involved cooperation among the independents to operate their own wholesale houses.

The cooperative association works something like this: the retailers mail in their orders, thus eliminating the need and expense of wholesale salesmen. The wholesaler operates the warehouse and delivers groceries on a regular schedule. The retailers provide the money to finance the wholesale house and either pay cash for their groceries or receive a week or ten day's credit. Most of the wholesale (cooperative) houses operate on very low expenses. The simple, average expense of four such wholesalers amounts to 4.4 percent of sales.[13]

A large share of the profit is returned to member stores as patronage dividends, and only a small proportion is carried to surplus. The expense percentage represents the margin charged the retailers.

The earlier houses developed mainly by handling dry groceries. Many today, however, have taken on fuller lines, including frozen foods, drugs, toiletries, and fresh produce. The retailer-owned wholesale grocers often have limited lines of goods under their own brands.

The second attempt to combat the advantages of the large chain food stores took the form of so-called voluntary wholesale organization. This movement has, by far, the larger growth and importance. A recent count showed 456 voluntary wholesalers with 59,000 affiliated retailers.[14] These associations are called voluntaries because they voluntarily associate with the wholesaler. The concept works this way: the wholesaler secures a group of retailers who agree to buy all or nearly all of their merchandise resources from him. The wholesaler, in turn, must furnish the retailers with merchandising assistance in operating their stores and gives them a franchise to use the sponsor's name on their stores. The most prominent of these voluntary groups are IGA, Red and White, and Clover Farm.

Because the retailers voluntarily submit their business to the wholesaler, the wholesaler is not faced with the necessity of providing salesmen. The wholesaler receives the orders from the affiliated retail stores, accompanied by signed blank checks for payment. The wholesaler's facilities, of late, have become the epitome of modern efficient operation. His buildings are one story on an assembly line or conveyor belt basis. He employs modern techniques of palletization and fork lift trunks.

On occasion the wholesaler employs merchandising men to help the retailers in such everyday problems as store operation, design, and layout of old or new facilities. Accountants are employed to aid the retailer in setting up records and to make out income tax statements. Both the cooperative and voluntary wholesale methods have aided the independents to maintain a stronger competitive position in the postwar era.

Table 8 shows the number of retailer-owned cooperatives reporting to the survey of the Federal Trade Commission in 1959. This total represents nearly a complete census of these organizations.[15] As can be seen from the table, the number of retailer-owned cooperatives has grown significantly in the 1948 to 1958 period, and the number of retail stores serviced by this method has grown even more rapidly.

Other interesting highlights from the Federal Trade Commission study of re-

---

[12] Paul D. Converse, "Twenty-five Years of Wholesaling—A Revolution in Food Wholesaling," *Journal of Marketing*, XXII, No. 1 (July 1957), p. 40.

[13] *Ibid.*, p. 47.

[14] *Ibid.*, p. 47.

[15] The Federal Trade Commission sent questionnaires to 182 firms. One was unincorporated, 16 proved not to be cooperatives, and 19 had moved without leaving forwarding addresses or had gone out of business. Federal Trade Commission, *op. cit.*, p. 159.

TABLE 8

MEMBERSHIP OF RETAILER-OWNED COOPERATIVES OPERATING IN 1958, BY
DECADE OF ORGANIZATION 1948 AND 1958*

| Decade | Companies Organized | | Members | | | Stores Served (Member and Nonmember 1958) |
	Number	Cumulative	1948	1958	1958 Cumulative	
1881-1890	1	1	2,072	1,723	1,723	1,723
1891-1900	1	2	1,063	1,091	2,814	1,091
1901-1910	1	3	130	300	3,114	304
1911-1920	12	15	5,889	5,556	8,670	5,661
1921-1930	26	41	6,383	8,000	16,670	9,348
1931-1940	38	79	4,465	5,376	22,046	5,632
1941-1950	44	123	4,325	7,823	29,869	7,980
1951-1958	13	136	...	1,273	31,142	1,364
Year not reported	10	146	809	1,033	32,175	1,180
Total	146	146	25,136	32,175	32,175	34,283

* Source: United States, Federal Trade Commission, *Economic Inquiry Into Food Marketing*, Part I (Washington, D.C.: United States Government Printing Office, 1960), p. 159.

tailer-owned cooperatives will now be reviewed.[16]

Total wholesale sales of the reporting cooperatives amounted to $544 million in 1948 and $2,031 million in 1958. Cooperative wholesalers owned by retail stores do 97 percent of their business with members; this contrasts sharply with the voluntary associations, which do a significant volume with nonmembers.

Between 1948 and 1958, their aggregate sales increased nearly ten times as much as those of all other general line wholesalers. Estimated retail sales of member stores of all cooperatives in the continental United States, increased from about $2.4 to $2.7 billion in 1948 to $7.6 billion in 1958. The retailer-owned cooperative has been a significant factor in the strengthening of the independents' competitive position.

Perhaps the single weakest factor in the cooperative wholesale ventures is the lack of stability which results from a rapid turnover of members. Less than half the members in the Federal Trade Commission 1958 study had belonged

to the same cooperative as long as five years. In spite of this weakness, however, the retailer-owned cooperatives have met, in large part, the objectives of their origination and use; they have enabled the independent merchant to combat the chains' tactics by supplying his merchandise requirements at a greatly reduced cost.

The threat of extinction posed by increasing direct sales from processors to chain stores and supermarket operators, plus the disappearance of many of their customers, caused several progressive wholesalers to establish "voluntary" groups of retail stores to which they would render special services and which would in turn be bound to their organizations with special ties.

The basic philosophy of both the retailer-owned cooperative and the wholesalers sponsored voluntary group is to make retailers better merchants. Their goal is one of operating good retail stores and selling at prices as low as the chains. That they have been successful is indicated by the ability of the independents in recent years to hold their share of the market reasonably well. The voluntary and cooperative wholesale organizations have been

[16]Federal Trade Commission, *Economic Inquiry Into Food Marketing, op. cit.*, pp. 157-169.

faced with the problem of supplying their customers with needed services and at the same time holding down their expenses to a comparable ratio to other competitive types of wholesalers. As can be witnessed, some success has been attained in this area.[17]

SUMMARY

The major focus of this paper has been on bigness. The large relative size of today's supermarkets has been reported and analyzed. The large corporate chain supermarkets now control a significant share of the food and grocery market. Whether by virtue of their size the large chains are able to exercise undue economic leverage on suppliers through integrative activities and/or whether these large chains are able to extract unduly high prices from consum-

---

[17]See Ralph Cassady, Jr., and Wylie L. Jones, *The Changing Competitive Structure in the Wholesale Grocery Trade* (Berkeley and Los Angeles: University of California Press, 1949).

ers remains to be determined. The fact that the ten largest chains sell almost 30 percent of all the food purchased at retail and that the three largest chains account for almost half the business done by all food chains is giving some substance to the hue and cry arising across the land that "there ought to be a law." Many suggestions are now being heard from consumer groups, farm organizations, and others that laws should be passed to keep supermarket chains out of the processing and production of food. Self-interested though these groups may be, they may force the food chains to give greater evidence and proof of their strident claims toward reducing food purchasers' costs.

As for the independents, in order to survive the mounting tide of competition from the food chains, they have formed voluntary and cooperative hybrid chains, thus emulating the successful practices of the chains. These tactics have enabled the independents to maintain a moderately successful competitive position in the postwar era.

D. CHANNELS OF DISTRIBUTION

20. Communication Networks in Intermediate Markets

F. E. BALDERSTON

I. INTRODUCTION

Most commodities move from points of production through successive stages of processing or manufacture and further stages of intermediate distribution before reaching points of final purchase. The final value of a commodity, in fact, is often analyzed by observing the amounts of labor and capital services that are added to it at each of these stages by the firm which owns it at each stage. The concept of value added has gained great currency in national income computations and other applications to cost and price theory. If there is pure competition and reasonably full information in all markets, it is assumed that the number of stages of ownership and of provision of services will be consistent with the costs and benefits of organizing the commodity flow in an optimal manner. Presumably, each operating enterprise or each potential entrant into a particular stage of the market can gauge the desirability of adding services to the commodity — and charging a margin which it is hoped will cover the costs of such services — on marginal considerations. The number of successive owners of a commodity, and the allocation of various functional types of effort among them, are not of much interest in the domain of purely competitive behavior. This unconcern extends, in fact, to problems of vertical integration of business enterprises, since it is possible to generalize from the marginal analysis that the performance of a particular set of activities by one firm as against two separated firms will not make any effective difference in the accumulation of value in a commodity under pure competition in all markets. Where economies of scale and potential monopolization of critical stages in the commodity flow are involved, the situation is somewhat less clear. If uncertainty and less than full information are also admitted as possibilities, the presumptions arising out of the theory of pure competition are still less adequate. However, insufficient attention has been paid to the development of explanatory hypotheses regarding vertical commodity flows. The present paper is devoted to some contributions toward this end.

The setting of the problem is this. Successive stages of dealing in a commodity are in general required on account of any of the following considerations: a.) an activity may need to be undertaken at a different scale — i.e., plant size — than that at which a preceding or a succeeding activity needs to be conducted; b.) changes in the *combinations* of commodities may be required from one stage to another; or c.) information and contacts need to be mobilized in order to connect disparate groups of actors in the complex of activities.

Students of marketing have developed the concept of the marketing channel, defined as the set of entities

From *Management Science*, Vol. 4, No. 1 (January 5, 1958), pp. 154-171.

that are brought into relation with one another in respect to a particular commodity flow. They have also pointed out that the set of activities required for effective commodity distribution can be broken down into functional classes. Some of the most important of these types of functional effort have to do with the establishment of contacts, the negotiation of transactions, or—more generally—the generating of information leading to transactions decisions. We will consider here some properties of communication networks in intermediate markets, with a view toward determining under simplifying assumptions what might be the optimal structure for such intermediate markets. Optimal structure is defined here as the proper adjustment of the number and types of intermediary agency to the numbers and types of supplier, to the numbers and types of customer, and to the type of marketing task which is called for by the characteristics of the commodity.

II. COMMUNICATION NETWORKS IN INTERMEDIATE MARKETS

A. THE CONTINUOUS-LINKAGE, ONE-COMMODITY MODEL

The simplest model of communication in an intermediate market restricts consideration to one commodity in which every supplier and every customer deals exclusively. The total commodity flow through the market is assumed to be given, in accordance with the basic cost conditions in the supplying industry and conditions of final demand facing the retail level or the ultimate transaction level in the market. As we shall concentrate on the communication network problem, we will also assume a standard order size and a single standardized method of shipment. Finally, wholesalers will be assumed not to carry any intermediate inventories. Their activities will be confined to the maintenance of contacts in the

communication framework, and the actual commodity shipments will be presumed to go from the supplying points to the customer points. The chief function of the wholesaler then will be to serve as a switchboard of a communication network between the suppliers and the customers. The suppliers will be taken as the group of producers of the commodity and the customers will be taken as a group of retail enterprises (if the commodity is a consumer good) or as a group of enterprises which make final sales of a raw material or other intermediate product to users of that product in production processes.

The heading of this section has indicated that this would be called a continuous-linkage model. The communication link between any two actors in the market will be assumed to be like a pipe line which is set up to connect any two points. Once built, it can carry variable flows of information (up to some maximum limit) but its current operating costs per time period will be assumed independent of the amount of information carried or the number of messages. To characterize a communication system in this way is to make a substantial abstraction from reality, as it is often true that each message between any two actors in a communication system has a separable variable cost of its own; thus, the total costs of an information flow depend on the magnitude of that flow, and there will be a problem of determining the optimal amount of information in respect to cost. We will, for the moment, neglect this problem.

The set of suppliers is assumed to be some given number S. Each of these suppliers has a certain amount of the commodity to sell in each time period and must be in touch with one or more of the members of the customer group in order to market this supply. The number of customers, also assumed given, will be called C. The number of intermediary agencies—i.e., wholesalers—will be W. In accordance with our assumption that the costs of a communication link are constant regardless of the amounts of information transmitted through it, we can assume that these costs are constant per time period. This constant cost per communication link is defined as q.

Although the continuous link is broadly enough defined to permit any two actors in the market who are so connected to exchange any type and amount of information, it is nevertheless true that the adequacy of the information in the hands of each actor depends on the number of other actors with whom he is connected.

1. *"Ideal" and "Adequate-Bargaining" Networks.* An *ideal* structure for the provision of full information would require that every actor in the market be connected with every other. For S suppliers and C customers, with no intermediary firms, the resulting network would be:

each supplier connected to every customer: $S \cdot C$ links

each supplier connected to every other supplier: $S \dfrac{(S-1)}{2}$ links

each customer connected to every other customer: $C \dfrac{(C-1)}{2}$ links

The sum of these links, multiplied by q, the constant cost per link, gives the total cost of the ideal network:

$$TC_1 = qSC + \frac{qS(S-1)}{2} + \frac{qC(C-1)}{2}$$

which reduces algebraically to

$$TC_1 = \tfrac{1}{2}q\left[(S+C)^2 - (S+C)\right] \qquad (1)$$

This is the communication network which exists, by assumption, in the pure theory of the perfectly competitive market.

Each actor may, however, be content to insist only that the communication network permit him to make a complete canvass of all actors on the opposite side of the market, for bargaining purposes. We are assuming that the actors operate in an atomistic manner in their bargaining relations. The linkages critical to any actor would then be those which could result in the completion of transactions—and these would necessarily be linkages with those on the opposite side of the market. The chief purpose of links with others on the same side of the market—in the absence of collusion—would be to verify the claims of those on the opposite side concerning bids or offers from one's competitors. Adequate protection in bargaining might still be afforded by a network connecting each actor with every actor on the opposite side. The total cost of such an adequate bargaining network, with no intermediaries, would be:

$$T_2 = qSC \qquad (2)$$

This "adequate-bargaining network" will be taken as a referent against which to compare the operation of the market when intermediaries are present. This network is less than "ideal," but it is clearly more elaborate, and more satisfactory in terms of information flow, than many networks involving *segmentation* of the market. In a segmented market, each supplier is connected only with a part of the customer group, and each customer is connected with part of the supplier group. Such partial segmentation of the market will be considered at a later point.

2. *Network Costs with Wholesale Intermediaries.* If a single wholesale intermediary connects all of the actors in the market, he will require S links to the suppliers and C links to the customers. The total costs of the system will then be:

$$T_3 = q(S+C) \qquad (3)$$

Every wholesale intermediary who enters the market will be assumed, for simplicity, to replicate this network, so that for any number of wholesalers, W, the total costs of the system will be:

$$T_4 = qW(S + C) \qquad (4)$$

3. *The "Indifference Number" of Wholesalers.* Given S and C, there is a number of wholesalers at which the costs of the indirect system would just equal the costs of the "adequate-bargaining" direct network. Setting $T_2 = T_4$, we find that this "indifference number" of wholesalers is:

$$W^* = \frac{SC}{S + C} \qquad (5)$$

When the number of wholesalers is less than W^*, the indirect system is less costly than the direct; if there are more wholesalers than W^*, the indirect system is the more costly. From the standpoint of the market as a whole, no indirect system would be set up whose costs exceeded T_2 and whose number of wholesalers exceeded W^*.

Note that the q's have no effect on the network, because in this model total costs are strictly proportional to the number of communication links, and this number is determined solely by sums and products of the numbers of suppliers and customers.

Some statements can now be made about the maximum number of wholesale intermediaries that can be supported in terms of total communication network costs. For very simple market structures involving low values of either S or C, no wholesale intermediary can be justified, as is shown by the Table. In the Table, S^* and C^* are any non-negative values. A minimum of two suppliers and two customers is required before one wholesaler can be introduced.

S	C	W^*
1	1	$\frac{1}{2}$
1	C^*	$C^*/(1 + C^*)$
S^*	1	$S^*/(1 + S^*)$
2	2	1

4. *A Condition of Symmetry.* More generally, defining the ratio of suppliers to customers as $r = S/C$ and substituting this ratio into equation (5), we have:

$$W^* = \frac{SC}{S + C} = \frac{C^2 r}{rC + C} = C\left(\frac{r}{r + 1}\right). \qquad (6)$$

The term $r/r + 1$ has a maximum value of $\frac{1}{2}$; this occurs where $r = 1$, that is, where the numbers of suppliers and customers are equal. Thus, for any given number of customers, W^* is largest where the market structure is *symmetrical*, and at this point the indifference number of wholesalers is one half of the number of customers.

5. *The Problem of Wholesaler Monopoly Power.* It is clear that the greatest improvement as compared with a system of direct links is secured by the operation of a single wholesale intermediary as a "switchboard" in the communication network, for the amount of saving from the installation of an indirect system is $qS \times C - q(S + C)W$.

If there were only one wholesaler, the opportunity for economic profits would be greatest. The maximum gain that the single wholesaler could secure would be:

$$M = q\,[SC - (S + C)]. \qquad (7)$$

Thus, a single wholesaler could set his margin so as to make his total costs plus his profits equal to the total costs of the system of direct links.

As the number of wholesale intermediaries increases, competition between them forces the potential monopoly profit toward zero. At some point, the number of wholesalers would be great enough so that this factor alone would enforce purely competitive conditions on each of them in setting his wholesale margin, and each wholesaler would set a margin which, at the volume he would secure, would just cover his long-run costs of operation.

In addition to this, there is an absolute upper bound on the total costs of

FIGURE 1
Total Network Costs and the Number of Wholesalers

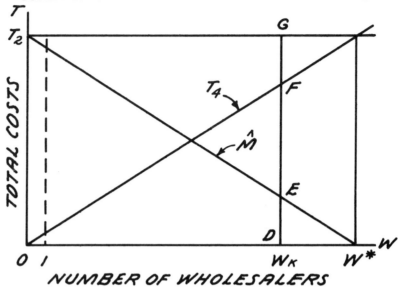

NUMBER OF WHOLESALERS

T_2 = TOTAL COST OF SYSTEM OF DIRECT LINKS

T_4 = TOTAL COST OF INDIRECT LINKS

W^* = "INDIFFERENCE NUMBER" OF WHOLESALERS

$\hat{M}$ = MAXIMUM VALUES OF PROFITS TO WHOLESALERS GROUP FOR EACH NUMBER OF WHOLESALERS, IN THE LONG RUN

the wholesale intermediaries, inclusive of economic profit. Relations between the total costs of the network and the number of wholesalers are portrayed in Figure 1. The ceiling on costs of the network involving wholesalers is seen to be T_2, the cost of the network of direct links between suppliers and customers. The costs of the network of "indirect" links, T_4, is a linear function of the number of wholesalers. The line M is a locus of amounts of greatest possible long-run profits (over and above linkage costs) to the wholesaler group, as the number of wholesalers increases. $\hat{M}$ is seen to be equal to zero when

$W = W^*$. For a number of wholesalers, W_k, the cost of linkages is DF, total economic profit is bb', and the total charges imposed on suppliers and customers (equal to the costs of the direct-link network) are DG.

6. *The Profits of Wholesalers and the Total Costs of the Network.* From the standpoint of total network costs to the suppliers and customers, gains from the existence of wholesale intermediaries are conferred whenever the total economic profits of the wholesalers, as a group, are less than $\hat{M}$. While it is clear that the profits can be at most equal to M (as in equation (7)) for one wholesaler

and that total wholesale profits fall to zero as the number of wholesalers approaches W^*, it is not obvious what the shape of the relation between total wholesaler profits and the number of wholesalers will be between these points.

The total costs of the network involving wholesalers, augmented by the total economic profits of the wholesaler group, are:

$$T_5 = M + qW(S + C) \qquad (8)$$

where

$$M = f(W). \qquad (9)$$

A necessary condition for a minimum of this function is

$$\frac{d}{dW}(T_5) = f'(W) + q(S + C) = 0$$
$$f'(W) = -q(S + C). \qquad (10)$$

It is already clear, from the discussion of boundary conditions on total profits, that $M = f(W)$ has negative slope. But the profit-function must also be *concave from above* for some part of its length in order that the total costs may have a minimum value. That is,

$$\frac{d^2M}{dW^2} < 0$$

Furthermore, the number of wholesalers for which T_5 is minimized *will be less than* W^* if the profit-function passes through the two end points (for $W = 0$, total 'profit' $= qSC$; for $W = W^*$, total profit $= 0$) and is negatively sloped and concave from above throughout its length.

This is demonstrated in Figure 2. The equilibrium number of wholesalers is W_E. But under these circumstances, the total costs of the network *rise* if new wholesalers, in addition to the W_E wholesalers already operating, attempt to enter the market. A curious fact about this equilibrium, however, is that it occurs when the economic profits of the wholesaler group are positive. A cost-minimizing solution, from the standpoint of the suppliers and customers, nevertheless permits the wholesalers to obtain positive long-run profits!

The gain function may, of course, not

FIGURE 2

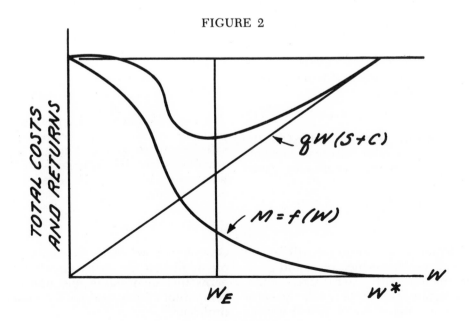

meet the severe conditions that are specified above. Instead of attaining zero only when $W = W^*$, the profit-function may reach zero at some smaller number of wholesalers. Nevertheless, provided that M is concave from above, our conclusion that W_E occurs at a level of positive profits remains true. Only when the profit function is *convex* from above $(f''(W)<0)$ will the equilibrium number of wholesalers be at the point of zero profit, wherever M cuts the horizontal axis.

7. *Wholesaler Entry and Equilibrium Structure.* Total network costs (inclusive of economic profits to the wholesaler group) are seen to be a minimum at some number of wholesalers, W_E, which is less than the "indifference number," W^*. The commodity flow, G, is defined in units of one dollar's worth of the commodity evaluated at (identical) f.o.b. prices at the supplying points. The wholesale margin per unit of commodity flow is therefore

$$h = \frac{qW(S + C) + f(W)}{G}, \qquad (11)$$

As G has been assumed to be given and constant, h is minimized where the numerator of equation (11) is a minimum — that is, where $W = W_E$. The supplier and customer groups are best served if the number of wholesalers stabilizes at W_E. Will this happen?

We may define the profits of the entering wholesaler as

$$B = hg - q(S + C). \qquad (12)$$

The following profit conditions for the entering wholesaler will lead to stable equilibrium in the wholesaler group at $W = W_E$.

$$\begin{array}{lll} \text{for } W < W_E, & B > 0, \\ \text{for } W = W_E, & B = 0, \\ \text{for } W > W_E, & B < 0. & (13) \end{array}$$

Whether these conditions will be met depends on the values of h and g, in combination with each other. First, some statements can be made concerning the manner in which h will vary as

the number of wholesalers increases. As is shown by equation (11), h depends solely on the number of wholesalers, under the assumption that all wholesalers receive the same margin per unit of business done. (Our lack of concern, at the moment, with the quality of information flows reinforces this assumption.) The rate of change of h with respect to W is

$$dh/dW = \frac{1}{G}[q(S + C) + f'(W)]. \qquad (14)$$

The same general slope conditions apply to h and to T_s, the total cost equation. The function must be generally U-shaped, and it must be concave from above in the neighborhood of its minimum at $W - W_E$.

As for the new entrant's market share, g, two limiting cases can be established. The first is that in which the new entrant is economically marginal — obtaining zero profits. Setting $g = g(W)$, we find that when every new entrant is marginal, regardless of the previous number of wholesalers, the function must be generally bell-shaped — convex from above. Specifically,

$$g = \frac{Gq(S + C)}{qW(S + C) + f(W)}, \qquad (15)$$

and

$$dg/dW =$$
$$Gq(S + C)\left(\frac{-[q(S + C) + f'(W)]}{[qW(S + C) + f(W)^2}\right) \cdot (16)$$

The second limiting case arises from the presumption that the entering wholesaler may be expected, at best, to obtain a market share proportional with those wholesalers already established. In this event, for any W,

$$g = \frac{G}{W}. \qquad (17)$$

On this proportionality assumption, and provided that the entering wholesaler earns the same margin per unit as his competitors, the entrant's economic profits are:

$$B = \frac{f(W)}{W}. \qquad (18)$$

These economic profits (over and above network costs), will be positive up to the point where $f(W) = 0$, which has been shown to be below or at the point where W reaches the indifference level.

The two limiting cases are shown in Figure 3. The shaded area in Figure 3 is the set of all points through which the function $g = g(W)$ may pass. All such functions must pass through point E, and if W_E is to be an equilibrium number of wholesalers, dg/dW must equal zero at that point.

More generally, from equation (12) we have

$$dB/dW = h\frac{dg}{dW} + g\frac{dh}{dW}, \qquad (19)$$

and, from conditions (13),

$$dB/dW < 0. \qquad (20)$$

The following statements can be made:

$$h > 0, \qquad g > 0;$$
$$dh/dW < 0, \qquad \text{for } W < W_E;$$
$$dh/dW > 0, \qquad \text{for } W > W_E.$$

As $dB/dW < 0$, it follows that, as W increases beyond W_E,

$$dg/dW < 0, \text{ and } \left|\frac{dg}{dW}\right| > \frac{dh}{dW}.$$

As dh/dW rises at an increasing rate with increases of W beyond W_E, it follows that $(d^2g/dW^2) > 0$ in this interval. Thus, $g = g(W)$ must be convex from above for the interval beyond $W = W_E$.

It would seem reasonable, also, that the entrant's market share should be high as the first entrants begin to compete with a monopoly intermediary, and that further entrants would win a smaller market share. That is, through the early part of the interval, $g = g(W)$ might follow generally the shape of the proportional market share curve. If this is the case, $g(W)$ must then have a flex point at $W = W_E$ in order to produce a stable equilibrium number of wholesalers at the minimum cost of the network system.

While it is possible that the actual empirical relation between the entrant's market share and the number of whole-

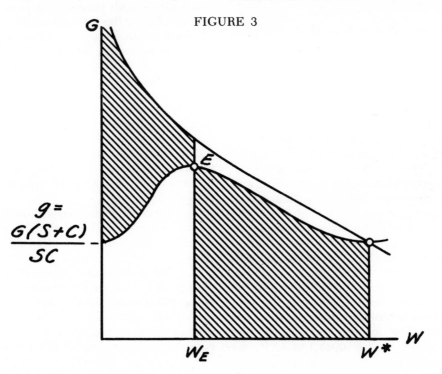

FIGURE 3

salers could meet the severe restrictions necessary to produce a stable equilibrium at the point of minimum total cost, there is no presumption that this *must* be so. We can only conclude that an increasingly sharp rate of decline in entrant's market share would be necessary to discourage entry under conditions of rising margin per unit of business. It would be providential if this rate of decline commenced precisely at the point where the number of wholesalers reached W_E.

This model of communication networks shows, then, that an optimum structure of the market does exist for the performance of communication tasks. This optimum involves long-run positive economic profit to the wholesaler firms. The structure may or may not stabilize at the optimum point, depending on (a) the shape of the function relating the wholesaler group's economic profits to the number of wholesalers, and (b) the shape and position of the relation between the entrant's market share and the number of wholesalers.

B. MODIFICATIONS OF THE NETWORK MODEL

Some of the most essential characteristics of communication problems in intermediate markets are brought out by the model just discussed, but other properties of these communication networks should receive some comment.

1. *Partial Segmentation of the Network:* When each wholesaler need not be connected with every supplier and every customer, but only with a part of each group, several new features of the network need to be taken into account.

Under the same assumptions as before concerning constant cost per communication link, entry costs for new wholesalers are reduced. If u is the proportion of suppliers covered, and v is the proportion of customers covered, then the cost function for the entering wholesaler is of course $q(uS + vC)$. If, for simplicity, the fractions u and v are assumed equal, the indifference number of wholesalers is W^*/u.

For any given u, total network costs therefore rise less steeply than before as the number of wholesalers increases. The relation between economic profits of the wholesaler group and the number of wholesalers will also change. The first wholesaler to enter the business will be connected to only a part of the supplier and customer groups. Later entrants will presumably link themselves to suppliers and customers not previously served. Every supplier will be connected with one wholesaler when $W = S/uS = 1/u$, and every customer will be so connected when $W = C/vc = 1/v$. Until this point is reached each wholesaler can exact a high margin for his services, but thereafter, the total economic profits of the wholesaler group should begin to fall rapidly, for the possibilities for economic profit depend not only on the degree of dependence that each supplier or customer has on the (limited) number of wholesalers with whom he is connected, but also on the total size of the intermediary group. Figure 4 is a comparison between the model first described and a model involving a partial segmentation of the network. It is so drawn as to show the minimum cost point in the latter case to be at a lower level of total cost than in the original model. To the extent that sheer numbers of wholesalers outweigh in importance the fewness of wholesaler connections to each supplier or customer, this cost reduction will take place.

The preceding discussion was based on the assumption that each wholesaler would set up a communication network of equal size and cost. Several factors will, however, cause wholesalers to change the size of their networks as competitive conditions change. The first few wholesalers to enter the business will have every incentive to set up as complete a communication network as

FIGURE 4

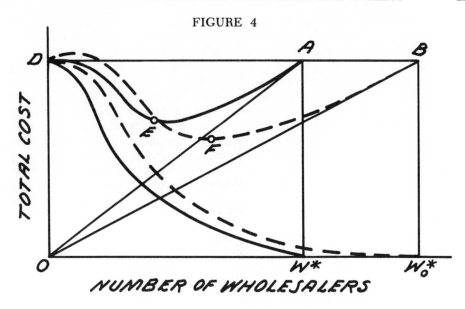

possible. Suppliers and customers not served in the initial phases will seek to obtain such service, and the wholesale margin, at the volume of business passing through each wholesaler's hands, will be high enough to yield substantial economic profits to each wholesaler and to provoke expansion of coverage by the established wholesalers as well as entry by new ones. As entry does occur, each supplier may be expected to divide his output (and each customer, his purchases) among the wholesalers connected to him. As a result, the yield per communication link will fall. In the winnowing-out of the preferred contacts between any one wholesaler and his suppliers and customers, the wholesaler will profit by dropping those suppliers and customers whose business (at the declining margins secured under increasingly competitive conditions) becomes unprofitable. Each supplier and customer benefits in terms of his effort-cost in communication by being in contact with a sufficient number of wholesalers to assure adequate market information, but not a number so large as to become overly burdensome in terms of *his* effort-costs of maintaining

the connection. Entrants are likely to fill the gaps in the segmented network until each supplier and customer is in contact with an adequate number of wholesalers, and in the meantime the size of each wholesaler's network is subject to shrinkage.

If suppliers have different output rates, the larger ones attract more wholesalers than do the smaller ones—and this larger number of wholesale contacts is needed by the supplier to assure adequate coverage of market opportunities. The same considerations hold for customers of varying size. In the nature of the case, therefore, large suppliers and customers come into possession of more complete market information and are also better protected against monopoloid behavior by their wholesalers.

The degree of interconnection or interlocking among all parts of the segmented network depends upon the amounts of mutual overlap between the networks of different wholesalers. It seems reasonable to expect that wholesalers will so distribute their communication links as to bring about substantial interconnection throughout the market, but institutional barriers may prevent this. On occasion, in these markets, there are special groups of suppliers or customers who are not considered "eligible" by established wholesalers, and whose business cannot be easily mixed with that of the dominant supplier or customer type. Institutional barriers of this kind are discussed in Part III.

2. *Variable Costs of Communication Links:* There are several types of cost variation in communication links between actors in the intermediate markets. First, networks made up of continuous links might be subject to economies or diseconomies of scale, so that for the individual wholesale intermediary, the cost of adding further links would depend on the number he already had. The effects of scale economies would be obvious: they could reinforce the position of a few established wholesale intermediaries and prevent entry on the equal terms previously postulated.

Another source of cost variation is in the establishment of different types of informational contact between supplier or customer and the intermediary. Personal sales calls, for example, are an alternative to telephone, teletype or mail contact. The degree of reliance on these methods of course varies, but their costs differ and so does their usefulness for certain parts of the communication task.

A third source of cost variation arises in the intermittent character of information flow in marketing networks – that is, the links can be considered ephemeral, not continuous. There are differences in the types of message and in the total burden of the message flow between a supplier or customer and his wholesaler. Each message will have a cost differing with the medium of transmission and the size and complexity of the message.

Analysis of intermittent, variable-cost message-flow – in terms of types and content of messages required for different types of transaction and in terms of opportunities for consolidation of messages when the flow is large – is reserved for separate treatment in a subsequent paper.

3. *Multiple Products: Directional Changes in Communication Flow:* A few characteristics of the content of message flows will, however, be treated here. First, it is often the case that suppliers produce, and customers buy and resell, a group of closely related products rather than a single commodity. In the extractive industries, these products are often produced under joint-cost conditions, with only partial control over the proportions of each product to total output. Wholesale intermediaries must then arrange transactions for each of the joint products. Fluctuations in relative demands or uncontrolled changes in the relative proportions of each product in the output flow lead to frequent adjustments in relative prices of the products. At any given time, prices of individual products may thus be moving in opposite directions. For the products in strong demand, *customers* will take the initiative in seeking supplies, while for those in over-supply, suppliers take initiative in seeking markets. The composition of the customer group is likely to be such that some customers absorb relatively more of one product than another, and in the supplier group, the composition of output is also likely to differ from one supplier to another.

The task of wholesale intermediaries is thus to match the differently-composed outputs of individual suppliers with the differently-composed demands of individual customers. Frequent reversals occur in the initiative taken by suppliers as against customers with respect to individual products. The result is that wholesale intermediaries benefit by being independent of either group, and therefore able to engage, simultaneously, in either market-seeking or output-seeking effort with respect to each product, and to reverse the direction of communication effort at will.

A wholesale firm that is operated as a subsidiary by a supplier or by a customer thus suffers a disadvantage as compared with independent operators. The supplier's wholesale subsidiary will find that for those products in strong demand, it cannot satisfy all customer requests from the supplier's own output but must seek elsewhere for them. Correspondingly, for products in oversupply, new customers must be sought. This difficulty may be overcome if the supplier is a very large scale, multi-plant firm, and if the wholesale subsidiary is able to embrace a wide group of customers whose local market requirements differ in product-composition. Also extreme flexibility in adding and dropping individual customers to and from the network may be helpful to such adjustment, but the *establishment* of contact is usually more difficult than the maintenance of a communication link once established.

The difficulty may also be avoided if a supplier's wholesale intermediary is empowered to buy freely from any supplier. However, wholesale representation on an integrated basis is usually arranged because the controlling firm wishes to secure special and exclusive attention to its marketing requirements. If the subsidiary must be able to buy freely from competing suppliers (when it is a wholesale subsidiary controlled by a supplier) or sell freely to competing customers (when it is a subsidiary controlled by a customer), the chief purpose of integrated wholesale representation cannot be achieved.

Frequent reversals in the direction of communication flow thus provide a rationale for autonomous operation of wholesale intermediaries. The chief exception to this is a protracted period of excess demand, or excess supply, for all parts of the product group. In this case, the direction of communication flow is the same for all of the products, and it is not subject to quick reversal. In a period of general excess demand, and

rising prices, customers may thus be impelled to integrate backward, and in a period of general excess supply, suppliers may integrate forward to control wholesale outlets. Uncertainty concerning the duration of the period of excess supply or excess demand does inhibit the development of forward or backward integration.

III. INSTITUTIONAL STRESS IN COMMUNICATION NETWORKS: PERCEIVED MODELS OF THE MARKET

1. ELIGIBLE PARTICIPANTS IN THE MARKET

The supplier and customer groups have been considered as objectively defined in the foregoing discussion. The wholesaler's task was to establish a communication network and participate in a flow of transactions decisions by means of it. The actual definitions of his supplier and customer groups are in the wholesaler's mind, and these definitions depend, as will be shown, on his perceived model of the operation of his enterprise and of the market as a whole.

At any given time, the intermediary may catalog the actors in the market into several types:

1. Suppliers and customers who are active members of his network;

2. Suppliers and customers who are *potential* members of his network and who are presently connected to other intermediaries of the same type;

3. Other intermediaries who are "competitors" — i.e., engage in the same type of operation, and may outbid the intermediary on any transaction or may seek to connect themselves with his suppliers or customers; and

4. Suppliers, customers, and intermediaries who are "outside" the trade. Some of the bases for exclusion will be discussed shortly, but the nature of the perceived model should first be examined.

2. THE LANGUAGE OF INFORMATION FLOW AND THE PERCEIVED MODEL OF THE MARKET

The communication network which characterizes the market supports a flow of information — information about the inventory positions, bids and offers of individual customers and suppliers, and detailed information concerning specific transactions which the wholesaler is working out with suppliers and customers. The information-flow thus contributes both directly and indirectly to the continuing flow of transactions decisions. The content of information required for those decisions is reduced by standardization of the details of proposed transactions so that only a small number of "cues" need be received by any actor participating in a transaction decision. This reduction of information content also permits the actors to focus on the critical factor or factors — e.g., a price bargain, or delivery date. The "lore of the trade" which is known to be important in many markets is in good part a set of customs determining the language of these "cues" to transactions decisions. Use of cues, or special language, provides one contrast to the complete mapping of all aspects of every alternative choice which is one of the classic postulates of rationality in economic decision-making. But this reduction of information content does permit each actor to process a greater number of alternative choices, for given effort, than he otherwise could.

To make the system of cues work effectively, it is necessary that every actor in the network know and utilize the same special language. Each actor must be able to form stable expectations concerning the meaning of these cues when others use them. This requires that each actor have a similar perception of what the market is like: what product or products are dealt in by the actors in the market, what normal functions they assume themselves and expect other actors to perform, and what factors lead to

changes in prices and the state of the market. As much bargaining is anticipatory, the last of these considerations is no less important than the first two.

3. THE PERCEIVED MODEL OF THE WHOLESALE ORGANIZATION

In addition to this perception of the operation of the market, which must be held in common with other actors in the market in order to make the language of "cues" effective, the wholesale intermediary has a perception of the form and content of his own organization. This perceived model of his organization must be compatible with the commonly-held model of the market, but it is defined more restrictively in a number of respects. For example, it is often true that dealings in a commodity take place in a number of regional market centers. These are connected together by actual or virtual inter-regional shipment of the commodity if transfer costs are not too large. The individual wholesaler in one regional center may, however, confine himself strictly to dealings with local customers, on account of his greater familiarity with this aspect of the trade, or because his organization's supply of capital or executive talent is limited. In numerous other respects, the activities of the firm may be a subset of the activities in which it could engage without violating the general model of the market. The firm's operations may be changed to include more of these activities that are compatible with the general model, but this requires a policy decision by the executive head of the firm.

The wholesale executive's perception as to what suppliers, customers and other wholesalers are excluded from the trade is thus seen to rest on two simplifying abstractions: (a) his model of the operation of his own enterprise, and (b) his model of the operation of the market as a whole. The first of these is a much less drastic constraining factor than is the second.

4. EXCLUDED ACTORS AND THE PERCEIVED MODEL

One exclusion resting on the general model is that of suppliers of commodities other than those dealt in together by wholesale intermediaries and by the customer group. It is not unusual for members of the customer group to buy some types of product from a completely different group of wholesale intermediaries than the one under study. Also, a by-product commodity produced by supplier firms may be channelled through wholesale markets other than those utilized for the bulk of the joint product group, if the set of customers for the by-product is different from the customer group which buys the rest of the products. But if the set of commodities that is produced by the supplier group is also handled, *in toto*, by the customer group, wholesale intermediaries tend to deal in all the individual commodities unless special intermediate handling is required for certain by-products which then go through the hands of specialists.

The wholesaler does not, therefore, view his potential supplier group as being composed of all possible sellers of all possible products. The expectations of the customer group also come into play in this connection. Customers form expectations (based on the general model of the market which they hold in common with other actors) as to the possible types of source for products entering to the assortments that they wish to accumulate. Wholesale intermediaries who wish to deal in a product which customers do not ordinarily expect them to sell therefore face a considerable task of educating their customers.

Stable expectations concerning what products move together through the market, and a common language of cues for transaction-decisions, are thus made possible by the general model of the market that is held in common by its participants. Suppliers of other commodities, customers whose activities are sharply different from those of the customer group as delineated in the model of the market, are excluded from consideration.

5. EVOLUTIONARY DEVELOPMENT OF THE PERCEIVED MODEL

The strength, precision, and degree of rigidity of this perceptual model may, of course, vary from one market to another and may change over time in the same market.

Time is in fact a necessary element in the development of the perceived model. It is the outcome of accumulated individual and joint experience in repeated solving of decision-problems. As actors in a market are involved in a succession of transactions decisions over time, the common elements of these decisions become recognized and then are taken for granted. This gives rise to the possibility of evolving the language of cues.

In addition, experience over time leads to the development of personal ties between actors. Loyalties therefore accumulate, for actors at successive stages of the market are in frequent contact with each other and have a substantial degree of mutual interdependence: all may suffer if the flow of goods through the market falls off, or if the communication networks are destabilized. Norms of behavior resulting from this experience become expressed in moralistic terms – as, for example, the characterization of the intermediary group as "legitimate wholesalers." These norms of behavior, in turn, are inculcated into the young executives of the wholesale intermediary firm who are the main source of potential entry to the trade.

The perceived model of the market thus acquires moral status and strength. It becomes the focus of personal and group loyalties, as well as conferring efficiency benefits on those who understand and adhere to it. The result is that the perceived model can continue to be a powerful force in determining how communication networks in the market will be formed, and how they will operate, even when the objective conditions which gave rise to this model have undergone substantial change.

6. ENVIRONMENTAL SHIFTS CAUSING STRESS IN COMMUNICATION NETWORKS

The objective conditions from which the market structure drew its original impetus may change in numerous ways. The active participants in the market — suppliers, customers, and wholesale intermediaries — may experience significant changes in the technology, capital requirements, or variable costs of their own operations. Changes such as these may arouse dissatisfaction with the types of arrangements for transactions which the market affords. The size distribution of the supplying industry may become more concentrated so that promotional strategy — branding, user-directed advertising, etc. — achieves new significance. There may be new entry by suppliers having a different technology and product-mix, in which some products customarily traded in the market are represented, but others are not. The new suppliers may find it convenient to use the facilities of the established market, but they may not be familiar with the special language of the trade or with its norms of behavior and so may find these an obstacle to successful entry rather than an inducement to conform. Entry by new types of customer may, for similar reasons, give rise to demands on the market for types of service which are outside the usual range of activities forming the agreed model of behavior.

One new type of customer is particularly challenging to the prevailing model: the firm which, under earlier circumstances, bought its requirements of the commodity at retail, from the firms that are "customers" in the whole-

saler's perceived model of the market, and which now desires to by-pass its former sources and buy from wholesale intermediaries. This situation can arise because the user firm has grown in response to the market conditions it faces and can now absorb shipments in the bulk amounts in which wholesalers buy and resell. Not only is this new type of customer different in credit standing and other business attributes from the established types of customer with whom the wholesale intermediary is accustomed to deal; but also the wholesaler will be regarded as competing with his own established customers if he by-passes them, and the stigma of illegitimate dealing will therefore attach to him.

Finally, changes in the economy at large and, particularly in consumer incomes, tastes and purchasing patterns may be an upsetting force. Sharp increases of consumer demand, for example, could give rise to the kind of transformation of a user-industry that leads to attempts at by-passing.

7. ADAPTATION OR DESTRUCTION OF THE PERCEIVED MODEL

The impact of these changes in environmental conditions on the market structure depends to a great extent on whether the changes are slow and sustained, or whether they are abrupt and possibly transitory. Experience with successive transactions over time gives rise to the perceived model of the market; slow, persistent changes in the basic conditions of the trade may bring about gradual adaptation. This adaptation may not occur, however, if the gradual shifts give rise to pressures that are not perceived throughout the market, but only by those firms whose survival would be most imminently threatened by the adjustments which may be necessary for the market as a whole. If the pressures for change thus accumulate, a sudden breakdown of the routine pattern of dealing may finally occur.

Also frequent is a rather abrupt change in environmental conditions that is of uncertain future duration and importance. In the face of such uncertainty, the established wholesale intermediary usually feels he has more to lose than to gain by dealing, say, with a new type of customer. The participants who benefit by it thus tend to defend their common model of the market against the incursion of the new type of customer. New entrants into wholesale trade are sometimes the vehicle of adaptation. Unlike the established firms, they have no customers whose loyalty may be impaired, or suppliers who may threaten to cut off supplies. The new entrants may, to be sure, be recruited through experience in the wholesale trade and may therefore be indoctrinated with its norms of behavior. But a new type of customer or a new type of supplier is an inviting target for the new entrant: he will not face competition from established operators in serving the new type of customer or supplier. New entrants, therefore, have a special role to play in accepting innovational opportunities that established firms avoid.

21. Major Channels of Distribution for Industrial Goods

W. M. DIAMOND

This chapter presents some of the findings of the empirical research bearing on channels of distribution for industrial machinery, equipment, and supplies. The data were secured through the use of interviews with major executives of manufacturing firms and through a questionnaire distributed to 485 producers of various lines of industrial machinery, equipment, and supplies. Attention is focused at this juncture upon the variety of major channels of distribution utilized in getting these product lines to the industrial user. The principal subject areas covered are: major channels used; company, market, and product line characteristics which appear to influence channel decisions; and changes occurring in major channels since 1945.

Because so many of the manufacturers make use of multiple channels in the distribution of their products, treatment of the data concerning secondary outlets for these lines has been reserved to Chapter V. Also included in Chapter V are the discussions of factors considered by manufacturers in making channel decisions, and the organizational location and structure of authority for making channel decisions.

The presentation of the material proceeds from the general to the particular; that is, presentation and analysis of the

findings applicable to the general class of products is presented first. This is followed with analyses relating to selected individual product lines where enough firms are represented to avoid disclosure of information pertaining to a particular firm. This plan of organization is followed throughout.

The tabulations in this chapter, as noted in Chapter II, reflect the presence of multi-line firms or divisions. Column headings in the tables are titled "company-product-lines" or "number of manufacturers' responses" in order to avoid confusion with distinct *kinds* of product lines, of which there are only 24 included in the study.

MAJOR CHANNELS OF DISTRIBUTION FOR ALL PRODUCT LINES

The term major channel of distribution refers to the chain of marketing institutions (including the maker of the product at one end and its user at the other) through which the greatest portion of the volume of a product line is moved, through title transfers, to the user of the item. It should be noted that the process of transfer of title is the real essence of the channel of distribution. Thus, the various types of agent middlemen discussed in Chapter III are a part of the channel of distribution for a product when they are used, even though they do not take title to the goods they sell, nor physically handle the product. The assistance of such middlemen in

From William M. Diamond, *Distribution Channels for Industrial Goods* (Columbus, Ohio: Bureau of Business Research, College of Commerce and Administration, Ohio State University, 1963), chap. 4, pp. 51-72.

the process of title transfer is the fundamental criterion for their inclusion in a channel of distribution.

Many firms are committed to the use of only one channel for the distribution of their products. However, the use of more than one channel for the same product line of a company is also frequently found in both the consumer and industrial goods areas in order to secure adequate coverage of different customer classes and geographic market segments. The product lines included in this study, while known to be of particular importance among the lines normally carried by general-line industrial distributors, are not limited to this single channel of distribution. In fact, it will be shown subsequently that a substantial number of individual company product lines in the area of industrial machinery, equipment, and supplies are sold through channels which do not involve the use of industrial distributors at all.

CURRENT MAJOR CHANNELS OF DISTRIBUTION FOR ALL PRODUCT LINES

The relative preference of the 156 manufacturers covered by this study for particular major channels of distribution is shown in Table 1. The figures in Table 1 refer to the *number* of individual company product lines, the major or total volume of which is sold through a particular channel. The percentage figures indicate the number of product lines distributed through the various channels, they do not refer to the actual volume or proportion of business moving through these channels.

Nearly one-half of all the product lines of the various producers was sold direct from factory to industrial distributors for resale. Distributors were involved, in one combination or another, in the marketing of 74.1 per cent of all the 220 product lines of the 156 manufacturers. This proportion points out the importance of the distributor in the over-all distribution pattern for machinery equipment, and supplies. However, the fact that over 25 per cent of the company product lines were marketed through major channels in which the distributor was not used at all indicates that these channels should always be considered by the manufacturer as possible alternatives in making channel decisions until eliminated or accepted through objective analysis relating to the specific situation.

The 6 distribution channels shown in Table 1 and illustrated in Figure 1 were the only ones reported in the survey with one exception, which has been eliminated from the data. The line in question was essentially a consumer good sold through retail hardware dealers with a very small proportion of industrial sales occa-

TABLE 1
MAJOR CHANNELS OF DISTRIBUTION FOR PRODUCT LINES OF 156 MANUFACTURERS OF INDUSTRIAL MACHINERY, EQUIPMENT, AND SUPPLIES

Major Channel of Distribution	*Company Product Lines*	*Per Cent of Total Product Lines*
	Number	*Per Cent*
Direct from factory to industrial distributor	107	48.7
Through manufacturers' agent to industrial distributor	37	16.8
Direct from factory to user	28	12.7
Factory sales branch to user	21	9.6
Factory sales branch to distributor	19	8.6
Through manufacturers' agent to user	8	3.6
Total	220	100.0

FIGURE 1

THE SIX PRINCIPAL CHANNELS OF DISTRIBUTION FOR INDUSTRIAL MACHINERY, EQUIPMENT, AND SUPPLIES

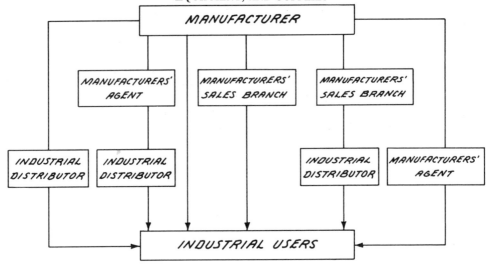

TABLE 2.

MAJOR CHANNELS OF DISTRIBUTION FOR INDUSTRIAL MACHINERY, EQUIPMENT, AND SUPPLIES, BY SALES-VOLUME SIZE OF REPORTING FIRM OR DIVISION

Size of Firm (Total Annual Sales Volume)	Total Number of Manufacturer Responses	Current Major Channel of Distribution					
		Factory to Distributor	Manufacturers' Agent to Distributor	Factory to User	Sales Branch to User	Sales Branch to Distributor	Manufacturers' Agent to User
(000 omitted)		Number of responses					
Under $1,000	48	20	22	3	0	0	3
1,000-4,999	69	36	10	8	2	8	5
5,000-9,999	32	16	5	6	2	3	0
10,000-19,000	32	18	0	6	6	3	0
20,000-49,999	19	10	0	2	4	3	0
50,000-99,999	10	4	0	1	4	1	0
100,000 and over	9	3	0	2	3	1	0
Total	220	107	37	28	21	19	8
		Per cent of responses					
Under 1,000	100	41.6	45.7	6.3	0.0	0.0	6.3
1,000-4,999	100	52.2	14.5	11.5	2.9	11.6	7.2
5,000-9,999	100	50.0	15.6	18.7	6.3	9.4	0.0
10,000-19,999	100	54.6	0.0	18.2	18.2	9.1	0.0
20,000-49,999	100	52.8	0.0	10.3	21.1	15.8	0.0
50,000-99,999	100	40.0	0.0	10.0	40.0	10.0	0.0
100,000 and over	100	33.3	0.0	22.2	33.3	11.1	0.0
Total	100	48.7	16.8	12.7	9.5	8.6	3.6

sionally made through these same outlets. Thus, it would appear that the potential channels available to a manufacturer of any product lines similar to those included in this study are rather effectively limited to the 6 channels shown.

CURRENT MAJOR CHANNELS BY SALES-VOLUME SIZE OF PRODUCING UNIT

The influence of sales volume size of the producing unit upon choice of the major distribution channel is shown in Table 2. Since a variety of different kinds of product lines appear in all but the very largest size classifications, the variation in channel usage among the various groups is related to sales volume. For example, while the factory to distributor channel is used by all size groups, it was relatively less important for the smallest and the two largest groups of producers. The sales size class of under $1,000,000 tended to make greater use of manufacturers' agents as a substitute for sales branches or a factory sales force selling to industrial distributors. This bears out well some of the general conditions for the advantageous use of agents noted in Chapter III, particularly with respect to small producers with limited financial resources selling in wide geographic markets. It should be emphasized that the agent is used primarily by these small firms in selling *to* distributors who in turn handle the sale of the product to users. When coupled with the 41.6 per cent of the product lines of firm with annual volume under $1,000,000 whose major channel was direct from factory to distributors, these data illustrate the overwhelming importance of the distributor to small manufacturing companies. Considering all combinations, the distributor was involved in some way in the distribution of 87.3 per cent of the company product lines produced by firms or divisions in the smallest sales size classification.

Conversely, no agents were used in the major channel of distribution of any firm or division with an annual sales volume greater than $10,000,000. As will be noted in Chapter V, agents are used by large firms as an element in secondary channels for their product lines, but among the larger firms included in this study the manufacturers' agent was totally excluded from the channel through which the greater portion of a line's volume was sold. When used, agents supplement rather than form a part of the major channel.

Use of the distributor in selling to the industrial user is also clearly related to the sales size of the producer. The following listing indicates the generally declining importance of the distributor with relation to the size of the producing firm or division:

	Per Cent of
Sales Volume	*Company-Product-Lines*
of	*Handled by Distributor at*
Producing Unit	*Last Stage of Channel*
87.3	Under to $ 1,000,000
78.3	1,000,000 to 4,999,999
75.0	5,000,000 to 9,999,999
63.7	10,000,000 to 19,999,999
68.6	20,000,000 to 49,999,999
50.0	50,000,000 to 99,999,999
44.4	100,000,000 and Over

Thus, like the manufacturers' agent, the industrial distributor is used in the major channel of distribution of proportionally more of the lines of small producers. The similarity, of course, ends here, since it is apparent from the above data that the distributor retains substantial importance as a major channel for even the largest manufacturers. The value of the distributor in reaching industrial users is reflected in this use of the channel by manufacturers of great size. The nonuse of agents in the major channels of large producers, however, and the declining importance of the distributors as the size of firm increases requires acceptance in both cases of the hypothesis that channel usage is associated with sales size.

There is also a strong relationship between sales size of producers and the adoption of sales-branch-to-user as a major channel, with an increasing proportion of the lines of larger producers being moved to the user through this form of direct sale with the exception of the very largest classification where the proportion drops off. Nevertheless, it should be noted that only 9.5 per cent of all the manufacturers' product lines had sales-branch-to-user as a major channel, and the lines of producers with under $10,000,000 annual sales showed a percentage use substantially under the figure. On the other hand, the lines of manufacturers who had more than $10,000,000 annual sales were all substantially above the 9.5 per cent figure in the proportional use of the sales-branch-to-user channel. The hypothesis that use of a channel of distribution is associated with sales size of the producer is again accepted in the case of the sales-branch-to-user-channel.

An interesting pattern is seen in the use of the direct-from-factory-to-user channel. Here there is an increasing use of the channel for the lines of manufacturers with up to just under $10,000,000

annual volume. Above $10,000,000 and up to $100,000,000 the use of factory-to-user drops off. This is explained by the sharply increased use of the sales-branch-to-user channel when volume exceeds $10,000,000 annually. In this case the return to proportionally greater use of factory to user by producers with over $100,000,000 annual volume is no doubt due to the nature of the lines involved. The two company product lines shown in this class in Table 1 are both produced by large steel manufacturers whose major volume of product goes to large processors. The general pattern of usage, nevertheless, shows a relationship between the channel and the sales size of the manufacturer providing ample basis for the acceptance of the hypothesis.

In the case of the sales-branch-to-distributor channel the hypothesis relating to sales size is rejected since no apparent relationship between the use of this channel and sales size of manufacturer is exhibited in the data, except that there is no use of this channel for the lines of the smallest class of producing units. No explanation for this lack of relationship is found in the data. However, a plausible inference is suggested, and that is that the sales branches used

TABLE 3
MAJOR CHANNELS OF DISTRIBUTION OF INDUSTRIAL MACHINERY, EQUIPMENT, AND SUPPLIES, BY
MAJOR USING INDUSTRY

Major Using Industry	Total Number of Manufacturer Responses	Major Channel of Distribution					
		Factory to Distributor	Manufacturers' Agent to Distributor	Factory to User	Sales Branch to User	Sales Branch to Distributor	Manufacturers Agent to User
			Number of responses				
Construction	18	12	3	3	0	0	0
Metalworking	92	42	16	19	4	6	5
Extractive	11	7	3	0	0	1	0
General Industry	79	38	10	6	12	10	3
Other[a]	14	5	2	0	5	2	0
Total	214	104	34	28	21	19	8
			Per cent of responses				
Construction	100.0	66.7	16.7	16.7	0.0	0.0	0.0
Metalworking	100.0	45.6	17.4	20.6	4.3	6.5	5.4
Extractive	100.0	63.6	27.3	0.0	0.0	9.1	0.0
General Industry	100.0	48.1	12.6	7.6	15.2	12.6	3.8
Other[a]	100.0	21.4	14.3	0.0	21.4	14.3	0.0
Total[a]	100.0	48.6	15.9	13.1	9.8	8.9	3.7

[a] Includes companies selling to specialized industry groups.

to sell to distributors probably are sales offices carrying no stocks since this would normally be expected of the distributor. Thus, except for the smallest firms, such sales offices could be established economically by manufacturers of all sales size classes.

MAJOR CHANNELS OF DISTRIBUTION IN RELATION TO SELECTED INDUSTRIES OF ULTIMATE USE

With the data on major channels arrayed by major using industry, the factory-to-distributor channel is heavily favored by manufacturers selling primarily to the construction and extractive industries (Table 3). Of 18 manufacturers' product lines where construction was the dominant using industry, none were sold through sales branches as a major channel. Also, none of the lines were sold through the agent-to-user major channel. These product lines consist primarily of relatively small unit value items such as hand tools, and the quantity purchased at one time by users is small. The industry involves a large number of these buyers, however, and the ability of the distributor to secure additional sales from other lines enables him, normally, to sell to the industry economically by spreading marketing costs across the multiple lines. The manufacturer, of course, can concentrate his sales from the factory by selling to distributors, and this concentration of effort makes it possible to use the factory-to-distributor channel economically, as was done for two-thirds of the lines going primarily to the construction industry.

Product lines sold to metalworking industries were distributed through all 6 channels, although the major channel for over 45 per cent of these lines was factory to distributor. Again, if lines sold predominantly to the extractive industry and to general industry (where no single group of producers was in the majority

as a user but rather the lines were sold to many different types of users, cutting across industry lines) are considered, 90.9 per cent and 60.7 per cent of the lines, respectively, were sold from factory to distributor, or through agents to the distributor.

Based on the channels used in the distribution of products to these four industry classifications it would appear (despite some absolute differences in percentages) that one of the basic hypothesis, namely, that the use of distribution channels is related to the using industry, must be rejected. This conclusion was reached because of the strong similarity in the pattern of channel usage for each industry group. It should be noted, however, that this similarity is believed due to the broad nature of the industry classification which may tend to obscure the predominance of a particular channel for reaching a segment of one of these industries. This qualification is prompted by the appearance of the data on the classification of "other" industry. Here the factory-to-distributor channel was used for only 21.4 per cent of the lines, the same proportion as for the sales-branch-to-user channel. Also, sales-branch-to-distributor was used for the same number of lines as agent to distributor. This industry classification includes lines sold to highly specialized industries such as railroads and public utilities. The lack of a truly dominant channel is believed due to the diverse nature of the users represented in the class. Thus, if metalworking, for example, were broken into subclasses such as electrical machinery, metal furniture, machinery (except electrical), transportation equipment, etc., it is quite possible that highly differentiated patterns of channel usage would appear among the various types of metalworking users. Such a detailed breakdown was not obtained through the survey, nor was it secured in the case of the initial interviews.

TABLE 4

MAJOR CHANNELS OF DISTRIBUTION OF INDUSTRIAL MACHINERY, EQUIPMENT, AND SUPPLIES, BY EXTENT OF MARKETING AREA

Extent of Marketing Area	Total Number of Manu- facturer Responses	Major Channel of Distribution					
		Factory to Distributor	Manufacturers' Agent to Distributor	Factory to User	Sales Branch to User	Sales Branch to Distributor	Manufacturers' Agent to User
		Number of responses					
National	177	95	28	18	14	15	7
Regional	35	10	6	8	6	4	1
Total	212	105	34	26	20	19	8
		Per cent of responses					
National	100.0	53.7	15.8	10.2	7.9	8.5	4.0
Regional	100.0	28.6	17.1	22.8	17.1	11.4	2.9
Total	100.0	49.5	16.0	12.3	9.4	9.0	3.8

TABLE 5

MAJOR CHANNELS OF DISTRIBUTION FOR TWELVE SELECTED PRODUCT LINES OF INDUSTRIAL MACHINERY, EQUIPMENT, AND SUPPLIES

Product Line	Total Number of Manu- facturer Responses	Major Channel of Distribution					
		Factory to Distributor	Manufacturers' Agent to Distributor	Factory to User	Sales Branch to User	Sales Branch to Distributor	Manufacturers' Agent to User
		Number of responses					
Abrasive Products	13	3	2	3	0	4	1
Cutting Tools	17	8	5	3	0	0	1
Fasteners	9	2	1	2	3	1	0
Materials Handling Equipment	21	10	1	3	3	2	2
Mechanical Rubber Goods	9	2	1	1	2	3	0
Metal Working Accessories	14	8	3	3	0	0	0
Power Transportation Equipment	17	7	1	3	1	5	0
Steel Products	12	7	0	3	1	0	1
Tools – Hand	26	16	7	1	0	2	0
Tools – Portable Power	8	7	0	1	0	0	0
Tools – Machine	25	7	10	4	1	1	2
Valves and Fittings	12	8	4	0	0	0	0
Other Lines	37	22	2	1	10	1	1
Total	220	107	37	28	21	19	8
		Per cent of responses					
Abrasive Products	100.0	23.1	15.4	23.1	0.0	30.6	7.7
Cutting Tools	100.0	47.1	29.4	17.6	0.0	0.0	5.9
Fasteners	100.0	22.2	11.1	22.2	33.3	11.1	0.0
Materials Handling Equipment	100.0	47.7	4.8	14.3	14.3	9.5	9.5
Mechanical Rubber Goods	100.0	22.2	11.1	11.1	22.2	33.3	0.0
Metal Working Accessories	100.0	57.1	21.5	21.5	0.0	0.0	0.0
Power Transportation Equipment	100.0	41.2	5.9	17.6	5.9	29.4	0.0
Steel Products	100.0	58.3	0.0	25.0	8.3	0.0	8.3
Tools – Hand	100.0	61.6	26.9	3.9	0.0	7.7	0.0
Tools – Portable Power	100.0	87.5	0.0	12.5	0.0	0.0	0.0
Tools – Machine	100.0	28.0	40.0	16.0	4.0	4.0	8.0
Valves and Fittings	100.0	66.7	33.8	0.0	0.0	0.0	0.0
Other Lines	100.0	59.5	5.4	2.7	27.0	2.7	2.7
Total	100.0	48.7	16.8	12.7	9.6	8.6	3.6

MAJOR CHANNELS OF DISTRIBUTION USED BY NATIONAL AND REGIONAL SELLERS

Manufacturers of products sold in a national market showed a much stronger preference for the factory-to-distributor route as a major channel than did those selling on a regional basis (Table 4). Product lines with sales concentrated in the smaller geographic area were more often sold direct from the factory to the user. Also, producers of regionally marketed lines made greater use of sales branches as an intermediate step between both sales made direct to users and sales made through distributors.

Since the data refer to major channels of distribution only, it is very probable that the greater total volume of sales going through distributors for nationally marketed lines obscures the importance of direct sales of these product lines in areas surrounding producing facilities. This is borne out by the fact, discussed in some detail in Chapter V, that a large proportion of the national lines have a secondary distribution channel of direct sale to the user. Also, the interviews with marketing executives of manufacturing establishments brought out that it is common practice to reserve the immediate territory about the plant for the company salesmen or even sales executives, while distributors are used in more distant areas.

However, the data do indicate that manufacturers of products for industrial use have a tendency, as do manufacturers of consumer goods, to increase their use of wholesaling institutions as the extent of the geographic market area increases.

MAJOR CHANNELS OF DISTRIBUTION FOR PARTICULAR PRODUCT LINES

While information on manufacturers' channel policies was received for 24 distinct product lines, the number of individual responses for several of these lines was so small that little separate analysis was possible. As a result, Table 5 shows a detailed breakdown of major channel usage for only 12 lines. Some comments are made in the section concerning individual lines included in the category "Other Lines" in Table 5, especially where the survey data are supported by interview findings, but in general, the following material relates largely to the lines listed separately in the table.

The data do not show conclusively that the choice of a major channel of distribution is directly related, in all cases, to the particular product line for which the channel is to be used because there is a strong preference for the factory-to-distributor channel shown for a majority of the lines. Neither is it indicated that the channel is not related to the specific product line, since in some instances the general emphasis on the factory-to-distributor channel does not appear. Note that less than 30 per cent of the manufacturers' lines in each of the following cases are moved through the factory-to-distributor major channel: abrasive products, fasteners, mechanical rubber goods, and machine tools.

The fact that in all other cases over 40 per cent of the manufacturers' lines have the factory-to-distributor major channel points up the basic similarity of the product lines; i.e., they are supply and equipment items sold in markets having similar characteristics and are especially suited to the operations of the industrial distributor.

The reasons behind the relative unimportance of the factory-to-distributor channel for abrasive products and the other lines mentioned above may be explained on an individual basis. In the case of abrasive products two important segments of the market are considered to be not best served through distributors. The first, and most important, of these market segments involves the sale of special-purpose grinding wheels or coated abrasives to producers who require them in large manufacturing operations. A second market segment involves producers of grinding machinery who install the abrasives as original equipment on their products. The number of these buyers is relatively limited. Also, the need for technical service on orders and the large volume sales involved dictate and facilitate the use of the factory-to-user, sales-branch-to-user, and agent-to-user channels. It should be noted in the case of abrasives, that where sales branches are used, their customers are primarily distributors rather than users although a substantial amount of sales to users is usually involved.

Sales to original-equipment manufacturers in large volume on a continuing basis account for the fact that 5 of the 9 manufacturers of fasteners used either the sales-branch-to-user or the factory-to-user major channel. When original equipment sales are of lesser importance, the larger proportion of sales as supply items involves the use of the distributor in the major channel. In general the same comments apply to the channel structure for mechanical rubber goods, although, as in the case of abrasive products, the sales-branch-to-distributor channel actually is more important.

The distributor is extremely important in the final sale of machine tools to the users. However, this line exhibits a greater use than any other of the manufacturers' agent in selling to the distributor. This appears to be attributable to three factors. First, the very small manufacturer who is not capable of developing and maintaining a factory sales forces uses the agent as an economical means of reaching the distributor. Second, for the manufacturer of a single item or small number of items constituting only a limited portion of a line, the manufacturers' agent provides an economical way of contacting the distributor with a full line in direct competition with full-line producers. Third, the agents operating in this field can supply the technical knowledge needed regarding the application of machine tools to the special processes of the user.

It may be noted that the use of the factory-to-distributor channel is greatest for those lines where original equipment sales and sales of special orders made to customer specification are least important. Hand tools, portable power tools, and valves and fittings are lines shown in Table 5 which illustrate this point particularly well. The opportunities for direct sale to the user of substantial quantities of these items on a regular basis are very limited relative to the large number of small replacement orders constituting the bulk of the market. Portable power tools, of course, require continuing service, but unlike large machinery items the service necessary is not highly technical in nature nor is the dollar volume large. An industrial distributor is in an ideal position to provide such service locally to numerous small accounts.

The hypothesis stated that the use of a particular channel was related to the product line. The data do not provide for conclusive acceptance or rejection of this hypothesis. Actually, it appears that channel usage is, in general, related to the broad type of product line. Since the lines included in this study consist of supply, equipment, and machinery items normally handled by industrial distributors as part of their line, the importance of these institutions is reflected in the data for all lines, where factory to distributor was the major channel used for nearly one-half of the total of 220 manufacturers' product lines. Exceptions to the general pattern, such as those mentioned above, are explained on the basis of particular market characteristics or characteristics of the producer.

CHANGES AND TRENDS IN MAJOR CHANNELS OF DISTRIBUTION

The policy of a specific manufacturer regarding the use of a particular channel of distribution is ordinarily long-run in nature such that once the commitment is made it is expected that the channel will be retained over a considerable number of years and perhaps indefinitely. There are exceptions to the general rule, of course, as when an agent is initially retained with the intent of switching later to the use of a factory salesman when the territory has been built up sufficiently to warrant the change. However, the examination of channel policies in force for any group of products over a period of years would anticipate results exhibiting a pattern of relative stability. This condition would appear to be related to a number of interconnected factors. Not the least among these factors, probably, is that of success as measured by profitable operations. Under such conditions there is little incentive for change, especially since known success with one channel must be compared with uncertain projections of probable degrees of success that might be achieved with other channels. Thus, uncertainty is also a factor since the risks attendant with failure are so potentially great; *i.e.*, the possibility that a change in channel policy could be utterly ruinous to the firm's total marketing effort.

A number of other important considerations are also involved. The actual dollar costs of building up effective relations with various elements of the channel are great enough to require serious consideration before any decision to change is made. The abandonment of a channel means the abandonment of these sunk costs and any future returns on them. The intangible goodwill of users and middlemen alike may be lost irrevocably. The preponderance of trade custom favoring a particular channel, and the general unawareness of available alternatives also may be seen as major factors limiting the frequency with which channel changes are made.

Also, as subsequently shown in Chapter V, channel policies are at the very least marketing policies formulated by the top echelon of that functional area within the firm. More frequently the channel decision is considered a top *corporate* policy area requiring the approval of the president of the company. Top level policy of this sort is directed at achieving long-run major organization objectives, and stability in the policy itself is requisite if these objectives are to be met. Finally, therefore, the very nature of channel policies implies a condition where only occasional adjustment will be undertaken by the individual firm.

NUMBER OF CHANGES IN MAJOR CHANNELS FOR PRODUCT LINES INCLUDED IN THIS STUDY

Of the total of 220 manufacturers' product lines, 24 showed a different major channel of distribution prior to 1945 from that which was currently in use. While this number represents only 10.9 per cent of the sample, it might be considered rather large in view of the preceding discussion. However, one important qualification should be noted. The change in major channel is not always a swift and dramatic one. Rather, it often reflects a gradual transition from one major channel to another with the original dominant channel being retained as a secondary outlet for the manufacturers' product line.

The 24 changes were distributed among 12 separate lines of equipment and supplies. These lines included abrasive products, cutting tools, fans and blowers, fasteners, hand tools, materials handling equipment, metalworking accessories, motors, portable power tools, power transmission equipment, pumps and compressors, and valves and fittings. No changes of major channel of distribution were indicated for the remaining 12 lines on which channel information was gathered. This latter group included some of the lines where a relatively large number of responses were received such as machine tools and steel products. Other lines where no changes were indicated and where 5 or more manufacturers were represented included mechanical rubber goods, precision measuring devices and tools, and safety equipment and supplies.

Considering the fact that the determination of distribution channels involves a policy decision at the top organizational levels, it may be concluded that the number of changes in major channel is indeed significant for the product lines in which the changes occurred, providing a basis for rejection of the hypothesis that the pattern of distribution channels for industrial machinery, equipment, and supplies has not varied significantly since 1945.

However, the available evidence concerning those lines mentioned above where no changes in major channel were indicated over the fifteen-year period suggests a degree of stability in the structure of major channels such that the hypothesis is accepted; *i.e.*, there is apparently no tendency toward the adoption of alternative major channels for machine tools, mechanical rubber goods, precision measuring devices and tools, safety equipment and supplies, and steel products. These lines do not exhibit greatly different patterns in channel usage from the other product lines included in the study with the exception of machine tools where manufacturers' agents are involved to a greater degree, on the average, than is the case with the other product lines. Three probable, interrelated explanations for this stability may be inferred. First, as in the case of all lines, detailed analysis including the use of comparative cost studies is not used for the purpose of isolating potential alternatives. Thus, some potential changes may be overlooked for lack of study of the problem. Second, it is doubtful that manufacturers of these lines have encountered any serious administrative problems connected with their use of a particular major channel such that the search for alternatives would be stimulated. Third, it would seem likely that the nature of the market for each of these product lines has not undergone sufficient

change to call for different major channels in order for the individual producers to reach their market effectively. Such changes in the nature of the market would include, for example, shifts in major geographic market areas, change in size and number of users, and changes in the attitudes and purchasing policies of users regarding buying through existing institutional arrangements. It is implicit in the succeeding discussion of the trends in channel usage and the reasons underlying the changes that are made that the changing character of a market may influence strongly the use of a particular channel.

TRENDS REFLECTED BY CHANNEL CHANGES

The basic importance of the industrial distributor as an element in the major channels of distribution for industrial machinery, equipment, and supplies has been documented at the outset of this chapter. While most of these relationships between manufacturers and distributors have been in effect for many years, it is important to note that where changes have been made by individual manufacturers since 1945, the trend continues to favor the adoption of distributors as a new element in the major channel of distribution. Of the 24 changes reported, 12, or 50 per cent of the total, involved the addition of the distributor where this institution had not been used before. In no case was the distributor dropped as a major channel. In 5 of the remaining 12 changes, the distributor had previously been involved and continued to be used, after the change in policy had been made. The distributor was retained as the final link with the user with the changes being made in the structure of the channel between the factory and the distributor. These involved, specifically, 3 changes from direct-from-factory-to-distributor to agent-to-distributor, one change, from agent-to-distributor to direct-from-factory-to-distributor, and one change from direct-from-factory-to-distributor to through own-sales-branch-to-distributor. The balance of 7 changes, wherein the distributor was involved neither before nor after, included 6 adjustments in direct selling from direct-from-factory-to-user to through own-sales-branch-to-user, and one change from direct-from-factory-to-user to agent-to-user.

Where sales branches were used, no changes were reported which showed their use being discontinued. While the principal reason is probably successful operating experience that would preclude any change, it should also be noted that it would be comparatively more difficult to make such a change than would be the case where agents or distributors were dropped because of the relatively large amount of fixed capital involved in a branch system, and because of the problem of relocating or terminating the employment of large number of sales, administrative, and clerical personnel. The inference then, is that manufacturers committed to branch distribution do not possess the flexibility for change that would characterize other channel arrangements.

The reasons given by respondents for having changed their channel policies were fairly consistent within each type of change. The most frequent reason cited for the addition of industrial distributors as the contact with the user was the ability to secure more complete market coverage with distributors. This consideration far outweighed the local inventory factor which was mentioned only twice. One firm gave no reason for having added distributors.

The addition of agents in place of factory sales forces selling direct to the distributor or to the user was made either to secure immediate sales increases through the use of better qualified agents, or to improve relations with distributors and users because agents were considered able to provide more product knowledge and market information (presumably leading to increased sales volume in the long run).

Sales branches had been added in all cases (8 in number) to provide regional or local inventories, and/or to improve service to users and distributors over what had previously been accomplished with a factory sales force or agents. While these two reasons might also logically be associated with distributors, it was pointed out above that market coverage rather than local stocks or service was most important to users of channels involving distributors.

SUMMARY

The dominant major channel of distribution for the industrial product lines included in this study was direct from factory to industrial distributor. In fact, the industrial distributor was involved in the major channel of distribution for 74.1 per cent of the 220 product lines of 156 manufacturers. In all, however, 6 distinctly different major channels were used in one degree or another, indicating that for the majority of these product lines there are probably alternatives always available that should be thoroughly considered before a commitment is made.

The sales size of the manufacturer appears to have a strong bearing on the channel chosen for a particular product line. The smallest producers, for example, tended to make greater use of the manufacturers' agent than did larger firms. In fact, no agents were used by firms or divisions with annual sales volume in excess of $10,000,000 annually. Likewise, there was a definite relationship between kind of major channel adopted and both the using industry for the product line, and the extent of the marketing area for the line.

Within individual product lines the relative importance of particular channels varied rather strikingly in some of channels used tended to be similar for the broad types of lines included in the categories of machinery, equipment, and supplies. Changes in major channels since 1945 were concentrated in 12 lines, with an equal number of lines indicating no changes at all having occurred. Thus, it would seem that some lines tend to show a much greater pattern of stability than others, due to a lack of any pressing reason for change.

The pattern of changes was strongly in favor of the adoption of the distributor, reinforcing the already strong position of that institution in the marketing of the particular lines of products included in this study. The reason most frequently cited for the addition of the distributor to the major channel was the desire of the manufacturer for more complete coverage of his potential market. By way of contrast, agents were selected primarily for their superior knowledge of the class of product as opposed to factory salesmen; and sales branches were established to provide local stocks, and to improve service to the user of the product.

E. FOREIGN MARKETING

22. Selecting Motion Pictures for the Foreign Market

RONALD CARROLL

THE LIMITED FOREIGN MARKET

The American motion picture industry depends on the foreign market for more than 40 per cent of its total revenue. In almost half of this foreign market the industry is either not permitted or does not find it profitable to release all the pictures it produces annually. Such limitations, imposed either by government decree or trade practices, exist in Argentina, France, Italy, Japan, Spain and Switzerland.

Economic conditions in many other countries—Austria, Belgium, Bolivia, Chile, Colombia, Denmark, Egypt, Finland, Germany, Haiti, Holland, Indonesia, India, Iran, Iraq, Israel, Lebanon, Norway, Pakistan, Paraguay, Peru, Portugal, Syria, Sweden, Turkey and Uruguay—make it undesirable to place certain pictures in them. These countries represent almost half of the foreign market for American motion pictures. The American motion picture company, is therefore, faced with a difficult and an important marketing problem: which pictures out of their annual production should be selected for distribution in each of these countries.

This problem is particularly complex because motion pictures are a unique mass consumption "merchandise." They are unique because each film is an original creation and differs in important aspects from all other films. Each

From *Journal of Marketing*, Vol. 17, No. 2 (October, 1952), pp. 162-71, by permission of the American Marketing Association.

film is the composite of numerous factors: story, direction, acting, music, color, etc. All together make a picture a success or failure in one or all markets of the world. Each separably might have a favorable or unfavorable influence on the ultimate monetary results somewhere in the world.

The "know-how" of distribution executives makes it possible to select pictures with some degree of accuracy for these restricted markets. However, no individual or group of individuals can be completely objective, and keep the relative value of all pictures at all times in mind. Certainly nobody can be right all the time. Since the selection of the wrong picture or pictures for a given country means the loss of a considerable amount of revenue it is natural that companies are interested in finding a scientific method to supplement the judgment and "know-how" of individuals. This article describes one approach to solving the problem of picture selection.

THE UNITED STATES AS TEST AREA

American motion pictures generally are first released in the United States. A study, therefore, was made to determine whether the monetary results of pictures in certain theatres or communities in this country could serve as an accurate index as to how these pictures would do in any or all of the restricted foreign markets. The hope was, for instance, that neighborhoods populated with people of Italian descent would serve as an index for Italy, French descendant neighborhoods for France, German for Germany, and so forth. However, this study only provided proof of the rapid adoption of American culture by foreign groups in the United States; it showed that there are no neighborhood theatres where box office results of motion pictures differed materially and consistently from the over-all results of these pictures in the entire nation.

The next step was a comparison of over-all results of pictures in the United States with over-all results of pictures in each foreign country. This study showed numerous substantial differences between the relative earnings of pictures here and in each foreign country. These differences were least pronounced between the United States and Great Britain and the British Dominions. But even in these instances they amounted to 30 per cent of the pictures checked, meaning that almost one out of three pictures made a substantially different profit showing.

As far as supplying reliable clues for business to be expected from foreign countries, the results of this study were definitely negative and proved that the business a picture does in the United States is not necessarily an indication of how it will do in the foreign market in general or in any country or group of countries in particular.

ANALYSIS OF FOREIGN BACKGROUND DATA

Therefore, a different approach to the solution of the problem was tried. Its purpose was to ascertain what business was done by the pictures released in the past in each country. The first step was the compilation and maintenance of a record which registered comparable figures by a representative group of pictures during a representative period of time in every country. Experience

had shown that during the first year of distribution motion pictures earn 60 per cent to 99 per cent of their total gross, depending on the country. Therefore, the gross of each picture at the end of one year of distribution was taken as the comparable figure.

In order to obtain a representative group of pictures these first-year grosses were compiled for a period as far back as was practical and economically and statistically sound. This means that the extraordinary business done by films during the war years and the immediate post-war period was disregarded. Also disregarded was business done by pictures in Austria and Germany prior to the currency reforms in these countries, the business done in Israel prior to the end of the Arab-Israeli war, etc. Figures were compiled on all important markets with the exception of Argentina and the Iron Curtain countries. Import restrictions made it impossible to release new pictures in Argentina between the summer of 1949 and the summer of 1951. During that two-year period a serious inflationary condition had changed business conditions. Therefore earning results of pictures released prior to 1949 became useless for comparison purposes with pictures released since the summer of 1951. However, it is hoped that with continued normal importation of American films into Argentina it will be possible to set up a similar record for that important market.

To date the compilation contains close to four-thousand first-year grosses from thirty-nine countries. This group of pictures becomes bigger and more representative each month as additional films complete their first year of distribution in various countries and are added to the record.

For each country a "base figure" is established. This "base figure" is the average first-year gross of all pictures recorded for that country. This figure changes slightly as new pictures are added. However, the larger and more representative the group of pictures is the smaller are these fluctuations. The first-year gross of each individual picture is compared with this "base figure," and pictures doing 1 per cent to 39 per cent of the average are rated as having done Very Poor business, 40 per cent to 79 per cent Poor, 80 per cent to 119 per cent Average, 120 per cent to 159 per cent Good, 160 per cent to 199 per cent Very Good, 200 per cent and over Excellent.

PICTURE TYPES

There is further refinement: Pictures are divided into six types: Action, Musical, Mystery, Drama, Drawing Room Comedy, Slapstick Comedy. An average also is established for each of these six type groups and by comparing the type averages to the over-all averages (the base figure), general audience preferences to types of pictures are obtained.

The six types of pictures mentioned above include the following categories of film:

The *action* group consists of what are usually known as westerns, war pictures, swashbuckling spectacles, such as *The Three Musketeers,* and outdoor adventure stories such as *King Solomon's Mines, Trader Horn, Tarzan* or *Lassie* pictures.

The *drama* and *musical* classifications are self-explanatory.

Drawing-room comedies are light and amusing films where the comic effect is mainly in the dialogue. Typical examples are the Spencer Tracy and Katharine Hepburn pictures such as *Woman of the Year* or *Adam's Rib,* and films such as *Ninotchka, Father of the Bride,* and *Father's Little Dividend.*

Mysteries include the usual crime and detective films and espionage pictures.

Finally, the *slapstick comedy* group consists of pictures in which the comic effect of the dialogue is supplemented by a great amount of comical action. Typical examples are comedies starring Red Skelton, Abbott and Costello, Laurel and Hardy, and the Marx Brothers.

Admittedly it is sometimes difficult to classify a picture. Some pictures are borderline cases. They can be classified either as action or drama *(Kim, Beginning of the End);* others are on the dividing line between the drawing room comedy and the slapstick group *(Reformer and the Redhead);* while others can be considered either as a musical or a drawing room comedy with music *(Grounds for Marriage, Strictly Dishonorable).*

Accordingly this refinement of classifying pictures by types has only secondary value especially since, as far as audience reactions to types of pictures are concerned, exceptions are the rule. For example, in Switzerland where dramas generally do better than musicals, a good musical always will be more successful than a weak or even mediocre drama.

POPULARITY OF PICTURE TYPES

Keeping in mind the qualifications cited above it is interesting to review the popularity of types of pictures on a world-wide basis and in the principal groups of countries.

The most successful groups of pictures on a world-wide basis are musicals. This statement is based on the fact that in twenty-three countries, representing about 70 per cent of the foreign market, musicals are the most popular of the six types.

In fifteen countries, representing about 50 per cent of the foreign market, action pictures are the most popular. On an over-all, world-wide basis they qualify as the second most successful group.

Using the same system of evaluation, dramas place third, drawing room comedies fourth, mysteries fifth, and slapstick comedies last.

It is not surprising that musical and action pictures are the two most successful types of pictures, for it is in these groups, especially the former, that we find films into which the most in pro-

TABLE 1
PICTURE-TYPE AUDIENCE PREFERENCE, BRITISH EMPIRE

Country	1st	2nd	3rd	4th	5th	6th
Australia	Musical	Comedies	Drama	Action	Mystery	Slapstick
Gr. Britain	Musical	Action	Drama	Mystery	Comedies	Slapstick
New Zealand	Musical	Drama	Action	Comedies	Slapstick	Mystery
S. Africa	Musical	Drama	Comedies	Action	Mystery	Slapstick

TABLE 2
PICTURE-TYPE AUDIENCE PREFERENCE, SCANDINAVIA

Country	1st	2nd	3rd	4th	5th	6th
Denmark	Action	Musical	Drama	Comedies	Slapstick	Mystery
Finland	Action	Drama	Musical	Comedies	Slapstick	Mystery
Norway	Musical	Action	Comedies	Drama	Mystery	Slapstick
Sweden	Musical	Comedies	Action	Slapstick	Drama	Mystery

duction and entertainment values has been put. Although the expenditure of money does not always produce its equivalent in picture quality and entertainment value, experience has shown that lavish or spectacular scenes and color usually help at the box office.

If we break the foreign market down into its principal groups of countries, we can find the pattern of picture-type audience preference for each group. Tables 1 through 7 show the pattern for seven different groups.

As can be seen in Table 1, musical pictures dominate in the British Empire. Interesting also is the fairly strong showing of mystery pictures in Great Britain; these usually are in fifth or last place in other countries. In Great Britain they rank fourth. On the other hand, comedies, both of the drawing room and slapstick type, show up weaker in Great Britain than in the Dominions.

The four Scandinavian countries (Table 2) seem to be divided into two equal groups, with Denmark and Finland preferring pictures with a more serious vein, while Norway and Sweden show preference for musicals and other lighter fare. In particular, dramas show up poorly in the latter two countries.

Action pictures dominate in the other Germanic European countries (Table 3). Otherwise it also seems divided into two equal groups with Austria and Germany preferring pictures with a lighter vein and dramas showing up better in the Netherlands and Switzerland.

In Latin Europe (Table 4), musical and action pictures show up as the most popular, with dramas a strong third. In Spain slapstick comedies were not rated

TABLE 3
PICTURE-TYPE AUDIENCE PREFERENCE, OTHER GERMANIC EUROPEAN COUNTRIES*

Country	1st	2nd	3rd	4th	5th	6th
Austria	Action	Comedies	Drama	Musical	Slapstick	Mystery
Germany	Action	Comedies	Musical	Drama	Mystery	Slapstick
Netherlands	Action	Drama	Musical	Slapstick	Comedies	Mystery
Switzerland	Action	Drama	Musical	Comedies	Slapstick	Mystery

* Switzerland has French and Italian speaking parts. Nevertheless she has been grouped with other Germanic countries as her German speaking section is the largest and also produces most of the revenue earned by American motion pictures in Switzerland.

TABLE 4
PICTURE-TYPE AUDIENCE PREFERENCE, LATIN EUROPE°

Country	1st	2nd	3rd	4th	5th	6th
Belgium	Action	Musical	Drama	Comedies	Slapstick	Mystery
France	Action	Musical	Drama	Comedies	Slapstick	Mystery
Greece	Musical	Action	Drama	Mystery	Comedies	Slapstick
Italy	Musical	Action	Drama	Comedies	Mystery	Slapstick
Portugal	Musical	Action	Drama	Slapstick	Comedies	Mystery
Spain	Musical	Action	Drama	Comedies	Mystery	

° Belgium, although partly non-Latin with its large Flemish section, and Greece have been placed in this group because the culture of these two countries seems predominantly Latin in character.

TABLE 5
PICTURE-TYPE AUDIENCE PREFERENCE, LATIN AMERICA°

Country	1st	2nd	3rd	4th	5th	6th
Brazil	Musical	Drama	Action	Comedies	Slapstick	Mystery
Chile	Musical	Action	Drama	Comedies	Mystery	Comedies
Colombia	Musical	Drama	Action	Mystery	Comedies	Slapstick
Cuba	Musical	Drama	Action	Mystery	Comedies	Slapstick
Mexico	Action	Drama	Musical	Mystery	Comedies	Slapstick
Panama	Musical	Action	Drama	Comedies	Mystery	Slapstick
Peru	Musical	Drama	Action	Mystery	Comedies	Slapstick
Puerto Rico	Musical	Drama	Action	Mystery	Comedies	Slapstick
Venezuela	Musical	Action	Drama	Mystery	Comedies	Slapstick

° As stated above, Argentina is omitted because comparable up-to-date figures are lacking.

because no representative data presently are on hand.

At first glance it would seem that musicals are the general box office favorite in Latin America (Table 5) with the exception of Mexico. This is true only with a certain qualification. Some musicals, such as those starring Esther Williams in lavish water ballet sequences, and those with semi-classical music, such as pictures starring Jane Powell and Mario Lanza, are successful. On the other hand, musicals with a typical United States background and predominantly featuring modern United States hit songs such as *Annie Get Your Gun, On*

The Town, Till The Clouds Roll By, Easter Parade, and *Three Little Words* are much weaker in Latin America than in other parts of the world. Remarkable are the strong showing of dramas which is even better than in Latin Europe and the fairly high rating of mysteries.

In the Near East (Table 6), as can be expected, action and musical pictures are the most popular. It is typical also that slapstick comedies show up better than the more sophisticated drawing room comedies.

Again, in the Far East (Table 7), we find action and musical pictures on top. The subtle humor of modern drawing-

TABLE 6
PICTURE-TYPE AUDIENCE PREFERENCE, NEAR EAST

Country	1st	2nd	3rd	4th	5th	6th
Egypt	Action	Musical	Mystery	Slapstick	Comedies	Drama
Iraq	Action	Musical	Drama	Mystery	Slapstick	Comedies
Lebanon	Action	Musical	Drama	Mystery	Slapstick	Comedies

TABLE 7
PICTURE-TYPE AUDIENCE PREFERENCE, FAR EAST

Country	1st	2nd	3rd	4th	5th	6th
Hong Kong	Musical	Action	Slapstick	Drama	Mystery	Comedies
India	Musical	Action	Slapstick	Drama	Mystery	Comedies
Indo China	Action	Musical	Drama	Mystery	Slapstick	Comedies
Indonesia	Action	Musical	Slapstick	Drama	Mystery	Comedies
Japan	Action	Musical	Drama	Slapstick	Mystery	Comedies
Malaya	Musical	Action	Slapstick	Drama	Comedies	Mystery
Philippines	Action	Musical	Drama	Mystery	Slapstick	Comedies
Siam	Musical	Action	Slapstick	Drama	Comedies	Mystery

room comedies seems completely lost on Far Eastern audiences as this type of picture is showing up very poorly. On the other hand slapstick comedies seem more popular in the Far East than in any other part of the world.

This type of picture record was supplemented by a Star Rating Form which registers the value of stars, again based on the percentage-average system. This method of star rating, of course, is simply a reflection of the performance of the pictures in which a star appeared in a given country. It does not necessarily record the actual popularity of the star in a country, for the star, as pointed out earlier, is only one of many factors influencing success or failure of a picture. As experience showed that this star-rating form gave little, if any, additional useful information it was discontinued and it seems that the only correct way of determining the popularity of a star in a given country would be by means of a direct audience poll.

The data gathered in this background record tell us what pictures were successful or unsuccessful in the past in each country. By comparing an as yet unreleased picture with a film or films of a similar type or with a similar cast we can make a fairly accurate estimate of its probable earning potential in a given country. However, here the basic difficulty faces us that although motion pictures are a mass consumption "merchandise" each picture is an original creation and must differ in important

aspects from all other films. Therefore only comparatively few films are so similar as to type, cast, story, direction, etc. that this procedure alone would give entirely reliable results.

CULTURAL SIMILARITY GROUPS

As pointed out previously the relative results of pictures differed between the United States and the other countries of the world. A study was made to find out whether a certain pattern or patterns could be established by comparing, country by country, the ratings of pictures which are based on the relationship of the first-year gross in a country to the proper "base figure" (the average of all first-year grosses in this country). As stated before, the ratings classify pictures as Very Poor, Poor, Average, Good, Very Good, or Excellent. The performance of a picture was considered as "similar" when it obtained the same or an adjoining rating (Very Poor and Poor, Poor and Average, Average and Good, Good and Very Good, Very Good and Excellent) in different countries. If its respective ratings were not adjoining (Very Poor and Average, Poor and Good, Average and Very Good, Good and Excellent) it would be considered "different."

The results of this study showed that there are only very few pictures which receive the same or similar ratings in all countries of the world. The majority of this group are weak pictures which failed wherever shown. There is one notable exception, the picture *Three Musketeers*. This is the only one of 126 MGM releases during the four years from September 1, 1946 to August 31, 1950 which obtained in all countries an Excellent rating, meaning that it did everywhere better than 200 per cent of average business.

Most of the pictures analyzed, however, showed different ratings in different countries. Here are a few examples picked at random:

Annie Get Your Gun did better than 200 per cent of average (Excellent) business in the British Empire and Scandinavia. On the other hand its rating in Portugal was only 103 per cent (Average).

Adam's Rib which did well in the British Empire and Scandinavia only achieved below average results in most of Latin America and in the Far and Near East.

Little Women which did Excellent business in the British Empire only did 22 per cent and 26 per cent of average or Very Poor business in Norway and Sweden respectively.

On the other hand *The Great Sinner* did poorly in the British Empire and was generally successful in Latin America.

It would be possible to go on reciting examples almost indefinitely to prove the apparent facts that only few pictures do "similar" business in all countries of the world and that most pictures do "different" business in different parts of the world. It seemed, however, that a definite pattern of "similar" countries could be developed.

The next step, therefore, was a study to determine whether there was a sufficient cultural affinity among various countries or groups of countries, so that the performance of a picture in one or more of them could be considered as an indication as to how this picture would do in another country belonging to the same cultural group. It was hoped that each group would contain at least one

country releasing all or most pictures. This country could then serve as a test area for all the other countries in that group.

In order to find a sound basis for this cultural group study, countries were considered as being a primary similarity group if at least 80 per cent of the pictures released in these countries had a "similar" rating with most of the "differences" showing a definite pattern. Such a definite pattern might be a marked preference for a star or a type of picture in one or more countries of the group. Countries which showed a picture rating similarity of from 70 per cent to 79 per cent were considered as belonging to a secondary similarity group.

The results of this study were most gratifying as they showed the following definite pattern of countries belonging to primary and secondary similarity groups:

1. Great Britain and its Dominions, Australia, New Zealand, and South Africa, form a primary similarity group. The "differences" are comparatively minor and show the following pattern:

Pictures starring Judy Garland and Mysteries are stronger in Great Britain than in the Dominions. Pictures starring Mario Lanza, Jane Powell and Red Skelton are weaker in Great Britain than in the Dominions.

2. The Scandinavian countries, Denmark, Finland, Norway and Sweden, form another primary similarity group which shows the following pattern of "differences":

Lassie pictures are stronger in Finland than in the other three countries. Musicals and comedies are stronger in Sweden and Norway than in Finland and Denmark. There is a marked preference for pictures starring Katharine Hepburn in Sweden.

3. The Germanic countries; Austria, Germany, and the Netherlands form another primary similarity group. There are only a few minor "differences" in this group.

The preceding Scandinavian group

and these three Germanic countries form a secondary similarity group.

4. The Latin countries of Europe, Belgium, France, Greece, Italy, Portugal and Spain are a primary similarity group which "differs" very markedly from the three preceding ones.

5. The Latin American countries are another primary similarity group which "differs" considerably from the first three groups but which on the other hand forms a secondary similarity group with the Latin countries of Europe.

This Latin American group shows a significant pattern of "differences" as far as musical pictures are concerned, as "USA type" musicals are weaker in Chile, Colombia, Peru, and Mexico, than in the rest of Latin America.

6. India and the Near Eastern countries Egypt, Iraq and Lebanon form another primary similarity group which "differs" very considerably from all other similarity groups.

7. The Far Eastern countries, Hong Kong, Indo-China, Indonesia, Japan, Malaya, the Philippines and Siam, form another primary similarity group which differs materially from all other groups. An interesting "difference" in this group is the considerable strength of war pictures in the Philippines.

Summing it up, this study established and confirmed seven primary similarity groups. In addition there are two secondary similarity groups, the Scandinavian-Germanic and Latin American-Latin European. This study also revealed three countries which showed no significant or consistent "similarities" with any other country. Interestingly enough the United States, Switzerland, and Israel, all countries with a multi-racial background, but with very strong national cultures, are in this latter category.

SELECTION PROCEDURE

Now to use the information collected. The ideal procedure to be followed when selecting a picture for a limited market country is (1) to check the past results of productions in the same type group and (2) to await the first-year results and ratings of this picture in other countries within the same primary or secondary similarity groups.

Because of the time element, the latter procedure frequently is impractical or sometimes even impossible. Therefore, it is necessary to look for a speedier method of establishing the market potential of a picture in the primary and secondary similarity group countries. Experience has shown that a definite interrelation exists between the "first-run key-city" grosses of a picture and the ultimate gross after one year of release. "First-run key-city" grosses are the grosses earned in premiere engagements of a picture in the large cities of a country. Thus, for example, the "key cities" of the Netherlands are The Hague, Amsterdam and Rotterdam, and the large downtown theatres of these cities are called its "first runs." Further research disclosed that under normal conditions pictures earn the same ratings based on first-run key-city grosses as they do based on complete first-year grosses. These results differ only when first-run key-city engagements are affected by extraordinary outside influences such as political disturbances, extremes of weather, local epidemics, unusually strong competition, etc. Because of these possible interference factors, the method of relying only on first-run key-city grosses in countries within primary or secondary similarity groups is not quite so reliable as the method using the full first-year grosses. However, because of the time element this short-cut method is being used in emergencies.

RESULTS OF METHODS USED

The methods outlined above have now been in use for about one year. So far they have proven themselves eminently successful. Several instances can be cited when local distribution executives relying on personal opinions advised against the release in their market of pictures which had been successful in countries within their similarity groups. They were overruled and the pictures proved to be hits in their countries also. On the other hand there are also numerous instances when local distribution executives, again relying on personal opinions, insisted on releasing pictures which had failed in countries of their similarity group. In such cases the fact that they were not overruled proved costly, as the pictures did disappointing business. As with all market analyses relying mainly on statistics, the methods outlined above become more reliable and accurate as additional figures are secured. There can be no doubt that their proper use, coupled with better selling, better exploitation, and improved quality of motion pictures now being produced will be reflected in a substantial increase of revenue earned in foreign markets.

CONCLUSIONS

In conclusion, the following can be stated:

(1) Results in the United States do not necessarily indicate the business a picture will do anywhere else in the world.

(2) Results in any one foreign country do not necessarily indicate the business this picture will do in all other foreign countries.

(3) Past results of pictures in a given country indicate the business that can be expected from similar type productions in the same market.

(4) Results in *certain* foreign countries are a very good index for other countries belonging to the same primary or secondary similarity groups.

23. Peasant Markets

SIDNEY W. MINTZ

On market days in Haiti the towns and the country market places gather thousands of peasants for hours of busy and noisy activity. The people come for gossip, courtship and the playing-out of personal rivalries, to visit a clinic or to register a birth; but above all they come for business – to sell the tiny surpluses of their little farms and to buy necessities. They press together in the ragged lanes among the stalls and the heaps of produce spread on the ground, inspecting and handling the displays of textiles, hardware, spices, soap and cooking oils, buying, selling and chaffering. Children push by hawking trays of sweets; farmers pull produce-laden animals through the crowds, calling loudly for the right-of-way. Trucks back up and turn around, their drivers honking horns, apparently oblivious of the people and the great piles of goods. There are vigorous arguments, sometimes ending in blows and arrests. In the very intensity of color, sound and smell the outsider is overwhelmed with an impression of confusion and disorder.

But for all its apparent anarchy the market place is characterized by an elaborate underlying order. Wherever they exist, peasant markets reveal a great deal about the societies they serve. They are a central economic institution in many countries where large numbers of small-scale farmers work

their own land. To follow the movement of marketers and stock through the system is an ideal way to begin to study the economy and to trace the distribution of economic and political power in the society.

In the simpler economies, wherein producers merely exchange local commodities, the market place may do little more than facilitate barter. In societies that use money but have fixed or traditional prices, the market place reflects that isolation from the world market; its transactions neither affect nor respond to economic events in the world at large. Where trade crosses national boundaries, links diverse regions and supports specialist traders, the market place takes on a new significance, joining local activities to the world outside.

As the underdeveloped areas of the world – for example, Jamaica, Haiti, Ghana, Nigeria, India, Burma, Indonesia – move more fully into the orbit of world trade, their market systems have been passing from the earliest of these stages to the next. The transition disrupts traditional relationships and creates new alignments and rivalries in the society, and these are nowhere more dramatically revealed than in the market place. It is here that the peasant trades his surplus for the necessities he cannot produce from his own holding, and it is the market place that determines, directly or indirectly, the prices at which the exporter will purchase the peasant's produce for delivery to the world market. In certain

From *Scientific American*, Vol. 203, No. 2 (August, 1960), pp. 112-22. Reprinted with permission. Copyright © 1960 by Scientific American, Inc. All rights reserved.

countries the connection that the market establishes between the peasant producer and the world market is the keystone of national development. Those who hold political power may use the peasant market system to try to educate, persuade, coerce and manipulate the peasantry, particularly with the aim of maintaining or increasing export production. The market places are primarily loci of trade, but they are also the arena where the diverse interests of the peasantry, traders and officials are pitted and exposed.

The study of the tangle of interests that animates the peasant market thus brings into the open numerous connections between regions, classes and interest groups. Traditional anthropological studies, which focus on small, local groups, cannot yield comparable insights into such large, differentiated societies as those of India and Nigeria or even Haiti. Courts and legislatures provide good settings for observation of the competing elements in a society. But the market place reveals far more because it allows these elements so much greater freedom to express themselves.

Though man has probably been a trader since the beginnings of society, his trading activities have not invariably produced market places. When the Spanish conquerors came to the New World, for example, they were stunned by the size and grandeur of such Aztec market places as Tlatelolco, where 50,000 traders assembled on market day. A wealthy merchant group, the *pochteca,* controlled trade and wielded considerable power, and also served as efficient spies for the military. But in the great contemporary Andean empire of the Incas the conquistadors found neither market places nor merchants. Instead of trade they found royal monopolies in gold, silver, coca and fine textiles. Thus while market places are not found everywhere, their very absence tells us something about a society. The presence of markets does not necessarily imply a particular course of

social development. Yet there are striking similarities among the peasant markets of the world, especially those of the new nations of Africa, Asia and tropical America.

Haiti is an older nation, with a history of political independence. But at its present stage of economic evolution this Caribbean republic is representative of the new nations that are emerging in the colonial regions of the world. Before the revolution of 1791-1804, Haitian slaves grew their food on plantation wastelands, selling surpluses in supervised market places. In the 1790's the French observer Moreau de Saint Méry described such a market place, where 15,000 slaves traded on market day. The revolution destroyed the plantations that had made the island of Saint-Domingue one of the richest colonies in history, and substantially eliminated the French planters. Gradually Haiti became a peasant country where small-scale landholders cultivated their subsistence crops for local sale and a few items for export. The cash they received paid for the soap, cloth, oil, metal tools and flour they needed and could not produce. The national government sustained itself almost entirely by taxes on imports and exports; the local government, by levies on dealings in the market place.

Today, 150 years later, nearly 90 per cent of the people live in the countryside, and 80 per cent of them work their own land. Haitian peasants still cultivate much of their own food and produce a small surplus destined for export or for consumption in the domestic economy through sale in the peasant market. By aiming at these three different production goals they try to minimize risk and to secure a reasonably stable subsistence. They further hedge their investment of time and capital by diversifying the cultivation of their land, and this accounts for the curiously cluttered look of their little plots. Like other Caribbean farmers, the Haitian peasant makes thorough use of his land:

he grows root crops underground, vines and creepers on the surface, grains above ground and trees and climbing vines in the air. Though technologically backward, the method provides a constant trickle of varied produce for the household where storage is difficult or impractical, a supply of craft and medicinal materials as required and a small quantity of items for sale at various times. It is upon this foundation that the Haitian market-system rests.

The peasant's wife most often handles the market transactions of the family, selling what the land has produced for sale and using the cash received to buy household necessities. Many peasant women become professional traders in this way. This further distributes the family's economic risks, since the men do the farming and the women do the trading partly as separate ventures.

Most of the trade in Haiti goes on in the nearly 300 officially controlled market places. In each region one or more central market-places services other, smaller centers. The larger centers are established in the towns; the satellite country market-places spring up overnight as little towns that last only through the day to gather in and to absorb the peasant buying-power. Market days are staggered, enabling itinerant buyers and sellers to move from one market to another. Most of the important market places are on well-traveled truck routes. Thus the markets form a network, and the produce bought in one is put up for resale—after bulking, processing and transport—in another. For example, pork purchased in one market is cut up, salted and shipped to the next, while rice, millet and maize are husked or ground between purchase and resale to increase their value. The whole system of market places constantly adjusts and readjusts to seasonal changes, to the success or failure of harvests, to the growth and contraction of production areas, to the expansion of roads and trucking.

Trade begins beyond the fringes of the market, where licensed tradesmen from the towns, called *spéculateurs*, maintain outposts at which they buy commodities for export. Peasant women on their way to market stop to sell their coffee, beeswax and sisal to the *spéculateurs*, and then proceed to market with the cash they have received. Because competition is heavy and supplies uncertain, *spéculateurs* do not always wait for the peasants to come to them. They often send illegal buyers called "zombies" or "submarines" to make purchases directly at the farms.

But it is in the tumult of the market place that most trading activity goes on. Only after many days of observing and classifying the actors and their activities does the underlying order become apparent. Sellers of the necessities that peasants come to buy are present each day in a given market place. Perishable foods come and go seasonally, but grains are nearly always available. Prices for different products fluctuate differently, perishables showing the greatest eccentricity, cloth and hardware changing very little from week to week, though perceptibly from season to season. Watching the market place each market day, one sees women dealing in the same goods always clustered together; grain sellers, cornmeal retailers and sellers of spice and sundries arrange themselves in rows. For the seller this permits a quicker check on the day's trade, on one's favored customers, and of course on prices. When sellers of the same stocks are together, the speed with which price is established, and with which it changes during the trading, is increased. Buyers of particular goods come regularly where the sellers are clustered.

Behind the facade of apparently uniform and competitive prices, however, there exists a relationship called *pratique*, in which the retailer gives her favored customers certain concessions in price or quantity or in the terms of credit in return for assurances of the customer's patronage when the market is glutted and prices are low. The retailer also makes *pratique* with her suppliers, thus assuring herself of a stock when certain commodities are scarce. Since *pratique* is a clandestine relationship, it can only be understood by carefully noting the details of many transactions.

Even the casual observer soon notices that the important heavy trade in perishables and the small-scale retailing of imports are carried on entirely by women. Men rarely trade; both sexes believe women are commercially shrewder than men. There are, to be sure, male traders, but with the exception of the peasant who has come to market to sell livestock or craft articles they are almost always townsmen. The peasant woman makes her entrance into the market as a trader on the most modest terms, first as her household's representative in the market, then perhaps with a small stake borrowed from relatives or other traders. In a country where a handful of grain makes a meal and a bit of land a farmer, a few pennies constitute operating capital for the middleman, and what one can carry in one's hands is enough stock to begin trading. If the woman is resourceful she may parlay her small stake in a series of small trading transactions to a sum sufficient to secure her status as a *revendeuse* (literally reseller).

Thousands of these women move from market place to market place, each dealing in small amounts, but together buying and selling vast quantities of stock. They live by connecting centers of supply and demand; their potential profit rests in the price differentials between regions and in their ability to contribute to the value of products by carrying, processing, storing, bulking and breaking bulk. They often render services at incredibly low cost. Thus salt retailers in one market place interpose themselves between truckers and consumers, breaking bulk and retailing salt for earnings that sometimes fall below five cents a day. If these services were not provided, consumers would have to buy in uneconomically large quantities, or truckers would have to sell in uneconomically small ones. The fact that consumers buy from them even though they sit only a few feet from the trucks that bring the salt is proof that the service they sell is worth buying. In their intermediary activities, the *revendeuses* scour remote countrysides. They buy basic commodities at their sources, where they are cheap, because the economic integration of the back country with the national economy is incomplete. Thus, by servicing buyers and sellers both, they help unite the peasant plot and the local market place with national currents of exchange, stabilizing general price levels and contributing to economic growth. The path to success is uncertain, but some few reach the top. The volume of a *revendeuse's* business may approach that of the famous "market mammies" of Nigeria, whose transactions amount to thousands of dollars a year. Though all apparently aspire to become city retailers, women with rural family-attachments incline to remain in the countryside and usually identify themselves with the peasantry.

For transportation from market place to market place the *revendeuses* depend upon the truckers. Demand is not sufficiently firm and centralized to give the truckers bulk cargoes to haul. It is not surprising, therefore, to discover that they are essentially passenger carriers, whose business it is to transport the *revendeuses* and their modest stocks. Trucking is a risky enterprise in a country where roads are few, maintenance facilities are poor and high taxes are levied against fuel and passengers. The trucker is a relatively new figure in the economy. His economic interests are at present firmly identified with those of the *revendeuses* and opposed to the *rentiers*, merchants and officials of the towns and cities. With the *revendeuses* he is against any forces aimed at the restriction and centralization of trade in Haiti. On the other hand, if the growth and evolution of the economy should make it possible for the trucker to profit by bulk transport, this general accord might well vanish.

In such an eventuality the truckers might find themselves allied with the townsmen. The *spéculateurs,* coffee processors, wholesalers and merchants, separately and in combination, all aim to encompass as much of the peasants' economic activity as possible. For although each peasant may be poor, the wealth that changes hands when thousands of peasants shop in the market place is considerable. Successful market places outside the towns constantly tempt the town merchants, particularly cloth- and shoe-sellers, who carry large stocks from their town shops into the country on market day. The townsmen would of course prefer that all peasant trading took place in towns, where markets could be centralized, and the small reseller subjected to more control. To that end they have inspired repeated attempts at restrictive legislation. In this they are joined by the *rentiers,* the value of whose property would appreciate with increase in town trade. The importers and exporters among the city merchants would prefer to see export production rise, even at the cost of subsistence crops.

Officials of the national government are often similarly disposed. Unlike the local governments, which are largely supported by taxes on market-place transactions, the national government derives its revenues chiefly from taxes on imports and exports. Hence the state officials want to see peasant agriculture producing more exportable goods. One could say that their aim is to maximize the peasantry's taxable income.

In the market place one sees the whole structure of official power: police, military, judicial, executive. All market places in Haiti are under some supervision by state officials, who carry on two major and familiar functions: maintaining order and collecting taxes and license fees. At the top this structure is tied to the ministries in the capital; at the bottom it embraces notaries, justices of the peace, soldiery and local political leaders. It is within the market place, in the regulation of concrete economic transactions, that the penetration of political control is seen at its most complete as well as its most trivial. State officials supervise the workers who clean and maintain the market place; they catch and imprison thieves; they stop fights. They are supported by the lowest ranks of political officials, the *chefs de section,* who come from the rural areas to the market place to oversee peasants from their neighborhoods. The peasantry's name for any official, no matter how lowly, is always *l'état.*

Traders are taxed or licensed for taking livestock to market, for butchering, for selling animals, for selling meat, for selling foods of any kind, for selling alcoholic beverages and tobacco, for dealing as intermediaries in all other agricultural products, for tethering beasts of burden and for the stands and sheds they use to display meat and other products for sale. This revenue goes largely to governments of the *arrondissements,* though part is drained off by the national government. Tax revenues are used for the operation of local governments, and to pay for tax collectors' salaries and the administration of the tax system.

Just as the political and commercial elements of the towns seek to centralize and control the markets, so the rural tradesmen seek to maintain the status quo. Their interests dictate a diffuse and open market in which ingenuity and intelligence enable them to compensate for lack of capital, and where they may hope to make the transition from perishable-produce dealers to hard-goods wholesalers or credit merchants.

The contention of these various groups, however, is ultimately intelligible only in terms of the behavior and power of the peasant, whose best interests do not lie decisively in either camp. In determining how he may maximize his cash income by transactions in the market place, he weighs the demand and prices of the domestic market against the opportunities offered by the export market. In striking a balance between the two alternatives he may incline toward the production of export goods to supplement his cash, but he is wary of export-market fluctuations which can deeply affect him and which he cannot control. His choices are not entirely free, for the various factions of the nation, especially those that favor increased production for export, exert considerable pressure upon him. As the source of his cash income, the market places are the peasantry's first line of defense against greater dependence upon the world market and a greater involvement with the officialdom of the state.

Apparently the alignments of interest that may be discerned in the peasant markets today have characterized Haitian society for many years. During the 19th century Haiti's seacoast towns sought to maintain economic hegemony over the inland towns. In the struggles of town merchants against the peasantry, and of the seacoast against the interior, climaxed by the capital's economic dominion over the nation, there are startling parallels with conflicts waged during the growth of capitalism in the nations of Western Europe. In both cases groups with vested economic interests sought to restrict the spread of competitive trading activity.

Thus study of an internal market-system may provide a lively vision of relationships among key economic and political groups in a society. Eventually it may be possible to compare internal market-systems in different societies as total systems, thereby revealing similarities and differences among the societies themselves that might otherwise be difficult to discover.

F. AGRICULTURAL MARKETING

24. Tobacco

J. F. THIGPEN AND A. G. CONOVER

The American farmer markets an average of more than 400 hours of labor in the tobacco he sells from an acre of land. It takes about a minute to examine and bid on that amount of tobacco at auction.

Some 850,000 farm families in 1953 — roughly 1 out of every 7 — in the continental United States and Puerto Rico marketed 2.1 billion pounds of tobacco, grown on 1.7 million acres. More than 90 percent of the tobacco was bought by about 20 major firms and their affiliates.

Americans paid around 5.2 billion dollars at retail for tobacco products in 1953. More than 1.6 billion dollars went for Federal tobacco taxes. Estimated State and municipal taxes amounted to more than 500 million dollars. Payments for transportation, processing and storage of leaf, manufacturing, distribution, imported leaf, and materials other than tobacco amounted to about 2.3 billion dollars. This figure includes profits of those engaged in the marketing process after purchase of leaf tobacco. United States farmers received approximately 800 million dollars from domestic manufacturers for the 1953 crop. In addition, they received around 300 million dollars for tobacco sold for foreign use.

About 25 percent of the United States crop is exported to foreign countries. The remainder is used by United States manufacturers. Foreign tobaccos imported in 1953 for blending with domestic tobaccos totaled about 7 percent of our consumption.

The manufacture of tobacco products of uniform quality depends on careful selection and blending of many different kinds and qualities of tobacco grown in different areas of this country and, for the large bulk of our products, in foreign countries.

Tobacco grown in this country and Puerto Rico is divided under Government standards into 6 major classes covering 26 types and a miscellaneous class covering minor types. Some types are divided into more than 100 grades and qualities. The different classes and types of domestic tobaccos can be grouped into those used primarily for cigarette and pipe and "roll-your-own" mixtures (flue-cured, Burley, and Maryland types); chewing tobacco and snuff (fire-cured and dark air-cured types); and cigars (filler, binder, and wrapper types).

Leaf tobacco is sold on the basis of physical inspection. There are no tobacco exchanges. The market is seasonal. Price information in most areas is that reported by Federal-State tobacco market news service from actual sales of tobacco.

The systems through which United States farmers sell their tobacco include auction markets; "barn door," or country, buying; sales by cooperatives and private dealers after delivery of tobacco by growers; and the "hogshead" market for Maryland tobacco at Baltimore. A substantial part of the cigar wrapper tobacco is grown by cigar manufacturers or under contracts with them.

More than 90 percent of our 1953 tobacco crop was sold on 171 "loose leaf" auction markets. Sales are conducted in

From *Marketing, The Yearbook of Agriculture* (Washington, D.C.: U.S. Department of Agriculture, 1954), pp. 438-46.

large, one-story warehouse buildings with skylights spaced across the roof to provide light. In 1953 there were 940 such warehouses, covering an area of more than 1,000 acres.

Before taking his tobacco to the auction, the farmer sorts it into lots based on color and other factors relating to grade and quality. Each lot of tobacco at the auction warehouse is placed on a separate basket or tray and weighed. A ticket on each basket shows the weight and the name of the grower and includes space for the Government grade, the price bid, and the buyer's grade.

The auction sale usually begins about 9 a.m. Federal inspectors enter the grade of the tobacco on each basket ticket ahead of the auction. The warehouseman, who acts as a commission merchant, makes the starting bid on each basket of tobacco. The auctioneer calls the bids. Usually 6 to 10 buyers participate in each auction sale. The ticket marker records the price bid and the buyer's name and grade on the ticket. Sales usually are made at the rate of 350 to 400 baskets an hour. The farmer can obtain payment for his tobacco at the warehouse office within a few minutes after the auction.

The farmer, who usually observes the sale of his tobacco, has a right — used seldom — to reject the bid on any basket of his tobacco.

About 4 percent of the 1953 tobacco crop was sold at the "barn door," about 2 percent through cooperatives or private dealers after delivery to warehouses by growers, and about 0.2 percent through the Baltimore "hogshead" market.

"Barn door" sales are made by individual negotiation between the farmer and the buyer. If deliveries are made to cooperatives or private dealers, the cooperative or dealer negotiates the sale on behalf of the farmer. On the Baltimore market the tobacco is packed in the hogshead by or for the farmer. Samples, drawn from each hogshead, are displayed by the grower cooperative or the commission merchant. Buyers in-

spect the samples and submit sealed bids. The farmer or his representative may reject the bids.

A farmer who rejects the sale of a basket of tobacco on the auction market runs the risk of a lower bid when it is reoffered. A farmer who rejects an offer for tobacco at the farm runs the risk that he will receive no other offer for some time. Although some growers of cigar tobacco and some Maryland growers hold their crops over from one year to another, to do so generally is not practical. The grower therefore is under pressure to sell at the price offered.

With the development of Federal price-support programs, loans have been made available for the various grades of tobacco at fixed rates. In areas served by the auction markets, a grower usually takes advantage of the loan if the buyer does not bid more than the loan. In other areas the grower usually sells before he knows the loan rates or prices. At best, he can only obtain an indication of the loan rate based on grading of samples. Final grades for loan purposes can be determined only after delivery of the tobacco to designated warehouses where it can be inspected fully.

Each grower who places tobacco under loan usually becomes a member of a grower association, which makes the loans under contract with Commodity Credit Corporation. The association is responsible for having the tobacco processed, packed, and stored, and for its sale. Tobacco placed under loans from the 1951, 1952, and 1953 crops averaged 277 million pounds.

Most tobacco is in a semiperishable condition when it is sold by farmers. Therefore, it must be moved promptly to central plants for handling and processing. Before tobacco can be placed in storage for necessary aging of about 2 years it must contain the right amount of moisture. Air-drying, fermentation, and steam redrying are used to fix the percentage of moisture.

In the steam redrying process, moisture is removed from the leaf and then put back in proper amounts. Steam re-

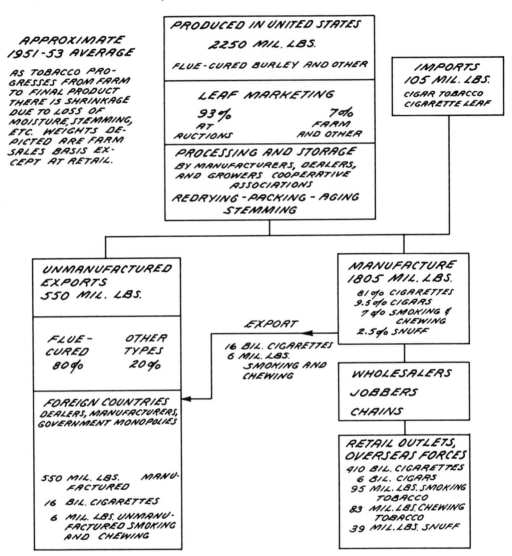

APPROXIMATE
1951-53 AVERAGE

AS TOBACCO PRO-
GRESSES FROM FARM
TO FINAL PRODUCT
THERE IS SHRINKAGE
DUE TO LOSS OF
MOISTURE, STEMMING,
ETC. WEIGHTS DE-
PICTED ARE FARM
SALES BASIS EX-
CEPT AT RETAIL.

PRODUCED IN UNITED STATES
2250 MIL. LBS.
FLUE-CURED BURLEY AND OTHER

LEAF MARKETING
93%   7%
AT   FARM
AUCTIONS   AND OTHER

PROCESSING AND STORAGE
BY MANUFACTURERS, DEALERS,
AND GROWERS COOPERATIVE
ASSOCIATIONS
REDRYING - PACKING - AGING
STEMMING

IMPORTS
105 MIL. LBS.
CIGAR TOBACCO
CIGARETTE LEAF

UNMANUFACTURED
EXPORTS
550 MIL. LBS.

FLUE-   OTHER
CURED   TYPES
80%   20%

FOREIGN COUNTRIES
DEALERS, MANUFACTURERS,
GOVERNMENT MONOPOLIES

550 MIL. LBS.   MANU-
                   FACTURED
16 BIL. CIGARETTES
6   MIL. LBS. UNMANU-
    FACTURED SMOKING
    AND CHEWING

MANUFACTURE
1805 MIL. LBS.
81% CIGARETTES
9.5% CIGARS
7% SMOKING &
    CHEWING
2.5% SNUFF

EXPORT
16 BIL. CIGARETTES
6 MIL. LBS.
SMOKING AND
CHEWING

WHOLESALERS
JOBBERS
CHAINS

RETAIL OUTLETS,
OVERSEAS FORCES
410 BIL. CIGARETTES
6 BIL. CIGARS
95 MIL. LBS. SMOKING
    TOBACCO
83 MIL. LBS. CHEWING
    TOBACCO
39 MIL. LBS. SNUFF

drying machines are used for the cigarette and smoking tobaccos (except for
most Maryland tobacco) and part of the
chewing and snuff tobaccos. Most of the
chewing and snuff tobaccos are air-
dried. Maryland tobacco dries on the
farm and usually is packed as delivered
by farmers. Most of the cigarette, smoking, and chewing and snuff tobaccos after processing are packed in hogsheads
that hold 800 to 1,500 pounds. Cigar leaf
tobaccos are conditioned by fermentation. Nearly all of the cigar tobacco is
packed in bales or boxes weighing 150
to 400 pounds.

Substantial amounts of tobacco used
in the cigarettes in this country are
stemmed at the redrying plants before
being packed for storage. The stems are
not removed from the remainder until
the tobacco is moved forward from storage for manufacture. Tobacco purchased for export usually is not
stemmed before shipment abroad.

The flavor, aroma, and quality of
United States tobaccos are prized in
many countries. United States exports of
tobacco annually range from 450 to 600
million pounds (farm-sales weight).
Tobacco frequently has ranked third

among our agricultural exports. Exports before the Second World War amounted to about one-third of the crop each year. Postwar exports have been a little above the prewar exports, but represent only about one-fourth of the crop, as domestic use has increased much more than exports. About 75 percent of our exported tobacco goes to countries of Western Europe, with small amounts to other European countries, about 15 percent to countries in the Far Pacific and Asia, and about 10 percent to countries in Africa and South America.

The upward trend in smoking of cigarettes of the United States "blended" type and of the English "straight Virginia" (flue-cured) type has made flue-cured the main export tobacco. Average exports of flue-cured at 433 million pounds (farm weight) during the 5 marketing years ending with 1953 were almost 20 percent above the prewar level. The total United States exports for the 5 years, averaging about 530 million pounds, exceeded prewar levels by about 14 percent. Burley exports at around 35 million pounds now equal nearly 3 times the small prewar figure. Dark-fired and air-cured tobaccos have lost ground and exports at around 43 million pounds now average just over half as much as before the war. Exports of cigar wrapper and binder and of Maryland tobacco are larger than before the war.

Foreign markets for United States tobacco in the postwar period have been affected adversely by foreign restrictions imposed primarily to save dollar exchange. Governments of tobacco-importing countries have been loath to reduce total imports because tobacco products are a major source of revenue. This has led them to favor other tobaccos even where preference of their domestic trade is for United States leaf. These policies along with favorable worldwide tobacco prices in recent years have encouraged expansion of tobacco production in foreign producing areas. Consequently, United States to-

bacco faces increasing competition in world markets.

About 93 percent of the tobacco used by American manufacturers is grown in this country. The rest consists of types imported primarily for blending with domestic tobaccos. This country usually ranks second or third among the world's importers. United States imports for consumption in 1953 were 105 million pounds. About three-fourths of United States imports are aromatic (oriental) cigarette tobacco, mainly from Turkey, Greece, and Syria, with smaller imports from several other countries. A fourth is cigar tobacco, mainly from Cuba, with small amounts from the Philippines and Indonesia.

The United States import duties on cigarette leaf and cigar wrapper have been reduced one-half and one-third, respectively, since 1947. A restrictive quota arrangement on Cuban tobacco was eliminated, and its preferential-duty status continued.

More tobacco is manufactured and consumed in the United States than in any other country, both in total quantity and per capita. With only about 6 percent of the world's population, the United States consumes nearly a fourth of the world's tobacco.

The tobacco manufacturing industry can be considered in three broad segments — cigarettes and smoking; cigars; and chewing and snuff. Several companies make more than one product.

More than 98 percent of the cigarette manufacture in the United States is concentrated in six companies. One factor in this concentration probably is the cigarette machine. Highly significant also are heavy investment in inventories of leaf tobacco sufficient for manufacturing requirements for about 2 years and large expenditures for advertising. Labor cost in manufacturing relative to the value of cigarettes is among the lowest for any industry.

Consumer expenditure of about 4.4 billion dollars in 1953 for cigarettes in the United States compared with total expenditures of 5.2 billion dollars for all tobacco products. The Federal Government and 41 State Governments collected about 2 billion dollars in taxes on cigarettes, compared with a total on all tobacco products of about 2.2 billion dollars.

Total output of cigarettes in the United States in 1953 was 423 billion— of which 16 billion were exported. In 1953, daily consumption of cigarettes averaged nearly 10 for each person, 15 years and older—more than twice as many as before the war.

In recent years there has been a steady and substantial gain of the "king size" cigarettes, which are about one-fifth longer and contain about one-sixth more tobacco than the standard size. There also has been a rapid gain in sales of filter tip cigarettes, although they still are a small part of total output.

Cigar manufacturing in the United States has shifted largely from hand to machine processes, but the shift has been slower and less complete than in the case of cigarettes. The greatest difference in mechanization of cigarette and cigar manufacture is the continuous feeding of tobacco and paper through the cigarette machine, whereas each cigar must be made individually through the machine from the leaf for the filler, the leaf for the binder, and the leaf for the wrapper. The output of a cigarette machine is 1,200 to 1,400 a minute. The output of a cigar machine is about 10 to 12.

In 1953, nearly 60 percent of the cigars were made by 8 companies, another 30 percent by some 40 companies, and the rest by a few hundred small firms. The manufacture of cigars employs about 40 percent more workers than does the manufacture of cigarettes.

Consumers spend about 560 million dollars annually for around 6 billion cigars. Around 50 million dollars represent taxes to the Federal Government and to 11 State Governments. Total consumption of cigars in 1953 was about 14 percent above the 1935-1939 average, but consumption per person was down about 5 percent and was only

about two-thirds of the 1925-1929 average.

Smoking tobacco, chewing tobacco, and snuff have been declining in relative importance over a considerable period of years. Output of smoking tobacco in this country in 1953 was 86 million pounds compared with an average of 161 million in 1925-1929. Similar output figures for chewing tobacco are 83 and 197 million pounds. The 1953 output of snuff was 39 million pounds, only a little below the 1925-1929 average. Annual tax receipts from smoking, chewing and snuff are about 20 million dollars.

Historically in this country taxes are levied on cigarettes with rates fixed on a per thousand basis. Taxes on cigars are levied on the basis of variable rates per thousand depending upon the prices at which the cigars are manufactured to retail. Taxes on smoking and chewing tobaccos and snuff are levied with rates fixed on a per pound basis. The current Federal tax rate on cigarettes is $4.00 per thousand. On cigars the rates vary from $2.50 per thousand for those retailing at 2½ cents each or less to $20.00 per thousand on those retailing for more than 20 cents each. On smoking and chewing tobacco and snuff the rate is 10 cents per pound. Taking into account the tobacco contained in the various products the approximate tax rates per pound would be $1.89 on cigarettes, 44 cents on cigars, and 18 cents on smoking, chewing, and snuff combined.

About 250 million pounds of stems and scrap and damaged tobacco which are not suitable or not needed for use in tobacco products are processed annually for use in fertilizers, insecticides, and other products. Some stems from tobacco are used in products in this country and some are exported for use in foreign countries.

Tobacco products are sold through approximately 4,500 wholesalers and more than a million retail outlets. Chain grocery stores and vending machines have become increasingly important channels for consumer purchases.

Part III

Marketing Operations

In Part I we briefly discussed the functional or task approach to the study of marketing. When we speak of marketing functions or tasks we are referring to those operations which are essential for exchange to take place. A consideration of the empirical research of factors influencing the performance of these tasks should lead to a clear understanding of the relationships between these tasks and market performance. Relevant questions are: What is the relationship between a salesman's self-perception and his success as a sales producer? How do the number of salesmen and the frequency of their calls affect sales? How does price and distribution policy affect advertising performance? etc.

To answer these questions and others like them in the fields of personal selling, advertising, sales promotion, pricing, financing, product development, purchasing and physical distribution we present the papers in sections A through H. Some of them report on the relationship between the level of the activity performed and market results and others give insights into the process by which determinations are made of the level at which an activity will be scheduled. In both cases we gain some additional awareness of the strategic considerations involved in making decisions about marketing operations.

The section devoted to research (I) deserves separate notice. Marketing research, best thought of as the data generating activity which produces inputs for marketing decisions, has experienced a manifold increase in interest and level of expenditures in the past decade. There has been an "explosion" in both the rate of increase of new techniques and areas of application; so much so that in the past decade two new journals, *Advertising Research* and *The Journal of Marketing Research*, have been created to disseminate the new materials. The technique areas which have contributed most to the heightened outpouring of valuable methodology and applications are operations research, computer sciences, experimentation, and the general area of behavioral sciences. While the former areas are commonly referred to as being quantitative in nature and the latter as being qualitative, any such division is arbitrary. Much of behavioral-science-oriented research is heavily statistical in nature. Indeed, considerable energy has been expended on computer simulation of human behavior. Our adherence to the qualitative — quantitative distinction is more for organization of material than an attempt to suggest a dichotomy.

A. SELLING

25. The Successful Salesman—As He Sees Himself

WAYNE K. KIRCHNER
AND MARVIN D. DUNNETTE

Personality tests, whether they be administered to salesmen, managers, or clerical help, are the most difficult kind of psychological tests to evaluate because they rely heavily upon the testee's own subjective answers. Though it may be true, under normal circumstances, that a man is the best judge of his own personality, it is a generally known and accepted fact that a job applicant is very likely to give answers on a personality test that will make him "look good."

In these circumstances it is difficult for him to be fully objective and, therefore, truthful in describing himself. He tends to put down what is most socially desirable. Aware of this limitation, psychologists are constantly searching for new approaches to personality testing that will minimize this social desirability factor and virtually force the person being tested to give as objective an answer as possible.

A relatively new approach that is now being used to achieve objective personality testing is the Adjective Checklist.* In this method, the person being tested is given a checklist consisting of 36 groups of five adjectives each. His task is to pick, from each group, the adjective most descriptive of himself and the one least descriptive of himself.

From *Personnel*, Vol. 35, No. 3 (November-December, 1958 (1), pp. 67-70, by permission of the American Management Association.
* The Adjective Checklist is copyrighted by M. D. Dunnette.

The adjectives used in the checklist have been equated statistically in terms of social desirability. (This was done by asking large numbers of people to judge the degree of favorability of a great many adjectives. From these judgments, an index of social desirability was obtained for each one.) In other words, the favorability or unfavorability of each adjective has been determined and expressed in numerical terms.

On the Adjective Checklist, those adjectives found to be most alike in social desirability are grouped together. Here, for example, is one group:

(a) Sturdy
(b) Handsome
(c) Tidy
(d) Intelligent
(e) Cheerful

These are all, obviously, favorable adjectives; their social desirability was found to be approximately the same. It is a difficult enough task for the person being tested to pick, from such a group, the two adjectives which he considers most and least like him. It is even more difficult for him to make himself "look good" on such a test.

ELIMINATING FAKING

Thus, the person being tested is forced to make an objective choice, thereby minimizing the social desirability factor. Consequently, the Adjective

265

Checklist provides a more subtle approach to personality testing than the suspect method of presenting only one list of adjectives to a subject and asking him to check those which best describe himself. In addition to providing a more objective description, the checklist should help, therefore, to minimize faking.

By means of the Adjective Checklist, the tendencies of various groups to make characteristic responses (i.e., to pick certain adjectives as most or least like themselves), can be observed. In the particular study under discussion here, responses to the checklist made by top-notch and less effective salesmen at the Minnesota Mining and Manufacturing Company were analyzed. The purpose was to see if the top-notch salesmen possessed a self-concept different from that possessed by the less effective salesmen. If so, the dif-

ferences could be used to size up sales applicants and to predict their ultimate selling effectiveness.

As part of a large sales research project, over 600 salesmen employed by 3M volunteered to take the series of tests being used to select sales applicants. One part of the study involved the filling out of adjective checklists. At the same time, measures of selling effectiveness were obtained for each salesman from his particular manager. In this way, the top-notch and less effective groups were identified. The two groups were then compared in terms of their answers to the various adjective combinations.

The adjectives selected most often by the top-notch and less effective salesmen as most descriptive and least descriptive of themselves are shown in the accompanying table, from which it will be seen that differences do exist be-

ADJECTIVES THAT DIFFERENTIATE BETWEEN TOP-NOTCH AND LESS EFFECTIVE SALES GROUPS

More Often Picked by Top-notch Salesmen As Most Descriptive	More Often Picked by Less Effective Salesmen As Most Descriptive	More Often Picked by Top-notch Salesmen As Least Descriptive	More Often Picked by Less Effective Salesmen As Least Descriptive
Successful	Unselfish	Scientific	Sharp-witted
Fair-minded	Leisurely	Mechanically	Directive
Uninhibited	Mechanically	inclined	Generous
Persistent	inclined	Original	Pleasure-seeking
Outspoken	Jolly	Reflective	Opportunistic
Opportunistic	Imaginative	Inventive	Clever
Spontaneous	Tough	Complicated	Emotional
Energetic	Tactful	Stolid	Thorough
Orderly	Unexcitable	Interests wide	Quick
Persuasive	Independent	Self-denying	Polished
Sociable	Loyal	Tough	Conventional
Wordy	Sentimental	Versatile	Attractive
Methodical	Unemotional	Tactful	Spunky
Thorough	Capable	Thrifty	Initiative
Unconventional	Musical	Mannerly	Trusting
Planful	Handy	Curious	Alert
Active	Contented	Sentimental	
Confident		Artistic	
Conventional		Reasonable	
Ambitious			
Stern			
Daring			
Competitive			
Excitable			

NOTE: The total number of top-notch salesmen was 86; the total number of less effective salesmen was 44. The less effective group is smaller because salesmen with less than two years' experience were eliminated from the sample as most were rated low in sales effectiveness. This, for the most part, actually reflected age, not ability, and would have tended to bias the sample.

tween the way top-notch salesmen see themselves and the way less effective salesmen see themselves. There are definite distinctions in the adjectives selected by the two groups.

Secondly, there seems to be an underlying logic in the adjectives chosen. For example, the adjectives selected most often by the top-notch salesmen as most descriptive of themselves tend to be adjectives that have the flavor of success about them. Top-notchers see themselves as persistent, thorough, confident, successful, opportunistic, persuasive, ambitious, and so on—all attributes usually believed to be desirable in a salesman. On the other hand, less effective salesmen tend to see themselves as a compound of qualities that, however worthy they may be, seem to have little direct bearing on successful salesmanship.

Some interesting deductions may also be made by comparing the adjectives selected by the two groups as least descriptive of themselves. Thus, the top-notchers do not see themselves as scientific, inventive, mechanically inclined, artistic, and so on. They are doers, rather than thinkers. By contrast, the less effective salesmen seem to shy away from adjectives that indicate resourcefulness, drive, or opportunism.

From these findings, we might form the hypothesis that better salesmen actually tend to see themselves as salesmen, whereas less effective salesmen do not. Logically, this makes good sense. A top-notch salesman *should* be one whose self-concept, or role in life, is focused on selling as a career and, in fact, as a total way of living.

Admittedly, the evidence for this hypothesis is not clear cut and is, at best, speculative. It does, however, tie in well with the idea sociologists have been stressing for years—that people are innately equipped to fit certain roles and that those who find their niche are the most successful.

The fact that better salesmen describe themselves differently from less effective ones and that these differences make sense may prove to be a valuable aid in sizing up new sales applicants and their chances of success in the field. Ultimately, with the checklist used in this study and others that will be derived from it, it may also become possible to provide more objective data on the personalities possessed by successful people in many other occupations.

26. Allocation of Sales Effort in the Lamp Division of the General Electric Company

CLARK WAID, DONALD F. CLARK, AND
RUSSELL L. ACKOFF

One of the authors of this paper was requested by the editor of *Operations Research* to prepare a more technical presentation of a case study he had published in 1955.* This request came shortly after the Conference on Operations-Research Education at The Johns Hopkins University in March of 1956. At this conference the need for *detailed* case histories, rather than highly rational reconstructions of OR projects, was recognized as serious in the field of education. Consequently, at the risk of boring professional analysts, but with the hope of assisting the novice, a detailed case history is presented here. It records the false starts, the blind alleys, and the tentativeness of the conclusions eventually reached. Not even those who worked on the project would do it over in the same way, knowing what they now know. The project raised more questions than it put to rest, but this, we believe, is the essence of scientific progress. Yet it should be pointed out, by way of anticipation, that even the tentative results were better than anything then available to management as a basis for decision making in the area involved. The results were used as recom-

mended and the outcome that was forecast has occurred in the eighteen months during which they have been used.

Publication of history of this sort would not be possible were it not for enlightened management, in this case that of the General Electric Company and of the Lamp Division in particular. We express our sincere appreciation to Mr. Donald Milham, Vice President and General Manager of the Lamp Division, for the encouragement and cooperation he displayed during this study and during preparation of this article.

BACKGROUND

In the summer of 1953 a Task Force was created by the General Manager of the Lamp Division of the General Electric Company to prepare what might be called a "Five-Year Plan" for the Division. The plan that evolved out of this research essentially did five things:

1. Set objectives for each of five years for each class of product.
2. Specified operating procedures by which these objectives should be attained.
3. Determined resources required to attain the objectives using these procedures.
4. Specified a new organizational structure for the Division.
5. Assigned authority and responsi-

From *Operations Research*, Vol. 4, No. 6 (December, 1956), pp. 629-47.
* Russell L. Ackoff, "The Allocation of Sales Effort," *Proceedings* of the Conference on *What Is Operations Research Accomplishing in Industry?* Case Institute of Technology, April, 1955.

bility for various types of decisions and actions required of management.

With slight modifications this plan was put into effect January, 1955.*

As part of the study of resources required it was necessary to determine how many additional salesmen would be required in each of the next five years. The need for additional salesmen grew out of the expanding market and out of the recommended organizational structure. In the new structure, three finished-product departments, each with its own marketing organization, were created. There had previously been only one sales department with each salesman offering all products. The creation of new departments resulted in the splitting of many accounts so that, in the future, salesmen from two or three of the product departments would have to call on the same account.

In order to estimate the number of additional salesmen required it was necessary to assume that the average number of accounts covered by a salesman was optimum. The shortage of time did not permit this assumption to be investigated. As a result, the plan contemplated the acquisition of a very large number of additional salesmen in each of the next five years.

The Task Force felt sufficiently insecure about these requirements to suggest, on completion of its work, that an OR project be initiated to determine the average number of accounts that *should* be assigned to salesmen. The recommendation was accepted. A team was formed, consisting of the three authors, ORVILLE ARMSTRONG (Market Research) and WALTER GLOVER (Finance) from the Division, and ROBERT F. WILSON and SHEILA SPAULDING from

---

* The work of the Task Force is described in "Five-year Planning for an Integrated Operation," by Walter S. Glover and Russell L. Ackoff, *Proceedings* of the Conference on *Case Studies in Operations Research*, Case Institute of Technology, pp. 38-47 (1956).

Case. The Lamp Division members of the team were not relieved of their other responsibilities during the project and so participated on a part-time basis. A management advisory group was formed of representatives from each function of the business. It was directed by MR. WILLIAM E. DAVIDSON (then manager of Sales Operations) to whom the team reported. Meetings were held with this group about once a month for each of the seven months that this study lasted.

FORMULATION OF THE PROBLEM

It seems apparent that a salesman's effectiveness depends on three things:

1. The way he allocates his time to the accounts for which he is sponsible and to prospective accounts.
2. The mixture and number of accounts assigned to him.
3. The personal characteristics of the salesman.

Optimization of sales effort would involve (at least) consideration of these three factors. Because of the limitations of time and funds, however, it seemed impractical to attack the problem on three fronts at once. Consequently attention was directed initially to allocation of the salesman's time to a specified set of accounts. Under the circumstances, findings in such a study would be easier to implement than findings relative to the other two factors. Once the study was begun, however, it was possible to obtain important information about the mixture and number of accounts that should be assigned to a salesman.

THE MEASURE OF EFFECTIVENESS

Ideally, the team would have liked to use as a measure of effectiveness of a salesman's effort the profit obtained from his sales. But since approximately

15,000 different products were involved it was decided to use 'dollar volume of sales per year' (hereafter referred to simply as 'dollar volume') as the measure of effectiveness. It was realized, of course, that increasing a particular salesman's dollar volume might decrease profit if simultaneously the product mix were to change in certain ways. But it seemed that, if average dollar volume of sales per salesman were to increase, total profit very likely would increase as well.

It was also realized that the manufacturing and distribution costs of an item, and hence the profit derived from its sale, depend on the volume and mix of products sold in any particular time period. Therefore, even if it were possible to extract from the books some profit figure for one time period, such a figure would not necessarily be applicable to another time period.

THE MODEL

Once the problem had been formulated and the measure of effectiveness specified, the team addressed itself to the following question: Ideally, how should the problem be solved? This question did not seem difficult to answer. First, one would want to obtain a curve or corresponding mathematical equation that would express the sales volume per customer as a function of sales time spent with that customer. It seemed reasonable to expect that such curves would be 'S' shaped, like a 'learning curve.' The 'plateau' of these 'sales-response curves' would represent the 'saturation' of the account with sales time. In fact, if sales time were increased beyond some 'supersaturation point' it seemed likely that sales volume would decrease: for example, the customer might be antagonized by excessive demands on his time by the salesman.

Thus, since each salesman has only a fixed amount of time available, the problem becomes one of allocating that time

to the accounts (each of which is represented by a sales-response function) in such a way as to maximize his total sales volume.

It was apparent that such curves could not be obtained practicably for *individual* accounts. For one thing, the computation would require data on both sales and salesmen's calls over a period of several years (seasonal and irregular variations make a period of less than one year undependable). For another, even if accessible, a set of thousands of individual curves would not be practicable to apply.

Consequently, a 'practical' revision of the model was made. If it may be assumed that those accounts which react to sales time in the same way can be identified and classified, then each account in the class can be represented by a point, that is, sales volume for a specified year may be plotted against total sales time spent with a customer during that same year. A curve may be fitted to these points to describe the responsiveness of the class of accounts. The nature of the curve anticipated is shown in Fig. 1. It was hoped that a wide enough range of 'time spent' would be found in a class to require little or no extrapolation—only interpolation.

If such a curve were obtainable for each class of accounts, this, then, could be used to represent each account in that class and the optimum allocation of time could be made for each salesman. It would be necessary, of course, to find classes of accounts whose sales-re-

FIGURE 1

VOLUME, TIME CURVE FOR ONE CLASS.

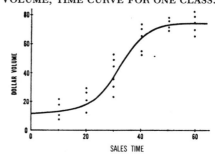

sponse curves were significantly different from each other.

If the slope of the sales-response curves were found to be decreasing monotonically within that range lying between 'reasonable' time per account on the one hand and supersaturation on the other, then it would be possible to employ a very simple iterative procedure yielding an exact optimum to this nonlinear programming problem.

In order to classify accounts a listing has to be made of account characteristics that might affect their responsiveness to sales time. Discussion with management and sales personnel yielded a list of nine possibly pertinent characteristics:

For All Accounts

1. Classes of lamps handled by the customer.
2. Number of customer's employees.
3. Total net sales.

4. Distance from G. E. salesman's office.
5. The population of the community in which the account is located.

For Distributors

6. The number and mix of distributors in the community.
7. Number of distributor's salesmen.
8. Nature of distributor's business (e.g., electrical, hardware, etc.).
9. Percentage of distributor's sales made to retailers.

The district with the best available call data (Sales District A) was selected for a trial research run. To obtain the required data on each characteristic of each of several hundred accounts in the district, it was necessary to go beyond company records. Salesmen in the district were given a set of questions concerning their accounts to which they

FIGURE 2

EXAMPLE OF PLOT OF DOLLAR VOLUME VS. NUMBER OF CALLS

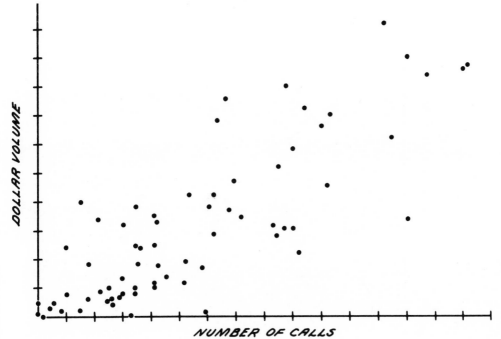

were to get answers by interviewing these accounts.

The sales-call reports which were available did not report the time spent on calls, or in preparation, travel, or waiting. Data available from a study done in 1942 made it clear that different types of accounts required different amounts of time. It was necessary, therefore, to design and conduct a time study of a sample of salesmen. Discussion of this study is deferred because, for reasons that were not known at this stage of the study, the time data were not required for the principal results. They did, however, yield some important side results that will be discussed below.

DATA ANALYSIS

Once all the required data on each account were obtained they were coded and put on an IBM card. It took more than a month, however, to get all the information on each account. In the meantime, what data were available on each account were used in a series of preliminary analyses directed toward obtaining a useful classification of accounts. These analyses may be summarized as follows:

1. First, with the most obvious classification of accounts (by type of business and product involved), annual dollar volumes were plotted against number of calls. The results were very disappointing, as is shown in Figures 2, 3, and 4, which are typical of the plots obtained. More sophisticated classification by use of combinations of characteristics yielded no better results.

2. Sales-response curves were arbitrarily drawn through subsets of points on the plots obtained in 1. Analyses of the characteristics of accounts falling about these curves failed to reveal any significant differences among these arbitrary subclasses of accounts.

3. A grid was superimposed on the plots and averages were determined for

FIGURE 3

EXAMPLE OF PLOT OF DOLLAR VOLUME
VS. NUMBER OF CALLS

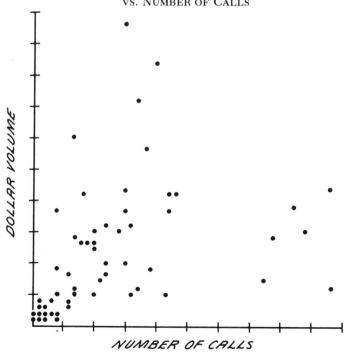

NUMBER OF CALLS

FIGURE 4

EXAMPLE OF PLOT OF DOLLAR VOLUME
VS. NUMBER OF CALLS

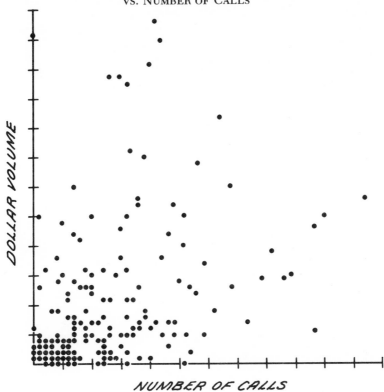

columns and rows, separately and in combination, with the hope that these "average" points would yield sales response curves. But none did.

In all, more than a hundred different plots were made while the complete data were being collected. The effort was fruitless. Once all the data were in and on cards, multiple linear and curvilinear regression analyses were run. Dollar volume was treated as the dependent variable. The only independent variable to which dollar volume was significantly related was number of calls. Not a single account characteristic turned out to be significant. It should be noted that this result did not even prove that increased numbers of calls *cause* increased dollar volume: it might have been that salesmen simply were calling more often on their larger accounts, whether necessary or not.

At first these results seemed to constitute an impasse. Initially only two explanations for the failure to obtain sales-response curves seemed possible:

1. Dollar volume is not affected by the number of calls.
2. The wrong account characteristics had been used.

The first explanation was untenable. Consequently, further attention was given by management, salesmen, and the research team to other possibly significant account characteristics. But this was to no avail.

During this vain effort to "save" the study, another possible explanation of the results obtained broke through to the team's consciousness: accounts were being saturated with sales calls and consequently the data obtained represented random fluctuations about the plateau of the sales-response curves. If this were so, it would follow that changes in numbers of calls per year (in the saturation region) should not be accompanied by changes in dollar volume.

The team set about at once to check this inference. Up to this point only sales and call data for 1953 had been used. Corresponding data for 1954 had just become available. Using both years, changes in dollar volume from 1953 to 1954 were plotted against changes in number of calls for the same years. One of the typical plots obtained is shown in Figure 5. All of the plots appeared equally random. The following hypothesis was then tested: There is no difference in average change in annual dollar volume between accounts that received an increased number of calls in 1954 and those which received a decreased number. Using the F-test, this hypothesis was confirmed for every class of accounts.

The same data were then converted into percentage change in dollar volume and number of calls, separately and in combination, and the same results were obtained.

The team went back to 1952 and made a similar study of 1952 and 1953 with the same results.

In the case of distributors (on whose accounts G.E. salesmen also make calls, i.e., "indirect" calls) the analyses were also made on direct and indirect calls separately; but again with the same results.

Two types of analyses were made in order to determine if the quadrant location of an account (in plots such as that shown in Figure 5 below) could be explained by the characteristics of the accounts as follows and with the results shown:

FIGURE 5

EXAMPLE OF PLOT OF DOLLAR VOLUME CHANGE VS. CHANGE IN NUMBER OF CALLS

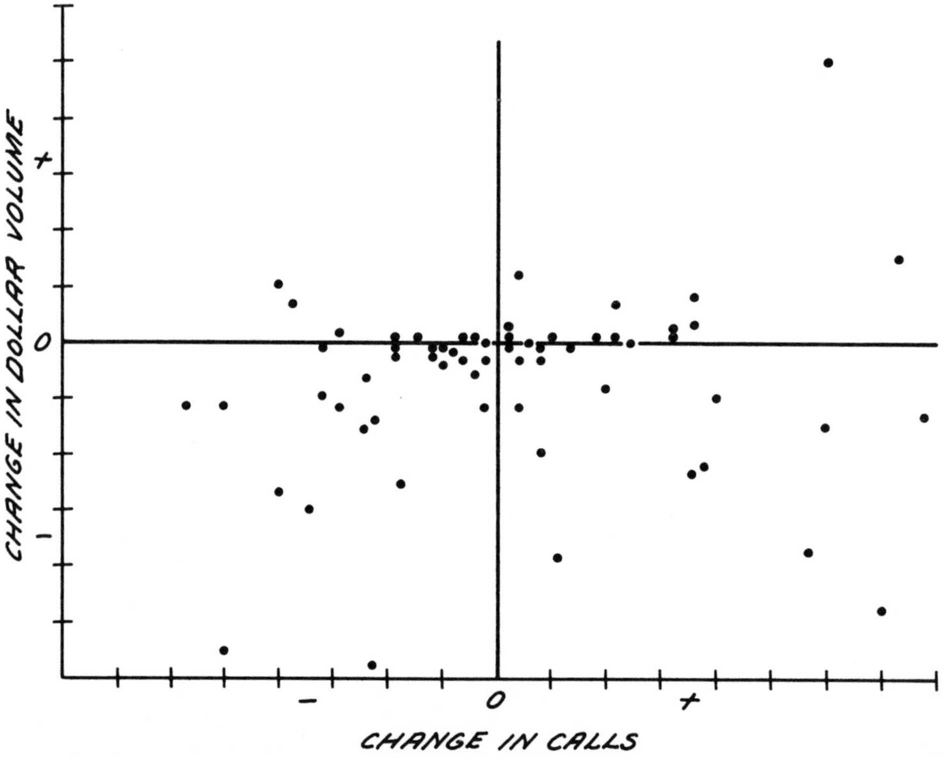

CHANGE IN CALLS

Class	(1)	(2)	(3)	(4)
1952-53	Increase	Increase	Decrease	Decrease
1953-54	Increase	Decrease	Increase	Decrease

1. The average and range of the values of each characteristic for each account in each quadrant were computed. Statistical analyses revealed no significant differences among quadrants with respect to any one or any combination of characteristics.

2. A small sample of salesmen, not aware of the basis of the grouping, was given a list of their accounts grouped by quadrants. They were asked to determine whether or not they could find any way of distinguishing among the groups. Such additional characteristics as the following were considered by the salesmen:

(a) Percentage (salesman's estimate) of customer's potential realized.

(b) Attitude of account's management toward him (rated on a five-point scale).

(c) Attitude of account's salesmen toward him (similarly rated).

(d) Knowledge of account's salesmen of G.E. lamps (also rated on a five-point scale).

Despite this "reaching" for characteristics none could be found that would distinguish among the four groups of accounts.

In a sense, the hypothesis of saturation had been confirmed. But probability and credibility are not always in agreement. In this case they were not. When plots such as the one shown in Figure 5 were shown to salesmen, they refused to accept the conclusion that changes in number of calls over the years shown would not have affected dollar volume. They were prolific with reasons why this was not so for a number of specific accounts, and hence would not accept the conclusion even though it applied to the "average."

A more credible proof had to be found. One was found. It went as follows: first, accounts were classified by whether they had an increase or decrease in number of calls in 1953 as compared with 1952. They were then subclassified by whether they had an increase or decrease in 1954. This yielded four classes of accounts, as shown in the above table.

A statistical analysis was performed to determine whether or not there was a significant change in average dollar volume between classes (1) and (2) and classes (3) and (4). No significant changes were found. The distribution of changes in dollar volume for each of the four classes of accounts is shown in Figure 6. This showed that accounts that received an increase (or decrease) in calls in one year were unaffected on the average by whether or not they received an increase (or decrease) in the succeeding years.

FIGURE 6

DISTRIBUTION OF DOLLAR VOLUME
CHANGE BY CLASS OF ACCOUNT
(DISTRICT A)

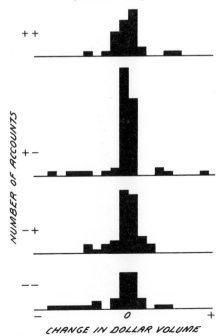

FIGURE 7

DISTRIBUTION OF DOLLAR VOLUME
CHANGE BY CLASS OF ACCOUNT
(DISTRICT B)

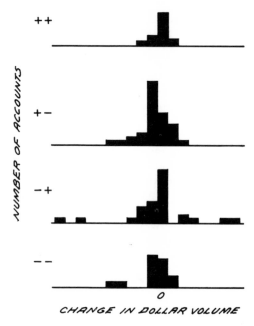

FIGURE 8

DISTRIBUTION OF DOLLAR VOLUME
CHANGE BY CLASS OF ACCOUNT
(DISTRICT C)

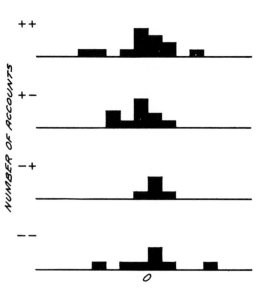

FIGURE 9

DISTRIBUTION OF DOLLAR VOLUME
CHANGE BY CLASS OF ACCOUNT
(COMPOSITE)

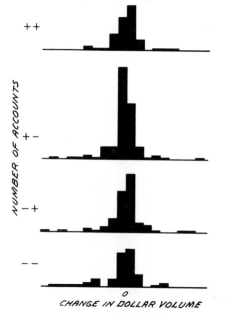

Although this result received reluctant acceptance on the part of some, easy acceptance by others, and rejection by a few, in the main it tended to be accepted. But the results were valid for only one sales district. In order to remedy this situation, corresponding analyses were performed for the other two sales districts for which data were available. The same results were obtained. They are shown in Figures 7 and 8. A composite distribution over the three districts is shown in Figure 9.

CONCLUSIONS DRAWN

What use could be made of these results? The problem of allocation of sales effort among accounts had not been and could not be solved with the available data, and time did not permit the generation of the required data. These results, however, could be used to make a more basic revision of allocation of sales effort than had been expected.

FIGURE 10

DOLLAR RETURN PER CALL
VS. NUMBER OF CONTRACTS

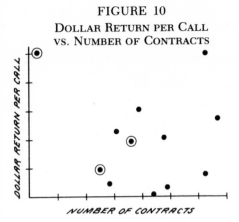

FIGURE 11

TOTAL LIST SALES VS.
NUMBER OF CONTRACTS

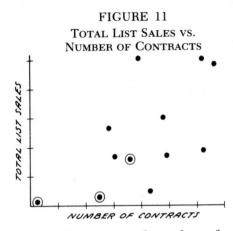

For the three-year period studied, the data indicated that, within the range of change in number of calls on accounts, there was no effect on the average dollar return from these accounts. This suggested that some reduction in number of calls could have been made without reducing sales. How could the amount of this reduction be determined? In other words, how much of a decrease in sales time could have been made without reducing the sales made to these accounts?

The maximum amount of reduction in calls that could be justified by the available data would result from cutting back, for each account, to the smallest yearly number of calls that it had received in the three-year period. If, for example, an account received 60 calls in 1952, 40 in 1953, and 50 in 1954, this rule says that, in 1954, the number of calls could have been cut to 40 for this account. It was assumed that any further cutback in calls would move the account off the sales-response-curve plateau and begin to decrease the dollar return from that account. *In the absence of knowledge* about the shape of the curve for any account, this assumption is a conservative one. A further reduction than this could probably have been made for many accounts without decreasing their dollar volume. The available data supported the hypothesis that the accounts were saturated with calls, but it did not indicate the extent of that saturation

beyond the range of number of calls made in the 1952-54 period.

For the three districts a computation was made of the reduction in calls that would have occurred in 1954 had this rule been followed. The average percentage reduction thus revealed is, unfortunately, a "classified" figure. It was, however, considerably larger than anyone expected. From this figure, it was easy to determine how many accounts, on the average, a salesman could handle, having reduced the indicated number of calls per account. This calculation showed, by generalization from the three sales districts, that the existing sales force was adequate to handle the increased number of accounts resulting from the reorganization of the Division and the anticipated increase in business for the first year of the "Five-Year Plan."

These results raised the question of whether or not heavier assignments to salesmen would affect total dollar return because of sales performance. Of the twelve salesmen in Sales District A, three were already carrying a larger number of accounts than the recommended average. These three were compared with the others with respect to total dollar volume and dollars of sale per call. As can be seen from Figures 10 and 11,* they have not only a higher

---

* The three dots furthest to the right represent the performances of the salesmen with greater than the recommended average number of accounts. The encircled dots represent the performances of

return per call on the average than the other nine salesmen, but also a higher total dollar volume. If these two groups of salesmen are considered to be random samples from the population of salesmen, these differences were not statistically significant. Analysis of the mix of accounts of these three salesmen as compared with the others did not reveal any significant differences.

The results, then, could be used to determine how many salesmen would be required for each of the three new finished lamp departments in each sales area.

CONTROLLING THE SOLUTION

A final approach to the problem was made by examining the relation between changes in number of calls over the three-year period (1952-54) and changes in dollar volume. This analysis ignored 1953; it concerned itself only with the *net* changes between 1952 and 1954. Although no (statistically) significant relation was found, there was some indication that, if a longer time period were taken, one might be discovered; i.e., that there might be a lag in the response of dollar volume to changes in number of calls. Consequently, if the recommended reduction in average number of calls per account were to be adopted, some control or checking procedure was required.

The procedure developed was a simple one, but it required the systematic maintenance of sales-call reports. It consisted of an annual multiple correlation analysis of changes in dollar volume that year with changes in number of calls for each of the preceding ten years. A routine prescription for this control was prepared for company personnel. If a significant correlation were found between dollar volume and separate or combined annual changes in calls, it would reveal any lag in response

personnel who have other responsibilities in addition to selling, and have no particular significance here.

and, hence, start to give data of use in constructing sales-response curves.

RELATED RESEARCH FINDINGS

The data collected made it possible to perform several important analyses on related aspects of sales effort. These are summarized here.

With the cooperation of salesmen in District A, a time study was made of one month's operations. In addition to the regular call report form, the salesmen filled out additional information for each call during the month of June, 1954. For each call the mileage, travel time, waiting time, and interview time were recorded. In addition the amount of "administrative time" in the office was recorded.

The sample thus obtained consisted of only nine from over three hundred salesmen, and for only one month (perhaps not even a typical one). No far-reaching conclusions could be drawn. Nevertheless, some of the patterns and relations were consistent enough in the sample to indicate the probability that they applied rather generally.

Some of the more interesting results were as follows:

1. Travel time was related to distance traveled only within wide limits. A more important factor was apparently the kind of territory. Calls in metropolitan areas consumed much more travel time than might be anticipated; those in "country" territories, much less. The time per call in the sample was almost identical, although the distance traveled per call was twice as great. In fact, the most stable estimate of travel time seemed to be a percentage of the total available time of the salesman, and not the distance traveled. The range of this sample was limited, with few individual calls representing more than 60 miles traveled. A test of a district involving greater distances between accounts was needed to confirm this result, since this result was obtained for a predominantly metropolitan district.

2. Waiting time was apparently an

insignificant proportion of the total, being about six minutes on the average and the same regardless of the type of call being made.

3. Interview time showed a rather stable relation to the type of account called upon. The average times of four major classes of accounts were tested for significance, and the differences were found to be significantly greater among the groups than within them. Differences in salesmen, in location of accounts, or in other characteristics tested did not seem to affect the average call time. These results also required examination by a further sample, and if similar results are found, they should be sufficient to support differences in direct-selling expense among these types of contracts.

4. "Administrative time" was a higher proportion of the total time than expected. However, this was the least reliable of the estimates, since it resulted from a sample of only nine full-time salesmen, whereas the call data came from a sample of over 1,000 calls.

The method of collecting and processing the data was as follows: The cooperation of the salesmen was elicited by a complete explanation of the basic purpose of the analysis. It was emphasized that this study was not a review of their own efficiency. They filled out a daily call report form indicating each call (including office time spent), the elapsed time of each interview, and the mileage. The net mileage and time for each call were computed by subtraction and punched on IBM cards.

RETURN PER SALES CALL BY TYPE OF ACCOUNT

It was possible to estimate the dollars sold per sales call for each type of account. This was equivalent to estimating the cost of sales by type of account, a type of data that had not previously been available to Division management. The cost per call could be estimated, as could the profit derived from a class of accounts. This provided an esti-mate of net return per sales dollar by type of account. Differences in "dollars per call" were as great as 8 to 1 among major account classes, and several hundred to one among minor account classes. These results indicated that the practice of allocating sales cost proportionately to sales (dollar) volume can lead to serious errors. Modification of this accounting procedure was suggested and steps were taken in this direction.

This analysis was extended to include calls on prospects that were converted into accounts. These "realized" prospects were classified in the same way as the accounts, and return per call was determined for both the sum of "before conversion" and "after conversion" calls per year, and "after conversion" calls alone. Two important results were obtained:

1. On the average, new accounts yielded considerably less return per call (in the first year) than old accounts.
2. Certain classes of new accounts, however, yielded more return per call in the first year than certain classes of old accounts.

This indicated that a reallocation of calls from certain types of established accounts to other classes of prospects could be expected to increase the productivity of sales effort.

OPTIMUM NUMBER OF CALLS ON PROSPECTS

The analysis described in the last section suggested the next one. A table was prepared listing the number of prospects and the number of calls made on them over the two-year period, 1952-53. A similar table with "doctored" data is shown in Table I. In the actual data as many as 40 calls had been made on a prospect.

It is clear from these "data" that a policy of a maximum of three calls per prospect yields the maximum return in

TABLE I
DIRECT PROSPECT ANALYSIS[a]

No. of calls	Cumulative no. of accts. obtained	Cumulative no. of prospects dropped	Cumulative totals, no. of calls	No. of calls per conversion
1	30	220	500	16.7
2	50	300	750	15.0
3	65	325	900	13.8
4	70	350	1010	14.4
5	72	370	1090	15.1
6	73	380	1148	15.7

[a] Total number of prospects called on (1952-3) = 500.

number of accounts per call on the average. If this policy has been followed, assuming that additional prospects of the same type could have been found, 248 calls (1148 − 900) would have been made on these prospects. This number of calls would yield an expected (248/13.8) or 18 accounts. The data in the table indicate that these calls obtained only eight (73-65) accounts. The policy of a maximum of three calls per prospect, then, could yield a 14 per cent increase in number of new accounts (from 73 to 83) with the same number of calls. The actual data indicated a possible increase of 11 per cent.

DIVISION OF TIME BETWEEN SALES AND SERVICE

On the call reports maintained in one sales district, several of the salesmen described their activity during the call. These activities were classified as sales (e.g., arranging sales meeting, writing orders, instructing customer's salesmen) or service (e.g., checking billings, taking inventory, changing source of supply). The data were incomplete and could not be assumed to be representative, but nevertheless indicated about an even division of the salesman's time between sales and service.

The appearance of this large percentage of time spent in servicing customers suggested the need for the systematic accumulation of more representative data. If this were substantiated by better data, it would indicate the possibility of having agents less expensive than salesmen perform at least some of the service functions — possibly a service representative working out of the district sales office.

RECOMMENDATIONS AND ACTION TAKEN

The recommendations which were submitted on the basis of this study were the following (as quoted from the final report):

Analyses of data on sales calls and sales volume from a sample of three sales districts showed that within the range of the number of calls currently being made on accounts, variations in the number of calls have no effect on sales volume. Specifically, the study indicated that (assuming the same mixture of sales and service calls) the number of calls required on the average to obtain 1954's volume of business could have been reduced by [X per cent]. Put another way, the average salesman could have carried [X/100 − X) per cent] more accounts in 1954 (an average of [Y]) without having affected the sales volume obtained per account.

This conclusion suggests that the

estimates for additional sales force requirements made by the Task Force be revised down. The present sales force is more than adequate to handle the increased number of accounts created by the reorganization of the Division into three lamp departments with separate sales forces.

In addition to this main result, several subordinate conclusions and recommendations were reached:

A study of the way salesmen spend their time indicates that a significant portion while on duty is not spent with customers. This suggests that additional time can be made available for sales both by decreasing time spent in the office and by more efficient use of this office time in planning sales activity. This study made only on one sales district should be extended to other districts before general conclusions are drawn.

A study of the responsiveness of prospects to calls in one sales district shows that by restricting the number of calls that are made on a prospect to [Z], an 11 per cent increase in the number of new accounts per year can be obtained (assuming that additional equally good prospects are available). This study should also be extended to cover other districts and other years (only 1952 and 1953 were studied).

A study of remarks made concerning the nature of calls made on accounts on a restricted sample of call reports shows that time is about equally divided between sales and service functions. Therefore, it may be possible to separate these functions so that highly skilled salesmen can be used to better advantage. *Before such conclusions could be drawn, a more systematic study would be required.*

The results and recommendations were presented orally to the Management Advisory Group who in turn arranged for their presentation to a large meeting of District Sales Managers. On the basis of these reports several actions were taken. The plan to add to the sales force the number of salesmen recommended by the Task Force was curtailed. District Sales Managers were urged to initiate salesmen-call reports on a regular basis. One of the new finished-product departments instituted call reports as a standard part of the salesman's operations. A new report form was designed by the research team, using the knowledge it had gained during the study. The District Sales Managers were encouraged to take the initiative in carrying out self-analysis along the lines indicated by the study.

At the end of the first year under the five-year plan, sales-volume objectives were met. The annual saving of *not* acquiring the additional number of salesmen originally recommended was approximately 25 times the cost of the study.

27. Selling as a Dyadic Relationship — A New Approach

F.B. EVANS

Very little is known about what takes place when the salesman and his prospect meet. The two parties meet in a highly structured situation, and the outcome of the meeting depends upon the resulting interaction. In this sense, the "sale" is a social situation involving two persons. The interaction of the two persons, in turn, depends upon the economic, social, physical, and personality characteristics of each of them. To understand the process, however, it is necessary to look at both parties to the sale as a dyad,[1] not individually. Specifically the hypothesis is: the sale is a product of the particular dyadic interaction of a given salesman and prospect rather than a result of the individual qualities of either alone. This approach to the selling situation is quite different from the ones typically found in business practice.

THE TRADITIONAL VIEW OF SELLING

Although salesman selection and evaluation cannot be undertaken with any significant degree of certainty (in spite of the large investments made in psychological test procedures), the emphasis in business is still placed upon finding ideal sales types. The salesman

is thought of as outgoing, bluff, hardy, and aggressive.[2] Salesmen, themselves, feel that the stereotype fits. Raymond W. Mack has suggested that salesmen are "money" oriented as opposed to technical people who are "work" oriented.[3] There is very little commitment to the job and no fixed behavior patterns. Mack further suggests that selling is an occupation one enters for status maintenance; a job into which are filtered the sons of managers, professionals, and proprietors who are unable to keep up with the standards set by their fathers.[4] It is also said that unlike many other professions even moderate success in selling depends upon a real liking for the job.[5]

Literally thousands of books and articles have been written about sales techniques but invariably these deal only with the salesman's point of view. Three approaches are common to these works. They are:

1. *The Sales Personality* — what the salesman must be. The salesman must develop a "sales personality" by self-appraisal and self-development.[6] The salesman must be mentally tough but

---

Reprinted from *The American Behavioral Scientist*, Vol. 65, No. 9 (May, 1963), pp. 76-79 by permission of the Publisher, Sage Publications, Inc.
[1] For a general discussion of dyad analysis, see M. W. Riley, *et. al., Sociological Studies in Scale Analysis* (New Brunswick, N.J.: Rutgers University, 1954).

[2] W. K. Kirchner and M. D. Dunnette, "How Salesmen and Technical Men Differ in Describing Themselves," *Personnel Journal,* 37, No. 11 (April, 1959), p. 418.
[3] Raymond W. Mack, Northwestern University, in an unpublished speech, "Who is the Salesman?," 1955.
[4] *Ibid.*
[5] Anne Roc, *The Psychology of Occupations* (New York: John Wiley & Sons, 1956), pp. 178-79.
[6] R. W. Husband, *The Psychology of Successful Selling* (New York: Harper & Brothers, 1953), pp. 260-270.

he must have more tact, diplomacy, and social poise than most other employees. He must be ambitious, self-confident, like people, thrive on responsibility, like to travel and want to be his own boss.[7]

2. *The Persuasive Salesman*—how to persuade or manipulate prospects. Some writers suggest a general approach, for example: a. Establish need for the product. b. Believability. c. Make materials attractive and positive. d. Repetition. e. Offer a variety of products or services.[8] Other writers concentrate on finding different ways to handle the various kinds of prospects. For example: regardless of type, all true prospects will buy from someone. Will it be you? It could be if you will learn to classify prospects and then use the methods, principles, and techniques that will permit you to handle the various prospects in the most profitable manner.[9]

3. The *Adaptable Salesman*—be whatever the prospect wants. For example: the good salesman is a chameleon and likes being one. He must be what the client wants, to make the client feel that he (the salesman) understands him,[10] and, the salesman must find a man's wavelength and tune in.[11]

INTERACTION STUDIES

BUSINESS STUDIES

Two sociological studies have dealt with retail saleswomen and restaurant

waitresses. Both have recognized the importance of the interaction between the client and the salesperson. Lombard studied twenty saleswomen in the children's clothing department of a large department store.[12] He found that salesgirls perceive customers who reject the merchandise as rejecting them and vice versa,[13] that customers in a hurry perceive salesgirls as not being interested in them,[14] and that the salesgirl who feels secure in beliefs about herself perceives the customer as someone who needs help.[15] She feels she has done her best when she helps the customer.

Whyte similarly pointed out the importance of the interaction between the restaurant waitress and her customers, and the waitress and the cook.[16] He found that the behavior of the waitress varies with the social status of the customer she serves.[17] The higher the social status of the restaurant's clientele, the less friendly and personal the waitress must act. The well adjusted waitress did not react to her customer's moods, etc. She controlled her behavior.[18] Whyte also noted, "if the cook and waitress have a fight or if the waitress clashes with her supervisor, then that waitress is likely to take out her aroused feelings on the customer through poor service or discourtesy. . . ."[19]

INTERVIEWING

As opposed to selling, most studies of interviewing in social research have dealt with the interaction problems of interviewer and respondent. The general assumption is that the more freely the information is given the more valid

[7]W. J. Stanton and R. H. Bushkirk, *Management of the Sales Force* (Homewood, Ill.: Richard D. Irwin, 1959), p. 126ff.

[8]W. E. Robinson, President, The Coca-Cola Company, "Fundamental Factors in Persuasion," *Industrial Medicine and Surgery*, June, 1956, pp. 269-72.

[9]J. W. Thompson, "A Strategy of Selling," *Salesmanship*, edited by S. J. Shaw and J. W. Thomson (New York: Henry Holt, 1960), p. 18.

[10]H. J. Leavitt, "Selling and the Social Scientist," *Journal of Business*, XXVII (April, 1954), pp. 41-43.

[11]H. S. Bell, *Championship Selling* (Englewood Cliffs, N.J.: Prentice Hall, 1959), p. 45

[12]George F. F. Lombard, *Behavior in a Selling Group* (Boston: Harvard, 1955).

[13]*Ibid.*, p. 207.

[14]*Ibid.*, p. 209.

[15]*Ibid.*, p. 227

[16]William F. Whyte, *Human Relations in the Restaurant Industry* (New York: McGraw-Hill, 1948).

[17]*Ibid.*, p. 92.

[18]*Ibid.*, p. 109.

[19]*Ibid.*, p. 18.

it is likely to be.[20] Anything that hinders the communication may bias the answers. The fewer such characteristics as age, sociometric status, and education the interviewer and respondent have in common, the more difficult the interview.[21] Similarly the interviewer's role expectations of the interviewee can bias the survey results.[22] The interviewer may record the answers that he thinks the respondent should (wants to) give rather than the correct ones.

The September, 1956 issue of the *American Journal of Sociology* was devoted to the problems of interviewer and respondent interaction. It showed that the relative ages and sex of the respondent and the interviewer affect the answers to questions used.[23] The least inhibited communication took place between young people of the same sex, the most inhibited between people of the same age but different sex.[24] Similarly a study of over 2,400 interviews showed that 90% of the respondents reacted favorably to being interviewed and found pleasure in the relationship and with the interviewer.[25]

It has also been shown that interview results can be biased by many other factors. Hyman has said that excessive social orientation of the interviewer is not conducive to superior performance.[26] In other words, too much rapport with the respondent is as bad as too little. And a study of 40 telephone interviews

showed that the results were biased if the interviewer said "good" after certain answers as opposed to saying "mmhmm."[27]

MEDICINE AND PSYCHOTHERAPY

A doctor's speech and manner are often an important part of his treatment of patients. Many patients are susceptible to *iatrogenicity,* doctor-induced illness.[28] In medical school the prospective doctor is taught the importance of not communicating his own anxieties to the patient.[29] What the doctor says and what the doctor *is* is an important part of the pattern of treatment.[30]

In psychotherapy, communication with the patient *is* the treatment, and every action of the therapist is an important part of the pattern. There is, accordingly, considerable discussion of the interaction situation in the psychoanalytic literature.[31]

OTHER INTERACTION STUDIES

Besides the areas of interviewing and medicine, many other studies in sociology and social psychology have dealt with variables which are important to two-person interaction systems.

It is a common psychological assump-

[20]Mark Benny and Everett C. Hughes, "Of Sociology and the Interview," *American Journal of Sociology,* LXII (September, 1956), p. 139.

[21]Robert L. Kahn and Charles F. Cannell, *The Dynamics of Interviewing* (New York: John Wiley, 1957), p. 11.

[22]Herbert Hyman, *et. al., Interviewing in Social Research* (Chicago: University of Chicago, 1954), pp. 83-117.

[23]Mark Benny, David Reisman, and Shirley A. Star, "Age and Sex in the Interview," *American Journal of Sociology,* LXII (September, 1956), pp. 143-52.

[24]*Ibid.,* p. 152.

[25]Charles F. Cannell and Morris Axelrod, "The Respondent Reports on the Interview," *American Journal of Sociology,* LXII (September, 1956), p. 177.

[26]Hyman, *et. al., op. cit.,* p. 282.

[27]Donald C. Hildam and Roger W. Brown, "Verbal Reinforcement and Interviewer Bias," *Journal of Abnormal and Social Psychology,* 53 (1956), p. 111.

[28]Robert P. Goldman, "Do Doctors Make You Sick?" *Custom and Crises in Communication,* edited by Irving J. Lee (New York: Harper, 1954), pp. 257-61.

[29]Brian Bird, *Talking with Patients* (Philadelphia: J. B. Lippincott, 1955), p. 63.

[30]Fillmore H. Sanford, "Interpersonal Communication" *Industrial Medicine and Surgery,* 25 (June, 1956), pp. 261-65.

[31]Harry Stack Sullivan, *The Psychiatric Interview* (New York: W. W. Norton, 1954); Dominick A. Barbara, "The Value of Non-Verbal Communication in Personality Understanding," *The Journal of Nervous and Mental Diseases,* 123, No. 3 (March, 1956); and H. L. Lennard, *et. al., The Anatomy of Psychotherapy: Systems of Communication and Expectation* (New York: Columbia University, 1960).

tion that the average person will often forego a wanted article if he has to face a negative emotional situation to get it, and if the emotional situation is pleasing and gratifying to him, he is likely to purchase articles which he would not otherwise buy.[32] Homans has pointed out that the more frequent the interaction between people, the stronger in general their affection or liking for one another, provided the relationship is mutually rewarding.[33] Similarly, studies have shown that an individual will prefer to interact with someone like himself rather than different if the interaction situation allows for mutual gain.[34]

Studies of military personnel have shown that there is less intense aggression directed towards an instigator of higher status (rank) than toward one of lower status.[35] And in social case work it has been noted that when the client's problems arouse anxiety in the caseworker, there is a risk that the worker will respond in relation to his own anxiety, and not to the client's needs.[36]

SELLING LIFE INSURANCE

Life insurance selling is considered to be one of the higher types of "creative" selling. It is highly rated among sales occupations. The life insurance agent is better liked and thought to be better trained, more honest, less aggressive, and less high pressured than the automobile or real estate salesman.[37] It is also an occupation where relatively few succeed in the long run; less than a quarter of the new inexperienced agents last through the first four years.

Rarely does the life insurance purchaser seek out either the agent or the company. The agent must locate the prospect and sell him upon his need for (more) insurance. Also, few people discriminate among the major life insurance companies in the United States. The typical view is that all the large companies are equally good and that their prices and services are identical.[38] The particular life insurance agent who contacts a prospect is the critical factor in determining whether or not a sale is made. Little life insurance would be sold without the actions of the salesmen.

DYADIC INTERACTION IN LIFE INSURANCE SELLING

In spite of the recognized importance of the relationship between the life insurance agent and his prospect almost no research has been done which focuses upon them as an interacting pair.[39] A study is now being conducted to examine the interaction situation of particular salesman-prospect dyads. The sample consists of approximately 125 established and successful salesmen and some 500 of their particular prospects, half of whom purchased from the agents and half of whom did not. The analysis will focus upon the dyads, successful outcomes versus unsuccessful outcomes.

The main hypothesis of this study is that the interaction in the dyad determines the results. The more similar the parties in the dyad are, the more likely a favorable outcome, a sale. The areas being studied include the social, economic, physical, personality, and communicative characteristics of both

---

[32]Charles Berg, *The First Interview* (London: George Allen and Unwin, 1955), p. 31.
[33]George C. Homans, *Social Behavior: Its Elementary Forms* (New York: Harcourt, Brace & World, 1961), pp. 186-187.
[34]Selwyn Becker (unpublished research report, Stanford University, 1959).
[35]John W. Thibaut and Henry W. Riecken, "Authoritarianism, Status, and the Communication of Aggression," *Human Relations*, No. 8 (May, 1955), p. 119.
[36]Francis B. Stark, "Barriers to Client-Worker Communication at Intake," *Social Case Work*, XL, No. 4 (April, 1959), p. 183.
[37]R. K. Bain, "The Process of Professionalization: Life Insurance Selling" (unpublished doctoral dissertation, University of Chicago, 1959, p. 342).

[38]Unpublished data, by the writer, 1959.
[39]Research on life insurance selling is commonplace but it has followed the traditional marketing methodologies. *Supra.*

TABLE 1
COMPARISON OF SOLD AND UNSOLD PROSPECTS' RECALL AND
ATTITUDES TOWARDS SALES AGENT WHO CALLED ON THEM

Interaction indicator	Sold (Percentage)	Unsold (Percentage)
Consider salesman a friend	31	6
Consider salesman an expert	67	55
Salesman liked me as a person	78	60
Salesman enjoys his job	95	75
Salesman enjoyed talking to me	98	71
Prospect knew salesman's name	76	32
Would introduce salesman to my business friends	92	78
Would introduce salesman to my social friends	89	79
Salesman represents the best company	20	10
Denied agent's call	0	20
Company A, not represented by salesman, is best	18	17
Total Dyads	(45)	(104)

parties. Also included are the salesman's role and the prospect's view of it, sales techniques, product and company knowledge, and the influence of third parties to the selling situation.

Although this study is only about one-third completed at this time, comparisons of the sold and unsold prospects (alone) indicate the importance of their reactions to the particular salesman who called upon them. Table 1 shows that prospects who purchase insurance know more about the salesman and his company and feel more positively towards them than prospects who do not buy.

The salesmen in this study have shown a high degree of role involvement. Most feel that they are salesmen 24 hours a day, not just for working hours; they feel they work no harder than people with office jobs, and are satisfied with the way their lives have turned out. They enjoy talking to prospects and typically discuss things other than insurance with the prospects.

Half of the agents view their job as being like that of a minister; the other half think it is more like a teacher's. None believe it is like other sales jobs.

They say that they hold the clients' interests higher than either a lawyer or tax accountant does. They do not feel that they are intruders upon the prospect's privacy and they claim not to be personally upset by a prospect's refusal to buy. Also they conform to rigid standards of dress which they think the role requires.

In spite of their role involvement these salesmen exhibited many conflicting attitudes. Less than 10% of them would like to see their sons follow in their footsteps. They claimed that they enjoyed meeting new people, yet over two-thirds of them said they would quit selling if they had to make only cold canvas calls. They feel they need introductions or referrals from past clients. Three-quarters of the agents indicated no interest in the professional C.L.U. degree, nor did they believe it would in any way help their selling.

Although the agents realize that they must please their prospects, they tend to deny the importance of the interpersonal relations. They say that their prospects are the kind of people they'd like to know better as friends, the kind they'd invite to a family party or to their

TABLE 2
INTERNAL PAIR SIMILARITY OF SOLD AND UNSOLD DYADS

Characteristic	Sold Dyads (Percentage)	Unsold Dyads (Percentage)	Total (Percentage)
Salesman same height or taller than Prospect	32	68	100
Salesman shorter than Prospect	28	72	100
Salesman same or better educated than Prospect	35	65	100
Salesman less educated than Prospect	23	77	100
Salesman and Prospect less than nine years apart in age	33	67	100
Salesman and Prospect more than nine years apart in age	25	75	100
Salesman earns same or more than Prospect	33	67	100
Salesman earns less than Prospect	20	80	100
Salesman and Prospect either both smokers or both non-smokers	32	68	100
Salesman and Prospect have different smoking habits	26	74	100
Salesman and Prospect have same religion	32	68	100
Salesman and Prospect have different religions	28	72	100
Salesman and Prospect have same political party	35	65	100
Salesman and Prospect have different political party	27	73	100
Prospect perceives Salesman's religion the same as his own	36	64	100
Prospect perceives Salesman's religion different from his own	28	72	100
Prospect perceives Salesman's political party the same as his own	48	52	100
Prospect perceives Salesman's political party different from his own	20	80	100
Total Dyads	30(45)	70(104)	100(149)

church's picnic. Still they claim that a prospect's age, religion, ethnic background, appearance, or whether he has children makes no difference to them. It seems quite unselective. The agents in the study are all married men with children, and the majority do not smoke.

The agents equate hard work with success. They want to tell the prospect what's best for him. They prefer to call on prospects at home, in the evening, and to talk to them in either the dining room or kitchen. A table is a handy sales tool. Some agents like to have the wife present when the sales presentation is made but most are indifferent on this point. In carrying out his role the salesman believes he knows the expectations and reactions of his prospects. In this he is only partially right.

The agent's training and his job expectations make him believe (or want to believe) that he can sell everyone. The agents tend to deny the importance of their interaction with particular kinds of prospects. However, analysis of the dyads available so far in this study points to the importance of certain similarities between the salesman and his prospect. Table 2 indicates that the successful dyads are more alike internally than the unsuccessful ones. The differences are small, but they are consistent.

The more alike the salesman and his prospect are, the greater the likelihood for a sale. This is true for physical characteristics (age, height), other objective factors (income, religion, education) and variables that may be related to personality factors (politics, smoking). It is also important to note that the perceived similarity for religion and politics is much higher and of greater importance to the sales than the true similarity.

SUMMARY AND CONCLUSION

Life insurance selling is commonly conceived of as depending upon the relationship between the salesman and his prospect yet the salesman-prospect dyad has rarely been studied. The traditional marketing approach to selling has been contrasted with interaction studies in sociology and medicine. Research is now being done on the salesman-prospect dyad. Some early results of this study indicate differences in the ways sold and unsold prospects viewed the particular salesman who called upon them, how the salesman views his role, and differences in pair similarity between sold and unsold dyads. Similarity of attributes within the dyad appears to increase the likelihood of a sale.

Much more basic research into various aspects of the selling situation will be needed before any definitive and practical results may be expected.

B. ADVERTISING

28. Cyclical Behavior of National Advertising*

DAVID M. BLANK

Although annual data on national advertising expenditures do not suggest much cyclical variability, examination of quarterly data shows that advertising is quite responsibe to swings in general business activity. For the postwar period, in fact, conformity between business cycles and cycles in advertising is very close.

There is a general tendency for peaks in national advertising to follow business-cycle peaks by several months, although the amount of this lag has shortened in recent years. On the other hand, troughs in national advertising at cycles seem to have preceded troughs in business in earlier periods, but this response of national advertising to changes in general business activity has slowed somewhat in the most recent period and is now about the same at cycle troughs as at cycle peaks.

The typical length of expansions and contractions in advertising is about the same as that for gross national product.

The expansions in advertising have been perceptibly larger than those in gross national product and in industrial production, except for 1958-60 when advertising increased only about as much as industrial production. Contractions in advertising typically exceed those in gross national product but are more modest than are those in industrial production.

Outdoor advertising and radio spot, whose rates of growth are the smallest of the media under study, have cyclical characteristics most typical of mature, slow-growing industries. On the other hand, network and spot television are characterized by cyclical behavior of the sort associated with rapidly growing industries. The three print media (business papers, magazines, and newspapers), whose rates of growth fall between the other two groups, also have cyclical characteristics that fall between the slow-growing and the fast-growing media.

INTRODUCTION

The advertising industry has reached substantial size; final estimates for 1960 indicate that advertising volume last year approached $12 billion. More interest is continually being evidenced in the economic behavior of this industry, both in terms of long-run and cyclical variability.[1]

There are substantial gaps in our knowledge of this industry, and the data that do exist are of somewhat variable quality. Yet some information concerning major sectors of the industry is available, although surprisingly little

Reprinted from *Journal of Business*, Vol. 35, No. 1 (January, 1962), pp. 14-27, by permission of the University of Chicago Press. Copyright 1962 by the University of Chicago.

* The author wishes to thank his associate, Charles Yang, of the Columbia Broadcasting System, for performing the many laborious calculations that underlie the data shown in this paper.

[1] See, e.g., Martin Gainsbrugh, "Better Economic Indicators for Industry," *The Conference Board Business Record*, February, 1961, p. 26.

TABLE 1
ADVERTISING EXPENDITURES,* 1948-60
(Millions of Dollars)

	1948	1949	1950	1951	1952	1953	1954	1955	1956	1957	1958	1959	1960
Grand total	$4,878	$5,202	$5,710	$6,426	$7,156	$7,755	$8,164	$9,194	$9,905	$10,311	$10,302	$11,255	$11,932
Total national	2,786	2,965	3,257	3,701	4,096	4,521	4,812	5,407	5,926	6,253	6,331	6,835	7,296
Total local	2,092	2,237	2,453	2,725	3,060	3,235	3,352	3,788	3,979	4,057	3,971	4,420	4,636
Business papers	251	248	251	292	365	395	408	446	496	568	525	569	609
Direct mail	689	756	803	924	1,024	1,099	1,202	1,299	1,419	1,471	1,589	1,688	1,830
Magazines	513	493	515	574	616	667	668	729	795	814	767	866	941
Newspapers	1,750	1,916	2,076	2,258	2,473	2,645	2,695	3,088	3,236	3,283	3,193	3,546	3,703
National	394	476	533	549	562	643	635	743	789	810	769	826	836
Local	1,356	1,440	1,542	1,709	1,910	2,002	2,060	2,345	2,447	2,474	2,424	2,720	2,867
Outdoor	132	131	143	149	162	176	187	192	201	199	192	193	203
National	89	88	96	101	109	119	126	130	136	134	129	130	137
Local	43	43	46	49	53	57	61	63	65	65	62	63	66
Radio	562	571	605	606	624	611	559	545	567	618	619	666	668
Network	211	203	196	179	162	141	114	85	61	64	58	44	43
National spot	121	123	136	138	142	146	135	134	161	187	190	206	210
Local	230	245	273	289	321	324	309	326	346	368	372	406	415
Television	15†	58	171	332	454	606	809	1,025	1,207	1,265	1,354	1,494	1,605
Network	7†	29	85	181	256	320	422	540	625	670	709	740	805
National spot	2†	9	31	70	94	146	207	260	329	352	397	486	520
Local	5†	19	55	82	104	141	180	225	253	244	248	267	280
Other media	968	1,030	1,147	1,291	1,438	1,555	1,636	1,870	1,984	2,092	2,064	2,206	2,338
National	509	540	610	693	766	845	894	1,040	1,115	1,184	1,199	1,278	1,364
Local‡	459	490	536	598	672	710	742	830	869	908	864	928	974

* Includes time, space, talent, and production. Figures may not add to totals because of rounding.
† Estimated.
‡ Includes all expenditures on advertising in local farm publications and local advertisers' expenditures on "miscellaneous."
Source: McCann-Erickson estimates, as given in *Printers' Ink*.

analytic work has been done even with this information. In this paper, we shall utilize the available data to examine the cyclical behavior of advertising.

Advertising is usually classified in several ways: first, in terms of the size of the area within which the advertiser sells and, second, in terms of the medium employed. The first classification essentially divides all advertisers into "local" and "national" categories, with retailers being the dominant local advertisers and national manufacturers the dominant national advertisers.[2] The second classification, relating to medium, comprises the various vehicles in which advertising is carried; the major media consist of the print media (newspapers, magazines, business papers), broadcasting (radio and television), outdoor advertising, and direct mail. Several of these media carry both local and national advertising (e.g., newspapers, radio, and television). Others carry only national advertising (e.g., magazines and business papers). Broadcasting is usually described as comprising three forms of advertising: national advertising through networks, national advertising placed directly on local stations (so-called national spot advertising), and local advertising placed on local stations.

ANNUAL VOLUME OF NATIONAL ADVERTISING

Study of the annual volume of advertising yields only modest evidence of any perceptible response of advertising expenditures to cycles in general business activity. At best, we can see only some slowdown in the rate of growth of advertising during three postwar recessions (1948-49, 1953-54, and 1957-58),[3]

most particularly in the 1957-58 recession during which total advertising remained essentially unchanged (Table 1).

When we compare national and local advertising, we find that local advertising has grown somewhat less than national advertising in the postwar period (117 per cent as against 153 per cent between 1948 and 1960), and that local advertising has been more sensitive to business declines than has national advertising.[4] The slowdowns in the rate of growth of local advertising were somewhat greater during the first two recessions, and local advertising actually declined during the third recession while national advertising increased slightly.

Examination of national advertising in eight major media shows somewhat more evidence of cyclical responsiveness than do estimates of aggregate national advertising. These media, which we will later examine in more detail, comprise network and spot television, network and spot radio, newspapers, magazines, outdoor, and business papers (Table 1). National advertising in these media accounted for almost 60 per cent of all national advertising in 1960.[5]

Nearly half these media show actual declines during years of general recession. National advertising in four media—business papers, magazines, outdoor, and network radio—fell during 1949. A fifth medium—radio spot—rose during 1949 but by less than the year before. National advertising in only three media—newspapers and the newborn network and spot television—

have a complete picture of the effect of this recession on advertising.

[4] The more rapid growth of national advertising in the postwar period is undoubtedly related to the decline in the personal sales function associated with the growth of supermarkets, discount houses, and self-service operation in general. These changes have imposed increasingly greater need on the part of manufacturers for pre-selling customers before they even enter retail stores.

[5] The major medium not included in this group is direct mail which accounted for an estimated 23 per cent of national advertising in 1960.

[2] Firms selling over a region larger than a metropolitan area are typically classified as regional advertisers and included within the "national" category.

[3] Throughout this paper, we exclude data for the 1960-61 recession. In view of the typical time lags involved, it will be several months before we can

shows no effects of the recession at all.

During the somewhat milder recession of 1953-54, annual amounts of national advertising fell in only two media—spot radio and newspapers. But national advertising in two other media —business papers and magazines— showed perceptible declines in rates of growth. Only the two television media and outdoor advertising showed no effects of the recession at all. The longer-run decline of radio networks, under the impact of television, was so great in this period that it is difficult to measure the effects of the recession.

In the 1957-58 recession, which was the most severe of the three, four of the media again showed year-to-year declines—business papers, newspapers, magazines and outdoor advertising. A fifth—spot radio—registered some slowdown in its rate of growth. Network radio renewed its long-run decline, after having registered an increase in 1957 for the first time in seven years. Network and spot television, however, showed little obvious effect of the recession; network television registered about the same increase as in 1957, while spot television increased more than in 1957. Both television media, however, had experienced their first major declines in rates of growth in 1957.

Thus, analysis of annual data for individual media shows more evidence of cyclical variability than does analysis of estimates for aggregate advertising. Yet annual data, even of individual media, do not permit a completely adequate portrayal of cyclical behavior. That annual data are inadequate for cyclical analysis is, of course, well known to business-cycle analysts. Despite this fact, however, most studies of the effect of business cycles on advertising still confine themselves to annual data.

The basic reason why annual data are inadequate is that recessions are typically short-lived, averaging about thirteen months for the seven downswings since 1920 (excluding the great depression) and about eleven months for the three completed postwar recessions. Calendar years in which recessions occur usually include some months of expansion, as well as some months of contraction, and always include some months at higher than trough levels and at lower than peak levels. As a result, comparison of succeeding calendar year totals will not show anything like the full amplitude of the cyclical variation of the industry in question. And, indeed, under proper circumstances, the peak or trough year may not even include the peak or trough month or quarter. As a result, timing measures can be completely distorted by the use of annual data.

Accordingly, we have developed data which permit us to study more carefully the cyclical behavior of most national advertising media; the data are seasonally adjusted quarterly figures for these media. Ideally, we should like to work with seasonally adjusted monthly data, but in the present case monthly data cannot be used. The available monthly data are somewhat erratic, even after seasonal adjustment. Presumably this defect could be taken care of by moving averages, say three or more months in duration, but two of the eight series we examined are available only in quarterly form. As a result, we are forced to use neither monthly data nor moving averages of monthly data but instead quarterly data for all series.

QUARTERLY DATA ON NATIONAL ADVERTISING

Five of the eight series—for network radio, newspapers, magazines, business papers, and outdoor—are derived from seasonally adjusted monthly data originally prepared by McCann-Erickson Advertising.[6] Two of the remaining

[6] Through each year, McCann-Erickson develops seasonally adjusted monthly indexes of these and other national advertising media from various kinds of current reports. Sometime after the end of a given year, more complete and more accurate

series—for network and spot television —are derived from gross billings data published by the Television Bureau of Advertising and then seasonally adjusted and corrected for level by use of FCC and McCann-Erickson data.[7]

The last series, that on spot radio, is based on data published by the Station Representatives Association. These data are seasonally adjusted by us.[8]

Close examination of the eight seasonally adjusted quarterly series reveals that one, advertising on radio networks, was subject to such a sharp downward trend throughout most of the postwar period that cyclical variation could not be readily observed. Accordingly, we have excluded this medium from any further analysis. This leaves seven national advertising media that we shall study for varying periods between 1948 and 1960.

---

annual data on these media are obtained. The ratio between the monthly average implicit in the final annual data and the average of the original adjusted monthly data is then used by McCann-Erickson as a correction factor for *each* month in the year. This procedure maintains the original month-to-month movements of the series, but changes the original December-January movement by the full amount of the correction in yearly levels. Yet the original data undoubtedly represent the only valid information available on month-to-month movement of the series in question. Adjusting the December-January change by the full correction for the entire year can, and sometimes does, result in erratic and highly misleading December-January movements. To avoid this unfortunate result, we employed a different correction procedure. We first linked the original monthly series together. We then applied to each month's adjusted index value a correction factor based upon the difference for that month between a twelve-month moving average, graphically interpolated between the final annual values provided by McCann-Erickson, and the twelve-month moving average of the linked index. This procedure results in annual totals approximately equal to the final McCann-Erickson values, yet maintains as closely as possible the original month-to-month movements of the series.

[7] The correction for level was performed in the same manner as for the McCann-Erickson series described in n.6.

[8] The data are corrected for level by the Station Representatives Association; unfortunately, the data do not permit the kind of correction that we have performed on the McCann-Erickson series.

Even these seven cannot be analyzed for the full three-cycle period. Network and spot television grew so rapidly before 1957 that the two earlier postwar recessions left no imprint on them. Quarterly data for spot radio are not available prior to 1955; therefore, study of this series as well is restricted to the last business cycle. Finally, the data for outdoor advertising are suspect for the period before 1956; analysis of this series is also restricted to the last cycle.

The three print media, for which we have adequate data for all three completed postwar cycles, accounted for 40 per cent of all national advertising in 1950 and 34 per cent in 1960. The seven media, for which we have data only for the 1957-60 cycle, accounted for 58 per cent of national advertising in 1960.

The first conclusion which examination of these data provides is that there is close conformity between the general business cycle and this somewhat restricted universe of national advertising (Table 2). Indeed, the three print media show complete conformity with all three cycles and all seven media show complete conformity with the 1957-60 business cycle.

The second general conclusion is that peaks in advertising lag peaks in general business activity (Tables 3 and 4). On average, the seven media lagged the 1957 and 1960 peaks in general business by about one quarter and the three print media lagged the four peaks between 1948 and 1960 also by a quarter.[9]

---

[9] Our aggregate measures throughout are simple unweighted averages of the behavior of the several media. We have tested various summary measures and have found that weighting would make little difference in the results.

The determination of turning points, as always, involves some element of judgment. In general, we have tried to follow National Bureau of Economic Research procedures, including the definition of the last point in a plateau formation as a turning point. For several turning points that appear early in our period of analysis, slightly different dates might have been chosen but our conclusions would have been little affected by such a shift in dating. In several cases toward the end of the period studies, knowledge of the institutional

TABLE 2
CYCLICAL PATTERNS OF ADVERTISING

	Contraction (Peak-Trough)					Expansion (Trough-Peak)				
	Period	Interval in Quarters	Total Change	Average Change per Quarter	No. of Qrs. Lead (−) or Lag (+) at Business Cycle Trough*	Period	Interval in Quarters	Total Change	Average Change per Quarter	No. of Qrs. Lead (−) or Lag (+) at Business Cycle Peak*
1946–48 expansion:										
Business papers						2d qr. '49	N.a.	N.a.	N.a.	+2
Magazines						2d qr. '49	N.a.	N.a.	N.a.	+2
Newspapers						1st qr. '49	N.a.	N.a.	N.a.	+1
Average for all media / Index of conformity†									N.a.	+1.7
1948-53 cycle:										
Business papers	2d qr. '49–3d qr. '49	1	− 6.9%	−6.9%	−1	3d qr. '49–4th qr. '53	17	77.9%	4.9%	+2
Magazines	2d qr. '49–4th qr. '49	2	− 11.4	−5.7	0	4th qr. '49–4th qr. '53	16	49.5	3.1	+2
Newspapers	1st qr. '49–3d qr. '49	2	− 5.8	−2.9	−1	3d qr. '49–3d qr. '53	16	45.1	2.8	+1
Average for all media / Index of conformity†				−5.2% +100	−0.7				3.6% +100	+1.7
1953-57 cycle:										
Business papers	4th qr. '53–3d qr. '54	3	− 2.4%	−0.8%	0	3d qr. '54–3d qr. '57	12	44.2%	3.7%	0
Magazines	4th qr. '53–3d qr. '54	3	− 7.2	−2.4	0	3d qr. '54–4th qr. '57	13	26.4	2.0	+1
Newspapers	3d qr. '53–3d qr. '54	4	− 4.3	−1.1	0	3d qr. '54–3d qr. '57	12	33.1	2.8	0
Outdoor	N.a.	N.a.	N.a.	N.a.		3d qr. '57	N.a.	N.a.	N.a.	0
Radio spot	N.a.	N.a.	N.a.	N.a.		3d qr. '57	N.a.	N.a.	N.a.	0
Television network	N.a.	N.a.	N.a.	N.a.		2d qr. '58	N.a.	N.a.	N.a.	+3
Television spot	N.a.	N.a.	N.a.	N.a.		3d qr. '57	N.a.	N.a.	N.a.	0
Average for all media / Index of conformity†		3.3		−1.4% +100	0		12.3		2.8% +100	+0.7
1957-60 cycle:										
Business papers	3d qr. '57–3d qr. '58	4	−10.1%	−2.5%	+1	3d qr. '58–3d qr. '60	7	17.3%	2.5%	+1
Magazines	4th qr. '57–3d qr. '58	3	− 7.4	−3.7	+1	3d qr. '58–2nd qr. '60	7	28.7	4.1	0
Newspapers	3d qr. '57–1st qr. '58	2	− 9.6	−4.8	−1	1st qr. '58–2nd qr. '60	9	21.7	2.4	0
Outdoor	3d qr. '57–1st qr. '59	6	−15.0	−2.5	+3	1st qr. '59–4th qr. '60	7	16.2	2.3	+2
Radio spot	3d qr. '57–4th qr. '58	5	− 6.7	−1.3	+2	4th qr. '58–4th qr. '60	8	13.7	1.7	+2
Television network	2d qr. '58–3d qr. '58	1	− 0.9	−0.9	+1	3d qr. '58–3d qr. '60	7	20.2	2.5	+1
Television spot	3d qr. '57–1st qr. '58	2	0.0	0.0	−1	1st qr. '58–4th qr. '60	11	50.0	4.5	+2
Average for all media / Index of conformity†		3.3		−2.2% +100	+0.9		8.0		2.9% +100	+1.1

* Business-cycle peaks—fourth quarter, 1948; second quarter, 1953; third quarter, 1957; second quarter, 1960; business-cycle troughs—fourth quarter, 1949; second quarter, 1954; second quarter, 1958.

† + 100 is assigned to each medium for conformity with the business cycle and −100 for non-conformity. "Conformity" is defined as an expansion in general business, or a contraction accompanying a contraction in general business, and vice-versa. "Non-conformity" would involve a contraction in the medium accompany an expansion in general business, and vice-versa.

Source: For business papers, newspapers, magazines, and outdoor, McCann-Erickson indexes, adjusted; for radio spot, station representatives association data, adjusted; for television network and spot, Television Bureau of Advertising data, adjusted.

TABLE 3
Timing of Cycles in National Advertising Media, 1948-60

Medium	No. of Quarters Lag° at Business-Cycle Peaks			No. of Quarters Lag° at Business-Cycle Troughs		
	1957 and 1960 Peaks	1948 and 1953 Peaks	All Four Peaks	1958 Trough	1949 and 1954 Troughs	All Three Troughs
Business papers	0.5	2.0	1.3	1.0	− 0.5	0
Magazines	0.5	2.0	1.3	1.0	0	0.3
Newspapers	0.0	1.0	0.5	1.0	− 0.5	− 0.7
Outdoor	1.0	N.a.	N.a.	3.0	N.a.	N.a.
Radio spot	1.0	N.a.	N.a.	2.0	N.a.	N.a.
Television network	2.0	N.a.	N.a.	1.0	N.a.	N.a.
Television spot	1.0	N.a.	N.a.	− 1.0	N.a.	N.a.
Mean lag, seven media	0.9	N.a.	N.a.	0.9	N.a.	N.a.
Mean lag, three print media	0.3	1.7	1.0	0.3	− 0.3	− 0.1

° From turning points in general business activity.

TABLE 4
Ranking of National Advertising Media by Amount of Lag at Business Cycle Peaks and Troughs, 1948-60

Medium	Rank at Peaks°			Rank at Troughs°		
	1957 and 1960 Peaks	1948 and 1953 Peaks	All Four Peaks	1958 Trough	1949 and 1954 Troughs	All Three Troughs
Business papers	2.5	2.5	2.5	4	1.5	2
Magazines	2.5	2.5	2.5	4	3	3
Newspapers	1	1	1	1.5	1.5	1
Outdoor	5	N.a.	N.a.	7	N.a.	N.a.
Radio spot	5	N.a.	N.a.	6	N.a.	N.a.
Television network	7	N.a.	N.a.	4	N.a.	N.a.
Television spot	5	N.a.	N.a.	1.5	N.a.	N.a.

° Media with shortest lag or longest leads ranked first. When two or more media have the same lag or lead, each is given the median rank of the group. Thus in the first column of the table, two media have the same lag at the last two peaks; these media are therefore tied for the ranks of 2-3. Accordingly, each is given the rank of 2.5.

The behavior of advertising at business-cycle troughs is less clear. The framework of the media in question is necessary for a logical choice of turning points. Thus, the third-quarter 1956 bulge in television network advertising is a function of coverage of the political conventions and has nothing to do with cyclical variation; similarly the drop in the fourth quarter of 1959 in radio spot, newspaper, and outdoor advertising is a function of the 1959 steel strike and the consequent cutback in automobile production and new-model advertising, a type of advertising which bulks large in these three media.

seven media lagged the 1958 trough by almost one quarter, on the average. The three print media, however, led the two cyclical troughs of 1949 and 1954 by 0.3 quarters but lagged the cyclical trough of 1958 by 0.3 quarters on the average. For all three troughs combined, the average lag of the three print media was essentially zero.

There seems to be a clear tendency for the typical time lag at cycle peaks to shorten in recent years. Thus, the three print media averaged a lag of 1.7 quarters in 1948 and 1953, but only 0.3 quarters in 1957 and 1960 (Table 3). On the other hand, the lag at cycle troughs seems to have lengthened over the period under study; in fact, the three print media actually led the cycle troughs in 1949 and 1954 by 0.3 quarters while they lagged in 1958 by about the same amount of time. In the 1957-60 cycle, the three print media had about the same lag at peaks and trough, as did all seven media.

When we turn to examination of the duration of the cycles in national advertising, we find little difference between the three print media and all seven national advertising media in average length of the last contraction and expansion (Tables 5 and 6). The three print media do show some evidence of slightly longer expansion and slightly shorter contractions than industrial pro-

duction in 1948-57, but about the same length as expansions and contractions in gross national product.[10] The three print media and all seven media show about the same duration in their last contraction and in their last expansion, and both show a duration lying somewhere between that for GNP and that for the Federal Reserve Board index.

With regard to the amplitudes of the cycles in national advertising, we find that the total percentage increase in the last expansion and the total percentage decline during the 1957-58 contraction were fairly similar for the three print media and for all seven media combined (Tables 7 and 8). In that most

---

[10] The duration of the last cycle in national advertising, relative to that of earlier cycles, is, of course, a function of the relative durations of the cycles in general business activity.

TABLE 5

DURATION OF CYCLES IN NATIONAL ADVERTISING MEDIA, 1948-60

(In Quarters)

Medium	Duration of Expansions			Duration of Contractions		
	1958-60 Expansion	1949-53 and 1954-57 Expansions	Three Expansions	1957-58 Contraction	1948-49 and 1953-54 Contractions	All Three Contractions
Business papers	7.0	14.5	12.0	4.0	2.0	2.7
Magazines	7.0	14.5	12.0	3.0	3.0	3.0
Newspapers	9.0	14.0	11.7	2.0	2.5	2.3
Outdoor	7.0	N.a.	N.a.	6.0	N.a.	N.a.
Radio spot	8.0	N.a.	N.a.	5.0	N.a.	N.a.
Television network	7.0	N.a.	N.a.	1.0	N.a.	N.a.
Television spot	11.0	N.a.	N.a.	2.0	N.a.	N.a.
Mean duration, seven media	8.0	N.a.	N.a.	3.3	N.a.	N.a.
Mean duration, three print media	7.7	14.3	12.1	3.0	2.5	2.7
Gross national product	9.0	14.5	12.7	2.0	3.0	2.7
Federal Reserve Board index of industrial production	7.0	13.0	11.0	5.0	4.0	4.3

TABLE 6

RANKING OF NATIONAL ADVERTISING MEDIA BY DURATION OF
EXPANSIONS AND CONTRACTIONS, 1948-60

Medium	Rank in Expansions°			Rank in Contractions°		
	1958-60 Expansion	1949-53 and 1954-57 Expansions	All Three Expansions	1957-58 Contractions	1948-49 and 1953-54 Contractions	All Three Contractions
Business papers	5.5	1.5	1.5	3	3	2
Magazines	5.5	1.5	1.5	4	1	1
Newspapers	2	3	3	5.5	2	3
Outdoor	5.5	N.a.	N.a.	1	N.a.	N.a.
Radio spot	3	N.a.	N.a.	2	N.a.	N.a.
Television network	5.5	N.a.	N.a.	7	N.a.	N.a.
Television spot	1	N.a.	N.a.	5.5	N.a.	N.a.

° Media with longest expansions or contractions ranked first. Media tied for the same rank are treated as explained in Table 4, n. °

TABLE 7

PER CENT AMPLITUDE OF CYCLES IN NATIONAL ADVERTISING MEDIA, 1948-60

Medium	1958-60 Expansion		Average of 1949-53 and 1954-57 Expansions		Average of All Three Expansions		1957-58 Contraction*		Average of 1948-49 and 1953-54 Contractions*		Average of All Three Contractions*	
	Total	Per Quarter	Total	Per Quarter	Total	Per Quarter	Total	Per Quarter	Total	Per Quarter	Total	Per Quarter
Business papers	17.3	2.5	61.1	4.3	46.5	3.7	−10.1	−2.5	−4.7	−3.9	−6.5	−3.4
Magazines	28.7	4.1	75.9	2.6	60.1	3.1	−7.4	−3.7	−9.3	−4.0	−8.7	−3.9
Newspapers	21.7	2.4	39.1	2.8	33.3	2.7	−9.6	−4.8	−5.1	−2.0	−6.6	−2.9
Outdoor	16.2	2.3	N.a.	N.a.	N.a.	N.a.	−15.0	−2.5	N.a.	N.a.	N.a.	N.a.
Radio spot	13.7	1.7	N.a.	N.a.	N.a.	N.a.	−6.7	−1.3	N.a.	N.a.	N.a.	N.a.
Television network	20.2	2.5	N.a.	N.a.	N.a.	N.a.	−0.9	−0.9	N.a.	N.a.	N.a.	N.a.
Television spot	50.0	4.5	N.a.	N.a.	N.a.	N.a.	0.0	0.0	N.a.	N.a.	N.a.	N.a.
Mean change, seven media	24.0	2.9	N.a.	N.a.	N.a.	N.a.	−7.1	−2.2	N.a.	N.a.	N.a.	N.a.
Mean change, three print media	22.5	3.0	58.6	3.2	46.6	3.2	−9.0	−3.7	−6.4	−3.3	−7.2	−3.4
Gross national product	16.6	1.8	34.4	2.3	28.4	2.1	−3.6	−1.8	−3.2	−1.3	−3.3	−1.4
Federal Reserve Board Index of Industrial Production	23.5	3.4	33.0	2.5	29.8	2.8	−12.4	−2.5	−8.2	−2.5	−9.6	−2.5

* Minus sign (−) indicates decrease.

TABLE 8

RANKING OF NATIONAL ADVERTISING MEDIA BY PER CENT CHANGE IN
BUSINESS CYCLE EXPANSIONS AND CONTRACTIONS, 1948-60

	Rank in Expansions°			Rank in Contractions†		
Medium	1958-60 Expansion	1949-53 and 1954-57 Expansions	All Three Expansions	1957-58 Contraction	1948-49 and 1953-54 Contractions	All Three Contractions
Business papers	5	2	2	2	3	3
Magazines	2	1	1	4	1	1
Newspapers	3	3	3	3	2	2
Outdoor	6	N.a.	N.a.	1	N.a.	N.a.
Radio spot	7	N.a.	N.a.	5	N.a.	N.a.
Television network	4	N.a.	N.a.	6	N.a.	N.a.
Television spot	1	N.a.	N.a.	7	N.a.	N.a.

° Media with largest total increases per business cycle expansion ranked first. Ties are treated as in Table 4.
† Media with largest total declines per business cycle contraction ranked first. Ties are treated as in Table 4.

recent cycle, national advertising increased about as much as industrial production, during the expansion phase, and about one and one-half times as much as gross national product. During the contraction phase (1957-58), the decline in national advertising was one-half to two-thirds as great as the decline in industrial production and two to three times as great as the decline in gross national product.

The total increase in the three print media in 1958-60 was only about half that experienced in the two preceding expansions, while the total decline in 1957-58 was slightly larger than in the preceding contractions. In these two earlier cycles, expansions in the print media exceeded those in industrial production and total output, while contractions in the print media fell between those in industrial production and total output. In terms of quarterly changes, both the expansions and the contractions in aggregate national advertising were characterized over the entire period by changes of about 2-4 percentage points per quarter.

CYCLICAL BEHAVIOR OF INDIVIDUAL NATIONAL ADVERTISING MEDIA

We can divide the seven national advertising media into three groups, defined in terms of their rates of growth

over the last decade. The two media with the smallest rates of growth were outdoor advertising (43 per cent between 1950 and 1960) and radio spot (50 per cent). The three print media have intermediate rates of growth — newspapers (59 per cent), magazines (82 per cent), and business papers (139 per cent). The two television media — network (847 per cent) and spot (1,545 per cent) — had by far the largest rates of increase over the decade (see Figure 1).

When we classify the media into these groups and examine their cyclical characteristics, we find that cyclical behavior is closely related to rate of growth.[11] Thus, both outdoor advertising and radio-spot experienced relatively short- or medium-length expansions (seven to eight quarters long in each case) and long contractions (five to six quarters long).[12] The total increase during expansions for both media was modest (14-16 per cent), relative to other media. Similarly, the relative amount of decline

[11] For the three print media, our characterization of cyclical behavior relates to all three completed postwar cycles. For the other four media, of course, our characterization relates only to the 1957-60 cycle.

[12] All descriptions of timing, duration, and amplitude as "fast" or "large", etc., are relative to the behavior of other media in the same business-cycle expansions or contractions. Comparisons of the same medium in different cycles will be affected by the lengths or amplitudes of the business cycles themselves.

FIGURE 1

QUARTERLY INDEXES OF NATIONAL ADVERTISING VOLUME IN SELECTED MEDIA AND
INDUSTRIAL PRODUCTION, 1949-60 (BASED ON DATA IN TABLE A, STATISTICAL APPENDIX)

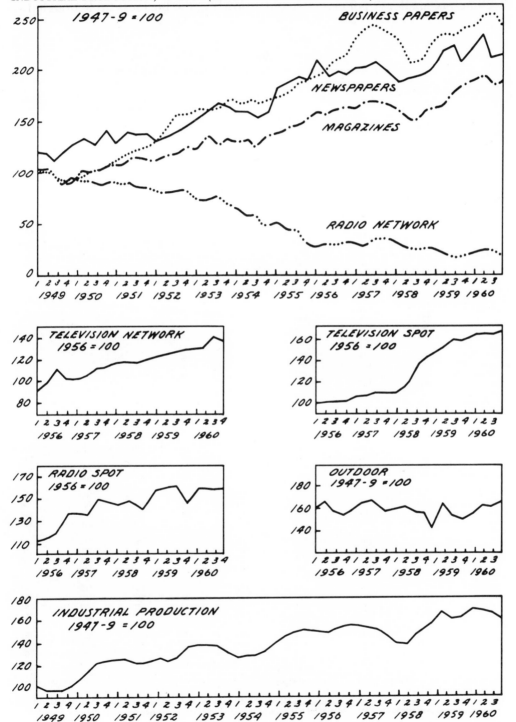

in outdoor advertising during the contraction was substantial (15 per cent). For radio spot, however, the relative decline was smaller (7 per cent). On the other hand, radio spot reacted quickly at the business-cycle peak in 1957 (zero lag), although less quickly in 1960, and slowly at the business-cycle trough (two

STATISTICAL APPENDIX

TABLE A°

QUARTERLY INDEXES OF NATIONAL ADVERTISING VOLUME IN SELECTED MEDIA, 1949-60

Year and Quarter	Business Papers	Magazines	Newspapers	Outdoor	Radio Network	Radio Spot	Television Network	Television Spot
1949:								
1st quarter	102		120		105			
2nd quarter	102	105	119		104			
3rd quarter	95	92	113		91			
4th quarter	96	93	125		98			
1950:								
1st quarter	100	103	132		97			
2nd quarter	103	102	136		98			
3rd quarter	103	104	129		93			
4th quarter	105	105	143		94			
1951:								
1st quarter	113	109	131		93			
2nd quarter	117	110	141		92			
3rd quarter	124	120	139		85			
4th quarter	128	119	140		83			
1952:								
1st quarter	137	119	135		80			
2nd quarter	146	122	139		77			
3rd quarter	157	123	143		78			
4th quarter	157	129	148		79			
1953:								
1st quarter	161	127	154		71			
2nd quarter	161	138	160		69			
3rd quarter	160	131	164		73			
4th quarter	169	139	163		65			
1954:								
1st quarter	165	135	159		62			
2nd quarter	169	137	161		56			
3rd quarter	165	129	157		58			
4th quarter	168	138	161		48			
1955:								
1st quarter	173	139	182		51	98		
2nd quarter	178	146	187		43	101		
3rd quarter	188	148	192		41	99		
4th quarter	190	151	190		31	103		
1956:								
1st quarter	194	159	208	159	28	113	92	99
2nd quarter	203	156	194	166	30	116	98	100
3rd quarter	208	160	198	156	29	121	110	100
4th quarter	212	161	195	152	32	136	101	101
1957:								
1st quarter	226	160	201	157	31	137	100	106
2nd quarter	233	164	202	164	28	136	103	106
3rd quarter	238	164	209	167	34	149	109	108
4th quarter	234	163	201	157	33	146	110	108
1958:								
1st quarter	231	157	189	158	32	143	114	108
2nd quarter	223	152	192	159	29	148	115	116
3rd quarter	214	151	193	155	27	144	114	130
4th quarter	219	160	196	157	26	139	117	137
1959:								
1st quarter	228	161	203	142	27	153	119	142
2nd quarter	234	167	219	163	23	157	120	147
3rd quarter	232	178	223	155	19	159	123	153
4th quarter	238	186	205	149	21	143	125	154
1960:								
1st quarter	240	190	217	153	22	157	126	159
2nd quarter	251	194	230	160	23	158	128	159
3rd quarter	252	184	212	159	23	157	137	157
4th quarter	242	188	214	165	17	158	134	162

° Note: 1947-49 = 100 for business papers, magazines, newspapers, outdoor and radio network; 1955 = 100 for radio spot; 1956 = 100 for television network and television spot.

Sources: For business papers, newspapers, magazines, outdoor and radio network, McCann-Erickson indexes, adjusted; for radio spot, Station Representatives Association data, adjusted; for television network and spot, Television Bureau of Advertising data, adjusted.

quarters lag in 1958). Outdoor advertising reacted slowly at both peak and trough. In general, most of these characteristics are those typically associated with mature industries that are growing relatively slowly.

At the other extreme lie the television networks and television spot. Both of these media have experienced short contractions (one to two quarters) and television spot has been characterized by a long expansion (eleven quarters). Expansions in both media were medium to large in amplitude (20-50 per cent); contractions were relatively small (0-1 per cent). Both networking and spot reacted slowly at peaks (one to two quarters lag) but more quickly at the 1958 trough (one quarter lead to one quarter lag).

In between lie the print media with more diverse experience. Contractions in business papers and magazines were of medium relative duration, while expansions were relatively long.[13]

The amount of expansion in business-paper advertising was relatively small in the last expansion (17 per cent) but fairly standard in earlier expansions (47 per cent average for all three post-war expansions). Magazine advertising experienced a large expansion in 1958-60 (29 per cent) as well as in earlier expansions (60 per cent average for all three). The last completed contraction in business-paper advertising was relatively large (10 per cent), but earlier contrac-

tions were quite mild (6 per cent average for all three recessions). On the other hand, the last contraction in magazines was mild (7 per cent), compared to other media, but the earlier contractions were more severe (9 per cent average for all three).

Newspapers had even more divergent experience, with a relatively long expansion in 1958-60 (nine quarters) but shorter expansions earlier, relative to other media (twelve quarters average for the three expansions). The last contraction in national advertising in newspapers was relatively short (two quarters) but the earlier contractions were fairly standard in length, relative to other media (a little more than two quarters average for all three contractions).

The magnitude of the last expansion in newspaper advertising was close to the average for all media (22 per cent), while the magnitude of the two earlier expansions was somewhat smaller than average (33 per cent for all three combined). All three contractions in national advertising in newspapers were about average for all media (10 per cent in 1957-58 and 7 per cent in all three contractions combined).

Thus, duration and amplitude measures of cyclical advertising behavior tend to conform fairly closely with the rate of growth of the medium under study. Timing measures, on the other hand, seem to be more closely related to the institutional characteristics of the several media, with the three print media tending to react quickly to changes in the business environment and the three broadcast media and outdoor advertising tending to react more slowly.

---

[13] The expansions were seven quarters long in 1958-60 and averaged twelve quarters in all three postwar expansions; the contractions were three to four quarters long in 1957-58 and averaged close to three quarters for all three postwar recessions.

29. How Advertising Performance Depends on Other Marketing Factors[1]

ALFRED A. KUEHN

The budgeting of advertising is frequently discussed as though the
appropriation were independent of
competitive behavior, product characteristics, price, retail distribution, and
the habits of potential customers. An advertising budget is commonly set as a
percentage of past or expected future
sales, in relation to the advertising-to-
sales ratio prevalent in the industry, or,
more recently, by estimating the expenditures required to achieve some desired sales or promotion objective.

Can we be more precise in our budgeting of advertising? Can mathematical
models sharpen our thinking about the
effects of advertising and guide advertising practice? How do consumer product
preferences, price, retail availability,
and costs of production influence the
payoff of advertising for competing
brands of a product? How should advertising appropriations be allocated
throughout the year for seasonal product
classes? This paper will discuss these
questions in some detail. It will outline
results of research which appear to
provide sound guides to advertising and
merchandising policy for low priced,
frequently purchased products distributed through retail grocery and drug
outlets.

MATHEMATICAL MODELS

Mathematical model building has
achieved prominence in recent years as
a means of studying a wide range of
complex problems: the effectiveness of
military weapons systems, the design of
nuclear reactors, production and inventory control in industrial operations,
prediction of voting behavior, and the
routing of vehicular traffic. In most of
these applications, the value of model
building has been demonstrated beyond doubt. In marketing and advertising the use of mathematical models has
generally met with less success, perhaps because of the difficulty model
builders encounter in understanding
the total merchandising system. Moreover, some aspects of marketing appear to be more complicated than the
problems solved by model builders in
other areas of business. This may be
misleading, however, since any problem understood and solved then appears simple.

I am personally convinced that working with models will help us understand
the mechanisms underlying the marketing process and enable us to make
better advertising and merchandising
decisions. A sound foundation of research on the behavior of consumers
and the interaction between merchandising variables is needed, however, to
reach this goal. Care must be taken to
weed out the unstated assumptions from
the hypotheses and factual evidence.
Results which at first appear reasonable

[1] From *Journal of Advertising Research*, Vol. 2,
No. 1 (March, 1962), pp. 2-10. Copyright © 1962
by Advertising Research Foundation, Inc. Based
on an address to the Eighth Biennial Marketing
Institute of the Minnesota Chapter of the American Marketing Association in Minneapolis, November 3, 1961.

are easy to achieve in model building; a more difficult task is to maintain internal consistency and to test the assumptions, implications, and predictions of the model. The latter requires concurrent empirical research. We are not likely to solve many advertising problems by theorizing alone. Nor, in my opinion, are we likely to solve the broader aspects of these problems until we take into account the interaction of a firm's advertising with other marketing factors.

To show how a model can help determine advertising policy, let us examine the budgeting implications of lagged (carry-over) effects of advertising and habitual brand-choice behavior by consumers for the purchase of a seasonal product.

TIMING OF ADVERTISING

Many products have a seasonal demand. Given this condition, how should a firm allocate its advertising appropriation throughout the year? This problem has been studied for low-cost grocery products. Two aspects of the problem appear most significant:

1. *Advertising Carry-over.* An advertising impulse is generally thought to have both immediate and delayed effects. Such evidence as is available suggests that the advertising impulse carries over to the future but decays with the passing of time. The rate of decay appears to vary with the type of advertising, sale-price advertising decaying rapidly, and institutional advertising declining more slowly (see Figure 1).

2. *Habitual Behavior in Customer Choice of Brands.* To what extent do consumers change their brand mix of purchases over time? There appears to be a high probability of a consumer's maintaining a relatively stable mix of brand purchases of grocery products from one month to the next. A study of frozen orange juice purchases indicated a decay rate in a consumer's brand purchase probability of approximately seven per cent per month, or a holdover due to habit, inertia or "brand loyalty" of about 93 per cent per month. This phenomenon is illustrated in Figure 2. Factors influencing the rate of decay include the extent to which consumers even consider buying brands which they do not currently purchase and the

FIGURE 1
CARRY-OVER EFFECTS OF TWO TYPES OF ADVERTISING

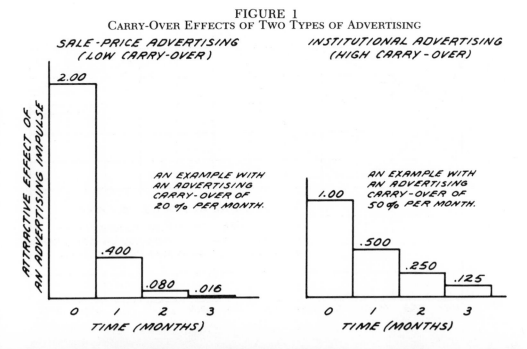

FIGURE 2

Effect of Habitual Buying Behavior upon a Consumer's Choice of Brands

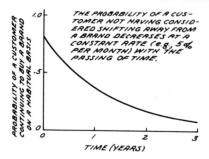

THE PROBABILITY OF A CUSTOMER NOT HAVING CONSIDERED SHIFTING AWAY FROM A BRAND DECREASES AT A CONSTANT RATE (e.g., 5% PER MONTH) WITH THE PASSING OF TIME.

extent to which their evaluation of such products on trial purchases is influenced unfavorably by a predisposition to favor the well-known previously-used brand.

Figure 3 shows a hypothetical seasonal sales curve together with three curves illustrating how firms should advertise in a competitive environment for various levels of advertising carry-over. The first curve shows the "optimal" advertising rate for the case assuming no advertising carry-over, the second assumes a 50 per cent carry-over from month to month, and the third curve assumes a 75 per cent carry-over. In each case it is also assumed that there is a high level of habitual purchasing in the choice of brand from month to month, namely, a 90 per cent holdover due to habit. Note that each of the advertising curves leads the sales curve: the greater the advertising carry-over the more the advertising cycle should lead the sales cycle. Note also that the

FIGURE 3

Optimal Advertising Budgeting at Competitive Equilibrium for a Seasonal Product with High Habitual Purchasing

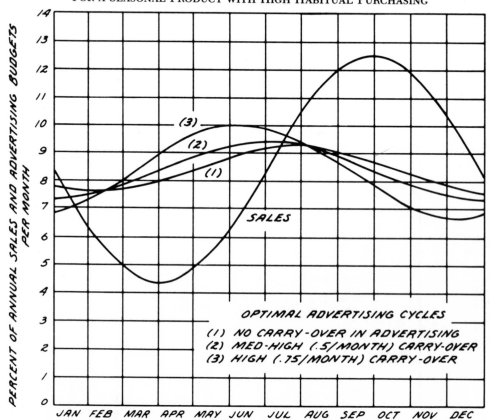

OPTIMAL ADVERTISING CYCLES

(1) NO CARRY-OVER IN ADVERTISING
(2) MED-HIGH (.5/MONTH) CARRY-OVER
(3) HIGH (.75/MONTH) CARRY-OVER

amplitudes of the advertising cycles are very small relative to the sales cycle. Whereas the sales cycle at its peak is three times the level of the trough, the peak-to-trough ratio for the "optimal" advertising response by a firm ranges from 1.25 (when there is no advertising carry-over) to 1.50 (when there is 75 per cent advertising carry-over). The ratio with 50 per cent advertising carry-over is 1.28, very close to that observed for no carry-over.

How can these "optimal" advertising curves help a merchandiser of grocery products budget his advertising? First we should recognize the meaning of the phrase "at competitive equilibrium" used in the title of Figure 3. This phrase reflects the assumption that each competitor in the market is independently budgeting his advertising expenditures at that level which will maximize his profits. This may not be true—perhaps some competitors are trying to maximize share of market, subject to certain profit constraints. If a firm's competitors were not to follow a policy consistent with maximizing profits, we could use the underlying advertising model to compute for the firm an "optimum" reaction to the advertising budgeting behavior established by competitors and, in general, obtain some relative advantage as a result. Only by outlining stated objectives for all competitors as we have done here with the assumption of competitive equilibrium, however, can we abstract generalized rules for advertising budgeting strategy from the model.

The "optimal" budgeting strategy illustrated in Figure 3 suggests that advertising for seasonal, habitually bought products *should* be budgeted relatively uniformly throughout the year, with the peak in advertising coming before the peak in sales. It also shows that these monthly appropriations are insensitive to the level of advertising carry-over in the range of 0 to 50 per cent per month, a range within which most advertising seems to lie.

Six additional assumptions underlie the above and subsequent analyses.

1. *Relationship of Consumer Planning-to-buy and Purchase Periods.* In the case of low-priced grocery and drug products there is apparently no substantial lag between a consumer's planning-to-buy and the actual purchase. Thus there is no need to determine the planning period during which time the consumer might decide upon the brand to be purchased, as distinct from the industry's sales period. This would probably not be true for major household appliances. If the planning period differs from the consumer purchase period, the sales curve should be replaced by a curve reflecting the brand *choice decisions* made in each time period.

2. *Price Level Throughout the Sales Cycle.* Gross margin from sales before advertising is assumed to be constant throughout the year. If it is not, the industry sales cycle should be replaced in the analysis by the cycle of total gross margin potential for the firm, that is, industry sales multiplied by the firm's gross margin apart from advertising.

3. *Effect of Advertising.* The sales cycle used in these analyses is assumed to be consistent with the advertising cycles computed for the industry. If the level of industry advertising influences total industry sales this assumption would be invalid. (However, if we were to know or assume some relationship as to the effect of industry advertising upon industry sales, a solution consistent with such a relationship could easily be computed.) For many established products, at least in the short run, it would appear that advertising has a greater effect in shifting consumers among brands than in influencing the level of total industry sales.

4. *The Influence of Other Merchandising Variables.* It is assumed that product characteristics, retail availability, and price of competing brands maintain a constant relative appeal to consumers throughout the sales cycle. In addition, the effectiveness of each

firm's advertising is assumed to be constant throughout the year.

5. *Influence of Advertising Upon the Retail Trade.* These analyses consider the influences of advertising only on the consumer. Advertising also has a short term effect upon the availability of retail space for special displays. Since advertising intended to influence retailers (including consumer advertising) should be budgeted proportional to current sales, consideration of this aspect of the problem would result in a revised optimal advertising cycle, a weighted combination of the sales cycle and the advertising cycles computed here.

6. *Growth of the Industry.* A stable industry is assumed in these analyses. Growth effects can be added, however, merely by increasing the plotted percentage budget of each month after the initial month by the rate of growth and renormalizing so that the sum of the percentages will again equal 100 per cent.

PRODUCTS WITH NON-HABITUAL BRAND CHOICE

In Figure 4 we see the same sales curve outlined in Figure 3, with three "optimal" advertising curves reflecting no advertising carry-over, 50 per cent

FIGURE 4

OPTIMAL ADVERTISING BUDGETING AT COMPETITIVE EQUILIBRIUM
FOR A SEASONAL PRODUCT WITH NO HABITUAL PURCHASING

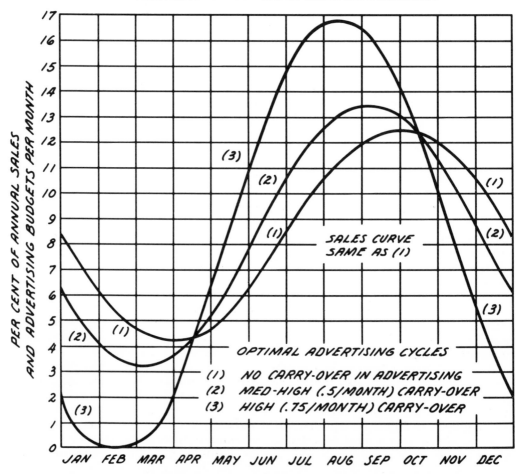

carry-over, and 75 per cent carry-over from month to month. The difference between advertising curves in Figures 3 and 4 results from the assumption in Figure 4 that consumer brand choice is *not* influenced by habit. In the earlier analysis, it was assumed that 90 per cent of each brand's monthly sales reflect a continuation of habitual purchases from the previous month.

For what types of products is habitual brand choice low? Likely candidates are infrequently purchased items with a low level of brand identification, and products which the consumer can to some degree evaluate first-hand. Some industrial goods might also meet these qualifications.

In summary, the optimal advertising cycle under competitive equilibrium is identical to the sales cycle if there is no advertising carry-over and no habitual purchasing of brands. Both advertising carry-over and habitual behavior by customers results in the advertising cycle leading the sales cycle.

Increasing the level of habitual purchasing by brand within a product class serves to *decrease* the amplitude of the "optimal" advertising cycles. In contrast, an *increase* in advertising carry-over results in an *increase* in the seasonal amplitude of advertising.

COSTS, PRICES, QUALITY AND DISTRIBUTION

Many variables influence the profitability of advertising, and thereby the "optimal" level of a firm's advertising appropriation. Some are: manufacturing and shipping costs, price and product characteristics relative to competition, the distribution and advertising expenditures of competitors, the relative effectiveness of each brand's advertising message and choice of media, price and advertising elasticities, and the growth rate of the industry coupled with the rate of return required on investments. Since so many variables influence the value of a firm's advertising, we are fre-

quently on shaky ground when making broad generalizations for the budgeting of advertising. These same considerations also limit the value of certain techniques of market testing advertising.

Since the various elements of marketing activity and consumer behavior are closely entwined, it would seem to be risky to study advertising without incorporating all of these factors into our analysis. This can be done by first building a model of consumer purchasing behavior and the influence of merchandising variables. Such a model might then be evaluated empirically, with respect to both its assumptions and its predictions. In addition, the theoretical implications of the model can be examined. I have attempted to construct such a model, much of which is contained in an earlier paper, "A Model for Budgeting Advertising" (Kuehn, 1961). More recently, the complete model has been incorporated in the Carnegie Management Game and in the C.I.T. Marketing Game for use as an educational tool and in research. The results outlined earlier for seasonality in advertising are included in this model. Similarly, the comments which follow are consistent with it and represent my current understanding of the interaction of advertising with other market variables.

PRICE AND RETAIL AVAILABILITY

Most advertising models ignore price and retail availability. Such models in effect assume price and retail availability to be equal for all brands. They also generally assume that no consumers would be attracted to an unadvertised brand. But we all know of the success of unadvertised brands whose appeal to potential customers is based primarily upon their price and retail availability. Given such assumptions within a model, price and availability would not be likely to appear as variables in the resulting advertising decision rules derived therefrom.

In practice, competing brands do

differ in retail availability. These differences are accentuated when we recognize that shelf space, location and special displays affect brand availability as much as does its mere presence in the retail outlet. There may also be differences in price. How do these factors influence the profitability of advertising?

Sales gain resulting from increased advertising expenditures is generally correlated with the availability of the brand. On the other hand, advertising can be an effective vehicle for obtaining increased distribution, shelf space and special displays. Consequently, we get some insight with respect to the classic problem of where to allocate additional funds for a brand: to areas where it is doing poorly? or to areas in which it is selling well?

Briefly, increased advertising where the brand is relatively strong generally appears to be more profitable in the short run, unless the brand is already near its maximum potential penetration of the consumer market. Expenditures in areas where the brand is weak must generally be looked upon as investment spending directed at obtaining distribution and shelf position. And these activities will succeed only if the balance of the sales program is closely coordinated with them. How frequently has a firm wasted its advertising or promotional budgets by failing to utilize its sales force concurrently to sell the retailer?

In allocating advertising dollars to regional or metropolitan markets, planners frequently must decide whether to allocate extra funds to some areas at the expense of others. Generally, however, they find it difficult to temporarily withdraw funds from areas in which a brand is doing poorly since they see the problem as one of survival. Under such circumstances, *pulsation* in advertising or promotion, coordinated with sales force efforts, offers better prospects of profits and gains in distribution than a continuous dribble of advertising. In many such cases, it would also appear desirable to withdraw funds from some territories to concentrate on others, a result contrary to that suggested by most advertising models. By concentrating on a few markets, a brand frequently has a better chance of forcing distribution and increasing its over-all short term profitability, thereby obtaining the means for subsequent investment expenditures in other territories. It can be expensive to hold one's own in every market simply as a matter of principle, especially if this prevents the brand becoming firmly established and profitable in any one region.

A brand with greater retail availability than its competitors will tend to have a favorable differential in consumer response to its advertising. Such an advantage can generally be translated into a somewhat greater profit differential, all other factors being equal. For example, if one brand in a two-brand market were to have twice the availability of its competitor (i.e., a situation in which the first brand would outsell the second by a 2:1 ratio if price and sales promotion levels were equal), its profitability at competitive equilibrium would be 2½ times that of its comparable rival given an inter-brand price elasticity of four. The relative increase in profits for the first firm under conditions of competitive equilibrium would be a result of increased advertising expenditures by the firm due to its stronger retail distribution.

A decrease in price also improves consumer response to the brand's advertising. However, a reduced unit profit due to the lower price accompanies the increased response to advertising. Thus, only if a firm has lower costs than its competitors should it price below competition at equilibrium. If a brand has both lower costs and certain advantages in terms of basic product attributes, however, it should in most cases apply its added gross margin to increased advertising and sales promotion rather than to price cutting. In general, a brand with *product* advantages as well as *lower* costs would charge a premium *price* under conditions of competitive equilibrium.

COMPETITIVE ADVERTISING

The effect of competitive advertising on a brand's optimal advertising budget depends on the relative strength of the brand's appeal to consumers in terms of its product attributes, price, and retail availability *as well as* on the effectiveness of its advertising story and its choice of media. If all competitors are about equal in these variables, we can easily compute the equilibrium price and advertising-promotion budgets in terms of the number of competitors (N), the industry price and advertising elasticities (η_p and η_a, respectively), the share-of-market price elasticity for brands (ϵ), the cost of manufacturing and distributing the product, and the probability (b_{pda}) of the consumer's brand choice being influenced in part by advertising or promotion:

$$\text{Price/unit} = \text{Cost/unit} \cdot \frac{\eta_p + \epsilon(N-1)}{\eta_p + \epsilon(N-1) - N},$$

and

$$\text{Sales Promotional Expense/unit} =$$
$$\text{Cost/unit} \cdot \frac{\eta_a + b_{pda}(N-1)}{\eta_p + \epsilon(N-1) - N}.$$

The industry price and advertising elasticities in the above expressions are consistent with the use of these concepts by economists. That is, all other factors being held constant, we have

$$D(p,a) = D(p_0,a_0) \left[\frac{p}{p_0}\right]^{-\eta_p} \left[\frac{a}{a_0}\right]^{\eta_a}$$

where $D(p,a)$ = industry demand at price p and advertising-promotion level a, where the industry price is the weighted average price of all brands in the market, each brand's contribution being weighted with respect to its share of market, and $D(p_0,a_0)$ = industry demand at some base price level p_0 and base advertising-promotion level a_0.

Thus an increase in industry price or a decrease in industry advertising expenditures will decrease industry demand. The larger the absolute values of the price and advertising elasticities, η_p and η_a, the greater is the sensitivity of industry demand to changes in industry price and sales promotional expenditures.

The term b_{pda}, which represents the probability of a consumer's choice of a brand being influenced by advertising, has no direct counterpart in economic theory. In effect, at any given time the market can be treated as being divided into two segments; the first contains $(1 - b_{pda}) \cdot 100\%$ of the market and is influenced only by the effects of price, product characteristics and retail availability; the second contains $b_{pda} \cdot 100\%$ of the market and is influenced by advertising *in interaction with* price, product characteristics and availability. Thus if b_{pda} is near 0, advertising will affect only a small portion of the market. But if b_{pda} is near 1, competitive advertising will influence virtually all consumers. Product classes in which the customer either cannot or will not evaluate the brands in terms of their intrinsic merits have high values of b_{pda}. This reflects the ability of advertising to project status, confidence, or other desirable attributes to the product.

The share of market price elasticity (ϵ) for brands also deviates from the economists' treatment of cross-product elasticity except in certain limiting cases. As noted in the above discussion of advertising, price has influence in both market segments. In each segment, the relative attraction of each brand in terms of the combined effects of product characteristics, retail availability and, in the b_{pda} segment, advertising appeals, is modified (multiplied) by its relative price appeal computed as $\frac{p_i^{-\epsilon}}{\Sigma\, p_i^{-\epsilon}}$. This might be thought of as "share of price appeal," the numerator being the brand's price taken to the negative power of the share of market elasticity, the denominator being the same term summed over all brands. Note that an increase in the price of a brand, all other brands holding price constant, will reduce its share of market. The greater the elasticity ϵ, the higher the brand shifting sensitivity of the market to the relative prices of competing brands.

The share of market price elasticity generally ranges between three and six, while the industry price elasticity is on the order of two or less. It follows that the equilibrium relationships indicated above suggest two things. First, the industry equilibrium level for pricing and promotional expenditures is much more sensitive to ϵ than to η_p. Second, the industry price elasticity plays a minor role in determining prevailing prices when several firms are competing in the market. Similarly, the effect of advertising on brand shifting, represented by b_{pda} ranging from 0 to 1, generally tends to influence prevailing industry advertising levels for mature products more than does the industry advertising elasticity η_a, whose value is frequently on the order of $\frac{1}{10}$.

In practice, individual competitors might be expected to deviate from these competitive equilibrium values, either because of goals other than profit maximization, the lack of price competition, or because of the absence of sound guides for implementing an appropriate budgeting policy. To evaluate the implications of such deviations from profit maximizing behavior by competitors, let us consider two promotional counterstrategies suggested by the decision rules derived from the merchandising model:

1. *Sub-optimal Advertising Expenditures by Competitors.* If all members of an industry are about equal with respect to operating costs, product appeal, retail distribution and promotional effectiveness, and if one's competitors *underspend* on advertising and other forms of sales promotion, then the firm could increase its profit by also spending less than the equilibrium rate. The optimal size of its reduction would be *less*, how-

ever, than that of the firm or firms initiating the underspending.

2. *Excessive Advertising Expenditures by Competitors.* If a firm's brand is equal in costs product quality, distribution, and advertising effectiveness to its competitors, and the latter *overspend* on advertising, the firm could increase its profit by reducing its expenditures below equilibrium. To do so, however, would also increase the competitors' profits and, on balance, competition would gain a relative advantage. Consequently it may be desirable here to compete with overspending by also overspending, reducing the profitability of the industry at least temporarily, but hopefully bringing one's competitors to their senses.

Note that a firm operating at a competitive disadvantage in terms of costs or product appeal cannot easily counter competitive overspending with an increased advertising budget. The weaker firm tends to be at the mercy of its stronger competitor. Insofar as the stronger firm is willing to absorb some reduction in profit, it can keep a weaker competitor "on the ropes" by overspending, or by engaging in more advertising research to improve its promotional effectiveness. If the weaker firm counters by overspending, it helps dig its own grave. Interestingly enough, the share of market held by a firm does not necessarily indicate its competitive strength. Under many conditions the model suggests that the stronger firm, to maximize its profits, should permit its weaker rivals to maintain a significant share of the market. The underdog position of the rivals is, however, fully apparent when profits are compared.

SUMMARY AND CONCLUSIONS

The above model decision rules do not make decision-making easy or contradict our thinking about optimal strategy. Instead, they quantify relationships generally discussed only in qualitative terms. By making explicit our assumptions about market behavior and examining their consequences, we can test and thereby understand advertising phenomena. The use of such models does not eliminate the need for managerial judgment, but rather assists it by providing a new set of reference points.

The model from which these results were derived is relatively complex when viewed in its entirety. This research was begun some seven years ago with a very simple model—a model which has been modified and extended repeatedly in the light of additional evidence. As a result of these experiences, I now feel reasonably confident that a very simple model cannot hope to portray the intricacies of marketing processes. This is not to say that we cannot gain insight from simple models, but rather that we must be very careful that the factors these models ignore do not have a large effect upon the specific problem being studied. Only rarely do we get sound decisions from a model whose assumptions are not in tune with reality.

Because of the complexities of consumer behavior and the merchandising process, it is difficult to state widely applicable marketing decision rules for the guidance of management. The simplicity of the above solution for the seasonality of advertising budgets, for example, holds only when there is stability in the relative distribution, product attractiveness, and price of competing brands. And the effectiveness of each brand's advertising message and choice of media must be constant throughout the year. When these conditions are not met, we can still determine a firm's optimal budget in terms of the expected changes in these variables, but the results cannot be easily generalized. To date we have not been able to derive simple equilibrium decision rules for market situations in which there are more than two types of firms, that is, n_1 brands having one set of product, cost and distribution characteristics, and n_2 brands each

having another common set of characteristics. The generalized rules available to us today are of limited value in practice. They serve to outline the broad aspects of the problem but, to solve any specific marketing problem, we must revert to the underlying detailed model.

What about the limitations of the model? First, there are difficulties in estimating some of the parameters and variables of the model. For example, it is not clear that we will ever be able to estimate very adequately the industry advertising and price elasticities. This being the case, we cannot make much practical use of the model in what appears to most marketing executives to be the simplest type of market—the situation in which a single brand virtually controls an entire product class. Our inability to estimate these parameters precisely is not a problem, however, in studying markets with multiple brand entries. Here the industry elasticities have only a very minor influence upon optimal merchandising decisions.

We must reckon with other inadequacies in the model. For example, we know little of the effect of advertising and sales force activity, along with the brand's share of market, in obtaining retail distribution and shelf space for a brand. The problem is accentuated by the fact that we do not yet have a good measure of the effects of display space and location upon retail sales. I have attempted to make plausible assumptions, where necessary, to incorporate these aspects of the marketing process into the C.I.T. Marketing Game. Future research, both empirical field studies and analyses within the framework of this game, should enable us to evaluate these relationships and incorporate improvements into the model. Such untested portions of the model require us to exercise extreme care in its application.

The model cannot be used mechanically. Analyses of the sensitivity of decisions to the untested assumptions are generally required. In some instances, these gaps in the model can be filled by management's judgmental estimates. This is often feasible because management is required to estimate only competitive ratios (e.g., the effectiveness of our advertising copy relative to that of competition) rather than absolute levels.

An interesting sidelight of this research is its implications for the field testing of advertising campaigns. It suggests that controlled market by market testing contains a variety of pitfalls. For example, it is *not sufficient* that we "control" market conditions throughout the period of the test, assuming that such control is in fact possible. We must also know the *level* at which each of the variables is being controlled. This suggests, as a minimum, that we would have to match territories.

A more promising approach is to build a model of the marketing process, obtain the needed market measures through continuous monitoring, and evaluate these market activity data regularly by estimating the parameters required to determine the effectiveness of competitive strategy. Is this far in the future? I don't think so. Will the costs of monitoring the market be too high? Not once we know how to use these data in developing improved marketing decisions.

Models will grow in importance as guides to marketing management. They will not, however, take over management's role, or preclude creative approaches to merchandising. All they can do is help direct management toward better use of the firm's resources. The ultimate success of a brand will still depend upon how well its total marketing program meets the physical and phychological needs of the consumer.

REFERENCE

Kuehn, Alfred A. A Model for Budgeting Advertising. In *Mathematical Models and Methods in Marketing* (Bass, Frank M. et al., Editors). Homewood, Illinois: Richard D. Irwin, Inc., 1961.

30. Radio Advertising

JAMES L. PALMER

A study of the use of radio as an advertising medium, made in October and November, 1927, revealed a number of interesting facts. The study was confined to metropolitan Chicago and consisted of one thousand personal interviews with owners of radio receiving sets. The objectives were to obtain facts about the size of the radio audience, about its attitude toward the use of radio for advertising, about its entertainment likes and dislikes, and about listening habits.

Following are the important conclusions reached through the study:

1. During the autumn of 1927 the largest number of radio sets was in operation daily between seven and nine o'clock in the evening. The peak was reached between eight and nine.

2. The number of sets in operation before seven and after nine in the evening was considerably less than between seven and nine — at least 25 per cent less. The hour between nine and ten had a somewhat larger listening audience than the hour between six and seven.

3. The radio audience reached its largest size between seven-thirty and eight-thirty in the evening. Approximately 60 per cent of all the receiving sets in Chicago were in use daily during this hour.

4. In the autumn months the average receiving set was in use between three and four hours a day. The average was slightly higher in midwinter and much lower in midsummer.

5. The total volume of radio listening in midsummer was about one-half that in the late autumn. It was about one-third more in midwinter than in the late autumn.

6. In the evening hours the average number of listeners per family slightly exceeded three. At all other times of day it slightly exceeded one.

7. Programs of national advertisers which were of high quality and which had been carried on over a long period of time had a large following among listeners. This applied both to classical and to so-called popular programs.

8. A substantial number of local Chicago programs classifying as stations features had a following which compared favorably with the best programs of national advertisers broadcasting over chains.

9. The great majority of listeners in Chicago owned multi-tube sets of one of twenty-five makes.

10. Four broadcasting stations in Chicago ranked far ahead of all others as advertising media. All others either had a scattered following throughout the city or confined their influence entirely to local groups of listeners. Each leading station appealed to all classes of listeners. No station had built up a large class following.

Reprinted from Journal of Business, Vol. I, No. 4 (1928), pp. 495-96, by permission of the University of Chicago Press. Copyright 1928 by the University of Chicago.

11. Sport events and musical programs far outranked all other types in popularity with all classes of listeners. Classical music compared very favorably with lighter forms of entertainment in popularity.

12. Listeners were about evenly divided between those who preferred local Chicago programs and those who preferred chain broadcasts originating in New York.

13. There was no appreciable body of sentiment opposed to the publicity or radio-hour type of advertising when programs were of high quality and the advertising factor was kept in the background.

14. There was strong sentiment against the use of radio for selling or shopping talks. This type of advertising nevertheless had a fairly substantial following among listeners.

15. Both the publicity and shopping talk types of radio advertising had directly influenced the purchasing of a considerable number of listeners.

C. SALES PROMOTION

31. Sales Promotion Decisions

EDWIN H. LEWIS

Those who have goods or services to sell may reach potential buyers in several ways. They may sell their products through a sales organization, either one in their own employ or under the control of an agent; the several customary advertising media may be used, or the seller may use some other promotional device such as a demonstrator or a trade show. These different methods of contracting prospective customers comprise the marketing activity known as sales promotion.[1]

Since several forms of promotion are available to sellers, it becomes necessary for them to choose the specific methods which will be used and to determine the manner in which these methods will be combined in order to reach the firm's operating goals. A company may decide to use one method alone or, more frequently, two or more in some combination. In addition, there are choices within the major classifications such as the choice of advertising media after it has been decided to use advertising.

The combination of selling methods

used in a given case may be called the "promotional mix."[2] Several questions, from an operations point of view can be raised concerning this mix. How are the ingredients and the proportions of the mix determined? What factors account for variations in the mix among types of products and companies and among product-lines and market segments within a company? How does a company determine when it has the correct mix? These are questions to which it is difficult to find answers in marketing literature.

During the past summer the author conducted a series of interviews with firms in the Twin Cities area in order to get some indication, at least, of possible answers to these questions and to gain some insight into the thinking which lies behind promotional-mix decisions.[3] Several things are apparent from this study:

(1) Manufacturers tend to think of the

From *Business News Notes*, No. 18 (Minneapolis: School of Business Administration, University of Minnesota, November, 1954), pp. 1-5.
[1] Like many terms, sales promotion does not have a standardized meaning. It is sometimes used to include certain forms of promotion which, strictly speaking, are not within the fields of either advertising or personal selling but supplement them and make them more effective. Retailers frequently use it to cover their special sales or other promotional activities. In this study the term refers to all selling methods used by a company. Thus it includes personal selling, advertising, and the other forms which selling activities may take.

[2] A similar concept, "marketing mix," has been developed and used by Professor Neil H. Borden of the Graduate School of Business Administration of Harvard University who has done some of the pioneering work in this field.
[3] Personal interviews were conducted with 38 manufacturers who have their headquarters in the Twin Cities. Most of these companies are leading firms in their fields, and the large majority sell in the national market. They represent a cross section of industry ranging from food and soft-goods lines to consumers' durables and industrial products. Among the lines covered were grainmill products, malt beverages, women's apparel, home furnishings and equipment, paper products, building materials, paint, and several types of machinery and industrial equipment. A varied group of consumer specialty products was also included.

several forms of sales promotion in terms of the job which each can do. The expenditures for each are, therefore, pushed to the margin, i.e., the point where additional expenditures would not bring further gain to the company.

(2) Expenditures for personal selling tend to be more stable and, therefore, fluctuate less than expenditures for advertising and the several miscellaneous forms of sales promotion.

(3) Advertising expenditures tend to be more rigidly controlled than selling expenditures. In some companies, personal selling expenses are not yet budgeted. Advertising expense almost invariably is. At least two factors seem to account for this difference: (a) Specific advertising costs, particularly media and production costs, can be determined fairly easily in advance, in most cases. Selling costs, in some fields at least, are much more difficult to predict and vary with customer requirements and market conditions. (b) Companies seem to have more confidence in their personal selling expenditures and will permit an expansion in them more readily than in advertising expenditures. Many feel that it is necessary to set advertising at a specific figure, which appears to be reasonable, and then hold it at that level. This seems to indicate a belief that advertising costs, unless carefully watched, tend to get out of hand.

(4) There is no agreement with regard to the best procedure for budgeting selling and advertising expense, but the general tendency is to use the task method (i.e., deciding what needs to be done and then estimating what it will cost) coupled with the per cent-to-sales approach. A percentage of gross margin may also be used as a control figure. In fact, the gross margin is frequently a major determinant of the amount spent for promotion. This is especially true when competition is essentially in terms of non-price factors.

(5) The companies contacted had little evidence that their promotional expenditures were at the optimum level. They seem more certain of their selling expenditures, however, than of their advertising expenditures. Very few thought that their personal selling costs were out of line, but many had reservations about the amount of advertising they were doing. This may be traced, in part, to the immediacy of personal selling results compared with the relatively long-run effects of national advertising.

(6) Companies selling consumers' goods frequently have a promotional mix in which advertising expense is high relative to personal selling. The advertising weight is heaviest when brand is of paramount importance and the product itself is relatively simple. Consumer products which can be sold though the use of strong emotional appeals tend to be heavily advertised. Packaged food products and malt beverages are typical of this group.

(7) Products for which the needs for dealer cultivation and merchandising at the retail level are substantial will have rather high personal selling costs relative to sales. Whether these costs equal or exceed advertising costs depends on the importance of brand identification. If the manufacturer needs to build brand acceptance and preference, advertising costs generally will exceed personal selling costs. If the product is one for which brand recognition among consumers is low, personal selling costs will exceed advertising costs. Branded soft-goods lines, consumers' durables, and some building materials frequently require a considerable amount of work with dealers.

(8) Industrial products almost invariably have personal selling costs which are substantially higher than advertising costs. The need to make many calls and to give customers considerable assistance both in arriving at a decision and in putting the product into use increases personal selling costs. Relatively little can be accomplished by advertising other than making the company and the product known to potential users. After

the acquaintance is made, the salesman and his technical assistants must carry the bulk of the load.

(9) Products which move into both consumer and industrial markets have considerably higher personal sales-to-advertising cost ratios when they are aimed at the industrial market. Paint is typical of this situation.

(10) Manufacturers of distributor brands typically do no advertising, and their contacts with customers are almost entirely on a personal basis. In fact, the total promotional costs in this field are very low relative to the volume of sales.

(11) The spectrum of advertising-to-personal selling ratios is very broad, and companies and products are arranged along it from one extreme to the other

(see the chart). Their position depends on such factors as: the need for brand identification, complexity of the product, scope of the market, channels of communication available, technical requirements of buyers, customer services, and the need for dealer merchandising.

(12) The promotional mix used by a company is not fixed over time, and the company may shift its position along the spectrum. This frequently occurs when it becomes necessary, for competitive reasons, to use more of one ingredient relative to the others. In the packaged food field, for example, many companies are putting greater emphasis than formerly on advertising and on the use of certain devices such as premiums in

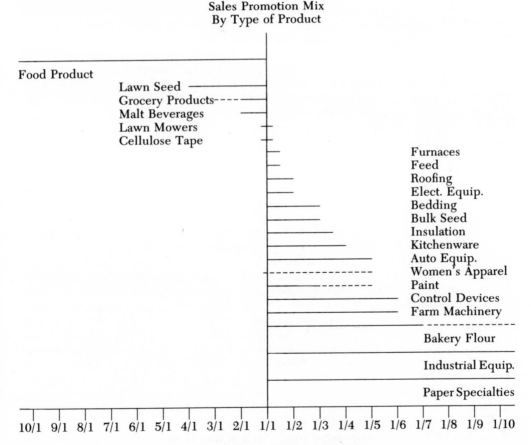

Sales Promotion Mix
By Type of Product

Ratio of Advertising to Personal Selling
(---- Indicates the Range of the Ratios)

order to develop a preference for their brands.

(13) Within a company, the mix varies by product line. The variation is great when the products go to quite different markets and involve different selling problems. Frequently, a company with a wide line of products will do no advertising at all for many of them. The key lines will be advertised on the assumption that the institutional advertising thus created benefits the other products.

BUDGETING SALES AND ADVERTISING EXPENSE

Several methods are used to predetermine probable personal selling expenditures, but one frequently used bases the estimated cost on the job to be done. The desired coverage of accounts is worked out including the necessary call frequencies, classified by type of customer. In the food field, for example, the number of potential retail calls is so great that manufacturers which attempt to do a merchandising job at the retail level must select the specific accounts to be covered. Furthermore, in this field the types of stores to be visited and the call frequencies tend to be approximately the same among competing firms. The growing competitive pressures in most commodity fields are forcing manufacturers to call at least as frequently as their competitors.

A number of firms indicated that they have about reached the saturation point in sales coverage. Their markets are being covered as thoroughly as is necessary and, consequently, no increases in their sales forces are anticipated. As the sales of these companies increase, selling expenses should show some decrease in relation to sales. In a few instances, companies which have been building their sales organizations during the post-war period state that they have not yet filled their sales personnel quotas but are planning to do so at the first opportunity.

Competitive pressures have forced some companies to up-grade their salesmen and to replace older salesmen with better-trained, higher-caliber men. As this becomes necessary, direct selling costs increase in terms of dollars but may not increase in relation to sales. Some firms have also increased commission rates in order to keep desirable salesmen and to maintain a compensation plan which is comparable with those used by competitors.

In the industrial field, particularly where men are on a straight salary, the ratio of selling expense to sales may be erratic and difficult to predict because of the firm's inability to forecast sales. For extended periods of time, these companies maintain the same organization, and the ratio of selling expense to sales rises and falls with the sales volume they happen to secure. One large company indicated that it has no dollar budget for field selling costs at all but uses a manpower budget. Plans are made in terms of the number of men needed to obtain the desired coverage.

The cost of alternative channels may serve as a guide and a control for direct selling costs in some cases. In the food field, for example, the customary brokerage fees may indicate the amount which a manufacturer can afford to spend for his own sales organization. This procedure is particularly useful where the manufacturer does not find it necessary to do a better job than would be done by a competent broker.

The control of selling costs for a new line presents special problems. One firm developed a plan which gave control of personal selling costs and also permitted the addition of new men when needed. It was determined that the acceptable range of selling expense to sales was 10 to 15 per cent during the early growth period of this product. Salesmen were hired until selling costs rose to 15 per cent of sales. The organization was then stabilized to permit the new men to become established. As their sales increased, direct selling costs gradually decreased until they were about 10 per cent of sales. New men were then added until the 15 per cent ceiling was reached again. This cycle was repeated until the sales organization was large enough to do an effective job of covering the market. Now that the product has become well established in the national market, costs have fallen below 10 per cent.

Like personal selling expenditures, advertising expenditures are most frequently established in terms of what is needed. In a few cases this results in a very flexible advertising budget which permits expenditures to be changed quickly to meet new conditions in the market. For example, the sale of malt beverages is strongly influenced by weather conditions. Budgets, therefore, are purposely kept flexible so that advertising impact can be adjusted to climatic changes.

At the other extreme are firms which use an advertising ratio based on physical units of output and which consistently hold to this ratio regardless of the specific needs of the market. In a few cases, where demand is very difficult to predict, advertising expenditures may be set entirely on the basis of the previous year's expenditures.

Many of the companies interviewed place in the hands of one person the responsibility either for all selling and advertising or for that portion which applies to a given line. This is a satisfactory way of controlling the sales promotion mix when the executive knows and appreciates the uses of each form of sales promotion. He is in a position to take full advantage of each and to coordinate the efforts employed in the several promotional media.

Most firms base their sales and advertising budgets on data prepared originally by these departments. In large companies, the controller may assemble the departments' requirements and work out an over-all budget. The department requests frequently are examined and discussed by a top management committee which in turn makes recommendations to the president or the board of directors. Sometimes a management committee will have the authority to approve a sales budget. In at least one case, it was found that the advertising budget is determined by the president, primarily on his own initiative.

The need for a sales budget is illustrated by the experiences of one firm which does a national business. This organization had not been budgeting sales expenditures and found that selling costs had risen to about 23 per cent of sales. It was felt that selling expense was excessive and could be cut in half. Costs were, therefore, budgeted at 12 per cent for 1954. Actual expenses are running a little under 15 per cent. Advertising expense has been cut by about two-thirds and selling expense by about 40 per cent. The personal sales-to-advertising cost ratio which formerly stood at 3 to 1 is now about 5 to 1. At the moment, the sales results of this mix appear to be satisfactory.

THE PROMOTIONAL MIX

The proportions in which companies use personal selling, advertising, and other forms of promotion vary widely among the several product fields. The Twin Cities sample included firms which, at times, have done no advertising at all. At the other extreme, were one or two companies in which personal selling has been of very minor importance. In each of these cases, however, the firms have increased the use of the less-favored promotional factor during recent years and are now depending on both advertising and selling in addition to other promotional devices.

Manufacturers of packaged food products rely heavily on all forms of promotion. The promotional mix varies, however, even among firms producing essentially the same type of products. Thus, some firms may have a 1 to 1 ratio of advertising to personal selling while others will have a ratio as high as 2½ to 1 in favor of advertising. One manufacturer of a specialty food product has very low personal selling costs but exceedingly high advertising costs. The resulting advertising-to-personal-sales ratio is far in excess of that found among manufacturers of similar products. Manufacturers of malt beverages also tend to lean toward advertising, and their advertising-to-personal-sales ratio approximates 2 to 1.

When the pulling power of a brand is important, as is true of packaged food, manufacturers use advertising as an attempt to develop a high degree of brand consciousness among consumers. Salesmen are used primarily for merchandising at the retail level and have the job of building good-will in the trade. Advertising is placed in the more expensive media such as general and women's magazines, television, and radio, with a high degree of frequency in order to create acceptance for the brand. When products are relatively simple, easily presented, and subject to strong emotional appeals, advertising can do an effective promotional job.

Among the products for which advertising and personal selling expenses are approximately equal are consumers' durables. Manufacturers of these products likewise need to develop brand preferences, and although there are technical differences among the products, these features can be highlighted in their advertising. Furthermore, durables frequently are sold under a policy of limited distribution and, therefore, the number of sales contacts is relatively low. Lawn mowers and heating equipment are characteristic of this group. Heavily advertised consumer specialties may also have a similar pattern.

At the other end of the scale are the various industrial products, most of which have promotional ratios heavily in favor of personal selling. Frequently, a number of carefully prepared personal contacts are necessary before the sale is made. One manufacturer of highly specialized industrial equipment, for example, indicated that his men make six calls, on the average, before a sale is completed. In addition, there is a very important service problem following the sale of these products which also requires personal contact.

Advertising may be helpful in making industrial products and their companies known to potential buyers but it cannot do much more than that. Also, the advertising media which can be used effectively in the industrial field are quite limited. The bulk of the advertising expenditures are for trade papers and direct mail with which considerable coverage can be obtained at a relatively low cost. This situation is quite the opposite of that prevailing in most consumers' goods.

Ratios of personal selling costs to advertising for industrial products are likely to be at least 6 to 1, and may be considerably higher. Some firms do practically no advertising and depend on their reputation in the field to prepare the way for salesmen. In one instance, a manufacturer of heavy equipment had a ratio which was approximately 1 to 1, but he pointed out that most of the advertising was institutional, and that advertising expenditures probably were too high.

Firms which sell in both a consumer and an industrial market advertise more heavily than those which sell exclusively to industrial users. This is true in paint, for example, where a firm of the former type may have a personal sales-to-advertising cost ratio of 2 to 1 while the latter may have a ratio nearer 5 to 1.

Building materials, which have a low degree of brand preference, have a promotional ratio which reflects this situation. The need in this field is to cultivate dealers and to persuade them to carry the line. A personal sales-to-advertising cost ratio of 2½ to 1 may, therefore, be a satisfactory mix for this type of product.

Private-brand business, of course,

creates special promotional problems. A manufacturer who limits output to private brands will typically do no advertising at all, although the distributor may induce him to do some advertising for the private brand.

CHANGES IN THE PROMOTIONAL MIX

In some instances, a company may work out a mix which appears to be satisfactory, and it may remain relatively unchanged for a long period. Generally, however, competitive pressures force manufacturers to re-examine the mix periodically and make changes dictated by market needs.

In the grocery products field, for example, advertising and sales promotion costs are increasing relative to personal selling costs. Selling costs are based on the necessary calls on selected customers. After this saturation point has been reached, selling costs will not increase further, and in relation to sales volume may actually decrease. The need for advertising and sales promotion grows, however, with the entrance of new brands and lines into the market. Attempts to influence choice by the use of premiums appealing to women and children and the extensive use of a wide range of advertising media indicates the need to keep brand names prominently before the buying public. As brand competition becomes more intense in this field, manufacturers are forced to find new and more effective ways of presenting their advertising message and to spend more money relative to sales to do it.

In another very competitive product field, malt beverages, total promotional costs per barrel are increasing as manufacturers of national brands compete among themselves in an attempt to get a larger share of markets which have been dominated by regional brands. Advertising costs per barrel which in 1953 were about $1.40, on the average, are now closer to $1.50. In addition, expenses for

personal selling are also increasing because of the need to maintain good working relations with establishments serving these products.

Some manufacturers of industrial equipment feel that their advertising has been excessive, and in certain cases steps have been taken to cut it. These decisions are not made on the basis of definite evidence of advertising results but in the belief that advertising costs seem to be too high.

One factor in the mix which is difficult to evaluate is the qualitative aspect of the several mix components. One large company had a product which had been unprofitable for a long period of time. Increased expenditures for advertising seemed not to make much difference in sales. It was, therefore, decided to reduce the advertising substantially in an attempt to cut promotional costs and place the product on a profitable basis. This was done, and sales of the product increased. The answer to this apparent paradox is that the agency devised a better campaign than had been used when the budget was substantially larger. A smaller amount of advertising was more effective simply because of better ideas.

DIFFERENCES IN MIX AMONG PRODUCTS AND PRODUCT LINES

Manufacturers with several product lines are not likely to use the same mix for every line. However, some do so purposely, and others have no satisfactory way of allocating promotional costs to individual lines.

The milling companies, as a case in point, have quite different personal sales-to-advertising cost ratios for their grocery products, bakery flour and feed lines. Advertising costs for bakery flour are very small, while advertising and sales promotion costs for family flour and packaged grocery products are substantially in excess of personal selling cost for these products. Furthermore, in relation to sales volume, personal selling costs for bakery flour are likely to be no more than one-fifth as large as the selling costs for grocery products. Personal selling costs for feed are larger than the advertising costs and will run 50 to 100 per cent above the advertising expenditures.

The markets for packaged grocery products and flour are very broad. These brands must be brought to the attention of prospective customers prominently and frequently. Advertising is the most efficient way to reach this national family market. Bakery flour, on the other hand, is sold to a limited number of buyers who have special technical requirements and who are primarily interested in price and quality rather than brand name. Advertising can do little to advance sales in this market. Feed, likewise, requires intensive personal selling, although brand preferences can be established among consumers through advertising. Consequently, the promotion ratio for feed lies between the ratios for grocery products and bakery flour.

As another illustration, a seed distributor has quite different mixes for the several items in the line. Products such as farm seed and garden seed, which are sold in bulk, have a personal sales-to-advertising cost ratio of about 3 to 1. On the other hand, products which are sold primarily to the ultimate consumer, such as lawn seed, have a mix which is the reverse. In this instance, advertising will be 3 or 4 times the personal-selling cost.

In general, sales promotion costs tend to be higher on high-gross margin lines than on low-gross margin lines. Several firms indicated that they calculate back from the selling price in order to see how much they can "afford" to spend for promotion. They have more leeway in the high-gross margin lines and, consequently, feel that they can spend more. This appears to be a fairly common procedure, even though expenditures are made in terms of the margin available rather than in accordance with the need

for promotion, or any evidence of the results of promotion.

As a case in point, advertising expenditures for women's apparel may range from 1½ to 5 per cent of sales. The highest percentages will be applied to items which have high gross margins and are less affected by price competition. One firm in this field, however, indicated that the same percentage is spent for all of its lines because it is felt that all should have about the same advertising support.

The seed distributor mentioned above has a promotional ratio for a hybrid-seed line which is 3 or 4 times the total percentage spent on bulk farm seed. In this case, the hybrid line is heavily advertised and is a specialty product with a substantial degree of product differentiation. It carries a higher margin than other products and can absorb a higher percentage of selling expense since apparently a relatively high price does not materially reduce unit sales.

Firms with many items in the line tend to advertise the key lines and not the others. The lesser brands thus ride along on the demand developed for the major products. This is done in paint and in some lines of home furnishings. In the case of one major Twin Cities company, this policy has resulted in loading a heavy advertising charge on the company's leading product. This puts a definite limit on the amount of advertising which can be done for this particular line. Actually, part of this advertising has an institutional effect, and the other lines benefit but bear no charge. If advertising costs were allocated in part to other lines, more could be spent on the major line since its sales are subject to further growth.

All company advertising tends to be institutional to some degree, and it is not always desirable to attempt to allocate the costs to individual lines, particularly since the procedures available for allocating costs are far from precise. In the industrial field, much of the advertising is frankly institutional, and often no attempt is made to promote individual products. Industrial companies develop a reputation for service and product performance. Advertising may facilitate obtaining leads, however, which are then used by salesmen.

The promotional mix for industrial products varies widely within the same firm. Selling costs are typically high in relation to advertising, but the ratio may be as high as 7 to 1 in some cases and as low as 2 to 1 in others. Industrial selling costs vary with the type of customer, the amount of service needed, the size of the order, and the selling methods used. A number of industrial companies indicated that they sell almost their entire output of one or more lines to one buyer. This situation typically results in low selling costs relative to sales.

The development of a satisfactory sales-promotion mix by an individual company requires continuous study of the market and the competitive situation in it. The optimum mix probably is seldom attained, but companies must continue to experiment with the several methods of sales promotion and to use them in various combinations in order to make their sales efforts more effective. In many product fields, selling costs are being forced upward by competitive pressures. The individual firm has no choice but to attempt to find the promotional mix which seems to give the best results.

32. Trading Stamps and the Consumer's Food Bill

MARKET ORGANIZATION AND COSTS BRANCH, AGRICULTURAL MARKETING SERVICE

One of the most controversial issues in today's fight for the consumer's dollar is the use of trading stamps. Discussions of this subject, either pro or con, have often been somewhat emotional in nature. This report, dealing with these "little pieces of gummed paper," is an attempt at an objective presentation of the effect of this promotional device on consumers.

Trading stamps have been given by stores since the end of the last century. Their importance, however, appears to run in cycles, reaching a peak during periods of keen competition. Stamps gained prominence during the years of depression when incomes were reduced and each business was competing vigorously to keep up its sales. Today, with incomes at an alltime high, competition for the consumer's dollar is again intense. Almost every type of business is offering lures of some kind — T. V. giveaways, door prizes, trips, coupons with which items can be purchased at a reduced price, and many kinds of special sales.

CHANGES IN THE FOOD BUSINESS

Traditionally, grocers have not used as many promotional devices as other merchants, although today they appear to be using them in ever-increasing numbers. This greater use has been caused by several factors. Among these is the fact that the retail food business is rapidly becoming a big business. The average size of retail grocery stores has increased so much that between 1948 and 1954 the number of stores with annual sales of over a million dollars more than tripled (26).[1] Though these supermarkets still represent a small percentage of the total number of grocery stores, they account for almost a third of total food sales.

To maintain the high volume necessary to successful operation, supermarkets have had to adopt big business methods. In early attempts to obtain volume, they stressed lower prices. These were effective against smaller stores but, as time went on and other supermarkets became the chief competitors, price differentials quickly narrowed. Other devices were then tried — larger and more attractive stores, air-conditioning, a greater variety of items including many nonfood items, parking lots, longer store hours, and check-cashing services. As these changes in practices, facilities, or services became more generally adopted, they, too, lost much of their promotional value.

U.S. Department of Agriculture, *Marketing Research Report No. 169* (Washington, D.C.: Government Printing Office, 1957), pp. 1-9.

[1] Italic numbers in parentheses refer to items in Bibliography, p. 330.

It was at about this point that trading stamps again began to assume importance and, today, they are given by stores in all parts of the country. The use of trading stamps was initially more prevalent in the East and Midwest but, in the last year or so, the practice has rapidly spread to almost all sections of the country. In addition to numerous independent supermarkets, superettes, and small chain groceries, several of the largest chains are now issuing stamps in some cities.

CHARACTERISTICS OF TRADING STAMPS AS A PROMOTIONAL DEVICE

Stamp companies usually license only one store of a kind within the same shopping area. This one retailer then has a promotional device that cannot be duplicated exactly by nearby competing food stores. Others can use a different kind of stamp, but stamp plans vary considerably in appeal and merit. Hence, the first grocer to adopt the practice generally has the advantage provided he has selected a leader in customer preference.

In many instances, the first dealer to use trading stamps has increased his volume of business significantly at the expense of competitors not giving stamps. Nonstamp-giving food stores have tried various appeals in an attempt to regain customers. One of the more usual lines of attack has been to emphasize the cost of trading stamps and to suggest that, because consumers finally pay the marketing bill, this added cost must also be paid by them. This attack is usually met by stores giving stamps with the claim that the cost is not being passed on, and that consumers are getting the equivalent of a cash discount.

Probably some consumers would be willing to forego all promotional efforts if this meant lower prices, but if such efforts are a part of modern-day merchandising, trading stamps may have a broader appeal than some other forms of promotion, as trips to Europe or door prizes. Such promotions are for the lucky few while trading stamps promise a tangible return to all who save them.

CONSUMERS' ATTITUDES TOWARD STAMPS

Most surveys made to determine reactions to trading stamps have shown that in localities where stamps are available, the majority of consumers save them. Two studies made late in 1956 showed that about 83 percent of all families in a midwestern city (16) were saving stamps, as were about the same proportion in a city in New York State (2). It is estimated that in 1956 about half of all families in the United States are saving trading stamps (20).

Another bit of evidence of consumer interest in trading stamps was provided during the 1965 election. One State passed a law that required payment of an annual license fee of $6,000 by any store issuing trading stamps. Enough consumers were unhappy about the law that it had to be included on the ballot for referendum. Some consumers were sufficiently disturbed to make public statements as, for example, "Selfish forces are trying to take away our right to save trading stamps (30)." Voters defeated this proposal by more than a 2 to 1 margin.

Bills have been introduced in many State legislatures which would, in effect, practically legislate or tax trading stamps out of existence. In 1955, 50 such bills were introduced to 24 State legislatures. However, only 2 of these were passed and neither is in effect today.

Though studies have shown that consumers are interested in saving stamps, they also have shown that stamps are seldom given as the main reason for shopping at a particular grocery store. Consumers say they choose food stores chiefly for convenience, quality of food sold (particularly meats), prices, and the kind of services offered. Only a very small percentage gave trading stamps as the principal reason for patronizing a particular store.

Consumer interest in saving stamps varies greatly in intensity. Some consumers approach stamp-saving with great enthusiasm, some can take it or leave it, and still others are antagonistic to the whole idea. The preliminary report of a current study *(16)* shows that the highest proportion of stamp savers are young married couples less than 40 years of age with 2 or more children, living in suburban areas and having incomes in excess of $3,000 a year. Consumers in this category, to a great extent, are the ones having the largest amount of personal debt. An article published late in 1956 on the use of consumer credit states that "consumers in the middle- and upper middle-income groups are most likely to have such debts. . . . These middle-income groups include many young couples with children who seem to have an almost insatiable capacity to consume the goods credit will buy and enough optimism to make them willing to take on debts. . . . Having children in the family not only increases the need for credit by increasing the number and quantity of goods and services required for living; it also increases the pressure to buy goods that may not be considered exactly essential *(14).*"

The insatiable desire of these young, middle-income families for more and more possessions may be an important underlying force that stimulates their interest in trading stamps. Though in debt, these families can save stamps and acquire still more goods without apparent expenditure of money.

Other reasons have been put forth for the appeal of trading stamps. One of these is that the accumulation of stamps satisfies the desire to save which still seems to be strong in our society. Also, stamp-saving makes consumers feel thrifty. Another reason sometimes given is that when consumers redeem stamp books for merchandise, they seem to get a great sense of satisfaction at having attained a goal.

Consumers appear to have varying opinions about and reactions to the effect of trading stamp plans on prices of food. In one study, about a third of the families interviewed thought prices of food had been increased by stores giving stamps, whereas almost half did not think so *(16)*. Families actively interested in saving stamps were less likely to think that stamps had increased food prices and appeared less concerned about any change that may have taken place than did those with less interest in saving stamps.

RETURNS CONSUMER GETS FOR STAMPS

Though some retailers redeem stamp books with cash or with merchandise from their store, more often stamps are exchanged for merchandise or gifts provided by the stamp company. These are usually articles of popular brands that range in appeal from personal items for each member of the family to household items that all can enjoy. They include articles that classify as necessities as well as those that are luxuries.

Recent catalogs from 2 leading stamp companies each offered a choice of about 500 items. Between two-thirds and three-quarters of these required from 1 to 3 books of stamps. Items offered in the 2 catalogs were very similar, but few appeared to be identical. If the item offered were a percolator, for example, the brands might differ. Or articles might be of the same make but of different size or with more or less trim. For the few items that could be identified as being the same or very nearly so, the number of stamps needed was the same even though the number of stamp books required was different.

Some stamp companies' catalogs have terminal dates and a new issue may have a different assortment of items or the same item may require a different number of books. In catalogs for the same company for 2 consecutive time periods, about a third more items were offered in the later catalog than in the earlier one. Of the 125 items that could be reasonably well identified as the same, 48 percent required the same number of books in both catalogs; 40 percent called for a larger number of books in the later catalog and 12 percent called for fewer. By and large, consumers appear to be satisfied with merchandise or gifts offered in exchange for trading stamps. Seventy-five percent of the persons interviewed in a recent study (16) indicated they were satisfied; 23 percent could not answer as they had not redeemed any stamps. Only 2 percent stated definite dissatisfaction. Reasons given for dissatisfaction were changes in number of books required, the article wanted was out of stock at redemption store, and the merchandise obtained seemed a small return for length of time required to fill the books.

If stamps were available only at a food store, it would take the average urban family who spends about $25 a week for food consumed at home about 5 to 6 weeks to fill a book of 1,500 stamps provided all food items were bought at the same store or at a store issuing the same brand of stamps (15). Thus, it would take from 5 to 18 weeks for such a family to save enough stamps to obtain any one of the majority of the items offered in the catalogs. In a recent catalog, to accumulate enough stamps to obtain the merchandise that required the largest number of books would take such a family around 2¼ years and an expenditure of about $3,000. These calculations are based on stamps being obtained for every purchase. At times, however, a consumer may forget to get them. Then, too, some stores give stamps only on request or only for certain kinds of purchases.

Stamps are generally given for multi-

ple amounts of 10 cents. In actual practice, therefore, the period required to fill a book of stamps may be longer than the 5 to 6 weeks indicated above.

On the other hand, stores may give double or even triple amounts of stamps to stimulate trade on slow days. Also, it is fairly common for other types of businesses in the same market area to give the same kind of stamps. If this happened to include a gasoline station, for example, a book would be completed in a shorter period of time.

MONEY VALUE OF STAMP BOOKS

Some consumers have little concept of the money value of a book of stamps. According to a recent study, about 45 percent of those interviewed said they didn't know. Others gave amounts ranging from $1 to more than $8 a book (16)

Stamp savers appeared to have a better idea of the money value of a book of stamps than nonsavers. Although about a third of those saving stamps gave no estimate of the value of a book of stamps, almost half estimated it to be worth between $2 and $4. This range seems to be in line with available information considering the variation in value per book of stamps even among redemption merchandise offered by the same stamp company.

Some indication of money values can be gained from a small pricing study made in Washington, D.C., in November 1956.[2] About 25 articles shown in a stamp company's catalog that could be reasonably well identified were priced in 4 large department stores and in 13 discount houses. Merchants in the District of Columbia do not have to follow manufacturers' list prices but, because dealers in many States do, such prices were included for comparison whenever available.

The items selected for pricing were

---

[2] This study was made by a member of the Market Organization and Costs Branch, Agr. Mktg. Serv.

TABLE 1

AVERAGE DOLLAR VALUE PER BOOK OF STAMPS AND RATE OF RETURN ON $150
EXPENDITURE BASED ON MANUFACTURERS' LIST PRICES AND AVERAGE DEPARTMENT
AND DISCOUNT HOUSE PRICES, WASHINGTON, D.C., NOVEMBER 1956

Item	Stores giving prices	Dollar value per book of stamps based on average—			Average rate of return[1]		
		List prices	Department store[2] prices	Discount house prices	List prices	Department store[2] prices	Discount house prices
	Number	Dollars	Dollars	Dollars	Percent	Percent	Percent
Portable mixer	13	3.74	2.53	2.40	2.49	1.69	1.60
Automatic toaster (A)	12	3.74	2.53	2.51	2.49	1.69	1.67
Automatic toaster (B)	5	3.74	2.70	2.70	2.49	1.80	1.80
Steam-dry iron	14	3.74	2.46	2.45	2.49	1.64	1.64
Roaster oven	6	3.46	2.63	2.45	2.31	1.75	1.63
Aluminum 4½ qt. dutch oven	3		4.07			2.71	
Dictionary	2		3.33			2.22	
All items priced	25						
Median value		3.74	2.98	2.51	2.50	1.99	1.67
Range in value		3.46−5.22	1.70−4.25	2.31−3.44	2.32−3.43	1.13−2.83	1.55−2.29

[1] Based on a rate of 1 stamp for each 10-cent purchase and an expenditure of $150 to fill a book of 1,500 stamps.
[2] Do not have to maintain manufacturers' list prices.

those most likely to be found in department stores and discount houses. As a result, proportionately more electrical appliances and housewares were included in the list priced than are usually found in trading stamp catalogs. This bias does not appear to be too important as such articles are among the most popular with consumers. Though all items were not available in all stores, several prices were obtained for most of them.

The number of books of 1,500 stamps required to obtain the items priced ranged from 1 to approximately 13 with about half calling for less than 3 books. The prices collected were averaged by type of outlet from which they were obtained—department stores and discount houses. To estimate the dollar value of a book of stamps, these average prices were divided by the number of books required for the particular item. For example, if the retail list price for an electrical appliance is $17.95 and it can be redeemed for 4⅞ books, 1 book would be equivalent to $3.74 or, assuming an expenditure of $150, a maximum return of about 2½ cents for each dollar spent to fill a book of stamps.

This small study shows the possibility of wide variation in the money value of a book of trading stamps (table 1). For example, based on manufacturers' list prices, the value of a book of stamps ranged from $3.42 to $5.22 with a median value of $3.74. This median value indicates that half of the items priced gave a return of between $3.42 and $3.74 and half between $3.74 and $5.22.

The percentage return based on an expenditure of $150 ranged from 2.31 to 3.48 percent for manufacturers' list prices and from 1.55 to 2.29 percent for discount house prices. If more than $150 worth of store purchases were required to fill a book of stamps, obviously the return would be lower.

Similar studies made in other cities have shown essentially the same variation.

IMPLICATIONS TO CONSUMER

Though it is difficult to show conclusively whether consumers are getting a bargain via trading stamps or are paying a premium for food, there are a number of things that can be considered in any attempt to evaluate a specific situation.

First, maintaining a trading stamp plan is an expense to a food merchant. It has been estimated that, on the average, the merchant pays about 2½ percent of his gross sales to the stamp company for the right to issue stamps, and for stamps, stamp books, and some advertising. In addition, dealers may incur other expenses, at least during the introductory stage. With the comparatively low markups on most foods, an extra cost of this magnitude must be offset in some way.

There are ways in which such costs may be partially or wholly offset without raising prices. These include, for example, reduction of unit costs by substantially increasing the quantity of merchandise sold, reduction of other forms of promotion, and stocking items other than food that have higher markups.

Though many retailers experience an increase in sales following the introduction of a stamp plan, the size of this increase can vary greatly. The first dealer in his immediate trade area to introduce stamps may have an increase in sales that will more than meet the entire cost of stamps. On the other hand, if the grocer already has a large share of his possible customers, there may be little or no increase in sales. Then, too, even though sales increase at first, they may not continue to do so if competing stores adopt trading stamps. In instances such as these last two cases, unless a retailer can save in other ways, all or part of the cost of the stamp plan must be passed on as higher prices, or he will have to take smaller profits or even a loss.

If any cost is passed on through increased prices, consumers may not share it equally. Those who do not save stamps may be paying part of the bill for those who do. Or if prices are raised only on luxury foods, the burden of cost may fall to a larger extent on those buying such products. Even if the entire cost of the stamp plan is passed on, again consumers may not be equally affected. In a recent study (16) in which many items commonly offered as redemption merchandise were priced, it was found that if prices were raised enough to cover the cost of a stamp plan (2½ percent of gross sales) a consumer purchasing an article at manufacturers' list price would be buying it on what amounts to a prepayment plan. If the item could be purchased at discount prices, a loss to the consumer would result. This statement is based on an average return and, because there is great variation in returns depending on the redemption merchandise selected, again an individual consumer may be affected differently.

Until more information is available on the effect of trading stamp plans on prices of foods purchased, no generalization can be drawn as to whether a consumer gets something for nothing, pays part, all, or even more than the cost of similar merchandise purchased for cash. It can vary from community to community, from store to store within the same community, and even within the same store at different periods of time. Hence, a trading stamp company's catalog or the redemption center should be shopped as carefully as if a cash purchase were being made. Consumers will have to evaluate grocery store prices and the merits of merchandise obtained for stamps the same as they would in any other buying situation.

BIBLIOGRAPHY

(1) Batten, Barton, Durstine, & Osborn, Inc., 1956. Why women select and shop in any one particular grocery store. Food Staff Presentation No. 19, 5 pp., illus., Feb.

(2) Batten, Barton, Durstine, & Osborn, Inc., 1956. Trading stamps and premium credit plans – the consumers pro and con. Food Staff Presentation No. 20, 31 pp., illus., Nov.

(3) Blatt, K. M., 1954. A study of retail trading stamp plans. Thesis submitted to Graduate School of University of Minnesota, 45 pp., illus. (Processed.)

(4) Bond, R. J., 1956. Summary information on trading stamps. U.S. Dept. Commerce, Business and Defense Serv. Adm., Business Serv. Bul. 182, 4 pp., Sept.

(5) Bureau of Business and Social Research, University of Denver, 1955. Effects of the use of trading stamps by the grocery trade in Denver, Colorado, spring 1954. Colo. Retail Grocers & Meat Dealers Assoc., 40 pp., illus. (Processed.)

(6) Business Week, 1956. Super Market Institute collects evidence on trading stamps. P. 54, Sept. 22. (Also see issue of May 19, 1956, p. 43.)

(7) Changing Times – The Kiplinger Magazine, 1956. Trading-stamp craze – silly or not? Pp. 11-13, Aug.

(8) Consumer Counsel to the Governor, Albany, N.Y., 1956. Summary transcript of representative state conference on store trading stamps, Oct. 2, 39 pp. (Processed.)

(9) Consumers Reports, 1956. What's behind the trading stamp boom? Vol. 21 (10): 506-509, Oct.

(10) Cross, Wilbur, 1957. Trading stamps become a sticky national question. Life, pp. 114-126, March 4.

(11) England, W. B., 1956. Operating results of food chains in 1955. Harvard Business School, Div. Res., 30 pp., Sept.

(12) Food World, 1956. The modern food department store, P. 15, Nov.

(13) Haring, Albert, and Yoder, W. O., 1957. Boom Business Res., School of Business, Indiana University, Supplement to Ind. Business Rev., pp. 36-43.

(14) Holmes, E. G., 1956. Who uses consumer credit? U.S. Dept. Agr., Agr. Res. Service, Household Econ. Res. Branch, 9 pp., Nov. (Processed.)

(15) Household Food Consumption, 1955., 1956. Food expenditures of households in the United States. U.S. Dept. Agr. Prelim. Rpt., 15 pp., Aug. (Processed.)

(16) Indiana University School of Business., 1957. Trading stamps in Indianapolis, Ind. Preliminary report of a study conducted at Indiana University between Sept. 1 and Dec. 31, 1956.

(17) Kroeger, Arthur, 1953-54. The response to trading stamp plans. Jour. Retailing, vol. 29(4): 171-172, 192-193.

(18) Livingston, J. A., 1956. Do trading stamps raise prices? Washington Post and Times Herald, p. A22, Dec. 21.

(19) _____, 1957. Trading stamps give BLS index problem. Washington Post and Times Herald, p. A17, Jan. 11.

(20) Market Organization and Costs Branch. 1957. Do trading stamps affect food costs? U.S. Dept. Agr., Agr. Mktg. Service, Mktg. Res. Rpt. No. 147, Jan.

(21) Meat and Food Merchandising, 1956. Trading stamps—friend or foe? Vol. 32 (6): 27-31, illus., June.

(22) Mehling, Harold, 1956. Trading stamps, the big lick and promise boom. Pageant, pp. 40-46, Dec.

(23) Mueller, R. W., 1956. Nation-wide survey finds . . . sales at mid-year up 6.5 percent—stamp plan power on wane. Progressive Grocer, vol. 35 (9): 72-77, Sept.

(24) Murphy, C. S., 1956. Memorandum concerning the trading stamp industry. Sperry and Hutchinson Co., 20 pp., Jan. (Processed.)

(25) Newsweek, 1956. 30 billion dollar trade stamp spree. Pp. 83-84, Sept. 24.

(26) Ogren, K. E., and Scott, F. E., 1957. Trends in marketing costs. Agr. Mktg., pp. 15-18, Jan.

(27) Super Market Merchandising, 1956. How to choose a stamp plan. Vol. 21 (7): 59, July.

(28) Trout, J. J., 1956. How trading stamps affect volume and earnings. Progressive Grocer, vol. 35 (8): 48-55, Aug.

(29) Vredenburg, H. L., 1956. Trading stamps. Bur. Business Res., Ind. Univ. School of Business, Ind. Business Rpt. No. 21. 159 pp.

(30) Wall Street Journal, 1956. Trading stamp curb. P. 1, Nov. 2.

33. Predicting Trademark Effectiveness

HARRY A. BURDICK, EDWARD J. GREEN AND
JOSEPH W. LOVELACE

Under the sponsorship of Raymond Loewy Associates we undertook the following study. The task which confronted us may be related in terms of a single question, namely: "How effective is a given trademark in comparison to six other trademarks, one of each of the product's leading competitors?" The question is a simple and reasonable one, undoubtedly of major significance to all advertisers. The answer is not so simple, mostly because the word "effective" is so difficult to define. In the following report, we will present the definition which we used and the correlates we found to this definition of effectiveness.

We decided that for a trademark to be an effective trademark it must have the following properties:

1. Salience—it must be readily seen and recognized.
2. Meaningfulness—it must convey, through associations, connotations which are favorable and significant to the observer.
3. Memory-value—it must be readily remembered by the viewer.

With these criteria, we set out to investigate the relative effectiveness of each of seven trademarks.

From *Journal of Applied Psychology,* Vol. 43, No. 5 (October, 1959), pp. 285-86.

METHOD

SUBJECTS

In all, 166 male Ss were tested. A proportion of these Ss (40) participated in the salience and meaning phase of this experiment. The other 126 participated in the meaning and memory-value phase of the experiment. All Ss were paid for their participation. The 40 Ss who performed in the salience aspect had vision corrected to 20/20.

MATERIALS

Official trademarks of seven companies were obtained. These were enlarged photostatically and the official colors applied by air brush. Ektachrome transparencies were prepared of each of the emblems. In the memory-value aspect of the study, all of the trademarks were presented on one slide. Four different arrangements of the trademarks were photographed for this, so that whatever effects position might have would be reduced. Ektachrome transparencies of the composites were produced.

SALIENCE AND MEANING PROCEDURE

Ss appeared in a testing laboratory individually. They were met by E, seated before a screen, and told that words would be flashed upon the screen. *S* was to report everything he saw. Slides were shuffled before each series to control the effect of position in the series. For each *S*, the point at which correct identification occurred was recorded by *E*.

The slides were shown through a matched pair of 300-v. projecting tachistoscopes which were placed 6½ ft. from the screen. The screen was held at constant illumination to reduce the reading of after-images. Preliminary investigation showed that no one recognized the trademarks at exposure intervals less than 1/50 sec. without repeated presentations. Therefore, our series began here, with all slides being presented at 1/50 sec., then all slides at 1/25 sec., all at 1/10, 1/5, 1/2, and 1 sec. After this part of the study was completed, *S* was given a ten-item copy of the Semantic Differential described by Osgood, Suci, and Tannenbaum (1957). He was shown each slide for as long as he wished and evaluated the trademark in terms of 10 seven-point dimensions. This is our operational definition of "meaning."

MEMORY-VALUE AND MEANING PROCEDURE

Groups met and were told they would be asked to view a number of slides. Half of the group was sent out of the room while the others remained. The ones remaining were provided with forms for the Semantic Differential and asked to turn the forms over and write on the back. The technique used to test memory-value was the Aussage technique.

One of the four transparencies containing a view of all the trademarks was presented to the group for 15 sec. Then *S*s were asked to write down all of the trademarks which they recalled. The procedure was duplicated for the other half of the group, using a second slide with different positional arrangement. After responses were made to the composites, each trademark was presented alone, and *S*s in the group were asked to

evaluate it on each of 10 dimensions of the Semantic Differential.

SALIENCE

Mean recognition thresholds were computed for each of the trademarks. Trademarks were then ranked, with the trademark having the lowest threshold receiving a rank of one.

MEANING

Following a recommendation of Osgood et al. (1957), the characteristics of evaluation, potency, and activity were taken to be most significant in designating "meaning." Good-bad, strong-weak, and active-passive were taken to be the focal dimensions of evaluation, potency, and activity. Scores on these dimensions were summed for each trademark, and a rank ordering from most to least along the dimension was obtained. The rank on the evaluation dimension was doubled, as Osgood et al. suggest, and added to the rank of the other two dimensions. A final rank order of the trademarks for the three dimensions combined was thus obtained.

MEMORY-VALUE

A score of seven was assigned to a trademark every time it was the first of the group which was written down by *S*, a six for each time it was second, and so on. If it did not appear at all, it was given a score of zero. From the totals of the summed scores, the trademarks were ranked in terms of the degree to which they stood out and were remembered by *S*. The trademark having the highest score was rank one, the second two, and so on.

Using a Spearman rho, rank order correlations were computed for each of the aspects of effectiveness with one another. On the basis of face validity, the memory-value aspect of our effectiveness definition was felt to be most critical. Hence the correlations of salience and meaning with memory-value were of special importance. Finally, a composite rank order was composed by combining the ranks of the salience and meaning dimensions, giving them equal weight, and this was correlated with the memory-value order. The matrix of correlations is presented in Table 1.

TABLE 1

INTERCORRELATION OF EFFECTIVENESS MEASURE

	V.T.	S.D.	Aussage
Visual Threshold	—	.77*	.75*
Semantic Differential		—	.82*
Aussage			—
V.T. and S.D. Combined			.94**

* Significant at .05 level.
** Significant at .01 level.

As can be seen in Table 1, all of the aspects correlate positively with one another. Of particular interest is the exceptionally high correlation between memory-value and the composite ordering of the salience and meaning aspects.

DISCUSSION

We feel that the results of this study indicate a great deal of power is to be obtained from a straightforward approach to a particularly practical but slippery problem. The approach has involved techniques taken from two subdisciplines of psychology, namely, the sensory and cognitive areas. Through an opportune choice of variables in these areas, we have demonstrated the significance of the variables for either an evaluation of an existing emblem or of an original, new trademark. This obviously does not mean that the most effective trademark, by this definition, will necessarily give rise to an increase in sales or connote integrity or honesty of the firm symbolized. But it is even more apparent that such desired ends are not to be fostered by making the trademark less visible or less favorable in its meaning. The first step toward "effectiveness" in this latter sense is the making of the trademark as effective as possible in salience, meaning, and memory-value.

SUMMARY

We have investigated the effectiveness of seven competing trademarks. Effectiveness is defined in terms of the salience, meaning, and memory-value of the trademark. The three characteristics were found to be positively related. Further, taking memory-value to be our major dependent variable, we have found that, through a combination of our salience and meaning measures, we were able to predict the memory-value with a high degree of success.

REFERENCE

Osgood, C. E., Suci, G. J., & Tannenbaum, P. H. *The Measurement of Meaning.* Urbana: Univer. Illinois Press, 1957.

D. PRICING

34. How Auto Firms Figure Their Costs to Reckon the Price Dealers Pay

DAN CORDTZ

DETROIT—Why do car prices keep going up?

"Administered prices" and exorbitant corporate profits are to blame, charges the United Auto Workers Union.

Wage increases have far outstripped gains in productivity, retort the auto manufacturers.

A puzzled public, which ultimately must foot the bill for either swollen profits or wages, is bombarded with "evidence" from both sides and not unnaturally ends up suspecting that both sides may share the blame.

The problem of rising prices and their causes is a vital and vexatious one—the more so in the auto industry because of its position as a mainstay of the economy and the evidence, growing stronger, that customers are starting to balk at higher price tags.

BID FROM WASHINGTON

So important is the auto pricing question regarded, in fact, that a Senate committee headed by Tennessee's Estes Kefauver has invited representatives of the U. A. W. and four auto companies to seek some answers.

It's highly questionable, however, that the hearings, scheduled for late January, will yield any conclusions satisfactory to all concerned. Indeed, the

From *The Wall Street Journal*, December 10, 1957, pp. 1ff.

extent to which they can even provide facts to help the public make up its own mind depends almost entirely on the Senators' ability to pry out figures on auto costs which the manufacturers traditionally guard even more closely than styling secrets.

On many occasions in the past, the car makers have sternly rebuffed demands by the U. A. W. for a "a look at the books" and there's no indication their attitude has changed.

But if company spokesmen are publicly tight-lipped on the matter, an occasional auto executive is willing to discuss—privately—the manner in which auto companies determine car prices and the factors that figure in that determination. Based on conversations with such officials, a cost breakdown has been obtained of the sort the Senators will be seeking—the share of car's price that goes for labor, for material, for overhead, for sales and administration and for profit.

A STATISTIC, A CONCEPT

Before examining the figures, however, two important points must be made. First, although the car makers frequently point publicly to their relatively modest margin of profit on sales, the really important statistic, and one which the successful auto executive never loses sight of, is the return on invested capital.

Secondly, the allocation of costs in every company is made on the basis of what is known as the "standard volume," a concept developed in the 1920's by General Motors executives and carried through by all companies — practically without modification — ever since. It works roughly like this: The company forecasts the market and its own share over a long period. It then builds plant capacity great enough to handle not only that volume but the added volume of peak years in the sales cycle. Standard volume is set as a percentage of that plant capacity and costs are allocated and prices figured on the basis of that volume.

Standard volume really amounts to the number of cars over which all costs shall be spread for the purposes of estimating per-car costs — and thus determining per-car prices. Because all costs — the value of unused plant and equipment as well as that being used — must be charged to standard volume, the per-car costs also include the cost of idle capacity.

What's the industry's calculated standard volume today? Estimates range all the way from 33% of capacity to 80%. "My guess," says one executive, "is that the industry as a whole has a total capacity today of 10 million cars and an aggregate standard volume of perhaps 55% of that, or 5.5 million cars." For comparison, actual output reached 7.9 million cars in 1955, fell to 5.8 million in 1956 and is expected to run about 6.2 million this year.

MAKING A CAR

With these points in mind, picture as an example of the pricing process an imaginary car-making division in the Ford-Chevrolet-Plymouth field. The cost figures to be used are those for an actual vehicle of one of the "low-priced three" but they illustrate the approximate costs of the others as well. This sample division's first concern with prices begins with the assignment to it

by the parent corporation of its "asset base" for the coming model year.

The asset base is the portion of the corporation's total assets on which the division is expected to return a profit. For illustration, say the sample division's asset base is set at $600 million. At the same time the division is also notified that its required return on its share of the corporate investment is 30% before taxes at standard volume. In other words, at year's end it is expected to have turned over to the corporation total earnings of $180 million on its standard volume, which we shall set at one million cars.

Before it has even started to estimate costs, therefore, the division has established the average profit it must make on its first million cars — $180 per car.

"It's not nearly as simple as it sounds," cautions a veteran official. "In fact, the complexities are unbelievable For competitive reasons, for instance, we may have to shave the profits thin on one model and get them back on another. Our profit on operations varies, too, and so we may be able to sell a stripped version of a certain model for very little profit, knowing we'll make it up on the extra-cost accessories."

Acknowledging these qualifications, however, the only way to get an understanding of pricing is to pick out a "typical" vehicle and break it down. Our example is a four-door sedan in the upper end of the division's price bracket which sells in Detroit, complete with radio and heater, for about $2,600 — including a full factory-suggested dealer markup and all taxes.

Just what does this car cost to build?

By far the most important factor in determining its cost is material, which, to the division finally assembling the car, includes not only parts purchased from outside suppliers but those fabricated by itself or another company division from raw materials bought by the corporation. Outside purchases, in this case, total $500 of parts. The other, or "inside transfer" parts, cost the assembling division $600—but the original cost to the company for raw material was only $300. The additional cost represents value added by internal manufacture and includes these items: $50 in productive labor costs of parts-making divisions; $25 in administrative costs; $75 in profits to the other divisions (which also have asset bases and required earnings) and $150 in "burden." This last charge, which also figures in the assembly division's costs, takes in all overhead expenses—including nonproduction labor such as maintenance men and time-keepers, amortization of plant and equipment, local taxes, utility charges, insurance and the like. Thus, final material costs as the car starts down the assembly line amount to $1,100.

DIRECT LABOR COSTS

The division's next cost consideration is that of direct, productive labor which, for the sample vehicle at the assembly division's level, is estimated at $75. This does not, of course, represent all the manufacturing labor in a motor car. Another $50, as was previously mentioned, is involved in the the labor cost of "inside transfer" material. And it is reasonable to assume that the labor costs of outside suppliers amounted to another $50. But to the car assembly division, these already have been covered in material costs. To the materials bill, productive labor adds only $75.

Finally is added the division's "burden" charges of $125, and the sum of material, labor and "burden" yields a "plant-level cost" of $1,300. Plant-level cost is nothing more than the actual cost of procuring and converting material into a finished car—with no allowance whatever for the division's costs of planning, administration or sales.

The first and most important item added to the plant-level cost is the required profit of $180. All other items are susceptible, to some degree, of reduction. But profit must be $180 if the required return on investment is to be met.

ADDING CHARGES

There follow these additional charges (which usually are figured in terms of a percentage of sales or plant-level costs but which are indicated here only in their actual dollar figures):

Freight, both inbound and outbound, $85. Inbound freight is the charge for materials and parts shipped into the assembling division's plants and is separate from the actual cost of materials. Outbound freight is the charge for delivering the car to the dealer in Detroit.

Tooling and engineering, which some executives argue should properly be charged to burden as a part of plant-level cost, $50.

Sales and advertising expenses, $50.

Administrative, commercial and miscellaneous charges, $65.

This last item, according to some officials, can hide a multitude of items. One cost frequently included, for example, is a warranty charge, about which the auto makers are extremely touchy. The manufacturers normally guarantee a new car against defects for a specified period and if a rash of part failures turns up it can be costly indeed.

"A competitor of ours got in trouble with a batch of bumpers last year," recalls an official of one of the low-priced three with obvious relish. "The original bumper cost only $13, but the cost of shipping a new one, paying the labor bill for replacing the faulty one, and then shipping the bad bumper back to the factory amounted to $27 a car."

It's probable that the miscellaneous item for our sample car contains a $15 charge for warranty costs based on past experience.

Another auto executive contends that some companies also add a "variance" factor, which is simply a bit of padding to cover possible errors in estimating other costs. This, he says, can range from 1% to 3 %. Although other officials dispute the existence of a variance factor, it could also account for about $15 of the miscellaneous item.

PRICE TO DEALERS

Here then is a recapitulation of the division's costs:

Materials, outside and inside	$1,100
Productive labor	75
Burden	125
Profit	180
Freight	85
Tooling and engineering	50
Sales and advertising	50
Administrative, etc.	65
Total sales price to dealers	1,730

All of the above costs, as previously indicated, are based on the standard volume. But they are affected in widely varying degrees if the division falls below or exceeds that figure.

For example, material and productive labor costs which vary in almost direct ratio to volume. Two million cars will require twice the material needed for one million. And barring the need for overtime operations, twice the labor costs also will be incurred.

Many of the other cost items, however, are less controllable and the major share of burden is rigidly fixed. Thus if sales reach only 800,000 cars, material and labor costs per car remain constant but burden charges could easily rise, for instance, to $145 per car from $125. The $20 of "unabsorbed burden" must, of course, come out of profits, which are further reduced by unit sales much smaller than planned. Whereas in our sample case example, $180 million would have been earned on sales of one million cars, profits would plummet almost 30% to $128 million on a 20% decline in sales.

IN REVERSE, TOO

The same leverage factor works in reverse, to the division's benefit, when sales go above standard volume. Over one million cars, for example, most of burden costs becomes a much smaller factor on each car so that profits per car accelerate rapidly. If, for instance, sales reach 1.2 million, it could reduce burden per car to $110 and the "overabsorbed burden" of $15 per car would then be added to profits. Earnings on such a 20% rise in sales would then total $234 million—a gain of about 30%.

Burden, of course, is not the only really fixed charge; administration costs, tooling and engineering also are relatively stable, too, but these costs do not remain as constant as burden when volume fluctuates. If, for example, a company sees that volume is going to fall short of standard volume, it can trim office expenses far more readily than it can cut its local taxes. The leverage, in short, stems from many fairly fixed charges, but burden is the most important single factor.

This uneven impact of volume on profits and sales is indicated by some figures from car sales in 1954 and 1955. Chrysler's unit sales, for instance, rose 79% from 1954 to 1955, but dollar profits zoomed 440%. Ford sales went up 31% in the same period, while profits soared 92%. The effect was less pronounced on G.M., where sales rose 32% and profits went up 48%. In 1956, the reverse effect was demonstrated. Chrysler sales dropped 32%, but profits plunged 80%. Ford sales fell 25%; Ford profits declined 46%. G. M. sales dipped 19%; its profits were off 29%.

It is this volatility that accounts for sharp peaks and valleys of auto company profits, exhibited so dramatically in 1956 and 1957 by Chrysler Corp., and this makes the auto industry the risky, high stakes game it is. The lever on profits is also responsible for decisions to make huge and costly investments in styling changes in an effort to cash in on lucrative "extra" sales.

"In 1956 we made only minor changes and fell more than 200,000 cars behind Chevy," explains a Ford Division official.

"Assuming that if we'd made a bigger change, we would have stuck close to Chevy, our lack of change cost us nearly all those 200,000 sales. And with all of them up in the range where it's mostly gravy, we could have financed a lot of tooling with those profits." That Ford learned its lesson is obvious. After spending $246 million for a 1957 model that's leading the pack, it plunged another $185 million into a broad alteration of the successful 1957 styling for its 1958 models.

The rapid rise of profits after standard volume is passed has one final consequence. Although it's practically unheard of for an auto firm to make a public price change in the middle of the model run, it is the auto makers' feeling they can well afford to give dealers special discounts and bonuses in the closing weeks or months of a model year to encourage them to cut prices and thus clear out any unsold cars.

"SUGGESTED" PRICES

As prices are set, however, the car's official price to the dealer is fixed at $1,730 — no matter what happens to volume. But, as every buyer is well aware, the invoice price is only the beginning of his tab. The factory first of all "suggests" (it cannot legally do more) a dealer markup of 31.6% of the invoice price — or, as it is usually expressed, 24% of the "factory-suggested list price," or, in the case of the sample car, $546.

In today's hotly competitive auto market, it's rarely possible for a dealer in the low-priced field to get that gross profit. Figures of the National Automobile Dealers Association suggest the markup on such a model is closer to $330. This varies widely, of course, depending on what a dealer is willing to shave to make a sale. As every car buyer knows, dealers often will snip charges here and there and sometimes will even cut their own take — on the theory that they'll make it up on greater

volume. This price snipping becomes more widespread, of course, toward the end of a model year.

Added to the invoice price which the dealer pays for the car, but not calculated in his markup, is an item labeled by various names (General Motors calls it E.O.H.: excise, overhead and handling) which is made up almost entirely of the 10% Federal excise tax. To the sample car price it adds another $180.

Dealer handling, which amounts to another $50 for the car used as an example, is another factory-suggested charge which the dealer may or may not be able to tack onto his price. It is simply a standard "make-ready" charge based on records of the time normally spent by retailers to prepare the car for delivery.

Finally, and inescapably, come state and local taxes, including licensing fees. In Detroit, these would total approximately $80. The grand total: $2,586.

WAGES AND PRICES

With all the items of cost thus in hand, what is indicated about the causes for price hikes?

First of all, it seems clear that wage increases can hardly explain away all the 1958 price rises which, for models similar to our sample, ranged this year from $85 to $135. Total direct productive labor costs of parts suppliers and the auto manufacturer amount in this case to only an estimated $175 — certainly no more than $200. Even adding in hourly-rated non-productive labor could hardly bring the U. A. W. labor bill to more than $300 to $320. Based on average auto worker wages of $2.47 an hour, this would indicate there are about 120 to 125 man-hours of hourly-rated labor in the sample car. If wages rose 18.6 cents an hour in the past year, as Ford Vice President Benson Ford asserted recently, this would have boosted costs less than $25 on the car.

"That's not the whole story, though,"

objects a company official. "When we raise the pay of our hourly-rated people, we also have to do the same for salaried workers. The total wage bill per car produced goes up by more than just the U. A. W.'s gains." This obviously is true. But even adding in, to the extent possible, equivalent percentage wage boosts for the rest of the company's employes produces an indicated cost increase of less than $40.

This estimate, moreover, ignores productivity rises which offset at least part of the higher wages. If wages go up, as we have estimated, by 12.5% and productivity gains 3% the effective increase in costs is but $30.

A SORE POINT

The question of productivity gains is a sore one in the auto industry. Company officials say the industry has accepted the principle of sharing equally with its workers the gains of productivity. The productivity gain it shares, however, is that of the national economy as a whole. The U. A. W., which insists productivity of auto workers has risen much faster than that of the total industrial community, charges that the companies share with the workers only the first 2.5% of productivity gains and pocket the rest. Auto men retort that productivity should not be shared on a strictly pro rata basis. The relative contribution of management and labor to the increase in productivity must also be taken into account, they contend.

"Besides," one economist adds, "the union is never content to accept the gain in productivity as its wage increase. If the U. A. W. is going to insist on a 9% wage boost, what difference does it make whether productivity has gone up 3% or 6%?"

Some industry spokesmen carry the "pay hike effect" argument back even further. They assert that the U. A. W., as a pace setter, inevitably touches off new rounds of wage increases among em-

ployes of their suppliers of raw materials and services — pushing up material costs as well.

CATCHING UP?

The union's rebuttal is twofold: It argues the steelmakers and other suppliers need not raise prices because of higher wages — high prices in steel, goes the union argument, are caused by the same "exorbitant" profits as are high prices in cars. Moreover, auto union officials note, steel workers' wages already are higher than those in the auto industry. The U. A. W., they claim, is not setting the pace but merely catching up with the rest of industry.

The factor of material price increases, incidentally, also fails to furnish a pivotal clue to car price rises. One source estimates the steel price increase earlier this year raised the cost of building our sample car by only $12 and costs for other materials, which altogether represent only 30% of car-making requirements, probably rose only slightly. Some commodities (copper, for example) have actually declined in price.

What of the union's charges about excessive profits? The total corporate profit in our sample car comes to $255, including the profits made by parts-making divisions in the company. This is barely 10% of the price the buyer pays for the car and less than 15% of the price the company receives from the dealer. Auto officials are far from apologetic about the figure.

"Sure, we make good money," says the head of one large car-making division, "but we sure don't steal it. The union doesn't recognize that just putting the car together isn't the whole thing — or even the most important thing. Management has to do the terribly hard job of making the right decisions, day in and day out, to keep the company running and provide production workers with jobs."

"CONSIDERING THE RISKS"

Executives are emphatic as well in denying their companies make an outlandish return on investment, which is their real concern. "Considering the risks involved in this business, the swings in the market and the gambling on styling, we don't make any more on our capital than other comparable industries," one auto man insists.

Consider the current rate of return. In 1956 General Motors earned before income taxes a 38% return on what it calls its "shareholders' net investment"—a figure composed of real estate, depreciated plant and equipment and net working capital. Ford, on the same basis, returned a little more than 24% before income taxes and Chrysler—in a dismal sales year—realized pre-tax profits of only 2.8% of shareholders' net investment.

Profits in 1955 were distorted by the fact that sales boomed so high standard volume levels were left far behind. In 1953, however, the last previous year when sales approximated 1956 levels, General Motors returned almost 60% on net shareholder investment; Ford, 36%; and Chrysler, nearly 37%. Net shareholder investment, of course, is much less than total assets. In 1953, for instance, G.M.'s net shareholder investment was slightly under $2.7 billion, while total assets were $4.4 billion.

Not one of the three, therefore, realized a return in 1956 as great as three years earlier. Does this demolish the union's case? Not in the opinion of the U. A. W. economists, who decline to comment on the price-profit argument now with the Washington hearings near but who have made their position clear in the past.

WHO'S FINANCING?

"The reason their return has declined," one explained awhile back, "is that they have added enormously to their plant and equipment so that they have a much higher base on which to figure return and our position is that the customers, not the stockholders, have financed that enormous expansion. They've added to the investment base out of profits instead of going to the securities market for additional funds."

It's true that, in the years since 1953, G. M.'s depreciated property, plant and equipment has risen from $1.5 billion to $2.9 billion, with almost all of the new investment financed out of profits. Similarly, Ford's plant has gone up from $872 million to almost $1.7 billion and Chrysler's has increased from $345 million to $613 million. But auto executives have a ready answer to the union's objection.

"It's all the stockholders' money," one insists. "I don't see how you can distinguish between money taken out of the investor's mattress and invested in new plant and the legitimate profits earned by the stockholders' money but left voluntarily in the business. The stockholder is, through his support of management, indicating his desire to reinvest some of his profits. How can you say he's not entitled to the same return on that reinvested money as on money he got from some other source and poured into the auto company's expansion."

"JUST GRAVY"

U. A. W. economists, however, do insist there is a distinction and assert that only the original investment can properly be termed "risk" capital. "The rest is just gravy," one argues. "You can't justify a high rate of return on that kind of money."

Auto men object strenuously, on the other hand, to the use of pre-tax figures in calculating their return. "We don't see half that money," they explain. "Our only real profit is what's left when Uncle Sam takes his." This is so, but for purposes of setting prices the auto companies use a profit figure which will yield an after-tax return they regard as satisfactory. The actual net profit on our sample car is about $125, but a charge of $255 must be passed on to the buyer to enable the company to come out with that net.

The U. A. W. is unimpressed with the industry's argument on pre-tax profits. "When they talk about what they pay out in wages, they're talking about pay before taxes," one unionist asserts hotly. "Our members don't pocket all of that $2.47 an hour. But when the companies are talking about their own income, they want to reduce it to net."

Because of consolidated reporting, it's impossible to determine how much profits per car have risen. But they have not gone up nearly as fast as auto company investment in physical facilities, as indicated by the declining rate of return between 1953 and 1956.

AN ASSUMPTION

Industry sources guesstimate the annual profit rise between 1953 and 1956 at around $18 to $20 for a car such as we have used in the sample. The calculation goes something like this: Assume our sample division's asset base doubled between 1953 and 1956 and that its return on that base declined, as did G. M.'s, from 60% to 38%. This assumption is drawn from the fact that the value of the property, plant and equipment of each of the Big Three in the period almost doubled. The asset

base of our sample car, therefore, would have been $300 in 1953, half of its $600 asset base now. A 60% return in 1953 would have been $180 million, or $180 per car on a million car sales. If the base then rises to $600 million, a 38% return in 1956 is $228 million, or $228 a car, on the same number of sales. This is a rise of 27%. Translating that increase in terms of the corporate per-car profit of $255 in the present sample car, the profit per car would have risen by $55 since 1953, an average annual rise of a bit more than $18.

To sum up: We have estimated that labor costs have accounted for perhaps $30 of the higher price tag. Material price increases make up another $12 of the greater cost, and the company has boosted its profit figure by $18. The total is $60, leaving a variety of miscellaneous charges to account for the additional $14 or so which has been added to the price of the car at wholesale. With wholesale prices up to $75, the dealer is expected to add $25 to his profit (although competition may not allow this) to jack up the price to the buyer by $100.

This, according to some auto officials, is about what has happened. One of them sums up the situation thusly:

"To be perfectly frank I don't see any place where you can start cutting. As long as we have general inflation—and I have to admit that we've helped further it—neither labor nor management is going to lag behind willingly. Prices are simply going to have to go on up until the buyers quit buying."

35. Advertised Specials and Local Competition Among Supermarkets

ROGER W. GRAY AND ROICE ANDERSON

A large proportion of the supermarket advertising dollar is spent for local newspaper advertising, which in most metropolitan areas of the United States has come to feature special prices on a select list of items. The investigation whose findings are summarized in this report has focused upon these advertised specials, in the hope of gaining some insight into a competitive device which has been growing in importance (1, p. 134, table 37). The findings reported here are relevant to some only of the many questions that might be posed regarding the practice. An obvious question concerns the extent to which prices on featured items are reduced from their regular levels; the clear indication is that they are reduced considerably. The relative importance of the featured items was also examined, but since we did not obtain any data on relative sales, this could only be inferred from stated assumptions whose validity was not tested. The inference drawn is that the specials can be quite important in the household food budget. Another question concerned the extent of correspondence between specials and over-all price levels from store to store. Do the special prices reflect any information about regular shelf prices? No very sharp general picture emerged here, but comparisons between certain

stores are suggestive of the different role and emphasis given to specials. A further question pertained to store strategy in the use of specials, insofar as this can be detected in the selection of items and prices. Awareness of the danger that we might presuppose it where no conscious strategy existed may have discouraged us in this quest, which in any event produced little evidence. The final question on which we sought evidence was whether the so-called "battle of the brands"[1] was manifest in specials advertising. The threatened brand franchises of manufacturers had been built largely upon advertising; *a posteriori* it seemed that they would be defended through advertising. The evidence suggests that they are being defended in the weekly specials, or even that a counterattack on behalf of manufacturer's brands is conducted here.

THE SAMPLE

The prices used in this analysis were obtained by direct enumeration in eight

From *Food Research Institute Studies*, Vol. III, No. 2 (Stanford, Calif.: Stanford University, May, 1962), pp. 125-40.

[1] A very common designation is that of "private labels" for what we refer to as retail brands; whereas manufacturer's brands are sometimes more loosely termed "name" brands, "major" brands, or even "advertised" brands in contradistinction to "private" labels. We follow Mueller and Garoian (1, p. 92) in distinguishing between retail brands on the one hand and, under the heading of manufacterer's brands, either manufacturer's or distributor's brands on the other.

stores in Palo Alto, California, during eight successive weeks, from January 20 to March 10, 1960. Since several of the chain stores have more than one outlet in Palo Alto, the eight stores represent thirteen retail outlets. Each of these is a supermarket, as defined by the Bureau of the Census in terms of annual sales volume of at least $500,000. The stores are located in various shopping centers in the city, and include most of the competitive possibilities for a resident who shops locally. We presume that a large proportion of the food purchases for the 50,000 inhabitants of Palo Alto are made in these stores. Large and small corporate chains, an independent, a member of a voluntary chain, and a consumer's cooperative are included in the eight firms represented.

The procedure for selecting the list of items to be priced each week began with the weekly newspaper advertisements. From these eight advertisements were selected items that we could confidently expect to find in all stores. This meant that we listed the well-known manufacturer's labels of most branded items, and also the more common cuts of meats or varieties of fresh fruits and vegetables. The problem of quality differences enters with any departure from identical branded merchandise. There is apparently no complete solution to this problem. There are several well-accepted brands of many common shelf items; it seemed unduly restrictive to accept no substitution among them. We accepted the retail stores' pricing practice as the guide in such cases; any pair of brands which were regularly priced the same in any given store were considered perfect substitutes. We also equated the same cuts of meat among stores, as well as the same varieties of fresh fruits and vegetables, despite our subjective feeling that important quality differences prevail. The U.S. Department of Agriculture inspects and grade stamps fresh meats: the stores in this survey sold only the "choice" grade.[2] We occasionally excluded fresh fruits or vegetables because of their conspicuously low quality, judging from appearances. Most of our tabulations show the meat and produce results separately, which allows them to be discounted or disregarded in view of possible quality differences, and also reveals different emphasis from store to store.

Also recorded from the advertisements, in order partially to compensate for the bias in favor of major manufacturer's brands that inheres in the aim to select generally available items, were "low-price specials" on items of lesser known manufacturer's labels, or more often retailer's labels. One of the stores, for example, might feature its own lowest price brand of canned fruits or vegetables; we then specified "lowest-priced No. 1 can of cut green beans," e.g., at the same time that Del Monte and its equivalents were also priced.

Without pretending to have solved the quality problem, we feel that interesting and useful results flow from our treatment of it, which accords considerable significance to brands, to common pricing practice, to grade labeling of meats, and to our own judgment of the appearance of fresh fruits and vegetables. Our procedure said in effect that all major manufacturer's labels that were priced together within stores were of equal quality. Similarly, the lowest priced labels of branded items were treated as being of equal quality. Finally, all meats of similar cut and with occasional exceptions all fresh fruits and vegetables were considered equal in quality.

The list of items priced during the fifth week of the survey is shown (chart), in order to provide some indication of the coverage of a list growing out of the procedure employed.

We also compared our list with the basic list of the U.S. Bureau of Labor

---

[2] Cf. 2 for illustration of the range of quality found within the U.S.D.A. choice grade.

Cereals and Bakery Products:

Flour° †
Biscuit Mix
Rice
Rolled Oats
Corn Flakes
Bread
Graham Crackers
Soda Crackers
Party Crackers
Oat Meal Cookies
Sandwich Cookies

Meats, Poultry, and Fish:

T-Bone Steak
Round Steak
Sirloin Steak
Porterhouse Steak
Chuck Roast
Cross Rib Roast
Standing Rib Roast
Ground Beef
Pork Chops
Bacon
Ham
Lamb Leg
Frankfurters
Canned Luncheon Meat
Frying Chicken
Frozen Fish Sticks
Frozen Meat Pies
Canned Salmon
Canned Tuna

Dairy Products:

Ice Cream
Butter
American Cheese
Cheddar Cheese
Cottage Cheese
Evaporated Milk
Instant Milk

Fruits and Vegetables:

(Frozen)
Strawberries
Orange Juice°
Vegetables
Fruit Pie
(Fresh)
Apples
Bananas
Oranges
Lemons
Grapefruit
Potatoes
Yams
Onions
Carrots
Lettuce
Celery Hearts
Cabbage
Tomatoes
Avocado
Cauliflower
Spinach
(Canned)
Peaches‡
Pineapple
Fruit Cocktail°
Pears°
Apricots°
Applesauce‡
Pineapple Juice‡
Corn°
Peas‡
Tomatoes°
Green Beans°
Tomato Juice°
Baby Food (strained)
Baby Food (junior)
(Dried)
Prunes
Beans

Other Foods:

Vegetable Soup
Meat Soup
Vegetable Soup Mix
Meat Soup Mix
Onion Soup Mix
Beans with Pork
Dill Pickles
Catsup
Instant Coffee
Coffee
Tea Bags
Cola Drink
Vegetable Shortening
Margarine‡
Lard
Mayonnaise
Salad Dressing
Peanut Butter
Cooking Oil
Sugar
Corn Syrup
Grape Jelly
Chocolate Bar
Pudding
Eggs
Gelatin Dessert

° Both a major manufacturer's brand and a low-priced brand were priced.
† This list does not include the complete description of the item, nor does it include several cases in which more than one variety of the same item was priced, apples for example.
‡ Only a low-priced brand was priced.

Statistics (B.L.S.)(3), from which official food price indexes are computed, in order to gain an objective indication of the extent of coverage of our list. There are 77 items on the basic B.L.S. list, between 60 and 71 of which appeared on our list from one week to another. In addition, of course, items appeared on our list, which contained from 90 to 103 items, that do not appear on the basic B.L.S. list.

The rules that were followed in preparing the list for enumeration were inherently not ironclad, but on the two occasions when the two authors prepared the lists independently they conformed very closely being exact duplicates excepting for two or three items. The advertisements change markedly even over a brief period, what with special holiday fare being featured at one time or store, canned goods at another, retailer's brands at another, or some individual manufacturer's brand at another, so the extent and coverage of the list is not always uniform. Only food items were included in our survey. Other items are important in the stores and are included in the advertisements. Availability of items was not a problem; in only one instance, obviously unintentional, was the advertised item not available at all, and in few instances was the supply exhausted before the time covered by the advertisement had elapsed. No adjustment was made if sales per customer were limited. Once or twice shelf supplies of a particularly attractive special were exhausted but were quickly replenished upon request. In the first two weeks of the survey we spot-checked prices after the specials period had expired, and learned that in every case the price went back to the higher "normal" level. We thereupon abandoned this check, on the assumption that this pattern would continue.

ARE SPECIALS REALLY SPECIAL?

The first question posed was whether the advertised specials incorporate *bona fide* price reductions. Occasionally, of course, items are listed in the advertisements at their standard prices, particularly when an advertising theme is being carried out, or perhaps "fillers" are being placed in the advertisements. On very rare occasions a featured item may even be priced above its standard price. But in the great preponderance of cases—92 per cent of all 1,546 observations of specials—the price of the item

was lower in the stores that advertised it than in those that did not. Our specials list contained a total of 225 items, each of these averaging nearly seven appearances to make the total of 1,546 observations. For each of the 225 items the average special price was compared with the average non-special price, and the mean of all these ratios was 78.6 per cent, indicating a saving of over 20 per cent for buying these items on special. Furthermore, the incidence of an item in the specials list, indicative of its "competitive focus," influences the degree of price reduction. At one extreme, 50 items appeared only once during the survey, and their average price reduction was 13.3 per cent; at the other extreme, 55 items appeared ten or more times each, and their average price reduction was 26.3 per cent. The remaining 120 items that appeared two to nine times each were reduced 22.5 per cent in price on the average.

It pays, not only to shop the specials, but also to keep posted on which items are being most widely and frequently featured. There may be a number of reasons for this. An item may be a traditional loss leader, selected to attract customers into the store in the hope that they will buy other items as well. Since legal problems arise, the store managers are reluctant to talk about loss leaders,[3] but items like vacuum packed major

---

[3] Since the period of our survey, a new California law, aimed at loss leaders, forbids the practice of limiting the number of items that will be sold to an individual customer. On at least one occasion, a competing store has sent a truck to haul away a large volume of an advertised special. One store in our group changed its competitive strategy drastically in the context of the new law and the attendant publicity given loss leaders. This store adopted the practice of listing items and prices that it considered to be loss leaders at other stores. Its own strategy was then to rely upon a 5 per cent discount on *all* merchandise in all purchases in excess of one dollar; and its advertising slogan became "Choose Your Own Specials." After a brief and unhappy experience, this effort to depart from the "specials game" was abandoned.

brand coffee at less than the wholesale price of green coffee beans in San Francisco, Gold Medal Flour at 39 cents when the regular price was 67 cents, or Best Foods Mayonnaise at 39 cents instead of 59 cents may belong in this category. This need not mean, of course, that the retail store is suffering any loss on such items, as the manufacturer or distributor may offer substantial price concessions (advertising allowances) to promote the product or forestall defections to private brands.

Another reason that certain items may be featured is that they are in abundant supply. The advertisements provide valuable information when spring lamb comes to market; or when fruit or vegetable harvests are in full swing, with perhaps bountiful crops of some and short crops of others; or when in a variety of other circumstances they call attention to abundance. Or the advertisements may be keyed to consumer preferences; the Lenten period, for example, occasioning the recurrence of certain types of items at certain times. The store that plans such themes may buy ahead in large volume and thereby obtain price concessions which are passed along to the consumer. The last two weeks of our survey period fell within Lent, which led several stores to feature Lenten treats or Lenten specials such as fish at below regular prices.

Competition itself may force lower prices on certain prominently featured items. The advertising copy is not prepared in a vacuum; on the contrary, close attention is given to what others are featuring and which of their specials seem to be winning customers. Pressure may be brought on the distributor — "You gave this special to our friends across the street; give it to us if you want to see it on our shelves" — or the store may absorb the cost of meeting the competition.

New products are also introduced in this milieu. New brands of instant coffee, for example, were brought out during the period of our survey. Introductory prices were placed on these and they were given considerable space in the newspaper advertisements and in the stores. Other established brands, to prevent inroads being made onto their franchise, retaliated in kind. Price wars flare up, from this or other causes, and may persist for a time to the delight of the observant consumer.

The price reductions are real and substantial; but it may be objected that chasing all over town to run down the various specials is worthwhile only when there is a gasoline price war too, or that even the time and effort consumed in trying to fit a menu to the specials is more than the saving warrants. How important and broadly representative and widely distributed are the specials?

THE COVERAGE OF THE SPECIALS

Economizing by purchasing specials obviously does not permit an unlimited range of choice. The typical weekly specials advertisement contains about 50 food items which seems trivial by comparison with the more than 5,000 food items carried in the store. But the specials are more important than their mere numbers indicate: a random selection each week of 50 items in a store for a 20 per cent price reduction would not be nearly so meaningful as the selection of prominent items, from a food budget standpoint, that is actually made.[4] The

[4] A limitation on measuring the importance of specials arises from the impossibility of saying how much value consumers place on "choice" or "variety" as such, as well as on a particular good or brand. One who has already selected presumably places no value on the discarded alternatives, but before the selection he may value (a) his known first choice or (b) the privilege of choosing from among many. Some discount houses that have added grocery departments have reversed the tendency of supermarkets to enlarge the range of choice, while preserving the other major features of supermarket merchandising.

TABLE 1

INDEX OF PRICES SHOWING THE EFFECT OF SPECIALS

| Store | Departments | | | Total |
	Meat	Produce	Other	
A	84.4	96.0	91.2	88.1
B	88.8	88.0	95.4	91.9
C	92.4	94.9	93.2	92.9
D	97.4	92.4	92.2	94.8
E	96.3	88.6	92.5	94.2
F	91.2	94.0	97.1	94.1
G	96.3	94.1	95.1	95.6
H	102.3	92.7	97.2	99.5

[a]The index number compares the cost of our list in the designated store, its specials included, to the same list in all stores *excluding* specials.

specials list comprised a large fraction of the list of items in the B.L.S. index, but this exaggerates the coverage of the specials, owing to the fact that the list was taken from the advertisements of all eight stores. Shopping in as many as three stores would be convenient in terms of their proximity but it would be scarcely reasonable to shop in all eight. More than 75 per cent of the 77 items in the basic B.L.S. list, accounting for more than 85 per cent of the relative importance, appeared each week in our own specials list. Any one of three clusters of three stores each that are located in convenient proximity accounted for upwards of 40 per cent of the items and 47 per cent of the relative importance. The average for an individual store, so extensive was the overlapping, was 26 per cent of the items and 33 per cent of the relative importance. And the specials list, as was mentioned earlier, understates the coverage of specials because we chose items with a view toward direct price comparison, thus omitting many. The buyer who has room to store some items, enough leeway in the budget, and enough menu flexibility to accommodate the specials, can make an important part of her food purchases from the advertised specials.

An index of the combined effect of price reductions *and* specials coverage is obtained by answering the following question: How do the prices of those items actually priced in a given store, about one-fourth of which were on special (see Appendix Table I) compare with their average non-special price at all stores over the eight-week period? The answer is shown, by stores and departments, in Table 1, where the average saving per store is seen to range from 0.5 to 11.9 per cent. This table suggests that the specials may reduce food bills up to 10 per cent, depending upon which one store she shops in, for the consumer who pays enough attention to specials for her shopping list to be made up of one-fourth specials and the remainder non-specials. This overstates the savings to the extent that our selection procedure favored specials more than the housewife is likely to; but it understates savings to the extent that consumers shop specials in more than one store.

THE SPECIALS AS AN INDEX OF STORE PRICES

The question arises as to the extent to which advertised prices reflect the general level of store prices. "We sell for less" is what the advertisements tend to suggest, and often to claim. Some of the advertisements do stress quality of course, and there is even some hint in the advertising that the specials are a

TABLE 2
REFLECTIONS OF NON-SPECIAL PRICES IN SPECIAL PRICES

| Store | Rank sum of | |
	Unweighted price index of items on special	Unweighted price index of items not on special
A	12	50
B	29	19.5
C	47	25
D	31	29
E	59	43
F	36	22
G	30	36.5
H	44	63

misleading guide to store price levels.[5] Such departures are exemplified by one store which repeatedly emphasizes the trim of its meat cuts in an obvious effort to justify higher prices by weight; while another store advertises "lowest every-day shelf prices" in an apparent attempt to persuade the consumer that its store price level is lowest, apart from the question of comparative specials.

The rankings of the unweighted price indexes of the specials and of the non-specials are compared in Table 2. The unweighted price index is simply the

$$\frac{\text{Sum of the prices of each item priced in each store each week}}{\text{Sum of the average prices of the same items in all stores all weeks}}.$$

The indexes were ranked each week, then simply summed, so that if a store had the lowest prices every week it would have a rank sum of 8, or highest prices every week a rank of 64, and the mean rank sum would be 36.

Store A has a much higher relative price level for items not on special than for featured items, as does Store H. Stores C and E display the opposite characteristics, and in general the spe-

cial prices provide a poor indication of price levels on items not featured.

There is some indication here, then, that if one shops the specials he had better stick to the specials and not trust them to lead him to the best bargains in general. No doubt the specials are intended in some degree as "come-ons," as this evidence suggests. We pursue the suggestion further by examining individual store data by departments and in some detail.

PRICING POLICY AND THE USE OF SPECIALS: A TWO-STORE COMPARISON

Stores E and A, an independent and a small chain, respectively, afford an interesting contrast in the use of specials and pricing policy for several reasons. As mentioned above, their specials price indexes diverge in opposite directions from their non-specials indexes. Both stores feature manufacturer's brands to the virtual exclusion of retailer's brands (see Appendix Table III). Both also emphasize meats, although from opposite standpoints: Store A was formerly almost exclusively a meat market that featured low-priced meats, which policy has carried over as the store expanded, becoming a small chain of large supermarkets with very large meat departments and heavy emphasis upon meat items in the specials, having by far the largest proportion of meat items in the ads of any store. (See Appendix Table III). Store E features a large meat department under separate management within the store. This meat department emphasizes the quality of its meats and makes no pretense of being low-priced. In the weekly advertisements, meats are frequently featured, with the second largest proportion of meat specials of any store, but nearly always at *regular* prices — certain cuts of beef for example were featured during every week of the survey and always at the same price, which was considerably higher than the average special price. And while we did not undertake an objective comparison of meat quality, it is our opinion, based upon a general *appearance* of quality and upon hearsay, that Store E sells a superior quality and better trim of meat than Store A, and indeed that these two stand at or near the opposite extremes in this regard among the stores studied.

In this light it is pertinent to look at the price indexes of these two stores by departments. Their rank totals and the arithmetic means of their weekly price indexes are shown in Table 3.

The contrasting meat policies show up clearly, Store A featuring low meat prices in its advertisements and selling meat at low prices, while Store E ranks highest in the advertised prices of meats, yet sells meats otherwise at about average prices. In both the produce department and the far more important "all other" category, Store A

displays a very pronounced contrast between its special and non-special prices. In the produce instance, the wider spread between special and non-special prices probably owes to the fact that perishable items need to be moved and clearly warrant special pricing for this purpose; yet this does not explain the discrepancy in rank totals, since all stores face the same problem.

If we focus attention on the price index comparisons instead of their rank totals, we find that buying non-specials in Store A is relatively much more costly than buying specials. Given the quality comparison problem in both meats and produce, plus the contrasting meat reputations of the two stores, and the fact that both feature well-known labels in the "all other" category, it seems fair to make the comparison rest heavily upon this latter category. This comparison suggests that one should buy specials at Store A and non-specials at Store E, as between these two stores; or perhaps a better reading of the data is simply "beware the thousands of non-specials at Store A."

SPECIALS STRATEGY

So clear is the indication that Store A must follow a deliberate policy of pricing other items high in order to support its specials merchandising that we pursue evidence on this point one step further. Many of the items that appear in the survey have a strongly modal price;

TABLE 3
COMPARISON OF STORES A AND E

Store	Meat		Produce		All Other	
	Special	*Non-special*	*Special*	*Non-special*	*Special*	*Non-special*
A (Rank totals)	17	13	25	53	14	63
E (Rank totals)	63	43	33	39	25	39
A (Price indexes)	73.4	93.3	64.2	107.8	76.8	103.9
E (Price indexes)	92.6	99.9	68.7	102.2	84.5	100.4

TABLE 4

NUMBER OF INSTANCES OF PRICES
HIGHER, LOWER, OR SAME AS MODAL
PRICE

Store	Higher	Same	Lower
A	206	110	55
B	74	215	140
C	93	183	134
D	46	222	164
E	132	194	92
F	110	220	127
G	100	187	136
H	126	184	100

the same, or what might be called the "standard" price appearing on many items in most stores. This is especially relevant where the product is identical—a branded can of peas or sack of flour—from store to store. Hence we omit fresh meats and produce again, and tabulate instances of prices on any non-special item, compared to the all-store all-period average non-special price of that item. For Store A, such a price was higher than average 206 times, the same 110 times, and lower 55 times. Moreover, Store A was the only store, as seen in Table 4, for which this price was higher than average more times than it was either the same or lower, and here it exceeded *both* other categories. The store with the *lowest* priced specials obviously maintained higher prices on its non-specials. For the bewildered and beleagured consumer, the simple maxim that it pays to shop the specials needs to be refined; it pays to shop the specials, but beware the non-specials, especially where the specials are best.

THE BATTLE OF THE BRANDS

One way to save on the grocery bills, according to a recent article in *Consumers Report (4)* is to purchase retailer's instead of manufacturer's brands. Reach for the Ann Page (A&P) instead of Krafts; or for the Town House (Safeway) instead of Del Monte. This prescription is admittedly an oversimplification,

which "does not reveal the full story of the brutal battle of the brands." Whatever the comparative merits of the products—which *Consumers Report* took for granted in this instance—it is clear from their encroachment onto store shelves that enormous gains have been made by the retailer's brands. But the proprietors of manufacturer's and distributor's brand franchises have contested the encroachment, as was to be expected, and the manner in which they have contested it was also predictable; these brand franchises had been established through advertising and they would be defended through advertising. One of the more important battlegrounds in this struggle has been the institution of the weekly special.

When a store stocks 5,000 different food items, plans a deliberate strategy of "synthetic competition," and has frequent opportunities to reflect advertising allowances from its suppliers, it is not only the consumer who may be bewildered into some rule-of-thumb basis for choice. The consumer research organization itself understandably prefers stating a useful rule-of-thumb to the apparently impossible task of naming the "best food buys," which are necessarily evanescent in this context. Nevertheless, we may despair too quickly of the possibilities of gleaning useful information from this complex.

It is not difficult to discern the battle of the brands in the weekly specials. One need only observe the contrasting participation in the weekly special institution between the stores that emphasize their own brands and those that emphasize manufacturer's brands. Only Store D, which alone accounted for half of the retailer brands featured in all advertisements, may be said from these to be a predominantly retailer brand store, for it alone mentioned its own brands more frequently than the manufacturer's brands. The manner in which this store employs the institution of the weekly special makes another revealing contrast with Store A, which is highly

TABLE 5

COMPARISON OF STORES A AND D

Description	A *lower* than D	Same	A *higher* than D
Total	296	172	393
No specials involved	88	109	229
Specials involved	208	63	164
Specials involved (meat excluded)	148	52	141

oriented to manufacturer's brands. In the present section we first focus upon this contrast.

A high proportion of the items in Store A's advertisements entered into our list by virtue of the fact that it features many standard cuts of meat and a high proportion of brand names among its specials. Store D, in contrast, placed a low proportion of its items on our list by featuring few meat cuts and a low proportion of brand names (see Appendix Table III). Our list may be said to have a bias in favor of Store A as an inevitable result of the procedure by which the list is formed. However, retailer brands do enter into the list among the lowest priced items (irrespective of brands) and also among the unbranded items. But the incidence of comparable items in each advertisement is no doubt a reflection, in part, of deliberate strategy; hence the degree of this bias may be small. One sense in which Store A uses the weekly special more than Store D, in other words, may be the deliberate selection of items that occur more frequently in all the advertisements and thus facilitate price comparisons. Of the items mentioned in Store A's advertisements, 56 per cent appeared in our lists, compared to only 34 per cent of those mentioned in Store D's advertisements.

A more important sense in which Store A uses the special more than Store D is manifest in the price comparisons. Store A reduces the prices of its specials more, relative to its own general price level, than does Store D, with the result that the specials price comparison is far different from the non-specials price comparison. Table 5 shows this contrast.

Comparing prices on all 861 observations over the eight weeks, Store D had lower prices more times than Store A. But these lower prices occurred predominantly in the list of items not on special at either store, whereas Store A had lower prices more frequently among the approximately half of all items which were on special at one or both stores. This latter contrast was considerably influenced by meats (which as noted earlier are very prominently featured by Store A), such that omitting meats from the comparison virtually eliminates the advantage that Store A has among the specials.

The contrast is confirmed and extended by measuring the extent of price reduction in the specials in terms of the weekly index value. In the important grocery category (exclusive of meats and produce), where many of the specials are nationally advertised brands, Store A has consistently greater price reductions on its specials. Its specials index averaged 27 points lower than its non-specials index compared to a 16 point difference for Store D, and these differences were quite consistent from week to week. Yet Store A has so much higher regular prices than Store D that its specials are not much lower priced than D's, the difference in index values being four points or less in six of the eight weeks. The *non*-specials index was always higher at Store A (higher than for *any* store), and in seven of the eight weeks was five points or more higher than D's.

TABLE 6
SPECIALS AND NON-SPECIALS PRICE INDEXES, EXCLUDING MEATS
AND PRODUCE, EIGHT-WEEK AVERAGES

Price indexes	A	B	C	D	E	F	G	H
Specials Price index	76.8	82.9	83.5	81.4	79.3	81.5	81.4	83.0
Non-specials Price index	103.9	98.9	100.0	97.7	100.4	100.5	99.6	100.1

In fresh produce the picture was much the same, only more extreme while less reliable because of a limited number of observations. While Store A has higher priced groceries, but lower prices on a limited number of grocery specials, it has much higher priced produce, but much lower prices on a very limited number of produce specials. In produce, A's specials index averaged 45 points lower than its non-specials index; while for Store D this difference averaged 26 points. The inherently greater variability in produce prices undoubtedly accounts for the higher differences —the pattern is much the same as in groceries. Stores D's advantage in the non-specials price index was slightly more than its disadvantage in the specials index.

In meats the comparison was quite different in two respects. Store A had a lower non-specials index, and with almost the same degree of reduction to its specials index, also a lower specials index. In addition, A had a much higher number and proportion of meat specials than any other store—40 per cent of the food items in A's advertisements were meats, compared to 15 per cent in D's advertisements.

The battle of retailer vs. manufacturer brands is of course virtually confined to items other than fresh meats and produce. Therefore, it is reasonable to abstract from the meat and produce comparisons in interpreting these results in terms of the battle of the brands.

There is some danger of distorting the scene on the brand battlefront by letting Stores A and D represent, respectively, retailer and manufacturer brands. We can guard against this danger by view-

ing the scene more broadly, having treated these stores as the leading protagonists in order to obtain a vivid picture. We first view, in Table 6, the two-store contrast in the setting provided by all eight stores. Store A stands out from all others in two major respects, its specials price index is distinctly lower than the cluster, and its non-specials index is distinctly higher than the cluster. Thus the store that promotes manufacturers' brand names is making more use of specials than others. Store D's non-specials index is lower than the cluster while its specials index is approximately in the middle. The store that promotes its own brands, like all the stores, prices its specials below regular prices, but has lower regular prices than other stores. Its specials in comparison with other specials are more modestly reduced—much more so than those of Store A.

That this contrast is manifest throughout the eight stores may be seen by dichotomizing them according to the proportion of retailer brands to other brands in their advertisements. Of the four stores with the lowest proportion, two had no retailer brands and the other two less than one-tenth as many retailer as other brands. Of the other four stores, all had more than one-fourth as many retailer as other brands, and one, Store D, had more retailer than other brands. The specials indexes and the non-specials indexes, both dichotomized in the above manner, are shown in Table 7.

The four manufacturer-brand stores had lower specials indexes and higher non-specials indexes, suggesting that they make more use of the weekly special as a competitive weapon than do the

TABLE 7

SPECIALS AND NON-SPECIALS PRICE INDEXES, EXCLUDING MEATS AND
PRODUCE, EIGHT-WEEK AVERAGES, FOUR "RETAIL-BRAND" STORES VS.
FOUR "MANUFACTURER-BRAND" STORES

Price indexes	"Manufacturer-brand" stores[a]	"Retail-brand" stores[b]
Specials price index	80.2	82.3
Non-specials price index	101.2	99.0

[a] Stores B,D,C,G.
[b] Stores A,E,F,H.

retail-brand stores. This is not to imply, however, that the best shopping strategy is to buy specials from manufacturer-brand stores and non-specials at retail-brand stores. The latter very frequently match (or even undercut) the manufacturer-brand specials of other stores with retailer-brand specials of their own. Our selection procedure did not equate retailer and manufacturer brands, hence it was biased against the retailer-brand stores, quality disregarded. It appears rather that the retail-brand stores are the better sources of non-specials *including* manufacturer-brands; and quite possibly also the better sources of specials, if one is willing to equate retailer and manufacturer brands. Since this willingness is implicit in the *Consumers Reports* prescription that we took as our point of departure in this section, it might seem that our attempt to refine the prescription has come to naught—one should, as they advised, buy in the retailer-brand stores. It still is not obvious how this would compare with buying specials almost exclusively in one or two stores that make the most of the specials technique. It is apparent that the consumer who watches the specials *in addition* to following the *Consumers Reports* advice will have a still lower food bill.

CONCLUDING REMARKS

This study scratches the surface of one segment of a major problem area—the continuing structural change in the food economy of the United States— which has attracted the interest of many economists. The famous A&P decision (5) elicited some of the most fascinating economic enterpretations of the present age (6, 7, 8, 9). More recently the Federal Trade Commission has completed an extensive study of the food marketing structure (10) which Hoffman had analyzed two decades earlier (11), and Mueller and Garoian (1) have updated the catalogue of structural changes, while undertaking also to interpret these in the light of contemporary price theory. Still no one pretends that the phenomenon is adequately understood, and Galbraith's contention (12) that orthodox price theory has little to contribute toward understanding this and similar structural changes in other industries, although widely challenged, can hardly be said to have been refuted. The most prominent aspect of the larger phenomenon has been the rise of the retail supermarket, the more recent appearance of which in other countries may also prove a harbinger of far-reaching changes in the structure of their food economies (13). The struggle of supermarkets to ascendancy in the United States food marketing structure has certainly involved them in conflict against the pre-existing retail food outlets, but it could not stop there. The struggle had to permeate the entire system of distribution because the various functions are closely interrelated. Latterly a focal point of the continuing struggle has been a contest between the larger corporate chains of supermarkets and manufacturers or distributors of food products in promoting their respective brand labels.

The evidence shown here has little direct bearing on the larger issues of industry performance, but in the course of the investigation we formed impressions, and asked further questions, that may be worth stating in this larger context. Advertising plays a key part in the drama, yet economists have less to say about its causes and consequences than about any other part. It is usually classified as a form of nonprice competition that emerges in a market structure where monopoly profits are attainable through product differentiation. In much advertising, price is not mentioned, and in a great deal more in which it is mentioned, price is treated as an incidental item of information. But it is also frequently a vehicle through which price competition is conducted, through the conveyance of price information or the announcement of price reductions or prices lower than those available elsewhere. Where rivalry is intense the specials advertisement can become an instrument of price warfare on a selected list of items. It can also blossom into virtual price competition: unintentional in the case of a firm that is drawn into a specials program by the actions of others, or where consumer strategy forces it; intentional in the case of a firm that sees in the practice an opportunity for covert price competition where overt price competition would be self-defeating. Arthur (14) has aptly referred to this form of rivalry as "synthetic competition," without intending to minimize the very real competition that sometimes emerges from it. We find at least the possibility that competition may be generated by a mechanism which is initially and overtly a departure from competition. "Synthetic competition" may take on the attributes of the real thing, as specials lists approach the full market basket in their coverage, and to the extent that the price variable is emphasized within and among

the lists. A question that Dirlam and Kahn asked, "Did A&P's bargaining force heavy advertisers . . . to forego advertising for price competition," and partially answered, "On the contrary, suppliers may well have responded by intensifying their advertising," (7, p. 129) leaves still open the possibility of increased price competition through advertising.

None of this is necessarily anomalous in the framework of market structure theory. Mueller and Garoian (1) for example have been careful to avoid so broad a reading of the evidence, or so narrow an interpretation of market structure, as would require a judgment of diminished competition. It may be that the range of alternatives confronting the grocery shopper has been enlarged, what with such broad changes in the shopping environment as have been wrought by the changing role of the automobile, and the expanding use of advertising; so that the relevant market structure has become more competitive, despite diminishing numbers of retail food outlets. This would suggest that more competitive performance could be rationalized in terms of orthodox theory simply by appropriately redefining the extent of the market, or otherwise refining the theory, and recognizing that even price competition requires communication.

At the same time it must be recognized that the particular form assumed by rivalry among firms, or individual firm policy, may be conducive toward results that are not predictable from structural considerations. We also deem it possible that the battle between retailer and manufacturer brands may interact with the inter-firm rivalry at the retail level and result in an intensification of competition beyond the mere addition of the forces taken independently. The evidence shown here says very little about these important issues; insofar as it barely suggest the relevance of specials to market performance, or the patterns of pricing strategy, or the

APPENDIX TABLE 1

PERCENTAGE OF ITEMS ON THE SPECIALS LIST THAT WERE ON
SPECIAL, BY STORES AND DEPARTMENTS

(Eight-week averages)

Stores	A	B	C	D	E	F	G	H
Meats	49.1	39.4	21.2	23.1	39.1	22.8	18.4	24.7
Produce	26.5	34.3	25.4	28.2	34.7	23.2	24.6	26.4
All Other	34.6	24.3	27.9	24.0	23.9	15.8	16.2	25.4
Total	35.3	28.6	27.1	24.6	28.3	18.1	17.8	25.6

APPENDIX TABLE 2

UNWEIGHTED PRICE INDEXES [a] BASED ON THE SPECIALS LIST

Item	A	B	C	D	E	F	G	H
				Specials				
Meat	73.4	76.6	79.0	79.4	92.6	81.2	77.7	79.6
Produce	64.2	67.7	72.5	72.5	68.7	72.9	65.5	62.6
All other	76.8	82.9	83.5	81.4	79.3	81.5	81.4	83.0
All products	74.9	79.4	81.8	79.3	84.5	80.7	79.1	81.6
				Non-Specials				
Meat	93.3	98.5	96.7	101.0	99.9	95.0	99.2	108.2
Produce	109.2	95.6	98.9	99.8	102.2	101.5	100.8	102.3
All other	103.9	98.9	100.0	97.7	100.4	100.5	99.6	100.1
All products	101.1	98.6	98.7	99.0	100.3	98.7	99.5	102.9
				Total				
Meat	82.9	89.8	91.9	95.9	96.8	91.5	95.5	101.7
Produce	97.4	85.3	93.2	91.4	90.2	94.9	92.8	93.9
All other	94.6	95.3	95.5	93.3	94.2	97.2	96.2	95.8
All products	89.9	92.8	94.2	94.1	94.8	95.2	95.7	97.6

[a]The unweighted price index for a given store and week =

$$\frac{\text{Sum of prices in that store of all items priced that week}}{\text{Sum of average prices of those items in all stores, all weeks}}.$$

The index numbers given here are averages, for the eight weeks, of those weekly indexes.

types of interaction that may occur here. But if it does suggest a greater emphasis upon price than contemporary structure theory would predict, or a higher level of performance than either the predictions of theory or the performance of the corner grocery store regime, it will have served its purpose.

After a much larger study than this one, Mueller and Garoian conclude at one point: "The preceding comments are not offered as conclusive proof that local retail market structures have, in fact, resulted in market behavior consistent with that which economic theory implies. Rather, we report it here simply to illustrate that scattered evidence suggests that such behavior may indeed exist" (*1*, p. 136). And at another point: ". . . [There has been] a generally downward trend in profit margins in these industries since prewar and postwar years. Moreover, profit margins of chains have not increased during this period even though grocery retailers are performing more functions than previously. This suggests that the food-retailing industry is also performing in

APPENDIX TABLE 3

SIZE AND COMPOSITION OF WEEKLY ADVERTISEMENTS
OF EIGHT STORES
(Eight-Week Averages)

Nature of advertising	A	B	C	D	E	F	G	H
Total items	59	57	85	68	53	35	46	63
Newspaper columns	8	9	12	13	7	6	8	9
Retailer brands	4	8	14	35	0	0	7	4
Manufacturer brands	32	32	55	19	35	23	23	41
Meat	24	13	17	11	18	11	9	12
Fresh produce	4	7	4	7	6	4	4	5
Non-food	1	7	14	8	5	2	7	6

an improved manner" (1, p. 154). It would overburden our meager evidence to claim that it does any more than lightly underscore the recognized limitations of market structure theory in interpreting one facet of performance. But it may underscore more heavily the conclusion that "additional research is needed to give a conclusive picture of the type of competitive behavior actually extant in local markets" (1, p. 136).

CITATIONS

1. Willard F. Mueller and Leon Garoian, Changes in the Market Structure of Grocery Retailing, Univ. of Wisconsin, Madison, 1961.
2. Newt Hawkinson, "What's a Meat Type Steer?" Wallaces Farmer, May 19, 1962.
3. U.S. Dept. Labor, Bur. Lab. Stat., Retail Prices of Food 1959-60, Bul. No. 1301, Nov. 1961.
4. "How to Save $200 a Year at a Supermarket," Consumer Reports, February 1961.
5. U.S. vs. The New York Great A&P Tea Co. 67 Federal Supplement 626, E.D. Ill. 1946.
6. M. A. Adelman, "The A&P Case: A Study in Applied Economic Theory," Quar. Jour. Econ., May 1949, pp. 238-57.
7. Joel B. Dirlam and Alfred E. Kahn, "Antitrust Law and the Big Buyer: Another Look at the A & P Case," Jour. Pol. Econ., April 1952, pp. 118-32.
8. M. A. Adelman, "Dirlam and Kahn on the A & P Case," Jour. Pol. Econ., October 1953, pp. 436-41.
9. Joel B. Dirlam and Alfred E. Kahn, "A Reply," Jour. Pol. Econ., October 1953, pp. 441-46.
10. Federal Trade Commission, Economic Inquiry into Food Marketing, Interim Report, June 30, 1959.
11. A. C. Hoffman, Large Scale Organization in the Food Industry, TNEC Monograph 35, Washington, 1940, pp. 89-90.
12. John Kenneth Galbraith, American Capitalism, The Concept of Countervailing Power, Boston, 1952.
13. Robert T. Davis, The Changing Pattern of Europe's Grocery Trade, Stanford, Calif., 1959, p. 292.
14. Henry B. Arthur, "Requirements of Consumers, Distributors, and Processors that Are Important to Farmers," Harvard University (processed) Dec. 1960.

36. Can Speculators Forecast Prices?

H. S. HOUTHAKKER

The role of speculation in the economic system is still a matter of controversy. In popular parlance the word has acquired an unfavorable connotation; most economists would probably say speculation is at best a necessary evil, though some would regard it as an unnecessary source of instability. One of the main issues in evaluating speculation is no doubt the degree of skill with which speculators can forecast prices: the more accurately prices are forecast, the less they will fluctuate, and the easier therefore the adjustments which interested parties have to make. Thus formulated the question leaves open to what extent the prices that actually emerge are in some sense optimal, for steadiness is only a minor characteristic of optimality. The very difficulty of defining optimality in a dynamic context, however, is a sufficient reason for separately considering speculators' success in predicting prices as they are. For this purpose we shall consider data concerning three important American commodity markets.[1]

In commodity futures markets a measure of the forecasting ability of speculators is not hard to find, for it is immediately reflected in their profits and losses. Except for hedgers, whose futures commitments are offset by commitments in the cash market, the buying and selling of futures contracts has no purpose other than to profit from changes in futures prices. The problem, then, consists in estimating and analyzing speculators' profits.

The best source of information on this subject would be the actual trading records of speculators, but these are rarely available. An important study based on data of this type was presented by Blair Stewart,[2] who made a detailed analysis of the accounts of about 9,000 customers of a nationwide brokers' firm during the period 1925-34. These accounts reflected almost exclusively speculative transactions in grain futures, mainly by non-professional traders. The most striking results were that nearly 75 per cent of the speculators lost money and that in the entire sample total losses were about six times as large as total gains. Since in the futures market as a whole gains and losses cancel out (apart from commissions, which in futures trading are small), the question arises by whom corresponding profits were made. Although the coverage of Stewart's material was not wide enough to give much information on this point, he seems to have thought it difficult to

Reprinted by permission of the publishers from *Review of Economics and Statistics*, Vol. 39, No. 2 (May, 1957), pp. 143-51. Copyright, 1957, by the President and Fellows of Harvard College.

[1] These results are part of an investigation of commodity futures undertaken at the Cowles Commission for Research in Economics with the valuable assistance of Lester G. Telser and supported by the Rockefeller Foundation. Further acknowledgments and details will be given in a forthcoming Cowles Foundation monograph.

[2] Blair Stewart, "An Analysis of Speculative Trading in Grain Futures," U.S. Department of Agriculture Technical Bulletin No. 1001, October 1949.

account for these heavy losses and to have suspected some unknown bias in his sample.

There were, in fact, two possible sources of bias. In the first place, prices in 1934 were much lower than in 1925, while the customers tended to prefer the long side. This effect, however, does not explain a great deal, since the trading experience of the shorts in the sample was not much less disastrous than that of the longs. A second source of bias may have been that the firm with which the accounts were held went bankrupt, which casts some doubt on the reliability of the advice it presumably gave to its customers.

If no actual trading accounts are available, estimates of gains and losses must be made from price movements and assumptions about commitments. This was done for speculators by Working[3] and for hedgers by Yamey[4] and others. The technique of the present paper is basically similar to theirs, but we were able to replace some assumptions about commitments by observed data and to consider a much longer period.

The method of estimating profits is based on monthly figures of open commitments and futures prices. The commitments are divided into three groups: (large) hedging, (large) speculative, and non-reporting. This division corresponds to the reporting requirements under the Commodity Exchange Act. Traders whose commitments in any one futures contract exceed the reporting limit (200,000 bushels in the case of wheat and corn and 5,000 bales for cotton) have to communicate their entire position to the Commodity Exchange Authority, which classifies futures commitments into hedging or speculative.[5] The remaining commitments

are those of small traders, and it is commonly assumed that they are predominantly speculative in nature. It also seems clear that the reporting traders (both hedgers and speculators) are almost exclusively professionals, and that the figures for non-reporting traders are representative of the small non-professional speculators.

To estimate profits and losses it was assumed that the commitments of a group of traders that existed at the end of a month were opened at the average price during that month and closed out at the average price during the following month. The profit or loss of that group was then found by multiplying the end-of-month position by the change in the average price. Thus if large speculators were long 10 million bushels of May wheat on March 31, and the average price of May wheat was $1.60 per bushel during March and $1.55 during April, then their loss on that position was put at $500,000. Commission charges have been ignored throughout. It need hardly be said that this estimation procedure is no more than approximate and could be improved in various ways, but it should be accurate enough for the purpose of this paper.

In the case of wheat and corn the calculation just described could be performed for each futures contract (i.e., delivery month) separately, thanks to a recent analysis of the Commodity Exchange Authority[6] which cross-classifies open contracts by future and group of traders.[7] Total profit or loss for each group was then found as the sum of the profits or losses in each futures contract, calculated by multiplying the position

---

is "spreading" or "straddling" positions, in which a long position in one or more futures contracts is offset by a short position in one or more other contracts.

[6] U.S. Department of Agriculture, "Grain Futures Statistics 1921-51," Statistical Bulletin No. 131 (July 1953).

[7] Some minor problems connected with the use of these figures will be discussed in the monograph mentioned in footnote 1.

---

[3] H. Working, "Financial Studies of Speculative Holding of Wheat," *Wheat Studies*, VII (July 1931).

[4] B. S. Yamey, "Investigation of Hedging on an Organized Produce Exchange," *The Manchester School*, XIX (1951).

[5] A special category of speculative commitments

in a future by the change in the average price of that future. This procedure will be referred to as Method A.

For cotton Method A could not be applied because a cross-classification is not available. It therefore had to be assumed that the percentage distribution of open commitments between futures was the same for all groups of traders, and hence the same as the distribution of total open commitments between futures, which is known from Department of Agriculture data.[8] The price change used was a weighted average of the changes in the average price of each future, the weights being given again by the percentage distribution of total open contracts between futures. This procedure, to be called Method B, was also applied to corn and wheat as a check. As may be seen from Table 5 the results from Methods A and B are not grossly different, although there are systematic discrepancies which will be discussed below.

The price data used were monthly averages of daily closing prices in Chicago (for grains) and New York (for cotton), obtained by courtesy of the Commodity Exchange Authority. Results are given by crop years, which start on July 1 for wheat, August 1 for cotton, and October 1 for corn. Open contract data for grains in the crop years starting in 1937-39 refer to the Chicago Board of Trade only, for 1946-51 to all United States markets combined. The first six months of the crop year 1946-47 had to be omitted in wheat because futures trading was still restricted by the aftermath of wartime measures. Open contract data for cotton are based on New York and New Orleans together in crop years beginning in 1937-44; for the remaining years they also include the insignificant cotton futures market in Chicago.

Despite the considerable variability of the entries in Table 1 certain broad conclusions may be drawn. In all three commodities the large hedgers lost and the large speculators gained. The small traders lost in the grains but did quite

---

[8] U.S. Department of Agriculture, *Cotton Futures Statistics* (3 issues covering 1937-45), and *Commodity Futures Statistics* (annual).

TABLE 1
NET PROFITS (+) OR LOSSES (−) OF THREE CATEGORIES OF TRADERS IN
COMMODITY FUTURES[a]
($ million)

Crop year[d]	Corn[b] Large hedgers	Corn[b] Large spec's	Corn[b] Small traders	Wheat[b] Large hedgers	Wheat[b] Large spec's	Wheat[b] Small traders	Cotton[c] Large hedgers	Cotton[c] Large spec's	Cotton[c] Small traders
1937-38	+ .46	+ .22	− .68	+ 21.93	+ .36	− 22.30	− 3.43[a]	+ .44[e]	+ 2.99
1938-39	+ 1.68	− .81	− .88	+ 5.91	− .45	− 5.46	− 3.80	+ .58	+ 3.22
1939-40	− 1.67	+ .56	+ 1.11	− 2.59	+ 1.70	+ .90	− 8.04	+ 1.59	+ 6.45
Sub-total	+ .47	− .02	− .45	+ 25.26	+ 1.61	− 26.87	− 15.27	+ 2.61	+ 12.65
1940-41	...	...	...	...	...	...	− 20.98	+ 2.04	+ 18.95
1941-42	...	...	...	...	...	...	− 9.39	+ 1.80	+ 7.59
1942-43	...	...	...	...	...	...	− 7.14	+ .82	+ 6.33
1943-44	...	...	...	...	...	...	− 1.84	+ 1.12	+ .72
1944-45	...	...	...	...	...	...	− 3.59	+ 1.41	+ 2.19
1945-46	...	...	...	...	...	...	− 79.77	+ 15.06	+ 64.71
Sub-total	...	...	...	...	...	...	− 122.72	+ 22.24	+ 100.48
1946-47	− .20	+ 6.12	− 5.92	+ 6.77[f]	+ 1.43[f]	− 8.20[f]	+ 11.00	+ 1.87	− 12.86
1947-48	− .36	+ 1.28	− .92	− 22.86	+ 13.39	+ 9.46	− 12.80	+ 3.35	+ 9.46
1948-49	+ 3.58	− .55	− 3.03	− .34	+ 1.56	− 1.22	+ 2.18	+ 1.85	− 4.02
1949-50	− 6.06	+ 2.56	+ 3.50	− 5.44	+ 5.10	+ .34	− 12.93	+ 7.28	+ 5.65
1950-51	− 5.52	+ 2.50	+ 3.02	− .47	+ .19	+ .66	− 34.11	+ 9.25	+ 24.86
1951-52	+ 2.00	− .27	− 1.73	− 9.19	+ 4.24	+ 4.95	+ 1.20	+ 4.13	− 5.33
Sub-total	− 6.56	+ 11.65	− 5.08	− 31.53	+ 25.54	+ 5.99	− 45.47	+ 27.73	+ 17.75
Grand total	− 6.09	+ 11.62	− 5.53	− 6.28	+ 27.16	− 20.88	− 183.45	+ 52.58	+ 130.88

[a] Figures may not check downward or across because of rounding.
[b] Computed by Method A (see text). Prewar years Chicago Board of Trade only; postwar years all markets combined.
[c] Computed by Method B (see text). Until August 1, 1945 New York and New Orleans only; thereafter all markets combined.
[d] Crop years start October 1 for corn, July 1 for wheat, August 1 for cotton.
[e] Excluding first two months.
[f] Excluding first six months.

TABLE 2
NUMBER OF MONTHS WITH PROFITS AND LOSSES

Months with:	Corn			Wheat			Cotton		
	Prices rising	Prices falling	Total	Prices rising	Prices falling	Total	Prices rising	Prices falling	Total
Large speculators' net profit	52	12	64	43	19	62	116	5	121
Large speculators' net loss	12	32	44	6	34	40	6	48	54
Small traders' net profit	51	8	59	38	9	47	99	15	114
Small traders' net loss	13	36	49	11	44	55	23	39	62
Total months	64	44	108	49	53	102	122	54[a]	178[b]

[a]Including one month in which large speculators broke even.
[b]Including two months in which prices did not change.

well in cotton, although it will be noted that of their total computed profit of $130.9 million no less than $100.5 million was made during the period 1940-46, which was excluded in the grains because of lack of data. In the case of the hedgers, only profits and losses on futures commitments are shown, which have to be offset against profits and losses in the cash market.

Most conspicuous in these results is the consistent profitability of the large speculators' transactions. In cotton they made a net profit in every year observed, and although in corn and wheat they lost in a few years, they never lost much. A tabulation of the monthly figures underlying Table 1 is shown in Table 2. It will be seen that the large speculators had net profits in 59 per cent of all months for corn, 61 per cent of all months for wheat, and 68 per cent of all months for cotton. If, to make the period for cotton comparable to the period for the grains, the crop years beginning in 1940 through 1945 are omitted, the percentage for cotton becomes 65 per cent. These scores are sufficiently different from 50 per cent to provide *prima facie* evidence of forecasting skill; some tests of this hypothesis will be presented below.

Less forecasting ability is apparent

from the results of the small traders. They gained in 55 percent of all months for corn, 46 per cent of all months for wheat, and 64 per cent of all months for cotton. Again leaving out the period 1940-46 the score for cotton drops to 61 per cent.

The main purpose of Table 2 is to show to what extent gains and losses are connected with a net long or net short position. Both large speculators and small traders are net long most of the time and therefore stand to gain when prices go up. During the period of observation cotton prices rose fairly steadily; wheat and corn prices declined on balance during each of the two sub-periods, though in corn the number of months with price rises exceeded the number with price falls. This behavior of prices explains a good deal of the discrepancy between small traders' results for grains and for cotton, especially when it is considered that in each of the three commodities small traders were net short about 20 per cent of the time. The latter figure, incidentally, shows that the traditional picture of the small speculator as an incurable bull, too ignorant to understand short selling, is incorrect. In fact, small traders do not appear to be less inclined to the short side than the large professional specula-

TABLE 3

PROFITS (+) AND LOSSES (−) OF THREE CATEGORIES OF TRADERS ON LONG
AND SHORT POSITIONS[a]

($ million)

	Large hedgers			Large speculators			Small traders		
	Long	*Short*	*Net*	*Long*	*Short*	*Net*	*Long*	*Short*	*Net*
Corn									
1937-40	− .84	+ 1.31	+ .47	− .47	+ .44	− .02	− 1.67	+ 1.22	− .45
1946-52	+ 11.28	− 17.85	− 6.56	+ 27.97	− 16.32	+ 11.65	+ 34.74	− 39.83	− 5.08
Total	+ 10.44	− 16.54	− 6.09	+ 27.50	− 15.88	+ 11.63	+ 33.08	− 38.61	− 5.53
Wheat									
1937-40	− 4.79	+ 30.04	+ 25.26	− 8.68	+ 10.29	+ 1.61	− 40.98	+ 14.11	− 26.87
1947-52	+ 30.82	− 62.36	− 31.53	+ 41.99	− 16.44	+ 25.54	+ 57.20	− 51.21	+ 5.99
Total	+ 26.04	− 32.31	− 6.28	+ 33.31	− 6.15	+ 27.16	+ 16.22	− 37.10	− 20.88
Cotton									
1937-40	+ 9.99	− 25.26	− 15.27	+ 5.23	− 2.62	+ 2.61	+ 22.54	− 9.89	+ 12.65
1940-46	+ 49.30	− 172.01	− 122.72	+ 61.70	− 39.46	+ 22.24	+ 219.78	− 119.31	+ 100.48
1946-52	+ 98.59	− 144.06	− 45.47	+ 98.83	− 71.10	+ 27.73	+ 250.77	− 233.02	+ 17.75
Total	+ 157.88	− 341.34	− 183.45	+ 165.75	− 113.18	+ 52.58	+ 493.09	− 361.21	+ 130.88
Total all commodities	+ 194.36	− 390.19	− 195.82	+ 226.56	− 135.21	+ 91.36	+ 542.39	− 437.92	+ 104.67

[a] The footnotes of Table 1 apply also to Table 3.

tors. In cotton small traders were net short in 38 months as against only 11 for the large speculators. In grains the pattern, though opposite to that for cotton, is not very marked (20 against 25 for wheat, 21 against 24 for corn).

On the other hand it is clear that the small traders are rather less successful when net short than the large speculators in similar circumstances. Thus in wheat, although prices fell in 53 out of 102 months, the small traders were short mostly in months when prices were rising, whereas the large speculators in that market were remarkably accurate in their choice of the short side. There is some evidence, particularly from the early postwar years, that small traders were unduly cycle-conscious and therefore unwilling to believe that high prices could last for long. In the end this Cassandra attitude often turned out to be correct, but by then the initial losses had sometimes so undermined the small traders' courage or their margins that they were no longer able to reap the fruits of their badly-timed foresight. This happened for instance in the corn market during the boom of 1947. In the wheat market of 1947, too, small traders were initially speculating against the rapid price rise, but after a long period of losses they reversed themselves and

made large profits from the tail end of the boom, only to lose again when prices broke early in 1948. If it is correct to explain the small speculators' actions by a belief that price rises will always be followed by falls, then the usual arguments about the destabilizing influence of speculation may require reconsideration.

In Table 3 the totals from Table 1 are analyzed by short and long positions. Apart from the difference in small traders' net profits noted previously, the general pattern is the same for the three commodities. The hedgers, who are nearly always net short in the futures markets, are the mainspring of profits for the other traders, who share in proportion to their net long position. In all three commodities the large speculators and small traders lost on balance on their short positions. It cannot be inferred from this that speculators would have done better to stick to the long side, for their short positions are often one half of a spread or straddle (i.e., they are offset by a long position in another delivery). Spreading is not only a means of saving on margin requirements[9] but it

---

[9] Because the differences between the prices of various contracts (also known as "spreads") are less volatile than these prices themselves.

is helpful in distributing different maturities between speculators according to their preferences.[10]

The essence of futures trading, however, is the transfer of price risks from the hedgers to the speculators in return for a risk premium, and this is clearly illustrated in Table 3. Even in wheat and corn, where prices fell during the period of observation, a risk premium was produced. As it happened the whole premium went to the large speculators, who in addition obtained some of the small traders' funds. In cotton the risk premium went to both large and small traders. Of course a net risk premium accrues to speculators only in the long run, and not necessarily in any given period of time.

The exact mechanism by which the risk premium is transferred cannot be described in this paper. Its principal component is a tendency for the price of a futures contract to rise from the inception of trading to the delivery date. The existence of this tendency, which is implied by Keynes's theory of "normal backwardation,"[11] can be statistically demonstrated in various ways.

The main implication for the present analysis is that in the long run no great amount of skill is necessary to make a profit in the futures market: all one has to do is to maintain a long position. In this way a trader, if he has enough patience and capital to cover temporary losses, will sooner or later secure his portion of the risk premium. If, moreover, he can predict short-term price movements more accurately than other speculators, and adjusts his posi-

tion accordingly, he may make a further profit at their expense. Conversely if he is outguessed by other speculators he may lose his share of the risk premium and more. There are consequently two kinds of skill: general skill, which consists only in being long and requires no information, and special skill, which involves a continuous adjustment to changes in current information. The two types of skill may be positive or negative: a negative general skill means a proclivity for the short side, whereas a negative special skill implies a tendency to be short when prices go up and long when prices go down.

The extent to which a category of traders possesses these two skills may be measured (ex post) from the following equation:

$$y_t = \alpha + \beta x_t + \epsilon_t$$

in which y_t is the net position of that category, at a certain time t (here, the end of each month); x_t is an index of the change in prices around time t (more particularly the index used to estimate gains and losses by Method B described above); and ϵ_t is a random disturbance. The general skill is reflected in the constant term α: it is clearly positive when the group tends to be long irrespective of price changes. The coefficient β measures the special skill. What matters for our purpose is not the absolute magnitude of the estimates of α and β, but rather their statistical significance, which can be found by comparing each estimate with its standard error.

It is important to realize that (I) is not a behavior equation; it is purely an ex-post relation. Estimates of α and β are given in Table 4, with standard errors in brackets. The number of observations and the correlation coefficient are also given. As an aid in judging significance we note that if α or β is "really" zero, its estimate has a 30 per cent chance of exceeding its standard error and a 5 per cent chance of exceeding twice its standard error. It is hardly

---

[10] J. M. Mehl, formerly Administrator of the Commodity Exchange Authority, ascribes the recent increase in spreading also to income tax considerations, since it permits the transformation of short-term into long-term profits. Cf. J. M. Mehl, *Futures Trading Under the Commodity Exchange Act 1946-54*, U.S. Department of Agriculture (December 1954) 20.

[11] J. M. Keynes, *Treatise on Money* (London, 1930), Vol. II, 142-44. See also J. R. Hicks, *Value and Capital* (Oxford, 1939), 137-39; and the monograph announced in footnote 1 above.

TABLE 4.

ESTIMATES OF α AND β IN EQUATION (I), WITH STANDARD ERRORS (IN
PARENTHESES) AND CORRELATION COEFFICIENTS

	Number of observations	Large speculators			Small traders		
		α	β	r	α	β	r
Corn[a]							
1937-40	36	4.20	+.0318	.0235	9.56	+.0206	.0082
		(.77)	(.232)		(1.42	(.430)	
1946-52	72	4.72	+.0416	.0927	7.58	−.2220	.2533
		(.52)	(.051)		(1.03)	(.101)	
Wheat[a]							
1937-40	36	4.87	+.2375	.3451	43.13	−.3370	.0462
		(.72)	(.111)		(8.18)	(1.250)	
1947-52	66	6.48	+.2024	.2950	10.51	−.0770	.0553
		(.84)	(.082)		(1.79)	(.174)	
Cotton[b]							
1937-45	94	62.2	+31.59	.3030	621.6	−90.56	.0879
		(5.3)	(10.42)		(54.4)	(106.99)	
1945-52	84	121.7	+16.57	.2646	153.2	+26.01	.0889
		(9.9)	(6.67)		(47.1)	(31.81)	

[a] Net position in millions of bushels, price changes in cents per bushel.
[b] Net position in thousands of bales, price changes in cents per pound.

necessary to go into further refinements since the results are rather clear-cut.

Table 4 shows that both speculators and small traders possess general skill, since all the estimates of α very considerably exceed their standard errors in all three commodities. A conspicuous difference appears in the measure of special skill, however. The estimates of β for the small traders all fall short of their standard errors and must therefore be regarded as insignificant, with the exception of postwar wheat where the small traders' special skill appears to be significantly negative. The special skill coefficients for the large speculators are significantly positive in wheat and cotton but not in corn, where they are positive but very small.

It seems clear, therefore, that there are real differences in the ability of large and small traders to forecast price changes. This implies also that the differences in profits and losses exhibited in Tables 1-3 are not wholly due to random causes.

We must now consider another aspect of relative skill. So far we have looked only at the total net position of a category of traders, that is to say at the net position in all futures contracts combined. Since, however, the prices of different deliveries do not usually move in an exactly parallel manner, there is also scope for skill in choosing the futures in which to be long or short; this might be called distributive skill to distinguish it from the sort of skill analyzed in Table 4.[12]

It is possible to estimate distributive skill by comparing results from the two methods used for estimating profits and

[12]In principle this distributive skill might also be divided into general distributive skill, leading to a long position in those contracts which *on the average* tend to go up most, and special distributive skill, consisting in an ability to buy those futures which *in a given period of time* will go up most or sell those which fall most. It does not appear, however, that different deliveries have markedly different rates of average increase in the long run. There would consequently be no scope for general distributive skill, and the distinction between general and special skill would be redundant here.

TABLE 5
ANALYSIS OF DISTRIBUTIVE SKILL
($ million)

	Large hedgers		Large speculators		Small traders	
	Method B	Method A − Method B	Method B	Method A − Method B	Method B	Method A − Method B
Corn						
1937-40	+.40	+.07	−.07	+.05	−.33	−.12
1946-52	−7.49	+.93	+11.32	+.33	−3.83	−1.25
Total	−7.09	+1.00	+11.25	+.38	−4.16	−1.37
Wheat						
1937-40	+25.04	+.22	+1.29	+.32	−26.33	−.54
1947-52	−32.59	+1.06	+22.99	+2.55	+9.60	−3.61
Total	−7.56	+1.28	+24.29	+2.87	−16.73	−4.15

losses in Table 1. Method A, used there for corn and wheat, was based on the actual distribution between futures of commitments of the three groups of traders, whereas Method B, used for cotton, was based on the assumption that the distribution between futures was the same for all three groups. By applying Method B to the gains, and subtracting the gains or losses it gives from those estimated by Method A, we will therefore obtain a measure of the gains and losses due to a more or less skillful distribution of a given over-all position between different deliveries.

Table 5 shows that Method B gives smaller profits (or larger losses) to the large hedgers and large speculators, and larger profits (or smaller losses) to the small traders. This would imply that the large traders have a positive distributive skill. The differences between the results from Methods A and B are not large, however, and the question arises whether they are not merely due to an accumulation of random errors. By way of a crude test[13] it was found that the large corn speculators showed evidence of positive distributive skill in 54 months out of 108, negative skill in 51 months, and equal results from Methods A and B in the remaining 3 months. The

small corn traders showed positive distributive skill in 43 months, negative skill in 62 months, and zero skill in 3 months. In wheat the large speculators showed positive skill in 56 months out of 102, negative skill in 41 months, and a tie in 5 months; for the small traders these figures were respectively 42, 59, and 1. On the basis of these figures the apparent positive distributive skill of the large speculators is not statistically significant; the apparent negative distributive skill of the small traders, on the other hand, cannot plausibly be attributed to random causes only.[14]

It appears, therefore, that the distribution between futures is one of the factors influencing the relative profitability of large and small traders' commitments. Further evidence on this point is provided by an analysis of the monthly profits and losses in corn and wheat for individual futures contracts. For this purpose futures have been grouped together according to their distance from maturity. Thus at the end of February the May future is regarded as 3 months distant from maturity, the July future as 5 months distant, and so on. The expiring future (in this case the March future) is consequently treated as one month

---

More refined tests could not be applied either here or in Table 2 because the distribution of gains and losses is not of the normal type.

[14] If distributive skill were really zero, so that positive and negative skill was equally likely, the standard error for each of the grains would be about 5 months.

TABLE 6
NET PROFITS AND LOSSES OF THREE CATEGORIES OF TRADERS BY DISTANCE FROM
MATURITY OF FUTURE CONTRACTS
(*$ million*)

Months from maturity	Corn			Wheat		
	Large hedgers	Large speculators	Small traders	Large hedgers	Large speculators	Small traders
1	−2.59	+4.37	−1.78	−1.04	+4.57	−3.53
2	−1.47	−5.29	−3.82	+8.90	+4.03	−12.93
3	+.59	−.23	−.36	+16.01	+4.13	−20.14
4	+3.85	−1.25	−2.61	−3.32	+5.25	−1.93
5	−.54	+2.57	−2.02	+5.73	+1.72	−7.44
6	−2.63	+3.13	−.50	−9.45	+5.00	+4.45
7	−1.87	+.48	+1.39	−5.68	+1.82	+3.86
8	−.84	−1.08	+1.92	−8.26	+1.33	+6.93
9	−.56	−.60	+1.16	−9.06	+.67	+8.39
10	−.03	−.77	+.80	−.16	−.71	+.86
11	−.01	−.27	+.28	+.06	−.67	+.61
Total	−6.09	+11.62	−5.53	−6.28	+27.16	−20.88
1-6	−2.79	+13.88	−11.09	+16.82	+24.71	−41.53
7-11	−3.30	−2.26	+5.56	−23.09	+2.45	+20.65

away. Then the profits and losses on all futures one month distant from maturity, 2 months distant, and so on, were added up. The totals appear in Table 6.

Although the results are not as clear-cut as they might be we can nevertheless find some indication of a difference in success according to the distance from maturity. The large speculators do better in the near futures (those close to maturity) than in the very distant ones, and the opposite is true for the small trader. The exceptions as regards the large speculators are the corn futures three or four months distant from maturity, in which they lose, in common with the small traders, and in which, consequently, the hedgers gain. The last two lines of Table 6 show that small traders lost twice as much in the near futures as they gained in the distant futures. It would be interesting to do the same analysis for cotton, but the data are not available.

It is not difficult to explain these differences. The price behavior of the near futures depends to a large extent on the magnitude and ownership of deliverable stocks at the relevant terminals (Chicago, Kansas City, and Minneapolis for wheat, Chicago for corn), and this is a matter on which non-professionals cannot easily inform themselves. Price movements in the more distant contracts, on the other hand, are influenced mainly by basic supply and demand factors such as crop prospects, the general economic outlook, or government policy. In evaluating the latter factors the professionals have no particular comparative advantage. Indeed it is often profitable for them to use their superior knowledge by taking a long or short position in the near futures, at the same time taking an opposite position in the more distant deliveries in order to limit their risks. We have already mentioned that such spreading accounts for a major part of the large speculator's operations. By taking the other side of the distant half of these spreads the small traders may then earn a risk premium from the professionals; the other side of the near half is more likely to be taken by hedgers, who rarely go into distant futures. This type of spreading is quite similar to hedging, which is based on hedgers' superior knowledge of the cash market.

Returning now to the question raised in the title we conclude that large speculators show definite evidence of forecasting skill, both in the long and in the short run. Since these large speculators are professionals whose existence depends on their skill, this finding is hardly revolutionary, edifying through it is to see virtue rewarded. The experience of the small traders indicates that they do quite well when they stick to the long side, where the theory of "normal backwardation" assures them of a profit in the long run, but they show no evidence of ability to forecast short-run price movements. It appears, moreover, that non-professionals would have done well to confine themselves to the more distant futures.

37. Improving Credit Evaluation with a Weighted Application Blank[1]

JAMES J. McGRATH

The weighted application blank is a familiar tool to most personnel managers and has proved to be a valid predictor of performance on many different types of jobs. The work of a personnel manager is similar to that of a credit manager in that both often use biographical information from application blanks to predict the future behavior of individuals. Since the prediction problems are similar, it is likely that the techniques of personnel selection would also be useful in evaluating applicants for credit.

PROBLEM

In the retail automobile business credit must often be extended to customers whose failure to fulfill their contract obligations represents potential losses to the dealer. When a sale ends in repossession of the automobile the dealer not only suffers a direct cash loss, but also the losses associated with increased clerical and handling costs and damaged public relations. If the professional credit man can accurately predict the risk involved in extending credit to certain individuals, the profit on credit sales can be materially increased. In this study an attempt was made to de-

velop a credit evaluation tool, using the weighted application blank technique, to assist in identifying unprofitable groups of credit customers. The objective of the study was to distinguish between good and poor credit risks by analyzing the items of information available at the time of application for credit.

PROCEDURE

The procedure was similar to that used in the item analysis of application blanks for personnel selection. Criterion groups of credit risks for new car sales were established by randomly selecting from the files of a large automobile dealership 100 records of credit customers who paid for their cars as agreed and 100 records of credit customers who did not pay for their cars and whose cars were repossessed. These cases were considered representative of the desirable and the undesirable types of credit customers. In each case the credit sale had been made from 12 to 18 months prior to the date of the study.

Since only data available at the time of the sale may be useful in prediction, the information on only two documents in each record was analyzed. These documents were the contract and the credit application blank. The contract contained 17 possible predictor items, such as percent down payment, number of installments, and trade-in allow-

[1] From *Journal of Applied Psychology*, Vol. 44, No. 5 (October, 1960), pp. 325-28. This study was supported in part by Human Factors Research, Incorporated.

ances. The application blank contained 45 possible predictors such as age, occupation, and income. These 62 items were subdivided into response categories, and the responses of the two criterion groups were tabulated. The original categories were then reorganized to simplify the items and to maximize the discriminatory power of the items where it was possible to do so. For each response category of every item the percentage difference between groups was tested for statistical significance. Twenty-four items significantly discriminated the good and poor credit customers.

A new selection of criterion groups was made consisting of 100 paying customers and 69 customers whose cars were repossessed. The 24 selected items were scored on the application blanks and contracts of these cross-validation groups. Separate scores were obtained from the contract items and the application blank items. These were then summed to yield a total score. Three different scoring systems were used:

Scoring System A: Each response category was weighted according to its degree of significance in discriminating the standardization sample. These weights ranged from 0 to 14.

Scoring System B: Each response category received unit weight (-1, 0, or $+1$) with the algebraic sign indicating the direction of discrimination.

A constant of $+1$ was added to these weights to eliminate the minus sign, yielding weights of 0, 1, or 2.

Scoring System C: Only those items which discriminated the standardization groups at the .01 level of confidence were scored, using the unit weights of Scoring System B.

RESULTS

With any of the three scoring systems, the mean score of the paying customers was significantly higher than the mean score of the repossession customers. The coefficients of correlation (biserial r's) between score on the selected items and the criterion were all significantly greater than zero well beyond the .01 level of confidence. These results are presented in Table 1. There was no significant difference between the correlation coefficients obtained by the different scoring systems. System B was not only the simplest scoring method, but yielded the highest validity. Neither the contract nor the application blank alone was as valid as the total score. The correlation between contract score and application blank score was .28, indicating that these two measures were largely independent of each other.

A table was then developed indicating the percentage of repossession and paying customers eliminated by each possible cut-off score, using Scoring System B. Table 2 shows that if all ap-

TABLE 1

MEAN SCORES ON THE 24 SELECTED ITEMS AND VALIDITY COEFFICIENTS FOR THE CROSS-VALIDATION SAMPLE

Scoring Method	MS Repossession Group	MS Paying Group	r_{bis} between Score and Criterion
Scoring System A	76.6	102.0	.54
Scoring System B	18.2	23.8	.58
Scoring System C	12.5	17.2	.52
"B" score on contract	5.3	7.5	.43
"B" score on application blank	13.0	15.9	.39

TABLE 2
ELIMINATION OF REPOSSESSED AND PAYING CUSTOMERS BY VARIOUS CUT-OFF SCORES USING UNIT ITEM WEIGHTS

"B" SCORE ON TOTAL SCALE	REPOSSESSED CUSTOMERS ELIMINATED (□ = 1%)	CUM. %	CUM. %	PAYING CUSTOMERS ELIMINATED (□ = 1%)	EVALUATION DECISION
39					
38			100	□	
37			99	□	
36			98	□	
35			97	□	
34			96	□□□□	
33			92	□□□	ACCEPT
32			89	□□	
31			87	□□□	
30			84	□□□□□□□	
29			76	□□	
28			74	□□□	
27	□□□	100	71	□□□□□□□□□	
26	□□□	97	61	□□□	
25	□	94	58	□□□□□	
24	□□□□□	93	53	□□□	
23	□□	88	50	□□□□	
22	□□□□□□□□□□□□	86	46	□□□□□□	EVALUATE FURTHER
21	□□□□□□□□	72	40	□□□□□□□	
20	□□□□□□	64	33	□□□□	
19	□□□□□□□□□□□	58	29	□□□□	
18	□□	46	25	□□□□□	
17	□□□□□□□	44	20	□□□□	
16	□□□□□□□□□	36	16	□□□	
15	□□□	26	13	□□□□□□	
14	□□□□	23	7	□□□□□□	
13	□□□□	19	1		
12	□□□□□□□	15	1		
11	□□□	7	1	□	
10		4	0		
9	□□□	4			REJECT
8	□	1			
7		0			
6					
5					

plicants receiving a score of 13 or less had been eliminated at the time of application for credit, 19% of sales ending in repossession would have been eliminated while sacrificing 1% of paid sales. It may also be noted that none of the customers who scored 28 or higher had his car repossessed. This rather select group of superior credit customers made a large proportion of the total purchases during the time period sampled.

DISCUSSION

The 24 selected items were demonstrated to have considerable validity for discriminating good and poor credit customers in a cross-validation sample. The estimate of validity was probably conservative. Every case in the sample had already been selected by the existing credit evaluation method as an acceptable credit risk. With an unselected sample, the validity of the selection device would likely be higher. These results were comparable to those obtained from similar studies (Myers & Cordner, 1957; Wolbers, 1949).

The cut-off scores indicated in Table 2 should be regarded as only suggestive, and should themselves be subjected to cross-validation. Then they may be used in the following way: a clerk can score the selected items for each credit applicant, rejecting all applicants who score below the lower cutoff, accepting all who score above the upper cut-off, and sending those who score in between to the credit manager for further evaluation. This procedure would not only improve upon the validity of the existing credit evaluation method, but would reduce the credit manager's work load and credit department operating costs.

An estimate of the net profit or loss resulting from the use of various cut-off scores can be determined provided certain information is available. This estimate may be derived from this simple formula:

$$S = Q \, M_q \, E_q - P \, M_p \, E_p - A$$

Where: S = estimated savings per credit sale using the weighted application blank

P = proportion of paying customers in the defined population of credit customers

Q = proportion on nonpaying customers in the defined population of credit customers

M_p = mean profit on credit sales to paying customers

M_q = mean loss on credit sales to nonpaying customers

E_p = proportion of paying customers eliminated by the cut-off score

E_q = proportion of nonpaying customers eliminated by the cut-off score

A = mean cost of administering and scoring the weighted application blank

As an example of the use of this formula, we may apply it to the present study in this way: Of total credit sales during the period covered by the study, ⅚ were paid as agreed. Therefore, P is estimated to be .83 and Q is .17. The mean profit on paid sales (M_p) was estimated to be \$350.00. The mean loss on repossessions (M_q) was estimated to be \$200.00. A cut-off score of 13 eliminated 1% of paid sales and 19% of repossessions, so Ep equals .01 and Eq equals .19. The mean cost of administration and scoring (A) was not more than \$0.50. Putting these values[2] into the formula, the net profit using a cut-off score of 13 would be \$3.05 per credit sale. With approximately 2,000 sales per year, the annual profit would be \$6,000.

A separate analysis of the results of this study was made in which the contract scores and the application blank scores were used as successive hurdles. That is, the applicant had to pass a cut-off score on both the contract and the application blank before being accepted. With this method, 13% of repossessions were eliminated without losing any paid contracts. Net increase in profit using this method was \$4.34 per credit sale (changing only the values E_p and E_q in the equation). It will be noted that when only nonpaying customers are eliminated and no paying customers are lost by using a particular cut-off score, the second term in the equation reduces to zero.

Using this dollar criterion to most profitable cut-off score may be determined. By transposing the equation, one may also estimate the degree of dis-

[2] With the exception of E_p and E_q hypothetical values have been used in place of the true values because of the confidential nature of such information.

crimination demanded by any instrument for it to be a profitable predictor. For example, if the incidence of nonpayment (Q) is low and the loss sustained from nonpaying customers $(M_q$ is low compared with the profit on paying customers (M_p), it is likely that a study of this sort would not be profitable in terms of the level of validity one may expect from such measures. This would allow an investigator to estimate beforehand his chances of developing a usable predictor.

SUMMARY

A method of personnel selection was applied to the evaluation of credit applicants. A weighted credit application blank was developed which significantly discriminated the good and poor credit customers in a cross-validation sample. A formula was presented which allows the profit obtaining from the use of any particular cut-off score to be estimated.

REFERENCES

Myers, J. H., & Cordner, W. C. Increase credit operation profits. Credit World, 1957, February.

Wolbers, H. L. The use of biographical data blank in predicting potentially good and potentially poor credit risks. Unpublished master's thesis, Univer. Southern California, 1949.

F. PRODUCT DEVELOPMENT

38. Consumer Versus Management Reaction in New Package Development

MILTON L. BLUM AND VALENTINE APPEL

The last decade has been one of radical change in packaging as it has in many other areas of commerical life. A real part of this packaging revolution has been the contribution which consumer research has made. In fact, the introduction of a new package without the benefit of consumer research evolution is becoming the exception rather than the rule. The study to be reported points up the importance of consumer research in such package development programs.

The writers' firm was engaged to conduct a preliminary packaging study for one of its clients. The client's objective was to develop a package for a new product line. The product was intended for use by men but to be bought by women as a gift.

The purpose of the study was to screen, from a group of 18 design renderings submitted, the designs which showed the most promise, and to indicate possible areas of design modification which might further improve the acceptance of the more promising of the design concepts. The principal intention was ultimately to evaluate the more promising designs further based upon three dimensional prototypes and larger samples of respondents.

Earlier research had detailed certain specifications which the ideal package should meet. Among these was the decision that the package should appear

both as masculine and relatively expensive. Moreover, women should prefer it as a gift for their husbands, and men should prefer to receive it as a gift for themselves.

The study was unusual in that not only consumers were interviewed. The client's management, and also the design firm which created the packages, agreed to evaluate the designs from what they considered to be the female consumer's point of view. There was, therefore, the opportunity to compare the judgments of designers, management, and consumers.

METHOD

The study employed four independent groups of raters: female consumers ($N = 80$), male consumers ($N = 39$), advertising and marketing executives of the client company ($N = 8$), and the industrial designers who created the packages ($N = 7$). Each of the members of these groups individually rated a total of 18 different package design renderings using Stephenson's (1953) Q sort technique. The 18 designs were rated in terms of the extent to which each design was perceived as: masculine or feminine, expensive or inexpensive, and appropriate or inappropriate as a male gift. The Q sort was performed by asking the respondent to arrange the renderings into seven scaled categories, each category being assigned a score ranging from one to

From *Journal of Applied Psychology*, Vol. 45, No. 4 (August, 1961), pp. 222-24.

seven. For each respondent, this resulted in a forced frequency distribution of scores for the 18 designs. This frequency distribution was perfectly symmetrical, approached normality in shape, and had a modal rating of four which was assigned to six of the 18 designs. The forced frequency distribution and the scores assigned to each category were as follows:

Frequency	1	2	3	6	3	2	1
Score		1	2	3	4	5	6	7

The advertising and marketing executives of the client company, and the members of the design firm Q sorted the same 18 designs only on the basis of the extent to which they believed that women would be willing to give each of the packages to their husbands as a gift. This made for a total of eight variables to be analyzed; three each for the male and female consumers, and one each for management and the designers. Because of the amount of time involved in rating the designs for each variable, it was not considered desirable to request the management and design groups to rate the designs on more than one variable only. The ostensible purpose of asking management and the designers to complete the ratings was primarily as a device to explain to them the method employed.

RESULTS

Each design was assigned an overall rating for each variable which was the mean score for the group evaluating the designs, and the mean scores were converted into ranks for each variable. To measure the extent of agreement and disagreement among the four groups of raters, the Spearman rank-difference correlations among the eight variables were calculated.

The correlations for the gift ratings between the men and women and between management and the designers were as follows: .58 between the men and women, and .55 between management and the designers. From this it can be seen that there was fair agreement between management and the designers as to which packages they believed women would be more likely to prefer as gifts for their husbands. There was also fair agreement between the men and women as to which designs they would like to give and receive. Both the male and female consumers, however, were in substantial disagreement with the other two groups on this point. The correlations between the consumers vs. the management and designer groups were as follows: $-.48$ between the designers and the women, $-.14$ between the designers and the men, $-.21$ between management and the women, and $-.42$ between management and the men. The reasons underlying this disagreement can be understood in terms of the matrix of intercorrelations among all eight variables as shown in Table 1.

Examination of this correlation matrix reveals two clearly defined clusters. The first cluster is composed of the gift ratings of management and of the designers, and of the masculinity ratings of the male and female consumers. The second cluster is composed of the gift and the expensiveness ratings of the consumers. The two clusters correlate negatively with each other. The one exception is the low positive correlation (.23) between the gift and masculinity ratings of the male consumers.

The reason for this disagreement, between the consumers on the one hand and management and the designers on the other, stems from the fact that these two groups were apparently using conflicting criteria in evaluating the designs. Management and the designers were evaluating the designs in terms of what the consumer perceived to be masculinity. Those designs which were perceived as being more masculine tended to be the same ones which designer and management groups thought the consumers would prefer. The ratings of the consumers, on the

TABLE 1

RANK DIFFERENCE INTERCORRELATIONS AMONG THE EIGHT VARIABLES
(N = 18 designs)

Variable	1	2	3	4	5	6	7	8
1. Masculinity-men								
2. Masculinity-women	.70							
3. Gift-designers	.44	.65						
4. Gift-management	.14	.67	.55					
5. Gift-men	.23	−.08	−.14	−.42				
6. Gift-women	−.23	−.21	−.48	−.21	.58			
7. Expensiveness-men	−.47	−.61	−.29	−.44	.47	.47		
8. Expensiveness-women	−.55	−.73	−.49	−.47	.41	.53	.92	

Note.—With 16 degrees of freedom a correlation of .47 is significant at the .05 level. A correlation of .59 is significant at the .01 level.

other hand, tended to vary as a function of what they considered to be the expensive appearance of the design.

In this particular case expensiveness and masculinity appear to be relatively incompatible criteria, the correlation between them being −.73 among the women, and −.47 among the men. Since the two groups of raters tended to use one of these criteria to the relative exclusion of the other, the gift ratings of the consumers tended to correlate negatively with the ratings of the client's management and of the designers who created the designs. This is not to say that masculinity was completely unimportant among the consumer samples. It is to say that of the two variables, masculinity and expensiveness, expensiveness was the more important. Actually, among the sample of males, masculinity assumes considerable importance when the effects of perceived expensiveness are partialed out or eliminated. The partial correlations between the gift ratings and the masculinity ratings, when expensiveness is partialed out, is: .58 for the men, and −.13 for the women. The inference to be drawn here is that masculinity does contribute to preference on the part of the men when the effects of perceived expensiveness are eliminated. In the case of the women, masculinity appears to play no role at all in contributing to preference.

DISCUSSION

The marketing implications of these findings are clear. Had the packaging decision been made on the basis of the recommendation of the design firm and on the pooled judgment of the client's marketing management, the net effect would have been to select designs which would have had the least appeal so far as the consumers sampled were concerned.

The result of the research was to outline specifications for the design group which would enable them to modify certain of the designs in ways which would cause them to be perceived by the consumer both as masculine as well as expensive.

These findings point up the contribution which consumer research can make to the company involved in new packaging plans. Without the kind of information which consumer research can provide, management decisions concerning new package development remain much more of a gamble than most manufacturers can afford.

REFERENCE

STEPHENSON, W. *The study of behavior.* Chicago: University, Chicago Press, 1953.

39. Planning A Holiday*

DONALD M. HOBART

Since it first became known that The Curtis Publishing Company was developing plans for a new publication, to be called *Holiday,* there has been considerable interest expressed concerning the marketing research activities which accompanied, aided and followed the launching. This is a brief review of those marketing research activities.

The launching of a new magazine is a long and complicated process—it takes time, thought and money. Magazines succeed primarily because of editors and editorial plans together with sound management and financing. It also seems equally clear that editors and editorial plans can produce better magazines *with* research than without it.

The research activity surrounding *Holiday* can be understood more easily by giving a quick picture of some of our company's postwar planning activities. A Postwar Discussion Committee was appointed representing all departments of the company. From these discussion meetings came definite assignments asking for reports on our present properties and preliminary reports on certain new areas of future operation which the discussion group and management felt were worthy of more attention. Two such areas were considered—new magazines and new products other than magazines, such as paper-backed books, of

which Bantam Books, Inc., is an example.

In approaching the area of new magazines we were influenced primarily by the fact that we wanted a large expanding market for mass circulation, and we did not want to fall into the error of putting out an imitation of any magazine now in existence. After much discussion it seemed clear that the field of travel, recreation, sports, entertainment and hobbies offered real possibilities for the future. So a man was assigned the job of bringing in a report on the field and of preparing preliminary plans, specifications and estimates. This report was accompanied by a very rough paste-up dummy covering the general idea. At this stage the project was known as Magazine "Y" and sometimes referred to as "Go" or "Play."

This preliminary report was submitted to our Postwar Action Committee, made up of the officers and department managers. It was decided to set up an experimental group to study in more detail such things as the market possibilities, the editorial formula, circulation possibilities and the physical properties of the book itself. Our Research Department moved into the situation in three major ways:

(1) We brought together, studied and analyzed all the information available from many sources on such things as the size of the pleasure, travel and recreation market in the past, in terms of dollar volume and the number of people interested. In addition we gathered all

From *Journal of Marketing,* Vol. 12, No. 1 (July, 1947), pp. 47-52, by permission of the American Marketing Association.
* Presented before the New York Chapter of The American Marketing Association.

the estimates and evidence of future trends. We saw that postwar America represented a travel and pleasure-hungry market—a market made up of millions of people who, weary of wartime work and restrictions, would be eager to satisfy that innate urge for fun and relaxation.

We knew that the travel and recreation market had always been an important one from the standpoint of dollar volume. We learned that it is perhaps far more important . . . and far more all-inclusive than many realize. It is a market which completely embraces many different industries and deeply penetrates into many others. Therefore, we found the task of measuring the dollar amount of the potential *Holiday* market a difficult one if we were to rely alone upon the industrial or trade statistics.

We decided upon a basic concept which was that the Holiday market would rightfully include all goods and services purchased by the consumer in satisfaction of his urge for fun and relaxation; and that the factor which motivates the spending is of primary importance-not the industry classification into which the product or service falls.

The total sales of the *primary* recreational classifications such as amusements, sporting goods and radio, were easily obtained, but the other classifications such as food, clothing, hotels and transportation, which owe an important share of their market to recreational spending, also deserved consideration. The difficulty arose in estimating the recreational share of total sales for these secondary classes. The statistics which were readily available, however, served as important guide posts to indicate the tremendous size of this market. During the prewar period—1929-1941, for example—Department of Commerce figures showed us that an average of over 5½ billion dollars per year was spent by the consumer for recreation (in the primary classes only) and for pleasure transportation. This meant that

without considering the secondary classifications, and during a period which included the greatest economic depression this country has ever experienced, $1 out of every $11 spent by the consumer went for having a good time.

If we gave recognition to recreational spending in the secondary classifications and if proper allowance was made for the pent-up demand for fun and relaxation current in America today, it appeared reasonable to conclude that considerably more than that $1 out of every $11 to be spent by the consumer in these postwar years would be motivated by the holiday urge.

(2) The Research Department, through its Development Division, also conducted two national personal-interview surveys among magazine readers. One survey among 2,500 men and women was on travel; the other of equal size was on recreation, sports, hobbies and entertainment. These surveys gave us a comprehensive and detailed analysis of typical magazine readers' tastes and plans for travel.

In the Travel Survey we found, for example, that:

Seventy-six per cent expected summer vacations after the war and that 90 per cent of these expected to go away from home. Two weeks was mentioned most often as the probable duration of their summer vacation. Thirty-eight per cent of the summer travelers expected to travel *outside the United States* within the next few years, and their first choices were Canada, Mexico, Alaska, the British Isles and South America— in that order.
Eighteen per cent expected winter vacations after the war, and 89 per cent of these planned to go away from home. Winter vacationers apparently expect to spend more time on their trips, for one month was mentioned most often as the probable duration. Thirty-two per cent of these winter travelers planned to go outside the United States on their winter vaca-

tions. Mexico was their first choice—then South America, the West Indies, Canada and Alaska.

In the Sports and Recreation Survey we learned that people were almost universally interested in active participation in a wide variety of sports and hobbies. Space does not permit giving any more of the figures, but these surveys served in large measure to confirm the belief at Curtis that Mr. and Mrs. America were not only interested in travel and recreation, but were also eager to find a magazine which would provide interesting and informative reading matter on these subjects.

(3) The Research Department was also able to bring to this experimental group years of experience in editorial research covering, among other things, the reaction of readers to various types of editorial and art appeals. Not that we would tell them what to do, but we could discuss with them our conclusions and reactions on many subjects vital to their plans.

After many, many months of work, with the cooperation of all departments of the company, the editorial group on Magazine "Y" produced its first dummy carrying the name *Holiday.*

More accurate preliminary recommendations were developed on specifications such as book dimensions, price, weight of paper, book size and print order. A cost and income analysis for a five-year basis was prepared, together with an operating budget for the coming year. The final plan for Magazine "Y," the necessary appropriation, all details of size, print order and newsstand dates were okayed by the company. Thus the magazine was born as an operating entity, but it still had no official name and its editorial and advertising staffs were not complete.

The story concerning the name is very interesting. Somewhere along the line someone suggested the name *Holiday.* As the editorial plans developed, it

seemed clear that the magazine was being edited to the holiday mood. That is the way you feel when you plan for or actually experience the pleasures of travel, recreation, sports or enjoy a hobby. The name *Holiday* expressed that mood so well.

When we checked on the copyright of the name, we found that it was controlled by the American Automobile Association, which had published a magazine by that name. We told them of our plans for a new magazine in the interest of travel and recreation. They were very cooperative and from them we secured control of the name "Holiday."

Shortly after this Research sent to the editorial group a complete analysis of the first dummy, item by item, based on our past experience in editorial research. Soon after, work was started on the second preliminary dummy. The editorial staff was enlarged—a Sales Manager was appointed and advertising representatives were employed. Circulation made its plans to handle the sale of *Holiday* through the Sales and Subscription Divisions.

The second preliminary dummy, using the same cover, was larger and showed internal changes. When it was completed, it was used by our advertising salesmen to sell advertisers and advertising agents, and by our Circulation Department to sell wholesalers, subscription workers and agencies on *Holiday.*

This second dummy was also used by the Development Division of the Research Department to secure potential consumer reaction to the finished product. A carefully controlled acceptance test was made during November 1945 among representative magazine reading homes to certain key cities throughout the country.

Copies of the dummy were placed in these selected homes, and people with whom the copies were left were told, quite frankly, the nature of the test and were asked to look at the magazine just as if it had come into the home by subscription or as the result of newsstand purchase. To eliminate bias they were not told that the test was being done for The Curtis Publishing Company. Field work was handled entirely by national interviewing organizations.

On the follow-up interview, made after the dummy had been in each home for a specified period of time, a complete record of observation and reading was made, plus (and most important) the answers to a series of attitude questions. Results were then turned over to *Holiday's* editorial department. Our subsequent editorial research surveys on identical material in actual published issues have shown nearly identical results with those obtained on this acceptance test.

And then the first issue — March 1946 — appeared in the mails and on the newsstands of the nation. But the job of the Research Department had only begun. Research had played an important part at *Holiday's* inception by obtaining and presenting the broad market facts essential to management. Now the idea was an actuality — a full-fledged, slick paper magazine being read in many thousands of subscriber homes throughout the country and being sold on newsstands in nearly every town and city in the nation. It was necessary to renew and redouble Research efforts to give this new publication the support it would require now that it was on the market.

One of the first questions we were asked after the first issue appeared was — "What *kind* of people are *Holiday* readers?" This question was a perfectly natural one for both editors and advertisers to raise and, of course, had been anticipated. We had, by this time, already completed a survey among *Holiday's* charter subscribers, but it was necessary to withhold this information until we could make a survey among the newsstand buyers and present the entire story at the same time. We waited until the second, or April issue, before

we attempted to conduct the newsstand survey, because we felt that there would be less possibility for curiosity buyers and collectors to distort the picture. The methods used in conducting both surveys were simple but effective.

The questionnaire mailing list for the Charter Subscriber Survey was compiled in December 1945, by selecting every fourth name from the subscriber file, which at that time contained about 29,000 names. This method of random selection insured a representative sample of the group. An especially designed and illustrated questionnaire, accompanied by a "personalized" letter with a masculine appeal, was addressed to the male subscribers and a letter designed for feminine interest was sent to the women on the list. Each mailing contained the letter, a questionnaire and a return envelope. No premium offer or follow-up was made, but 4,460 questionnaires were returned, which represented a 62 per cent response.

The same questionnaire which was used in the Charter Subscriber Survey was inserted in 10,000 newsstand copies of the April issue, together with a similar letter and a return envelope. The distribution of these newsstand questionnaires conformed very closely to the actual newsstand distribution of the magazine.

The questionnaire sets were sent to the Curtis circulation branch offices in 101 cities geographically representative of the country. The number of sets sent to each of these cities was in direct proportion to that city's newsstand copy allotment. Then, in order to insure a proper sample within each city, the local Curtis representative "tipped" the questionnaire sets into copies of *Holiday* on selected newsstands throughout his territory. Every care was taken to see that this distribution of newsstand questionnaires was in proper proportion to the single copy distribution of the magazine within each city.

Here, again, the response was good, but considerably lower, as you might expect, than in the Charter Subscriber Survey which had been conducted through the mails. Over 1,500 newsstand buyers of this April issue completed the questionnaire and mailed it back to us, thereby providing a better than 15 per cent return.

The findings of these combined surveys indicated that April newsstand buyers were generally the same kind of people who made up our initial charter subscriber group. They were younger in age, as we suspected, since those who would subscribe to a new type magazine as yet unpublished would naturally come from the older and more substantial segment of our population. Then, too, many of the younger element of the population were still in the service or just returning to civilian life in December 1945 and had little chance for representation among our first charter subscribers.

Here are just a few highlights from the survey. The median family income of the April *newsstand buyers of Holiday* was $4,679, which may be compared to the median figure for our charter subscribers of $6,308 . . . the same type people — only the charter subscribers, being older, have higher incomes.

The median age of the initial charter subscribers was 46 years and for the newsstand group 32 years. Sixty-one per cent of the charter subscribers had attended college. To prove the statement that the April newsstand buyers were the same *kind* of people, but younger, we found that 65 per cent of this group had been college students.

The breakdowns for occupations again showed a marked similarity of types. For example, 25 per cent of the male charter subscribers were in the professional and semi-professional classification, while 29 per cent of the male April newsstand buyers were in that occupational group; 41 per cent of the male charter subscribers were either proprietors, managers or company officials and 28 per cent of their younger

contemporaries in the newsstand group were in similar positions.

Both charter subscribers and newsstand buyers alike are active people interested in travel, sports and other recreational activities. Ninety-eight per cent of the charter subscribers mentioned one or more outdoor sports in which they like to participate, whereas 99 per cent of the newsstand buyers indicated interest in exercise out-of-doors. About 85 per cent of both the first charter subscribers and the April newsstand buyers have hobbies, and nearly 80 per cent of both groups said they had visited one or more of ten foreign countries, popular among travelers, which were listed in the questionnaire.

The question of circulation naturally arose soon after the first issue appeared. How many net paid copies? Where had they been sold? And how were they sold — subscription or newsstand? It was too early for a published ABC report, so the job of analyzing preliminary circulation reports fell to the Research Department. For obvious reasons, a statement on this subject will have to be on the ultra-conservative side. That is only good business for any publisher with a new magazine.

The pre-publication announcement to the advertising world was that *Holiday* expected to have 300,000 net paid circulation on the first issue. The records of the Circulation Department were checked and it is now a published fact that the average for the first three issues was over 400,000. And in order to prove the complete national coverage of *Holiday* as a magazine we obtained a breakdown of the circulation by states which shows a very close correlation percentagewise to the buying power of the nation when compared with standard indices. So we found that this new magazine, *Holiday*, though still in its infancy, had already formed a marketwise circulation distribution pattern.

As in the case with all new products, *Holiday* is going through a period of careful study. Many opinions of *Holi-*

day, admittedly both pro and con, have been offered by the experts who would have edited the book differently. Much constructive criticism, voluntarily given, has been received and digested. Much of this will be reflected in future changes. But as valuable as this expert advice has been in planning for immediate changes, the most important evidence on this subject had to come from the consumer.

This evidence was in the form of reader mail (of which we fully recognized the limitations) and continuing editorial research among readers of *Holiday* in the homes of subscribers and newsstand buyers. These surveys, which are made on every issue, follow our usual traffic surveys, using the methods of going through the book item by item with readers and checking those items seen, read part and read in full. We also secure the degree to which each item is liked or disliked. This is done through a series of general attitude questions and through certain supplementary questions about the book. Because of the importance of speed, returns are reported by wire from the field and are then analyzed by the Development Division of the Research Department. The findings are then presented in report form, for use by the editorial group and by management.

In addition to these monthly traffic surveys, we have recently initiated a series of small but, we feel, highly important tests of consumer preference on layout, illustration, titling and other mechanical features of the magazine. We have also carried out a panel study of the issue-by-issue purchasing habits of first issue single copy buyers. This has been of assistance in predicting such factors as the inevitable audience turn-over and drop-out rate of "novelty" buyers.

The significance of these plans for continuous editorial research must be apparent to all marketing research men. It means that *Holiday* editors and Curtis management have at hand research which will lead to constant product improvement.

All of us in marketing research know that no new product, especially a new magazine, can be produced in a perfect state. As proof of this, just think back to the first issues of most now successful magazines. Improvement and perfection of a product takes time. Research can add much to hasten the day.

G. PURCHASING

40. Deliberations of a Chain Grocery Buying Committee

DONALD G. HILEMAN and
LEONARD A. ROSENSTEIN

The importance of the buying committee as the key to the purchasing function in today's food stores cannot be taken lightly. Few items gain admission to the nations supermarkets without the express consent of the buying committee.

How does the buying committee operate? What is appraised by the buying committee? Who, within the buying committee, carries the weight of evaluation? What factors are evaluated in determining the products to accept? Do certain factors carry more weight than others?

The answers to these questions are paramount in any analysis of the workings of the buying committee. To obtain these answers, a tape recording was made of a chain grocery-buying committee at its regular meeting.

FACTORS CONSIDERED

The session was democratic. While the committee operates on a majority basis, in almost every case unanimity of opinion seemed to prevail. The comments of the branch manager, the merchandise manager, and the buyer appeared to carry the greatest weight; yet any serious objection or comment on the part of any member was given consideration. The merit of the comment

From *Journal of Marketing*, Vol. 25, No. 3 (January, 1961), pp. 52-55, by permission of the American Marketing Association.

was usually far more important than who made it.

The majority of the committee devoted very little time before the meeting to a study of the proposals. The buyer (making the presentation) was expected to be completely informed about all facets of the product under consideration. All quantitative material covering price, markup, movement of the product under consideration, and *all* competitive products carried was presented to the committee at the time of meeting.

Many factors were discussed or mentioned by the committee in evaluating a new product. No member of the committee appeared to be aware of the importance of *all* of the factors, nor was each factor mentioned for every product.

At some time during the study of the thirteen products presented to the committee, each of the factors listed in Table 1 was mentioned. No check list was followed. Some items were discussed at great length, while others were casually mentioned. The specific product under discussion dictated the factors to be discussed.

It is not practical to attempt an individual analysis of each of the factors listed in Table 1. The discussion followed no formal outline on a factor-by-factor basis, and there was no uniformity of policy or practice for each item under discussion. Rather, it was a discussion of all factors relating to the product and their interplay.

SPECIFIC PRODUCT CONSIDERATIONS

Certain observations can be made concerning the specific items considered at this particular buying session.

Two of the products accepted were cigarettes—one a new king-size menthol filter, and the other an accepted premium-priced cigarette with a new flip-top box. Strong advertising support and probable consumer demand

TABLE 1

FACTORS CONSIDERED BY THE BUYING COMMITTEE

Product Characteristics	Miscellaneous Factors	Merchandising
Newness	Difference in store size	Store demonstrations
Differentness or uniqueness	Test market results	Merchandising allowances
Taste appeal	Warehousing considerations	Distribution allowances
Quality aspects	Transportation considerations	Point-of-purchase materials
Mass appeal vs. limited appeal	Diet fad	Special displays
Shelf life	Shelf space & back-room inventory	Uniqueness of merchandising
Evaluation of personal sampling	Company image	Free goods
Convenience aspects	Brand image	Consumer allowance
	Season of year	General office merchandising recommendations
Packaging	Integrity of supplier —past experience	
	Consumer demand	Special promotional allowances
Size of container	Variation in demand between areas of company	
Shelf stacking properties	National vs. private label	*Advertising*
Number of items to case	Length of time product on market	Length of campaign
Novelty aspects of package or container	Branch unwillingness to pioneer	Frequency of campaign
Similarity of size to existing competition		Media selection and impact
Consumer demand and acceptance of size	*Competitive Aspects*	Advertising allowances
		Copy:
Profit Area	Completeness of competitive lines now stocked	Use of product
		Tie-in with other products
Cost	Competitive stores carrying new product	National vs. localized advertising
Anticipated profit (in per cent)		Co-operative advertising
Prepricing		Complete line vs. product advertising
Inventory costs		
Competitive pricing of same item		
Markup in relation to product group		
Markup in relation to store averages		
Guaranteed sale		
Fair traded		

seemed to be major reasons for acceptance. Some members of the committee questioned the market for the premium cigarette in this area, but they were in the minority.

A blue and perfumed liquid starch, which had been rejected at a previous buying session, was accepted when consumer demand caused store managers to ask for its reconsideration. The particular brand was well advertised. One size in a competitor's white liquid starch was discontinued.

One manufacturer's new 40-oz. refrigerator jar of prune juice was adopted, due to the demand for its quart size. Consumer demand for large containers of prune juice was the primary factor, with the new container a plus factor. Consideration of this new size container caused analysis of all prune-juice sales. When it was found that the manufacturer's quart size far outsold the quart size of a competitor, the latter's quart size was dropped.

Acceptance of a chiffon pie mix was affected by the fact that there was nothing quite like it in the store, its quick preparation with no cooking, its use as a favorable diet food, and a major schedule of magazine advertising. Concern for space, the seasonal demand of the product, and the rate of demand for various flavors caused the committee to take on only lemon chiffon and chocolate, and to reject strawberry and butterscotch.

Packaged, shredded, sharp cheddar cheese and cubed sharp cheddar cheese with toothpicks included were accepted, when the manufacturing organization was recognized for its unique merchandising ideas; yet it was not thought of particularly as being in the cheese field. The committee felt that only one advertisement in *Life* was not enough to promote these products. The committee's acceptance that this was a quality product, and that it performed a service for the consumer, were the primary considerations. In addition,

a sales guarantee and provision for a demonstrator for two days in each store were other important factors in obtaining placement in the chain's larger stores.

The committee rejected four products —coffee-cake mix, sliced apple thins, rootbeer candy, and pine-oil disinfectant—because it felt that these products offered nothing particularly new and that they held little consumer appeal in this area. In none of the four instances was there much advertising support for the product.

After considerable debate, a pre-priced, fair-traded tooth paste—with the price appeal of two giant tubes at a new low price—was rejected. The reasons: nationally accepted brands offered a greater advertising allowance; these same brands used national advertising more extensively; and the particular product under consideration had not been recommended by the general office's merchandising department.

Likewise, a new liquid detergent in a plastic dispenser received considerable comment. Concern for the durability of the plastic container caused the committee to adopt a wait-and-see attitude toward the item. The stores carried a complete line of detergents, and this product offered nothing new other than the container. The fact that the advertising would reach only a small part of the branch marketing area helped to cement the decision not to accept the product at this time.

The committee discussed extensively several items of a complete line of premium-priced canned chicken products. It respected the company for its quality products but felt that the company had not supported its line with sufficient advertising in recent years. The company, however, was embarking on a new promotional program including spots on several TV programs which the committee members regarded favorably, and the possible effectiveness of this new promotional program was thoroughly discussed.

A decision as to acceptance and distribution policy was tabled until the next session.

IMPLICATIONS

ADVERTISING IS THE CATALYST FOR MUCH OF THE DISCUSSION OF A BUYING COMMITTEE

Most of the members of this committee appeared to be "advertising wise." They seemed to have a keen sense about media. This was especially true in the case of television, where they were very much aware of talent, station, and time. They were not copy experts, but appraised copy in the light of "will it sell?"

It is true that not all of the products presented at this meeting were discussed in terms of the advertising program behind them. Products were accepted with little or no advertising to back them, whereas other products having fairly substantial advertising to support were rejected. However, the appraisal of advertising was along the lines of its influence in creating demand, not merely acceptance of the brand or product.

ONCE IT IS ON THE SHELF, PRESSURE IS PLACED UPON THE PRODUCT

Once admitted to the store, the product soon discovers its new home is less than heaven. The instant a new item in a product category is presented to the buying committee, every older item now on the shelf has the spotlight of appraisal turned upon it. There was evidence from this meeting that many products are evaluated only when attention is focused on the product category by the presentation of a "new" product to the committee.

At this time there is no salesman available to defend the marketing position of the "old" product. Advertising campaigns, or promotions designed to hypo the sales of the old product, cannot be presented to the committee. Attention is focused on the old as well as the new product; and, if the old product fails to meet the expected performance standards, it may be "axed." Discontinuance is a part of the routine of the seller; he does not feel called upon to warn the supplier. He does not need to offer an extension of time during which the manufacturer may devise a sales-stimulating program to regain former sales levels.

"LIMITED SHELF SPACE" IS NOT THE OGRE IT IS MADE OUT TO BE

The murderous competition for chain store shelf space has led chains to adopt the attitude of "we just don't have room for that item—our space is limited." This appears to be a safe defense against the bombardment of new items being presented to the buying committee.

Yet the chains recognize that their competitive position is related to the astuteness with which they place new and different items throughout their stores. If limited shelf space were the dominant reason for refusing to accept the new item, it is obvious that in order to add a new item (and this refers to size of package as well as product definition), something would have to be discontinued in order to make room. Interestingly, of the six items accepted for placement at this meeting, four were taken on without dropping anything from the present line of products carried.

Of course, items are discontinued in order to provide shelf space for new items—this takes place even when the new item is not acceptable to the chain. There is a physical limit to the number of lineal feet available for display, but it is apparent that the reason of "limited shelf space" may have been exaggerated.

PROFIT MOTIVE IS NOT NECESSARILY
THE PREDOMINANT INFLUENCING
FACTOR

The buying committee must balance the interests of the consumer, the manufacturer, and their own company in selecting an item to be sold in their stores. Their first and foremost responsibility is to make a profit on the products they sell.

There is, however, an awareness of the needs, interests, and desires of Mrs. Consumer. The committee knows well the composition of its market and the needs of its customers. Satisfaction of these needs will contribute to the ultimate profit of the chain. While the markup must conform to store averages and product group averages, certainly consumer satisfaction and demand can override strict profit considerations.

COMPANY IMAGE AND BRAND IMAGE
ARE IMPORTANT FACTORS

When a strongly established brand name is attached to what qualifies as a new item, regardless of whether it is a new product or a new size, the new item wins a better hearing. This does not imply that this is the major consideration. If many other factors are good, brand image will help the decision.

The committee members were aware that brand demand and brand acceptance are two distinct ideas. Many products have consumer acceptance without having consumer demand. The presence of what the committee felt was a favorable brand image eased their problem of decision making.

In general, at this buying session certain factors appeared each time a product adoption occurred. Basically, there was an element of newness—of something different. The item did not duplicate in type, size, or price an item already carried in the stores. The presence of a "gimmick" or something a little extra in the way of packaging helped. And the existence of supporting advertising, not only in introducing the product but in continual promotion, carried a great deal of weight in influencing favorable decision.

41. Analysis of Vendor Selection Systems and Decisions

GARY W. DICKSON

The problems associated with deciding how one vendor should be selected from a number of potential alternatives recently has received a substantial amount of consideration by people in the purchasing profession. From the purchasing literature, it is fairly easy to abstract a list of at least 50 distinct factors (characteristics of vendor performance) that are presented by various authors as being meaningful to consider in a vendor selection decision.[1] Each authority suggests about five or ten items, and close analysis shows considerable variation in the factors that are considered appropriate for the evaluation of potential suppliers.

Not only is there little agreement upon what factors should be considered when selecting a vendor, there has been little attention focused upon the way in which the nature of the purchase affects the decision. It seems very reasonable to assume that the factors considered when selecting a vendor for nuts and bolts are not the factors that are appro-

priate when selecting a supplier for a computer. Furthermore, no system has been developed to show how, in any particular instance, the pertinent factors should be weighted relative to one another.[2] Should price, for example, be considered more important than the vendor's perceived ability to meet quality standards? Does the same relationship between price, quality, and all other pertinent factors hold for all purchases, or are the importance relationships between the factors that are considered in the vendor evaluation and selection also a function of the item to be purchased?

Since the effectiveness of a purchasing decision is a direct function of selecting the proper vendor, the above questions are important. Regardless of whether a purchasing department has a formal vendor analysis system or an informal system resting only upon the buyers' experience and judgment, it is important to know what factors on which to evaluate vendors and how to weight these factors relative to one another.

Before work can progress on the problem of relative weighting of factors, some preliminary information descriptive of the factors themselves must be obtained. In an attempt to obtain a list of factors in current use for vendor evaluation, a survey was made of both firm and individual vendor selection

From *Journal of Purchasing*, Vol. 2 (February, 1966), pp. 5-17. Copyright February, 1966 by the National Association of Purchasing Agents, Inc. Reprinted with the permission of the National Association of Purchasing Agents, Inc.

[1] The following sources provide good examples of the disparity in the factors suggested for the evaluation of potential suppliers: **Evaluation of Supplier Performance** (New York: National Association of Purchasing Agents, 1963), pp. 11-18; Department of Defense, **Armed Services Procurement Regulations** (Revised March, 1965), Section 1-903, p. 165; and **Moving Ahead With Chrysler, A Supplier's Guide** (New York: The Chrysler Corporation, 1964), p. 29.

[2] **Evaluation of Supplier Performance**, *op. cit.*, p. 8, recognizes the importance of factor weightings but presents no system for determining the weightings.

TABLE 1

ATTRIBUTES OF FIRMS REPRESENTED IN THE SAMPLE*

Characteristic	Median
Size of organization	794 Employees
Size of purchasing department	6 Employees
Number of buyers	4 Employees
Annual sales volume	$13,000,000
Annual purchasing volume	$4,600,000

*Because 32 of the organizations represented in the survey did not sell a product, a ratio between the median sales and purchases is not appropriate. In general, the purchases of the non-selling organizations tended to be somewhat smaller than those of firms selling a product. For the organizations for which the figure is meaningful, purchases represented approximately 50 per cent of total annual sales.

TABLE 2

PERCENTAGE OF THE PLACEMENT OF ORDERS PRECEDED BY REQUESTS FOR QUOTATION BY DOLLAR VOLUME AND BY NUMBER

Class	By Dollar Volume Frequency	By Number Frequency
90% and over	30	17
75% under 90%	22	16
50% under 75%	28	26
15% under 50%	36	36
6% under 15%	15	34
under 6%	16	29
Total Responding	147	158
Median	56%	31%

TABLE 3

FACTORS USED IN VENDOR RATING SYSTEMS

Factor	Per Cent of Systems Using Factor
Quality of product	96.6
Price	93.9
Delivery, dependability of promises	93.9
Service	81.8
Technical capability	63.6
Financial strength	51.5
Geographical location	42.4
Reputation	42.4
Reciprocal arrangements	15.1
Other factors	12.1

practices. Although this survey was primarily of a descriptive nature (how vendors are selected), many implications of a normative nature (how vendors ought to be selected) can be drawn from these data. The research reported here provides a foundation for further research on the relative weighting of appropriate factors and should be of interest to buyers, purchasing agents, and purchasing management for a number of other reasons.

The survey provides a great deal of information about the vendor selection practices of others, since both firm practices and individual opinions are reported. Also, a specific and detailed list of factors for vendor evaluation is presented and evaluated. Using this list, the reader can compare his values concerning factor importance with the consensus of the survey respondents in four specific cases. Finally, some generalizations both descriptive of current practice and helpful in developing suggested vendor selection systems are presented.

QUESTIONNAIRE RESEARCH

To gather the information desired concerning the selection of vendors, data were obtained from purchasing agents throughout the United States and Canada by means of a mail questionnaire. Since there was no available list of the whole population of purchasing agents, the membership list of the National Association of Purchasing Agents was used in the selection of a random sample to which to send the questionnaire. From this list, the names and business addresses of approximately 300 potential respondents were obtained.[3] After several pre-tests, a four-page questionnaire consisting of three

[3] The sample size was based upon economic considerations, trading off cost versus the volume of information to be obtained. The original request to the National Association of Purchasing Agents was for approximately 300 names, of which 273 were provided.

parts evolved. Parts I and II were concerned primarily with information descriptive of the respondents' businesses and the vendor selection practices of these firms. The third part of the questionnaire examined the decision behavior of the individual purchasing agents in the selection of a vendor. The return from the initial request letter sent to the 273 purchasing agents was 113 questionnaires (41.4%). Fifty-seven persons returned a second questionnaire sent to all non-respondents, bringing the total response up to 170 (62.3%).

SAMPLE CHARACTERISTICS

The respondents represented typical commercial organizations throughout the country, with the exception that manufacturing perhaps was overrepresented (67.8% of the firms represented were engaged principally in this activity). Both large and small firms were included in the sample with about equal representation. Roughly 20 per cent of the firms fell in each group and 60 per cent of the sample was made up of intermediate size organizations. These categories were determined by measuring both sales volume and number of employees. About 22 per cent of the respondents stated that they were operating as a subsidiary of a larger organization and that their answers referred to local operations. All other respondents' answers were for the main purchasing department of their organization. Table 1 shows the median figures for a few of the characteristics of the firms represented in the sample.

VENDOR SELECTION PRACTICES BY FIRMS

The second part of the questionnaire explored how firm practices and procedures influence the process of selecting a supplier. As might be expected, it appears that those orders which involve large dollar volumes are subject to the most attention by purchasing agents.

TABLE 4
INFORMATION RETAINED ON VENDOR PERFORMANCE

Type of Information	Frequency	Per Cent
Delivery experience	77	45.8
Defective material experience	75	44.6
Repair service rendered	38	22.6
Technical service rendered	35	20.8
All service rendered	30	17.8
None of the above	59	35.1

Asking for the submission of bids from prospective suppliers on some orders but not on others gives an indication of which orders receive particular attention. Table 2 shows that respondents felt that the request for the submission of bids (and therefore more detailed analysis) is associated with the economic value of the order. The first category in Table 2, for instance, states that 30 of the respondents estimated that 90% of the *dollar volume* of orders placed by their firms were preceded by bid requests, whereas the second column shows that only 17 felt that 90% of the *number* of all their orders were treated in this manner. Examination of both the frequency distributions and their medians reflects the emphasis on purchases involving large dollar amounts.

Only 44 (19.6%) of the firms represented had a formal method of vendor analysis, i.e., a rating system based upon written procedures. Table 3 shows the factors used to rate potential vendors by the existing systems.

Somewhat surprisingly, over one-third of the responding firms stated that they kept no formal records of vendor performance for use in subsequent vendor selections. The information that is retained, however, consists, in general, of the same factors mentioned in the vendor rating systems. Table 4 depicts the availability of information on vendor performance. As in the rating systems, the emphasis on quality, delivery, and service is apparent.

In response to a question about the obligation to place an order with the low bidder, only 19 persons (11.9%) said they felt such an obligation. Although this question actually deals with individual rather than firm practices, it was included in the section on organizations because its response is related directly to previous data. Those respondents who answered negatively were asked for the factors that they felt would override a low bid. Table 5 shows that the the factors named reinforce the previous emphasis upon quality and delivery as factors that are critical to vendor selection decisions.

TABLE 5
FACTORS MENTIONED THAT WOULD OVERRIDE LOW BID

Factors	Frequency
Quality	84
Delivery	84
Service	38
Past experience	32
Reputation	12
Facilities	11
Technical ability and services	11
Financial responsibility	8
Failure to comply with specifications	6
Multiple sources of supply	3

An examination of these three separate and somewhat independent indices of factors pertinent to vendor evaluation and selection (existing rating systems, retained information, and special circumstances that would lead to overriding a low bid) yields a remarkably consistent list of important factors. The ability of potential vendors to meet quality standards and delivery schedules stand out as the two most critical factors in the vendor selection process. Price, service, financial position, technical capability, and past experience appear as factors of secondary importance.

This analysis of firm vendor selection practices, however, gives only one view of the way vendor characteristics are evaluated. So far, the influence of the item to be purchased upon the selection of the vendor has not been considered. The effect of the individual who chooses the vendor also has been only touched upon. To further analyze the vendor selection decision and to allow for comparison with the results indicated from organizational practices, the third part of the questionnaire examined individual opinions about the selection of vendors in four specific instances.

VENDOR SELECTION OPINIONS BY INDIVIDUALS

The cases that were selected to be used in the examination of vendor selection decision-making by individuals (which appear as Exhibit 1) were designed to be widely variable with regard to the items to be purchased and also with respect to the background of the purchasing situation. These cases had to be concise enough to present considerable information to the respondents while at the same time fulfilling the constraint of limited length. A list of 23 factors that might possibly be of importance when evaluating potential vendors was abstracted from the purchasing literature and used in the test of the evaluative criteria in vendor

selection. The factors used are shown in Exhibit 2.

EXHIBIT 1
CASES USED IN THE STUDY OF VENDOR SELECTION DECISION-MAKING

CASE A: A large company whose principal product is industrial chemicals has scheduled the repainting of the interior walls of its manufacturing plant. The painting is complicated due to the fact that all painted surfaces are subject to severe chemical fumes which tend to make paint deteriorate. Fortunately the surfaces to be painted are of a common substance, cement. It is estimated that 10 barrels of paint will be sufficient for the project. The necessary labor will be furnished under contract by a reliable painting firm.

CASE B: The purchasing agent of a large university has received a requisition for the purchase of 200 desks. The desks are to be used by faculty in their soon-to-be completed office building. It has been the university's policy to furnish all new office facilities with metal furniture.

CASE C: A very large aerospace manufacturer has received a substantial contract to build an orbital laboratory. This five-man satellite, to be used for astronomical research, will orbit the earth at a mean distance of 500 miles. Once the satellite is in its orbit, its position will be stabilized under computer control. The computers will be subcontracted. The complexity of the computer and manufacturing tolerances are such that only firms known to be experienced in precision micro-electronic manufacturing and use of materials such as phenolics, platinum, beryllium, and stainless steel are to be considered. Only two computers are to be built for the orbital laboratories which are to be launched two years from the awarding of the prime contract.

CASE D: A division of a large aerospace corporation is faced with the problem of contracting for art, makeup, and printing services for a five-volume, 2500-page training manual for the company's supervisory and engineering personnel. The manual will contain 2000 illustrations. Due to the fact that the company is revising its operating procedures, it is necessary that all manuals be completed within ten weeks of the date the contract is awarded.

EXHIBIT 2
LIST OF FACTORS USED IN THE STUDY OF VENDOR SELECTION DECISION-MAKING

Factor

---

1. The net price (including discounts and freight charges) offered by each vendor.
2. The ability of each vendor to meet quality specifications consistently.
3. The repair service likely to be given by each vendor.
4. The ability of each vendor to meet specified delivery schedules.
5. The geographical location of each vendor.
6. The financial position and credit rating of each vendor.
7. The production facilities and capacity of each vendor.
8. The amount of past business that has been done with each vendor.
9. The technical capability (including research and development facilities) of each vendor.
10. The management and organization of each vendor.
11. The future purchases each vendor will make from your firm.
12. The communication system (with information on progress data of orders) of each vendor.
13. The operational controls (including reporting, quality control, and inventory control systems) of each vendor.
14. The position in the industry (including product leadership and reputation) of each vendor.
15. The labor relations record of each vendor.
16. The attitude of each vendor toward your organization.
17. The desire for your business shown by each vendor.
18. The warranties and claims policies of each vendor.
19. The ability of each vendor to meet your packaging requirements for his product.
20. The impression made by each vendor in personal contacts with you.
21. The availability of training aids and educational courses in the use of the product of each vendor.
22. Compliance or likelihood of compliance with your procedures (both bidding and operating) by each vendor.
23. The performance history of each vendor.

Explicit case situations were used for several reasons. In order to make the factor ratings meaningful, it was necessary to put each respondent in a similar purchasing situation. The four cases accomplished this by describing the circumstances under which the purchase was made, the items to be purchased, and the organization making the purchase. The wide variety of items and purchasing situations employed (see Exhibit 1) made it difficult for respondents to relate their training and experience to all four cases. Therefore, a side benefit from setting a common frame of reference for the respondents was to remove as much bias as possible from personal experience and training. Varied purchasing cases also were necessary to allow the analysis of the way in which the nature of the purchase affects the vendor selection decision.

The actual mechanics of completing the decision-making part of the questionnaire were straightforward. Each respondent was asked to read each case and to put himself in the position of the purchasing agent responsible for the selection of a vendor to supply the items described by the case. The respondent then was requested to rate the importance *he* would attach to each of the factors (characteristics of potential vendors) listed, i.e., "evaluate the factors on the basis of whether the factor is of extreme, considerable, average, slight, or of no importance relative to other listed factors when considering potential vendors in *this purchasing situation.*" The importance rating of each of the 23 factors was scored on a 0-4 basis with the "no importance" box established at zero and progressing in sequence to the "extreme importance" box. Thus, for each combination of respondent, factor, and case, a score was obtained. The analysis of the responses to the decision-making section of the questionnaire can most clearly be presented in two parts — the first dealing with aggregate factor importance, and the second treating the influence of the purchased item.

FACTOR IMPORTANCE

Table 6 shows the aggregate ratings of the 23 factors over all four cases. The ratings are almost exactly in accordance with the findings from the analysis of firm practices. As in the previous section, the ability to meet quality standards and delivery schedules are rated as the most important factors to consider in the selection of a vendor. A point of interest is that price ranks sixth in importance when all four cases are evaluated together. One deviation from the previous findings is that the service factor is given a relatively low rating. A possible explanation for this positioning is that the four cases selected were atypical with regard to service requirements. Looking only at the aggregate ratings, however, tends to mask some-

TABLE 6
AGGREGATE FACTOR RATINGS

Factor	Mean Rating	Evaluation
Quality	3.508	Extreme Importance
Delivery	3.417	
Performance History	2.998	
Warranties & Claims Policies	2.849	
Production Facilities and Capacity	2.775	Considerable
Price	2.758	Importance
Technical Capability	2.545	
Financial Position	2.514	
Procedural Compliance	2.488	
Communication System	2.426	
Reputation and Position in Industry	2.412	
Desire for Business	2.256	
Management and Organization	2.216	Average
Operating Controls	2.211	Importance
Repair Service	2.187	
Attitude	2.120	
Impression	2.054	
Packaging Ability	2.009	
Labor Relations Record	2.003	
Geographical Location	1.872	
Amount of Past Business	1.597	
Training Aids	1.537	
Reciprocal Arrangements	0.610	Slight Importance

TABLE 7

THE MOST IMPORTANT FACTORS BY SITUATION

Importance Rank	CASE A: Paint	CASE B: Desks	CASE C: Computer	CASE D: Art Work
1	Quality	Price	Quality	Delivery
2	Warranties	Quality	Tech. Capability	Prod. Capacity
3	Delivery	Delivery	Delivery	Quality
4	Perf. History	Warranties	Prod. Capacity	Perf. History
5	Price	Perf. History	Perf. History	Communication System

what a number of variations in the factor ratings. A better analysis can be made by examining the rating case by case, so that the influence of the item being purchased becomes apparent.

THE INFLUENCE OF THE TYPE OF PURCHASE

Table 7 shows the five factors rated most important in each of the four purchasing situations used in the questionnaire. Despite the variations from case to case, the ability of potential vendors to meet quality standards and delivery schedules, and the fact that they have performed well in the past were considered of major importance in every instance. Price, it should be noted, does not appear in the top five factors in either Case C or D. In Case D (Art Work), it just missed the list, being sixth, but in Case C (Computer), price was rated 19th. In other words, in the case involving a highly complex product and presumably a government contract, price was felt to be of minor importance, relative to the other selection factors, in the vendor evaluation process.

Price was not the only factor to show wide swings in importance between the four cases. Technical capability, repair service, and warranties also were adjudged by the respondents to be very important for some of the purchases and to be unworthy of much consideration in other instances. The factors showing the most consistency in their position in

the four cases were: (1) the ability to meet quality standards, (2) the ability to meet delivery schedule, (3) financial position, (4) performance history, and (5) reciprocal arrangements.

Analysis of variation in the factor ratings implies that agreement among individuals on factor importance seemed to be a function of factor position on the importance continuum. In other words, respondents agreed on which factors were important and which were very unimportant but could not place the intermediate factors in any consistent way. The most significant point is that agreement was shown where it counts most, i.e., on the factors believed to be critical for the selection of the proper vendor in each case.

In the four cases presented, the item to be purchased and, therefore, the decision to choose a particular vendor varied in complexity. The aggregate importance ratings reflect this fact. Table 8 shows the average importance ratings for each case and Table 9 presents a frequency distribution of the factor ratings, case by case. In the latter table, the frequency in each class represents the number of factors that had a mean rating within the class limits.

Examination of Tables 8 and 9 shows that more factors were rated as being highly important in the cases involving complex products. In the Computer case (Case C), for example, sixteen factors were of considerable or extreme importance, whereas in the case involving

TABLE 8
MEAN FACTOR RATINGS BY CASE

Case	Mean Rating
A: Paint	2.058
B: Desks	2.025
C: Computer	2.860
D: Art Work	2.337

TABLE 9
FREQUENCY DISTRIBUTION OF FACTOR RATINGS BY CASE

	Number of Factors with Mean Rating in Each Class			
Class	CASE A: Paint	CASE B: Desks	CASE C: Computer	CASE D: Art Work
3.5 under 4.0	1	0	3	1
2.5 under 3.5	5	5	13	6
1.5 under 2.5	14	14	6	13
.5 under 1.5	3	4	0	3
under .5	0	0	1	0
TOTAL	23	23	23	23

a relatively simple product, Paint, only six factors were rated in these categories. The behavior pattern of the respondents indicated that one or two factors may be used to make a vendor selection decision for a relatively routine purchase but in a more complex situation, a larger amount of information was believed necessary. Although more factors were rated as being important in the complex situations, the question still is unanswered as to whether they all are used in the actual vendor selection.

SUMMARY OF QUESTIONNAIRE FINDINGS

The study of firm vendor selection practices and the opinions of purchasing agents in four vendor selection cases lead to similar conclusions about what factors are important in the decision to select a source of supply. There appear to be three factors that are crucial in the choice of a vendor: the ability to meet quality standards, the ability to deliver the product on time, and performance history. The latter is difficult to assess because it presupposes past experience with the vendor and it also subsumes a number of other factors. There are a number of other factors that may be critical to a particular vendor selection decision but, because of the nature of the item being purchased, these vary from purchase to purchase. Price, financial strength, technical capability, service ability, warranties, and production facilities and capacity are examples of this class of factors. In some instances, a number of these "second level" factors may be important in selecting a vendor, while in other cases only one or two may join the "first level" factors as the basis for the decision.

A few generalizations may be made about which factors are important to consider in any particular vendor selection. The more complex (technically) the product being purchased, the more factors are likely to be considered, and, in these cases, price is likely to be relatively unimportant. Conversely, in purchases of ordinary products ("nuts and bolts" type purchases), price generally is the primary factor that is considered.

Other than reputation, intangible factors such as attitudes, impressions, and desire for business were given very little weight in the selection of a vendor. Reputation, while not rated of high importance in any instance, became of intermediate importance when the item to be purchased grew in complexity. This implies that a vendor's reputation in the industry enhances his chances of getting an order, especially when the product is technically complex. Other factors, such as the amount of past business, labor relations record, packaging ability, and geographical location probably are important only in isolated instances. Reciprocity was completely downgraded by the respondents as an item to be considered in the selection of a vendor. Only in unique instances (depending on the industry or on the individuals involved in the purchase) would reciprocal arrangements be likely to make any difference in the vendor selection decision.

IMPLICATIONS OF THE SURVEY FINDINGS: VENDOR SELECTION SYSTEMS

As we have seen, the nature of the item to be purchased has a major influence on the factors that are considered when selecting a supplier. Individual disagreement on the relative factor importance appears to have a much smaller effect on the choice of factors since it occurs primarily on factors of intermediate importance. These results have implications that directly affect the development of formal vendor selection systems. Since a number of firms have such systems (or are developing them), it is useful to relate the findings of this research to the general systems that have been designed to aid in the vendor selection decision.

Analysis of the results concerning the way in which individuals influence the vendor selection decision offers particular encouragement to those persons in purchasing who support the development of formal vendor selection systems. Enough agreement was found

among the respondents on the factor importance ratings to suggest that the "first" and "second" level factors listed in Table 6 (including every factor down to and including "Reputation and Position in the Industry"[4]) could be used as a standard list forming the basis for the construction of a general vendor selection system. In other words, any existing or proposed system (formal or informal) should include these factors.

The implications of the findings concerning the influence of the purchased item on the vendor selection decision hold less promise for the development of a general vendor analysis technique. Using a descriptive approach, we have evolved a normative list of factors to serve as the basis for a formal vendor analysis system. Unfortunately, the descriptive approach is not a valid one to determine how these factors *ought to be* manipulated, i.e., weighted, to make the optimal vendor selection. The basis for this statement, of course, is the fact that a majority opinion on a course of action will not necessarily produce the optimal result. There is, however, a very fruitful (and valid) approach to the solution of the problem of how the factors ought to be weighted. The basis for this approach is an examination of the cost relationship between various levels of suboptimal performance on each factor employed in the system. This approach to analyzing vendors is known as the "Cost-Ratio" plan.[5]

Thus, in any one situation, there is some hope of manipulating the factors in an optimal way. In this study, though, it was found that the factor importance relationships (in a descriptive sense at least) were different for each of the four

---

[4] There are several reasons that three factors below the "Considerable Importance" level are suggested for inclusion. In the first place, there is a natural break in importance scores below these factors. More important, however, is the fact that each of the suggested factors appeared in the ten most important factors for at least one of the four cases.

[5] *Evaluation of Supplier Performance, op. cit.*, pp. 11-20.

purchase types. This implies a practical problem that must be faced by any universal vendor analysis system, i.e., the weighting system may need to be unique for each purchase. The difficulties in determining and actually manipulating such a vast number of importance relationships very likely would negate the utility of such a complex system. About the only way this dilemma can be resolved is to test for the existence of classes of purchases that would have common factor importance relationships. This could be accomplished by studying a number of common purchasing situations and the associated factor performance cost structures.

This study, by presenting a common list of factors to be used in the vendor analysis process, should be useful in adding to the universality and rationality of vendor selection practices. However, the implications of the findings cast some serious doubts on the development of a universal system for vendor analysis that is appropriate over the entire range of purchasing situations and whose practical limitations do not outweigh its advantages for increased profitability through effective vendor selection.

H. PHYSICAL DISTRIBUTION

42. Physical Distribution Costs: A Two-Year Analysis

RICHARD E. SNYDER

A year ago, in its January 1962 issue, DISTRIBUTION AGE published the results of the first comprehensive "modern-day" survey especially designed to throw light upon the physical distribution cost load borne by the business sector of our economy. Carrying 1960 P-D cost ratios for eight broad categories and 20 subgroups of expenses expressed as percentages of net sales in seven manufacturing industries, the report of findings was accorded an eager reception, indicating the desirability of further exploration along these lines. Thus DISTRIBUTION AGE now presents the 1961 counterpart of the study published a year ago.

Perhaps the most immediate impression to be gained from an inspection of the industry cost figures shown in Table 1, which summarizes data for eight major categories of P-D expense, is that the

From *Distribution Age* (January, 1963), pp. 45-56.

ratios (to net sales) for the latest year covered, 1961, reflect a general pattern of shrinkage by comparison with those for the preceding year. (Table 1 also shows averages of the ratios for the two years covered. Individual firms may find these 2-year average ratios more valuable than single-year ratios, for budgeting purposes.)

We have already pointed out that statistical data expressed in terms of *annual* results for only two years in sequence do not necessarily represent absolute *trend* indications. (See "Technical Notes.") It usually requires a *third* observation in a given annual series to suggest a trend tendency, as such, in conformity with the ancient law of the triangle. Of course, a series of *monthly* observations, properly charted, may give a signal of either a rise, or a drop, in the whole-year level for the second year of a two-year span (by comparison with the first year) long before the actual re-

TABLE 1. RATIOS TO NET SALES, FOR 8 MAJOR CATEGORIES OF PHYSICAL

Expense Element	Food & Food Products Industry			Machinery (Elec. & Non-Elec.) Industry			Chemicals, Petroleum & Rubber Products Industry		
	1960	1961	2-Year Avg.	1960	1961	2-Year Avg.	1960	1961	2-Year Avg.
TOTAL PHYSICAL DISTRIBUTION EXPENSE RATIO TO NET SALES (X)	34.42	29.60	32.01	11.40	8.83	10.02	25.95	21.72	23.80
Common Carrier Expense	10.18	9.63	9.91	8.15	5.29	6.72	10.32	9.31	9.81
Private Trucking Expense	7.50	5.95	6.73	1.22	.84	1.03	4.51	3.47	3.99
Public Warehousing Expense°	2.37	1.89	2.13	.29	.35	.32	1.55	1.09	1.32
Private Warehouse Expense	5.70	4.02	4.87	.51	.53	.52	3.91	2.88	3.39
Materials Handling Expense	2.59	2.34	2.46	.42	.36	.39	1.43	1.41	1.42
Shipping Room Expense	3.98	3.88	3.93	.58	.95	.76	2.61	2.41	2.51
Over-Short & Damage	.33	.27	.30	.12	.02	.07	.26	.19	.23
Selected Administrative Expense	1.77	1.62	1.68	.11	.49	.21	1.36	.96	1.13

° Public Warehousing ratios for 1960 included the effect of local distribution charges. The 1961 ratios exclude such charges.
(X) All totals relating to 2-year average figures are additive.

398

sult for the second year has been toted-up. Broad-gauge industry-wide cost figures, however, are seldom available for short-term periods.

SALES TRENDS ON COST PATTERNS

People whose jobs require them to grapple with problems of cost control know that the movement of the sales trend not only can, but usually does, have a marked influence upon the cost pattern, and they take care to note significant divergences as between the sales trend and the cost trend in any given situation. This is because the rate of change in net sales, from one period to the next, may not be—and usually is not—the same as the rate of change in costs. Thus, if sales rose and costs remained unchanged, the cost ratio to sales would show a drop. Conversely, if sales declined and costs held steady, the cost ratio to sales would show a rise. If sales rose sharply while costs declined, the cost ratio would show a significant reduction, and if sales declined sharply while costs increased, the cost ratio would show a significant upturn. If sales hold steady, the movement of costs in relation thereto is determined either by management policy or the business cycle, or both.

Astute managements will require a steady flow of statistical information regarding *trend changes* on both sides

of the Sales: Cost equation. But this is not enough! In addition, there must be cognizance of other factors which bear upon the individual company picture, from outside. These very often play a larger part than any others in influencing top management strategy and tactics.

We have already alluded to the survey finding of a broad, general downside move in manufacturers' P-D costs between 1960 and 1961. The fact that this move was so widespread throughout the accounts, *despite* some significant differences in the size and characteristics of the survey samples for the two years covered, strongly suggests that the stated result was produced by the action of a basic and pervasive economic force. We shall now enlarge upon this point.

In broadly-reasoned terms we see the 1961 drop in physical distribution costs as a *lagged adjustment to general business cycle moves*. Each month since December 1947 this analyst has compiled a general business cycle index which measures the monthly rate of change in the total physical volume of goods produced, transported, and sold in the United States. By the nature of its composition, this index makes a close approach to being an index of physical distribution, as such, and we have therefore found it useful in connection with special studies relating to this field. Its application to the present discussion will soon be made clear.

DISTRIBUTION EXPENSE IN 8 MANUFACTURING INDUSTRIES

Paper & Paper Products Industry			Primary & Fabricated Metals Industry			Wood Products (Including Furniture) Industry			Textiles Industry					
1960	1961	2-Year Avg.	1960	1961	2-Year Avg.	1960	1961	2-Year Avg.	1960	1961	2-Year Avg.	1960	1961	2-Year Avg.
19.93	16.60	18.13	33.14	26.43	29.23	17.27(R)	15.81	15.99	16.15	NA	NA	NA	10.22	NA
4.56	5.60	4.98	5.51	5.14	5.32	9.15	8.81	8.46	5.42	NA	NA	NA	5.27	NA
4.39	2.54	3.45	5.87	3.53	4.70	2.82	2.46	2.64	.10	NA	NA	NA	1.83	NA
2.44	1.40	1.92	–	.58	–	.10	.10	.10	1.00	NA	NA	NA	–	NA
2.85	2.01	2.43	11.30	9.53	10.42	.70(R)	1.00	.85	5.74	NA	NA	NA	.74	NA
1.41	1.27	1.34	1.61	1.51	1.56	1.08	1.09	1.09	1.00	NA	NA	NA	.80	NA
3.55	3.01	3.28	3.33	2.49	2.91	1.75	1.43	1.59	2.17	NA	NA	NA	1.12	NA
.21	.20	.20	.02	.02	.02	.22	.13	.17	.01	NA	NA	NA	.01	NA
.52	.57	.53	5.50	3.63	4.30	1.45	.79	1.09	.71	NA	NA	NA	.45	NA

NA Not available.   (R) Revised.

FIGURE 1
COMPARATIVE TOTAL P-D COSTS BY INDUSTRY
RATIOS TO NET SALES FOR 1960, 1961, AND 2-YR. AVERAGES

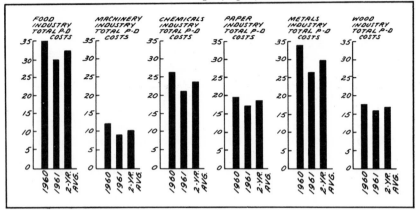

P-D TRENDS IN LINE WITH MANUFACTURING

The annual level of any measurable business activity is determined, in the last analysis, by the respective monthly contributions to the year's total. Where monthly rates of change keyed to the previous year are used, the 12-month average of such rates determines the whole year's percentage of increase or decrease. For the record, the annual levels of our business cycle index for the 1958-1961 period showed the following year-to-year percentages of change in total physical activity: 1959/1958 + 9.9; 1960/1959 + 2.6; 1961/1960 + 1.1. (Also for the record, here are the comparative year-to-year percentages of change in total gross product (deflated) of all U. S. manufacturing concerns: 1959/1958: + 11.4; 1960/1959: + 1.9; 1961/1960: + 1.2.)

Although the annual index figures are interesting in themselves, even more so is the monthly rate of change pattern out of which they evolved. In May of 1959 (that notorious year of the "sell 'em big and to hell with the costs" hysteria), the monthly rate-of-change index topped off a major cyclical peak at a point nearly 19% above the comparable level of 1958. The ensuing slowdown did not terminate in a major cyclical bottom until March of 1961. It prevented the 1959

whole-year result from reaching higher than + 9.9, and held the 1960 and 1961 levels to respective gains of only 2.6% and 1.1%, as is indicated above in Figure 1.

PERIOD OF NEW INDUSTRIALIZATION

The period of this business cycle downsweep, as measured in terms of monthly rates of change, was of sufficient duration (21 months) so to stimulate not only a new cost consciousness on the part of businessmen generally, but also to enable them to formulate and install cost reduction programs in depth. This was a period of great new progress in the fields of automation, mechanization, and transportation techniques. While their sales fluctuated uncertainly and the number of their production workers declined, manufacturers spent more money for new plants and equipment in both 1960 and 1961 than they spent in the 1959 boom year. (These references bespeak the performance of all U. S. manufacturers combined.) Therefore, it would have been astonishing, to say the least, if, by the end of 1961, the fruits of these developments had not manifested themselves as widespread reductions in the ratios of physical distribution to net sales, the signs of which stand out like a sore thumb in the DISTRIBUTION AGE survey findings for that year.

As a final reference to the lead-lag relationship between business cycle moves and physical distribution cost adjustments, we cite the actual performance of a small cluster of manufacturing concerns for which we have P-D cost figures extending back over 10 years. These data show a neat 12-to-18-month lag between the top-off point of a major business cycle rise and a discernible cutback in P-D costs. Costs, after a sharp rise, tend to remain stuck at the higher levels until a deterioration of business conditions forces management action to reduce them. (Or so it seems!)

Further expansion of the universe of physical distribution cost statistics eventually should enable us to define more precisely the cyclical patterns of such costs in specific industry areas. Meanwhile, we present (on the following pages) the industry-by-industry analyses of the cost patterns developed by the latest survey.

AN INDUSTRY-BY-INDUSTRY ANALYSIS OF COST RATIOS

Table 2 illustrates how the six industries (for which 2-year data are available) ranked in terms of highest to lowest *total* P-D cost ratios to net sales for both 1960 and 1961 as well as on the basis of the 2-year averages. The vertical listing of these industries in this tabulation follows the same order as the horizontal listing does across the top of Table 3.

These figures show that there was no change in the ranking structure between 1960 and 1961 with respect to the relative levels of total P-D cost ratios to net sales. In the following commentaries on the individual industry performances with respect to specific categories of expense, the emphasis will be on the 1961 vs. 1960 changes *within* each industry rather than on inter-industry comparisons (and contrasts). This is because each of these industrial groups possess individual operational characteristics which differ from the others. Even though they are all competing for a share of the consumer dollar and therefore have many problems in common, they never could be poured into the same cost mold. Moreover, although they are all influenced by business cycle fluctuations, the degree of their sensitivity thereto may show considerable variance during any given phase of the cycle.

TABLE 2
INDUSTRY RANKINGS BY TOTAL P-D COST RATIOS TO NET SALES

	1960		1961		2-Year Averages	
Industry	Total P-D Cost Ratio	Rank	Total P-D Cost Ratio	Rank	Total P-D Cost Ratio	Rank
Food & Food Products	34.42	1	29.60	1	32.01	1
Machinery (Elec. & Non-Elec.)	11.40	6	8.83	6	10.02	6
Chemicals, Petroleum & Rubber Products	25.95	3	21.72	3	23.80	3
Paper	19.93	4	16.60	4	18.13	4
Primary & Fabricated Metals	33.14	2	26.43	2	29.23	2
Wood Products	17.27	5	15.81	5	15.99	5

TABLE 3. Detail of Cost Ratios for Individual

Expense Element	Food & Food Products Industry			Machinery Elec. & Non-Elec. Industry			Chemicals Petroleum & Rubber Products Industry		
	1960	1961	2-Year Avg.	1960	1961	2-Year Avg.	1960	1961	2-Year Avg.
Common Carrier Expense – Total	10.18	9.63	9.91	8.15	5.29	6.72	10.32	9.31	9.81
Rail shipping expense	6.02	5.63	5.82	1.18	1.04	1.11	5.14	4.76	4.95
Truck shipping expense	2.79	2.80	2.80	5.75	3.60	4.68	3.50	2.94	3.22
Water transportation expense	.82	.83	.83	1.00	.51	.75	1.21	1.33	1.27
Air transportation expense	.55	.37	.46	.22	.14	.18	.47	.28	.37
Private Trucking Expense – Total	7.50	5.95	6.73	1.22	.84	1.03	4.51	3.47	3.99
Truck drivers' pay	2.03	1.55	1.79	.50	.32	.41	.84	.70	.77
Equipment leasing charges	3.75	2.97	3.36	.69	.40	.54	2.73	1.98	2.36
Depreciation of equipment	.89	.78	.84	.01	.09	.05	.32	.29	.30
Truck maintenance and supplies (including license fees, insurance and taxes)	.83	.65	.74	.02	.03	.03	.62	.50	.56
Public Warehousing Expense (including accessorial charges)°	2.37	1.89	2.13	.29	.35	.32	1.55	1.09	1.32
Private Warehouse Costs – Total	5.70	4.02	4.87	.51	.53	.52	3.91	2.88	3.39
At distribution and sales centers	3.52	2.31	2.92	.11	.11	.11	1.59	1.07	1.33
Depreciation	1.04	.75	.90	.11	.10	.11	.60	.31	.45
Total overhead, including payroll and maintenance	1.14	.96	1.05	.29	.32	.30	1.72	1.50	1.61
Materials Handling Expense – Total	2.59	2.34	2.46	.42	.36	.39	1.43	1.41	1.42
Freight handlers' pay	.97	1.17	1.07	.17	.16	.16	.54	.51	.52
Material handling equipment depreciation	.91	.60	.75	.03	.03	.03	.47	.49	.48
Material handling equipment maintenance & supplies	.71	.57	.64	.22	.17	.20	.42	.41	.42
Shipping Room Costs – Total	3.98	3.88	3.93	.58	.95	.76	2.61	2.41	2.51
Payroll	2.05	2.20	2.13	.35	.51	.43	.53	.55	.54
Supplies (including cartons, strapping, etc.)	1.37	1.46	1.41	.16	.28	.22	1.45	1.43	1.44
Overhead	.56	.22	.39	.07	.16	.11	.63	.43	.53
Over-Short and Damaged Goods (Warehousing and Transportation)	.33	.27	.30	.12	.02	.07	.26	.19	.23
Selected Administrative Expenses Related to Distribution Costs – Total	1.77	1.62	1.68	.11	.49	.21	1.36	.96	1.13
Management: Vice President of Traffic	.34	.40	.37	.05	.13	.09	.99	.60	.79
Department Heads	.60	.38	.49	.03	.09	.06	.19	.20	.20
Clerical	.83	.82	.82	.03	.10	.06	.18	.10	.14
Other°°	–	.02	–	–	.17	–	–	.06	–
TOTAL (X)	34.42	29.60	32.01	11.40	8.83	10.02	25.95	21.72	23.80

° Public Warehousing ratios for 1960 included the effect of local distribution charges. The 1961 ratios exclude such charges.
°° Not included in the 1960 survey cost accounts.

THE FOOD INDUSTRY

Total P-D costs of food industry, as represented by the survey participants dropped to 29.60% of net sales in 1961 from 34.42 in 1960. Total common carrier costs – the biggest element in the food industry expense picture – declined to 9.63 from 10.18 in 1960. Running counter to this were fractional

EXPENSE ITEMS IN MAJOR CATEGORIES

Paper & Paper Products Industry			Primary & Fabricated Metals Industry			Wood Products (Including Furniture) Industry			Textiles Industry			Transportation Equipment Industry		
1960	1961	2-Year Avg.	1960	1961	2-Year Avg.	1960	1961	2-Year Avg.	1960	1961	2-Year Avg.	1960	1961	2-Year Avg.
4.56	5.60	4.98	5.51	5.14	5.32	9.15	8.81	8.46	5.42	NA	NA	NA	5.27	NA
2.52	2.80	2.66	1.74	1.64	1.69	4.18	5.07	4.62	.65	NA	NA	NA	2.16	NA
2.04	2.60	2.32	2.78	2.52	2.65	3.97	3.71	3.84	3.77	NA	NA	NA	1.44	NA
–	.20	–	.80	.79	.79	1.00	–	–	.50	NA	NA	NA	1.55	NA
–	–	–	.19	.19	.19	–	.03	–	.50	NA	NA	NA	.12	NA
4.39	2.54	3.45	5.87	3.53	4.70	2.82	2.46	2.64	.10	NA	NA	NA	1.83	NA
2.52	1.36	1.94	3.04	1.79	2.42	1.35	1.16	1.25	.10	NA	NA	NA	.72	NA
1.77	.96	1.36	.19	.24	.21	.64	.66	.65	–	NA	NA	NA	.63	NA
–	.01	–	.60	.35	.48	.24	.25	.25	–	NA	NA	NA	.22	NA
.10	.21	.15	2.04	1.15	1.59	.59	.39	.49	–	NA	NA	NA	.26	NA
2.44	1.40	1.92	–	.58	–	.10	.10	.10	1.00	NA	NA	NA	–	NA
2.85	2.01	2.43	11.30	9.53	10.42	.70(R)	1.00	.85	5.74	NA	NA	NA	.74	NA
–	–	–	6.25	4.57	5.41	.50(R)	.40	.45	3.00	NA	NA	NA	.21	NA
.23	.30	.27	1.05	.97	1.01	.10	.12	.11	.65	NA	NA	NA	.11	NA
2.62	1.71	2.16	4.00	3.99	4.00	.10	.48	.29	2.09	NA	NA	NA	.42	NA
1.41	1.27	1.34	1.61	1.51	1.56	1.08	1.09	1.09	1.00	NA	NA	NA	.80	NA
.84	.70	.77	.71	.69	.70	.75	.73	.74	.80	NA	NA	NA	.58	NA
.38	.50	.44	.80	.74	.77	.15	.15	.15	.10	NA	NA	NA	.10	NA
.19	.07	.13	.10	.08	.09	.18	.21	.20	.10	NA	NA	NA	.12	NA
3.55	3.01	3.28	3.33	2.49	2.91	1.75	1.43	1.59	2.17	NA	NA	NA	1.12	NA
1.01	.91	.96	1.39	1.34	1.36	.75	.70	.72	.84	NA	NA	NA	.63	NA
1.67	1.50	1.58	1.17	.75	.96	.52	.35	.44	.29	NA	NA	NA	.37	NA
.87	.60	.74	.77	.40	.59	.48	.38	.43	1.04	NA	NA	NA	.12	NA
.21	.20	.20	.02	.02	.02	.22	.13	.17	.01	NA	NA	NA	.01	NA
.52	.57	.53	5.50	3.63	4.30	1.45	.79	1.09	.71	NA	NA	NA	.45	NA
–	.03	–	3.50	1.88	2.69	.15	.11	.13	.13	NA	NA	NA	.23	NA
.30	.29	.30	–	.46	–	.20	.28	.24	.20	NA	NA	NA	.12	NA
.22	.24	.23	2.00	1.23	1.61	1.10	.35	.72	.38	NA	NA	NA	.09	NA
–	.01	–	–	.06	–	–	.05	–	–	NA	NA	NA	.01	NA
19.93	16.60	18.13	33.14	26.43	29.23	17.27(R)	15.81	15.99	16.15	NA	NA	NA	10.22	NA

(X) All totals relating to 2-year average figures are additive.
NA Not available.　(R) Revised.

increases in truck and water transportation expense, while rail and air costs followed the downside pattern. The overall private trucking expense ratio registered 5.95 in 1961 compared to 7.50 in 1960, and all four components of this expense showed declines.

Public warehousing charges amounted to 1.89% on net sales in 1961 against 2.37 in 1960 (see footnote to Table 3) while total private warehouse costs skidded to 4.02 from 5.70 in 1960 with all three of the component expenses participating in the drop.

On the materials handling side, total expense fell to 2.34 from 2.59 in 1960 because of sharp reductions in depreciation and maintenance charges which more than offset a rise in freight handlers' pay.

The food industry's total shipping room expense showed a comparatively small decline — from 3.98 in 1960 to 3.88 in 1961. The shipping payroll and supply cost ratios moved upward against a meat-ax cut in overhead, the latter development explaining the drop in the total shipping room cost ratio. The over-short & damage ratio dropped to 0.27 in 1961 from 0.33 in 1960.

Administrative expenses related to the physical distribution function totaled 1.62% of net sales in 1961 compared to 1.77 in 1960. The only significant drop in this expense category was shown by the "Department Heads" ratio which read 0.38 for 1961 vs. 0.60 for 1960.

THE MACHINERY INDUSTRY

As set up for survey purposes, the machinery industry covers manufacturers of electrical machinery as well as those making non-electrical machinery.

This industry's total P-D cost ratio to net sales amounted to 8.83% in 1961, down from 11.40 in 1960. Its 1961 total common carrier cost ratio fell off sharply to 5.29 from 8.15 in 1960 with all four of the specific expenses in this category showing declines. The heftiest reduction centered on truck shipping charges which dropped to 3.60 from 5.75 in 1960.

In the private trucking area, total costs for this function came to 0.84% on net sales in 1961 compared to 1.22 in 1960. Truck drivers' pay and equipment leasing charges, when combined, show a 1961 ratio of only 0.72% to net sales against a similarly-combined figure of

1.19 for 1960. The depreciation and maintenance ratios, though small, both showed increases in 1961 over 1960.

Public warehousing charges accounted for a higher ratio in 1961 than in 1960, 0.35 to 0.29. (See footnote to Table 3.) Total private warehouse costs in the machinery industry showed a slight increase to 0.53% on net sales in 1961 compared to 0.51 in 1960. The prime mover was a moderate rise in overhead.

The total materials handling cost ratio dropped to 0.36 in 1961 from 0.42 in 1960, due chiefly to a cutback in equipment maintenance and supplies expense.

A contrast was provided by a strong upward move in shipping room costs, with the total expense ratio jumping to 0.95 in 1961 from 0.58 in 1960. This development at the overall shipping cost level stemmed from similar action by the ratios applying to payroll, supplies, and overhead. The O-S&D ratio almost faded out at 0.02 in 1961; down from 0.12 in 1960.

The machinery industry's cost ratio reflecting total administrative expenses related to physical distribution zoomed upward to 0.49% of net sales in 1961 from 0.11 in 1960. The four components of this ratio provided concerted support for this move.

THE CHEMICALS INDUSTRY

As structured for purposes of the survey, the "Chemicals" industry encompasses not only chemicals, but also petroleum and rubber products manufacturers. The total P-D cost ratio to net sales for this industrial complex amounted to 21.72 in 1961 compared to 25.95 in 1960. Common carrier expense was the dominating element in the cost picture, amounting to 9.31% on net sales in 1961 against 10.32 in 1960. Of the four expense items within this category, the water transportation cost ratio alone showed an increase in 1961, rising to 1.33 from 1.21 in 1960. The 1961 ratio covering total private trucking costs dropped to 3.47 from 4.51 in 1960, with all four components declining.

Public warehousing expense accounted for 1.09% of the net sales dollar in 1961; down from 1.55 in 1960. (See footnote to Table 3.) The total private warehouse cost ratio reading for 1961 was 2.88 against 3.91 for 1960. The movement of the three underlying expense elements was unanimously on the downside.

Total materials handling expense at 1.41 was almost even with the 1960 ratio of 1.43. Of the three component items, only depreciation showed a rise, to 0.49 from 0.47 in 1960. Total shipping room costs dropped to 2.41 in 1961 from 2.61 in 1960. Within this expense category, a slight rise was shown only by payroll costs. The O-S&D ratio dropped to 0.19 from 0.26 in 1960.

The total administrative cost ratio fell to 0.96% of sales in 1961 from 1.36 in 1960. In the detailed breakdown of these costs, the department heads payroll ratio showed a fractional rise.

THE PAPER INDUSTRY

The paper (and paper products) industry posted a total P-D expense ratio to net sales of 16.60 in 1961; down from 19.93 in 1960. The most outstanding development in this industry's cost picture was a rise in the total common carrier expense ratio which advanced to 5.60 in 1961 from 4.56 in 1960. In support of this move, rail shipping costs rose to 2.80 from 2.52 in 1960; common carrier trucking expense increased to 2.60 from 2.04; and water transportation showed a ratio of 0.20 for 1961 against a zero reading for this expense in 1960. The total private trucking expense ratio declined to 2.54 in 1961 from 4.39 in 1960 due to sharp decreases in the ratios for truck drivers' pay and equipment leasing charges. The truck maintenance-supply cost ratio—a minor factor—showed a rise in 1961.

The public warehousing expense ra-

tio dropped to 1.40 in 1961 from 2.44 in 1960. (See footnote to Table 3.) This move was accompanied by a decline in the total private warehouse cost ratio which registered 2.01 in 1961 against 2.85 in 1960 on the strength of a sharp cutback in overhead. Depreciation charges rose to 0.30 from 0.23 in 1960.

Total materials handling costs fell to 1.27% of net sales in 1961 from 1.41 in 1960. Large reductions in freight handlers' pay and equipment maintenance offset a rise in depreciation charges.

In the shipping room, costs showed a general decline and the total shipping room expense ratio dropped to 3.01 from 3.55 in 1960. The O-S&D ratio held steady.

Total administrative costs germane to the P-D function rose moderately to 0.57 in 1961 from 0.52 in 1960 with the contributing items showing only slight changes.

THE METALS INDUSTRY

Survey findings for this industry are based on returns from primary metals concerns, fabricated metal products companies, and companies with both primary and fabricated metal operations. The total P-D cost ratio for this industry accounted for 26.43% of the net sales dollar in 1961 compared to 33.14 in 1960. Common carrier expenses totaled 5.14% on net sales in 1961 against 5.51 in 1960. Rail shipping costs dropped to 1.64 from 1.74 in 1960, and the common carrier trucking ratio slipped to 2.52 from 2.78 in 1960. Water and air transport cost ratios remained basically unchanged.

The total private trucking expense ratio dropped sharply to 3.53 in 1961 from 5.87 in 1960 due to drastic reductions in truck drivers' pay, depreciation charges, and maintenance costs. Equipment leasing costs showed a small rise.

Public warehousing in 1961 commanded 0.58% of the net sales dollar. (No comparative registered for 1960.) Total private warehouse costs amounted

FIGURE 2

COMPARATIVE 1961 PHYSICAL DISTRIBUTION COST RATIOS TO NET SALES
FOR EIGHT MAJOR EXPENSE CATEGORIES IN SEVEN MANUFACTURING INDUSTRIES

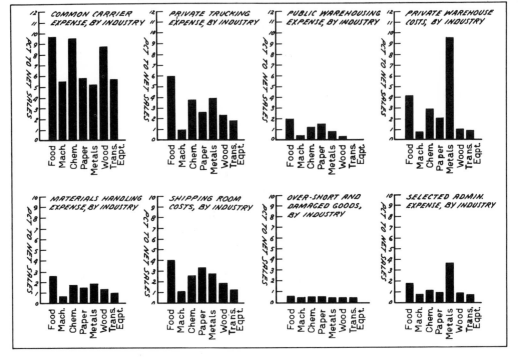

to 9.53% of net sales in 1961; down from 11.30 in 1960. The components of this expense category showed a unanimous downturn in 1961.

The total materials handling expense ratio registered 1.51 in 1961 against 1.61 in 1960. Slight declines were posted by all three expense items within this group. Shipping room costs in 1961 showed a general decline, with the total ratio for this expense dropping to 2.49 from 3.33 in 1960. The O-S&D ratio held steady at 0.02.

Administrative expenses related to physical distribution functions totaled 3.63% on net sales in 1961 compared to 5.50 in 1960. The ratios applying to management and clerical pay showed sharp declines.

THE WOOD PRODUCTS INDUSTRY

Survey returns from this industry cover companies in the "lumber and wood products" group as well as manufacturers of wood furniture. The combined total P-D cost ratio to net sales dropped to 15.81 in 1961 from 17.27 in 1960.

Total common carrier expense amounted to 8.81 in 1961 compared to 9.15 in 1960. Rail shipping expense rose to 5.07 in 1961 from 4.18 in 1960 while the common carrier trucking expense ratio showed a moderate decline. The total private trucking cost ratio slipped to 2.46 in 1961 from 2.82 in 1960 with truck drivers' pay and maintenance costs leading the way down.

The public warehousing expense ratio remained at 0.10 in 1961, unchanged from the published result for 1960. (See footnote to Table 3.) Private warehouse costs totaled 1.00% on net sales in 1961 compared to a revised 1960 ratio of 0.70, the revision being necessitated by an inadvertent omission of a ratio amounting to 0.50, applicable to the "distribution and sales centers" account. The

1961 comparative for that account is 0.40. Private warehouse overhead and depreciation cost ratios both showed increases in 1961.

In the materials handling category, the total cost ratio was 1.09 for 1961 against 1.08 for 1960, with the three component expenses showing almost no change. On the shipping room side, the total cost ratio dropped to 1.43 in 1961 from 1.75 in 1960, with all three expense elements in this group showing downside moves. The O-S&D ratio for 1961 registered 0.13 against 0.22 for 1960.

Administrative expenses associated with physical distribution activities totaled 0.79 in 1961 against 1.45 in 1960.

TRANSPORTATION EQUIPMENT INDUSTRY

1961 P-D cost ratios for the transportation equipment industry — a newcomer to the latest survey — will be found in Tables 1 and 3. Consistent with the broad pattern of results for the other industries covered, the chief element of P-D expense in this big industry is seen to be common carrier costs, followed by private trucking costs. The other catego-

ries of expense in the transportation equipment industry, listed in order of importance in terms of ratios to net sales, are: shipping room costs, materials handling costs, private warehouse expense, administrative expenses, and O-S&D charges.

SIX-INDUSTRY COMPOSITE RATIOS*

Table 4 sets forth composite expense ratios applying to the six industries which provided comprehensive basic data in the surveys for both 1960 and 1961. These ratios were derived by developing a consolidated 6-industry dollar total for each expense category and percenting each of these totals to the aggregate net sales total.

While the percentages shown are self-explanatory, it should be kept in mind that they reflect only the industry data gathered in this survey, and that these data are *not* to be interpreted as being necessarily representative of, or applicable to, *total U.S. sales* of the same industries.

---

* The six industries covered are: Food, Machinery, Chemicals, Paper, Metals, and Wood.

TABLE 4

COMPOSITE PHYSICAL DISTRIBUTION EXPENSE RATIOS TO NET SALES

Expense Element	% of Net Sales	
	1960(R)	1961
Total Physical Distribution Expense Ratio to Net Sales	26.20	22.55
Common Carrier Expense	9.14	7.86
Private Trucking Expense	4.88	3.75
Public Warehousing Expense	1.36	1.11
Private Warehouse Costs	4.58	3.92
Materials Handling Expense	1.59	1.53
Shipping Room Costs	2.71	2.64
Over-Short and Damaged Goods	0.22	0.16
Selected Administrative Expenses Related to Distributive Costs	1.72	1.58

(R) Consolidated 1960 ratio figures covering 7 industries, as published in last year's survey report, were revised to exclude the Textile Industry which did not supply sufficient data for inclusion in the survey for 1961.

COMMENTS & TECHNICAL NOTES

PURPOSE OF THE SURVEY

Basic intent of these studies is that of bringing into being various arrays of statistics showing the relative importance of selected distribution costs as related to the net sales of manufacturing concerns in the specific industrial classifications designated. It is the essential purpose of any "costs-of-doing-business" survey to provide the business manager with a master tool for measuring the cost side of his business in such a way as to make it possible for him to see wherein his own operation is comparatively weak or strong, i.e., by comparison with the "industry" averages. It thus gives him a basis for ferreting out waste; for expense and sales budgeting; for realistic pricing; for appraising buying efficiency (including the purchase of transportation services); for developing improved inventory controls; for negotiating loans and discounts; and, in general, getting a better all-around grip on his business.

By bringing the real facts out into the open, the cost survey contributes to business stability. It helps to dispel suspicions and misunderstandings as to "what's going on." Every enlightened businessman knows that his toughest competition comes from incompetent rivals who do not know their costs. These people are the ones who, out of fear, desperation, or ignorance, throw markets into chaos by ill-considered price cutting. (**General deterioration of product quality standards is often seen as a direct reflection of distressed conditions under which price fighting has become the order of the day. John Ruskin, the famous English author and critic, wrote: "There is hardly anything in this world that some man cannot make a little worse and sell a little cheaper, and the people who consider price only are that man's lawful prey.")**

Where distribution costs are concerned, the meaning is clear: If you lower the quality and the price of your products and yet are unable to reduce the costs of distributing them, you are simply sapping the life-blood of your business. Cost survey findings, if properly used, may go a long way toward promoting more efficient *control* of costs, and the degree to which such control is exercised very often determines the relative profitability of a given business operation.

In a series of monthly articles appearing in DISTRIBUTION AGE over the past ten months we have indicated various specific applications of cost survey figures in connection with such functions as: Comparing individual company figures with cost survey averages; using the cost survey ratios in setting up a "cost model" for a company which does not have a broad-gauge cost accounting schedule; deriving company dollar cost estimates by applying the industry cost averages to the company's net sales; setting-up charts of accounts from listings used in actual cases; measuring physical distribution costs per employe; viewing, and breaking down, the P-D cost dollar as a separate entity, independently of the net sales factor; budgeting sales as a preliminary step to budgeting physical distribution costs; and, budgeting physical distribution costs: a) in relation to net sales, and, b) in terms of costs as such.

DISTRIBUTION AGE, through these past efforts and its sponsorship of the new survey of manufacturers' P-D costs, confides its belief that the process of *illumination* conduces toward nobler ends than does the process of *elimination*.

SURVEY METHOD AND COVERAGE

The method employed in gathering survey data involved the use of a questionnaire which called for both dollar and percentage figures expressing, in the first instance, actual outlay for the

TABLE 5
RESPECTIVE RANKINGS OF INDUSTRIES

Industry	Rank in Terms of Number of Observations Reported		Rank in Terms of $ Volume of Sales		Rank in Terms of Number of Employes	
	1960	1961	1960	1961	1960	1961
Food & Food Products	1	2	2	2	4	5
Machinery (Elec. & Non-Elec.)	2	4	3	4	1	3
Chemicals, Petroleum & Rubber Products	3	3	1	1	3	2
Paper	4	7	6	5	6	6
Primary & Fabricated Metals	5	1	4	3	2	4
Wood Products	6	5	7	7	7	7
Textiles	7	NA	5	NA	5	NA
Transportation Equipment	NA	6	NA	6	NA	1

various physical distribution functions listed, and, in the second instance, the ratios to net sales represented by the given dollar amounts. The portion of the questionnaire devoted to these elements is reproduced herein. The questionnaire also provided spaces for the entry of information reflecting company sales size, the accounting period covered, total number of persons employed, the geographical area served by each company, and its industry affiliation. Questionnaires were mailed to the entire DISTRIBUTION AGE manufacturer subscriber list.

Returns in the latest survey, covering 1961 operations, were received from manufacturing concerns in 33 states. This compares with a 32-state response in the previous survey applying to 1960. In terms of total returns received, the latest survey produced 65% more than the preceding survey.

OPERATING CHARACTERISTICS

When the reporting companies were grouped into eight industrial classifications, six of which provided data in the surveys for both 1960 and 1961, it was possible to discern the relative "weights" contributed to the survey findings by the various manufacturing sectors represented. The respective rankings in terms of the number of statistical observations summarized, dollar sales volume, and number of employes are shown in Table 5.

TABLE 6
PERCENT OF CALENDAR VS. FISCAL YEAR
RETURNS BY INDUSTRY

Industry	Calendar Year		Fiscal Year	
	1960	1961	1960	1961
All Firms	52%	66%	48%	34%
Food & Food Products	27%	43%	73%	57%
Machinery (Elec. & Non-Elec.)	69%	79%	31%	21%
Chemicals, Petroleum & Rubber Products	54%	73%	46%	27%
Paper	77%	88%	23%	12%
Primary & Fabricated Metals	67%	65%	33%	35%
Wood Products	50%	75%	50%	25%
Textiles	100%	NA	—	NA
Transportation Equipment	NA	50%	NA	50%

TABLE 7
PERCENT OF REPORTING FIRMS, BY SALES
VOLUME CATEGORY

Industry	Sales Below $5 Million		Sales Above $5 Million	
	1960	1961	1960	1961
All Firms	43%	48%	57%	52%
Food & Food Products	64%	71%	36%	29%
Machinery (Elec. & Non-Elec.)	26%	32%	74%	68%
Chemicals, Petroleum & Rubber Products	16%	23%	84%	77%
Paper	70%	40%	30%	60%
Primary & Fabricated Metals	27%	55%	73%	45%
Wood Products	80%	62%	20%	38%
Textiles	25%	NA	75%	NA
Transportation Equipment	NA	38%	NA	62%

Tables 6, 7, and 8, in turn, reveal the industrial group patterns with respect to calendar vs. fiscal year accounting periods, sales volume classifications, and the geographical scope of each industry's distribution, showing comparative data for both 1960 and 1961.

From the four tables shown we derive these summary conclusions relating to noteworthy changes in survey sample characteristics: In terms of numbers of usable statistical observations reported, the Primary & Fabricated Metals Industry, which ranked fifth in 1960, took over the top position in 1961, dropping the Food Industry to second place. With respect to comparative industry sales volumes represented by the survey returns, the Chemicals-Petroleum-Rubber Industry group held first place in both years and Food remained in second place. As to numbers of employes, the Transportation Equipment Industry—a newcomer to the 1961 survey list—was in first place while the Machinery Industry's first place position of 1960 was exchanged for third place in the 1961 employe count. (See Table 5.) . . . With regard to accounting periods covered by the survey returns, there was a marked increase in the proportion of calendar year reports (vs. fiscal year reports) received in 1961, by comparison with 1960. (See Table 6.) . . . When sorted into two broad sales volume categories,

TABLE 8
GEOGRAPHICAL SCOPE OF DISTRIBUTION, BY INDUSTRY

Industry	Both U. S. & Foreign		U. S. (Natl.) Only		Nearby States Only		Local Only	
	1960	1961	1960	1961	1960	1961	1960	1961
All Firms	52%	52%	28%	27%	16%	19%	4%	2%
Food & Food Products	15%	35%	34%	26%	38%	29%	13%	10%
Machinery (Elec. & Non-Elec.)	91%	79%	9%	21%	—	—	—	—
Chemicals, Petroleum & Rubber Products	58%	64%	32%	23%	10%	13%	—	—
Paper	15%	34%	46%	44%	31%	22%	8%	—
Primary & Fabricated Metals	82%	47%	18%	29%	—	24%	—	—
Wood Products	40%	38%	60%	24%	—	38%	—	—
Textiles	50%	NA	25%	NA	25%	NA	—	NA
Transportation Equipment	NA	72%	NA	21%	NA	7%	NA	—

i.e., companies with sales below $5 million and those with sales above that level, returns in the 1961 survey show a small rise in the proportion of smaller firms to 48% of the total compared to 43% in 1960. Thus, the proportion of reporting firms with sales above $5 million dropped to 52% in 1961 from 57% in 1960. Industries showing increases in the relative proportions of smaller firms represented in the 1961 survey were Food, Machinery, Chemicals, and Metals. In the case of the latter three, however, larger firms greatly exceed the smaller, by actual count. The Paper and Wood Products Industries showed 1961 increases in the proportions of larger firms reporting by comparison with 1960. (See Table 7.)

In reporting the geographical scope of their distribution fields the participating companies, when classified into broad industry groups showed a narrow overall range of variance between 1960 and 1961. The "All-Firms" pattern indicates that 52% of the total number of firms reporting (in both surveys) served U. S. as well as foreign markets; 27% reported only U. S. (national) distribution in 1961 vs. 28% in 1960; 19% confined their distribution to nearby states in 1961 against 16% in 1960; and a mere 2% reported that they served only local markets in 1961 vs. 4% reporting this in 1960. Industry-by-industry variations, however, were much wider. (See Table 8.)

TECHNICAL NOTES

Having acknowledged the breadth of the field from which the survey returns were drawn and the chief characteristics of the participating industrial groups, it remains for us—prior to dealing with the ratio analysis section of this report—to stress several "technical" points which have an important bearing upon the proper interpretation of the survey findings, by users thereof.

NOTE A. First, it must be empha-sized that the survey P-D cost ratios presented in this report reflect the experience of the reporting companies only, and are not to be interpreted as being necessarily representative of, or applicable to, total U. S. sales of these same industries. Moreover, it should be understood that variations between the ratios for the two years covered, i.e., 1960 and 1961, do not necessarily reflect absolute *trend* changes, or tendencies. This is true for two reasons: 1) *annual* figures for just two years may, or may not, indicate a *trend*, as such; 2) the 1960 and 1961 survey data were not derived from exactly the same groups of reporting firms. Any commentaries in this report on the ups and downs of various expense ratios as between 1960 and 1961, in reference to specific industry performances, must be read with these qualifications in mind.

In short, we ask that you please think of these survey findings as "pilot study" results, definitive within the avowed scope and limitations of the areas covered.

NOTE B. All ratio-to-net sales figures contained in this report are *medians*. A median may be defined as the midpoint of an array of figures listed in order of descending size, or value. If eleven figures are listed in this fashion, the sixth figure from the top is the median. If the figure array contains an *even* number of items, say twelve, then the median is found by averaging the values of the sixth and the seventh items. Being the midpoint of a series, the median is less affected by extreme values than is the arithmetic average.

NOTE C. Ratio figures applying to manufacturers' Public Warehousing expense for 1960 included the effect of local distribution charges. The figures for 1961 *exclude* such charges. In the 1961 Administrative Expense schedule, the listing of expense categories called for "Other" expense of an administrative nature to pick up overhead allocations. The 1960 schedule did not include this.

I. RESEARCH

(1) Qualitative

43. Science and Truth in Marketing Research

ALFRED POLITZ

While the bulk of consumer and dealer surveys, which form so important a part of marketing research, are primarily descriptive (for example, studies of brand distribution and most studies of advertising media), there is another, more ambitious, kind of research — one that aspires to predict consequences of marketing action, to solve marketing problems. The kind of result it yields can be expressed like this:

If the marketer will do so-and-so, the consumer's reaction will be such-and-such. Or, vice versa, if the marketer wishes the consumer to do such-and-such, the marketer must do so-and-so.

The ideal of this kind of research is to enable the manufacturer to increase the share of the competitive market held by his brand, and to do so as economically as is possible. It is with such research that this article is concerned.

OBSTRUCTIVE FALLACIES

The development of predictive and problem-solving research is frequently held back by notions taken over from journalism, psychology, or statistics.

Reprinted by permission of the publishers from *Harvard Business Review*, Vol. 35 (January-February, 1957), pp. 117-26. Copyright, 1957, by the President and Fellows of Harvard College; all rights reserved.

Some of these, while slowing the progress of marketing research, are not so serious because they can easily be shown to be inappropriate or superficial. A more fundamental kind of obstacle is the traditional idea, so plausible few stop to question its logic, that marketing research does not produce true results unless it gets the "truth" from the consumer.

SELF-DEFEATING TRUTH

Wanting nothing but the "truth" from the consumer appears on the surface a commendable objective, and indeed there are some phases of marketing research where one would, as a matter of course, try to get a "true" answer from the respondent — particularly in the exploratory stage of formulating a research project. But too often the whole thrust of marketing research is based on the fallacious assumption that somewhere in the consumer's mind resides the "truth," and that is what is needed to solve a marketing problem. It is presumed that the task of the skilled researcher is to bypass the consumer's conscious and unconscious blocks, to avoid partial, rationalized, or mistaken responses, and to obtain actual opinions, attitudes, motives.

Apart from the difficulty of achieving

such a goal, it is more than possible for successful pursuit to end in self-defeat! For example:

A housewife interviewed in January may have the "true" opinion that she will buy a General Electric refrigerator in the summer. Her true motives may be the desire to get what she considers the best shelf arrangement. The stimuli presented during the interview, in the form of questions or discussion, lead only to responses denoting her preference for General Electric.

Yet in August, when she decides to buy a refrigerator, she cannot withstand the temptation to shop around and look at a variety of brands. She will read the literature of different companies. Also, she will be exposed to different sales arguments in advertising and in the stores themselves. Cubic feet of space, shelf arrangements, and many other things will act as new stimuli on her.

In the end, she will buy, say, a Frigidaire instead of a General Electric, and for reasons which were nonexistent in her conscious and unconscious mind at the time of the interview.

In sum, the interview may have succeeded in obtaining the "true" opinions, attitudes, and motives of the respondent at the time. However, this "truth" did not predict her actual buying behavior—the way she reacted when making her purchasing decision. The point is that to predict reactions one must study reactions, and these are not the same as opinions, attitudes, motives; the latter are of interest only to the extent that they happen to reveal reactions. Reactions are results, not causes, and they reflect many stimuli other than attitudes, motives, preferences; the latter cannot be assumed to be the determinants of what consumers will do.

However, just because marketing research cannot depend on getting the "truth" from the consumer, it does not follow that truth is unimportant. Rather, to be creative, research must be predictive; and to be predictive, it must find the truth. The difficulty is that the truth which advanced marketing research must obtain is not hidden in the consumer's mind; indeed, it is frequently nonexistent there.

Thus, a well-designed survey aims at an arrangement of interviewing conditions from which the researcher, in the end, can *calculate* the truth of how consumers will act, irrespective of the correctness or incorrectness of their responses to interview questions. In short, the truth to be obtained by the researcher is objective; it is of a higher order than any possible "true" opinions, motives, attitudes, or preferences hidden in the consumer's mind.

DELIBERATE INFLUENCE

This "truth" dogma leads to another fallacy which stands in the way of marketing research reaching its full potential. If the objective is the "truth" in the consumer's mind, then it is necessary that the respondent remain uninfluenced by the interview. The reasoning behind such a stipulation runs this way:

The respondent has opinions and motives that prevail under his natural living conditions. These must be brought to light in their natural form. If the fact that the respondent is interviewed in itself changes this arrangement, then the interview produces a biased or untrue picture.

The "don't influence" stipulation, like the "truth" dogma in general, has an enormous eye appeal from a nonanalytical viewpoint. The implication of ethics and cleanliness brings a substantial amount of emotion to such postulates. Therefore their eradication is difficult. But if consumer research is to lift itself to the level of research in the natural sciences, then it has no room for an assumption so unrealistic as the one which underlies the "don't influence" stipulation.

There is good reason to avoid any *unnecessary* bias, and this is all the more important when the attempt is to discover factual things such as past behavior and current characteristics and reactions of people. But, particularly when it comes to opinions, attitudes, or preferences, every interviewer is bound to exert some influence; the interview is an experience, and as such it cannot take place in a vacuum. So it is hoping for the impossible to try to obtain the full "truth" directly from the consumer.

Moreover, so long as the "truth" in the consumer's mind is not the kind of truth the researcher seeks, it makes sense to acknowledge influence as inevitable and to make use of it for the larger purpose of getting material which can in fact be used as the basis of prediction. In other words, it may be worthwhile to shape the interview for the deliberate purpose of bringing influence to bear and studying the consumer's reactions to it.

For example, in the refrigerator survey mentioned above, the researcher's task is *not* the unearthing of a true opinion or true motive existent in the respondent at the time of the interview. Rather, the task is to create circumstances during the interview which sufficiently resemble the circumstances which will be present when the respondent actually goes out to buy—even to the extent of such stimuli as sales arguments concerning various refrigerators and visual demonstrations of "live" refrigerators.

Of course, it is possible that in some cases no set of stimuli of sufficient similarity can be created. But this simply means the problem does not lend itself to predictive research. In any event, it should be evident that an interview related to "true" preferences, opinions, or motives does not meet the requirement of experimental design; it cannot be depended on for full answers, and may in fact lead to misinformation.[1]

[1] See Alfred Politz, "Questionnaire Validity Through the Opinion-Forming Question," *Journal of Psychology*, July 1953, pp. 11-15.

PROBLEM SOLVING

If consumer surveys are to predict consumer behavior in a way which will help management to make marketing decisions, they should be able to come up with quantitative findings. As well as being more useful, this is a requisite of the scientific approach. It is also one more reason why definite reactions to stimuli must be studied rather than opinions, attitudes, and preferences, which as such cannot be reduced to weights or measures.

As a corollary, in order to get such results the method must be rigorously scientific. This means, among other things, that it must be experimental— that is, it must start with a hypothesis and then test the validity of that hypothesis under controlled conditions. Only by formulating a research design to do these things will the researcher be sure of getting reactions to stimuli that are meaningful.

REACTIONS TO STIMULI

Because we are not seeking the solution in the respondent's mind, but in his reactions, the questions put to him do not usually contain any verbal reference to the problem itself. Rather, the researcher must figure out what question or combination of questions to ask so that the reactions produced will provide the information which he needs.

Actually, a well-designed questionnaire usually looks dull, harmless, unrevealing; seemingly it misses the main points. Thus, an outsider looking at an automotive questionnaire has no reason to be impressed with the question: "What makes of cars do you see here in this neighborhood?" He cannot imagine of what use the results can be. Such a question, however, is quite logically related to the objective of measuring the effectiveness of styling, according to the following rationale:

"More attractive-looking" cars tend to

catch more people's eyes than "less attractive-looking" automobiles. As new cars hit the market, year after year, they impress the public as being good-looking or not good-looking on a scale which ranges approximately from beautiful down to indifference. (New cars are rarely considered ugly.) Within this range, it appears reasonable to assume that an attractive-looking car gets more attention, i.e., is seen more often, than an indifferent-looking car.

One may then reason as follows: if we put a given number of good-looking cars and indifferent-looking cars into the same neighborhood, then the good-looking cars will be estimated by the public as being more numerous than they actually are, and the indifferent ones as being less numerous than they actually are.

This suggests, in turn, the possibility of comparing the "visibility" of various makes of automobiles in the public's eye with the actual number of each make passing the public's eye.

The simple question, "What makes of cars do you see here in this neighborhood?" provided, in 1951, an instrument for a comparison of the leading makes of lower-price cars. It turned out that, for every 100 cars of a specified make on the road, "A" had a visibility index of 50, "B" of 80, "C" of 100. This suggested that the looks of an automobile, taken as one of the sale factors, made "A" comparatively inefficient, and of course style changes were called for on the part of that manufacturer.

It should be noted that the role of attractiveness seemingly is not considered in the questionnaire. The crucial question is aimed at simple reactions, not at complex preferences. Further, it should be noted that, while the phenomenon under study is of a psychological nature, in agreement with the roles of scientific research the result is not a mere mention of attractiveness of styling but a quantitative statement expressed in the ratio 5 to 8 to 10.

EXPERIMENTAL DESIGN

It is unfortunate that well-designed consumer research which contributes most to the improvement of a marketer's position is so zealously guarded by secrecy. From the viewpoint of competitive needs, this secrecy is respectable and essential. Nevertheless, it is regrettable that in consequence consumer research in its most advanced form is the least publicized, and therefore the least known, development in the social sciences. The writer is convinced that this advanced consumer research is about as close to the experimental level of the natural and exact sciences as any social science can hope to be.

The frailty of consumers' opinions, memories, and motives, the presence of their unconscious and conscious biases, and the semantic uncertainties of the meaning of verbal responses, all can be bypassed by the expedience of experimental design. As indicated above, in an experiment one tries to find or create a set of circumstances under which a specific effect becomes measurable. More precisely:

An experiment is a deliberate arrangement of circumstances under which one specific difference, the "effect," can be attributed to the presence of another specific difference, the "cause." The presence of the term *difference* indicates that besides the fundamental problem of arrangement, there is also the secondary problem of efficiency. Efficiency within the arranging operation is aimed at making the differences as sharp as possible for measurement purposes.[2]

An outstanding recent example of ingeniously designed experiments in the natural and exact sciences can be

---

[2] Concerning this point of efficiency within the design, credit is due to Ronald A. Fisher of the statistical school in England; cf. *The Design of Experiments* (New York, Hafner Publishing Company, 6th Edition, 1951).

found in the work of Karl Von Frisch, who discovered how one honeybee informs another member of its community about the location of a food supply— its angle from the hive's exit as well as the distance.[3] The imagination and the elegance with which Von Frisch designs his experiments reminds one of the classical experimental work which led to the measurement of the speed of light.

While the bees tell one another certain things, they do not tell the entomological researcher anything; he has to find out from their actions or reactions. If Von Frisch can get insight into what sends the bees to the flowers without benefiting from any verbal responses on the part of the bees under study, the marketing researcher should find it relatively easy to design experiments which give him genuine insights into what, consciously or unconsciously, activates the consumer.

The researcher can do this, however, only if he recognizes his own field as being important enough to warrant designs of its own. The situation is difficult or even hopeless if he depends on, or waits for, psychology or mathematics or some other discipline to do the creative work for him in his consumer field. Engineers of course make use of the sciences of metallurgy, electronics, mathematics, and so on; yet it is the existence of specific design problems which makes engineering a science of its own. Similarly, consumer research has its specific design problems which should make it a science of its own. For example:

In a survey designed to measure the effect of making a national soft drink available for the first time in large bottles like competing soft drinks, we measured the percentage of consumer purchases under two sets of circumstances.

1. Buying to have on hand *at home,*

where the main factors for the selection of brand were preference for the brand and convenience of the large bottles. Here, because competitors had large bottles and this company did not, some consumers could be expected to sacrifice their brand preference for the convenience of the large bottles.

2. Buying for on-the-spot consumption *away from home,* where the main factors for selection of brand were preference for the brand and availability of the brand. Here the large bottle was not an issue, but some consumers would have to give up their preferences because the brand they preferred was not available.

We did find a considerably lower percentage of the at-home market going to the brand in question than of the away-from-home market. From our figures we could compute the rise in the percentage of home purchases which would result if consumers were free to follow their preference, that is, without being held back by having to buy in small bottles.

The success of the design lay in identifying the three interrelated factors of availability, convenience, and brand preference, and in perceiving the possibility of measuring the effect of the size factor on purchases by comparing two natural situations in which it happened to be respectively present and absent.

USE OF QUESTIONNAIRES

In consumer research the experimental design is the blueprint for a procedure by which information about the causal relationship between people and goods, and hence the appropriate marketing moves, can be obtained from observation and verbal responses, irrespective of the "truth" of the responses.

The more conventional way is to set the stage, say, by actually selling dish towels in a store or sample of stores; to deliberately introduce a variation in the circumstances representing the factor to be measured, say, a different price; then

[3] *The Dancing Bees* (New York, Harcourt, Brace and Company, 1955).

to observe the results, say, sales of *x* number of dish towels at the price under test compared with *y* number at the regular price (either in the same stores before the variation in price or in other "control" stores where the price has not been varied); and thus to measure the effect of the change in the one, supposedly causal, factor of price.

The difficulty is that this kind of experimentation often cannot be done on a large enough scale, short of prohibitive expense, to overcome the distortion caused by uncontrolled factors — shifts in the weather, promotion by competitors, etc. — or by lack of comparability between the situations being weighed against one another.

Fortunately — though not many researchers recognize this as yet — the same kind of design can be carried through with verbal responses. The idea is that consumers' reactions can be weighed against an actual variation in circumstance such as is occurring or has already occurred in the normal course of events (obviously more realistic than something staged); and that if a definite pattern shows up, it can be presumed to be the effect of the actual variation. (Further cross analysis can be applied to rule out alternative sources or directions of cause.)

This can be done in enough mass, and with enough care so respondents do not realize what they are being questioned on, to remove the distortions inherent in the "staged" experiment — and at much less cost relative to the value of the findings secured. Thus, a questionnaire can be the instrument for an experiment designed to obtain the information relevant to a problem, irrespective of the ability or willingness of the respondents to be accurate.

In such consumer research a very productive part of the experiment is the utilization of cross reference between two or more questions. While the latter has been used for decades in opinion and market research, its full potentialities have been given too little attention.

For years and years the "truth" dogma has obscured our view, prevented us from realizing that two answers, incorrect or meaningless or useless in and of themselves, can lead to correct, meaningful, and useful conclusions. There is no meaning in the letter "M"; there is no meaning in the letter "F," or "A," or "O"; but there is a useful message in the combination of the letters, "FOAM."

TRUTH FROM NONTRUTH

Suppose we want to find out what automobile manufacturers can do in relation to consumers' notions of "pickup," i.e., acceleration. Consumers are interested in the pickup of their cars. However, in delving into the problem one soon discovers that consumers hardly know whether or not a car has pickup. They often give credit for pickup to a car which has little of it, and vice versa. Thus, we first had better clarify in our own minds the various elements related to the concept of acceleration:

Motion is change of position. Acceleration is not motion; it is a change of motion — a change of a change. Being a magnitude of the second order, it is understandable that the human mind may have difficulty in estimating it. All estimates are comparisons. Superficially speaking one may assume the motorist compares the speed of the first instant with the speed of the second instant. However, the already weak estimates of speed combined with the even weaker estimate of time elapsed from the first to the second instant may allow enormous errors *if another impression-creating agent enters the field.*

Can there be such an agent? Acceleration is closely associated in the motorist's mind with the concept of power. It is also seen as an achievement, as the result of an effort. If two men alternately lift the same dumbbell, the first one with all the signs of strain, the other with all the signs of ease, the observer is inclined to give the latter credit for superior strength—this in spite of the fact that both men succeeded in lifting the same weight.

The estimate of strength differences, then, apparently is due to a comparison between efforts rather than results only. What is the effort on the part of the motorist to achieve acceleration? Pressing down the accelerator! This conjecturing leads us to the recognition of a possible psychological mechanism: *the easier it is to press the gas pedal down, the greater the acceleration appears to be.*

The recognition of this possibility is formalized into the hypothesis: *if the actual acceleration of two cars is equal, then the motorist tends to give credit for acceleration to the car with the softer accelerator spring.* Now we are ready to design an experiment as follows:

In some part of the interview the respondent is asked whether his car has good pickup. In another part of the interview the ease of handling the car is discussed—steering wheel, gear shift, brake, ease of pressing and holding the gas pedal down, etc. The answers to the question of pickup in itself are vague and useless. So are the answers to the question of the ease that accompanies the depression of the gas pedal.

But note that there is no distortion due to lack of control or of comparability. The stimuli consisting of these questions are similar from interviewer to interviewer, from interview to interview. The similarity is achieved by the rigor of the questionnaire—asking the same simple questions in the same direct way, rather than open-ended probing for deep-seated opinions.

The rigor can be afforded because the illusion that the interview has to obtain a "true" answer from a given respondent is dispensed with; the answers are reactions, and all we need to do is to observe and measure them as reactions. In fact, the less "true" they are in this case, the more revealing they are, as the rest of the experiment will show.

Next we cross tabulate the answers to the two questions in different ways and find this significant pattern:

Among motorists who report that it is somewhat difficult to push and keep their accelerators down, 26% give their cars credit for good pickup. Among motorists who report that it is easy to press and keep their accelerators down, 61% give their cars credit for good pickup. This means one of two things: (1) either a soft accelerator spring contributes substantially to the motorist's estimate of his car's acceleration, or (2) most automobiles equipped with a soft spring also have a high actual acceleration rate.

The problem is cornered but not yet solved. We can identify the right alternative through simple engineering data. And it turns out that among car models with high acceleration, stiff and soft accelerator springs occur in approximately the same proportion as they do among car models with low acceleration. Hence, the second alternative must be wrong.

In effect—without the difficulties of staging—we now have thousands of motorists who have been subjected, under real-life conditions, to driving cars of varying horsepower and accelerator springs, and we can measure their reactions to variation in these factors. (As in the case of style visibility, cited earlier, the variation of actual circumstances— makes of cars on the road or horsepower and spring strength— takes the place of the staged variation of dish towel price.)

Now the problem has lost its last freedom. It is solved. The motorist has told us, without realizing it, that the softness or stiffness of the accelerator spring is largely responsible for his conviction that his car has or does not have satisfactory pickup. Consequently, in the effect on consumers, the softness of the spring is the equivalent of additional horsepower. The recommendation to automobile manufacturers is obvious.

This experiment involves a recognition of the relationship between two questions, which can be analyzed statistically. Such productive relationships between questions cannot be expected to occur accidentally; they must be designed as tests of hypotheses.

RESEARCH EFFICIENCY

The construction of productive questionnaires requires that the market researcher not confine himself to psychological and statistical activity. He must be familiar with the marketing problems in order to develop useful hypotheses.

This procedure is parallel to research in the natural and exact sciences. A chemist does not simply mix ingredients and then wait to see what happens. He starts with a hunch, with an idea, with a hypothesis. He designs an experiment whose possible outcome he visualizes. He mixes the ingredients systematically under the conditions of his design. He thinks of the results first, and then establishes the conditions which either bring about the results, or rule them out. This point deserves emphasis and re-emphasis. It makes research more purposeful and hence more productive.

Of course, following a definite plan does not preclude the possibility of unforeseen discoveries. This, again, is true of the creative researcher whether in the natural and exact sciences or in marketing. But the fact remains that it is wasteful to play with interesting questions just in order to see whether something unforeseen will result.

To be efficient, then, marketing research must have clear objectives and definite designs. However, it also must be practical in the details of the design. Here the utmost sophistication is called for — not because the main essentials are abstruse, but because there are so many snares and pitfalls which are not foreseen through unfamiliarity with the

vagaries of human nature. While many of the difficulties yield to common sense, the trouble lies in realizing that common sense must be applied.

THE LEARNING FACTOR

To make the results of an experiment projectable to actual marketing moves, the experiment must provide the same conditions as reality, or at least conditions of sufficient similarity. If any important aspect of reality is ignored, the experiment will yield invalid results. Thus:

One soft drink company used to do itself a lot of damage by consumer research which looked deceivingly valid to an outsider. It started with the assumption that an improvement in taste would lead to an improvement in its market share. To discover what taste would be more "satisfactory" to consumers, the company developed two or three flavors, and interviewers carried samples to consumers. Two or three bottles of each flavor were left in a household, and the members were invited to report which formula was preferred. The flavor winning the greatest number of votes was supposedly the most satisfactory.

While the experiment sounds plausible, one aspect of reality was overlooked — the soft drink company referred to above forgot to take into account the problem of *learned* taste. It had been testing taste preferences as if they were innate and stayed with a person. Most taste preferences, however, are conditioned by experience; that is, they are learned. Preferences for soft drinks, and particularly for the cola-type drinks, are acquired through training over a period of time.

Regular investigations of the soft drink field, conducted by the writer's organization, have revealed that taste selected by the invalid procedure described above is the taste of beginners. People like it at first contact, but frequent contacts with other flavors lead eventually to a preference for these harder-to-learn tastes.

Many healthy looking product tests of taste fail because they have not taken this practical detail into account. One may easily visualize what would happen if the decision about introducing cigarettes in a market where they had never been used were based on a survey like the one above. Since the first cigarette tastes bad to most people, and reasons other than taste preference make a person smoke a second and a third, all subjects exposed to the experiment of trying just one cigarette would react negatively; and an unsophisticated piece of consumer research would conclude that cigarettes could not be sold in the new market.[4]

Another, somewhat similar, error is to forget that when a fashion or trend develops, it will lead people to buy things they are not interested in today. But this too, like learning, is a part of reality; and, again like learning, it takes time. It is not enough to be skillful at measuring; one must take into account the nature of what one is measuring. In short, to provide realistic conditions, the research design itself must provide enough time to uncover developing changes.

CONTINUING RESEARCH

The learning factor just discussed is not the only reason research efficiency can be increased by being conceived of as a continuing process. Of course, some kind of change is involved in most marketing situations, and a second survey in the same area often reveals more than the first one because it indicates progress or lack of progress. But, even beyond this, is the fact that the logic of questionmaking favors a sequence of surveys.

After a survey is finished and interpreted, every researcher has experienced the feeling that he could now construct a better questionnaire if only he had a second chance. This does not necessarily mean that mistakes were made the first time; but every question is based on assumptions, and after the survey is finished, some of the assumptions are proved while others appear to be unsupported. In light of the knowledge gained, one could always design a more efficient questionnaire.

Sometimes it is possible to achieve this very point by dividing a single survey into several phases. Where feasible, this research design is better because one has the answers to Question No. 1 before formulating Question No. 2. The situation is analogous to the game of "Twenty Questions," where each answer can be used to direct all subsequent inquiry into more profitable channels. If a player had to pre-develop a set of questions with the hope that a combination of the answers would tell him the correct object, he most likely would be forced to set up 200 questions.

As an obvious example in marketing research, think how many fewer questions have to be asked and how much sharper focus can be put on the problem if one can find out first why consumers buy a product, and then what advertising appeal to use, than if one has to try to do both in one single set of interviews.

All this suggests that the total marketing research operation be thought of as a series of interrelated surveys, each of which may be split into subsamples concerned with different topics. So envisaged, research has little in common with the one-shot survey procedure, which so often is characterized by overexpectation and underproductiveness.

[4] For the role of motivation in learning see C. I. Hovland, "Human Learning and Retention," in *Handbook of Experimental Psychology,* edited by S. S. Stevens (New York, John Wiley & Sons, Inc., 1951), p. 629.

ADVERTISING EFFECTIVENESS

The efficiency of research depends on far more than details of method or organization, however. The clarity with which marketing objectives are crystallized and then translated into research designs can make all the difference in whether a project produces useful information or not. There is no point in measuring reactions if they are not reactions which reveal the marketing results that are being sought. To take one area for illustration — because it happens to be one of the toughest as well as most important areas for research — let us consider the matter of advertising effectiveness.

Once upon a time it may have been possible — as in mail order selling, where tests can be made under rigid controls — to isolate the net effect of the advertising effort and measure it as such. But in the modern world the difference in impact between two advertising messages is obscured by the fact that consumers are affected by the cumulative power of previous advertising, sales promotion, distribution, competitive activities, and so on. To decide the question is almost impossible through opinion or motive hunting.

Here is where advanced marketing research comes to the rescue. It recognizes that the specific advertising objective is not to create a general climate of good will but to get consumers to act or react in a certain way. Thus, to use what would seem to be a very simple example, the purpose of a sign on a gas station is to get motorists' attention so they will stop there to buy gasoline.

Unfortunately, it is at this point that many research projects purporting to measure advertising effectiveness make a serious mistake: they seem to rest on the notion that generation of pleasure is practically synonymous with successful advertising. But it is not the function of advertising to be liked — anymore than it is the role of teaching to be liked (though it is desirable of course that

advertising, as well as teaching, not be *dis*liked). The real function of advertising is to stimulate purchase, and its ability to win out in the market place is not necessarily enhanced by its ability to generate any kind of psychic satisfaction.

PLEASURE VS. ATTENTION

To substantiate the controversial dictum just made, let us look at an actual case involving gas station signs. The Socony Mobil Oil Company was considering methods of increasing the efficiency of its communication with motorists. Among other things, the research turned to an examination of whether to continue identifying the company's gas stations by the traditional sign of the "Flying Red Horse," or by a sign simply featuring the letters "M-O-B-I-L." It can be agreed that:

● It is the purpose of a gasoline station sign to inform the motorist at the greatest possible distance about the locations of the station or, more particularly, about the availability of a specific brand of gasoline.

● A picture of a flying red horse surely can be used for this purpose. If used repeatedly, it will gradually be associated with a specific gasoline.

● The same holds true of the name "Mobil." If the name is shown repeatedly, it too will become associated with a specific gasoline.

In comparing the relative efficiency of the two identification devices, the lay person is inclined to rate the picture of the flying red horse higher because of its entertainment value, because of the fact that it undoubtedly conveys more pleasure than a simple sequence of letters. This lay opinion is more likely to be confirmed than refuted by marketing surveys that confine themselves to using conventional techniques. In fact such surveys show strong emotional preferences for the traditional station signs featuring the flying red horse.

However, the advanced researcher must take into account factors that would hardly be accessible to the self-analysis of the lay person and that likewise would be impenetrable by even the most skillful prober of opinion:

(1) A printed word is as much a visual symbol as a picture.

(2) A word, being closer to the verbalizing mind, is more easily remembered.

(3) The fact that a word can be written and (more important) spoken makes it a vehicle for communication among consumers, for hearsay and word-of-mouth advertising.

Leaving aside the more profound problem of word-of-mouth advertising, one may confine oneself to the elementary question: Is the pleasure-creating picture of a flying red horse or the communicable word "Mobil" more efficient in impressing on the traveling motorist that here is a station where he can buy the specific brand of gas we want to sell? After almost airtight evidence for the need of changing the station signs had been accumulated, a closing experiment of the following nature was designed:

An automobile equipped with a movie camera was driven along roads where Mobilgas and other gas stations were located. As the camera moved along, it photographed every gasoline outlet on the way. After the film was developed, the number of Mobil stations and other brands was equalized. To avoid bias, the selection was random.

Various audiences were invited to see the movie thus prepared and afterwards every member in each audience was requested to tell what brands of station signs were on the road, and approximately how many of each he thought there were. The frequency of the flying red horse sign was underestimated down to about one-half of that of its most efficient competitor.

The outcome of this experiment is not surprising. What it shows is not an exception, but a typical instance, in advertising. The world of real life has very little resemblance to the world of the advertising workshop.

Out on the road the motorist sees many signs showing babies, landscapes, soft-drink bottles, smiling faces, words. He also sees real scenes of houses, clouds, pedestrians, stoplights. If, within this multitude of impressions, he also sees a picture of a flying red horse, this perception has little opportunity to "sink in" and to arouse emotional responses. It is more realistic to describe the impression created as very faintly pleasant, near to complete indifference.

The same situation prevails when a person is going through a magazine or watching television. Surveys which probe opinions, particularly in situations which give opportunity for personal feelings, do not measure what happens in the outer world, where advertising must appear and in the end do its work.

This brings us back to the point already made and emphasized so often throughout this article: survey results are bound to be misleading unless the research experiment simulates conditions as they are in the real world and measures reactions rather than opinions and attitudes.

NEUTRALITY OF RANDOMNESS

Finally, there is the total efficiency which comes from combining the advantages of a survey large enough to achieve randomness and the advantages of getting cause-and-effect relationships through the design of the experiment. Let us look at another survey made for the Socony Mobil Oil Company, which may serve to sum up this whole approach to advanced marketing research:

At the time, 1947, the major gasoline companies were engaged in a campaign to convert consumers to higher-octane, premium-price gasoline. Data were needed to judge the efficacy of this policy as well as its prospect for continued success.

To obtain results predictive of consumer behavior a questionnaire was designed on which appeared the very simple question, "Would you say that your car tends to knock?" Such a question is meaningless with respect to an individual respondent. As any interviewer is aware, the difference between a "yes" and a "no" can be minute. The motorist knows that there were occasions when his car did knock and others when it did not. He must generalize. Does his past experience add up to a general "yes" or a general "no"? A smile or a change in the pitch of the interviewer's voice is sufficient to change a "yes" into a "no." There is no truth one way or the other.

Yet the point is that the question as expressed in the present tense does require a definite answer. The lack of precision does not matter, if there are enough interviews (6,000 in this case) so the interviewers' smiles and nonsmiles, the respondents' underestimates and overestimates, get frozen into the neutrality of randomness. We do not have the "truth" from each individual respondent, but we do have an over-all measure of respondents' reactions under realistic conditions of use.

But what do their reactions mean? Are they, then, an indication of perception of the differences between octane numbers on the part of consumers, or do they simply reflect advertising claims and preferences established over a period of time? This could not have been decided if the original design of the experiment had not been clearly formulated: Do consumers recognize and appreciate the performance of higher-octane numbers *regardless of other affecting circumstances?*

The year 1947 happened to be characterized by a lead shortage. In this situation the various brands of gasoline provided a wide range of actual octane numbers, which were typical neither of their octane ratings in the past nor of their current advertising. Thus we had our actual variable against which to compare consumers' reactions about knocking, under nearly ideal conditions of control.

So we asked the further simple question, "What gasoline are you using most often?" Through cross reference to this question, the answers to the primitive knocking question took on definite meaning. The following relationship was established:

- Among the users of Brand A gasoline, 30.2% said their car knocked.
- Among the users of Brand B gasoline, 17.1% said their car knocked.
- Among the users of Brand C gasoline, 7.5% said their car knocked.

This rank order (actually we carried it through for six brands) turned out to match exactly the rank order of actual octane numbers. Thus, although the individual motorist produced only an almost meaningless "yes" or "no," we could reach the definite conclusion that the effort to increase octane numbers was worthwhile from the standpoint of consumers' perception.

CONCLUSION

In being faced with problems which do not exist in other fields, problem-solving consumer research finds itself in the same lonesome position as that of a certain king in the Middle Ages. This king also faced a design problem.

As the story goes, he had ten manufacturers who minted his silver coins. Each coin was to weigh 16 grams. Eventually, it was discovered that one of the manufacturers was minting coins weighing only 15 grams. But no one knew which of the manufacturers was the culprit.

The king called a meeting and had each of the ten men submit a sample of ten of the coins he had produced. A spring scale was available. However, there was one difficulty — somewhat unusual in this instance, but wholly typical of the quandary marketing research often finds itself in. It was impossible to make more than a single weighing.

The king had no "traditional sciences" to turn to. Yet he was able to design an experiment such that he could determine which manufacturer was producing the underweight coins. He took a different number of coins from each manufacturer—from one to ten—and the number of grams by which the total weight was short immediately identified the guilty party!

Marketing research must approach its survey problems in the same scientific spirit manifested by this king. He did not ask the "truth" from his ten respondents, but uncovered it through objective measurement.

44. Projective Techniques in Marketing Research

MASON HAIRE

It is a well accepted maxim in merchandizing that, in many areas, we are selling the sizzle rather than the steak. Our market research techniques, however, in many of these same areas, are directed toward the steak. The sizzle is the subjective reaction of the consumer; the steak the objective characteristics of the product. The consumer's behavior will be based on the former rather than the latter set of characteristics. How can we come to know them better?

When we approach a consumer directly with questions about his reaction to a product we often get false and misleading answers to our questions. Very often this is because the question which we heard ourselves ask was not the one (or not the only one) that the respondent heard. For example: A brewery made two kinds of beer. To guide their merchandizing techniques they wanted to know what kind of people drank each kind, and particularly, what differences there were between the two groups of consumers. A survey was conducted which led up to the questions "Do you drink _____ beer?" (If *yes*) "Do you drink the *Light* or *Regular?*" (These were the two trade names under which the company marketed.) After identifying the consumers of each product it was possible to find out about the characteristics of each group so that appropriate appeals could be used, media chosen, etc.

From *Journal of Marketing*, Vol. 14, No. 5 (April, 1950), pp. 649-56, by permission of the American Marketing Association.

An interesting anomaly appeared in the survey data, however. The interviewing showed (on a reliable sample) that consumers drank *Light* over *Regular* in the ratio of 3 to 1. The company had been producing and selling Regular over Light for some time in a ratio of 9 to 1. Clearly, the attempt to identify characteristics of the two kinds was a failure. What made them miss so far?

When we say "Do you drink *Light* or *Regular?*" we are at once asking which brand is used, but also, to some extent, saying "Do you drink the regular run-of-the-mill product or do you drink the one that is more refined and shows more discrimination and taste?" The preponderance of "Light" undoubtedly flows from this kind of distortion.

When we ask questions of this sort about the product we are very often asking also about the respondent. Not only do we say "What is _____ product like?" but, indirectly "What are *you* like?" Our responses are often made up of both elements inextricably interwoven. The answers to the second question will carry clichés and stereotypes, blocks, inhibitions, and distortions, whenever we approach an area that challenges the person's idea of himself.

There are many things that we need to know about a consumer's reaction to a product that he cannot tell us because they are to some extent socially unacceptable. For instance, the snob appeal of a product vitally influences its sale, but it is a thing that the consumer will not like to discuss explicitly. In other cases the consumer is influenced by motives of which he is, perhaps, vaguely aware, but which he finds difficult to put into words. The interviewer-respondent relationship puts a good deal of pressure on him to reply and to make sense in his reply. Consequently, he gives us stereotypical responses that use clichés which are commonly acceptable but do not necessarily represent the true motives. Many of our motives do not, in fact, "make sense," and are not logical. The question-answer relation demands sense above all. If the response does not represent the true state of affairs the interviewer will never know it. He will go away. If it does not make sense it may represent the truth, but the respondent will feel like a fool and the interviewer will not go away. Much better produce a cliché and be rid of him.

THE NATURE OF PROJECTIVE TESTS

Still other kinds of motives exist of which the respondent may not be explicitly conscious himself. The product may be seen by him as related to things or people or values in his life, or as having a certain role in the scheme of things, and yet he may be quite unable, in response to a direct question, to describe these aspects of the object. Nevertheless, these characteristics may be of great importance as motives. How can we get at them?

Clinical psychologists have long been faced with a parallel set of problems. It is quite usual for a patient to be unable or unwilling to tell the therapist directly what kinds of things are stirring in his motivational pattern. Information about these drives are of vital importance to the process of cure, so a good deal of research has been directed towards the development of techniques to identify and define them. The development of projective techniques as diagnostic tools has provided one of the most use-

ful means to uncover such motivations, and the market-researcher can well afford to borrow their essentials from the therapist.

Basically, a projective test involves presenting the subject with an ambiguous stimulus — one that does not quite make sense in itself — and asking him to make sense of it. The theory is that in order to make it make sense he will have to add to it — to fill out the picture — and in so doing he projects part of himself into it. Since we know what was in the original stimulus we can quite easily identify the parts that were added, and, in this way, painlessly obtain information about the person.

Examples of these tests come readily to hand. Nearly everyone is familiar with the Rorschach Test, in which a subject is shown a series of ink-blots and asked to tell what they look like. Here the stimulus is incomplete in itself, and the interpretation supplied by the patient provides useful information. This test yields fairly general answers about the personality, however, and often we would like to narrow down the area in which the patient is supplying information.

The Thematic Apperception Test offers a good example of this function. Let us suppose that with a particular patient we have reason to suppose that his relation to figures of authority is crucial to his therapeutic problem. We can give him a series of pictures where people are shown, but where the relationship of authority or the characteristics of the authoritarian figure are not complete. He is asked to tell a story about each picture. If in each story the subordinate finally kills the figure of authority we have certain kinds of knowledge; if, on the other hand, he always builds the story so the subordinate figure achieves a secure and comfortable dependence, we have quite different information. It is often quite impossible to get the subject to tell us these things directly. Either he cannot or will not do so. Indirectly, however, he will tell us how he sees authority. Can we get him, similarly, to tell us how a product looks to him in his private view of the world?

APPLICATION OF PROJECTIVE TEST IN MARKET RESEARCH

Let us look at an example of this kind of thing in market research. For the purposes of experiment a conventional survey was made of attitudes toward Nescafé, an instant coffee. The questionnaire included the questions "Do you use instant coffee?" (If *No*) "What do you dislike about it?" The bulk of the unfavorable responses fell into the general area "I don't like the flavor." This is such an easy answer to a complex question that one may suspect it is a stereotype, which at once gives a sensible response to get rid of the interviewer and conceals other motives. How can we get behind this facade?

In this case an indirect approach was used. Two shopping lists were prepared. They were identical in all respects, except that one list specified Nescafé and one Maxwell House Coffee. They were administered to alternate subjects, with no subject knowing of the existence of the other list. The instructions were "Read the shopping list below. Try to project yourself into the situation as far as possible until you can more or less characterize the woman who bought the groceries. Then write a brief description of her personality and character. Wherever possible indicate what factors influenced your judgement."

Shopping List I
Pound and a half of hamburger
2 loaves Wonder bread
bunch of carrots
1 can Rumford's Baking Powder
Nescafé instant coffee
2 cans Del Monte peaches
5 lbs. potatoes

Shopping List II
Pound and a half of hamburger
2 loaves Wonder bread
bunch of carrots
1 can Rumford's Baking Powder
1 lb. Maxwell House Coffee (Drip Ground)
2 cans Del Monte peaches
5 lbs. potatoes

Fifty people responded to each of the two shopping lists given above. The responses to these shopping lists provided some very interesting material. The following main characteristics of their descriptions can be given:

1. 48 per cent of the people described the woman who bought Nescafé as lazy; 4 per cent described the woman who bought Maxwell House as lazy.
2. 48 per cent of the people described the woman who bought Nescafé as failing to plan household purchases and schedules well; 12 per cent described the woman who bought Maxwell House this way.
3. 4 per cent described the Nescafé woman as thrifty; 16 per cent described the Maxwell House woman as thrifty. 12 per cent described the Nescafé woman as spendthrift; 0 per cent described the Maxwell House woman this way.
4. 16 per cent described the Nescafé woman as not a good wife; 0 per cent described the Maxwell House woman this way.
   4 per cent described the Nescafé woman as a good wife; 16 per cent described the Maxwell House woman as a good wife.

A clear picture begins to form here. Instant coffee represents a departure from "home-made" coffee, and the traditions with respect to caring for one's family. Coffee-making is taken seriously, with vigorous proponents for laborious drip and filter-paper methods, firm believers in coffee boiled in a battered sauce pan, and the like. Coffee drinking is a form of intimacy and relaxation that gives it a special character.

On the one hand, coffee making is an art. It is quite common to hear a woman say, "I can't seem to make good coffee," in the same way that one might say, "I can't learn to play the violin." It is acceptable to confess this inadequacy, for making coffee well is a mysterious touch that belongs, in a shadowy tradition, to the plump, aproned figure who is a little lost outside her kitchen but who has a sure sense in it and among its tools.

On the other hand, coffee has a peculiar role in relation to the household and the home-and-family character. We may well have a picture, in the shadowy past of a big black range that is always hot with baking and cooking, and has a big enamelled pot of coffee warming at the back. When a neighbor drops in during the morning, a cup of coffee is a medium of hospitality that does somewhat the same thing as cocktails in the late afternoon, but does it in a broader sphere.

These are real and important aspects of coffee. They are not physical characteristics of the product, but they are real values in the consumer's life, and they influence his purchasing. We need to know and assess them. The "labor-saving" aspect of instant coffee, far from being an asset, may be a liability in that it violates these traditions. How often have we heard a wife respond to "This cake is delicious!" with a pretty blush and "Thank you—I made it with such and such a prepared cake mix." This response is so invariable as to seem almost compulsive. It is almost unthinkable to anticipate a reply "Thank you, I made it with Pillsbury's flour, Fleischman's yeast, and Borden's milk." Here the specifications are unnecessary. All that is relevant is the implied "I made it"—the art and the credit are carried directly by the verb that covers the process of mixing and processing the

ingredients. In ready-mixed foods there seems to be a compulsive drive to refuse credit for the product, because the accomplishment is not the housewife's but the company's.

In this experiment, as a penalty for using "synthetics" the woman who buys Nescafé pays the price of being seen as lazy, spendthrift, a poor wife, and as failing to plan well for her family. The people who rejected instant coffee in the original direct question blamed its flavor. We may well wonder if their dislike of instant coffee was not to a large extent occasioned by a fear of being seen by one's self and others in the role they projected onto the Nescafé woman in the description. When asked directly, however, it is difficult to respond with this. One cannot say, "I don't use Nescafé because people will think I am lazy and not a good wife." Yet we know from these data that the feeling regarding laziness and shiftlessness was there. Later studies (reported below) showed that it determined buying habits, and that something could be done about it.

ANALYSIS OF RESPONSES

Some examples of the type of response received will show the kind of material obtained and how it may be analyzed. Three examples of each group are given below.

Descriptions of a woman who bought, among other things, Maxwell House Coffee. "I'd say she was a practical, frugal woman. She bought too many potatoes. She must like to cook and bake as she included baking powder. She must not care much about her figure as she does not discriminate about the food she buys."

"The woman is quite influenced by advertising as signified by the specific name brands on her shopping list. She probably is quite set in her ways and accepts no substitutes."

"I have been able to observe several

hundred women shoppers who have made very similar purchases to that listed above, and the only clue that I can detect that may have some bearing on her personality is the Del Monte peaches. This item when purchased singly along with the other more staple foods indicates that she may be anxious to please either herself or members of her family with a 'treat.' She is probably a thrifty, sensible housewife."

Descriptions of a woman who bought, among other things, Nescafé Instant Coffee. "This woman appears to be either single or living alone. I would guess that she had an office job. Apparently, she likes to sleep late in the morning, basing my assumption on what she bought such as Instant Coffee which can be made in a hurry. She probably also has can [sic] peaches for breakfast, cans being easy to open. Assuming that she is just average, as opposed to those dazzling natural beauties who do not need much time to make up, she must appear rather sloppy, taking little time to make up in the morning. She is also used to eating supper out, too. Perhaps alone rather than with an escort. An old maid probably."

"She seems to be lazy, because of her purchases of canned peaches and instant coffee. She doesn't seem to think, because she bought two loaves of bread, and then baking powder, unless she's thinking of making cake. She probably just got married."

"I think the woman is the type who never thinks ahead very far—the type who always sends Junior to the store to buy one item at a time. Also she is fundamentally lazy. All the items, with possible exception of the Rumford's, are easily prepared items. The girl may be an office girl who is just living from one day to the next in a sort of haphazard sort of life."

As we read these complete responses we begin to get a feeling for the picture that is created by Nescafé. It is particu-

larly interesting to notice that the Nescafé woman is protected, to some extent, from the opprobrium of being lazy and haphazard by being seen as a single "office girl"—a role that relieves one from guilt for not being interested in the home and food preparation.

The references to peaches are significant. In one case (Maxwell House) they are singled out as a sign that the woman is thoughtfully preparing a "treat" for her family. On the other hand, when the Nescafé woman buys them it is evidence that she is lazy, since their "canned" character is seen as central.

In terms of the sort of results presented above, it may be useful to demonstrate the way these stories are coded. The following items are extracted from the six stories quoted.

Maxwell House	Nescafé
1. practical frugal likes to cook	1. single office girl sloppy old maid
2. influenced by advertising set in her ways	2. lazy does not plan newlywed
3. interested in family thrifty sensible	3. lazy does not plan office girl

Items such as these are culled from each of the stories. Little by little categories are shaped by the content of the stories themselves. In this way the respondent furnishes the dimensions of analysis as well as the scale values on these dimensions.

SECOND TEST

It is possible to wonder whether it is true that the opprobrium that is heaped on the Nescafé woman comes from her use of a device that represents a shortcut and labor-saver in an area where she is expected to embrace painstaking time-consuming work in a ritualistic way. To test this a variation was introduced into the shopping lists. In a second experiment one hundred and fifty housewives were tested with the

TABLE 1
PERSONALITY CHARACTERISTICS ASCRIBED TO USERS OF PREPARED FOODS

If They Use	No Prepared Food (Maxwell House alone)		Nescafé (alone)		Maxwell House (plus Pie Mix)		Nescafé (plus Pie Mix)	
They are seen as:	Number	Per Cent	Number	Per Cent	Number	Per Cent	Number	Per Cent
Not Economical	12	17	24	32	6	30	7	35
Lazy	8	11	46	62	5	25	8	40
Poor Personality and Appearance	28	39	39	53	7	35	8	40
N =	72		74		20		20	

form given above, but a sample was added to this group which responded to a slightly different form. If we assume that the rejection in the first experiment came from the presence of a feeling about synthetic shortcuts we might assume also that the addition of one more shortcut to both lists would bring the Maxwell House woman more into line with the Nescafé woman, since the former would now have the same guilt that the Nescafé woman originally had, while the Nescafé woman, already convicted of evading her duties, would be little further injured.

In order to accomplish this a second prepared food was added to both lists. Immediately after the coffee in both lists the fictitious item, "Blueberry Fill Pie Mix" was added. The results are shown in the accompanying Table I.

It will be seen immediately, in the first two columns, that the group to whom the original form of the list was given showed the same kind of difference as reported above in their estimates of the two women. The group with an additional prepared food, however, brought the Maxwell Coffee woman down until she is virtually undistinguishable from the Nescafé. There seems to be little doubt but that the prepared-food-character, and the stigma of avoiding housewifely duties is responsible for the projected personality characteristics.

TABLE 2

The woman who buys Nescafé is seen as:	By Women Who Had Instant Coffee in the House (N = 32)		By Women Who Did Not Have Instant Coffee in the House (N = 18)	
	Number	Per Cent	Number	Per Cent
Economical°°	22	70	5	28
Not economical	0	0	2	11
Can not cook or does not like to°°	5	16	10	55
Plans balanced meals°	9	29	2	11
Good housewife, plans well, cares about family°°	9	29	0	0
Poor housewife, does not plan well, does not care about family°	5	16	7	39
Lazy°	6	19	7	39

° A single asterisk indicates that differences this great would be observed only 5 times out of 100 in repeated samplings of a population whose true difference is zero.
°° A double asterisk indicates that the chances are 1 in 100. We are justified in rejecting the hypothesis that there is no difference between the groups.

RELATION TO PURCHASING

It is still relevant to ask whether the existence of these feelings in a potential consumer is related to purchasing. It is hypothesized that these personality descriptions provide an opportunity for the consumer to project hopes and fears and anxieties that are relevant to the way the product is seen, and that they represent important parts of her motivation in buying or not buying. To test this hypothesis, a small sample of fifty housewives, comparable in every way to the group just referred to, was given the original form of the shopping list (Nescafé only). In addition to obtaining the personality description, the interviewer, on a pretext, obtained permission to look at her pantry shelves and determine personally whether or not she had instant coffee of any brand. The results of this investigation are shown in the accompanying Table II.

The trend of these data shows conclusively that if a respondent sees the woman who buys Nescafé as having undesirable traits, she is not likely to buy instant coffee herself. The projected unacceptable characteristics go with failure to buy, and it does not seem unwarranted to assume that the association is causal.

Furthermore, these projected traits are to some extent, additive. For instance, if a respondent describes the woman as having one bad trait only, she is about twice as likely not to have instant coffee. However, if she sees her as having two bad traits, and no good ones (e.g., lazy, cannot cook), she is about three times as likely not to have instant coffee as she is to have it. On the other hand, if she sees her as having two good traits (e.g., economical, cares for family), she is about six times as likely to have it as not.

It was pointed out earlier that some women felt it necessary to "excuse" the woman who bought Nescafé by suggesting that she live alone and hence could not be expected to be interested in cooking, or that she had a job and did not have time to shop better. Women who had instant coffee in the house found excuses almost twice as often as those who did not use instant coffee (12 out of 32, or 42 per cent, against 4 out of 18, or 22 per cent). These "excuses" are vitally important for merchandizing. The need for an excuse shows there is a barrier to buying in the consumer's mind. The presence of excuses shows that there is a way around the barrier. The content of the excuses themselves provides valuable clues for directing appeals toward reducing buying resistance.

CONCLUSIONS

There seems to be no question that in the experimental situation described here:

(1) Motives exist which are below the level of verbalization because they are socially unacceptable, difficult to verbalize cogently, or unrecognized.

(2) These motives are intimately related to the decision to purchase or not to purchase, and

(3) It is possible to identify and assess such motives by approaching them indirectly.

Two important general points come out of the work reported. The first is in the statement of the problem. It is necessary for us to see a product in terms of a set of characteristics and attributes which are part of the consumer's "private world," and as such may have no simple relationship to characteristics of the object in the "real" world. Each of us lives in a world which is composed of more than physical things and people. It is made up of goals, paths to goals, barriers, threats, and the like, and an individual's behavior is oriented with respect to these characteristics as much as to the "objective" ones. In the area of merchandizing, a product's character of being seen as a path to a goal is usually very much more important as a determinant of purchasing than its physical dimensions. We have taken advantage of these qualities in advertising and merchandizing for a long time by an intuitive sort of "playing-by-ear" on the subjective aspects of products. It is time for a systematic attack on the problem of the phenomenological description of objects. What kinds of dimensions are relevant to this world of goals and paths and barriers? What kind of terms will fit the phenomenological characteristics of an object in the same sense that the centimetre-gram-second system fits its physical dimensions? We need to know the answers to such questions, and the psychological definitions of valued objects.

The second general point is the methodological one that it is possible, by using appropriate techniques, to find out from the respondent what the phenomenological characteristics of various objects may be. By and large, a direct approach to this problem in terms of straightforward questions will not yield satisfactory answers. It is possible, however, by the use of indirect techniques, to get the consumer to provide, quite unselfconsciously, a description of the value-character of objects in his environment.

45. Another Look at Two Instant Coffee Studies

CONRAD R. HILL

Judging from the momentum of published reports, the use of motivation research as an advertising tool has languished considerably since the faddish frenzy of the early fifties. Despite this gradual fade-out, one — Mason Haire's study of instant coffee — continues to stand out and earn kudos and footnotes from research writers (Selltiz *et al*, 1959). The purpose of this article is to assess this "classic" article (Westfall, Boyd and Campbell, 1957, p. 135) so far as practical advertising and marketing problems are concerned.

Haire's premise is that advertising research methods which rely exclusively upon direct questioning of consumers usually elicit mere rationalizations about product attributes. Therefore, in order to uncover the more important but latent attitudes, projective techniques are required.

Haire suspected that "dislike for the flavor of instant coffee" was just a ready rationalization. To test this notion he showed different grocery lists to two groups of 50 housewives each. Group One was asked to describe the housewife who made up the following shopping list:

"Pound and half (*sic*) of hamburger
Two loaves of Wonder bread
Bunch of carrots

From *Journal of Advertising Research*, Vol. 1 (1960), pp. 18-21. Copyright © 1960 by Advertising Research Foundation, Inc.

One can Rumford's Baking Powder
Nescafé instant coffee
Two cans Del Monte peaches
Five pounds potatoes" (Haire, 1950, p. 651)

Group Two was asked to describe a housewife who made up a list identical to that above except that "Maxwell House Coffee (Drip Grind)" replaced "Nescafé instant coffee."

Before recapitulating Haire's findings in Table 1 let's take a closer look at the suspected cultural stereotype that Haire discusses — dislike for the flavor of instant coffee. His respondents were asked, "Do you use instant coffee?" If the answer was "No," they were then asked, "What do you dislike about it?" Obviously this question introduces bias because it assumes that non-users are non-users due to dislike, which may or may not be true.

A better question would have been, "Have you used instant coffee within the past week?" or some other question that would have avoided the defensive sting of a direct accusation. What's more, Haire should have asked for likes as well as dislikes. Failure to look at the other side could load his data seriously.

As Haire's Table 1 shows, "flavor" as a determinant of respondents' underlying attitudes toward instant coffee failed to arise in the depth situation. Instead, attitudes were pitched in terms of value judgments about the shopper. This is

TABLE 1
MENTIONS BY USERS AND NON-USERS OF INSTANT COFFEE
(After Haire, 1950)

The woman who buys Nescafé is seen as:	By Women Who Had Instant Coffee in the House (N = 32)		By Women Who Did Not Have Instant Coffee in the House (N = 18)	
	Number	Per Cent	Number	Per Cent
Economical†	22	70	5	28
Not economical	0	0	2	11
Can not cook or does not like to†	5	16	10	55
Plans balanced meals*	9	29	2	11
Good housewife, plans well, cares about family†	9	29	0	0
Poor housewife, does not plan well, does not care about family*	5	16	7	39
Lazy*	6	19	7	39

* An asterisk indicates that differences this great would be observed only five times out of 100 in repeated samplings of a population whose true difference is zero.
† A dagger indicates that the chances are one in 100. We are justified in rejecting the hypothesis that there is no difference between the groups.

not surprising because that is what he asked for. The instant coffee shopper is viewed as lazy and as failing to plan her household duties and purchases. On the other hand, the regular coffee woman shines with the positive, culturally approved, housewifely virtues. Haire's follow-up pantry check revealed that instant users tended to be more tolerant of the instant coffee shopper, whereas the non-users were more negativistic. From these findings, Haire concluded that these "underlying attitudes" influence the decision to buy or not to buy instant coffee, that the only way to unearth these important attitudes is by projective research, and that direct questions cannot bring forth the "real" information so necessary for effective advertising campaign appeals.

As this critique suggests, that is one whale of a supposition. Negative attitudes toward sinners do not prevent most of us from sinning; negative attitudes toward instant coffee may not prevent us from buying it.

COMMENTS ON METHODOLOGY

Haire's failure to describe his sample design makes it difficult to assess the validity of his computational methods.

Overlooking this basic consideration, there are other methodological questions that may be legitimately raised. Even if we grant that attitudes toward instant coffee and instant coffee users are synonymous — which they are not — Table 1's presentation suggests other weaknesses.

Because the Table 1 presentation offers gross analysis, it doesn't really tell us very much. Needed are determinants of relationships between the attitudes of users and non-users by age, income, family size and so forth. This is impossible with a sample of 50, because there are not enough respondents for the cells demanded in cross-tabulations. In other words, it is statistically unwise to draw conclusions and inferences from two respondents per cell.

As for the pantry check, we learn there were 32 users and 18 non-users of instant coffee. Projecting that ratio to the universe as Haire did with other findings, are we to assume that instant coffee enjoyed 64 per cent market penetration in 1950?

Another methodological criticism involves the selection of classes in Table 1's stub. Do these meet the research criterion of being mutually exclusive? For instance, could it be that "good housewife, plans well, cares for her family" and "plans balanced meals" represent a single "planning" dimension, and not two as Haire suggests? In other words, do they overlap?

If so, then the findings may be heavily loaded with articulate respondents, that is, those who harped on the same theme with only slight variations. Additional discussion of this aspect follows.

Because Haire's objective was to reveal the presence of underlying attitudes toward instant coffee, Table 2's division of responses into favorable and unfavorable categories seems better suited for analysis. Note particularly the bracketed percentages listed under "Per Cent of Mentions." Rather than base respondent mentions upon the N of respondents, the new base is taken as the total mentions made by both users and non-users. In this manner it is possible to compare relationships between the groups. As Table 2 indicates, they are not as dramatic as those in the original presentation.

The average number of mentions by non-users (33 by 18) and by users of instant coffee (56 by 32) is roughly equal at 1.8 per respondent. In order to assess that statistic, however, we need to know the ranges as well. That is, did a small but vocal minority contribute the bulk of the mentions to the detriment of a larger but mute group? Such a statistic would provide clues for an understanding of the attitude classes in Table 1's stub.

BIAS BY BAKING POWDER?

Refer back to the grocery list used. Note that Rumford's Baking Powder immediately precedes the coffee item. Is it possible that baking powder, as a symbol of the good cook, could have subtly biased the responses? It may have exerted a strong "contrast effect" so that instant coffee assumed a shameful role in obvious contradiction to the stereotype of what constitutes a good cook.

TABLE 2

FAVORABLE AND UNFAVORABLE MENTIONS
BY USERS AND NON-USERS OF INSTANT COFFEE
(Revision of Haire's Table 1)

The woman who buys Nescafé is seen as:	By Women Who Had Instant Coffee in the House (N = 32)			By Women Who Did Not Have Instant Coffee in the House (N = 18)		
	Number	Per Cent of Subjects	Per Cent of Mentions	Number	Per Cent of Subjects	Per Cent of Mentions
Economical	22	69	(39)	5	28	(15)
Good housewife, plans well, cares about family, plans balanced meals	18	56	(33)	2	11	(6)
Total Favorable Mentions	40	125	(72)	7	39	(21)
Not economical	0	0	(0)	2	11	(6)
Lazy	6	19	(10.5)	7	39	(21)
Poor housewife, does not plan well, does not care about family	10	31	(17.5)	17	95	(52)
Total Unfavorable Mentions	16	50	(28)	26	145	(79)
Total Mentions	56		(100%)	33		(100%)

An analysis of respondents' verbatim reports published by Haire augments that suspicion. That is, in the ambiguous evaluative situation, respondents seem to have searched the list for items to serve as guides. For example, one respondent resolved her ambiguity in this fashion:

". . . she must like to cook and bake as she included baking powder. . . ."

Another rationalized baking powder in terms of other items:

". . . canned peaches, instant coffee . . . all the items with the exception of Rumford's are easily prepared items."

It seems safe to conclude that baking powder did prejudice the case against instant coffee, but it is impossible to know to what extent.

WESTFALL, BOYD AND CAMPBELL STUDY

This second study of attitudes toward instant coffee was conducted seven years later by the above Northwestern University researchers. After first qualifying respondents as to recency of coffee-making, they asked:

". . . the last time you made coffee — did you use percolator, drip method, vacuum method, instant coffee, or some other method?"

Next they asked respondents to match 19 personality dimensions (the best cook you know, the worst cook you know, etc.) to each of the coffee preparation methods. This technique, the authors suggested, would reveal underlying attitudes toward instant coffee.

Generally, their findings agree in direction but not degree with Haire's. For example, "dislikes to cook," "thrifty," "cares for family" and "good planner" proved to be in good agreement. But Westfall's "poor cook" dimension had smaller differences between users and non-users than did Haire's. Surprisingly, "laziness" proved to be similar for users and non-users of instant coffee in Westfall's findings.

This last finding, contradicting as it does expectations that users and non-users should react differently to "lazy" attitudes, suggests a common weakness of forced choice research techniques. There's simply no way of knowing to what degree forcing elicits rationalizations rather than true attitudes. And unless attitude intensity is measured, superficial responses must be accepted as equally valid as expressions of rigid attitudes. Consequently, the "laziness" dimension may be as much a rationalization as "dislike for flavor."

FORCE OF HABIT

Despite projective researchers' apparent ability to reveal underlying attitudes that are ostensibly more sophisticated than those elicited by direct questioning, there is no basis upon which to evaluate the worth of those "revealed" attitudes. In several reported studies, different researchers probing for underlying attitudes about identical products have unearthed disparate findings.

Therefore the suspicion emerges that these so-called underlying attitudes may be rationalizations also — but at a slightly more sophisticated level; that is, they may be less ready rationalizations about cultural stereotypes that do not necessarily impinge on decisions to buy or not to buy a given product. What's more, these underlying attitudes may be rationalizations for habitual or routinized behavior.

Pursuing this notion of habit, we know that psychology has well documented the fact that resistance to change usually increases with age. Therefore, in order for advertising researchers to assess properly opportunities for new products, or to understand their share-of-the-market for established products, they should consider seriously, much more seriously, the workings of neophobia (fear of the new) as a sales deterrent. This assumes sharper meaning if we remember that one objective of advertising established impulse items is to reinforce conditioned brand responses. Therefore, research for any brand in a given product line needs to measure as accurately as possible the drag of previous conditioning and how that drag is distributed among competitors market by market.

This is to suggest, then, that Haire and Westfall failed to tap anything of significance so far as "true attitudes" toward instant coffee are concerned. Both studies made it easy for respondents to report superficial attitudes that may actually represent the weight of habit, not subconscious attitudes as implied. It is hoped that this suggestion casts the concept of depth research into a new focus.

REFERENCES

Haire, Mason. Projective Techniques in Marketing Research. *Journal of Marketing*, Vol. 14, No. 5, April 1950, pp. 649-656.

Selltiz, Claire, Marie Johoda, Morton Deutsch and Stuart W. Cook. *Research Methods in Social Relations.* New York: Henry Holt & Company, 1959.

Westfall, Ralph L., Harper W. Boyd and Donald T. Campbell. The Use of Structured Techniques in Motivation Research. *Journal of Marketing*, Vol. 22, No. 2, October 1957, pp. 134-139.

46. A Televised Test of Subliminal Persuasion

MELVIN L. DeFLEUR and
ROBERT M. PETRANOFF

Efforts to use subliminal stimuli for persuasive purposes have received a considerable amount of attention in recent months. Reports in the press and in popular books that subliminal devices used in connection with motion pictures have been successful in promoting certain commercial products have stirred the imagination of political leaders to the point where several members of Congress have asked such bodies as the Federal Communication Commission to regulate the use of subliminal devices on television. The Commission has not instituted such a regulation, but it has announced that if authority is needed to control this technique, it will be requested from Congress. Such groups as the National Association of Broadcasters have recommended to their members that subliminal stimuli not be used in connection with commercial broadcasts.

The research which has resulted in the present controversy is more than half a century old. The experimental study of discrimination on the basis of imperfectly perceived stimuli, or stimuli perceived without conscious awareness, goes back at least to 1898. Adams has summarized the major findings of seventy-six such studies of "behavior without awareness." He concludes that subjects in widely varying experimental settings have been able to discriminate,

to a degree greater than chance expectation, among many different types of stimuli (both auditory and visual) which were presented to them below their threshold of awareness. Adams comments that "Behavior without awareness of the kind described . . . can easily be obtained even as a class exercise."[1]

By 1939 the phenomenon of subliminal perception was so well established by experimental psychologists that interest in the process waned. It was not until these experimental findings were translated into attempts at persuasion through subliminal communication that popular interest materialized.

A CLOSED CIRCUIT TEST OF SUBLIMINAL COMMUNICATION

Can the television screen be used as a medium for the presentation of messages at a subliminal level? That is, is it possible for individuals to perceive messages presented subliminally when they are superimposed over the complex stimuli of a television program? This question poses the problem of subliminal *communication*. It can best be answered in reasonably controlled settings such as closed circuit laboratory sessions, where subjects can be placed

From *Public Opinion Quarterly*, Vol. 23 (Summer, 1959), pp. 168-80.

[1] J. K. Adams, "Laboratory Studies of Behavior without Awareness," *Psychological Bulletin*, Vol. 54, 1957, pp. 383-405.

in experimental situations. The problem of subliminal *persuasion* is another matter. If television does indeed provide a medium for communication without awareness, is it possible to stimulate people to perform specific acts on the basis of this communication? The latter problem is the more controversial and the more difficult to answer. It was approached through a test on a commercial television station which will be described in detail in the next section.

In designing a test of subliminal communication with an ordinary television set as a medium, one experimental study from psychology is particularly relevant. In 1939 Miller[2] brought subjects into a black-painted room and seated them before an opaque "mirror screen." Each subject was told that the experiment was designed to study "clairvoyance." He was asked to concentrate on the screen in lieu of a crystal ball and attempt to guess which of five cards (each with an abstract symbol on it) the experimenter was concentrating on. Actually, behind the opaque screen was a projector with a low-intensity light which presented to the subject one of five abstract symbols (star, square, triangle, wave, and circle). These were individually projected onto the back of the opaque screen at an intensity below the level of awareness of the subjects.

The subjects were able to discriminate among these five symbols to a de-

gree significantly greater than chance. When told that weak images of the stimuli had actually been presented to them during the trials, the subjects were surprised and incredulous. A variety of complications were introduced into the experiment, but the general findings remained the same.

The similarity between the "opaque mirror screen" and the ordinary television screen suggested that a similar procedure might be used to establish whether subjects could discern such stimuli when they were superimposed over a program. The same five abstract symbols were prepared on slides. The program content was a full-length feature motion picture. In two similar sessions, a total of twenty-five subjects chosen from courses in social psychology viewed the feature film under conditions similar to home viewing; that is, the subjects sat in a semi-darkened room and viewed an ordinary home receiver. The feature film was interrupted every fifteen minutes, and the subjects privately recorded their guesses as to which of the five symbols they had been viewing. Note that the subjects were aware that symbols were being presented. Their task was to guess *which* of five possibilities was being superimposed during a given fifteen-minute period. The subjects were not allowed to discuss the matter among themselves.

The results of these sessions are presented in Table 1. The unit of observation is number of fifteen-minute trials. Technical difficulties forced the discarding of several of the initial trials, but

[2] James G. Miller, "Discrimination without Awareness," *American Journal of Psychology*, Vol. 52, 1939, pp. 562-578.

TABLE 1

EFFECTS OF CLOSED-CIRCUIT SUBLIMINAL COMMUNICATION WITH FIVE ABSTRACT SYMBOLS SUPERIMPOSED OVER A TELEVISED MOTION PICTURE

	Number of 15-minute Trials	Number of Correct Identifications	Per Cent Correct
Experiment 1	27	9	33.3
Experiment 2	76	26	34.2
Total	103	35	34.0°

° Significantly greater than the chance expectation (of 20 per cent correct) beyond the .05 level.

a total of 103 opportunities were available for the twenty-five subjects to guess which of the five symbols had been presented. If no communication had taken place and chance had dictated the results, the expectation would be that 1 out of every 5 guesses would be correct, for a total of 20 per cent of the trials. Actually, 34 per cent were correctly guessed, a performance significantly greater than the chance expectancy.

We can conclude, then, that this small pilot study yielded results consistent with the bulk of more highly controlled experimental studies of the discrimination of stimuli presented below the level of awareness. The addition of the complex stimuli of a television program does not present an insurmountable complication.

A TELEVISED TEST OF SUBLIMINAL PERSUASION

The second phase of the present study has as its purpose a test of the degree to which subliminal messages, presented at low intensity to audiences during regularly televised programs, are influential in stimulating them to engage in two forms of behavior: (1) viewing a particular program as a result of subliminal suggestion; (2) buying certain food products as a result of exposure to subliminal stimuli, and as a result of exposure to subliminal stimuli in combination with regularly scheduled "commercials."

In testing the feasibility of subliminal persuasion, it is important that the behavioral task posed for the audience is not too difficult. The most feasible method of persuading an audience to act on the basis of subliminally presented stimuli is to tap into already established habit patterns, or to suggest a response which is very simple and easy for the subject. For example, one trial of subliminal messages on television was reported in the press. The station involved was said to have superimposed the message "Write to Station . . . ," specifying their call letters. This demands a really complex response on the part of the audience. The potential complier must first find writing materials, then compose a letter or post card message. He must then find a stamp and see that the letter or card gets to a mail box. It is little wonder that the experiment was reported as a failure; such an attempt at persuasion required too complicated a response.

The commercial television station cooperating in the present experiment had a program arrangement which made the first of the experimental messages much more feasible in this respect. Television station WTTV, Channel 4, Indianapolis, regularly broadcasts a feature motion picture from 8 until 10 P.M. each weeknight, Monday through Friday. This motion picture is followed by a fifteen-minute news program featuring Frank Edwards, a widely known news analyst. An experimental message with the simple suggestion "Watch Frank Edwards" could thus be continuously broadcast during the two-hour period immediately preceding the news program.[3] Such a subliminal message solicits a response which makes minimum demands. It merely requires that the respondent remain supinely in his easy chair and

_____

[3] Several methods of producing the subliminal messages were tried, but the final technique used in the closed-circuit and on-the-air experiments consisted of projecting a 2-inch by 2-inch slide into the vidicon film camera at a level equal to 1.00 per cent of the normal picture being projected. This image was then superimposed over the feature film (at 100 per cent gain) by producing a "split super" on the control-room switching panel. The slides were made up with white letters on a black background and, when switched into the outgoing circuit, were kept at the 1.00 per cent level—or a 100 to 1.00 ratio. The authors wish to express their gratitude to Mr. Floyd Malott, chief engineer for television at the Indiana University Radio and Television Service, and to Mr. Carl Onken, former chief engineer for WTTV, for their cooperation and technical assistance.

continue what he is in fact already doing, watching a particular television channel.

One simple way to test the hypothesis that such a subliminal message will have a persuasive effect on its audience is to obtain "before" and "after" measurements of the size of the news program's audience. The statistical and other significance of any increase in audience size due to the experimental treatment can then be evaluated. This was in fact the research plan followed, the details of which are presented below.

But we must consider other forms of response. Of greater interest, of course, are messages which persuade the respondent to purchase some specific item. Such commercial applications of subliminal communication constitute one basis for current public debates regarding the ethics of this process.

Possibly, food products constitute the most universal commercial items for any given audience. The remaining phases of the research, then, explore the ability of subliminal suggestions, broadcast over a five-week period during the regular two-hour motion picture program outlined above, to increase the sales of specific food items in the area reached by the television signal.

The wholesale distributor for the Independent Grocers' Alliance for south-central Indiana, John Figg, Inc., agreed to furnish reliable information concerning the "normal" sales of a variety of food items to the residents of south-central Indiana and the sales of these food items during the experimental periods. The firm also agreed to synchronize some of its own television advertising with subliminal messages suggesting that the audience "Buy Product X." With this cooperation, it was possible to test the efficacy of subliminal messages in stimulating the purchase of several selected food items.

With the ability to synchronize ordinary television advertisements with subliminal messages, it was possible to test the effects of subliminal messages both singly and in *combinations* with more usual persuasive techniques. For example, the food distributor regularly advertised some particular food item as a "special of the week," during which time that particular food could be obtained at a special low price in all of the IGA stores in south-central Indiana. This "TV Special," as we can call it, was routinely broadcast during the "commercial" segment of the Frank Edwards program. This programing allowed a presentation of a subliminal message to "Buy Product X" each night for five days during the two-hour feature movie, followed by a TV Special which showed that this food could be obtained at a special bargain price at any IGA store in the area. The idea of this combination was that a subliminal message might be capable of building up a vague urge for Product X which could be given specific direction by the TV Special. Thus it was hypothesized that a combination of subliminal and ordinary persuasion would significantly increase sales of the food item involved.

Similarly, during the experimental weeks in which the subliminal message was the suggestion to "Watch Frank Edwards," a combination of persuasive techniques was possible. The subliminal persuasion to watch the news analyst theoretically increases the audience size. This should expose a larger number of people to the TV Special of that particular week. Thus, by an indirect process, the subliminal message should increase the sale of the food item involved.

These variations of subliminal suggestions and combinations of subliminal persuasion and TV Specials represent a rather complex design. Table 2 may make more clear the nature of the experimental treatments, the hypotheses involved in each, and the measure of effect used to evaluate the tenability of each hypothesis. It will be seen that the hypotheses concern the effects of subliminal persuasion to watch a particular program and buy specific products, and

TABLE 2
SUMMARY OF FIVE-WEEK EXPERIMENTAL PROGRAM

Experimental Condition	Hypothesis	Test of Effect
	First Experimental Week	
Subliminal suggestion to "Buy Product A" broadcast for five nights during feature film.	Subliminal persuasion alone will increase sales of the food product in the area reached by the TV signal.	The amount of increase in the sale of Product A in the area.
	Second Experimental Week	
Subliminal suggestion to "Buy Product A" broadcast for another five nights during feature film, followed by TV Special sale on Product A on the following news program.	Subliminal persuasion in combination with ordinary advertising of product at reduced price will increase the sale of Product A to a greater degree than ordinary advertising alone.	The amount of increase in the sale of Product A during the second week, checked against the effect of ordinary advertising as a control.
	Third Experimental Week	
Subliminal suggestion to "Watch Frank Edwards" broadcast during feature film for five nights. Also, TV Special on Product B broadcast during news program.	The increase in size of audience watching Frank Edwards as a result of subliminal suggestion will increase exposure to the TV Special on Product B and thereby increase the sale of Product B to a greater degree than if there were no subliminal suggestion.	The amount of increase in the sale of Product B during this experimental week, checked against the effect of the TV Special alone, as a control.
	Fourth Experimental Week	
Subliminal suggestion to "Watch Frank Edwards" continued for another five days during feature film. Also, TV Special on Product C broadcast during news program.	The audience size of the Frank Edwards program will significantly increase because of the ten two-hour broadcasts of the subliminal message during the third and fourth weeks. The effect will be to increase exposure to the TV Special on Product C, and thereby increase sale of Product C to a greater degree than by a TV Special alone.	A comparison of regular audience surveys made three months before the fourth experimental week and at the end of the fourth experimental week. The amount of increase in the sales of Product C during the experimental week checked against the effect of a TV Special alone, as a control.

Experimental Condition	Hypothesis	Test of Effect
	Fifth Experimental Week	
Subliminal suggestion to "Buy Product D" broadcast during the two-hour feature film for a five-day period. Also, TV Special on Product D broadcast during news program.	The combination of (1) the increased audience size from the conditions of the third and fourth week, (2) the subliminal suggestion to buy Product D, plus (3) the TV Special on Product D will increase the sales of Product D to a significantly greater degree than the increase due to a TV Special alone.	The amount of increase in the sale of Product D during the experimental week, checked against the effect of a TV Special alone, as a control.

of combinations of these subliminal efforts with more ordinary persuasive techniques. The measures of effect consist of checks on increases in the sale of the food items involved and checks, through viewer surveys, on increases in audience size for the news program involved.

A word should be said about the selection of the food items. Since there are obvious seasonal variations in the buying patterns of food items, the foods selected were staple items used in almost every household. Two kinds of preserved meats were involved, and two kinds of vegetable oils. Product A was bacon, product B was frankfurters, product C was shortening, and product D was margarine. Although, ideally, the *same* food item would have to be used for all tests to control variations in response to specific food products, this was impossible because what occurs during one week will have an effect on the sales of that food during the following week. While there are dangers from an experimental point of view in changing food items from week to week, it will be seen that no special problems of interpretation were introduced into the *present* research because of this.

THE FINDINGS

The first set of findings from the commercially broadcast test is summa-

rized in Table 3. The first row of the table shows the increase over "normal sales" resulting from the first experimental week. The increase is negligible, indicating that the subliminal message alone had no measurable effect as a persuasive device. The remaining experimental conditions, which represent various combinations of subliminal and more ordinary persuasive techniques, show rather substantial effects. Increases in sales range from 282 per cent to *over 500 per cent!* The question arises immediately as to the possible statistical significance of such dramatic changes in sales. To provide significance tests based on normal probability sampling, a stable measure of the variability of each normal sales array would be needed. The present estimates of normal sales are based on simple six-week averages and can lay no claim to being random samples of weekly sales figures. Longer-term estimates open the possibility of error due to seasonal variation. Ordinary tests of significance, then, cannot be used to evaluate the size of the sales increases. However, one estimate of the variability of an array is provided by its *range*. For each of the products in Table 3 the range between the greatest and smallest "normal" weekly sales is shown. It can be seen that, in each of the instances of a substantial increase in sales, the increase far exceeds the range of its correspond-

TABLE 3

EFFECTS OF SUBLIMINAL PERSUASION, AND COMBINATIONS OF SUBLIMINAL
PERSUASION AND MORE ORDINARY PERSUASIVE TECHNIQUES

Experimental Condition	Average Number of Units Sold per Week for Normal 6-week Period	Number of Units Sold during Experimental Week	Range°	Per Cent Increase above Normal Sales
1 week of subliminal promotion of Product A	6,143	6,204	6,026	1
2 weeks of subliminal promotion of Product A, with TV Special on Product A during second week	6,143	17,304	6,026	282
1 week of subliminal suggestion to "Watch Frank Edwards," with TV Special on Product B during same week	2,073	9,418	741	454
2 weeks of subliminal suggestion to "Watch Frank Edwards," with TV Special on Product C during second week	4,451	24,120	5,364	542
2 weeks of subliminal suggestion to "Watch Frank Edwards" followed by 1 week of subliminal promotion of Product D, with TV Special on Product D during same week	5,413	27,510	6,400	508

° Computed by determining the difference between the greatest and smallest number of units sold per week for the 6-week period of normal sales.

ing six-week array of normal sales. This indicates that these increases are all *highly unlikely* to be chance variations. We may conclude, then, that the combinations of subliminal messages and ordinary persuasive techniques were responsible for substantial increases in the sale of these products in the experimental area.

We must now consider the question as to the relative effects of the sublimi-nal component in these combinations of experimental treatments. That is, when a subliminal message is employed in combination with a more ordinary persuasive technique and a substantial effect occurs, can the effect of the subliminal message itself be partialed out? One method of determining this is to establish the degree of effect that is likely to result from the use of the more ordinary persuasive device alone. In

TABLE 4
EFFECTS OF THE TV SPECIAL ON THE SALE OF PRODUCTS WITH NO
SUBLIMINAL PROMOTION

Product	Average Number of Cases Sold per Week for Normal 6-week Period	Number of Cases Sold during TV Special Week	Range°	Per Cent Increase above Normal Sales
E	86	1,550	108	1,802
F	26	763	69	2,934
G	24	812	24	3,383
H	44	843	49	1,916

° Computed by determining the difference between the greatest and smallest number of cases sold per week for the 6-week period of normal sales.

terms of the present problem, this means establishing the increase in sales which is likely to occur when a product is given special advertising on a TV Special with no subliminal message in combination.

Table 4 summarizes the increases in sales that occurred for four food products which were given special advertising via the same TV Special procedure used in the experiment. These four food products were advertised shortly before the beginning of the present experiment. It is clear that the TV Special *without any subliminal aids* is capable of stimulating substantial increases in sales. Each of the increases shown in Table 4 exceeds the range of variability in its corresponding six-week period of normal sales. In fact, these increases are of such a substantial nature that their occurrence by chance is a remote possibility.

On the basis of this evidence we must conclude that the large sales increases which occurred after the experimental treatments, as shown in Table 3, were solely due to the ordinary advertising techniques involved in those treatments. This means that in terms of persuading an audience to purchase several standard food items, subliminal persuasion failed completely to produce any noticeable results, when used either singly or in combination with more ordinary techniques in a variety of ways.

We may now turn to the remaining

test of the effectiveness of televised subliminal persuasion. While the act of going to a store and purchasing specific food items may be regarded as relatively complex, the other behavior form under consideration is extremely simple—compliance with the suggestion to "Watch Frank Edwards." It requires only the viewer remain passively in front of his set and continue watching a particular channel. No muscular movement, decision, outlay of funds, or any other overt behavior form is involved in such compliance. If subliminal persuasion has any effectiveness, it should be capable of stimulating responses of this type.

Regularly scheduled audience surveys for all programs broadcast in the Indianapolis area are conducted by a commercial polling agency (American Research Bureau, Inc.). From data provided by these surveys, the degree to which the subliminal experimental broadcast increased the audience size for the Frank Edwards newscast could be determined. A "before" measurement of audience size was provided by a survey completed on April 14, three months before the experiment. On the basis of 216 tabulated diaries, the daily viewing trends for the Frank Edwards program (during a five-day period) were obtained for the Indianapolis area. A comparable "after" measurement of the daily viewing trends, based on 206 tabulated diaries, was obtained for the five-

TABLE 5
EFFECTS OF SUBLIMINAL PERSUASION ON INCREASING THE AUDIENCE
SIZE OF A NEWS PROGRAM

Day of Week	"Before"*		"After"†	
	Per Cent of Potential‡ Audience Viewing Program	Per Cent of Sets in Use	Per Cent of Potential‡ Audience Viewing Program	Per Cent of Sets in Use
Monday	4.6	45.8	2.9	46.0
Tuesday	5.6	44.5	1.5	44.7
Wednesday	4.6	44.0	2.9	43.2
Thursday	4.6	43.0	2.4	41.7
Friday	3.7	50.0	5.3	42.6
Weekly average	4.6	45.5	3.0	43.6

*Data for week ending April 14.
† Data for week ending July 13.
‡ Potential audience refers to the total number of television receivers in the survey area.

day period ending July 13, the end of the fourth experimental week.

The data obtained from these two surveys are summarized in Table 5. Comparison of the weekly averages of the proportions of the potential audience who were viewing that particular program show that the two-week subliminal effort to boost the size of the audience had no measurable effect. In fact, the size of the audience suffered a slight decline! Comparison with somewhat similar news programs offered at the same time on other channels in the Indianapolis area showed that this was not due to a seasonal decline in audience attendance to news programs.

In terms of the data as a whole, then, it is clear that it was possible in laboratory settings to achieve subliminal communication. However, the present attempt to translate this into subliminal persuasion was not successful. The present experiment attempted to avoid some of the difficulties involved in previous attempts to apply subliminal devices to television. That is, it attempted to couple the subliminal suggestion to actions that were very easy for the audience, or to actions which they regularly perform anyway. In the case of the simple action form,

there was not only a failure to increase the audience size but a slight decline in viewing which was not due to seasonal variation. No causal relationships are suggested. In the case of the subliminal attempts to persuade the audience to purchase particular food items, there was no evidence of increase in the sale of these items due to a subliminal message alone. There was evidence of dramatic increases in the sale of food items promoted with combinations of subliminal and ordinary persuasive devices. However, the increases which occurred were actually smaller than those which usually occur with the use of the ordinary advertising techniques alone. The subliminal component of those combinations, then, had no discernible effect.

COMMENTS

Several matters should be kept in mind in evaluating the results of this experiment. It would be premature to conclude that we do not need more experimentation with subliminal techniques of persuasion before we can fully evaluate their effectiveness. It is entirely possible that the one- and two-week exposures used in the present experiment were not enough. Perhaps the presentation of a message for a year or more would eventually predispose an audience to a given form of action. However, in addition to the negative findings of the present research, there are several other considerations which suggest that subliminal messages may be ineffective persuasive devices.

First, subliminal communication is a very *inefficient* form of communication at best. Although laboratory experiments do show "greater-than-chance" results, this often means only that a small percentage of subjects were able to distinguish a few more messages than they would have if they were just guessing. Messages presented in the ordinary way, at the level of awareness, are vastly more efficient for communicating.

Second, a frequently heard assumption regarding subliminal messages should be considered carefully. It has been widely assumed that because people are not aware of subliminal messages, they are somehow "helpless" against their suggestions. However, as a normal part of learning, audiences have developed "mental callouses" against many forms of persuasion. Such audiences may not be aware of their own behavior in this respect. There is perhaps just as much reason to assume that these protective habits would operate to *resist* subliminal persuasion as there is reason to assume that they would be ineffective against it.

Third, the whole notion of subliminal persuasion appears to be based upon an outmoded "psychological model," assuming that people will respond immediately and directly to any stimulus that is presented. As many students of communication have pointed out, this confusion is widespread in popular discussions of the influence of mass media on their audiences. It is incorrectly assumed that portrayals of violence and crime on television stimulate youngsters immediately and directly to be delinquents, that liquor advertising leads directly to alcoholism, etc., etc. A number of communication studies have shown that even simple acts such as trying a new food product, subscribing to a magazine, changing from one cosmetic to another, or prescribing a new drug to a patient are not simple S-R phenomena, but are imbedded in networks of social relationships.

Fourth, a last factor should be considered before attributing great persuasive power to subliminal messages. In a sense, subliminal messages have been a part of our everyday world for many decades! All of us are surrounded by a complex symbolic world in which advertising messages are thrust at us from every conceivable source. We are the target of messages from match covers, billboards, magazines, handbills, mailed folders, radio, television, and newspapers, to mention only a few. The ordinary individual could not possibly attend consciously in a month to the tidal wave of persuasive messages he encounters in a day. He may dimly perceive the content of *some* of these messages, even though they scarcely command his awareness, but we do not fear that he will be helplessly driven to buy every product whose message he perceives in such a marginal way.

Finally, while no single research project can be regarded as definitive or conclusive in such a complex matter, there was *absolutely no evidence whatever* that the subliminal messages broadcast in the present experiment had the slightest effect in persuading the mass audience. This was true even though the suggested acts were of a simple nature, of a type carried out normally by the mass audience as a matter of routine.

These considerations suggest that the current controversy with regard to the ethics of subliminal persuasion may be without factual basis. Those who have feared subliminal persuasion as an insidious process are probably more concerned than the facts warrant.

(2) Quantitative

47. Some Correlates of Coffee and Cleanser Brand Shares

SEYMOUR BANKS

A theory of market demand for brands must consider two major elements: first, the choice process within the mind of the consumer; and second, the marketing environment in which purchase takes place. This paper describes a model of market demands for brands of convenience goods and reports the results of a test of this model.

All discussion of demand in this paper is in terms of ratios, i.e., a brand's share of the market. If one attempted to deal with demand in an absolute sense, these ratios would have to be multiplied by a base which would consider such factors as the importance of the product in consumers' budgets and the level of national income. This is a task far greater than seems desirable at the moment, and one which is not necessarily required for realism. Many businesses consider primary demand trends to be out of their control, and evaluate their relative success in terms of selective demand position.

The general demand model may be written:

$$P_i = f_c(A_1, A_2, \dots) + f_1(B_1, B_2, \dots) + f_m(D_1, D_2, \dots) + f_m(E_1, E_2, \dots)$$
$$ C_i R_i W_i M_i$$

where P_i is a brand's share of the market. Market share is taken to mean a brand's share of the total volume of sales

From *Journal of Advertising Research*, Vol. 1, No. 4 (June, 1961), pp. 22-28. Copyright © 1961 by Advertising Research Foundation, Inc.

of the given product class in a certain geographical area.

The terms on the right of the equation are of two types. The first term (C_i) deals with consumer evaluation of the intrinsic attributes of a brand, and the remainder with the marketing efforts of the component elements of the channel of distribution: R for retailer, W for wholesaler and M for manufacturer.

The A's in the consumer term of the above equation are criteria by which consumers evaluate the intrinsic qualities of various brands of a given type of merchandise. For coffee, these qualities might include flavor, flavor consistency, bouquet, type of grind, and size and type of package. These criteria will differ from person to person in number and importance. Furthermore, since judgment is subjective, individuals with identical criteria may have different evaluations of a given brand. The evaluation of each brand on all criteria considered by a consumer leads to a consolidated judgment of that brand at that time.

This mental evaluation of brands by a consumer can be visualized as an archipelago with some peaks rising out of a sea while others are visible below the surface. Sea level corresponds to a level of acceptability for brands of a given product. The peaks represent scalar evaluations of the qualities of the various brands at a given time. Brands are considered acceptable in the sense that, by their intrinsic qualities alone, they would be considered as possible purchases. For example some brands of coffee may not be acceptable because they have too mild or too strong a flavor or do not come in the desired grind.

But the above picture holds only temporarily. As time passes, brands may lose their acceptability, either because their qualities have actually deteriorated or because other brands have been improved. Brands previously unacceptable may rise to acceptability by product improvement. A scouring cleanser, for example, which was changed from an abrasive to a detergent increased sales considerably.

Then too, the *level* of acceptability is subject to change. In times of shortage, consumers take almost any brand. But in a buyer's market, they will not accept substitutes for favored brands.

A purchase is made from among the acceptable brands but is not mechanically determined by an evaluation of value, either ordinal or cardinal. An acceptable product may cease to be bought because the customer who used it previously desires a change for change's sake. This satiation phenomenon appears to be random and is relevant only for individual decision; its effect probably washes out in groups (Banks, 1950).

The number of brands considered depends in part upon the extent of the consumer's experience and in part upon the nature of the product. The more experienced the consumer, the more brands he knows, but limits are imposed by attention and memory. Generally the consumer is more familiar with convenience goods than with shopping goods. In the case of shopping goods like appliances, a complete picture of brands is seldom available—the consumer shops not only to learn which brands are for sale, but often to discover the criteria by which he might evaluate the brands he has discovered.

The term of the demand equation starting with R represents selling effort by retailers for each brand considered.

The B's represent their performance of activities like special displays, demonstrations, recommendations to consumers, services rendered (large stock, credit and repair), return privileges, etc., on the brands he carries. The next term deals with efforts of wholesalers to push different brands, training courses for retailer salesmen, demonstrations, special price or credit concessions and so on. Finally, we have the term which represents the selling efforts of the manufacturers for each of their brands.

The rather simple assumptions implied by the form of equation used are not really satisfactory in representing the effect of a manufacturer's sales efforts. A sound marketing program calls for working at several levels simultaneously. Manufacturers merchandise new consumer advertising campaigns to wholesalers and retailers; retailers are affected by advertising campaigns addressed to the general public; price changes affect margins throughout the channel of distribution. The manufacturer's selling efforts and those of his wholesalers and retailers are often closely related. Because of this, the plus signs in the equation should be interpreted as general logical conjunctions rather than as arithmetical additions. Possibly multiplication signs would represent reality more closely.

Customers, retailers, wholesalers and manufacturers vary greatly in scope of activity and our equation must not be interpreted as giving equal weight to each of the terms. Formally, the f_c, f_r, f_w and f_m in the equation represent quite general functions of the factors inside the brackets.

METHOD

Two research techniques which are often used to determine the effect of marketing variables upon sales of brands are experimentation and regression analysis. In the first, the researcher controls the way in which the independent variables affect his test units. One example might be a sales test of a new package design versus an old, each package being used in a comparable sample of stores.

In the regression procedure, the researcher assumes a simple relationship between the market share of a brand and prices, promotional efforts, point of purchase advertising, etc., for it. The assumption is that the market share of a brand can be expressed as an equation, usually linear, which is of the form:

Brand share = a (price of the brand)
+ b (consumer's prefer-
ence rating) + etc.

By mathematical techniques we choose values of the coefficients a, b, c, etc., which best fit the observed facts. The researcher cannot control factors such as preference ratings for all the brands, but his mathematical procedures enable him to estimate the effect of each while the effects of the others are accounted for statistically. The regression procedure has administrative advantages, but will not yield the functional relationship among the variables studied.

The user of regression analysis assumes that:

1. The values of the independent variables are fixed and may be looked upon as population parameters. Often particular values are deliberately chosen.
2. For a given set of values of the independent variables, the resulting values of the dependent variable are normally distributed.
3. That the sample be drawn by a process of random selection (Anderson and Bancroft, 1951).

The research situation which we shall discuss has an additional complication in that all variables, both independent and dependent, are subject to error. Bartlett (1949), and more recently Acton (1959), have discussed procedures for dealing with this type of situation, but it should be noted that few appli-

cations have appeared in the literature.

In evaluating the results of tests of significance of regression coefficients, caution will be used. In a numerical example presented by Bartlett (1949), the 95 per cent confidence interval of the regression coefficient is 16 per cent larger, assuming both variables are subject to error, than when assuming the independent variable is stated or measured without error.

Our data were collected in early December 1950 from 165 Chicago housewives selected by area sampling procedures. Blocks were chosen at random and four respondents picked at random in each block. Purchases were measured about a week before information was collected on other variables but it was felt that the situation prevailing at the time of purchase could not differ materially from that a week later.

For both scouring cleanser and coffee, the interview covered the respondent's knowledge and use of the various brands, preference ratings on the brands she knew, and brands, quantities, and place of her last purchase. Information was also obtained on possibilities for exposure to advertising in terms of ownership of a radio or TV set, subscription or regular readership of magazines and Chicago newspapers. Respondents were classified into high, medium and low economic strata on the basis of the 1940 rent data for the block in which they lived; this last rating was subject to revision by the interviewer after inspection of the household furnishings and equipment.

The respondents were asked to state their preferences for brands of scouring cleanser and coffee by means of a thermometer rating device. One-half of the respondents made preference statements before the question of purchases was raised and the other half made similar preference statements after the interviewer had determined the brands on hand. The two preference distributions differed insignificantly; from which we inferred no bias induced by the order of questioning and the returns of both halves were combined.

Only the highest preference ratings made by respondents were considered. If a respondent placed several brands in the highest category she used, each brand received an equal fractional share of the rating. The sum of these ratings for all respondents gave the total number of highest-choice ratings per brand. This procedure is described elsewhere (Banks, 1950).

To obtain data on purchases, the interviewer asked to see all containers of the last purchase under the guise of obtaining code numbers. Only when the containers were reported destroyed (e.g., when coffee packed in bags had been put into canisters and the bag discarded) were housewives asked to tell what brand they had bought last. Brand shares were of total amount bought in last purchases.

After discussing brand preference and purchase with a respondent, it was easy to discover where her last purchase of scouring cleanser and coffee had been made. The interviewer then went to the designated store or stores (not infrequently the scouring cleanser and coffee were bought in different stores) as soon as possible after finishing a given block assignment of interviews, and for each of the brands carried observed the price (in cents per package for scouring cleanser, in cents per pound for coffee), the amount of stock displayed, and the presence of promotional effort and point of purchase displays.

The formal model of demand discussed at the beginning of this article must be simplified drastically for empirical research because it deals with a very large number of variables, most of which are extremely difficult to measure. The model became, after appropriate simplification, one of multiple linear regression. The following equation was set up to study the forces affecting market shares of brands of scouring cleanser and coffee.

$$P_1 = aX_1 + bX_2 + cX_3 + dX_4 + eX_5 + fX_6 + gX_7, \text{ where}$$

P_1 = Each brand's share of the sample's last purchase of the product.

X_1 = Consumer preference in terms of number of highest ratings per brand.

X_2 = Average price in cents per unit.

X_3 = Store coverage =
$$\frac{\text{No. stores stocking each brand, weighted by number shopping these stores}}{\text{Total number of users}}$$

X_4 = Index of stock display =
$$\frac{1 \ (\text{no. good shelf displays}) + 2 \ (\text{no. special displays}) \times 100}{\text{Total number of ratings}}$$

X_5 = Index of promotional effort =
$$\frac{\text{No. stores where brand carried offers of price deals or premium} \times 100}{\text{No. of stores stocking}}$$

X_6 = Index of Point of Purchase Advertising =
$$\frac{\text{No. stores where brand had POP effect} \times 100}{\text{No. of stores stocking}}$$

X_7 = Dollar expenditure for advertising in the three major media (newspaper, radio and magazines), Chicago, June through November 1950.

a,b,c,d,e,f,g are the regression coefficients which were computed mathematically.

Information on consumer advertising expenditures was obtained from three sources. A. C. Nielsen Company made

SEYMOUR BANKS

available (in private correspondence) radio, newspaper and magazine advertising expenditures for brands of scouring cleanser and coffee in metropolitan Chicago from June through November 1950. This was satisfactory for scouring cleanser but gave no information on advertising of chains' private brands of coffee. The Chicago *Tribune* made available unpublished data on total advertising expenditures of these chains in Chicago in newspapers during this period. Some chains were willing to state, also in private correspondence, what share of their local advertising budget was allocated to their private brands of coffee; for the others, a sample of newspapers was selected and the ratio of space found to be allocated to their brands of coffee was used as the share of their total advertising budget allocable to their private brands of coffee.

RESULTS

The data were analyzed to determine first, how successfully—as measured by the coefficient of multiple correlation—

the research model fitted the actual purchase pattern; and second, the relative importance of the different elements of the model, as measured by the size of their regression coefficients.

First we considered how closely each factor separately was related to brand shares. For this we examined the simple correlations. For both coffee and scouring cleanser, consumer preference rating and store coverage, themselves highly correlated, showed the highest simple correlation with market shares. For scouring cleanser, promotional effort was highly correlated with market shares, while advertising expenditure was poorly correlated. The reverse was true for coffee. For both products, advertising expenditure was more highly correlated with store coverage than with market share or any other variable.

Table 1 shows the regression coefficients which permit direct evaluation of the relative effect of the independent variables on the dependent variable, brand shares.

For the scouring cleanser equation, all coefficients were significant at the

TABLE 1

REGRESSION COEFFICIENTS BETWEEN BRAND SHARES AND
SEVEN MARKETING ACTIVITIES

Marketing Activity	Cleanser (N = 9) (Multiple R = .999)	Coffee (N = 21) (Multiple R = .792)
Brand Preference (a)	.368°	1.108†
Average Price (b)	− .436°	− .202
Store Coverage (c)	.150°	.609
Stock Display (d)	.224°	− .364
Promotional Effort (e)	.416°	.067
POP Advertising (f)	− .242°	− .207
Advertising Expenditure (g)	.143°	− .536°

° Significant at the five per cent level.
† Significant at the one per cent level.

For Cleanser:
$$P_1 = .368X_1 - .436X_2 + .150X_3 + .224X_4 + .416X_5 - .242X_6 + .143X_7$$
For Coffee:
$$P_1 = 1.108X_1 - .202X_2 + .609X_3 - .364X_4 + .067X_5 - .207X_6 - .536X_7$$

five per cent level of confidence. The most important factors in determining market shares of brands were price, promotional effort and brand preference. As might be expected, price is negatively related, while promotional effort and brand preference are positively related to market share. One apparent anomaly was that point of purchase advertising was negatively related.

For coffee, the regression model produced a coefficient of multiple correlation of .972, significant at the one per cent level of confidence. However, in contrast to the scouring cleanser data, only two of the marketing factors studied, brand preference and advertising expenditure, were found to have significant effects upon the share position of brands of coffee, while store coverage approached significance.

For scouring cleanser it was observed that there were relatively high correlations between the brand preference ratings and several of the variables measuring marketing activity. The question arose—need we consider preference at all in such a demand equation?

The question was answered by dropping preference as an independent variable and noting what happened to the fit of the regression equation. This made little difference: R^2 dropped from .9997 to .9903, a change of less than one per cent. The reason for this may be found in the results of the regression of these marketing variables on the preference. Ninety-three per cent of the variance in preference for brands of scouring cleanser was accounted for by variance in the six external marketing variables. All of the regression coefficients were significant beyond the five per cent level, with those of price, promotional effort and stock display being highest. Differences among these three were not significant.

For coffee, on the other hand, dropping the preference variable reduced R^2 from .9456 to .6063, a change of 35 per

centage points. Although the six-variable regression equation without preference for various brands of coffee still yielded a statistically significant multiple correlation coefficient, it is clear that these customers were more sensitive to the qualities of coffee brands than to the qualities of cleanser brands.

The linear equation based on six marketing variables did a satisfactory job of "explaining" shares of brands of scouring cleanser and coffee. However, there are advantages in reducing the number of variables. Other sets of regression equations were developed, using only the three marketing variables found to have the strongest relation to brand shares.

For scouring cleanser, the three used were price, store coverage and promotional effort. These three variables were quite effective in fitting the data; R^2 dropped from .9903 to .8892, only 10 per cent.

Because of the ease with which this three-variable equation could be computed, it was applied to various segments of the total sample. On the basis of information collected during the interview, respondents could be classified in the following ways: by income group; by whether they were exposed to much advertising; and by whether they shopped mostly at chain or independent stores.

Income was determined from 1940 Census rent data and modified by interviewer's evaluation of homes. To be considered as being "exposed to much advertising" they had to be exposed to three advertising vehicles other than radio programs. Type of store usually shopped was determined by questioning.

In a cross-classification of respondents by income level and stores shopped (see Table 2), it was found that the low income groups patronized independents to a much greater degree than did the two upper income groups. This was largely because few chains have units in the Negro and low income areas. There was no clear relationship between income and availability to advertising exposure.

Even when the total sample was split up, the regression coefficients for the scouring cleanser data remained significant except for respondents shopping at independent grocery stores. Promotional effort and distribution apparently were more important than price in "explaining" variations in scouring cleanser brand shares for the entire sample as well as for its different segments. However, all three coefficients were still significant beyond the one per cent level.

Between the various segments of the sample, some differences in importance of the three variables did emerge. Apparently chain store shoppers were more susceptible to promotional offers and deals for brands of scouring cleanser than housewives who shopped at independent stores; for the latter, availability was the most important factor. Those open to advertising exposure were equally affected by the store distribution of brands and the use of promotional effort.

Price also had a strong effect. Promotional effort was the only variable among the three tested to affect market share among those respondents not available to heavy advertising exposure.

Income seemed to have no effect upon the weights of the variables in the demand equation. This seems plausible since scouring cleanser is relatively cheap. It is interesting to note that disguised price reductions—in terms of special deals or offers—had a much stronger effect upon scouring cleanser brand shares than did actual price differences. This was equally true for all income groups.

A three-variable regression model was also fitted to the coffee data using the variables found to have highest correlation with market shares: price, store coverage and past six months' advertising expenditure.

It was found to yield a statistically significant fit, the coefficient of multiple correlation was significant at the one per cent level. However, the fit of the three-variable equation for coffee was substantially poorer than that for scouring cleanser. There are at least two reasons for this: the greater diversity of marketing patterns among the 21 brands of coffee than among the nine brands of scouring cleanser; and the greater importance of brand quality for coffee than for scouring cleanser.

For the entire sample, only store coverage had a statistically significant relation with market shares of coffee brands. Neither price nor advertising expenditure was found to have a significant effect upon market shares when the other two factors were held constant

The three-variable model was applied to various segments of the sample and statistically significant fits were obtained among chain store shoppers, those advertising prone and those in the high income group. Probably these three subgroupings overlapped so that the same respondents showed up under different headings.

Although the data were not statistically significant, an interesting situation held among the "manufacturer's brand" buyers. Among those people who bought a manufacturer's brand (Hills Brothers, Chase & Sanborn, Stewarts, etc.), advertising actually appeared to have a negative relation with sales. Examination of the raw data indicated that, during the period studied, Maxwell House was spending 40 per cent of the total advertising volume in Chicago for these six brands, but was receiving only 16 per cent of their total sales. In contrast, Manor House was spending only nine per cent of the total advertising volume, but receiving almost 30 per cent of total sales.

CONCLUSIONS

The more general model discussed at the beginning of this paper has illustrative value for teaching purposes.

TABLE 2

REGRESSION COEFFICIENTS BETWEEN CLEANSER BRAND SHARES AND
THREE MARKETING ACTIVITIES: BY STRATA

	Regression Coefficients			
Group	Average Price	Weighted Store Coverage	Promotional Effort	Multiple Correlation Coefficient
Entire Sample	− .291†	.491†	.603†	.943†
Chain Store	.083	− .049	1.016†	.977†
Independents	− .045	.601*	.343	.832*
Adv. Prone	− .338†	.587†	.530†	.938†
Non-Prone	− .037	.164	.831†	.936†
High Income	.044	.210	.837†	.919†
Medium Income	.974	.130	.867†	.935†
Low Income	.029	.162	.809†	.909*

* Significant at the five per cent level.
† Significant at the one per cent level.

It formulates problems of demand in marketing terms by dealing with market share data obtained by differentiated brands whose owners compete with all the tools in their respective arsenals. Students are thus presented with a device for considering the major variables affecting sales.

The demand model easily accommodates the familiar discussion of convenience, shopping and specialty goods. For example, the demand model for convenience goods would likely show store coverage, point of purchase display and promotional effort to be most important in affecting sales. On the other hand, for specialty goods preference would probably be the only variable of major importance.

The model tested by the data presents more of a mixture of values. Such a regression model can approximate the importance of various factors affecting market shares, and the relationships between these factors. Surveys are less helpful on this point since people seldom can evaluate the relative importance of the factors impinging upon their purchase decisions.

The results of regression analysis should be considered as first approxima-

tions for several reasons. Foremost is the fact that they show only co-variation, not cause and effect. The regression analysis is useful to point out the factors to be used in experimentation, but should not be considered as a substitute for it.

Findings from the regression model hold only for the range of observations available in the data. Promotional effort was found to have a stronger relationship than price with brand shares of scouring cleanser. But the range of prices was quite narrow, 8.6 to 12.9 cents per can. Whoever breaks through these limits may well find price to have a great effect upon market shares.

Another caution in the use of the regression analysis is that it yields only over-all relationships. In any market, some brands are declining in market shares, others are rising, while still others are merely holding their own. The regression procedure gives coefficients which are actually averages of the coefficients for the individual brands. These results may not apply to any one brand.

Marketing strategies usually call for manipulating several variables simultaneously. Manufacturers merchandise their coming advertising campaigns to their retailers, who respond by improving stock holdings and displays and by putting up point of purchase advertising sent them. Private brands are usually offered in only a few stores; but in these stores they are usually given the best locations, largest stock displays and massive point of purchase advertising displays. Manufacturers' brands, especially in convenience goods, tend toward 100 per cent coverage but with less prominence of display within stores. Regression analysis is not the best way to cope with these different relationships between several independent variables.

Finally, regression analysis is a quantitative procedure and uses essentially quantitative evaluations of data. It is quite likely that many relationships are distorted by the units we use to express these quantities. Advertising is the most important case in point though the problem also arises with premiums and deals. If the effect of advertising were proportional to expenditure on it, then the firm which spent the most for advertising would sell the most product. However, this does not happen (Borden, 1942). Advertising effect depends not only upon magnitude of expenditure but also upon the motivating power of the copy and upon the media used. Failure of advertising expenditure to correlate with sales does not mean that advertising is ineffective, but may mean only that the measuring procedure failed to evaluate properly the strengths of various campaigns.

Implicit in the model presented is the assumption that all variables act instantaneously. This assumption is open to serious doubt. An effort was made to take different time lags into consideration by considering advertising expenditures for the previous six months, while all other variables were assumed to be acting at the time of the research.

This was a guess. It was found that the correlation of brand sales with the previous year's advertising was slightly higher than with the data of the shorter period, but the improvement was not significant. The varying time lag of different variables is certainly one of the most important matters of concern to marketing directors yet little or no research has been devoted to it.

I have said much of the limitations of the regression model but little of its value. I believe it offers real advantages. For relatively little expenditure, a substantial amount of material can be collected and evaluated. The simple correlations between market shares and the independent marketing variables will give a picture of the marketing strategies being used for the brands of a given product class, plus relationships between consumers' appreciation of the qualities of brands and external marketing variables. Finally, the findings of the multiple regression analysis can be considered a first approximation of the relative importance of these marketing variables — especially if more faith is put in findings of no effect than in findings of much effect.

REFERENCES

Acton, F. S. *The Analysis of Straight Line Data*. New York: John Wiley and Sons, 1959, Chapter 5.

Anderson, R. L. and T. A. Bancroft. *Statistical Theory in Research*. New York: McGraw-Hill Book Company, 1951.

Banks, Seymour. The Relationships Between Preference and Purchase of Brands. *Journal of Marketing*, Vol. 15, No. 2, October 1950, pp. 145-157.

Bartlett, M. S. Fitting a Straight Line when Both Variables are Subject to Error. *Biometrics*, Vol. 5, 1949, pp. 207-212.

Borden, N. H. *The Economic Effects of Advertising*. Chicago: R. I. Irwin, Inc., 1942, Chapter 8.

Ezekiel, M. *Methods of Correlation Analysis, 2nd ed*. New York: John Wiley and Sons, 1941, Chapter 21.

48. A New Way to Determine Buying Decisions

EDGAR A. PESSEMIER

SOME QUESTIONS

If we raise the price of our brand, what share of the market are we likely to lose if competitors do not follow suit? Or, if we fail to follow a general price increase, what additional share of the market can we expect to obtain?

Of the buyers lost to competing brands, what brands will they tend to buy? How resistant are the buyers of our brand and competing brands to switching to a new brand?

Effective answers to such questions would help to reduce the guesswork entering into management's decisions concerning price, product design, and promotional activities. So, a pilot study was carried out to see if useful answers could be obtained.

The results were so promising that there is every indication that the experimental method employed can be very useful to marketing management.

Both the advantages and limitations of experimental studies of consumer behavior are well known.[1] When experiments are conducted in the market, realism is preserved and the subjects

From *Journal of Marketing*, Vol. 24, No. 2 (October, 1959), pp. 41-46, by permission of the American Marketing Association.
[1] See, for example, Edward Hawkins, "Methods of Estimating Demand, *The Journal of Marketing*, Vol. 21 (April, 1957), pp. 430-438; and Harper W. Boyd, Jr., and Ralph Westfall, *Marketing Research* (Homewood, Ill.: Richard D. Irwin, Inc., 1956), pp. 79-102.

respond naturally. However, the location of the experiment may make it impossible to control all the important variables, and conditions of observation may prevent the accumulation of accurate data at reasonable cost. On the other hand, it is relatively simple to conduct experiments in a controlled environment. The principal weakness is the artificiality of the setting, and the fact the individual is aware that his conduct is under surveillance.

Therefore, it seemed desirable to use simple approximations of the market. Experiments were designed which permitted people to make simulated shopping trips. Their goal, as on a real shopping trip, was to maximize the satisfaction that could be obtained from a combination of merchandise and money.

Each participant was told how much money he had available to spend, the assortment of brands available in each class of goods for which he was "shopping," and the price of each item. The means by which he could maximize his satisfaction were defined by the funds and assortments available on each shopping visit. If he "bought" foolishly, he "acquired" a group of items and an amount of "change" from his purchase that gave him less than maximum satisfaction. Careful buying reduced the chances of making a poor choice and increased the reward of having made a wise choice.

After each experiment one "shopper,"

selected on a random basis, was given the actual items and change called for by the selections made during one of his shopping trips. Emphasis on price was somewhat exaggerated by listing the items and their prices in a manner that encouraged comparison. However, failure to pay off on every shopping trip tended to offset this bias. The procedure followed created a fairly close parallel to real shopping conditions.

THE STUDY

Business-administration students at the State College of Washington were selected as subjects. The first step was to ask the 103 subjects which brands of tooth paste and cigarettes they customarily purchased for personal use.

The second step was to prepare "assortment sheets" which listed all the brands available at the student book store in the selected classifications, plus an additional item in each classification labeled "A New Brand." The regular prices at which these items could be purchased were also noted. The basic assortments used in the experiments were those that the student would have found at a point in time in a retail store in which he frequently shopped. To eliminate the positional bias of a brand on a sheet, a brand's position in a column was changed from sheet to sheet.

Three separate experiments were conducted: experiment X, experiment Y, and experiment Z.

For the X experiment, the price of each subject's preferred brands was increased a different amount on each of ten successive shopping trips. Thus, he was faced with deciding whether he would continue to purchase his preferred brands, or whether he would switch to some other brands.

In the Y experiment, each subject faced the same condition with respect to his preferred brands; but he was given only one other item, "A New Brand," to which he could switch in each classification.

In the Z experiment, the price of each subject's preferred brands was held constant, but all other brands in a classification were reduced by varying amounts on each shopping trip.

When the three sets of ten assortment sheets had been prepared for each subject, the subjects were assembled in groups of about thirty-five. They were shown samples of the merchandise, told about the method of paying off on a shopping trip, given instructions for handling the sets of sheets, and then asked to make simulated shopping trips at normal shopping speed, checking items that would maximize the value to them of a "mix" of merchandise and money. At the conclusion of each experiment, one subject was selected at random to receive the merchandise and change called for by his decisions on one of his shopping trips.

ANALYSIS OF RESULTS

Before considering how the consumer responds to his own brand, a seller should know something about the attitudes of buyers toward various classes of goods, and especially the particular class of goods to which his product belongs. Patterns of brand loyalty can be derived for the X experiment for individual classes of goods. Figure 1 shows the brand-loyalty profile, or cumulative percentages of buyers switching brands at various price increases, for two classes of goods: tooth paste and cigarettes.

The flatter the curve, the higher is the brand loyalty, since larger price increases were required to encourage brand switching and fewer buyers were willing to switch. For tooth paste, for which buyers have a relatively low degree of brand loyalty, 53 per cent of all buyers could be switched to a second-choice brand with a 3-cent increase in the price of their favorite brand. In the case of cigarettes, a 5-cent increase was called for to get 58 per cent of the buyers to switch brands. Also note the

FIGURE 1

COMPARISON BY CLASSES OF GOODS OF THE CUMULATIVE PERCENTAGES OF BUYERS
WHO SWITCHED BRANDS AS THEIR PREFERRED BRANDS INCREASED IN PRICE

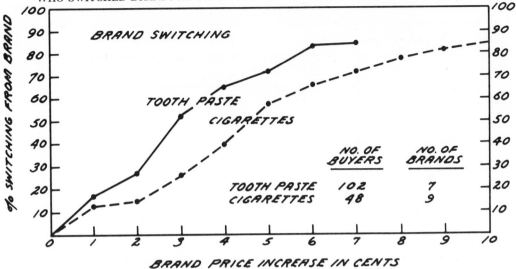

relative impact of 1-cent and 2-cent increases in price.

For each class of goods, a sizable number of buyers have very low brand loyalties. These individuals switch, on the smallest increase in price; but then there is a substantial fall-off in the number who will switch until buyers are faced with a price increase larger than 2 cents. Therefore, in many cases, it may be wiser to make a 2-cent rather than a 1-cent price increase.

However, there is a good deal of variation from brand to brand in the behavior of buyers faced with increasing prices, as will be shown later. Decisions with respect to a given brand could not be made without looking at its marketing characteristics.

In Figures 2 through 5, brands are lettered in alphabetical order, beginning with the brand holding the largest market share and proceeding through the less popular brands. Patterns of the type developed in Figures 2 and 4 will be referred to as brand-switching patterns.

Detailed findings in the X experiment for tooth paste and for cigarettes will be given.

TOOTH PASTE

BRAND SWITCHING

Figure 2 shows that tooth paste Brand A has a very strong position in the market but that few buyers of this brand continued to buy it when it had to be purchased at the maximum premium of 7 cents. On the other hand, Brand B has a good deal smaller share of the market than Brand A; but those who prefer Brand B were very loyal to it.

Surprisingly, those who switched from this brand did not switch to the leading Brand A as readily as to Brand E which holds a very small share of the market. In the minds of users, apparently the characteristics of Brand B and Brand E were similar. If Brand E is trying to expand its market, the current users of Brand B, in spite of their generally strong loyalties, may be susceptible to being switched to Brand E. On the other hand, if Brand B is trying to switch

FIGURE 2
COMPARISON OF BRAND-SWITCHING PATTERNS
FOR INDIVIDUAL BRANDS OF TOOTH PASTE

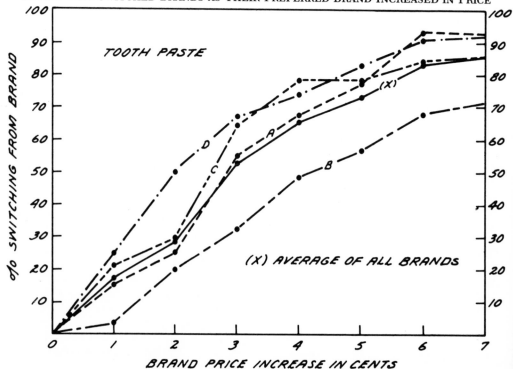

BRAND	ORIG. PRICE	NUMBER PREFERRING BRAND	DID NOT SWITCH	SWITCHED TO
A	31¢	40	A	B C D E
B	31¢	25	B	A C E F
C	31¢	14	C	A B D E F G
D	31¢	12	D	A B C E
ALL OTHERS	31¢	11		A B G
7	TOTAL	102		5 0 5 10 15 20 25 30 35 NUMBER OF BUYERS

buyers to itself, appeals to the types of customers who buy Brand A and the lesser brands would probably be most effective.

The brand-switching pattern of Brand C indicates that it is a product with moderate acceptance whose users are not particularly strong in their loyalties. The most distinguishing feature of Brand C's pattern is the fact that several buyers of this brand were willing to switch to Brand G which was "A New

FIGURE 3
COMPARISON BY BRANDS OF THE CUMULATIVE PERCENTAGES OF TOOTH PASTE
BUYERS WHO SWITCHED BRANDS AS THEIR PREFERRED BRAND INCREASED IN PRICE

Item." As a group, the buyers of Brand C were more venturesome than those who bought the other popular brands.

Apparently brand-switching patterns for a classification, if available at regular intervals, could reveal significant trends in consumer attitudes. If these patterns are viewed in the light of the changing prices, products, and promotional policies of the various brand sellers, it should be possible to draw useful conclusions about the effectiveness of these policies and to adjust marketing methods to meet changing conditions.

BRAND LOYALTY

Figure 3 shows brand-loyalty profiles. Each curve represents the cumulative percentage of those who switched to a second choice brand at various increases in the price of their preferred brand. The steep curve for Brand D shows that the buyers of this brand could be switched to a second choice brand by a relatively small increase in the price of their preferred brand. The seller of this brand would lose 25 per cent of his market share if he increased his price by 1 cent and if other sellers failed to follow his lead.

In contrast, the seller of Brand B could raise the price of his brand under similar conditions, and expect to lose only 4 per cent of his customers to other brands.

Figures 2 and 3 indicate that, in general, there is a relationship between how "loyal" buyers are to a brand and the share of the market held by the brand. Occasionally, however, a brand that holds a small share of the market may have a large proportion of unusually loyal buyers. This may be explained in either of two ways. The brand might have developed a product image or special features that are unusually effective in satisfying a relatively small segment of the market; or the product could be one with a rather wide appeal that is new and growing in market position. Either of these conditions could account for the relative strength of Brand B.

CIGARETTES

BRAND SWITCHING

Some of the same conditions that appear in the tooth paste classification were found for cigarettes. Figure 4

FIGURE 4

COMPARISON OF BRAND-SWITCHING PATTERNS
FOR INDIVIDUAL BRANDS OF CIGARETTES

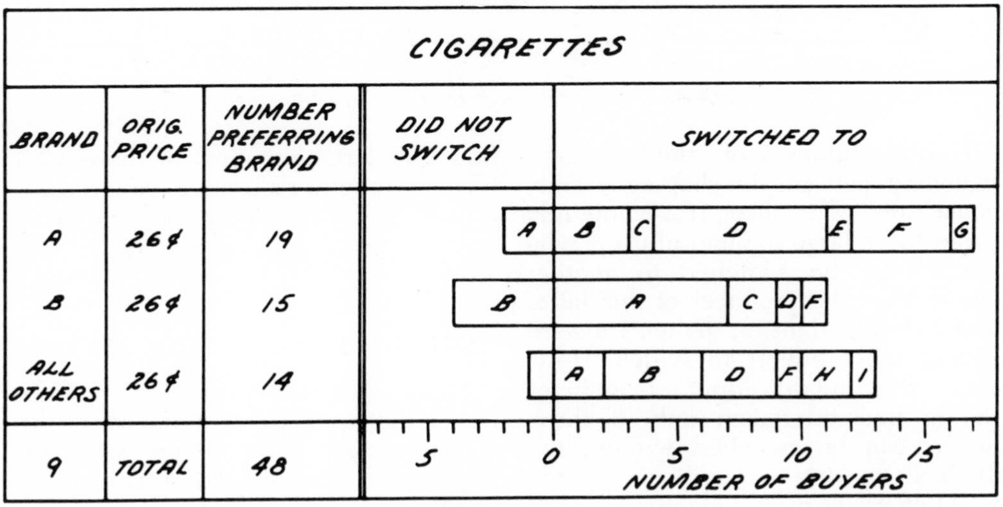

shows that the leading Brand A was not able to hold many of its customers through the full 10-cent range that its prices were increased. However, unlike the leading brand in the tooth paste classification, those who switched to a second choice brand tended to select a brand ranking below the two most popular brands.

Brand B, the second ranking in popularity, had users who were relatively loyal; but, of those who did switch, Brand A obtained an unusually large share. In other words, Brand A was fairly vulnerable to lesser brands, while Brand B was vulnerable to the leading Brand A.

BRAND LOYALTY

The brand-loyalty profiles in Figure 5 for Brands A and B reveal some facts relevant to the above question. As Brand A's price advances 1 and 2 cents, buyers remained rather loyal; but for price increases of 3 or more cents loyalty fell off rapidly.

In the case of Brand B, the opposite was true. Users who could be switched tended to switch in relatively large numbers when the price was increased 1 cent, but were lost in smaller numbers as the price continued to advance. By comparing brand-switching patterns with brand-loyalty profiles, a seller may

FIGURE 5

COMPARISON BY BRANDS OF THE CUMULATIVE PERCENTAGES OF CIGARETTE
BUYERS WHO SWITCHED BRANDS AS THEIR PREFERRED BRANDS INCREASED IN PRICE

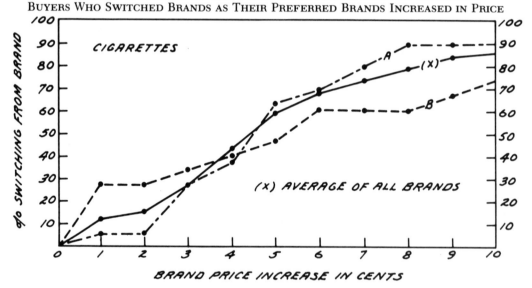

The usefulness of these brand-switching patterns in shaping promotional policies is clear. If a competing brand has a large number of users who can readily be switched to another brand, then the producer of this latter brand should slant his policies toward getting these buyers to switch. However, this modification of policies should be undertaken only if these buyers can be switched without the producer making extraordinary promotional efforts or price reductions.

find that large numbers of those who buy a competitor's product have a willingness to switch to his brand; and these buyers show low brand loyalty.

IMPLICATIONS OF THE STUDY

Many additional types of information can be obtained by experiments of the sort described. The sample size will depend on the desired reliability. A fixed sample or panel seems desirable, particularly if data are collected as often as once a year, and if the subjects are paid on the basis of one shopping trip per data-collecting contact.

Simulated shopping trips can be set up by substituting photographic reproductions of a price-marked assortment for each assortment sheet. By preparing standard sets of reproductions in advance, the whole procedure for conducting simulated shopping trips could be improved. To simplify handling data and increase their accuracy, buying decisions could be recorded on a medium that can be processed electronically.

The implications from this study are important. It demonstrates that large amounts of significant data about consumer behavior can be gathered rapidly at low cost by controlled experiments. And the experiments show that the types of information obtained could be especially helpful in making marketing decisions.

49. Input-Output Relations of the Auto Industry

FEDERAL RESERVE BANK OF CLEVELAND

The relative importance of the auto industry in the American economy is indicated by its contribution to the fluctuations of a number of major economics series.[1] If industries closely allied to autos were also taken into account, the role of autos obviously would be correspondingly larger. In this connection, 1963 data indicate that car sales, accessory equipment including tires, petroleum products, and the various services and fees associated with purchasing and maintaining automobiles, amounted to about 8.3 percent of Gross National Product, as compared with "auto product" as such, which accounted for 4.2 percent of Gross National Product.

This type of measurement, however, throws little light on the interindustry relationships in which the auto industry is involved; such relationships should be examined in order to improve understanding of both direct and indirect factors surrounding the role played by the auto industry in the economy. In recent years, development of input-output tables has facilitated the study of such industrial interrelationships. Pioneered by Harvard economist Wassily Leontief, the input-output approach reveals, for a particular industry, both the utilization of goods and services from supplying sectors and the distribution of its output to other industries and final markets.

A comprehensive set of input-output tables, pertaining to the American economy of 1947, was published in 1952 by the Bureau of Labor Statistics. In 1964, a new, preliminary set of tables for the 1958 economy was issued by the Office of Business Economics of the U.S. Department of Commerce.

Since input-output tables indicate the detailed interdependence of industries, they are, in essence, studies of production functions; in other words, input-output tables indicate how much output can result for individual industries, given certain quantities and combinations of inputs. Because the tables represent only a single year, however, they provide a technological portrait of the economy only at a particular time.

The input-output approach has several advantages. For the individual firm, the tables are useful in comparing the distribution of the firm's output with that of the entire industry in order to ascertain relative marketing emphasis. Also, the tables can show the permeating effects of factor price changes, particularly labor costs. In addition, it is possible to trace the effects of foreign trade on the domestic economy through examination of the inputs and outputs of those industries involved in foreign competition. Finally, since the tables indicate the requirements for increases in production, they can be especially important in times of national mobilization.

On the other hand, the tables possess certain inherent constraints. The most

From *Economic Review* (January, 1965), pp. 19-27.
[1] See "Some Perspective on Autos," *Economic Review*, Federal Reserve Bank of Cleveland, January, 1965.

CHART 1
ALLOCATION OF AUTO INDUSTRY OUTPUT TO FINAL DEMAND

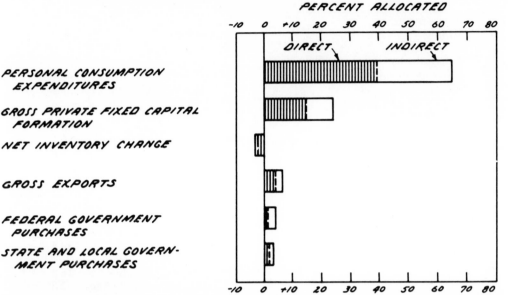

Source of Data: Table B, "The Interindustry Structure of the United States; A Report on the 1958 Input-Output Study," *Survey of Current Business*, November, 1964, Office of Business Economics, U.S. Department of Commerce.

important, perhaps, is the assumption that all industries have a constant cost function, or in other words, that the cost per unit of output does not vary with changes in aggregate production. Also, it is implicitly assumed that price changes in particular factors of production will not induce the substitution of other factors. Moreover, there is the implication that technical coefficients of production do not change appreciably over time, which they probably do in a number of cases. The latter is an important consideration because of the lag that usually exists between the year to which the figures pertain and the publication date of the tables.

DIRECT INPUTS AND OUTPUTS

A concise picture of the auto industry, based on 1958 relationships, can be obtained by selecting appropriate items from the standard input-output tables.[2]

_____
[2] The tables are shown in "The Interindustry

Auto industry purchases from and sales to various industrial groups are indicated in Table 1.[3] In addition, the input side shows the value added by the auto industry while the output side reveals the distribution of output according to final demand.[4]

_____
Structure of the United States; a Report on the 1958 Input-Output Study", *Survey of Current Business*, November 1964, Office of Business Economics, U.S. Department of Commerce.
[3] The industry is officially described as the "Motor Vehicles and Equipment Industry" in the 1958 Input-Output Tables. References to the industry in this article utilize the designation "autos".
[4] "Inputs" do not include capital equipment. All capital purchases are treated as final expenditures and are included in the "gross private fixed capital formation" category of final demand of the supplying industry. (See output side of Table I.) This is done for two reasons: (1) it is consistent with procedures used in the National Income Accounts, and (2) since capital equipment obviously will produce output for more than one year, the relationship between capital purchases and output in a particular year will not be stable.

As an illustration of how capital equipment is treated in the input-output tables, assume General

TABLE 1
INPUT-OUTPUT SCHEDULE FOR THE AUTO INDUSTRY

Input	Percent	Outputs	Percent
Purchases from:		Sales to:	
Mining	0.1	Agriculture	0.2
Construction	0.3	Mining	*
Auto industry	29.0	Construction	*
Other manufacturing	30.1	Auto industry	29.0
Transportation, com-		Other manufacturing	0.4
munications, & pub-		Transportation, communi-	
lic services	2.6	cations, & public	
Wholesale & retail		services	0.4
trade	3.1	Wholesale & retail trade	0.7
Finance, insurance, &		Services	4.8
real estate	0.7	Govt. enterprises	0.1
Services	2.7		
Govt. enterprises	0.2	Total sales	35.6%
Other industries	2.1		
Total purchases	70.9%	Final demand	
Value added	29.0%	Personal consumption	
		expenditures	39.2
		Gross private fixed	
		capital formation	15.2
		Net inventory changes	−2.3
		Gross exports	3.9
		Federal government	
		purchases	1.3
		State & local govt.	
		purchases	1.9
		Total final demand	59.2%
		Transfers to other industries[a]	5.0%
TOTAL INPUTS[b]	99.9%	TOTAL OUTPUTS[b]	99.8%

*Negligible
[a]Refers to the output of goods considered secondary to the industry, that is, those that would not come under the definition of goods produced by the "Motor Vehicles and Equipment Industry". Such goods are treated in this manner, rather than being redefined as the primary output of another industry, because of the difficulty of isolating the inputs necessary for the secondary goods. The assumption is made that the secondary output of an industry is a constant portion of its total output.
[b]Totals are less than 100 percent because of rounding.
Source: Tables 1 and 2 in "The Interindustry Structure of the United States; a Report on the 1958 Input-Output Study," Survey of Current Business, November 1964, Office of Business Economics, U.S. Department of Commerce.

It should be noted that although only 39.2 percent of the auto industry's output was distributed to consumer final demand, this figure represents

Motors buys a computer from Sperry Rand and sells a locomotive to New York Central Railroad. The purchase of the computer will be classified under the "gross private fixed capital formation" heading of final demand for the "Office, Computing and Accounting Machines" industry. But the transaction does not affect the accounts of the automotive industry. The sale of the locomotive will be classified in the same way, but for the "Motor Vehicles and Equipment" industry.

only direct sales to consumers and does not include intra-industry transactions, for example, sales of bodies and accessories by subcontractors, for the purpose of furthering the production of other final demand goods. Chart 1 shows both the direct and indirect allocation of the auto industry's output to various final demand categories. Including the indirect aspect, it can be seen that 64.7 percent of the industry's output was devoted to personal consumption expenditures. (Note that the parts of the bars on the left side of Chart 1 correspond to the final demand portion of "Output" in Table 1.)

It is evident from Table 1 that in terms of both inputs and outputs, the manufacturing sector of the economy is important to the auto industry. Table 2 (A,B) shows the distribution of the sources of manufacturing inputs as well as the distribution of outputs to manufacturing. The auto industry provides to itself 29.5 percent of its total input requirements and nearly half of its requirements from manufacturing industries (29.5 percent compared with 59.1 percent). The remaining half of requirements from manufacturing industries is distributed widely among several industries. On the output side, virtually all of the auto industry's production allocated to the manufacturing sector is self-consumed.

The relatively high consumption by the auto industry of its own production should perhaps be explained. Automotive manufacturing can be characterized

generally as the assembling of components produced by either a firm's own subsidiaries or by independent manufacturers. Since the output of a component firm or division (producing, for example, sparkplugs, batteries, engines, frames, etc.) is considered final production from the viewpoint of the firm itself, there occurs a disproportionate amount of intra-industry sales. The high proportion of auto industry output allocated to self-consumption thus refers to sales of components rather than industry usage of cars or trucks.[5]

---

[5] Only two other industries consume more of their own output than does the auto industry—"Broad and Narrow Fabrics, Yarn and Thread Mills" which consumes 33.9 percent of its own output and "Primary Nonferrous Metals Manufacturing" which consumes 29.6 percent. (See Table 1, "The Interindustry Structure of the United States; A Report on the 1958 Input-Output Study," *Survey of Current Business*, November 1964, Office of Business Economics, U.S. Department of Commerce.)

TABLE 2

AUTO INDUSTRY AND SELECTED OTHER INDUSTRIES

	Direct Purchases as % of Total Inputs of Auto Industry A	Direct Sales to Other Industries as % of Total Output of Auto Industry B	Direct Purchases as % of Total Output of Named Industry C	Direct and Indirect Requirements Per Dollar of Delivery to Final Auto Demand D
Manufacturing				
Motor vehicles & equipment	29.5%[a]	29.0%[a]	29.0%	$1.43
Primary iron & steel manufacturing	8.5	0	10.3	0.20
Other fabricated metal products	3.5	0	12.5	0.06
Stampings, screw machine products & bolts	3.0	0	18.8	0.05
Rubber & miscellaneous plastics products	2.8	0	9.1	0.05
Misc. electrical machinery, equipment & supplies	1.5	°	21.0	0.02
Primary nonferrous metals mfg.	1.1	0	2.6	0.05
Metalworking machinery & equipment	1.1	0	7.0	0.02
Glass & glass products	1.0	0	10.6	0.02
Misc. fabricated textile products	0.7	0	6.6	0.01
Machine shop products	0.6	0	8.4	0.01
General industrial machinery & equipment	0.6	0	2.8	0.01
Radio, TV, & communication equipment	0.5	0	1.9	0.01
Aircraft & parts	°	0.2	0	°
Farm machinery & equipment	0.1	0.1	0	°
Nonmanufacturing				
Wholesale & retail trade	3.1	0.7	0.7	0.08
Business services	2.4	°	2.3	0.05
Gross imports of goods & services	2.3	0	4.9	0.06
Transportation & warehousing	2.0	0.4	1.2	0.07
Electric, gas, water & sanitary services	0.5	0	0.5	0.03
Business travel, entertainment & gifts	0.4	0	1.5	0.02
Auto repair & services	°	4.8	0.1	°
State & local government enterprises	°	0.1	0.1	0.01
Livestock & livestock products	0	0.1	0	°
Other agricultural products	0	0.1	0	0.01

°Negligible
[a]Conceptually, the direct purchases of an industry of its own output should equal the industry's direct sales to itself. However, a slight deviation is incurred because of computational procedures.
Source: Tables 1, 2 and 3 in "The Interindustry Structure of the United States; A Report on the 1958 Input-Output Study," **Survey of Current Business,** November 1964, Office of Business Economics, U. S. Department of Commerce.

CHART 2

HYPOTHETICAL EXAMPLE OF THE RELATIONSHIP BETWEEN
DIRECT AND INDIRECT REQUIREMENTS AND FINAL AUTO OUTPUT

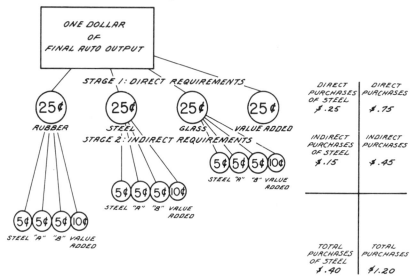

Of the various industries that contribute to automotive production, many are highly dependent on this industrial buyer. Table 2 (C) lists various industries and the percentage of their output going to the automotive industry. Excluding the fact that the automotive industry is its own biggest supplier, the industry is the biggest single customer of the output of four other industries: Rubber and Miscellaneous Plastics Products; Stampings, Screw Machine Products and Bolts; Metalworking Machinery and Equipment; and Miscellaneous Electrical Machinery, Equipment and Supplies.

ADDITION OF INDIRECT REQUIREMENTS

Through utilization of the particular input-output table that shows total requirements (both direct and indirect) for various industries, it is easy to ascertain the effect that a change in production of one industry will have on others. For example, as Table 2 (D) indicates, a one dollar increase in final demand of the automotive industry will necessitate a 5-cent increase in the output of the rubber industry, a 20-cent increase in primary iron and steel manufacturing, a 7-cent increase in transportation and warehousing, and an 8-cent increase in wholesale and retail trade. Total requirements (both direct and indirect) per dollar of delivery to final demand of the automotive industry amount to slightly over $2.65.[6]

At first glance, it may appear inconsistent that it should require $2.65 of goods and services to produce one dollar of final demand. However, it must be kept in mind that the requirements' figure represents the total sales activity that leads to a specific amount of final output; the one dollar addition to final demand is the increment to Gross National Product while the $2.65 is the financial sum of the intermediate steps in the production process that led up to the final demand output.

A simple hypothetical illustration can show the difference between direct and indirect requirements. Assume that the

---

[6] Table 3, 1958 Input-Output Study, *Survey of Current Business*, November 1964, Office of Business Economics, U.S. Department of Commerce.

auto industry obtains all of its direct requirements from only three industries: rubber, steel, and glass. (See Chart 2.) These industries, in turn, obtain their direct requirements from the steel industry and two other industries. Thus, in stage 1, one dollar of auto output might necessitate 25 cents each of rubber, steel, and glass output.[7] In stage 2, however, 25 cents of rubber production requires 5 cents each of steel, industry "A," and industry "B." The same holds true for obtaining 25 cents worth of steel and glass. Therefore, considering only these first two simple stages, the hypothetical illustration would show that one dollar of final auto output necessitates 25 cents worth of steel directly and an additional 15 cents worth of steel indirectly. Also, the total purchases involved in order to produce one dollar of final auto output add up to $1.20.

MEASUREMENT OF IMPACT ON OTHER INDUSTRIES

The auto industry ranks 7th out of 82 industries in relation to the amount of total requirements needed per unit of delivery to final demand. (See Table 4.) However, of the industries listed in Table 4, the auto industry contributes more to final demand than any other industry with the exception of "food and kindred products."[8]

In view of the industry's absolute contribution to the economy and the relatively high amount of total requirements

needed per unit of auto output, it can be concluded that changes in demand for automotive products would have more pervasive effects on the economy than would changes in demand for other products. This becomes especially important since it is known that changes in the demand for autos are more likely to take place than are changes in most consumer products. Since the replacement of a car is not an immediate necessity for most people, automotive purchases can be postponed in a recessionary period. For example, the industry's final sales declined to 4,244,000 units in 1958 from 6,115,000 to the previous year.[9]

The pervasiveness of automotive manufacturing also can be demonstrated by

---

[9] *Ward's Reports.*

TABLE 3
PARTIAL EXAMPLE OF STAGE 2
COMPUTATION

One Dollar of Final Auto Output
Stage 1
Direct Requirements:
Steel $.08543
Rubber .02788
Glass   .01001
Stage 2
$.08543 of Final Steel Output:
Steel $.01940
Rubber .00027
(e.g., .08543 × .00318, which is rubber sales to steel per dollar of steel output)
Glass   .00001
$.02788 of Final Rubber Output:
Steel $.00006
Rubber .00086
Glass   .00018
$.01001 of Final Glass Output:
Steel   −0−
Rubber$.00004
Glass   .00048

Source: Table 2, in "The Interindustry Structure of the United States; a Report on the 1958 Input-Output Study," *Survey of Current Business*, November 1964, Office of Business Economics, U.S. Department of Commerce.

---

[7] The figures used for illustrative purposes here and in Chart 2 are much larger than would actually be found for individual industries involved in the second stage. In most cases the figure for an individual industry would be a fraction of a cent, in the context shown above. However, for all 82 industries the cumulative effect would not be negligible. See Table 3 for an example, using actual figures at the second stage for only three industries.

[8] Table A, "The Interindustry Structure of the United States; A Report on the 1958 Input-Output Study," *Survey of Current Business*, November 1964, Office of Business Economics, U.S. Department of Commerce.

looking at the value added of the industry relative to other industries. Value
added, which is mainly comprised of
labor costs, capital consumption allowances, and profits, represents what the
industry adds to its total purchases to
achieve its own final output. Since an
inverse relationship exists between
value added and dependence on other
industries, a low value added figure indicates a relatively greater involvement
with other industries. Of the 82 industries listed in the 1958 input-output
tables, only 7 have a lower value added
per dollar of gross output than the auto
industry.

Although there are 7 industries with a
lower value added figure than the auto
industry, an argument can be made that
automotive production has a greater
diffused effect on the economy. This can

be accomplished through examination
of how much of an industry's inputs is
being supplied by a particular number
of contributors.

Chart 3 shows the auto industry and
the 7 industries with lower value added
figures in relation to the percentage of
their direct requirements provided by
their 4 leading supplying industries. It
can be seen that all of the 7 other industries have more of their requirements
provided by only 4 suppliers than has
the auto industry. The significance of
Chart 3 is that relative to other industries low in value added, the needs
of automotive production are spread
throughout the economy. Consequently,
a change in the industry's output would
tend to have more widespread effects
than would a change in the output of an
industry that has a high value added and

CHART 3

DIRECT REQUIREMENTS PROVIDED BY THE FOUR LEADING SUPPLYING
INDUSTRIES TO THE INDUSTRIES HAVING LOWEST VALUE ADDED

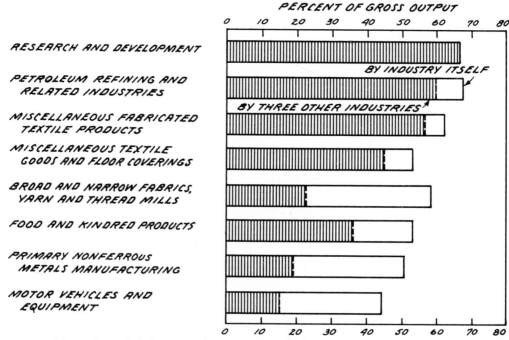

Source of Data: Table 2, "The Interindustry Structure of the United States; A Report on the 1958
Input-Output Study," *Survey of Current Business*, November, 1964, Office of Business Economics,
U.S. Department of Commerce.

obtains most of its supplies from only a few sources.

SUMMARY

The pervasive impact of the auto industry has been shown through examination of several factors revealed in the input-output tables. Automotive production is highly dependent on other manufacturing industries; the total requirements, both direct and indirect, for a unit of auto output are quite high; the high ratio of total purchases to total inputs (which is the same as a low value added/inputs ratio) also contributes to

the diffused economic effects of the industry. This is particularly significant in that a comparison of the 1947 and 1958 tables indicates that the percentage of personal consumption expenditures attributed to the industry has virtually doubled (1.67 percent compared with 3.17 percent).[10]

---

[10] The industrial categories in the 1958 tables are quite different from those utilized in 1947. However, reference to the Standard Industrial Classification codes indicates that the 1958 category of "Motor Vehicles and Equipment" is equivalent to the 1947 categories of "Motor Vehicles," "Truck Trailers," and "Automobile Trailers." Therefore, the output of the single 1958 category was compared with the aggregate output of the three 1947 categories.

TABLE 4

INDUSTRIES RANKED IN ORDER OF HIGHEST TOTAL REQUIREMENTS, DIRECT AND INDIRECT, PER DOLLAR OF DELIVERY TO FINAL DEMAND

Industry	Total Requirements
Office supplies	$3.17407
Business travel, entertainment, and gifts	3.02038
Research and development	3.00884
Miscellaneous fabricated textile products	2.99101
Broad & narrow fabrics, yarn & thread mills	2.78866
Food and kindred products	2.66911
Motor vehicles and equipment	2.65126
Miscellaneous textile goods and floor coverings	2.58047
Apparel	2.54437
Metal containers	2.44158
Wooden containers	2.41874
Livestock and livestock products	2.41749
Lumber & wood products (except containers)	2.41471
Paints and allied products	2.40278
Ordnance and accessories	2.40194
67 other industries	lower values

Source: Table 3, in "The Interindustry Structure of the United States; a Report on the 1958 Input-Output Study," *Survey of Current Business*, November 1964, Office of Business Economics, U.S. Department of Commerce

(3) Operations Research

50. A Heuristic Program for Locating Warehouses[*]

ALFRED A. KUEHN and MICHAEL J. HAMBURGER

I. THE WAREHOUSE LOCATION PROBLEM

Regional warehouses may perform a variety of functions in the distribution of a manufacturer's products. These include: (1) the reduction of transportation costs relative to direct shipment to customers by permitting bulk or quantity shipments from factory to warehouse; (2) the reduction of delivery costs by combining products manufactured at several factories into single shipments to individual customers; and (3) the improvement of customer relations by decreasing delivery time relative to direct factory shipment, thereby permitting customers to reduce their inventories. It should be noted, however, that there are substantial costs associated with the operation of a regional warehouse system.

The problem at issue may therefore be phrased as follows: determine the geographical pattern of warehouse locations which will be most profitable to the company by equating the marginal cost of warehouse operations with the transportation cost savings and incremental profits resulting from more rapid delivery. A heuristic computer program which appears to be capable of generating reasonably good solutions to this class of problems will be described in the following sections, after a brief discussion of the heuristic approach to problem solving. A mathematical formulation of the warehouse location problem is given in Appendix I. A comparison of the heuristic program with several alternative approaches to the problem is contained in Appendix II.

II. THE HEURISTIC APPROACH TO PROBLEM SOLVING

Simon [27] has referred to heuristics as rules of thumb selected on the basis that they will aid in problem solving. In an earlier paper, Simon, in collaboration with Newell and Shaw, used the term "heuristic" to denote "any principle or device that contributes to the reduction in the average search to a solution" ([21], p. 22). Making use of the latter definition, a heuristic program can be defined (after Tonge [29]) as a problem-solving program organized around such principles or devices. Simon [27] has distinguished between such programs and algorithms on the basis that *only* the latter guarantee solution of the problem to a desired degree of accuracy. We do not believe that this is the most appropriate way to characterize heuristic programs. There are many solution procedures referred to as

Reprinted by permission, with minor editorial revisions, from *Management Science*, Vol. IX, No. 4 (July, 1963), pp. 643-66.

[*] This research has been supported to varying degrees by the Graduate School of Industrial Administration and IBM and Ford Foundation Fellowships. While a number of individuals have offered valuable comments in reviews of earlier drafts of this paper, the authors particularly acknowledge the suggestions and encouragement of W. W. Cooper and Ralph L. Day of Carnegie Institute of Technology.

algorithms which do not guarantee solutions to a desired degree of accuracy, but rather, as is possible with the heuristic warehouse location program, provide only upper and lower bounds to the solution (for example, the fictitious play method for solving matrix games [17]). Furthermore the definition of algorithm generally used by mathematicians (for example, Courant and Robbins [8], p. 44) is "a systematic method for computation." Such a definition would include all computer programs.

We prefer to look at heuristic programing as an approach to problem solving where the emphasis is on working towards *optimum solution procedures* rather than *optimum solutions.* This is not to say that we ever expect to obtain an optimum solution procedure. The requirement of optimality would, in fact, be contradictory to the concept of using heuristic techniques. Heuristic techniques are most often used when the goal is to solve a problem so the solution is described in terms of acceptability characteristics rather than by optimizing rules (Tonge [29] p. 232).[1] The traditional operations research approach has been to search for optimum solutions. The heuristic approach differs in the following ways:

1. Explicit consideration is given to a number of factors (for example, computer storage capacity and solution time) in addition to the quality of the solution produced.

2. The evaluation of heuristic techniques is usually done by inductive rather than deductive procedures. That is, specific heuristics are justified not because they attain an analytically derived solution (for example, an optimum) but rather because experimenta-

tion has proved that they are useful in practice ([27], p. 11).

Recent interest in the heuristic approach to problem solving has led to the development of computer programs designed to: compose music [15], play checkers [24], play chess [5, 18, 20], discover proofs for theorems in logic and geometry [22, 12], design electric motors and transformers [14], and balance assembly lines [28].

III. A HEURISTIC PROGRAM FOR LOCATING WAREHOUSES

The heuristic program which we propose for locating warehouses consists of two parts: (1) *the main program,* which locates warehouses one at a time until no additional warehouses can be added to the distribution network without increasing total costs, and (2) *the bump and shift routine,* entered after processing in the main program is complete, which attempts to modify solutions arrived at in the main program by evaluating the profit implications of dropping individual warehouses or of shifting them from one location to another. The three principal heuristics used in the main program are:

1. *Most geographical locations are not promising sites for a regional warehouse; locations with promise will be at or near concentrations of demand.*[2]

The use of this heuristic in searching for and screening potential warehouse locations permits us to concentrate upon substantially less than $1/100$ of 1 percent of the United States and thereby eliminate mountains, marshes, deserts, and other desolate areas from consideration. To be sure, the program may as a result miss a good location. In

---

[1] These points have been discussed in more detail elsewhere in the context of a theory of human problem solving and choice (See, for example, Simon [26], pp. 196-207 and pp. 241-74, March and Simon [19], chaps. vi and vii, and Cyert, Dill, and March [9].)

[2] Baumol and Wolfe [4] also consider only a limited number of places at which to obtain warehouse space. However, their problem considers only the leasing of warehouse space and consequently the number of available locations is already limited and no heuristic is required to restrict the alternatives to be considered.

FIGURE 1

FLOW DIAGRAM.

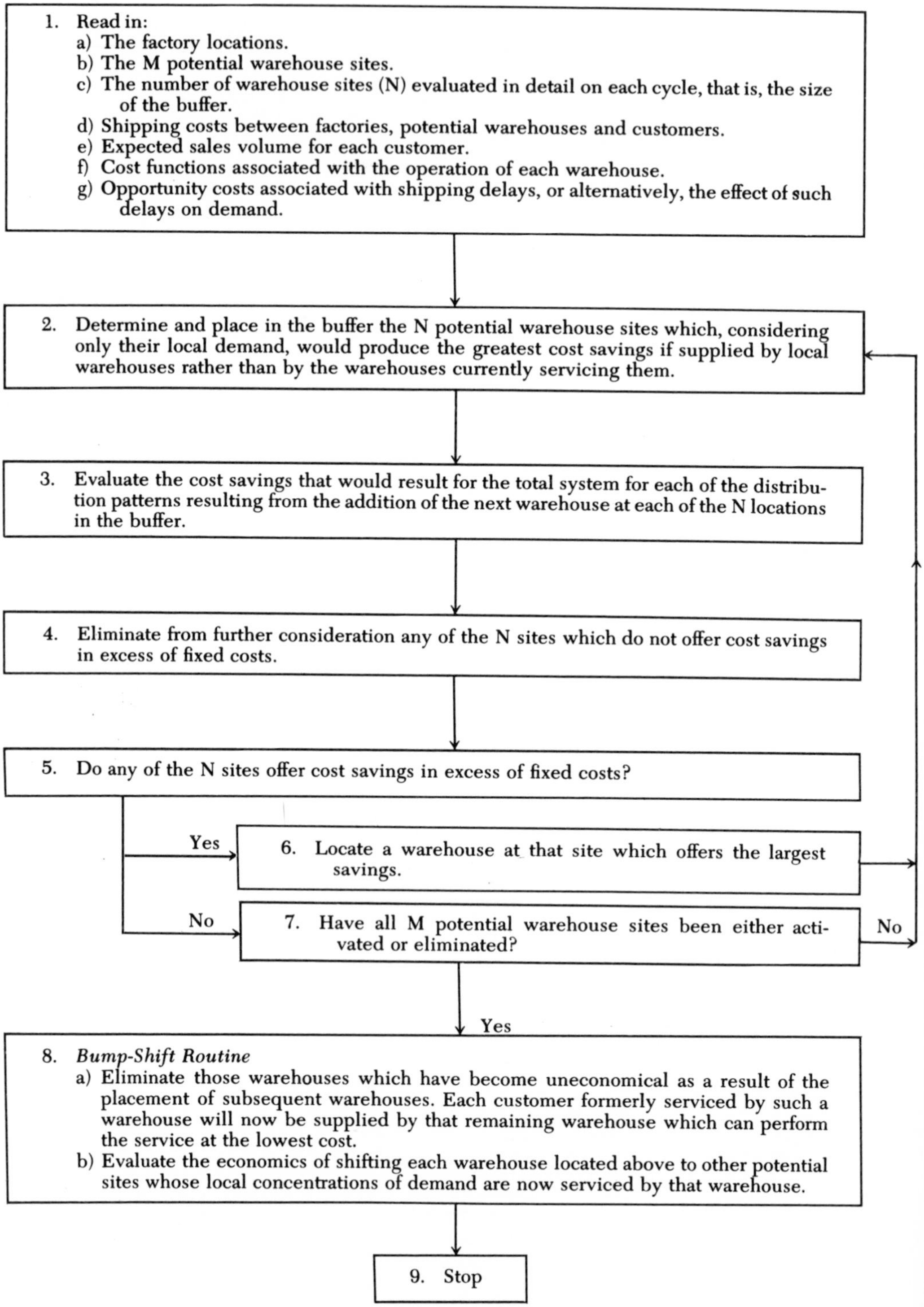

1. Read in:
   a) The factory locations.
   b) The M potential warehouse sites.
   c) The number of warehouse sites (N) evaluated in detail on each cycle, that is, the size of the buffer.
   d) Shipping costs between factories, potential warehouses and customers.
   e) Expected sales volume for each customer.
   f) Cost functions associated with the operation of each warehouse.
   g) Opportunity costs associated with shipping delays, or alternatively, the effect of such delays on demand.

2. Determine and place in the buffer the N potential warehouse sites which, considering only their local demand, would produce the greatest cost savings if supplied by local warehouses rather than by the warehouses currently servicing them.

3. Evaluate the cost savings that would result for the total system for each of the distribution patterns resulting from the addition of the next warehouse at each of the N locations in the buffer.

4. Eliminate from further consideration any of the N sites which do not offer cost savings in excess of fixed costs.

5. Do any of the N sites offer cost savings in excess of fixed costs?

Yes

6. Locate a warehouse at that site which offers the largest savings.

No

7. Have all M potential warehouse sites been either activated or eliminated?

No

Yes

8. *Bump-Shift Routine*
   a) Eliminate those warehouses which have become uneconomical as a result of the placement of subsequent warehouses. Each customer formerly serviced by such a warehouse will now be supplied by that remaining warehouse which can perform the service at the lowest cost.
   b) Evaluate the economics of shifting each warehouse located above to other potential sites whose local concentrations of demand are now serviced by that warehouse.

9. Stop

general, however, computer time is put to much better use in screening and evaluating a definite number of concentrations of demand than in searching blindly for a possible profitable desolate location. (If management or the program operator is interested in evaluating any specific locations of this type, they can be entered as alternatives.)

2. *Near optimum warehousing systems can be developed by locating warehouses one at a time, adding at each stage of the analysis that warehouse which produces the greatest cost savings for the entire system.*

The use of this heuristic reduces the time and effort expended in evaluating patterns of warehouse sites. Thus, if there are M possible warehouse locations, the above heuristic would reduce the number of cost evaluations necessary from 2^m to approximately $N (M' + 1) < NM$ where N is the size of the

intermediate buffer, discussed further below, and M' is the number of warehouses located. One can think of several classes of examples in which this heuristic would not work very well. However, such situations appear to occur only rarely in practice.

3. *Only a small subset of all possible warehouse locations need be evaluated in detail at each stage of the analysis to determine the next warehouse site to be added.*

To insure adding that warehouse location producing the greatest cost savings we could evaluate completely each of the remaining potential warehouse sites. The time required by such an approach can, however, be reduced very substantially with the addition of only slight risk with a good, easily computed method of screening potential sites. The heuristic used for screening calls for N of the M potential warehouse

TABLE 1
HEURISTIC SOLUTIONS TO SAMPLE PROBLEMS
FACTORY LOCATION: INDIANAPOLIS
Fixed Costs of Warehouses

$7,500		$12,500		$17,500		$25,000	
Warehouse Located at Each Stage	Cost of System at Each Stage	Warehouse Located at Each Stage	Cost of System at Each Stage	Warehouse Located at Each Stage	Cost of System at Each Stage	Warehouse Located at Each Stage	Cost of System at Each Stage
Main Program		Main Program		Main Program		Main Program	
No warehouses	$1,248,688	No warehouses	$1,248,688	No warehouses	$1,248,688	No warehouses	$1,248,688
Philadelphia	1,075,120	Philadelphia	1,080,120	Philadelphia	1,085,120	Philadelphia	1,092,620
Los Angeles	910,514	Los Angeles	920,514	Los Angeles	930,514	Los Angeles	945,514
Seattle	876,429	Seattle	891,429	Seattle	906,429	Seattle	928,929
San Francisco	861,967	San Francisco	881,967	San Francisco	901,967		
Houston	850,645	Houston	875,645	Houston	900,645	Bump-Shift Routine	
Chicago	839,853	Chicago	869,853	Chicago	899,853		
New York	830,424	New York	865,424			No change	$ 928,929
Detroit	824,721	Detroit	864,721				
Denver	819,073	Kansas City	860,484	Bump-Shift Routine		Improvements Not Found by the Heuristic Program	
Pittsburgh	815,818	Atlanta	859,125	Replace Houston with		None known	
Washington, D.C.	813,321	Cleveland	858,764	Dallas	$ 896,864		
Kansas City	809,827	Bump-Shift Routine					
Boston	808,203			Improvements Not Found by the Heuristic Program			
Atlanta	801,845	Drop Detroit	$ 857,725				
		Replace Philadelphia with Washington		None known			
Bump-Shift Routine			856,257				
Drop Denver	$ 801,748						
Improvements Not Found by the Heuristic Program		Improvements Not Found by the Heuristic Program					
Replace Houston with		Replace Houston with					
Dallas	$ 800,163	Dallas	$ 854,672				

locations $(M > N > 1)$ to be evaluated in detail at each stage (see step 3, Figure 1, Flow Diagram). The N potential warehouse sites chosen at each stage are those which, considering only local demand, would result in the greatest cost savings (or smallest increase in costs) if serviced by a local warehouse rather than by the system existing in the previous stage (see step 2, Flow Diagram). In other words, it is assumed that at any stage we can do reasonably well by locating the next warehouse in one of the N areas chosen on the basis of local demand and related warehousing and transportation costs.

In the detailed evaluation of each of the N locations placed in the buffer at each stage, the program either eliminates the site from further consideration, assigns a warehouse to that location, or returns the location to the list of potential warehouse sites for reconsideration at later stages in the program (steps 4, 6, and 7, respectively, in the Flow Diagram). Any site whose addition would not reduce total distribution costs is eliminated from further analysis in the main program. Of those sites which reduce total costs, that location which affords the greatest savings is assigned a warehouse; all others are returned to the list of potential warehouse sites. When the list of potential warehouses is depleted, all sites having been either eliminated or assigned a warehouse, the program enters the Bump and Shift Routine.

The Bump and Shift Routine is designed to modify solutions reached in the main program in two ways. It first eliminates (bumps) any warehouse which is no longer economical because some of the customers originally assigned to it are now serviced by warehouses located subsequently. Then, to insure the servicing of each of the territories established above from a single warehouse within each territory in the most economical manner, the program considers shifting each warehouse from its currently assigned location to

the other potential sites (original list) within its territory. It should be noted that this routine does not guarantee that each territory will in fact be serviced in the most economical manner (this deficiency is illustrated below with reference to several sample problems).

The basic steps in the heuristic program are summarized in the Flow Diagram, Figure 1. Before going on to examine the results obtained in applying this program to several sample problems, let us discuss briefly the heuristics used in handling the shipping cost data (see step 1d, Flow Diagram). The inclusion of lists of actual transportation costs and delay times (or distance) between all potential shipping points as data might appear to be unwieldly relative to the Shycon-Maffei approach [25] since locating M customers and warehouses by longitude and latitude takes only M computer locations whereas up to $M^2/2$ locations are required for recording all shipping costs. In practice the problem is not nearly so unwieldy and produces some compensations: For example in many cases a priori judgments can be made that customers in certain geographical regions will not be serviced from potential warehouses in other regions. Thus, in one of the sample problems discussed below, we do not consider shipping from warehouses in Eastern cities to the West Coast since the factory is located in Indianapolis. In addition, customers can frequently be aggregated into concentrations of demand (for example, metropolitan chain grocery and wholesaler warehouses) because of close geographical proximity. The program also automatically eliminates from the search list potential warehouse sites and warehouse-customer combinations that no longer offer promise of cost reduction. As a result, by the time that the program has located two or three warehouses, the list being searched is frequently reduced by 90 percent. The reduction in list size continues as more warehouses are added, speeding up the analysis on each cycle. These heuristics make the use of actual costs computationally efficient (computation times for 12 sample problems are outlined in the following section). They also permit us to: (1) avoid the errors associated with the use of air miles as a basis for approximating shipping costs; and (2) solve large-scale problems, involving, for example, several factories, 10 products, at least 200 potential warehouse sites, and more than a thousand concentrations of demand.

IV. SAMPLE PROBLEMS

The operation of the program will be illustrated with reference to 12 sample problems. The problems represent all combinations of three sets of factory locations—(1) Indianapolis, (2) Jacksonville, Florida, (3) Indianapolis and Baltimore—and four levels of fixed warehouse costs—$7,500, $12,500, $17,500, $25,000—for each warehouse in the system. Each of the sample problems considers only a single product. Transportation costs and costs associated with shipping delays are assumed to be proportional to the railroad distance between shipping points.[3] For purposes of illustration, bulk shipping rates from the factory to warehouses are evaluated at $0.0125 per mile per unit, whereas the sum of the shipping and delay costs from warehouses to customers is considered to be $0.0250 per mile per unit. To further simplify the 12 distribution problems analyzed in this paper, the variable costs of operating the warehouses

are assumed to be linear with respect to the volume of goods processed.[4] Consequently, these costs do not affect the optimal warehouse system and need not be further considered in the sample problems.[5] The size of the buffer (N) was equal to five in each of the 12 sample problems.

The market structure considered in the sample problems consists of 50 concentrations of demand scattered throughout the United States. Twenty-four of these centers of demand are treated as potential warehouse sites. The metropolitan population of each of these areas was used to represent sales potential, a population of 1,000 representing one unit of demand (see Table 4).

The results obtained for each of the 12 cases are shown in Tables 1 through 3. These tables summarize:

1. The warehouse locations selected by the main program, in the order of selection.
2. The modifications introduced into the main program solution by the bump-shift routine.
3. Alterations to the heuristic warehouse network which are known to lower total distribution costs.

---

[3] Railroad distances between cities were obtained from the *Rand-McNally Cosmopolitan World Atlas* (Chicago: Rand McNally & Co., 1951), p. 193. It should be noted that the simplifying assumption of linearity of transportation and delay costs with respect to railroad mileage is strictly a matter of convenience in making the cost data available to the reader. In practice, actual shipping costs and delay times would generally be read into the computer.

[4] The 12 sample problems were not specified so as to fully test the generality of the program. The simplification of linear warehousing cost functions was incorporated in the test problems so that the heuristic solutions obtained might subsequently be compared with optimal solutions developed by the application of integer programing. Such a comparison has not yet been made since we are not aware of the existence of an integer programing routine capable of solving a problem of that size.

[5] It should be noted that the heuristic program, in addition to being able to treat the case where both shipping costs and the variable and fixed costs of warehousing vary throughout the country, can determine which of several different types of warehouses (some of which might include packaging facilities) and transportation systems should be used to service each concentration of demand. The program can also be employed to locate regional factories, choosing among alternative factory sites for which production costs are specified.

TABLE 2

HEURISTIC SOLUTIONS TO SAMPLE PROBLEMS
FACTORY LOCATION: JACKSONVILLE
Fixed Costs of Warehouses

$7,500		$12,500		$17,500		$25,000	
Warehouse Located at Each Stage	Cost of System at Each Stage	Warehouse Located at Each Stage	Cost of System at Each Stage	Warehouse Located at Each Stage	Cost of System at Each Stage	Warehouse Located at Each Stage	Cost of System at Each Stage
Main Program		Main Program		Main Program		Main Program	
No warehouses	$1,832,861	No warehouses	$1,832,861	No warehouses	$1,832,861	No warehouses	$1,832,861
New York	1,602,504	New York	1,607,504	New York	1,612,504	New York	1,620,004
Los Angeles	1,376,900	Los Angeles	1,386,900	Los Angeles	1,396,900	Los Angeles	1,411,900
Chicago	1,239,864	Chicago	1,254,864	Chicago	1,269,864	Chicago	1,292,364
Seattle	1,211,687	Seattle	1,231,687	Seattle	1,251,687	Seattle	1,281,687
Washington, D.C.	1,169,916	Washington, D.C.	1,194,916	Washington, D.C.	1,219,916	Washington, D.C.	1,257,416
St. Louis	1,143,998	St. Louis	1,173,998	St. Louis	1,203,998	St. Louis	1,248,998
Cincinnati	1,123,224	Cincinnati	1,158,224	Cincinnati	1,193,224	Cincinnati	1,245,724
Houston	1,106,239	Houston	1,146,239	Houston	1,136,239		
San Francisco	1,098,949	San Francisco	1,143,949			Bump-Shift Routine	
Denver	1,096,245			Bump-Shift Routine		No change	$1,245,724
Detroit	1,093,780	Bump-Shift Routine		No change	$1,136,239	Improvements Not Found by the Heuristic Program	
Pittsburgh	1,092,163	No change	$1,143,949	Improvements Not Found by the Heuristic Program		None known	
Atlanta	1,091,374	Improvements Not Found by the Heuristic Program		None known			
Bump-Shift Routine		None known					
No change	$1,091,374						

None known

TABLE 3

HEURISTIC SOLUTIONS TO SAMPLE PROBLEMS
FACTORY LOCATIONS: BALTIMORE AND INDIANAPOLIS
Fixed Costs of Warehouses

$7,500		$12,500		$17,500		$25,000	
Warehouse Located at Each Stage	Cost of System at Each Stage	Warehouse Located at Each Stage	Cost of System at Each Stage	Warehouse Located at Each Stage	Cost of System at Each Stage	Warehouse Located at Each Stage	Cost of System at Each Stage
Main Program		Main Program		Main Program		Main Program	
No warehouses	$899,770	No warehouses	$899,770	No warehouses	$899,770	No warehouses	$899,770
Los Angeles	735,164	Los Angeles	740,164	Los Angeles	745,164	Los Angeles	752,664
Seattle	701,079	Seattle	711,079	Seattle	721,079	Seattle	736,079
New York	672,666	New York	687,666	New York	702,666	New York	725,166
San Francisco	658,205	San Francisco	678,205	San Francisco	698,205	Bump-Shift Routine	
Houston	646,882	Houston	671,882	Dallas	691,772	No change	$725,166
Chicago	636,091	Chicago	666,091	Chicago	690,980	Improvements Not Found by the Heuristic Program	
Denver	630,442	Kansas City	661,853			None known	
Detroit	626,481			Bump-Shift Routine			
Kansas City	623,114	Bump-Shift Routine		No change	$690,980		
Cleveland	620,405	No change	$661,853	Improvements Not Found by the Heuristic Program			
Atlanta	617,337	Improvements Not Found by the Heuristic Program		None known			
Bump-Shift Routine		Replace Houston with Dallas	$660,268				
Drop Denver	$617,116						
Improvements Not Found by the Heuristic Program							
Replace Houston with Dallas	$615,531						

4. The total distribution costs at each stage of the heuristic solution and for the warehouse network which incorporates subsequent improvements.[6]

In each of the four cases in which an improvement upon the heuristic solution was discovered, the improvement consisted of replacing a warehouse in Houston with a warehouse in Dallas. This improvement was not found by the shift portion of the bump-shift routine since Dallas was not being serviced from the Houston warehouse. The shift routine as currently programed considers as alternatives only those warehouse sites which are located within the territory served by the warehouse under examination. The rationale for limiting the alternatives considered in this fashion was (1) it provided a convenient method of identifying most of the nearby unactivated warehouse

---

[6] The improvements upon the heuristic solutions tabulated for four of the 12 problems have been found by evaluating the modifications in the heuristic distribution network which, upon inspection, appeared most likely to result in lower distribution costs. Approximately 25 types of modifications were tested, but only one resulted in a minor improvement in four of the problems. To determine the optimal system by complete enumeration would require the evaluation of the 2^{24} possible ways of locating up to 24 warehouses. With an IBM-704, which could perform approximately one such evaluation per second, this operation would take more than six months of continuous operation per problem. Testing all combinations of three and four warehouses, which would probably be sufficient to insure finding the optimal network for any one of the two least interesting cases (those problems in which, because of high fixed warehousing costs, the heuristic program locates only three warehouses) would require approximately four computer hours. The use of integer programing offers more promise. Once such a computer program is available, it should be feasible to test the sample problem solutions we have found for optimality in one iteration by using the heuristic solutions as the initial basis for the integer program. This points to another possible application for heuristic programing. Insofar as heuristics can be used to develop an advanced starting basis for an integer programing problem, a substantial reduction in the total computation time required to reach an optimum may be possible.

sites, and (2) computation time would be minimized by not considering the realignment of regions at this point in the program.

The shift routine as specified above cannot be applied directly to multiple product systems in which different mixes of products might be shipped to the customer from different warehouses since the regions for the different product mixes will not necessarily be identical. A simple heuristic now being programed to treat the multiple product problem considers shifting the warehouses located by the main program to all sites specified in the input as "neighboring warehouse sites." That is, the neighboring warehouse sites of each potential warehouse location are specified in the input to the program and are evaluated as alternatives in the shift routine. Since this routine does not make use of the concept of warehouse territories, it will also correct errors of the Dallas-Houston variety when applied to problems involving only a single product. (This routine will increase computation time in most cases.) It will not, however, correct for less-localized deviations of the main program solution from the optimal warehouse network.

In considering the development of new or more elaborate bump-shift routines (or, the inclusion of such devices in the main program to be performed after the addition of each warehouse) it is desirable to determine the improvements which might be expected. In the 12 sample problems discussed above, the improvements upon the main program solution developed in the bump-shift routine and through subsequent analysis never amounted to more than 0.5 percent. If future research indicates that the main program solution is generally near-optimal, it would give strong support to the use of the three basic heuristics in the main program and limit the gain to be expected in searching for corrective routines.

Some support for the heuristic which selects warehouse sites to be placed in the buffer is obtained by reference to

TABLE 4
SALES POTENTIAL OF CONCENTRATIONS OF DEMAND
USED IN SAMPLE PROBLEMS
(POPULATION IN THOUSANDS)

Concentrations of Demand	Sales Potential	Concentrations of Demand	Sales Potential
Albuquerque, N.Mex.	146	Knoxville, Tenn.	337
Amarillo, Texas	87	Los Angeles, Calif.*	4,368
Atlanta, Ga.*	672	Louisville, Ky.	577
Baltimore, Md.	1,337	Memphis, Tenn.*	482
Billings, Mont.	31	Miami, Fla.*	495
Birmingham, Ala.	559	Mobile, Ala.	231
Boston, Mass.*	2,370	Nashville, Tenn.	322
Buffalo, N.Y.*	1,089	New Orleans, La.*	685
Butte, Mont.	33	New York, N.Y.*	12,912
Cheyenne, Wyo.	32	Oklahoma City, Okla.	325
Chicago, Ill.*	5,495	Omaha, Nebr.	366
Cincinnati, Ohio*	904	Philadelphia, Pa.*	3,671
Cleveland, Ohio*	1,466	Pittsburgh, Pa.*	2,213
Columbia, S.C.	143	Portland, Oregon	705
Dallas, Texas*	615	Richmond, Va.	328
Denver, Colo.*	564	St. Louis, Mo.*	1,681
Des Moines, Iowa	226	St. Paul, Minn.*	1,117
Detroit, Mich.*	3,016	Salt Lake City, Utah*	275
Duluth, Minn.	253	San Antonio, Texas	500
El Paso, Texas	195	San Francisco, Calif.*	2,241
Fargo, N.Dak.	38	Seattle, Wash.*	733
Houston, Texas*	807	Spokane, Wash.	222
Indianapolis, Ind.	551	Tucson, Ariz.	49
Jacksonville, Fla.	304	Washington, D.C.*	1,464
Kansas City, Mo.*	814	Wichita, Kansas	222

* Potential warehouse sites.
Source: *The World Almanac* (New York: *New York World-Telegram and Sun*, 1960).

the frequency distribution of warehouses selected for activation in the 12 sample problems from each of the positions in the five-place buffer used in the analysis. This distribution is tabulated in Table 5, the buffer positions representing the rank of the potential warehouse sites in terms of their cost savings considering only local demand (step 2, Figure 1, Flow Diagram).

COMPUTATION TIME

The time required to reach a solution for the 12 sample problems in the main program totaled 72 minutes on an IBM-650 with RAMAC disc storage. The in-

TABLE 5
FREQUENCY DISTRIBUTION OF WAREHOUSES SELECTED
FOR ACTIVATION FROM EACH POSITION IN THE BUFFER

Position in the Buffer	Number of Warehouses Located from Each Position	Percentage of Total Warehouses Located from Each Position
1	48	49.0%
2	15	15.3
3	15	15.3
4	10	10.2
5	10	10.2

dividual problems required an average of 2 minutes setup time and 30 seconds per warehouse located. Experimentation with and analysis of the heuristic program indicates that computation time increases at a much slower rate with increases in problem size than is the case with linear programing algorithms designed to handle fixed cost elements. It appears that the problem setup time increases linearly with the product of the number of warehouses, the number of products, and the number of customers (concentrations of demand). The time required for locating warehouses increases approximately linearly with the size of the buffer (N), the number of products, and the number of customers, but almost negligibly with the number of potential warehouse sites. The effect of multiple factories on setup time is at most linear; if capacity constraints are not operative the effect is substantially less than linear. Surprisingly, increasing the number of factories actually tends to decrease the total warehouse location time since there is no effect upon the time required to locate individual warehouses and the total number of warehouses located will generally be reduced.

Accurate time estimates for the bump-shift routine are not available since only an inefficient routine was operating when the IBM-650 at Carnegie Tech was replaced. Processing the 12 sample problems with this version of the bump-shift routine required a total of one hour. We would expect an efficient computer routine to perform this operation in 10 to 15 minutes since comparable reductions in computer time were achieved in the revision of the main program.

EXTENSIONS AND APPLICATIONS

Improved heuristics in terms of reduced computation time and/or more nearly optimum solutions of the warehouse location problem will probably be forthcoming. The six-minute solution time on an IBM-650 in itself probably suggests to the reader that additional check and bump-shift routines might be interspersed between the location of individual warehouses; after all, the difference in cost between six minutes and even six hours of computation time on an IBM-650 is negligible relative to the cost savings that might be achieved in the sample warehouse network problems studied. It is not clear, however, that such approaches will on the average improve upon the solutions generated by the existing heuristic program if at least four warehouses are located. Care must also be taken to avoid the chase for optimal solutions to simple problems and thereby miss the actual problem of business—the solution of large-scale problems containing many customers buying various mixes of a full product line, many potential warehouse sites, alternate warehouse types with different cost structures, several factories and, perhaps, a number of potential factory sites.[7]

Two warehouse network problems

---

[7] It should be noted that the distribution of order-shipment mixes of products can be treated by considering each geographical concentration of demand as several concentrations at the same location, each concentration representing a given mix of products of a given total size. Insofar as discrete distributions can be used to approximate the empirical distributions, the specification of the problem can be greatly simplified. The number of computer locations required to store each of these mixes would then be reduced substantially from that which would be required if each of the mixes were treated as the demand at an individual geographical location. An interesting aspect of this treatment of the problem is that the total warehouse network would be established with full recognition of the fact that customers will not necessarily receive all of their shipments from a single warehouse if all factories do not produce all products. An order of packaged detergents and toilet bar soap, for example, might be received from one warehouse if it consists largely of detergent and from another if the order is primarily composed of bar soaps. Similarly, not all products will necessarily be stocked at all warehouses. In the distribution of appliances, for example, yellow refrigerators, for which there is a relatively small demand, might be stocked in only the larger warehouses.

containing many of the above complexities are now being examined, one representing the distribution of a variety of grocery-drug type consumer products, the other a line of consumer appliances. In both cases the problem is of such magnitude that the solution time could easily come to several hours on an IBM-7090 computer unless the problem is simplified beyond the level now thought to be desirable. Furthermore, in view of some uncertainty as to the actual nature of warehousing costs, it appears prudent to make several runs with different warehousing cost functions to determine the sensitivity of the heuristic warehouse solutions to the cost functions. It is in this context that the advantages of improved solutions to test problems must be evaluated relative to increased computer time requirements. Additional check or bump-shift heuristics increasing computer time on test problems from six minutes to six hours would increase the IBM-7090 time per run from 3-6 hours to 180-360 hours, time which might well be better spent in testing the sensitivity of the solutions to variations in warehouse cost structures and in providing an improved model of demand through greater detail in the description of product mix and size of customer orders.

It has been suggested that the heuristics might be applied by eliminating warehouses rather than adding them. That is, a warehouse is assumed to be operating at each potential site at the start of the program. Warehouses would then be eliminated one by one on the basis of cost savings. It is not clear how the quality of solutions produced in this manner would compare with those developed from the heuristic program outlined in this paper. In terms of computation time, however, it seems likely that the current program would be the more efficient when the number of warehouses located is less than half the number of potential sites being considered. This seems to be generally the

case in industry although situations could, no doubt, be found where this is not true (for example, the firm which is interested only in considering the possibility of closing existing warehouses).

Once we know the optimal solutions to the test problems (through the application of integer programing, using the heuristic solution as a starting basis), we will be in a better position to evaluate the potential gains possible through the use of improved heuristics. In addition, knowledge of the optimal solution should provide sound direction as to the type of heuristics which offer most promise in correcting the deviations inherent in the current program.

V. SUMMARY

A heuristic program was developed and applied to several warehouse location problems. The results suggest that a heuristic approach to this class of problems may be quite profitable in practice, producing near-optimal solutions within acceptable limits of computer time.

The use of heuristics in solving these problems has two prime advantages relative to the currently available linear programing formulations and solution procedures: (1) computational simplicity, which results in substantial reductions in solution times and permits the treatment of large-scale problems, and (2) flexibility with respect to the underlying cost functions, eliminating the need for restrictive assumptions. It also offers an important advantage relative to the simulation technique of Shycon and Maffei in that it incorporates a systematic procedure designed to generate at least one near-optimal distribution system while providing approximately the same flexibility in the modeling of the problem.

The proposed heuristic program permits fast screening and evaluation of alternative types of warehouses, transportation systems, and warehouse locations. It should, however, be emphasized that this program is not the end of the road. It may some day become practical to solve large-scale warehouse location problems with optimizing algorithms given continued development of computer hardware and linear programing techniques. Heuristic programing, too, is capable of improvement and such developments will probably be forthcoming as a result of the large amount of research on heuristic models and computer programing now being carried on at the RAND Corporation, Carnegie Tech and elsewhere.

APPENDIX I. MATHEMATICAL FORMULATION OF THE WAREHOUSE LOCATION PROBLEM

The problem can be expressed mathematically as follows:

$X_{h,i,j,k}$ = the quantity of good h $(h = 1, \ldots, p)$ shipped from factory i $(i = 1, \ldots, q)$ via warehouse j $(j = 1, \ldots, r)$ to customer k $(k = 1, \ldots, s)$.

$A_{h,i,j}$ = the per unit transportation cost of shipping good h from factory i to warehouse j.

$B_{h,j,k}$ = the per unit transportation cost of shipping good h from warehouse j to customer k.

$C_{h,j}(\Sigma_{i,k}X_{h,i,j,k_4})$ = total cost of warehouse operation associated with processing good h at warehouse j. Without loss of generality we may express this function as the sum of $S_{h,j}$ and F_j defined below.

$D_{h,k}(T_{h,k})$ = explicit or imputed cost due to a delay of T time units in delivery of good h to customer k. When the customer imposes a maximum delivery time (constraint), D becomes infinite whenever the indicated limit is reached.[8]

F_j = fixed cost per time period of operating warehouse j. Note that this is a planned fixed cost to be incurred and not a sunk cost.

$S_{h,j}(\Sigma_{i,k}X_{h,i,j,k})$ = semivariable cost of operating warehouse j per unit of good h processed, including variable handling and administrative costs, storage costs, taxes, interest on investment, pilferage, and so on (the homogeneous portion of the very general function $C_{h,j}$).

$Q_{h,k}$ = quantity of good h demanded by customer k.

W_j = capacity of warehouse j.

$Y_{h,i}$ = capacity of factory i to produce good h.

Z_j = 1 if $\Sigma_{h,i,k} X_{h,i,j,k} > 0$ and zero otherwise (that is, ΣZ_j = the number of warehouses used).

[8] The effect of delay in supplying customers has been treated above as an "opportunity cost" since this simplifies the notation and is consistent with current research practice. However, an alternative formulation which reflects management's view of the problem more accurately is to have delivery times affect demand.

The problem then becomes one of minimizing total distribution costs, an objective function of the form

$$f(X) = \Sigma_{h,i,j,k}(A_{h,i,j} + B_{h,j,k}) X_{h,i,j,k}$$
$$+ \Sigma_j F_j Z_j + \Sigma_{h,j} S_{h,j}(\Sigma_{i,k} X_{h,i,j,k})$$
$$+ \Sigma_{h,k} D_{h,k}(T_{h,k}),$$

subject to constraints of the following form:

$$\Sigma_{i,j} X_{h,i,j,k} = Q_{h,k}$$

(customer k's demand for product h must be supplied),

$$\Sigma_{j,k} X_{h,i,j,k} \leq Y_{h,i}$$

(factory i's capacity limit on good h cannot be exceeded).

$$I_j (\Sigma_{h,i,k} X_{h,i,j,k}) \leq W_j$$

(the capacity of warehouse   cannot be exceeded),

where $I_j(\Sigma_{h,i,k} X_{h,i,j,k})$ is a function which denotes the maximum inventory level associated with the flow of all goods from all factories to all customers serviced through warehouse j.

REFERENCES

1. Balinski, M. L. "Fixed-Cost Transportation Problems," *Naval Research Logistics Quarterly*, Vol. VIII (March, 1961), pp. 41-54.
2. Balinski, M. L., and Mills, H. "A Warehouse Problem," prepared for: Veterans Administration; Mathematica, Princeton, New Jersey, April, 1960.
3. Baumol, W. J. *Economic Theory and Operations Analysis.* Englewood Cliffs, N.J.: Prentice-Hall, Inc., 1961, pp. 410-13.
4. Baumol, W. J., and Wolfe, P. "A Warehouse Location Problem," *Operations Research*, Vol. VI (March-April, 1958), pp. 252-63.
5. Bernstein, A.; Roberts, M. de V.; Arbuckle, T.; and M. H. Belsky. "A Chess- Playing Program for the IBM 704," *Proceedings of the 1958 Western Joint Computer Conference*, pp. 157-59.
6. Charnes, A., and Cooper, W. W. "The Stepping Stone Method of Explaining Linear Programming Calculations in Transportation Problems," *Management Science*, Vol. 1 (October, 1954), pp. 49-69.
7. Charnes, A., and Cooper, W. W. *Management*

8. Courant, R., and Robbins, H. *What Is Mathematics?* Oxford University Press, 1941.
9. Cyert, R. M.; Dill, W. R.; and March, J. C. "The Role of Expectations in Business Decision Making," *Administrative Science Quarterly*, December, 1958.
10. Dantzig, G. B. "Application of the Simplex Method to a Transportation Problem," T. C. Koopmans (ed.), *Activity Analysis of Production and Allocation* (Cowles Commission Monograph No. 13). New York: John Wiley & Sons, Inc., 1951, chap. xxiii.
11. Ford, L. R., and Fulkerson, D. R. "Solving the Transportation Problem," *Management Science*, Vol. III (1956), pp. 24-32.
12. Gelernter, M., and Rochester, N. "Intelligent Behavior in Problem-Solving Machines," *IBM Journal of Research and Development*, Vol. II (October, 1958), pp. 336-45.
13. Gomory, R. E. "An Algorithm for Integer Solutions to Linear Programs," Princeton-IBM Mathematics Research Project, Technical Report No. 1, Princeton University.
14. Goodwin, G. H. "Digital Computers Tap Out Designs for Large Motors Fast," *Power* (April, 1958).
15. Hiller, L. A., and Isaacson, L. M. *Experimental Music.* New York: McGraw-Hill Book Co., Inc., 1959.
16. Holt, C. C.; Modigliani, F.; Muth, J. F.; and Simon, H. A. *Planning Production, Inventories, and Work Force.* Englewood Cliffs, N. J.: Prentice-Hall, Inc., 1960.
17. Kemeny, J. G., and Thompson, G. L. "The Modified Fictitious Play Method," *Dartmouth Mathematics Project Report*, 1958.
18. Kister, J.; Stein, P.; Ulam, S.; Walden, W.; and Wells, M. "Experiments in Chess," *Journal of the Association for Computing Machinery*, Vol. IV (April, 1957), pp. 174-77.
19. March, J. G., and Simon, H. A. *Organizations.* New York: John Wiley & Sons, Inc., 1958.
20. Newell, A.; Shaw, J. C.; and Simon, H. A. "Chess Playing Programs and the Problem of Complexity," *IBM Journal of Research and Development*, Vol. II (October, 1958), pp. 320-35.
21. Newell, A.; Shaw, J. C.; and Simon, H. A. "The Processes of Creative Thinking," the RAND Corporation Paper, P-1320, August, 1958.
22. Newell, A., and Simon, H. A. "The Logic Theory Machine," *IRE Transactions on Information Theory*, IT-2 (September, 1956), pp. 61-79.
23. *Rand-McNally – Cosmopolitan World Atlas.* Chicago: Rand-McNally & Co., 1951.
24. Samuel, A. L. "Some Studies in Machine Learning Using the Game of Checkers,"

IBM Journal of Research and Development, Vol. III (July, 1959), pp. 210-29.

25. Shycon, H. N., and Maffei, R. B. "Simulation —Tool for Better Distribution," *Harvard Business Review*, November-December, 1960, pp. 65-75.

26. Simon, H. A. *Models of Man*, New York: John Wiley & Sons, Inc., 1957.

27. Simon, H. A. "Modeling Human Mental Processes," *Proceedings of the 1961 Western Joint Computer Conference.*

28. Tonge, F. M. *A Heuristic Program for an Assembly Line Balancing Problem.* New York: Prentice-Hall, Inc., 1961.

29. Tonge, F. M. "The Use of Heuristic Programming in Management Science," *Management Science*, Vol. VII (April, 1961), pp. 231-37.

30. *The World Almanac*. New York: New York World-Telegram and the Sun, 1960.

Part IV

Marketing and Society

In this, the concluding part of the book, we consider topics having to do with the impact of the marketing system on costs, efficiency, ethical standards, effects of public policy and legislation and an assessment of the system.

To begin, the costs which have resulted from changes in model characteristics in the automobile industry are studied. In the section on ethics (B), the market effects of deceptive packaging and the ethical posture of purchasing agents are studied.

One of the most sensitive areas in all of marketing is that which deals with private entrepreneurs and public officialdom. The issue of public interest versus freedom in the market place is and will probably continue to be hotly debated for some time. The landmark duPont-General Motors case is examined in terms of the economic issues involved in the article which opens section C. It is followed by an appraisal of dealer margins when the legislated constraint of resale price maintenance or quality stabilization are imposed.

Section (D) completes this collection with a critical evaluation of an exhaustive study of efficiency in the food industry.

A. COSTS AND EFFICIENCY

51. The Costs of Automobile Model Changes Since 1949

FRANKLIN M. FISHER, ZVI GRILICHES, and CARL KAYSEN

I. INTRODUCTION: AIMS OF THE STUDY

This paper reports estimates of the costs to the consumer of the changes in private automobile specifications that took place during the 1950's. Throughout we concentrate on the costs that would not have been expended if cars with the 1949[1] model lengths, weights, horsepowers, transmissions, and other specifications had been produced in every year. As there was technological change in the industry, we are thus assessing not the expenditure that would have been saved had the 1949 models themselves been continued, but the expenditure that would have been saved had such cars been continued but built with the developing technology.

We count as costs not only the costs to the automobile manufacturers themselves of special retooling for new models, but also the direct costs of producing larger, heavier, and more powerful cars, plus the costs of automatic transmissions, power brakes, and the like. Finally, we include the secondary costs not paid out by the automobile companies but paid nevertheless by the

consuming public in the form of increased expenditures for gasoline necessitated by the "horsepower race."

This procedure clearly counts as "changes" *all* changes in those specifications which directly relate to the appearance of performance of the automobile. We do not count alterations in design of the car that do not *directly* change the package the consumer thinks he is buying. Thus, we assume that horsepower is a dimension of the car that enters directly into the utility function of the car buyer, but that engine displacement is not. This is not to say changes in engine displacement are not relevant: it is to say such changes are relevant only insofar as they influence one of the performance or appearance variables under consideration.

We have mentioned a consumer's utility function. The use of this concept carries with it the clear implication that the changes we consider may all have been desired by the car-buying public.[2] The question thus naturally arises: why not cost only those changes which were essentially "frills"? Why include in the estimates such things as automatic transmissions that were quite arguably improvements? The answer is that there is always a presumption of consumer sovereignty in the market economy and that it would be wholly arbitrary for us to say "this change was an improve-

---

Reprinted from *Journal of Political Economy,* Vol. 70, No. 5 (October, 1965), pp. 433-51 by permission of the University of Chicago Press. Copyright 1965 by the University of Chicago.
[1] 1949 is the earliest year for which all necessary data are available. It will be evident from the data that choice of 1950, 1951, or 1952 as the base year would not substantially alter the results.

[2] We say "may," not "must," for the market in question is far from perfect.

ment, and this was unnecessary" without detailed information on the utility functions of consumers. If tailfins were a frill, what about increased horsepowers? What about *extremely* increased horsepowers? Where there are costs, there are likely to be benefits as well, and, while the automobile market is not perfectly competitive, it seems likely to us that for most of the period in question the car manufacturers were giving the public what it wanted, save perhaps for overshooting in some respects.

We thus wish to avoid having this study taken as an indictment of the automobile companies. We are rather in the position of one who observes another man drinking various liquors. We do not blame the bartender for anything save that he occasionally gives the man more than he asks for of some expensive drink; nor do we question the man's right to drink; nor do we distinguish between "good" liquors and "bad." We do, however, present the bar bill. Since the argument is sometimes advanced that the resources spent on automobile model changes could be put to better use in the public sector,[3] it is clearly worth investigating the order of magnitude of the resources involved.

Section II considers the direct costs of model changes as well as the effect on advertising expenditures. Section III discusses retooling expenditures, and Section IV gasoline consumption. The results are combined and summarized in the final section, where we return to the question whether the estimated costs were worth incurring.

II. DIRECT COSTS AND ADVERTISING EXPENDITURES[4]

In this section we present estimates of the increases in consumer expenditures on automobiles associated with the changes in size and horsepower that have occurred since 1949. We discuss here how much more it cost to produce the, say, average 1958 car, given the 1958 levels of costs and technology, than it would have cost (at 1958 prices and with 1958 retooling expenditures) to produce a car of 1949 average specifications with the average 1949 level of "attachments." We shall treat the additional cost of the 1958 technology (above the 1949 level) — and the cost of retooling — in Section III. The "cost" estimates in this section consist of estimates of the increase in price due to increases in size and horsepower; the increase in expenditures due to the wider use of automatic transmissions, power steering, and power brakes; and the increase in price due to the increase in advertising expenditures above the 1949 levels.[5]

Only the effects of changes in size and horsepower present a difficult estimation problem, and hence only the solution to this particular problem will be discussed in some detail here. Ideally a group of engineers and cost accountants could produce the appropriate estimates of what it would cost to produce an average 1949-specifications car in each of the subsequent years. Unfortunately, we lack both the specialized knowledge and the resources required for such calculations. Instead, we make use of the apparent close relation between selected dimensions (specifications) of an automobile and its price at a point in time to estimate what the price would have been, at the same point of time, for a car with a different set of specifications.[6]

[3] See, for example, J. K. Galbraith, *The Affluent Society* (Boston: Houghton Mifflin Co., 1958), p. 352 and elsewhere.

[4] We are indebted to G. S. Maddala for research assistance with this section. Some of the computations reported in this section, originally designed for other purposes, were supported by a grant from the National Science Foundation to the University of Chicago to allow Griliches to engage in econometry studies of technological change.

[5] The last item belongs more properly in the section dealing with the cost of a given "technology" but is discussed in this section for reasons of convenience.

[6] For a more detailed discussion of the problems associated with relating cross-sectional differences in the price of a commodity to differences in

Table 1 presents the results of annual regressions of the logarithm of car prices (list) for different makes and models on the horsepower, weight, and length of these cars, and on a set of classificatory ("dummy") variables for other "qualities" such as whether a car has a V-8 engine, whether an automatic transmission is included in the list price (is "standard" equipment), and so forth. As can be seen from these results, the use of three numerical variables (horsepower, weight, and length) and several dummy variables explains, on the average, 90 per cent or more of the cross-sectional variance in the logarithm of list prices at a point of time. While the coefficients of particular dimensions are not very stable, the direction of their change over time (for example, the fall in the relative "price" of horsepower[7] and length) is consistent with other evidence and what we know about the industry.[8]

The regressions presented in Table 1 are used to estimate what would have been the list price of a car with the specifications of the average 1949 car each year since 1949 [9] This series and that of the average list prices of the cars actually produced move closely together until about 1954 when they begin to diverge, the difference (shown in col.

[1] of Table 2) reaching its maximum in 1959 and then declining slightly. During the 1956-61 period the difference between the average list price of the cars actually produced and the predicted price for the average 1949 car averaged approximately $450 per car, or about 17 per cent of the actual average list price.

The calculated price differences shown in column (1) of Table 2 are subject to several reservations. First of all they are based on list prices and may not represent the trend of actual prices adequately. In particular, if actual prices paid fell relative to list prices, the actual difference in price will be overestimated by our procedure. If, for example, discounts from list price increased from zero in 1949 to an average of about 15 per cent in 1960, then the average figure given for 1956-61 should be about $380 per car rather than the estimated $450.[10] On the other hand, we have priced *all* cars at their four-door sedan prices, not taking into account the faster growth in the number of higher priced station wagons, convertibles, and other car models. Since our equations make per-

---

"quality," dimensions, or specifications see Z. Griliches, "Hedonic Price Indexes for Automobiles: An Econometric Analysis of Quality Change" (Bureau of the Budget-NBER Price Statistics Review Committee Staff Report No. 3, printed in the United States Congress, Joint Economic Committee, *Government Price Statistics*, Hearings . . . January 24, 1961, [Washington, Government Printing Office, 1961], pp. 173-96), and the literature cited there.

[7] In particular, the fall in the relative "price" of horsepower clearly stems from the technological change in horsepower-engine size relation studied explicitly in Sec. IV below.

[8] Similar regressions were also run in linear form (rather than the semi-log form reported here) and using "piston displacement in cubic inches" as an additional variable without any improvement over the reported results. The "insignificance" of the displacement variable is due to its extremely high correlation with horsepower. Since

we are primarily interested in costing horsepower, we introduce it here directly rather than going through a circuitous procedure such as that necessary in Sec. IV.

Estimates were also made using several cross-sections at a time, imposing the condition that the various slope coefficients be the same for different years, but allowing the level of average prices ("technology") to shift "neutrally" over time, by assigning a separate constant term for each cross-section. The results were similar to those reported here and, since they do not lead to substantially different estimates or interpretations, are not reproduced here. Some of these estimates have been presented in Z. Griliches, "Hedonic Price Indexes . . . ," *op. cit.*

[9] In view of the form of our regressions, if profit margins and wholesale-retail markups are roughly constant in percentage terms, or at least uncorrelated with the various specification variables, this is also an estimate of "costs."

[10] For data on discounts see A. F. Jung, "Price Policy and Discounts in the Medium- and High-priced Car Market," *Journal of Business*, October 1960, pp. 342-47.

TABLE 1

COEFFICIENTS OF SINGLE-YEAR CROSS-SECTIONAL REGRESSIONS RELATING LOGARITHM
OF NEW UNITED STATES PASSENGER-CAR PRICES TO VARIOUS SPECIFICATIONS,
ANNUALLY 1950-61

Model Year	No.	Constant	H	W	L	V (Coefficients* of)	
1950	72	1.2709	.158 (.048)	.0484 (.0285)	.832 (.115)	−.024 (.014)	.892
1951	55	1.4329	.117 (.054)	.017 (.031)	.818 (.116)	.012 (.013)	.909
1952	51	1.7174	.097 (.042)	.105 (.030)	.578 (.127)	−.020 (.015)	.927
1953	54	1.9328	.113 (.044)	.103 (.038)	.471 (.136)	−.034 (.020)	.891
1954	65	2.3766	.202 (.037)	−.026 (.042)	.398 (.106)	−.024 (.014)	.857
1955	55	2.4570	.118 (.059)	.095 (.050)	.202 (.128)	−.050 (.026)	.871
1956	87	2.3359	.065 (.027)	.163 (.027)	.192 (.079)	−.052 (.016)	.907
1957	95	2.7370	.051 (.013)	.059 (.017)	.171 (.057)	−.011 plus significant (.010) coefficients for T, A, P, B	.967
1958	103	3.0389	.007 (.018)	.142 (.026)	−.073 (.092)	.005 plus T, A, P, B (.021)	.906
1959	87	3.1077	.052 (.013)	.103 (.017)	−.068 (.065)	−.031 plus T, A, P (.016)	.939
1960	78	2.9723	.052 (.009)	.059 (.020)	.065 (.073)	−.017 plus T, A, P, C (.011)	.951
1961	99	2.2530	.026 (.011)	.132 (.017)	.309 (.080)	.011 plus T, P, C (.012)	.940

* Dependent variable—logarithm of "list" (advertised delivered) price. Logarithms to the base 10. To convert the results to natural logarithms multiply all coefficients by 2.3. The resulting coefficient, if multiplied by 100, would measure the *percentage* impact on price of a *unit* change in a particular specification or "quality," holding the other specifications constant.

H, advertised brake horsepower, in 100's.

W, shipping weight in 1,000 pounds.

L, over-all length, in hundreds of inches.

V, 1 if the car has a V-8 engine; 0 if it has a 6-cylinder or less engine.

T, 1 if the car is a hardtop; 0 if not.

A, 1 if automatic transmission is "standard" equipment (included in price); 0 if not.

P, 1 if power steering is "standard"; 0 if not.

B, 1 if power brakes are "standard"; 0 if not.

C, 1 if the car is designated as a "compact"; 0 if not.

Source: *Specifications and prices, 1949, 1951-53:* Annual statistical issues (March 15) of *Automotive Industries* and annual issue of *Automotive News Almanac, 1954-60:* Various issues of National Automobile Dealers Association's *Used Car Guide,* Washington, *1955-58:* Data are from the February issue of the corresponding year. For 1954 models, figures are taken from July, 1959, issue; for 1959 models, from January, 1959, issue; and for 1960, from December, 1959, issue. *1950 and 1961: Red Book: Official Used Car Appraisals* (Chicago: National Market Reports, Inc.). November 14, 1956, and January 1-February 14, 1961. Some 1961 data are also based on *Car Fax* (Vol. VI, No. 1, 1961 ed., New York). Power brakes data for some years are taken from various issues of *World Automotive Yearbook.* Prices of automatic transmissions, power steering, and power brakes are taken from various issues of *Automobile News Almanac* and from October 1-November 14, 1958, issue of the *Red Book.*

Production Data: 1956-60 by model years by makes is taken from *Automotive Industries,* March 15, 1961. 1961 model-year data are from *Automotive News,* August 7, 1961. For 1955 it was assumed that the model year began in November of the previous year; for 1954 that the model year was January-October; model-year production by makes was computed from monthly production figures by make given in the 1955 and 1956 March 15 issues of *Automotive Industries.* For 1949-53 it was assumed that the model year coincided approximately with the calendar year; calendar-year production data by makes were taken from *ibid.* Data on models within makes and on V-8 engine, automatic transmissions, and power steering and brakes installations were available only for calendar years based on registration data (*Ward's Automotive Yearbook,* various issues). These data were transformed into percentages of a particular make, and these calendar-year within-make percentages were used to break down the model year production figure by makes to arrive at model-year production figure by makes *and* models. For 1961 we used 1960 calendar-year data on models within makes to break down the 1961 model-year production data by makes.

TABLE 2

TOTAL "DIRECT" COSTS OF AUTOMOBILE CHANGE SINCE 1949

Per Car Cost of Increase in

Model Year	Size and Horsepower[*]	Use of Optional Equipment			Advertising Expense	Total	Total Passenger Car Production (000's)	Total "Direct" Cost of Model Change† ($ Millions)
		Automatic Transmission	Power Steering	Power Brakes				
	(1)	(2)	(3)	(4)	(5)	(6)	(7)	(8)
1950	$-13	$12			$-3	$-4	6,659	-27
1951	17	33	$ 2		-2	50	5,331	267
1952	58	38	9	$ 1	0	106	4,337	460
1953	11	35	22	3	0	71	6,135	436
1954	160	55	21	7	3	246	4,359	1,072
1955	279	70	23	9	10	391	6,201	2,425
1956	377	72	14	9	14	483	6,295	3,040
1957	518	86	25	10	13	651	6,218	4,048
1958	410	86	31	9	16	553	4,256	2,354
1959	520	87	30	9	14	660	5,568	3,675
1960	447	75	31		13	575	6,001	3,456
1956-60 average							584	3,315

Source: See Table 1

[*] The regressions presented in Table 1 were used to predict the price of a car with average 1949 specifications. The specifications of the average 1949 car used in these predictions were: horsepower—104.24, weight—3,289.5 pounds, length—200.84 inches, and traction with V-8 engines—0.4067.

† Col. (6) × col. (7).

centage changes in price depend on changes in absolute specification levels, a higher "true" average price would lead also to a higher estimate of the difference.

Third, these and later calculations are based on "predictions" from statistically estimated equations that do not fit the data perfectly and hence are subject to error. The probable magnitude of this error can be calculated, however. The standard error of the regression line (the "standard" prediction error at the mean levels of the independent variables) is quite high for any one year. It averaged about $170 in the 1956-61 regressions. Thus, there is some doubt whether any *one* particular annual difference is statistically significantly different from zero. The consistency in the sign of these differences leaves little doubt, however, about their significance for the 1956-61 period as a whole. The quoted figures should thus provide a good estimate of the orders of magnitude that are involved here, since in no case were the average 1949 specifications outside the range of the observed variation in the specifications of later model-year cars. We are always interpolating rather than extrapolating to get at our "predictions."

The next set of "cost" estimates is very simple. Columns (2)-(4) of Table 2 present the estimated cost (per car) of the increased use of automatic transmissions, power steering, and power brakes. In each case we took a time series of list prices, a time series on the increase in the percentage use of these items (since 1949) as optional equipment (not already included in the price as "standard" equipment), and computed the "cost" per car as the product of these two series. Again, these "costs" reach their peak in 1958 or 1959.

Column (5) of Table 2 presents the estimated increases in advertising expenditures associated with the above-described model changes. We took a time series of advertising expenditures per car (for calendar years) from *Advertising Age*. These data are of doubtful quality but are used for lack of a better source. The main difficulty here is to devise a measure of the 1949 *quantity* of advertising per car in subsequent prices. We attempt to approximate such a measure by inflating the 1949 average advertising expenditures per car by the implicit GNP deflator. This deflator probably rises less than advertising *rates*, but the real cost of reaching and informing a particular consumer must have fallen somewhat during this period. Television rates, for example, have clearly not risen in proportion to the increase in the number of viewers. If anything, these calculations probably underestimate the "real" increase in the *quantity* of advertising per car. We estimated the "cost" of increased advertising as the difference between current advertising expenditures per car and the 1949 advertising expenditure level in current prices. Again these "costs" reach their peak in 1958.

The total direct cost of model changes (col. [8]) is estimated for each year by totaling the above described estimates (col. [6]) and multiplying them by the annual passenger-car production figures (col. [7]). For 1956-60 these costs averaged about $3.3 billion annually. This is probably an underestimate since we have left out of our calculations such other changes as the optional purchase of higher horsepower engines, power seats, power windows, various optional "trim" items, and so forth. On the other hand, allowing for the growth of discounting would reduce this figure to about $2.8 billion annually. In addition, the "prediction error" (two standard deviations) associated with these figures could lead them to be too high *or* too low by about $1.0 billion.

III. RETOOLING EXPENDITURES[11]

The most obvious cost of automobile model changes is the expenditure by the automobile manufacturers for the new tools, jigs, and dies needed to produce new models. Were models to remain unchanged, such expenditures would clearly be reduced to the level necessary to replace existing equipment as it wears out.

Of course, such expenditures on the physical equipment of production are not the only ones directly associated with model changes. There are, in addition, the costs of research and development and of design of the new models. Unlike the expenditures for retooling, however, the latter costs are not available, and we shall thus not be able to include them in our estimates. The exclusion of these costs, however, is not *wholly* undesirable. In the preceding section and in the following one we charge as "costs" expenditures that could have been avoided by producing cars with 1949 specifications *with the current technology*. It would clearly be inconsistent to charge also the costs of securing that technology. Since the development in which we are interested has been largely in engine design (see the next section), taking the form of reducing the "cost" of horsepower, it seems likely that the costs of securing that technology are a much larger part of research and development and design costs than of retooling expenditures. It follows that we are largely avoiding double counting here.[12]

It may appear, however, that we are double counting by including retooling expenditures as well as the direct costs discussed in the last section. Retooling expenditures are costs to the automobile companies and are presumably reflected in the prices of new cars which we already used in the regressions and computations of the previous section. It

[11] We are grateful to Lloyd Dollett, of the Securities and Exchange Commission, for his courtesy and assistance. The computations in this section were performed by Felicity Skidmore. We are indebted to members of the Harvard Research Seminar in Quantitative Economics for suggestions.

[12] Since we are not estimating "secondary" costs other than gasoline consumption, we feel safe in saying that the inclusion of retooling expenditures leaves our estimates on the low side.

seems to follow that we have already included retooling expenditures (and research and development and design costs) implicitly in our estimates of direct costs. This is not the case, however. We used the regressions of the last section to estimate the direct costs of producing cars with 1949 specifications with current technology. But the costs of retooling (which are reflected in our regressions) are also reflected in such estimates. Hence our estimated direct cost for 1949 specification cars are *overestimates* of the costs that would have been incurred had no model changes taken place, since in the latter event the prices of all cars would have been lower because of the elimination of retooling costs. It is thus not double counting to add retooling expenditures at this point.[13]

As our estimates of retooling expenditures, we took the expenditures for special tools included in additions to plant and property reported by the automobile firms to the Securities and Exchange Commission[14] and charged by them to current costs. The relevant figures are available by calendar year; for the most part we have interpreted them as applicable to the model year following that calendar year.[15] The figures are available for the full period we consider, save that the Ford figures are only available beginning with the 1953 model year, and figures for Studebaker are not available before the merger with Packard. These problems were handled as follows:[16]

Ford.—In 1953, Ford retooling expenditures were 10 per cent of the total. We have added 10 per cent to the totals for the preceding years.

Studebaker.—In 1954, expenditures by Packard were 1.3 per cent of the total (adjusted to include Ford). In 1955, expenditures by Studebaker-Packard were 3.7 per cent. We therefore added 2.4 per cent to the total for each year before 1955.

Clearly, the first adjustment is the only one of any importance; it seems conservative in view of higher Ford expenditures in later years.

To allow for normal replacement of worn-out equipment, we ignored the fact that 1949 was a year of substantial model change and assumed that all expenditure for that model year was for replacement of worn-out equipment; this yielded an upper limit of $190 billion for normal replacement expenditures. Taking into account model changes in 1949, $150 billion seems more than ample as an estimate of normal replacement expenditures (especially in view of the expenditure of only $175 million on retooling in 1950) and we used this figure adjusted for changes

---

[13] One qualification is necessary. If the recoupment of retooling costs in car prices is correlated with specifications, we have already counted some of it. In view of the semi-logarithmic form of our regressions, however, this effect will cancel out if it is roughly proportional to car price. This seems likely, since retooling expenditures per car are probably greater for high-priced models. In any case, such a bias in our results cannot be large, for despite the hugh increase in retooling expenditures over the period, our regressions show declining "prices" for specifications even after technological change in engine design practically ceased (as evidenced by our results of the next section). Moreover, the double counting engendered by this effect applies only to a part of the full retooling expenditure. We therefore feel fairly safe in neglecting it.

[14] Form 10K, Schedule V.

[15] The only exceptions are Willys-Overland and Nash and later American Motors, which report for

the year ended September 30. (Neither of these is a large part of the total, and the first is clearly negligible.) We have still assumed that such expenditures took place at the *end* of the reporting year and were for the *following* model year. This seems clearly to have been the case since about 1955 but is less certain before that time. Readjustment to account for this (if needed) would be only one of timing and would make very little difference in the industry totals in any case.

[16] Figures for Hudson in 1953 and Kaiser in 1950 are also missing. We did not bother to adjust the totals for this, because the first figure was clearly only about 1 per cent of the total at the most, and the second was much less.

TABLE 3

RETOOLING COSTS OF MODEL CHANGES SINCE 1949

| Model Year | Millions of Current Dollars | | Cost Per Car* (Current Dollars) (3) |
	Total Expenditures for Special Tools (1)	Retooling Costs Attributable to Model Changes (2)	
1950	175.3	19.6	2.9
1951	208.5	45.2	8.5
1952	262.8	81.7	18.8
1953	419.5	246.5	40.2
1954	439.1	263.5	60.5
1955	632.7	469.2	75.7
1956	523.3	336.2	53.4
1957	947.3	771.7	124.1
1958	827.8	625.7	147.0
1959	745.8	532.1	95.6
1960	756.5	536.6	89.3
1961	896.5	678.9	125.6
1956-60 average	760.1	560.5	98.9

*Production data 1950-60 from Table 2; 1961 estimated production from *Automotive News*, August 7, 1961.

in the wholesale price index for metal-working machinery. The resulting costs and costs per car (including 8 per cent for taxes that would have been saved) are presented in Table 3.

IV. GASOLINE CONSUMPTION[17]

A. THE DATA

This section deals with the saving in gasoline consumption that would have been effected had the "horsepower race" not occurred—had 1949 specifications been continued. To estimate this saving requires detailed data by model on miles per gallon performance of automobiles. The only such data available are the figures on miles per gallon during the period of ownership reported by Consumers Union and Consumer Research (principally the former) for 185 different models tested over the period 1948—July, 1961.[18]

B. FUEL ECONOMY AND ENGINE SIZE

There has been considerable technological progress in engine design over the last fifteen years. In particular, as the automobile manufacturers moved toward higher and higher horsepower cars in the middle and late fifties, they also redesigned engines to secure

[17] We should like to thank our research assistants, Stephen A. Resnick and David Shapiro, who secured most of the data here discussed; George Delehanty, who computed the weights for the relative importance of makers' models within automobile makes; and Felicity Skidmore and Cynthia M. Travis, who performed most of the computations directly relevant to gasoline consumption. The materials in this section of the study are based on work done for other purposes under a grant from Resources for the Future, Inc., to Massachusetts Institute of Technology to allow Fisher to study quantitative aspects of the economics of supply and demand in the petroleum industry.

[18] Other reported data are generally either for constant-speed tests, or highly aggregated.

higher horsepower for a given engine size. This had the dual effect of reducing the extra gasoline consumption attendant on horsepower increases and (as noted in Sec. II) of reducing the direct cost of horsepower. Accordingly, we had to find someway of measuring such progress in engine design in order to estimate the gasoline consumption that would have occurred had cars with 1949 horsepowers been built in each successive year *with the developing technology.*

Since the available test statistics for any given year are too scanty to allow us to analyze each year's models wholly separately (as in Sec. II)—our solution was a compromise between the need for enough data to perform any analysis and the impossibility of pooling the test data in any simple way because automobiles with different types of transmission cannot be simply lumped together for such purposes. We proceeded to break the problem into two parts: the relation of engine size to gasoline consumption and the effect of horsepower on engine size. The former relation was studied by pooling all test data for cars with a given transmission; the latter effect was studied by analyzing engine data for each successive year separately. This procedure involved the assumption that technological change was largely restricted to changes in engine design or in the type of transmission employed (we were able to use a moderately fine breakdown by transmission types) rather than acting to alter the effects of existing transmissions without changing their type.[19]

Consumer Reports each year presents a statistic which they term "Fuel Economy Factor" and which we shall denote by *F*. This statistic is "the cubic feet of cylinder volume swept by the pistons

on their suction strokes while the car travels one mile in high gear."[20] If engine displacement *(D)* is measured in cubic inches and the number of engine revolutions per mile in top gear is denoted by *R*, then:

$$F = \frac{R}{2}\left(\frac{D}{1728}\right). \qquad (1)$$

R, in turn, is dependent on wheel size and axle ratio, while *D*, as we shall see, is highly correlated with horsepower for a given engine type. Statements in *Consumer Reports* clearly imply that, if these data are segregated by type of transmission, they should be related to F[21]. This indeed turns out to be the case.

As already stated, F is defined for the performance of the car in its top gear. It would be possible to construct similar variables which measure performance in lower gears, but these would of course be almost perfectly correlated with F, for either manual or automatic transmissions, given the limited number of forward gears. However, even if we were to use such similar variables for lower gears, it would still be incorrect to regress gasoline consumption on them, pooling observations for cars with a different number of forward gears; the distribution of mileage over the different forward gears will not be the same for a car with four such gears as for a car with three or two. It follows that the coefficients in such regressions will be different for cars with a different number of forward gears. This being so, our data must be segregated by the number of forward gears before F can be used as the only "displacement-type" variable in the regression.[22] Accordingly, we

---

[19] Visual inspection of the residuals from our regressions seems to bear this out, as there does not seem to be any tendency for the scatter in the relation of gasoline consumption to engine size, given transmission type, to change over time.

[20] "U.S. Autos 1961," *Consumer Reports*, XXVI, No. 4 (April, 1961), 176.

[21] *Ibid.*

[22] F can be used also as the sole explanatory variable in the regressions, because such other variables as automobile weight enter principally into the determination of the characteristics and especially the size of the engine.

segregated the data into 2-speed automatics, 3-speed automatics, 4-speed automatics, manuals without overdrive, and manuals with overdrive. Fortunately, the test data are sufficiently numerous to support the ensuing analysis.[23] We therefore regressed gallons per 10,000 miles of car travel (denoted by G) on F for each of the five transmission categories.

As already remarked, the true relationship we are seeking is one between

statistically significant) correlations.[24] On the other hand, the relative stability of this distribution will depend on how much choice is left to the driver as to when to shift gears. We should, therefore, expect to find higher correlations for automatic-transmission cars than for manual-transmission cars, other things being equal. A similar argument leads us to expect higher correlation for 2-speed automatics than for 3-speed ones, for 3-speed automatics than for 4-speed

TABLE 4

REGRESSIONS OF GASOLINE CONSUMPTION (G) ON
Consumer Reports' FUEL ECONOMY FACTOR (F)

Transmission Type	Regression Equation	r^2	Number
2-speed automatic	$G = 214 + 2.38^{\circ}F$ (0.287)	.748	27
3-speed automatic	$G = 248 + 2.18^{\circ}F$ (0.179)	.693	68
4-speed automatic	$G = 380 + 1.54^{\circ}F$ (0.359)	.368	35
Manual without overdrive	$G = 240 + 1.79^{\circ}F$ (0.388)	.422	31
Manual with overdrive	$G = 308 + 1.68†\,F$ (0.648)	.233	24

$^{\circ}$ Significant at 0.1 per cent level.
† Significant at 2 per cent level.

G and variables similar to F reflecting performance in various gears as well as during idling periods. Given our segregation by transmission type, such variables are almost perfectly correlated with F, and we thus use F alone. However, the goodness of fit of the true relationship—and, therefore, of our estimated one as well—clearly depends on the stability of the distribution of mileage over the various forward speeds or gears (and, less importantly, of the distribution of time between idling and motion) over the tests reported. Since this distribution is not very stable, we expect to find somewhat low (though

ones, and for cars with manual transmissions than for those with overdrive.[25]

All these predictions as to the relative size of the R^2's are borne out by the results (Table 4). Their agreement with our predictions gives us some confidence in their relevance.

C. ENGINE SIZE AND HORSEPOWER

The present section is concerned with the effects of horsepower on F, our

---

[23] For the period 1949-61, there are almost no tests of semi-automatic transmissions, but the number of cars with such transmissions is negligible.

[24] Cf. comments on test statistics in "Roadtest Report on the Full-size 'Low-priced' V-8's," *Consumer Reports*, XXVI, No. 2 (February, 1961), 107.
[25] Since the variability of the distribution of mileage over forward speeds can be expected to be relatively high (*celeris paribus*) when the number of forward speeds is large and the amount of shifting among them consequently great.

measure of engine size.[26] These effects are assumed to operate only on engine displacement, *D,* the principal determinant of *F,* an innocuous assumption as the number of engine revolutions per mile, *R,* the other variable in equation (1), does not vary greatly from model to model.

As our measure of horsepower, we take "maximum advertised horsepower" (as in Sec. II), despite the fact that this variable is based on stripped engine performance rather than on actual power delivered to the rear wheels.[27] We considered the effects of transmission characteristics in the previous section. Moreover, if advertised horsepower is what the car-buyer thinks he is buying, it is advertised horsepower whose cost we wish to ascertain.

For a given type of engine and given engine efficiency, engine displacement *(D)* and horsepower *(H)* are theoretically proportional. Actual engines, however, were redesigned during the 1950's to permit the construction of high-horsepower engines at relatively lower displacement.[28] Accordingly, we did not pool observations from different years but estimated instead the relationship separately for each year.[29]

The fact that, for a given engine type, horsepower and displacement are roughly proportional implies that technological change takes the form of shifting a ray through the origin. Not all developments in engine design, however, can be applied to all horsepowers. Hence, while the points for a given engine type lie on a ray through the origin, not all points on that ray can represent actual engines. Successive technological changes which are aimed at higher horsepower engines become applicable at successively higher horsepower levels. Thus our regressions, save for the early years, are estimates not primarily of the relationship between displacement and horsepower for a given engine type but of the relationship between engine design and horsepower.[30] We are estimating the effect of higher horsepower on the availability of displacement-horsepower ratio reducing techniques. The fact that we obtain such a good fit leads us to accept a linear form for that relationship, and our faith in it is further bolstered by the fact that in every year the range of horsepowers covered in the data is extremely wide. Further, the 1949 horsepowers are all inside that range, so that we shall be interpolating between actual figures in applying our results to them.

It is important to realize that the relationship between *D* and *H* is exactly what we want. To take a given engine type and extend the line for high-horsepower cars backward toward the origin would give a most misleading overestimate of the extent to which the developing technology could have been used to effect gasoline economies at 1949 horsepowers. The engine redesigns for high-horsepower cars simply could not have been applied to these lower levels. Our estimates provide precisely the required information: the extent to which advances in engine design are applicable at given horsepowers.

---

[26] We are indebted to A. R. Rogowski, of the Department of Mechanical Engineering at M.I.T., for preliminary discussion of some of the technical matters covered in this section. He is emphatically not to be held responsible for our opinions, conclusions, results, or especially errors, nor for the evidently rudimentary state of our information on automotive mechanics.

[27] Cf. "U.S. Autos 1961," *op. cit.,* p. 176.

[28] This redesign took the form largely of raising compression ratios and of shifting the torque-rpm curve. The rising octane content of gasoline also helped.

[29] The observations in these computations were on engines rather than on cars. We eliminated observations on other models produced by a given company that had the same engine.

---

[30] Since the correlation between horsepower and displacement is so high for each year, and this is the relationship of interest, there is no need to introduce the effect on compression ratios as an explicit step.

TABLE 5

REGRESSIONS OF DISPLACEMENT (D) ON MAXIMUM ADVERTISED HORSEPOWER (H)

Model Year	Regression Equation	r^2	No.
1948	$D = 0.738 + 2.30^{\circ}H$ (17.0) (0.155)	.880	32
1949	$D = 6.24 + 2.17^{\circ}H$ (12.0) (0.106)	.938	30
1950	$D = 6.29 + 2.14^{\circ}H$ (13.8) (0.120)	.908	34
1951	$D = 11.4 + 2.04^{\circ}H$ (11.1) (0.0963)	.930	36
1952	$D = 30.0\dagger + 1.80^{\circ}H$ (11.1) (0.0900)	.917	38
1953	$D = 70.3^{\circ} + 1.42^{\circ}H$ (12.2) (0.0946)	.851	41
1954	$D = 82.2^{\circ} + 1.26^{\circ}H$ (14.1) (0.0987)	.798	43
1955	$D = 112^{\circ} + 0.938^{\circ}H$ (10.8) (0.0595)	.883	35
1956	$D = 103^{\circ} + 0.950^{\circ}H$ (10.4) (0.0505)	.912	36
1957	$D = 108^{\circ} + 0.860^{\circ}H$ (11.1) (0.0472)	.910	35
1958	$D = 109^{\circ} + 0.856^{\circ}H$ (11.6) (0.0444)	.921	34
1959	$D = 101^{\circ} + 0.914^{\circ}H$ (10.4) (0.0390)	.945	34
1960	$D = 109^{\circ} + 0.851^{\circ}H$ (19.2) (0.0783)	.797	32
1961	$D = 73.4^{\circ} + 1.07^{\circ}H$ (12.2) (0.0564)	.914	36

°Significant at 0.1 per cent level.
†Significant at 1 per cent level.

The results of these regressions are presented in Table 5.[31] We report standard errors for the constant terms, as the question of whether the regression line passes through the origin is obviously of interest. These results show a clear pattern. Starting with the expected ray through the origin in 1948, there is a slight decline in the slope to 1950-51, without much change in intercept. From 1952 to 1955, the slope diminishes rapidly and the intercept rises

---

[31] We present the results for the model years 1948-61 inclusive since the pattern seems of interest.

substantially.[32] From 1955 through 1961 the coefficients remain roughly constant.[33]

This pattern is to be expected from the preceding discussion. Starting with the ray through the origin which represents the displacement-horsepower relation for a given engine type, minor improvements took at first the form of lowering the slope of that ray slightly (making horsepower cheaper in terms of displacement). With the start of the horsepower race, this effect was accompanied by the introduction of new rays, with lower slopes, attainable only at higher .and higher horsepowers. The result in regression terms is depicted schematically in Figure 1, with R_1, R_2, and R_3 representing three engine types, representative of a whole spectrum of techniques (largely higher compression ratios and efficient use of high octane gasoline) available at higher horsepowers. The dashed portion of each ray represents that part of the ray which is unavailable, while the dotted circle shows the range of observations on the ray. BC is the resulting estimated regression line. As the horsepower race progressed, new rays became available to the right of R_3 at higher horsepowers, while existing techniques were used to

---

[32] Note that this change in the slope coefficients reflects itself (roughly) as a change in the direct cost of horsepower already reported in Sec. II.

[33] This pattern is not simply the result of sampling fluctuations. The hypothesis that all the regressions are from the same true relationship is emphatically rejected by covariance analysis, the relevant F statistic being 28.9, whereas the probability of observing an F even as high as about 2.1 if the hypothesis were true would be .001 (with 26 and 468 degrees of freedom). Moreover, such significant inhomogeneity is not merely due to the behavior of the intercepts. A further test of slope equality only yields an F statistic of 29.1, whereas the probability of observing an F even as high as about 2.7 if the slopes were all the same would be .001 (with 13 and 468 degrees of freedom). It is thus apparent that our results reflect real changes in structure for the period as a whole (similar tests would doubtless fail to reject the null hypothesis of no structural change for 1955-60).

FIGURE 1

ILLUSTRATION OF TECHNOLOGICAL
CHANGE IN THE HORSEPOWER-
DISPLACEMENT RELATIONSHIP

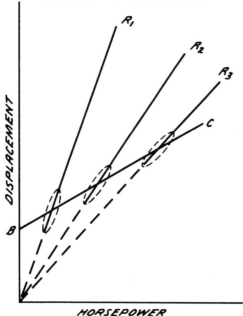

produce higher horsepower engines at
given displacements. The effect of all
this was to shift *BC* upward and lower
its slope. Finally, with the slackening
of the horsepower race and the introduction of the compact cars, existing
techniques were used to produce the required lower horsepower engines, thus
sliding the dotted circles back toward
the origin, shifting the regression line
BC downward and raising its slope
slightly.

The magnitude of these effects is of
some interest. Our results indicate that
a car in the 80-90 horsepower range
(slightly below the range encountered
for most low-priced cars) would have
had a roughly constant displacement
up until 1961 when a very moderate
decline in displacement would have
occurred. At 100 horsepower, displacement fell from about 230 cubic inches in
1948 to 194 cubic inches in 1960 and
180 in 1961. At 200 horsepower, however, displacement fell from about 460

cubic inches in 1948 to about 280 in
1960 and 1961. At higher horsepowers,
the fall was, of course, greater. In all
cases, most of the reduction occurred in
the 1951-55 period.

D. GASOLINE   COSTS   OF   MODEL
CHANGES

The relations summarized in Tables 4
and 5 were used to estimate the saving
in gasoline consumption that would
have been expected had 1949 specifications been continued. First, we estimated the gasoline consumption per
10,000 miles of each actually produced
automobile model. Where Consumer
Union test data were unavailable, we
estimated ("predicted") it from the appropriate equation in Table 4, using
"fuel economy factors" computed from
published engine displacement and
rpm data. These "predictions," together
with the actual test data, where available, were then aggregated to produce
comparable figures for company brand
names such as Chevrolet, Ford, and
Dodge, using (as in Sec.II) weights constructed from model-year production
data where available and from calendar-
year registration data otherwise.[34]
These figures were in turn averaged to
secure average figures for the industry
for each model year, 1949-60, using as
weights actual production data by brand
name, where available, or registrations
as of July 1 of the year following the
close of the model year.

To estimate the gasoline consumption
that would have been incurred by cars
with 1949 specifications, we took first
each 1949 model's horsepower and used
the results of Part C of this section to
estimate what the model's displacement

---

[34] The basic assumption in the latter case was
that the *internal* distribution of each brand name
over the various maker's models it included was
the same for the calendar year as for the model
year. This involved a host of minor problems of
comparability between successive year's models
too numerous to discuss in detail. The registration data are collected by R. L. Polk & Co., and
reported in several trade journals.

would have been in each successive year. From these estimates we selected as the displacement figure for each year the minimum of the displacements estimated for that model from 1950 to the year in question and the actual displacement for 1949. These displacements were then transformed into fuel economy factors using equation (1) from Part B and assuming that engine revolutions per mile in high gear would have been the same as in 1949. The resulting values of F were then transformed into gasoline consumption per 10,000 miles by use of the results of Part B of this section.

These estimated gasoline consumption figures were aggregated into brand-name figures using the 1949 weights. The results were then aggregated in turn into industry figures using registrations of 1949 cars as of July 1, 1950.[35] The resulting estimates of miles per gallon performance for both the actual and the constant 1949 specification cars are given in Table 6 for model years 1949 through 1960.

TABLE 6
MILES PER GALLON PERFORMANCE OF NEW ACTUAL AND
CONSTANT 1949 SPECIFICATION CARS

Model Year	Miles Per Gallon, New Actual Cars	Miles Per Gallon, New 1949 Specification Cars	Extra Cost of New Actual Cars Per 10,000 Miles[*] (Current Dollars)
1949	16.4		
1950	16.4	16.7	3.1
1951	15.7	16.9	12.5
1952	16.0	17.1	11.4
1953	16.1	17.2	11.7
1954	15.6	17.3	18.4
1955	15.1	17.4	26.8
1956	14.8	17.7	34.6
1957	14.5	17.9	42.4
1958	14.4	17.9	43.2
1959	14.3	18.0	44.3
1960	15.3	18.0	30.6
1961	15.2†	18.5	37.2‡

[*] Valued at prices in Table 7 (below).
† 1960 weights used.
‡ At 1960 prices.

[35] We assume here and below that the distribution of 1949 cars by brand names would have been preserved had 1949 specification been continued. Since brand market shares have not changed very much, this is not an important assumption.

Table 6 shows that, while gasoline mileage was declining from 16.4 miles per gallon in 1949 to 14.3 miles per gallon in 1959, it could have been rising to 18.0 miles per gallon had 1949 specifications been continued. Even the rise to 15.3 miles per gallon that occurred with the introduction of the compacts in 1960 fell far short of the actual 1949 level, let alone the level that could have been achieved. In money terms, the average owner of a 1959 car (the most gasoline-consuming model year) was paying about $44 per 10,000 miles more for gasoline than would have been the case with 1949 specifications — about 20 per cent of his total gasoline expenditures. For high-price high-horsepower cars, the additional cost was even greater.

Unlike the costs discussed in the last two sections, the costs of extra gasoline consumption do not terminate with the building and sale of the car; they continue over the life of the automobile. We must therefore estimate the total gasoline consumption of that part of the car *stock* consisting of cars built after 1949 that would have been avoided in each year with constant 1949 specification.[36]

To construct estimates of gasoline consumption by actual post-1949 cars for each year, we took the average gasoline consumption by brand name and model year derived above and multiplied them by the registration figure for that brand name and model year as of July 1 of the year in question. The basic assumption used in the construction of estimates of the gasoline consumption of the constant 1949 specification car stock was that the history of these cars

[36] We must make here some assumption about the change in gasoline consumption over the life of a car. Since we are primarily interested in the *difference* between the gasoline consumption of the actual car stock and of one made up to 1949 specification cars, we have only to assume that the effect of age on gasoline consumption is linear and the same in both cases, so that with the same age distribution of cars in the car stock, the difference in gasoline consumption will be unaffected.

TABLE 7

GASOLINE CONSUMPTION COSTS OF MODEL CHANGES SINCE 1949

Year	Extra Gasoline Consumption by Post-1949 Cars (Million Gals.)	Average Per Post-1949 Car (Gals.)	Per Cent of Actual Gasoline Consumption by Such Cars	Average Retail Price of Gas Including Tax (Current Dollars Per Gal.)*	Gasoline Costs of Model Changes	
					Per Post-1949 Car (Current Dollars)	Millions of Total Current Dollars
1950	45.4	14.7	2.6	.2776	4.1	12.6
1951	126.1	15.1	2.7	.2815	4.3	35.5
1952	362.4	27.2	4.7	.2856	7.8	102.0
1953	542.7	29.8	5.2	.2969	8.8	161.1
1954	797.4	33.7	5.8	.3004	10.1	239.5
1955	1,237.7	42.1	7.2	-3007	12.7	372.2
1956	1,906.7	53.6	9.1	.3093	16.6	589.7
1957	2,523.6	62.7	10.5	.3196	20.0	806.5
1958	3,025.4	69.3	11.5	.3138	21.7	949.4
1959	3,642.0	77.0	12.7	.3149	24.2	1,146.9
1960	4,189.0	83.3	12.6	.3213	26.8	1,345.9
1956-60 average						967.7

*One cent per gallon added (see text) to figures for 1950-58 in American Petroleum Institute, *Petroleum Facts and Figures, 1959*, p. 379; 1959-60 *Platt's Oilgram Price Service.*

would have duplicated the actual history of the 1949 models, so far as the distribution in any year t of such cars over brand names is concerned.[37]

The resulting estimates of gasoline consumption by post-1950 cars for both the actual and the 1949 specifications car stock assume that cars were driven 10,000 miles per year, on the average. However, the Bureau of Public Roads and the American Petroleum Institute estimate the actual average mileage of passenger cars at somewhat less than this, their estimates ranging between about 9,000 and 9,500 miles per year.[38] There is no need for great precision here, and we took 9,250 miles as the relevant figure for every year.

We valued gasoline consumption at the current retail prices for regular gasoline, including tax,[39] adding one cent

per gallon as an adjustment for the higher price of premium grade gasoline.

The resulting estimates are given in Table 7. However, they do not tell the whole story. As mentioned earlier, gasoline consumption costs of model changes last throughout the life of the car. Thus, even if the 1962 and all later model years were to see a return to 1949 specifications, the additional gasoline expenditures due to the 1950-61 model changes would continue for the next decade at least. Assuming an average car life of ten years, and discounting the future at 10 per cent (surely an ample rate), the present value in 1961 of such expenditures (at 1960 prices) is about $7,109.5 million.

V. TOTAL COSTS AND CONCLUSIONS

The various components of costs estimated in previous sections are brought together in Table 8 and graphed in Figure 2.

What can we say about these figures?

First, let us ask whether our estimates are likely to overstate or understate the costs to the economy of model changes since 1949. The answer seems to be that our estimates understate the cost. Aside from items previously discussed, we

[37] Other assumptions as to the composition of the car stock over brand names would have been more difficult to apply in practice and would make little difference to the totals. To assume that the total number of cars would have been less than actually was the case would have given a higher estimate of costs.

[38] American Petroleum Institute, *Petroleum Facts and Figures, 1959* (New York, 1960), pp. 252-53.

[39] We include taxes here as elsewhere as we are measuring expenditure by car owners. Taxes were about 7-10 cents per gallon during the period.

FIGURE 2
Total Estimated Costs of Model Changes Since 1949

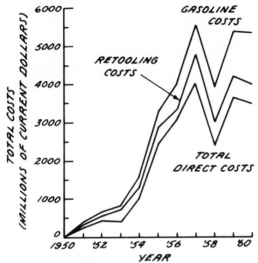

TABLE 8
Total Estimated Costs of Model Changes since 1949
(Millions of Current Dollars)

Year°	Total Direct Costs (1)	Retool-ing Costs (2)	Gaso-line Costs (3)	To-tal Costs † (4)
1950	− 27	20	13	6
1951	267	45	36	348
1952	460	82	102	644
1953	436	246	161	844
1954	1,072	264	240	1,576
1955	2,425	469	372	3,266
1956	3,040	336	590	3,966
1957	4,048	772	806	5,626
1958	2,354	626	949	3,924
1959	3,675	532	1,147	5,354
1960	3,456	537	1,346	5,339
1956-60 average				4,843
Present value in 1961 of future gasoline costs already committed‡				7,110

°We have combined model-year and calendar-year figures. The actual timing of the various elements of the total is slightly different.
† Total may not equal sum of components due to rounding.
‡ Due to lack of data at time of writing, we do not present complete estimates for 1961. Preliminary estimates using 1961 figures presented in earlier sections indicate that costs in that year (including gasoline costs) continue well above $5 billion.

have not attempted to estimate such possibly important secondary costs as the added traffic and parking problems due to greater car length, or the costs in

human life and property damage that may have resulted from higher horse-powers.[40] Further, newer model cars (especially as automatic transmissions became more and more widespread) tended to have higher repair costs than would presumably have been the case with 1949 specifications. None of these items have been included in our estimates.

Moreover, while we argued in Section III that the exclusion of design and research and development costs was in part an avoidance of double counting, it is clear that large elements of such design and research and development costs hardly contributed to the technological change involved in our estimates. One need only mention the expenditures that Ford must have incurred in the introduction of the short-lived Edsel to realize that we have failed to include some sizable items in our analysis.

Next, we have assumed throughout that the number of cars would have been unchanged had 1949 specifications been continued. This may or may not be a good assumption, but it is difficult to argue that *more* cars would have been sold. It follows that, if anything, our results fail to cost the extra cars that were in fact produced.

Finally, in choosing the 1949 model year as a standard for specifications, and in resting our analyses on the actual costs and gasoline consumption of domestically produced cars, we have not asked whether a more stringent standard could not be derived from the experience of various European car producers. Our cost estimates rest on the historical experience of the domestic industry. Had we chosen a European small-car standard, estimated costs clearly would have been higher.

---

[40] Potentially at least, these costs could be estimated. Some parking garages charge a higher fee for longer cars, and insurance claims paid presumably could be analyzed for variation with specifications, other things being equal. This would be a full-scale undertaking, however.

For all these reasons, it seems to us that our estimates must err considerably on the low side, even after the greatest benefit of the doubt is given to the stochastic nature of our estimates. The order of magnitude of the cost of model changes is clearly greater than that indicated in our figures. On the other hand, we have not attempted to assess monetary benefits. For example, the increases in horsepower and in the use of power steering and automatic transmissions may have led to an increase in the average speed of automobile travel of about 10 per cent.[41] Assuming that in the base period the average speed was about 30 miles per hour, that approximately 9,000 miles were traveled by a car per year, and that on the average there were about 1.5 passengers per car, we get an estimate of 45 man-hours saved per new car year. Valuing these hours at $1.00 per hour[42] leads us to a guess of $45 as the annual per car benefit from the time-saving aspects of higher speeds. This is a large figure, of the same order of magnitude as our estimate of the costs of increased gasoline consumption per car, and would similarly persist throughout the life of the car. It is hard to think of many additional "benefits" of this sort. Their existence, however, is indicated by the apparent willingness of consumers to pay for at least some of these changes.

The costs of model changes since 1949 were thus a substantial part of expenditures on automobiles, especially in the last half of the 1950's, our estimates running about $5 billion a year.[43] Were such costs worthwhile? It is difficult to say. There is a presumption that consumer purchases are worth the money paid, yet one might argue that the fact that our figures for the late 1950's (about $700 in the purchase price per car, or more than 25 per cent, and $40 per year in gasoline expenses) will probably seem surprisingly high to consumers[44] is an indication that the costs in question were not fully understood by the consuming public.

On the other hand, one must not press such an argument too far. We have repeatedly stated that, in every model year considered, the *average* 1949 specifications lay inside the actual range of specifications encountered. The clear implication is that consumers could have bought such cars had they wished. Moreover, such items as automatic transmissions, power brakes, and power steering were separately available and had prices of their own. It is thus extremely hard to claim that at least some of the costs of model changes were not explicitly reflected in the prices set before consumers. Indeed, the only elements of such costs that were obviously not explicitly stated were the costs of retooling and advertising and (possibly) gasoline costs. Thus consumers knowingly purchased more costly cars than those with 1949 specifications, even in the presence of *some* explicit cost differential in favor of the latter.

All in all, save for the understatement of costs involved and the possibility that such costs were not fully understood by car-buyers, the model changes of the last decade seem to have been largely those desired by the consuming public, at least until the last years of the horsepower race. There are thus grounds for believing that car owners (at the time of purchase) thought model

---

[41] This and the following figures are purely illustrative. We have been unable to find a consistent set of national data on this topic. The following calculation is only intended to indicate the possible magnitude of such benefits. These estimates are probably on the high side.

[42] This relatively low figure is used, since a substantial fraction of these passengers are women and children who are not in the labor force.

[43] These figures include tax and are thus measures of expenditures by consumers. At factory costs they would still be over $4 billion a year.

---

[44] The Automobile Manufacturers Association clearly regards them as extremely high (see letter of Harry A. Williams [its managing director] in *The Nation*, February 17, 1962, p. 128).

changes worth most of the cost. The general presumption of consumer sovereignty thus implies that these model changes *were* worth their cost.[45] How heavily that presumption is to be weighted in the presence of some cost understatement or in the presence of advertising directed at the formation or changing of tastes[46] is not a question that can be readily decided. Nor, indeed, is it obvious in retrospect that a referendum among the same car owners on the desirability of model changes would now reveal (or would have revealed in 1949) the same preferences for model change that seem to have been revealed in the historical market place.

It is thus not easy to decide whether the costs reported in this paper were worth incurring. Unlike some other examples of product change, the issue seems difficult enough to be worth raising. No one would deny that the shift from the horse and buggy to the automobile and the change from the kerosene lamp to the electric light were worth their respective costs.[47] Such improvements were so large and obvious that the issue is easy to decide. Whether this is true of some or all of the changes from the 1949 automobile specifications seems to us to be at least an open question.[48]

---

[45] Indeed, one of the authors has used some of the same calculations to measure the improvement in the *quality* of automobiles since 1949 (see Griliches, "Hedonic Price Indexes . . . ," *op. cit.*).

[46] Or in the presence of external diseconomies of consumption in the case of some of the non-costed items mentioned earlier in this section.

[47] Cf. Williams, *op. cit.*, and *Barron's Weekly*, January 11, 1962, p. 7.

[48] "The 1949 car . . . was pretty advanced transportation for its day" (Williams, *op. cit.*).

B. ETHICS

52. Deceptive Packaging: Are the Deceivers Being Deceived?

JAMES C. NAYLOR[1]

The tremendous emphasis placed upon packaging as a wedge to success in the consumer market in recent years has resulted in certain packaging techniques which have been questioned on an ethical basis. The most outstanding of these is the practice known as "deceptive packaging." Briefly defined, deceptive packaging involves a deliberate attempt to mislead the consumer regarding some aspect of the product (usually quantity) by using packages specifically designed to convey a false impression concerning this product attribute (e.g., making the package oversize). The extent to which this practice has become prevalent is difficult to state, although the fact that in recent months a Senate subcommittee was formed to inquire solely into this particular problem would attest to its frequency of occurrence.

From the point of view of consumer psychology, the problem is not primarily one of ethics, but rather of determining what effect deceptive packaging has upon the consumer, per se. First, does he realize that he is being deceived? Second, what is the effect of the deception upon his perception of the product (a) if he feels he has been deceived, or (b) if he is not aware of any deception? The purpose of this study was to experimentally investigate a case of deliberate deceptive packing in an attempt to provide answers to some of these questions.

METHOD

The independent variable chosen for study was package quantity. Through the cooperation of a local potato chip manufacturer, it was possible to obtain 144 experimental twin packs which were filled to specified weight requirements. The normal contents of a regular twin pack in terms of weight was 9 ounces. The experimental twin packs were of three weights: 9 ounces (control packs), 8 ounces, and 7 ounces. The experimental packs were all filled with chips from the same batch in order to assure equal treatment. All were packaged in regular twin pack containers in a normal manner. The only difference between the experimental packs was in terms of quantity as determined by weight. Two retail outlets were selected for distribution: a medium-sized independent grocery located in a suburban area (Store A) and a large chain store market (Store B) in more metropolitan surroundings.

Procedure. Because of possible ill feeling which might have been generated toward the donor company, it was not feasible to have the experimental packs actually purchased by the consumer. Thus, a procedure was adopted in which the experimental packs were given, free of charge, to any person willing to participate in the experiment. An observer was stationed with a supply of

From *Journal of Applied Psychology*, Vol. 46, No. 6 (December, 1962), pp. 393-98.
[1] The author wishes to acknowledge the data collection efforts of G. Croft Henry, John Mitchell, and Don Shumaker, members of the research field team.

the 7-, 8-, and 9-ounce experimental packs within view of the normal store display. Any consumers who "purchased" (i.e., clearly selected from the display) a twin pack of the donor brand were approached by the observer and asked as to their willingness to cooperate in a university study of consumer preferences. They were told that they would receive a sample pack free of charge on the condition that they were to "compare the contents of the two packs (regular versus experimental) in terms of personal preference." This preference would be obtained by a follow-up 10-minute interview in their own home within 3 days.

If the customer was agreeable to this, he or she was then given one of the experimental packs as a gift (the three weights were distributed in random order) and a time and day for the

TABLE 1
Sample Questionnaire Used in the Interview

AGE_____   SAMPLE_____

SEX_____

1. Was this the first time you have purchased this brand?   Yes____ No____
2. Do you usually purchase this brand?   Yes____ No____
3. Do you expect to purchase this brand again?   Yes____ No____
4. What did you like most about this brand?_____
5. What (if anything) did you like least about this brand?_____
6. Please circle the point on the scale that expresses your reaction to each pack.

  a. How well did you like the contents of the regular pack?

         1   2   3   4   5   6   7   8   9
      —|—|—|—|—|—|—|—|—|—
       terrible   poor   average   good   excellent

  b. How well did you like the contents of the sample pack?

         1   2   3   4   5   6   7   8   9
      —|—|—|—|—|—|—|—|—|—
       terrible   poor   average   good   excellent

7. If both were available for purchase the next time you went to the store, which would you buy?

      ____ sample pack
      ____ regular pack
      ____ either
      ____ neither

8. List three words that describe the two packs.

      a. Sample pack: _____
      b. Regular pack: _____

9. Which pack had the most in it?

      ____ regular pack
      ____ sample pack
      ____ same

subsequent interview were agreed upon.

A reminder slip with the time and date for the interview was made out and stapled to the sample (free) pack. This slip also served to provide the basis for differentiation between the sample and the regular pack.

Distribution of packs was done only between the hours of 4:00 P.M. and 9:00 P.M. on Thursdays, Fridays, and Saturdays. Twenty-four experimental packs were distributed every week—eight of each weight. This procedure was continued for a 6-week period. To prevent staleness of the experimental chips, they were obtained from the donor once every 2 weeks in lots of 48 (16 of each weight). Thus, over the 6-week period a total of 144 experimental packs was distributed—48 of each weight class. The first 3 weeks of distribution was in Store A, the remainder in Store B.

Interview. The interview itself consisted of having the consumer fill out a short, nine-item questionnaire (see Table 1). The first five items were for the purpose of obtaining information desired by the donor company, and Questions 6 through 9 were designed to obtain preference information as a function of perceived deception. Any requests for additional insight into the experiment on the part of the consumer at the time of the interview were refused. However, a promise to mail a short explanation at the conclusion of all interviews was made where desired. All such requests were subsequently honored.

Interviewers. The distribution of packs and the subsequent interviewing of consumers were done by a three-man research team consisting of a senior psychology graduate student and two undergraduate psychology majors.

RESULTS

SAMPLE CHARACTERISTICS

Only six customers declined to participate in the survey when approached by the observer, making the total acceptances 144 out of 150. This represents a loss of only 4%. Out of the 144 customers who agreed to participate, however, 26 were lost during the interview phase—primarily due to absences as a function of summer vacation. Thus, the final data sample consisted of 118 consumers. Table 2 shows the age and sex characteristics for the 114 people who responded to these two interview questions.

As indicated in the table, the sample was predominantly female. A chi square test was performed on the sample frequencies to determine if the relative proportion of males and females differed for the three experimental groups. The results clearly indicated that they did not ($\chi^2 = .167$, $df = 2$, $p > .99$). In addition, a simple analysis of variance test was made to test for age differences. The mean ages for the three experimental groups were not significantly different ($F = .04$, $df = 2/113$).

TABLE 2
BREAKDOWN OF CONSUMER SAMPLE IN TERMS OF AGE AND SEX

	Experimental group			
Criterion	9 ounces	8 ounces	7 ounces	Total
Age *M*	36.7	37.5	38.7	37.6
Age *SD*	10.7	12.3	7.7	10.2
Male	6	4	5	15
Female	35	31	33	99
N	41	35	38	114

TABLE 3
FREQUENCY OF PEOPLE JUDGING EXPERIMENTAL OR
REGULAR PACK AS HEAVIEST AS A FUNCTION OF
EXPERIMENTAL PACK WEIGHT

$(N = 118)$

Weight of experimental pack	Pack judged heaviest		
	Experimental	Regular	Equal
9 ounces	9	4	30
8 ounces	5	8	22
7 ounces	7	8	25

Note.—$\chi^2 = 3.121$, $df = 4$. $p < .50$.

In order to discuss the results of deceptive packaging, it was necessary to have some indication of the extent to which the weight shortages in the sample packs were perceived by the consumers. Table 3 shows the frequencies of the responses to the categories of Question 9 on the questionnaire. Regardless of experimental pack weight, the majority of the responders indicated the two packs as being equal in contents. A chi square test of significance showed no significant shift in proportions as the contents of the experimental pack was decreased ($\chi^2 = 3.121$, $df = 4$, $p < .50$).

It was possible to obtain two judgment scores for each person—his judgment for the regular pack and his judgment for the experimental pack—from Question 6. A difference score was then computed for each individual using the following formula: Experimental Pack Scale Value—Regular Pack Scale Value.

This resulted in a score indicating

FIGURE 1
PREFERENCE IN FAVOR OF THE CONTENTS OF THE EXPERIMENTAL
PACK AS A FUNCTION OF THE EXPERIMENTAL PACK WEIGHT

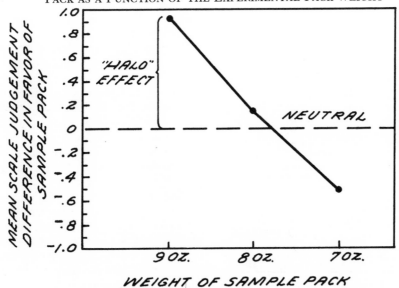

the degree to which the contents of the experimental pack were preferred over those of the regular pack. The mean of these scores was then computed for each group (see Figure 1). When the two packs were of equal weight a marked preference was indicated for the experimental pack. When the experimental pack was 1 ounce less, however, the preference for it was only slight, and when there was a 2-ounce difference the regular pack was substantially preferred. An analysis of variance of these judgment differences (see Table 4) indicated that the decrease in preference for the experimental pack as a function of its weight was statistically significant at the .05 level ($F = 4.58$, $df = 2/115$).

A second measure of the effect of weight on preference was obtained by

analyzing the responses to Question 7. Table 5 shows the distribution of responses to the alternatives presented by this question. The response alternative "neither" only attracted a total of four responses and was therefore eliminated in the analysis. When the packs were of equal weight, the majority of the consumers stated that, if given a choice, they would purchase the experimental chips. With a 1-ounce weight differential the plurality response changed to "would buy either," and with a 2-ounce difference the plurality response was in favor of the regular pack. A chi square test indicated that this change in preference was significant at the .05 level ($X^2 = 10.203$, $df = 4$).

A third analysis of package preference was obtained through the descriptive adjectives applied to each pack in Question 8. A total of 109 different adjectives or adjective phrases were used by the consumers in describing the two packs. These phrases were given to 10 judges (psychology graduate students) who rated each of them for favorability on a five-point Thurstone rating scale. The phrases and their resulting mean scale values are shown in Table 6. The analysis of variance reliability for the ratings was .96, and the difference between rater zero points was significant at the .01 level ($F = 23.95$, $df = 108/792$).

Each person was then assigned two mean scores on the basis of the adjectives used to describe the regular and experimental packs using the favorability scale value for each adjective. The difference between these two means was then computed as follows: ($\bar{X}$ adjective scale value for experimental pack) $-$ ($\bar{X}$ adjective scale value for regular pack).

This resulted in an adjective preference score for the experimental pack for each person. The mean of these adjective preference scores was then computed for each group (see Figure 2). The same pattern of preference as a function of experimental pack weight

TABLE 4

ANALYSIS OF VARIANCE OF THE DIFFERENCES IN THURSTONE JUDGMENTS OF PREFERENCE BETWEEN REGULAR AND EXPERIMENTAL PACKS AS A FUNCTION OF EXPERIMENTAL PACK WEIGHT

($N = 118$)

Source	df	MS	F
Weight	2	22.0	4.58*
Error	115	4.8	
Total	117		

* $p < .05$.

TABLE 5

DISTRIBUTION OF PREDICTED NEXT PURCHASE CHOICE AS A FUNCTION OF EXPERIMENTAL PACK WEIGHT

($N = 118$)

	Predicted choice		
Weight of sample	Buy experimental	Buy either	Buy regular
9 ounces	22	2	11
8 ounces	13	12	6
7 ounces	12	8	15

Note.—$\chi^2 = 10.203$, $df = 4$, $p < .05$

TABLE 6
SCALE VALUES OF DESCRIPTIVE ADJECTIVES USED TO DESCRIBE SAMPLE AND REGULAR PACKS

Mean scale value	Words or phrases	Mean scale value	Words or phrases
4.6	Crispy, Delicious	2.9	More tender, Saltier, Shorter, Same
4.5	Very tasty, Crisper		
4.4	Very very good, Very fresh, Excellent, Superb	2.8	Not too oily, Brown edges
		2.7	Milder, Small, Not as large
4.3	Scrumptious, Very good, Fresh	2.6	Not as thin, Unsized, Greasy but good, Less salty
4.2	Tastier, Crisp (as usual), Tasty		
4.1	Always good	2.5	Stronger taste, Average, Rough, Heavier, Too thin
4.0	Good taste, More crisp, Crisp, Full of goodness		
		2.4	Darker
3.9	Good color, Flavorful, Better flavor, Appetizing	2.3	Too well done, Ordinary, Thicker
3.8	Lighter, Good, Flavorsome, Good smell, Better taste	2.2	Not tender, Cheesy taste, Too brown
3.7	Better, Clean taste, Crunchier	2.1	Too small, Not enough shortening, Too salty
3.6	Wholesome, Satisfying, Good size, Richer, Crisp edges		
		2.0	Less flavorful, Heavy texture, Not very good, Not as crisp
3.5	(None)		
3.4	Good oil, Not greasy, Tangy, Not too salty	1.9	Oily, Burnt, Green, Scanty amount
3.3	Well done, Large, Thinner, Uniform size, Thin, Greaseless, Smooth texture	1.8	Hard, Not crisp, Unseasoned
		1.7	Flat
		1.6	A little greasy, Mealy
3.2	Digestible, Bigger, Lighter color	1.5	Greasy, Undesirable
		1.4	Slightly stale, Greasy taste
3.1	Done, Less oily, Dryer	1.3	Bitter, Limp, Tasteless, Too greasy.
3.0	Brown, Not burnt, Palatable, Salty, Smooth		

was found with the adjective values as had been found previously with the Thurstone judgments. As the weight of the experimental pack contents was decreased, the preference for that pack was also decreased. The analysis of variance on the means in Figure 2 indicated that they were not significantly different from one another ($F = .34$, $df = 2/115$) even though the differences were in the expected direction.

DISCUSSION

Deception in packaging can occur in two general ways. First, a consumer may be deceived at time of purchase and subsequently discover this deception at the time of product consumption. Such a case may be considered a "purchase deception." Second, a consumer may be deceived at time of purchase and not discover the deception at all. The latter may be considered a "consumption deception." Since the data from Question 9 indicated that even following the actual consuming of the chips people were not aware of any shortages, the results of the study may be considered as applying to a consumption deception and not to a purchase deception.

From an ethical point of view the consumption deception is the most severe, since the consumer, unaware of anything amiss, will supposedly continue to be satisfied with his purchase. With a purchase deception, however, he is overtly aware of having been taken advantage of and is thus able to modify his

FIGURE 2

MEAN DIFFERENCE IN SCALE VALUES OF ADJECTIVES USED
TO DESCRIBE EXPERIMENTAL AND REGULAR PACKS
AS A FUNCTION OF EXPERIMENTAL PACK WEIGHT

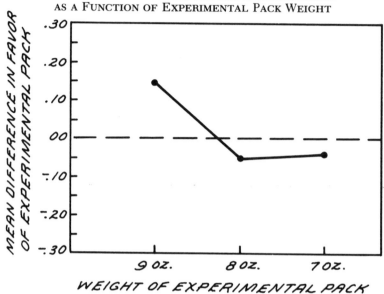

WEIGHT OF EXPERIMENTAL PACK

subsequent buying behavior to avoid a repeat deception. The results of the several preference indices computed in this study, however, indicate that even in the case of a consumption deception there is created a dissatisfaction with the product, even though the source of dissatisfaction cannot be identified by the consumer! As the contents of the experimental pack were decreased, there was a related decrease in product preference for the experimental pack. This occurred for all three indices — significantly so for two of them. The non-significance in the third case may have been a function of limited variance due to the use of a five-point Thurstone scale in scaling the adjectives.

The fact that the experimental pack was markedly preferred with all indices when it was the same weight as the reg-ular pack was probably a function of (a) the fact that it was free, and (b) an aura of "If it's something new, it must be better" surrounding the free pack. The end result was to produce a halo effect (see Figure 1) which accounted for the experimental pack preference.

If indeed the answers to Question 7 were true predictors of future buying decisions, the fact that a consumption deception had occurred would result in a decrease in purchases for the pack having a weight shortage, and this decrease would be related to the degree of deception involved. While such extrapolation of buying behavior on the basis of questionnaire responses is sometimes dangerous, the implications should be obvious to those engaged or planning to engage in a program of package deception.

53. Ethics in Purchasing: A New Look

ROBERT J. HOLLOWAY and TOD WHITE

Purchasers are probably more familiar with the problems of maintaining high ethical business standards than are other businessmen. The reason is obvious: they are in the center of the market exchange process where the temptations facing businessmen seem to be at their peak. Even if they wanted to ignore the problem, purchases could not entirely do so.

The problem of immoral conduct seems to be a natural one which arises from competitive conditions. It occurs in sports as well as in business. It occurs in communistic countries when supply is inadequate and buyers are tempted to bribe the suppliers. It occurs in our country where the seller and the buyer are each expected to gain advantage from the exchange process. The incentives are substantial from the personal as well as the company standpoint. We place high values on goods and positions in our society. Our aspirations in this direction underlie a good deal of our overall behavior. This is no indictment against our system, for the same materialism exists in most every place in the world. We do, however, need to be cognizant of this fact as we appraise the conduct of businessmen today.

The subject of businessmen's ethics has sustained a revival in recent years. A Consumer Advisory Committee was appointed by President Kennedy during the past year. Many universities have strengthened courses having to do with ethics. The attorney-general's office has increased its activities. Somewhat uniquely, Westinghouse Electric Corp. in 1961 asked four distinguished Americans to serve as a Board of Advice, in part to appraise the corporation's procedure for assuring that employees acted according to high standards of business conduct.

Various groups have drawn up codes of ethical conduct. For years the purchasing profession has had such a code. It is quite likely that many businessmen do not have a well-defined code. Our research suggests that some purchasing people are either not aware of their code or for some reason they disagree with various segments of it. It is difficult to attain complete agreement with philosophical matters. It would be expected to find differences from group to group and from society to society. Nevertheless, it would be expected that on most issues, businessmen would agree as to what is ethical and unethical.

One of the many articles which has been directed to the subject of codes is that of Austin's Code of Conduct for Executives. Austin treats matters of price-fixing, conflicts of interest, incentives, and suggests solutions to some of the problems. He concludes: "If business management is to be a profession, it must meet the basic requirements of

From *North Central Purchaser*, Vol. 10, No. 10 (October, 1963), pp. 48ff.

the professions. One of these requirements is an internally developed code of conduct that can be and is professed as the code by which the members of the profession will live."[1]

ETHICS AND PURCHASING

A great deal has been written on the topic of purchasing ethics. Heinritz has made many thoughtful statements on the subject as have other purchasing notables. There have been some self-analyses among purchasing people. There has been criticism of the selling profession, also. The market exchange process, after all, works in two directions. The salesman has persuasive techniques to apply to the buyer and the buyer has certain resources at his command.

The purpose of this paper is neither to eulogize the purchasing staffs nor to suggest that business corruptness is threatening the world. Instead, the purpose is to describe a new way to examine business behavior. It is, then, a kind of a new look at purchasing ethics.

A PILOT STUDY IN ETHICS

The Twin City Association of Purchasing Agents Board of Directors, in May of this year, authorized a pilot study to be undertaken in cooperation with the School of Business of the University of Minnesota. The results of this study are based entirely on returns from Twin City Association members and their buyers. The contribution of funds, the counsel of some members, and the cooperation of several hundred businessmen have made this pilot study possible.

The idea for this study came indirectly from psychologist Leon Festinger's theory of cognitive dissonance. Briefly, this theory states that two cognitions are dissonant if the obverse of one would follow from the other. A cognition is any knowledge, belief, or attitude. For example, one cognition may be that you enjoy smoking cigarettes. Another cognition may be that you have read that cigarette smoking causes cancer. These cognitions are dissonant so you probably attempt to eliminate or reduce the dissonance. One way would be to stop smoking. Another way would be to switch to pipe smoking. Still another way would be to discredit the research upon which the cancer scare was based. Take another example: you may have a golf date this afternoon but it begins to rain. Dissonance is created by this situation. You can reduce it by saying to yourself, "Oh well, I had a lot of work that should be finished." Or, "My golf has been terrible lately and a layoff may do me good." The point is that because the cognitions are dissonant, you attempt to reduce the dissonance.

Another psychologist, Judson Mills, applied the same concept to cheating. He found in an experiment with children, that those who did not cheat when tempted became more severe in their attitudes toward cheating; those who cheated became more lenient. The idea was that dissonance was created by the cheaters because they did something they knew was wrong in order to get a good grade. Good grades and cheating are dissonant: the dissonance was reduced by lowering their standards of cheating.

DISSONANCE AND PURCHASING

It appeared plausible to us that moral and immoral behavior could be examined in a business setting in a similar way to the cheating experiment. There are, of course, more limitations to this kind of study but the idea was worth further exploration. If we found an analogous situation in business, we would have a rather dramatic way to illustrate what happens to those persons who behave in an unethical manner.

[1] Robert W. Austin, "Code of Conduct for Executives," *Harvard Business Review*, Vol. 39, No. 5, September-October, 1961, p. 53.

The hypothesis of our study was as follows: buyers who behave unethically will become more lenient in their attitudes toward business practices whereas ethical buyers will become more severe. That is, a buyer who is tempted by a bribe would like the bribe but would like to remain ethical. If he accepts the bribe, his attitude toward business practices will be lowered as he attempts to reduce the dissonance between these conflicting cognitions of reward and wrong-doing. The ethical buyer gives up a reward and so he, too, has dissonance. He reduces his dissonance by raising his standards. Thus, we believed that we would find attitude changes based on the behavior of buyer involved.

The importance of the study to businessmen is obvious. If the theory is correct, honest businessmen become more honest and dishonest businessmen become more dishonest. There is an importance for the classroom, also. If the theory works out, we can demonstrate to the students what happens when they yield to a temptation in a business situation. We have tried this in two classes and have attained good results.

PROCEDURE

First, a pilot test among a few buyers was conducted. The results from this preliminary test enabled us to make a number of improvements in the questionnaire. Then, purchasing employees were given the questionnaires. These were filled out independently by the individual buyers and were sent to the University in sealed envelopes so that complete anonymity was maintained.

The questionnaire consisted of three parts.

PART I

A list of statements, each of which had to be graded on a scale ranging from "approve" to "disapprove," was given to each buyer. These statements were based on the Purchasing Code of Ethics. The responses to the statements in Part I permitted us to measure the buyer's standards or attitudes toward various business practices.

Example: "Buyers should never substitute materials for items which are requisitioned by employees without notifying the employee of the substitution."

0	1	2	3	4	5	6
Completely approve						Completely disapprove

PART II

Three situations were next presented to each person. He indicated whether he would under these circumstances, make an ethical or an unethical decision. This enabled us to classify him accordingly.

Abbreviated example: "As a buyer, you are seeking bids on a machinery purchase. One supplier has offered you his vacation facilities. He asks, in return, that you provide him with information concerning the other bidders in order that he might be low bidder if he so desires."

Will you accept the offer? Yes...... No......

PART III

Another list of statements similar to those in Part I was then given to each buyer. The answers to Part III gave us after-measure of his attitudes. The after-measure was then compared to his pre-measure in Part I.

RESULTS OF THE STUDY

A total of 342 buyers took part in the experiment. This total number was divided into two conditions with Condition I having 149 and Condition II having 193 buyers, respectively. The only difference between the two conditions was the order of the statements presented.

As it turned out, order of presentation was important as Conditions I and II had some consistent differences which apparently resulted from the order. Further work will be necessary to equate the two sets of statements.

CONDITION I

Part I Set "A" statements
II The 3 situations
III Set "B" statements

CONDITION II

Set "B" statements
Same 3 situations
Set "A" statements

Buyers responded to the three ethical situations by making moral decisions in the majority of cases. In each situation, however, a substantial number made unethical decisions.

In the "Country Club Membership Bribe Situation," buyers were evenly split on their "feeling proud" about being selected for the membership. Two out of three buyers said they would feel guilty about accepting the offer. One in five thought his wife would object if he did not accept the offer. Almost half the buyers thought acceptance of the membership would cause him to feel obligated to the supplier. The principal question — Would the buyer accept the bribe offer? — resulted in one-fourth of the buyers accepting the offer.

The second situation — "Bribe of Vacation Facilities" — resulted in rejection by nine out of ten buyers. Buyers indicated they were well aware of the implications involved in this situation.

Approximately one-fourth of the buyers accepted the "Gift" as a token of appreciation in the third Situation. Somewhat surprising was the division of opinion on the question: "Is the gift a bribe for future contracts rather than a token of thanks?" Fifty-five percent thought the gift was a bribe and forty-five percent considered it a gift.

Buyers expressed their opinions on two sets (A and B) of statements (ten pre-situation and ten post-situation). On some of these statements there was general agreement. On others, however, there was little unanimity. This is interesting, because if all buyers knew the Purchasing Code it would be expected that there would be rather general agreement on all statements. Buyers agreed that they disapproved of testing a "phony" product in order to mislead the competition. They disagreed, though, on the matter of "stepping on another's toes in order to promote one's own interests."

An interesting sidelight of the study was the definite opinions buyers have concerning selling practices. A number of the statements had to do with selling-initiated actions. Buyers definitely expect sellers to conform to a code. It would be interesting to compare the attitudes of buyers and sellers toward the same set of ethically-oriented statements!

The main hypothesis was concerned with the changing of attitudes toward business practices once a person commits himself to an unethical or to an ethical decision. That is, do buyers become less ethical when they make an unethical decision? Do they become more ethical when they make an ethical decision? The results of the study were not conclusive but they certainly were suggestive.

The best supported parts of the hypothesis was that **unethical buyers lower their standards**. In Table 2, it is clear that the buyers who made three unethical decisions did substantially lower their standards. The results are not as clear regarding those who were ethical although some support for this hypothesis can be seen. As pointed out previously, the order of presentation made quite a difference although the conclusions are the same.

It is interesting to examine the scores

TABLE 1

	Country Club Membership Bribe Situation	Vacation Facilities Bribe Situation	Gift Temptation Situation
Ethical	250	304	245
Unethical	92	36	96

TABLE 2

Number of Points of Change Between Pre- and Post-Ethical Attitudes

	Condition I	Condition II
0 Unethical Decisions	+ 1.4	− 2.3
1 Unethical Decisions	+ 0.9	− 2.9
2 Unethical Decisions	+ 1.3	− 2.2
3 Unethical Decisions	−13.7	−12.2

(−) indicates the buyers lowered their standards
(+) indicates the buyers raised their standards

TABLE 3

ATTITUDE SCORES AND UNETHICAL DECISIONS

	Condition I		Condition II	
	Pre	Post	Pre	Post
0 Unethical Decisions	38.0	39.4	40.8	38.5
1 Unethical Decisions	36.8	37.7	38.3	35.4
2 Unethical Decisions	34.1	35.4	35.2	33.0
3 Unethical Decisions	28.0	14.3	31.1	18.8

(A possible score was 60 points)

on the attitude tests and on the situations. As a person makes more unethical decisions, note how his standards of conduct drop. This is clearer than we had anticipated.

The results presented in Table 3 also suggest that it might be possible to predict behavior on the basis of the attitude scores. If we are able to improve the statements sufficiently, it may be possible to predict behavior as well as to measure results from behavior.

LIMITATIONS

Any pilot study has a number of limitations which should be examined. For example, perhaps buyers do not indicate in a test how they actually would behave in a real situation. Secondly, the statements and the situations still need a good deal of refinement before we can

place complete confidence in them. Thirdly, the sample sizes in some instances were too limited for one to draw conclusions which could be upheld by statistical procedures. There are other limitations, but these suggest the kinds of problems which existed with the study. Despite these, we felt that the results are definitely worthwhile reporting to the purchasing field.

COMMENTS

The results of the study indicate that the technique described in this report may prove to be a useful way of dramatizing the importance of making moral business decisions. Much work remains to develop the instruments to a point of adequate reliability, but the Twin City Association of Purchasing Agents-University of Minnesota pilot study is a move in the right direction. Future attempts will likely be made to generalize the procedure so that it can be used with any businessman. If that materializes, it may be possible to compare ethical behavior among age groups, occupations, incomes, positions, and size of firm, for example. The potential seems substantial to us and we hope that a contribution toward business conduct can eventually be made.

We would appreciate any suggestions. Some purchasers have already indicated ways in which the study could be made more realistic and hence more effective. Finally, we would like to express our gratitude to those in purchasing who helped make the study possible.

The surveys on pp. 519 and 520 will give you an opportunity to compare your ideas about ethics in purchasing with those of The Purchasing Agents Association.

HOW DO YOUR IDEAS ABOUT GIFTS COMPARE WITH THOSE OF PA's FOR CONTRACTING COMPANIES?

TAKE THIS SURVEY AND SEE

Tables 4 and 5 are from a thesis written by University of Minnesota graduate student, Donald C. Reioux, as part of his requirements for a Masters Degree. Answer the questions below in Table 4; then turn to Table 5 and see how your ideas compare with the Upper Midwest PA's for Contracting Companies who filled out the survey.

TABLE 4

Please check your answer to the following questions.

	YES	NO
1. Does your company have a policy regarding acceptance by your employees of gifts from suppliers?	( )	( )
1a. Do you believe a purchasing agent should be allowed to accept free luncheons from suppliers?	( )	( )
1b. Do you believe a purchasing agent should be allowed to accept gifts from suppliers?	( )	( )

1c. If you believe he should be allowed to accept gifts from suppliers, what is the dollar amount of gift you would limit from any one supplier? (Circle answer).
No Gift $3-$5 $5-$10 $10-$25   Other

	YES	NO
2. Do you, to the best of your knowledge, feel that your purchasing agent follows your prescribed rule?	( )	( )
OR: If you do not have a rule, does your purchasing agent accept gifts?	( )	( )
3. Do you believe your company receives benefits from allowing your purchasing agent to accept gifts?	( )	( )

What benefit does your company receive?

	YES	NO
4. Do you believe the practice of a purchasing agent owning stock in a company supplying your firm to be proper or ethical?	( )	( )

5. If you found one of your employees had accepted "lavish or extravagant gifts" over and above any limitation you may set, which of the following actions would you take? (Circle answer.)

a. Discharge the employee
b. Reprimand the employee
c. Suspend the employee
d. Do nothing

e. Promote him
f. Any other action
g. Get new supplier
h. Reprimand supplier

	YES	NO
6. Do you believe the practice of gift giving between buyer and supplier is quite well established in the construction industry?	( )	( )
7. Do you believe the practice of "kickbacks" or "payola" is prevalent in the construction industry as it applies between buyers and suppliers?	( )	( )

8. Do you believe that the construction industry as compared to other industries has, (1) more, (2) about the same or (3) lesser amounts of the practices of gift-giving, payola, and kickbacks.
Answer _____

TABLE 5

1. Does Company have policy, etc.

	YES to Q. 1			NO to Q. 1					
	Yes	No	Total	Yes	No	Total	28	30	58
1a.	26	2	28	26	4	30	38	20	58
1b.	15	13	28	23	7	30	38	20	58

1c. Amount of gift, etc.

No Gift	$3-$5	$5-$10	$10-$25			
20	30	5	3			58

2. Does P.A. follow rules			24	4	28
OR:					
Does P.A. accept gifts			19	11	30
3. Do you receive benefits			28	6	34

New Contracts	New Ideas	Good Buys	No Benefit
10	3	2	13

4. Owning stock in supplier	8	50	58

5. Action taken for "lavish" gifts
   a. Discharge (11)
   b. Reprimand (10)
   c. Suspend (20)
   d. Do nothing (2)
   e. Promote (0)
   f. Other (15)
   g. Get new supplier (12)
   h. Reprimand supplier (2)

6. Practices established in industry	44	14	58
7. "Kickbacks" or "Payola" established	18	40	58

8. Compared to other industries
   a. More (20)
   b. Same (15)
   c. Less (23)

C. PUBLIC REGULATION

54. Economic Issues in the du Pont-General Motors Case

ALFRED NICOLS

The Supreme Court ruled in June, 1957, that the 23 per cent stock ownership in General Motors Corporation held by the du Pont Company was in violation of the antimerger clause of the Clayton Act.[1] Because this decision has already established a precedent for subsequent cases and because the reasoning of the Court raises significant economic questions, a critique from the viewpoint of economic analysis seems justified.

Du Pont's original stock investment of $25,000,000 in General Motors was acquired in December, 1917,[2] as part of an expansion plan motivated by the decision of the United States government in 1907 to manufacture explosives for itself. Thus du Pont was under the necessity of finding and developing new markets for its basic raw materials when Durant, then engaged in a battle for control of General Motors, requested financial and managerial assistance from du Pont. Later in 1920, when Durant, at that time president of General Motors, experienced severe financial pressure, du Pont purchased more stock and took over Durant's obligations, though this necessitated that it borrow money for the first time in its history.

In 1923 du Pont sold the additional stock it had acquired in 1920 to Management Securities, a corporation organized by General Motors to provide additional incentive to its principal executives. The chief executive officer of General Motors made the bonus awards subject to the approval of the Finance Committee, which consisted in 1919 of seven members, five of whom were from du Pont. By 1937 the committee had expanded to fourteen, du Pont having six representatives. So far as the board of directors of General Motors was concerned, du Pont never had more than six members of a total which varied from twenty-nine to thirty-five. Several years after Durant stepped down, Alfred P. Sloan became president of General Motors and introduced the "Sloan Plan," which gave each general manager of the operating divisions complete authority over hiring, buying, programming production, pricing, and selling.

The antitrust action under discussion was initiated by the government in 1949. The main allegation was that through du Pont's control of bonus systems and placement of key officials, a privileged status as a major supplier to General Motors was gained. Second, this alleged "control" enabled du Pont to impose a division of fields which gave to du Pont full responsibility for the manufacture and sale of tetraethyl lead and the refrigerant "Freon," both of which had been developed by General Motors' research.

The defendants countered that the evidence demonstrated that du Pont

Reprinted from *Journal of Business*, Vol. 33, No. 3 (July, 1960), pp. 227-51, by permission of the University of Chicago Press. Copyright 1960 by the University of Chicago.

[1] *United States* v. *E.I. du Pont de Nemours and Company et al.*, 353 U.S. 586 (1957). The government proceeding was instituted to enjoin alleged violations of Secs. 1 and 2 of the Sherman Act and Sec. 7 of the Clayton Act.

[2] 353 U.S. 586, 601.

had not been successful in selling all its products to each of General Motors' divisions; that the General Purchasing Committee, functioning from 1922 to 1931, was instituted not to favor du Pont but better to compete with the unified purchasing power of the Ford Motor Company. Of the 709 contracts let by the committee, only 14 had gone to du Pont, while 13 du Pont applications had been rejected. Furthermore, the agreements over tetraethyl lead and "Freon" were typical of joint industrial research; General Motors had similar agreements with other companies in other areas.

The trial court found that the evidence did not support the government charge, since there was no restraint upon competitors of du Pont or limits upon the freedom of General Motors to develop its chemical discoveries. Since there had been no restraint of trade over thirty years, "there is not, nor has there been, any basis for a finding that there is or has been any reasonable probability of such a restraint within the meaning of the Clayton Act."[3]

The Supreme Court, however, reasoned that "the primary issue is whether du Pont's commanding position as a supplier of automobile finishes and fabrics was achieved on competitive merit alone, or because its acquisition of General Motors' stock, and the consequent close relationship, led to the insulation most of the General Motors' market from free competition."[4] The Court was impressed by the fact that du Pont, connected to General Motors by the stock interest, supplied a larger proportion of General Motors' requirements than those of any other competitor.

Several factors influenced the Supreme Court. First, it said that du Pont did not achieve its commanding position as a supplier to General Motors until after the stock purchase (this statement appears to be in conflict with the evidence). Second, General Motors' principal paint supplier, Flint Varnish and Color Works, had sold out to du Pont in 1918. Only after this did Fisher body, the division of General Motors most resistant to du Pont "sales pressure," succomb; by 1947 Fisher was purchasing from du Pont in proportions comparable to the other divisions. Third, the Taskob report of 1917 and the actions of Haskell (a retired du Pont vice-president who became a General Motors executive and kept himself closely informed of both du Pont's sales as well as its competitors' sales to General Motors) demonstrated that du Pont's concern in General Motors went beyond mere interest in a profitable investment.

The discussion which follows will attempt to analyze the reasoning of the Court in the light of what theoretical and empirical economic knowledge tell us on the matters at issue. In the first section, I discuss what du Pont's intent may have been in acquiring General Motors' stock—the question being whether the intention was to "foreclose" a key market to du Pont's competitors or simply to make what has proved to be an excellent investment. In the second section the unusual definition adopted by the Court of the market in which monopolization tended to take place—a definition in terms of "buyer requirements" rather than economic characteristics of the goods produced—is examined and shown to be crucial both for this decision and for future cases.[5] The third section is largely a review of the evidence on the basis of which the Court concluded that "foreclosure" of the market took place, in the course of which it will be pointed out that what the decision apparently concluded to be a highly significant omen of improper du Pont influence—its "dominant supplier" position for a

---

[3] *United States* v. *E. I. du Pont de Nemours and Company et al.*, 126 F. Supp. 235, 300 (1954).
[4] 353 U.S. 586, 588.

[5] See *Matter of Crown Zellerbach Corp.*, Federal Trade Commission (FTC) Docket No. 6180 (December 26, 1957), and *United States* v. *Bethlehem Steel Corp. and the Youngstown Sheet and Tube Co.*, 168 F.Supp. 576 (...8).

number of commodities purchased by General Motors—is a widespread institution in the automobile trade as well as in other trades where no ownership relationship exists. Finally, the fourth section deals with the question of what the appropriate remedy should be, both in general and in this case, if it is accepted that such a stock interest does injure competition by foreclosing markets to competitors of the supplier company.

I. INTENT AND RESULTS

Du Pont's stock ownership was alleged to have led to the insulation of most of General Motors' market from free competition.[6] That such a policy should have been pursued by du Pont as part of profit maximization seemed obvious to the Court. General Motors was the "colossus" of the automobile industry. There is no question that du Pont officials wanted the business. Raskob, du Pont's financial expert, referred to the advantage of the stock interest several times;[7] du Pont salesmen called attention to the "family relationship." Also, it is a fact that several du Pont officials were transferred to key positions in General Motors, including Haskell, who,

as vice-president, "set up lines of communication within General Motors to be in a position to know at all times . . . [which of] du Pont['s] products . . . [or of their] competitors were being used."[8]

However, an effort simply to sell to General Motors would not necessarily imply that du Pont sought control of General Motors' policy in order to become the preferred supplier. Nor can it be established that du Pont's purchase of General Motors' stock in 1917 was for the purpose of insuring that du Pont would perforce be in a position to supply a predominant share of General Motors' requirements for finishes, fabrics, and other products. Finally, the transfer of management officials and even the activities of Haskell do not represent conclusive evidence as to du Pont's interest.

A. THE THEORY OF INTERCORPORATE CONTROL

Optimal policy for du Pont in view of its ownership of some General Motors' stock obviously depends upon the proportion of its holdings relative to the total stock outstanding. Consider the two limiting cases. First, assume that du Pont's ownership was 100 per cent and that du Pont had partial monopoly power. The problem is not only simplified but actually non-existent when the automobile industry is competitive, because in such circumstances, if du Pont sought to extract a greater than normal return from the sale of intermediate products, its automobile-manufacturing activities would yield less than competitive returns. A possibility of extracting extra profits for du Pont exists only when General Motors possesses monopoly power; here, however, rational policy would dictate pricing intermediate products at marginal costs[9]

[6] 353 U.S. 588.

[7] E.g · "Our interest in the General Motors Company will undoubtedly secure for us the entire Fabrikoid, Pyralin, paint and varnish business of those companies" (353 U.S. 602). A letter from Pierre du Pont, then president of General Motors, to Lamont du Pont referred to the amount of finish and fabric business du Pont was securing from the various General Motors' divisions: "With the change in management at Cadillac, Oakland and Olds, I believe that you should be able to sell substantially all of the paint, varnish and fabrikoid products needed. . . . A drive should be made for the Fisher body business. Is there any reason why they have not dealt with us?" (Government Brief, Sup. Court pp. 35-36). A letter from R. R. M. Carpenter (brother-in-law of Pierre du Pont) stated: "We would like to present to the General Motors Company in the proper way the subject of entering into negotiations with us for the supplying of all the artificial leather and rubber which they use" (ibid., p. 37).

[8] 353 U.S. 603.

[9] Cf. Jack Hirschleifer, "On the Economics of Transfer Pricing," Journal of Business, XXIX (July, 1956), 172, 175.

(i.e., du Pont should sell to General Motors at *lower* prices than to the latter's competitors).

Second, assume that du Pont, while owning no stock, controlled General Motors' purchasing. Its policy under such circumstances might be to so influence the direction of these purchases as to enhance du Pont's profits. Again, if the automobile industry is competitive, General Motors must buy at competitive prices to survive. The choice problem emerges only where General Motors is in possession of monopoly power—du Pont might seek to divert the monopoly profits from automobile manufacturing. Since it owns no stock, the way to carry out the redistribution of profits is through charging non-competitive prices to its "creature."

The third case corresponds to the relationship that actually obtained, with du Pont owning 23 per cent of General Motors' outstanding stock. While General Motors is, of course, not the only automobile producer, its purchases presumably constitute a substantial portion of du Pont's total sales. Since profits of the automobile manufacturer were large, it is to be presumed du Pont sought to share them. Consequently, "control" of General Motors might be expected to be sought by du Pont in order to place it in the position of being able to secure the finish and fabrics business on its own terms. That is, it would attempt to transfer profits by simply charging higher prices than its competitors.

But the evidence did not indicate that du Pont exacted non-competitive prices; hence, there must have been either an absence of du Pont "control" or an absence of large profits. Since the automobile industry has been extremely profitable during the past forty years—whether due to monopoly or innovation is immaterial for the issue—it would seem to follow that du Pont did not control General Motors' purchasing policies. For, had it possessed such control, it would have been expected to transfer General Motors' profits directly to itself

through charging higher than competitive prices for the intermediate products sold to General Motors rather than sharing such profits with the remaining three-fourths of the shareholders. Since du Pont appears to have exercised its "control" only at competitive prices and profits—and in spite of its very large investment in a business whose custom it already had—its objective may have been merely a desire to participate in a growing industry.

B. DU PONT'S ACQUISITION AND GROWTH PATTERN

The question of whether or not du Pont "purposely employed its stock interest"[10] to achieve its present status as General Motors' dominant supplier was critical to the issue because, in contrast with straightforward integration cases, the two companies were not merged. The Court attached considerable significance to the pattern of acquisition and growth[11] followed by du Pont after the decision by the United States government to manufacture its own explosives in 1907. The company, seeking new markets for its basic raw material, made a number of acquisitions at more advanced stages of production: purchase of stock in General Motors appeared to assure it of at least one principal buyer of paint; the subsequent purchase of General Motors' interest in the Flint Varnish and Color Works removed the one main competitor for the General Motors business (Flint had been the principal supplier).

This evidence does not make it obvious that the stock purchase was to insure that du Pont would secure a predominant share of General Motors'

---

[10] *United States* v. *du Pont*, 353 U.S. 606.
[11] Cf. also the Federal Trade Commission in its complaint against Pillsbury (FTC Docket No. 6000, 1953), where its function was interpreted as halting the trend to oligopolistic or monopolistic competition. See, in addition, *Report of the Attorney-General's National Committee To Study the Anti-trust Laws* (Washington, D.C.: Government Printing Office, 1955), p. 124.

requirements for finishes, fabrics, and other products. First, du Pont had already been the major supplier of fabrics to various General Motors' divisions prior to the stock purchase in 1917.[12] It began manufacture of coated fabrics in 1910 and by 1916 practically every automobile producer was a purchaser of its "Fabrikoid" for upholstery. Prior to the investment in General Motors, du Pont supplied substantially all the coated-fabric requirements at Buick and one-third of the Oakland requirements. It supplied all of Cadillac's requirements of coated fabrics for interior trim, though the top business went elsewhere. It is significant that after the stock investment no consistent change in the pattern of purchases from du Pont emerged. They varied from year to year, depending upon what du Pont offered relative to its competitors.

In 1916, paints and varnishes had been selected as one of the five lines in which du Pont would diversify. By the end of the year, pursuing that policy, Harrison Brothers & Company was acquired. During the next few years additional concerns were added, with most of the expansion along "trade sales" lines (i.e., paints used for application to houses, fences, and other items of general maintenance). By the end of 1917, du Pont was studying the possibility of branching out into the "industrial" lines, which were the paints applied by manufacturers on items for sale "where it appeared that du Pont's technical and chemical and research abilities could be more useful."[13]

Du Pont did not become a manufacturer of automotive finishes until it acquired Flint Varnish and Color Works in the middle of 1918. The latter firm, located near the General Motors plants, had since 1910 met all General Motors' requirements with the exception of Cadillac, as well as supplying other automobile manufacturers. Yet the immediate consequences of its purchase by du Pont was directly contrary to the government hypothesis — not only did Flint fail to secure the Cadillac business but it also lost half of the Oakland business and, by 1923, all of General Motors' finishing varnish business. Furthermore, the total amount of business generated by General Motors' purchases of finishes and fabrics was insignificant in comparison with the $25,000,000 invested: Flint's sales to General Motors and Chevrolet in 1917 were $905,305.[14]

A consistent pattern of acquisition in the areas where du Pont provided the basic raw material, coupled with evidence showing "intent" on the part of du Pont to gain the exclusive business of its customers, was considered presumptive evidence by the government that its dominant-supplier position was not due to "competitive merit." While evidence of intent to profit from monopoly power is not considered essential it is relevant. It would be possible to argue, however, that all that was necessary was a showing that du Pont had the "power" to foreclose the market. But what would constitute power in the absence of outright ownership through vertical integration? The Court chose to look for evidence of expressed intent, which it found in letters by the du Pont management indicating what was desired in the way of increased sales. From expressions of intent to secure a greater market share, it was inferred that they possessed the power.

However, the relevance of such letters is questionable — would the du Pont officials be expected to favor reducing the amount of their business with General Motors? Any supplier — stock interest or no stock interest, actual or potential — wants to increase its share of the market for its products. The issue was not whether du Pont's goal was to expand its business with General Motors, but, rather, whether a substantial market could be foreclosed by virtue of

---

[13] Du Pont Brief, Dist. Court, p. 121.

[14] General Motors Brief, Sup. Court, p. 6, n. 5.

a 23 per cent stock interest. Although the Court clearly was not willing to make stock acquisitions a per se violation—it is difficult to see how it could have done so in view of the wording of the law, which states that stock purchases for investment are permissible—it is not apparent from its decision how a firm supplying the major requirements of a buyer could legally carry out acquisition.

One further point: It seems strange that the concern for intent should relate to a period when General Motors was not the large, important factor in either the automobile industry or the economy that it is today. In the years following the famous Raskob report, which predicted that the stock interest would divert business to du Pont, General Motors experienced a period of extensive organizational change and growth: Durant, the president and founder of General Motors, faced bankruptcy in 1921, which so threatened the existence of the corporation that du Pont, through the first bond sale in its history, had to come to its aid; Sloan became chief executive officer and instituted his plan for divisional autonomy;[15] and, ultimately, General Motors increased its market share in the automobile industry from 10.8 per cent in 1917 to 45 per cent of the market in recent years. The corporation had thus become a very different entity from that which depended back around 1920 for financial support on du Pont.

Consider the problem that will be present in future cases of this nature. What kind of evidence will refute the inference that stock acquisition is sufficient to create a dominant-supplier status? Suppose that both stock interest and a "commanding position as supplier" are present. Is it valid to infer that the first is the cause of the second? If this is to be the interpretation of the courts, almost every stock acquisition is a per se violation whenever the buyer is in the position of being the supplier or potential supplier. The absurdity of such reasoning is illustrated when applied to the 1949 purchase by Chrysler of the Briggs Manufacturing Company,[16] which for many years had been its principal body supplier. Even though there was no injury to competitors, it might be argued on the basis of the thesis just discussed that potential competition would be injured, since newcomers would be denied the possibility of securing a portion of the business formerly held by Briggs.[17]

Neither the government's case nor the decision by Justice Brennan conclusively established an "intent" by du Pont to control General Motors. Both the absence of evidence of non-competitive prices and the alternative "investment" explanation for the stock acquisition which is supported by contemporary documents and in particular by the "Five Industry Plan"[18] suggest

---

[15] "General Motors operates on what is recognized as a decentralized system of management. By decentralization, I mean we believe in giving the responsibility with the maximum authority necessary to discharge the responsibility as far down in the echelon of authority as we possibly can. The heart of our management technique is the operating divisions . . . the general manager has complete authority over that particular operation. . . . He lays down his own program of production. He buys his own materials. He hires his own people" (*United States* v. *E. I. du Pont de Nemours and Company et al.*, 126 F. Supp. 235 [1954], Transcript of Record 2445 [Sloan], quoted in General Motors Brief, Dist. Court, p. 27). See also Peter F. Drucker, *Concept of the Corporation* (New York: John Day Co., 1946), pp. 46, 56.

[16] In his testimony before a congressional committee, Sloan observed that Chrysler had "bought their bodies up to a few years ago, but they found that they could not continue that. So they took over the Briggs Manufacturing Company, who [*sic*] were making their bodies and made it a component part of themselves, for greater coordination, closer connection engineeringwise, and advantages in other ways" (U.S. Senate Committee on the Judiciary, Subcommittee on Antitrust and Monopoly, *A Study of the Antitrust Laws*, Part 7: *General Motors* [84th Cong., 1st sess.] [Washington, 1956], p. 3526).

[17] Cf. *American Tobacco Co.* v. *United States*, 328 U.S. 781 (1946).

[18] Du Pont Brief, Dist. Court, p. 119.

that undue emphasis was placed on a single motive—particularly in the light of General Motors' rather small and volatile market position at the time of the acquisition.[19]

II. THE RELEVANT MARKET

Determination of a "tendency to monopoly" must specify the market in which the tendencies are claimed to be manifest.[20] Automobile finishes and fabrics were identified as the appropriate "line of commerce" by the Supreme Court because they "have sufficient peculiar characteristics and uses to constitute them products sufficiently distinct from all other finishes and fabrics."[21] Reference was made to the Van Camp-American Can case:[22] du Pont's alleged control of General Motors could foreclose market opportunities for competing suppliers of automobile finishes and fabrics. The alleged tendency to monopoly in both cases rested on an implicit assumption of horizontal monopoly and monopsony.[23] Apparently, the Court felt that buyers in the canners' market had no alternative to American Can Company as a supplier and, consequently, that the discriminatory prices would have substantially lessened competition. But the reference as applied to the General Motors—du Pont relationship

is misleading. While monopolistic tendencies resulting from discrimination on the part of American Can would clearly have to take effect in the can buyer's or packers' market, monopolistic tendencies resulting from the du Pont stock interest in General Motors obviously did not apply to the market for automobiles but rather to the market for finishes. In the latter, General Motors was but one buyer among many.

It was, therefore, necessary for the Supreme Court to do what the district court had failed to do: make a finding of fact as to the market in which competition would be foreclosed. The Court ruled that autombile finishes were a separate line of commerce because "Duco" (du Pont's paint) (1) represented a significant advance over varnish[24] and (2) differed from other products because it was patented. On this basis, every improvement on a process would create an additional "line of commerce." But, what was even more astonishing, when the Court conceded that "Duco" was superior, it resolved what was said to be the "primary issue." Thus the use of "Duco" by General Motors originated in its superiority rather than the stock interest! However, the finding that a patent differentiates a product is no longer relevant—the patent expired in 1944. While it was in effect, du Pont issued two hundred and fifty licenses; in fact, it did so to everyone who applied. Furthermore, merely patenting a product does not necessarily eliminate competition—in spite of the patent, Cadillac, Oldsmobile, Ford, and Chry-

---

[19]See Federal Trade Commission, *Report on Motor Vehicle Industry* (Washington, D.C., 1939), p. 27.

[20]Justice Brennan referred to *Transamerica Corp. v. Board of Governors,* 206 F.2d, 163 169 (1953): ". . . It is the purpose of the Clayton Act to nip monopoly in the bud. . . . In order to determine the existence of a tendency to monopoly in . . . any line of business the area or areas of existing effective competition in which monopoly power might be exercised must first be determined."

[21]353 U.S. 593.

[22]*Van Camp and Sons Co.* v. *American Can Co.,* 278 U.S. 245 (1929). Discrimination by American Can tended to create a monopoly in the "packing and selling of food products in cans." The illegal effect was not in the market for cans but in the forward market—canning.

[23]Cf. Bork, "Vertical Integration and the Sherman Act," *University of Chicago Law Review* XXII (1954), 196.

[24]353 U.S. 595 In approving the majority's decision, one economist commented: "The mere fact that the latter was a patented product is at least presumptive evidence that it is significantly differentiated from other finishes. Moreover each such differentiated product has a distinct market." Whether the relevant market embraces a single product or a group of closely related products "is necessarily a policy question depending upon what degree of monopoly power is regarded as permissible" (R. W. Harbeson, "The Clayton Act: Sleeping Giant of Antitrust?" *American Economic Review,* XL [1950] 92, 100). ˴

ler all found suitable substitutes for "Duco."[25]

A. BUYER REQUIREMENTS

In finding that automobile fabrics constituted a separate market, the Court cited the testimony of Nickowitz, who was in charge of du Pont's fabric sales. He referred to the difference which existed between the furniture and automobile industries with respect to their purchasing. Selling to different buyer requirements precluded the development of a standard price, for each manufacturer used a different construction. The critical element, therefore, was the buyer's requirements; where they differed, the market was a separate "line of commerce." That this represented a departure from traditional judicial practice was indicated in the dissent's reference to the United Shoe Machinery case: "The problem of defining a market turns on discovering patterns of trade which are followed in practice"; further reference was made to cellophane, where determination of the competitive market depended "on how different from one another are the offered commodities in characteristics and use, how far buyers will go to substitute one commodity for another."[26]

This difficulty of market definition is illustrated by considering automotive purchases of textile constructions other than imitation leather and coated fabrics—for example, cotton, which accounts for a far greater proportion of the fabrics entering into an automobile than

do those sold by du Pont.[27] Now, although there are differences between the gray cloth sold to the converting trade and that sold to industrial buyers such as the automobile industry, the market is competitive.[28] Prices behave differently in the two markets; the market for industrial cotton fabrics involves close personal relationships.[29] On this basis, the Supreme Court might have ruled that such a market was a separate "line of commerce" from that of textile constructions in general. However, textile economists, buyers, and sellers would not agree; lateral adaptation of machines is such that, should one firm or group of firms specializing in industrial fabrics seek monopoly profits, immediate and satisfactory substitution of alternative sources of supply by buyers would result.[30] Since entry is easy, the result is that monopoly, like crime, does not pay. Automobile manufacturers have not been exempt from competing with other buyers of cloth.

By the Court's test, any special requirement would seem to make the market separate. Therefore, a request for some special steel by Chevrolet would not only put it in a different market but would give it monopsony power. But if, for purposes of Section 7 of the Clayton Act, the buyer's special requirements define the frontiers of the relevant market, the problem is not monopoly. Each buyer would have his own special market, depending on the

---

[25] 126 F.Supp. 292. The government's position was that "Duco" was especially developed for the automobile. Though it had to be adapted, the story is quite different: "It was a logical outgrowth of du Pont's lacquer business and upon its discovery du Pont turned, not to its alleged 'protected' market in General Motors, but quite naturally to its existing customers, for the old type of lacquers—principally the furniture and novelty makers" (Flaherty [the discoverer], Record 4284, cited in du Pont Brief, Sup. Court, p. 78).
[26] 353 U.S. 649.

[27] General Motors Brief, Dist. Court, p. 80. The type of fabrics sold by du Pont constitute less than 5 per cent of the total upholstery and trim in General Motors' automobiles.
[28] Of this industry, Wilcox says: "In general producers are numerous, small, and widely scattered, that entrance is unobstructed, that production shows little concentration, and that prices are flexible and profits low" (*Competition and Monopoly in American Industry* [TNEC Monograph 21 (Washington, D.C., 1941)], p. 31).
[29] Reavis Cox, *The Marketing of Textiles* (New York: Textile Foundation, 1938), pp. 192-97.
[30] See J. Backman and M. R. Gainsbrugh, *The Economics of the Cotton Textile Industry* (New York: National Industrial Conference Board, 1946), p. 117.

unique characteristics of his particular demand for which the various suppliers would compete. As a monopsonist, it would be expected that he would extract the monopsony return and discriminate on the basis of differences in costs of the suppliers. This, of course, is the typical picture of events under monopsonistic competition. How useful is it for antitrust purposes?

As a limiting case, the special requirements test has analytical usefulness in that it reveals the implications of market definition in terms of buyer requirements and uses. However, a most obvious shortcoming, strikingly indicated here, is that it completely ignores the opportunities of suppliers to turn to other markets. For example, 75-85 per cent of du Pont's total sales of the *same* finishes have gone to other industrial users.[31] The picture is the same with fabrics: du Pont's Fabrics Division had about 10 per cent of the national market at the time of the complaint; 80-85 per cent of its sales went to non-automobile buyers, such as furniture manufacturers, theater-seat manufacturers, bookbinders, and other trades.[32] General Motors took four-fifths of the remaining 15-20 per cent which went to the automobile industry. As du Pont's sales to the automobile industry and to General Motors approximated 2 per cent and 1.6 per cent, respectively, of the total market,[33] the data suggest that General Motors, rather than representing a separate market, was merely a substantial customer in a much larger market. Neither du Pont nor any other supplier of automobile finishes and fabrics appeared dependent for survival on the automobile buyers. Nor were the latter dependent on the suppliers.[34]

Justice Brennan insisted on viewing the market in terms of the automobile industry rather than in terms of the two intermediate products—finishes and fabrics. He appears to have repeated the mistake made in the Columbia Steel case,[35] where foreclosure was thought to have depended on the amount of rolled steel *consumed* in the eleven Western States in which Consolidated Steel sold. Actually, the proper market, in terms of the foreclosure possibilities, was that in which Consolidated *bought* rolled steel —a national market.[36] The minority's comment here is appropriate:

. . . The record appears deficient on such crucial questions as the characteristics of the products, the uses to which they were put, the extent to which they are interchangeable with competitors' products, and so on . . . [Nor are we] told what these peculiar characteristics are. . . . Arbitrary conclusions are not an adequate substitute for analysis of the pertinent facts contained in the record.[37]

Market definition in terms of the buyer's special requirements seems injudicious in another way. The Court was asked to judge whether the stock interest portended some reasonable probability of a tendency to monopoly. Yet it surveyed only the demand characteristics. It is not proper to predict monopoly consequences unless the conditions promoting control over supply are

---

[31] Du Pont Brief, Dist. Court, p. 97.

[32] 353 U.S. 652.

[33] General Motors Brief, Sup. Court, p. 8.

[34] But the government was not so ingenuous as the Supreme Court. It had stated in its Brief that a finding of the relevant market was unimportant, since the case was "similar to a patent tying case, where the only question is whether the volume of

trade restrained is appreciable" (Reply Brief, p. 34). Even though du Pont's competitors may have had ample opportunities in other markets, the fact that a substantial volume of commerce was isolated from competition made the extent of the rest of the market immaterial. But, as indicated in its efforts to define the relevant market, the Supreme Court did not agree. Had it done so, mergers would have become per se violations (cf. *Pillsbury Mills, Inc.*, FTC Docket No. 6000 [1953] and *Report of the Attorney-General's Committee*, pp. 121-22).

[35] *United States* v. *Columbia Steel Co.*, 334 U.S. 495 (1948).

[36] See "The Market: A Concept in Anti-trust," *Columbia Law Review*, LIV (1954), 599.

[37] 353 U.S. 649, n. 30.

spelled out in detail. Assuming arguendo that du Pont had effectively foreclosed the General Motors market, the Court might have seen a "tendency to monopoly" in predatory behavior. By diverting profits from its sheltered market to "subsidize" its activities in competitive markets, du Pont might, in time, have achieved monopoly. But such activity necessarily requires that the sheltered market be monopolistic; and, if that condition were met, it would have been simpler for du Pont merely to have had the "monopsonistic" General Motors not buy from other suppliers. In any case, no evidence was presented of predatory behavior[38] in the more general market for industrial finishes. And, in view of the Court's market finding, it would hardly have been relevant.

The Court's concern was foreclosure of opportunities to du Pont's competitors to supply automotive finishes and fabrics. But if du Pont's stock interest represented "a tendency to monopoly" in this market, General Motors' competitors as buyers would also be foreclosed the advantages of competitive supply. Though both the chemical and the automobile industries may have regarded the market for auto finishes as a distinct market, it does not follow that suppliers manufacturing paints for other uses in related markets could not offer adequate substitutes. It is not altogether irrelevant that Chrysler turned to Pittsburgh Plate Glass to supply its finishes[39] and that Ford was able to develop its own sources of supply through vertical integration.

Not only were alternatives available but they were developed in related markets. Indeed, the government's position here is somewhat contradictory in that, while claiming the market to be "sufficiently different," its theory of control asserts that, when Ford and Chrysler were able to turn to suppliers other than du Pont, the stock interest of the latter prevented General Motors from securing a superior product.[40] If Ford and Chrysler had purchased "Duco" because of its superiority to other available products, it follows that, when they shifted to another supplier, they were compelled to do so by the alleged competition. But the very fact that "competition appeared" indicates that, despite du Pont's resolution of a problem that had vexed the automobile industry for years,[41] General Motors' rivals found it possible to develop new sources of supply.

In a general sense the availability of substitutes can be tested not only by the record of the consumers but also by the responses of rival products to changes in prices and quality.[42] To what extent do prices move in the same direction? What have been the changes in relative sales? What are the public utterances of the managements of the different companies with respect to interproduct sub-

---

[38] Cf. *United States* v. *Corn Products Refining Co.*, 234 Fed. 964 (S.D.N.Y. 1916), appeal dismissed, 249 U.S. 621 (a sirup manufacturer sought to force its supplies on candy manufacturers by purchasing a candy factory which it threatened to use in competition). It might have been expected that du Pont would have used the profits from its "protected" market to eliminate rivals in competitive markets. See also *United States* v. *Aluminum Co.*, 148 F.2d 416, 436-38 (2d Cir. 1945).

[39] 353 U.S. 634.

[40] "The industry is highly competitive and neither Ford nor Chrysler could afford to permit General Motors to steal a march. But when competitive products appeared the Ford and Chrysler market fell off much more sharply than the General Motors market. The answer is not that Duco was not as useful to them, but that, not having the stock incentive to support continued buying, they went where competitive conditions led them as soon as competition appeared" (Government Reply Brief, Sup. Court, p. 21).

[41] Sloan testified that "in those days, the most important problem we faced, from the standpoint of the quality of the car, from the consumer's point of view, was the finish of the car" (Du Pont Brief, Dist, Court, p. 77). Fisher said that up to the development of "Duco" the industry had been finishing autos with varnish which was expensive, hard to use, and gave little satisfaction to the user (*ibid.*, p. 77).

[42] Cf. Professor George W. Stocking's analysis of the cellophane case, "The Cellophane Case and the New Competition," *American Economic Review*, XLV (1955), 29.

stitution? In this particular instance the degrees of separation of the market for automobile finishes from that of paints in general is to be tested by considering the movement of prices in each of the two markets and the extent to which they responded to changes in costs of raw materials. Where did Ford and Chrysler go when they sought to free themselves from dependence on du Pont? Were du Pont and other manufacturers of automobile finishes insulated from product improvements in the field of finishes and fabrics in general?

In sum, Justice Brennan's definition of the relevant market appears arbitrary, inconsistent, and dubious. The arbitrariness was indicated not so much in the judgment that automobile finishes represented a separate "line of commerce" where no such finding of fact had been made by the district court but, rather, in the stress on the buyer's special requirements. No rational basis was provided for restricting the market finding to the buyer. Logically, it is analogous to attributing the determination of market price solely to demand. That du Pont's competitors might have had ample opportunities for the sale of industrial finishes and fabrics was completely and unreasonably brushed aside without further discussion.

The definition was inconsistent in that "Dulux," a refrigerator finish, and other industrial finishes not used exclusively by the automobile industry[43] were included among the sales of automotive finishes. Similar procedures were followed in computing the purchases of fabrics.

Finally, the definition was dubious because, if the foreclosure possibility is anything more than a per se condemnation of vertical integration, it has to rest on the substantial position of General Motors as a buyer of the two products.

In that case, not only is the alleged "tendency to monopoly" not eliminated by relief which separates du Pont from control, but the problem is more properly viewed in terms of buyer dominance, or monopsony. While Sherman Act cases have found vertical integration illegal in cases involving abuses or intent to monopolize,[44] the Court at least implicitly recognized the prior existence of horizontal monopoly as the necessary prerequisite for the so-called leverage effect.[45] The obvious parallel for these proceedings was the very substantial market occupancy of General Motors as an automobile producer.

B. AUTOMOBILE FINISHES AND FABRICS AS THE "LINE OF COMMERCE"

The district court found that du Pont produces thousands of products and that, despite its sales efforts over a period of forty years,

the record discloses numerous instances in which General Motors rejected du Pont products in favor of those of one of its competitors. The variety of situations and circumstances in which such rejections occured satisfied the court and there was no limitation whatsoever upon General Motors' freedom to buy or refuse to buy from du Pont as it pleased.[46]

It seems likely that, had there been coercion of the General Motors division managers to purchase du Pont products, evidence would exist of loud and bitter protests by, and even perhaps disciplinary action against, those seeking to

---

[43] General Motors' 1947 purchases from du Pont's Finishes Division amounted to $18,938,229, of which $12,224,000 went for "Duco" and thinners and solvents associated with it, $3,179,000 for "Dulux," and $3,535,000 for other finishes.

[44] United States v. American Tobacco Co., 221 U.S. 106 (1911); United States v. Reading Co., 226 U.S. 324 (1912); United States v. Corn Products Co., 234 Fed. 964 (S.D.N.Y. 1916); appeal dismissed, 249 U.S. 621; United States v. Reading Co., 253 U.S. 26 (1920); United States v. Yellow Cab Co., 332 U.S. 218 (1947); United States v. Paramount Pictures, Inc., 334 U.S. 131 (1948).
[45] Bork, op. cit., p. 196.
[46] 126 F.Supp. 324.

exercise independent judgment. Further, as with most vertically integrated operations, it might have been expected that du Pont would have disposed of its entire output to General Motors,[47] permitting the latter to meet peak-demand requirements with outside purchases when necessary.[48] Partial integration always places the burden of adjustment to fluctuations in demand on the independent suppliers.[49]

The consideration of only two products (see Table 1) by the Supreme Court may be attributed to its finding of the appropriate "line of commerce." Once it was satisfied that automobile finishes and fabrics had "sufficient peculiar characteristics and uses," it simply had to conclude that *that relationship* would have the effect proscribed by Section 7. The House Committee report on amended Section 7 had stated that the purpose of the bill was "to protect competition in each line of commerce."[50]

Subsequent cases have condemned mergers where competition is substantially lessened or a tendency to monopoly created in "any" line of commerce out of a number of lines of commerce.[51]

The decision as to what process or product to choose is never simple. Decision-making is "ideal" and therefore simplest when all other things are equal — the familiar *ceteris paribus* condition of classical economists. Thus, where alternatives are physically identical so that the only basis for preference is price, the competitive model is applicable. But industry does not always present such simple choices. As an illustration, consider the competition between alcohol and glycerine for use as an antifreeze agent in automobile engines. General Motors' research concluded on a basis of its findings that glycerine was the superior product for such a purpose, although alcohol was cheaper.[52] Thus Kettering, who was head of General Motors' research, used nothing but glycerine. On the other hand, of forty-four car manufacturers, twenty-nine recommended alcohol, while five favored glycerine. It cannot therefore be said that one product was necessarily inherently superior — the decision of which to choose rested, it would seem, upon the weights assigned to the different qualities desired.

The government, on the contrary, sought to make it appear as though the issues were always clear cut. Thus, because du Pont pushed alcohol and evidence was produced that du Pont was able to have the official General Motors' approval of glycerine eliminated, it was inferred that there was no case for alcohol as the better product and that preferential treatment had been given du Pont. Obviously, such a conclusion had little if any substance to back it up in the

---

[47] See Donald Moore, "The Automobile Industry," in *Structure of American Industry*, ed. W. Adams (rev. ed., New York: Macmillan Co., 1954), p. 298.

[48] That du Pont sought such an arrangement but did not get it creates a strong presumption against the government's contention of control and preference. Carpenter, of du Pont, wrote Pierre S. du Pont, president of General Motors: "From another point of view, if an arrangement could be made, especially at this time, whereby the du Pont Company could secure all of the artificial leather and rubber business, we could operate our plant, I believe, on a fairly economical basis, thus getting considerably lower costs (which the General Motors Company would secure the advantage from) and we would not be compelled to operate at a considerable loss all the time. . . . It seems uneconomical, from the general du Pont pocketbook point of view, not to be able to make some arrangements whereby we could run our artificial leather plants fairly full, and in the long run it would not cost the General Motors Company any more money" (Government Brief, Sup. Court, pp. 37-38).

[49] Nickowitz testified that, when Ford entered the fabrics market, it was to "take advantage of bulges or their own shortcomings" (Du Pont Brief, Sup. Court, p. 202). Cf. also Federal Trade Commission, *Report on Corporate Merges and Acquisitions* (Washington, D.C., May, 1955), p. 116.

[50] H.R. Report No. 1191, p. 8.

[51] *United States* v. *Bethlehem Steel Corp. and Youngstown Sheet and Tube Co.*, 168 F. Supp. 576 (1958), and *Matter of Crown Zellerback Corp.*, FTC Docket No. 6180 (1957).

[52] General Motors Brief, Sup. Court, p. 93.

absence of an absolute standard as to a quality test.

III. FORECLOSURE AND THE CUSTOMER-SUPPLIER-RELATIONSHIP

Evidence of market foreclosure seemed to the Supreme Court to be indicated by two tests. First, there was the change in Fisher Body's purchases. Although by 1926 the major part of the stock of Fisher Body had been purchased by General Motors, the Fisher brothers retained management control until 1947. By that time, instead of stubbornly resisting du Pont sales pressure, "the proportions of its requirements supplied by du Pont compared favorably with the purchases by other General Motors divisions." Second, du Pont was the dominant supplier: "the bulk of du Pont's production has always supplied the largest part of the requirements of the one customer in the automobile industry connected to du Pont by a stock interest."[53] An analysis of each of these as an indication of foreclosure follows.

A. FISHER BODY

In 1926 a breakdown of General Motors' dollar purchases showed that "only Fisher Body of [all] the General Motors divisions was obtaining any substantial proportion of its requirements from du Pont's competitors."[54] Not until General Motors obtained 100 per cent control of this company did the "proportion of its requirements supplied by du Pont compare favorably with the purchases made by the other General Motors divisions."[55] But the relevant evidence referring to fabric purchases represented a departure from the findings of fact made by the trial court.

The government rested its case on the 37 per cent of Fisher's requirements that du Pont had supplied in 1926 compared with the situation existing in 1947-48. In 1926 Fisher Body accounted for 63 per cent of General Motors' requirements. Chevrolet, which at that time was buying 27 per cent of the total, switched over to du Pont "after an unfortunate experience with competitive products during the preceding year."[56] The result was that, in this particular year, 37 per cent of Fisher's purchases and 55.5 per cent of all General Motors' purchases were made from du Pont. The government commented: "The 55.5 per cent figure mentioned in the General Motors brief is a percentage made up by combining a controlled and uncontrolled market and meaningless."[57]

The 1926 figure relied on by the government was an arbitrary one. The lower court noted that the percentages purchased by the automobile divisions from various suppliers fluctuated from year to year:

In 1918 du Pont had difficulties in maintaining color uniformity and Oakland purchased from competitors. In 1922 Oakland purchased its entire requirements of coated fabrics from du Pont, but in 1923 began to purchase from competitors. By 1925 du Pont again received about one third of its coated fabric business. In 1926 it converted to uncoated combined top material and purchased from du Pont competitors.[58]

These variations, which occurred so regularly, are hard to reconcile with the government's selection of only one year as its base, and they are certainly not consistent with the government's hypothesis of du Pont control.

However, the Supreme Court accepted the 1926 base and compared figures for that year with those repre-

[53] 353 U.S. 606.
[54] Ibid., p. 605.
[55] Ibid.

[56] General Motors Brief, Supreme Court, p. 69, n. 47.
[57] Government Reply Brief, p. 21, n. 8.
[58] 126 F.Supp. 235, at 298.

TABLE 1°

GENERAL MOTORS' PURCHASES OF SELECTED SUPPLIES, 1947-48

Product	GM Purchasing Unit	Du Pont's Share of Total (Per Cent)†	Dollar Purchases from du Pont	Total Dollar Purchases	Year
Total finishes	Corporation	71	$18,938,229	$29,673,229	1947
Topcoats ("Duco" and thinner)	Chevrolet	100			
	Pontiac	100			
	Buick	100	12,224,798	19,756,798	1947
	Fisher Body	33			
	Oldsmobile	None	....	....	1947
	Cadillac	None	....	....	1947
Undercoats	Chevrolet	100			
	Buick	100			
	Pontiac	100	3,534,000	....	1947
	Fisher Body	Minor			
Exterior refrigerator	Frigidaire	75	3,179,225	....	1947
Interior refrigerator	Frigidaire	None	....	....	1947
Washer	Frigidaire	None	....	....	1947
Dryer	Frigidaire	None	....	....	1947
Rubbing compounds	Corporation	Very little	200,000	....	1947
Chassis enamel	Corporation	Very little	....	....	1947
Motor enamel	Corporation	Buick only	....	....	1947
Interior enamels	Corporation	Very little	....	....	1947
Radiator and heater	Harrison Radiator	None	....	....	1947
Insulating varnish	Delco-Remy	None	....	....	1947
Exterior diesel	Electromotive	Major	....	....	1947
Interior diesel	Electromotive	None	....	....	1947
High-tension lacquer	Packard Electric	None	....	....	1947
Low-tension lacquer	Packard Electric	None	....	....	1947
Total fabrics	Corporation	40	$ 3,700,000	$ 9,250,000	1948
Combination uncoated	Fisher Body	50	....	....	1948
Interior coated	Fisher Body	33⅓ or less	....	....	1948
Upholstery and trim	Chev. Commercial Body	30	600,000	2,000,000	1948
Diaphragm	AC Spark Plug	Chevrolet only	....	2,000,000	1948
Light-truck upholstery	GM Truck & Coach	33	....	....	1948
Heavy-truck upholstery	GM Truck & Coach	None	....	....	1948
Bus seats	GM Truck & Coach	None	....	....	1948
Synthetic rubber coated	Delco Electromotive	None	....	....	1948
Synthetic coated insulating	Electromotive	None	....	....	1948
Sheet stock	Delco	None	....	....	1948
Vinyl tape	Packard Electric	None	....	....	1948
Coated glass	Packard Electric	50	....	....	1948
Other products					
Chemicals (solvents)	Corporation	12	....	3,622,000	1947
Acrylic acid	Corporation	Minor	....	....	1948
Brake fluid	Corporation	None	....	ca. 2,000,000	1948
Rubber cement	Fisher Body	None	....	1,000,000	1948
Anodes	Corporation	‡	....	1,200,000	1947
Adhesives	Corporation	‡	....	3,000,000	1947

°Compiled from du Pont's and General Motors' briefs, *United States* v. *E. I. du Pont de Nemours and Co. et al.,* 126 F. Supp. 235 (N.D. Ill. 1954), and Government Brief, *United States* v. *E. I. du Pont de Nemours and Co. et al.,* 353 U.S. 586 (1957).

†Little significance can be attached to these particular percentages, since they varied from year to year, depending upon the competitive offerings of different suppliers. To illustrate: In 1926 du Pont furnished 50 per cent of Fisher Body's requirements of combined uncoated fabrics; in 1932 the Fisher Body business went to Haartz for a variety of reasons and remained there for the next fifteen years. Through the years 1948-50, du Pont was again meeting Fisher Body's requirements up to 50 per cent, but in 1951 du Pont's share was reduced to 33½ per cent.

‡Less than 1 per cent.

senting 1947-48 to verify its hypothesis that by this time "Fisher Body was just another department of General Motors, buying 65.5 per cent of its fabrics from du Pont in 1947 and 68 per cent in 1948."[59] In so doing, the government overstated the figures for "Fabrikoid,"

[59] Government Reply Brief, Supreme Court, p. 68.

"Fabrilite," and "Cavalon," as supplied by du Pont, in its assumption that all such material "is used *solely* for upholstery and trim." The government also understated the purchases by General Motors from du Pont's competitors by its assumption that "only those purchases by General Motors . . . shown under the heading 'Imitation Leather' were used for upholstery and trim." It should be noted that the lower court had refused to accept certain of these procedures. Instead it found that "in the fabrics field General Motors purchased approximately 40-50 per cent of its requirements from du Pont for the years 1946-47."[60] As this finding does not significantly differ from the 1926 purchases, there is little evidence of the alleged collapse of Fisher resistance.

The discrepancy between the government's estimates of 65.5 per cent and 68 per cent as accepted by the Supreme Court and the district court's finding of fact in terms of 40-50 per cent is explained by the arbitrary and unjustified procedures followed by the government. For one thing, it did not include all the purchased made by General Motors from du Pont's competitors—it excluded those which were expressed in yards rather than dollars, even though the price per yard varied widely. And, in any case, the figures were compiled from incomplete data contained in the reports of a du Pont salesman to his home office. This same salesman, Nalle, when on the witness stand estimated that du Pont had received approximately 40 per cent of Fisher's business in 1948.

The government also arbitrarily excluded substantial purchases of convertible-top materials from a competitor of du Pont on the grounds that such fabrics were not manufactured by du Pont. The trial court had not found with the government on this score: coated fabric was not used only for upholstery and trim but also for head linings, winter fronts, seat covers, top materials, case coverings, spring boots, sheet stock, work clothing, and curtains.[61] Over the years it appears that the percentages supplied by du Pont have fluctuated, depending on the quality of du Pont's product and that of its competitors.

A curious aspect of the government's procedure, and also the Supreme Court's acceptance of it, is that, beginning with a delineation of the relevant market as "automobile finishes and fabrics," the market was further restricted to "imitation leather" for upholstery and trim. When it is recalled that the issue was whether du Pont obtained a "captive market" in General Motors for fabrics, this procedure is highly suspect. The issue was fabrics, not a specialized product used only for upholstery and trim. The lower court refused to make such a distinction,[62] ruling that the terms "coated fabrics" and "imitation leather" are used interchangeably [and that] these separate headings . . . were used merely to permit recording in accordance with personal preference in usage of terms, and that in collecting and presenting the figures contained in GTX 1343A, General Motors included under both headings fabrics that were competitive with those offered by du Pont.

B. MAJOR SUPPLIERS

The government did not consider alternative reasons for General Motors or for any automobile firm to choose to concentrate on a dominant supplier. Du Pont had pointed out that where a product was not a technically difficult one to manufacture, and where price rather than quality or service was the major consideration, the company failed to achieve outstanding success.[63] In such circumstances a buyer was likely to distribute his purchases among a number of suppliers. On the other hand, where quality and service were of primary importance, and where the product was not a simple one to prepare and service, a dominant-supplier relationship might be expected to develop. The difficulties encountered in meeting technical problems in novel situations often lead to very close relationships between supplier and customer. The complementarily logically implies exclusiveness.

The difficulties experienced by the

---

[60] 126 F.Supp. 235, at 301.
[61] *Ibid.*, p. 300.

[62] *Ibid.*, p. 301.
[63] Du Pont Brief, Dist. Court, p. 113.

automobile industry with finishes seem to point directly to the development of a major-supplier relationship. Though the industry had been characterized by the assembly-line and mass-production techniques, "one great problem remained, for as late as 1922-24 automobiles were still painted with the same kind of paint and in much the same way as carriages and buggies had been painted for many years. A new type of finish had to be found—a finish which would last as long as the automobile itself and a finish which could be applied on the assembly line in a matter of hours."[64] In the early 1920's it took up to thirty days to apply as many as twenty-three separate coats of paint and varnish on a single automobile. "The problem of where to house thousands and more thousands of slowly drying automobiles became acute." Not only were large amounts of working capital tied up until delivery of the cars but it was found that the paint would not stand up under the heat of three months of summer sun.

Kettering, head of General Motors Research Division, approached a number of paint manufacturers, and only du Pont showed any interest in developing a special lacquer for automobiles. "This was due to the fact that about two years earlier Flaherty, the chief chemist of du Pont, had discovered a procedure for producing a lacquer with a high solids content—all previous lacquers had low solids content requiring the application of many coats when used in colors."[65] The new lacquer subsequently became known as "Duco." With its use, "painting time of an Oakland body came down from 336 hours to 13½ hours; material costs were lower; the floor space necessary for painting operations was substantially reduced; the number of bodies being painted at one time was reduced from 2400 to 600; inspectors' rejected

were cut from 20 per cent to 2 per cent of daily production."[66]

The change was clearly revolutionary and, according to Sloan, solved "the most important problem we faced, from the standpoint of the quality of the car, from the consumer's point of view."[67] When, after several years of development, the lacquer had been adapted to the automobile, and du Pont's Williams had gone from division to division in an effort to persuade them to substitute the new lacquer for varnish,[68] Pierre S. du Pont, then president of General Motors, "at the request of the Paint and Enamel Committee asked the du Pont Company to stop all negotiations with other possible consumers and all plans for selling these products in the open market."[69] Irénée du Pont turned down this request because they "had already started a number of small users in business and [could not] now cut them off from their source of supply." Du Pont was not only marketing this lacquer to other automobile manufacturers but had for some time been selling it to the auto-refinishing trade and to manufacturers of furniture, brush handles, novelties, and pencils.[70]

During the twenties, Ford "was losing its leadership in the low-priced field to Chevrolet,"[71] due partly to the company's insistence on clinging to its traditional black finish. But, with the advent of the thirties and the competitive necessity for shifting to a synthetic enamel finish, du Pont for a temporary period supplied up to 50 per cent of Ford's paint requirements. Henry Ford, however, did not like the idea of having his company dependent upon a supplier so

---

[64] Sloan, Record 2995-97, cited *ibid.*, p. 86. See also testimony by L. P. Fisher, Record 1009-17, and Kettering, Record 3591-93.

[65] Du Pont Brief, Dist. Court, p. 87.

[66] *Ibid.*, p. 89, n. 8.

[67] *Ibid.*, p. 77.

[68] Williams, the du Pont man who worked closely with each of the General Motors divisions, testified at the trial how he had spent more than two years going from division to division, from plant to plant, spraying fenders and bodies with "Duco," and talking with plant superintendents, production engineers, and plant managers (*ibid.*, p. 87; Record 4159-65, 4182, 4236-37).

[69] 126 F. Supp. 235, at 289.

[70] See n. 25 above.

[71] *United States* v. *duPont*, 353 U.S. 634.

closely tied to a major competitor. Consequently, he "issued instructions that the Ford Motor Company was not to purchase any more material from the du Pont Company."[72] Later, with the accession of Henry Ford II, the Ford Motor Company again purchased a portion of its finish needs from du Pont. Chrysler also purchased "Duco' until the early thirties, when, following a policy of concentrating on suppliers "to whom it would be the most important customer," it turned to Pittsburgh Plate Glass for its requirements.[73] Given the status of the competition among the "Big Three," it is not surprising that General Motors' competitors sought alternative sources of supplies.[74]

Decisions by both Ford and Chrysler to take steps to assure themselves of reliable suppliers "were in response to a fact of life in auto production,"[75] as is borne out in the testimony of automobile men. In this industry it is essential that materials be ready for the assembly line "at the right time and in the right quality."[76] Sloan illustrated this point by distinguishing the sale of men's shirts at Marshall Field's, for example, where, if you do not "get the right quality or the right delivery, it has little effect on their business, . . . [and] the automobile business, [which] industry and production-wise is a continuous operation. You cannot ship the car unless the car is complete, and any serious shortage of material stops the whole plant operation."[77]

Actually, in order to establish whether du Pont owed its commanding position as a supplier to its interest in General Motors, two questions should have been asked by the Court: (1) To what extent did General Motors use dominant suppliers which held no ownership interest in the corporation? (2) To what extent did Ford and Chrysler use dominant suppliers?

1. It is evident that General Motors used dominant suppliers in the absence of a stock relationship—particularly where quality and service factors were not easily reproduced. Differences between suppliers with respect to their reliability, quality of product, and location led to close customer-supplier relationships; the corporation has at one time or other purchased all or the greater part of its requirements of steel bars, coal, brass and copper sheets, screws, tubing, leather, car frames, and tires from a single source.[78] It purchases 100 per cent of its white paint from National Lead, a du Pont competitor;[79] 100 per cent of its glass from Libby-Owens-Ford;[80] and after negotiation of the rubber contract with United States Rubber in 1931, it bought up to 60 per cent of its tires from that company.[81]

2. The automobile producers other than General Motors, as well as many other industrial firms, use major suppliers. For example, Briggs supplied Chrysler with bodies until it was acquired by the latter in 1949; Borg-Warner until recently supplied the major part of Ford's requirements for transmissions; Firestone is the major supplier of tires to Ford;[82] Goodyear is the sole supplier of tires to Chrysler;[83] Pitts-

---

[72] Ibid.

[73] Ibid.

[74] In the recent Bethlehem Steel merger decision, the Court observed that the "opportunities for a price squeeze on the independent are enhanced, since the supplier may shift his profit between rope wire and wire rope in such a manner as to narrow or eliminate the independent's margin of profit on wire rope" (*United States* v. *Bethlehem Steel Corporation and the Youngstown Sheet and Tube Co.*, 168 F.Supp. 576, 611). The most desireable source of supply was a producer which did not compete with it.

[75] Du Pont Brief, Sup. Court, p. 99.

[76] Ibid.

[77] Ibid.

[78] Ibid., p. 195.

[79] General Motors Brief, Dist. Court, p. 78.

[80] U.S. Senate Committee on the Judiciary, Subcommittee on Antitrust and Monopoly, *Bigness and Concentration of Economic Power: A Case Study of General Motors Corporation* (Senate Report No. 1879 [84th Cong., 2d sess. (Washington: 1956)]), p. 31.

[81] General Motors Brief, Dist. Court, p. 165.

[82] 126 F. Supp. 235, at 329.

[83] Ibid.

burgh Plate Glass is the dominant supplier of both finishes and glass to Chrysler;[84] both Atlas and Montgomery-Ward secure 100 per cent of their supplies from United States Rubber;[85] Westinghouse has for many years "purchased its entire requirements of refrigerator finish from du Pont."[86] On a basis of these facts, it is not unreasonable to conclude that the switch of both Ford and Chrysler from du Pont may have had little to do with "competitive merit." The strength of the hypothesis that they shifted for other reasons is demonstrated by their pursuit of identical policies with respect to other material needs.

Table 1 roughly illustrates the extent of du Pont's participation in General Motors' business. Attempts made during the trial to construct a table showing the annual variations of du Pont's participation had to be abandoned because of incomplete data. The government objected to listing some of the products, contending that du Pont was not competitive and that "it was only where the products were competitive that the preference could operate."[87] Inferences following from this reasoning would be that, if a General Motors division purchased from a competitor, the product must have been superior to du Pont's (i.e., du Pont was not competitive); but, whenever the business was given to du Pont, it was not that its product was superior but that the preference was operative. Unfortunately, neither the government nor the Supreme Court outlined the terms in which the "competitive merit" hypothesis might have been verified.

If Ford and Chrysler had continued to purchase "Duco," General Motors' purchases might have been conceded to be based on "competitive merit." But, in completely rejecting the "special reasons" argument for the switch, the government contended that, because the automobile industry is "highly competitive," Ford and Chrysler were forced to shift their custom from "Duco" when competitive products appeared, whereas General Motors remained a "captive." This is to deny without evidence that "Duco" was at least as good as the alternatives adopted by the other two major automobile producers.[88] Furthermore, the government ignored the fact that 33 per cent of the finishes purchased by General Motors came from competitive suppliers, the dollar value the purchases—about $9,500,000 in 1947—being almost as much as Chrysler bought from Pittsburgh Plate Glass. In addition, 50-60 per cent of the fabrics purchases also came from competitors. It is, therefore, not strictly correct to claim that General Motors failed to adopt competitive products when they appeared; it merely did not do so to the extent of its rivals.

The three major automobile producers represented about 80 per cent of the market for automobile finishes and fabrics. If all three had continued to purchase from du Pont, the latter most certainly would have had a strong-supplier status—assuming the Court's definition of the market in terms of automobile finishes and fabrics. The finishes were an important item in the competitive sale of the automobile, and failure of either quality or delivery due to labor troubles, inertia in the absence of competition, or inability to come to terms because of the dependence of the entire industry on this one supplier might have well caused costly interruptions to assembly-line production.[89]

---

[84] General Motors Brief, Dist. Court, p. 101.
[85] *Ibid.*, p. 166.
[86] 126 F. Supp. 293.
[87] Government Reply Brief, Sup. Court, p. 10

[88] That the du Pont product was not inferior is suggested by 1947 sales of "Duco" to the value of $3,446,000 to the smaller automobile manufacturers.
[89] Pratt, who was both chairman of the General Purchasing Committee and head of the Accessory Divisions, wrote: "If it is possible to use the product from more than one company I do not

Competitive automobile manufacturers, in fact, gained by shifting, not only as a result of encouraging additional sources of supply, but in providing competition for du Pont. In addition, Ford and Chrysler sought suppliers that looked to them and were not related to their major competitor by ownership.[90] It was characteristic that each manufacturer chose a different means to implement its objective: Ford produced the bulk of its requirements; Chrysler developed a major supplier; while General Motors determined on a two-source supply policy.[91] The success of each of these policies effectively destroyed the probability that du Pont would ever wield monopoly power.

The government claimed that competition drove Ford and Chrysler to other suppliers. Part of this assertion is correct. But the same competition also drove a substantial part of the General Motors business from du Pont. Each of the buyers had to develop new sources of supply in order to escape dependence on a single source. General Motors differed only in the absence of *one* of the factors: it did not need to seek a supplier unrelated to its competitors. Thus the only reasons that should have compelled it to switch suppliers were the usual competitive ones of quality, service, and price. Apparently, for at least three of the corporation's divisions — Oldsmobile, Cadillac, and Fisher Body — these reasons were compelling.

The government's theory of foreclosure logically required du Pont inferiority. Otherwise no reason would have

existed for General Motors to switch suppliers. Yet in its Reply Brief the observation was made that salesmen had to sell to General Motors on the basis of merit: "There was no other way for General Motors to know what products were competitive, and it was only where the products were competitive that the preference could operate."[92] Aside from the ambiguity of the concept "competitive," this statement is inconsistent with the argument that an independent General Motors would have followed the same path as Ford and Chrysler. If du Pont's products were competitive, that would certainly be at least consistent with those two purchasers having switched suppliers for other reasons.

Not only was no evidence of du Pont inferiority produced but the case rested on unsupported assertions that du Pont "was unable to sell to others"[93] and that it was unable to "build up a comparable demand." These claims are, however, refuted by the facts, viz., when Ford bought from the outside, its principal supplier was du Pont.[94] Nor does it follow that du Pont's failure to sell to Ford and Chrysler proved a lack of competitive ability. Ford also has ceased purchasing the bulk of its transmissions from Borg-Warner and General Motors Hydramatic Division. Its decision to produce this equipment for itself came about for a number of reasons and without prejudice to the outside supplier's service, quality, and price. Similarly, Chrysler decided to discontinue the purchase of frames for its Dodge and Plymouth passenger-car lines after the completion of the 1959 model run in order to manufacture for itself.[95]

The present example of General Mo-

---

think it advisable to give any one company all of the business, as I think it is desirable to always keep a competitive situation, otherwise any supplier is liable to grow slack in seeing that you have the best service and price possible" (Government Brief, Sup. Court, pp. 122-23).

[90] This consideration apparently was no cause of apprehension among the major refrigerator manufacturers, who exclusively filled their requirements for exterior finish with du Pont (126 F. Supp. 293).

[91] *Ibid.*, p. 277.

[92] Government Reply Brief, Sup. Court, pp. 9-10. But it also said: "It is noteworthy that du Pont's relationship with General Motors made it unnecessary for it to compete pricewise" (Brief, Sup. Court, p. 60, n. 11).

[93] Brief, Sup. Court, p. 21.

[94] Du Pont Brief, Sup. Court, p. 202.

[95] *Wall Street Journal*, July 28, 1958.

tors' Chevrolet, Buick, and Pontiac divisions in buying "Duco" also requires comment. In any large organization which practices divisional autonomy, differences of opinion as to the merits of respective products may be frequent. Witness the debate within General Motors as to the respective advantages of the various automatic transmissions.[96] The fact that Cadillac and Oldsmobile do not use "Duco," while Chevrolet, Buick, and Pontiac do (as well as Nash, Hudson, Willys, Ford, and Chrysler), indicates that the divisions were free to make their own decisions as to what product to use. Chevrolet, Buick, and Pontiac have continued to buy "Duco," partly because of better service from near-by du Pont plants.[97]

Although Ford and Chrysler made different supplier decisions from the one followed by General Motors, the extent of the difference should not be exaggerated. Nor does it follow that the courses Ford and Chrysler chose would have been optimal for General Motors. The fact that they differed between themselves suggests that General Motors' decision was not necessarily the result of the du Pont stock interest. Ford and Chrysler also use different tire manufacturers, plate-glass suppliers, and parts manufacturers. General Motors' reliance upon suppliers other than those used by its chief competitors is consistent with its independence of those dominant suppliers.

Nor is it a persuasive rebuttal to argue that du Pont's uneven success in selling to General Motors can be accounted for simply because "it did not seek to obtain 100 per cent of General Motors trade,"[98] when no explanation is provided as to why the trade should have been sought for certain products and not others. There is no explanation either of why du Pont secured 70 per cent of the finish business, 40 per cent

of the fabrics business, and none of the white-lead business. Favoritism based on control could have given du Pont the entire market for each of the many products du Pont sought to sell to General Motors. To argue that the failure to gain the entire business was only due to not seeking it creates doubt as to whether any operational test would have refuted the government thesis.

IV. INCIPIENT MONOPOLY

Market foreclosure creating a tendency to monopoly may operate at either of three different levels. Thus, as applied to this case, (1) General Motors' freedom to buy might have been restricted; (2) General Motors' competitors might have been denied access to necessary supplies or else have faced discrimination; or (3) du Pont's competitors might have been barred from necessary outlets. It is obvious that (2) and (3) cannot exist at the same time; General Motors' competitors could not lack necessary sources of supply while suppliers lacked necessary market outlets. Accordingly, the government argued that it was du Pont's competitors which were foreclosed. But there was nothing more than speculation upon the foreclosure opportunities: no evidence of a competitor which had actually been foreclosed was introduced.[99]

Du Pont would have "foreclosed" the market in the sense of the word used here, assuming that it had the power, only if and when its products were not superior to those of competitors. In finding the market for automobile finish distinctive, the Court cited the du Pont brief to the effect that "Duco" represented a significant advance in its field.

---

[96] General Motors Brief, Sup. Court, p. 93.
[97] 353 U.S. 632.
[98] Government Reply Brief, Sup. Court, p. 9.

[99] The government suggested that the du Pont investment in General Motors provoked the sale of Flint Varnish and Color Works to du Pont (Government Brief, Sup. Court, p. 140, n. 44). But, if it represented an injury to competition that is illegal under the Clayton Act, it is difficult to conceive of any acquisition in an imperfect market that would not be illegal.

But, with a superior product, there would be no need to foreclose the market. The only products for which du Pont might have chosen to foreclose the market would be those in which there was no demonstrated superiority—those where it lacked technical advantage and where price rather than quality and service was the chief consideration. Thus, had du Pont possessed foreclosure ability, it might have been expected to assume exclusive-supplier status with respect to General Motors' use of these less important products. A study of Table 1 will show that the evidence does not support the above hypothesis, based on the government's reasoning—rubbing compounds, rubber cement, materials for seats of motor busses, diaphragm fabric for spark plugs, chemicals, adhesives, etc., were all supplied to the corporation by du Pont's competitors.

The Court's ruling that General Motors' market share of more than 40 per cent was sufficiently large for du Pont effectively to foreclose the markets appears obvious and clear cut. This assumes, however, that there is a clear understanding as to the *meaning* of competition and monopoly and that it is known what a "reasonable probability" *means*. But what is the basis for determination? Would a merger of two mills in the highly competitive textile industry lead to a prediction of monopoly? Economists would say that such a merger implies no anticompetitive effects. What, then, is the difference in the General Motors situation? Is it not the fact that the relative market share of any two textile firms is not likely to be great enough to be of any particular significance, whereas the share of the market held by a corporation such as General Motors is highly important? Therefore, the *sine qua non* for predicting that there is a reasonable probability that competition will be reduced is the large market occupancy of General Motors.

The difficulty here is that the applicable legislation, the Clayton Act, deals with symptoms rather than causes. The actual power in this instance remains with General Motors. If that power were objectionable when exerted in favor of du Pont, it would be *equally* objectionable if the stock interest were eliminated. General Motors may continue to give its business to du Pont; on the other hand, it may choose to foreclose the market to automobile-finish suppliers at any time simply by integrating, as Ford has done. Nor would integration be illegal if no merger were involved. The Clayton Act aims only at foreclosure and the resulting alleged monopoly which takes the *merger* route. Other routes are, however, permissible.[100] The law is effective not in preserving competition—whatever that may be—but in preventing the mergers of monopolists and oligopolists. Mergers are not illegal when the competitors are relatively small, that is, in terms of current economic theory, whenever monopoly elements are absent. It follows that the test of incipient monopoly is the presence of considerable monopoly power. But, since the Clayton Act was initially aimed at incipient monopoly, how is it to be effective if it does not become operative until monopoly elements are present?

If we are to avoid reaching the point of banning all mergers, we are forced into a dilemma. Either, (1) as a consequence of Ford's integration and Chrysler's policy of favoring major suppliers, a General Motors' merger with a dominant supplier cannot with any reasonable probability lead to monopoly, because monopoly is already present by the standards of market occupancy, or (2) there can be no tendency to monopoly because, in spite of the vertical acquisition, the automobile industry is effectively competitive. Either approach is unsatisfactory to professional economists. The first would make the law against incipient monopoly impos-

---

[100] Cf. comments of Louis B. Schwartz in *Report of the Attorney-General's Committee*, p. 128.

sible to enforce on the grounds that there was no incipient monopoly, only monopoly; the second is consistent with the view that oligopoly and competition are compatible. To the extent that oligopoly and monopoly are identical, competition cannot be reduced; to the extent that oligopoly is competitive,[101] vertical acquisition cannot represent a tendency to monopoly because suppliers have alternative outlets and buyers have alternative sources of supply.

The only way out of this dilemma would be to rule that *all* mergers necessarily violate law. But the reason for going this far is not compelling, for not every merger substantially lessens competition and tends to monopoly. There is no reason to believe that du Pont's stock interest in General Motors created a reasonable probability that du Pont's refrigerator enamel, "Dulux," for example, would become the sole product in that market. The government could argue so only on grounds that the arrangement foreclosed the market to *some* supplier of refrigerator enamel.

As it is widely believed that American *manufacturing* industry is characterized by oligopolistic elements,[102] vertical acquisitions are likely to become a per se violation. An acquisition by an oligopolist cannot help but foreclose a substantial share of the market if the recent cases are any guide.[103] But there is a

paradox. Their illegality must rest on incipient monopoly at one or the other levels of production.[104] Frustration of vertical integration, therefore, can have no favorable competitive effects. Section 7 is applicable, however, only in markets where competition must have been substantial—where incipient monopoly is the result of the acquisition, not the required condition for predicting a tendency to monopoly. Economic theory has always held that, at its weakest, oligopoly signified monopoly tendencies and, at its strongest, actual monopoly. Consequently, acquisition by an oligopolist cannot cause a tendency to monopoly. The tendency was really inherent in the oligopoly. The competitiveness of the markets for automobile finishes and fabrics depends as much upon the intensity of competition among the buyers as it does among the sellers. The effort to place du Pont on an equal basis as a supplier with its competitors will hardly make that market competitive. As both sides of the market remain oligopolistic, the tendencies to monopoly and monopsony persist.

V. CONCLUSIONS

One comes away from an analysis of this case with the view that, aside from matters of detail, such as those involved in mistaking a misleading calculation of du Pont's share of General Motors' purchases, a number of important issues were left unresolved. First, there is the matter of the determination of the "relevant market." The Court asserted that

---

[101] It is difficult to find any consensus on the competitiveness of this industry. Wilcox *(op. cit.)* does not place it among his competitive industries; Mason has, in one instance, observed that it is competitive ("The Current Status of the Monopoly Problem," *Harvard Law Review*, LXII [1949] 1282); cf. also Federal Trade Commission, *Report on the Automobile Industry*, 1939, p. 1074. Stigler classifies it as a monopoly *(Five Lectures on Economic Problems* [New York, 1950], p. 49), but, more appropriately, the government in this case said: "The industry is highly competitive" (Reply Brief, p. 21, n. 7).

[102] See, e.g., J. K. Galbraith, "Monopoly and the Concentration of Economic Power," in *Survey of Contemporary Economics*, ed. H. Ellis (Philadelphia, 1948), p. 118.

[103] I.e., Crown Zellerbach's merger with St. Helen's Pulp and Paper Co. and the abortive mer-

ger attempt between Bethlehem Steel and Youngstown Sheet and Tube.

[104] In his very fruitful discussion Bork *(op. cit.,* p. 200) commented: "Vertical integration is not a useful tool for economic analysis. Such integration confers no ability to alter market price, does not impede entry, and adds nothing unique to the ability to employ predatory tactics. . . . The idea of horizontal monopoly is sufficient to the tasks of the Sherman Act, and presents in the guise of market definition, problems enough for judicial ingenuity." The caution is equally applicable to Section 7.

automobile finishes and fabrics have sufficiently "peculiar characteristics and uses" to make them a line of commerce, ignoring the fact that the core of the government's case rests on the finding of additional paint supply sources by Ford and Chrysler. The availability of alternative supply sources is strong evidence that, in the paint business, du Pont was competitive with other paint manufacturers. Similarly, there is good reason to believe that du Pont is competitive with a wide range of fabric manufacturers. Second, neither the Court nor the government came to grips with the implications of the doctrine of "substantiality." If the General Motors market was so "substantial" that the competing suppliers could not survive after the du Pont investment, those suppliers must initially have been dependent on the corporation. Either of two situations would have had to exist: (1) General Motors was the only buyer of automobile finishes and fabrics (or the other markets were closed to the suppliers because of reliance upon integrated operations or dominant suppliers) or (2) there were only a few large suppliers who could not easily replace the General Motors market. Had it been otherwise, as in the case of a large number of small suppliers, any *one* would have had no difficulty in disposing of its entire output to the remaining buyers, representing up to 50 per cent of the total market. But, where there are only a few large suppliers, the situation must initially have been one of oligopoly.

If, on the other hand, General Motors was but one relatively small part of a large market of buyers (e.g., as in its purchase of *cotton* fabric), competitive opportunity could not have been effectively foreclosed. Competitive oppor-tunity can only be denied in the first case, that is, where General Motors, in effect, is the *only* buyer of the product. But, if this were so, suppliers must of necessity have depended on the General Motors market in the absence of a du Pont stock investment in the corporation. More significantly, General Motors would have enjoyed monopsony power so that it could have played one supplier against the other. It logically follows that, if du Pont's alleged "control" implied a substantial lessening of competitive opportunity for other suppliers of finishes and fabrics, those suppliers must initially have been at the mercy of such a dominant buyer.

And this leads to the third problem: Neither the Court nor the government took the time to specify the market in terms of *both* buyers and sellers. The well-known, and much-abused, "supply-and-demand" relationship might as well have never been discussed during the last fifty years. Had the Court looked closely at the buyers, the nature of the firms, how they manufactured their cars and assembled their materials, it could not seriously have believed the issue would be resolved simply by ordering the end of du Pont's control of General Motors in the interests of competition. Whatever the ensuing changes in the supplying and purchasing of automobile finishes and fabrics, there is no reason to expect economic welfare to be substantially enhanced. Nor is there reason to hail the decision as a victory over "bigness,"[105] for not only was it not on trial but it also escaped unscathed from the battle.

[105] See Joel B. Dirlam and Irwin M. Stelzer, "The du Pont-General Motors Decision: in the Antitrust Grain," *Columbia Law Review*, LVIII (1958), 25.

55. Dealer Margins Under Resale Price Maintenance*

STANLEY C. HOLLANDER

A standard hypothesis concerning resale price maintenance is that manufacturers who use the practice will probably increase their dealer margins over time. The hypothesis rests upon a belief that the desire to win dealer favor is one of the main reasons, if not the only one, that leads manufacturers to support retail prices. Since retailers' attitudes are considered important, this argument holds, the producing firms will compete for retail support by establishing ever increasing margins.[1]

Over a century ago, a British bookseller noted how the retail margin could become a competitive weapon under resale price maintenance:

> If all booksellers could be induced to . . . allow no discount from the published prices . . . and if it were the general custom of the publishers to allow to the bookseller an average discount of 30 per cent, it would be possible for any one publisher to induce the booksellers to take a special interest in promoting the sale of his publications, rather than those of other houses, by allowing them a larger discount than they usually obtained . . . At their trade sales, Messrs. Longman and Co. allow about 30 per cent discount to purchasers, and rarely give the extra advantage of charging 25 books as 24 or 13 as 12; whereas Mr. Murray [a leading price maintenance advocate] in common with two or three other publishers, allows at his trade sales 33 /3 per cent discount, and gives the extra advantage of charging 25 books as 24, and very often 13 as 12 . . . a main reason why the bookseller is subjected to the system of protection, which he is assured is for his exclusive benefit, is, that the practice of competition is found to produce a rich return to the underselling publisher in proportion as the privilege is withheld from the retail bookseller.[2]

But oddly enough, the 110 years that have passed since this book dealer's protest was made have seen relatively little empirical research on margin behavior under resale price maintenance. Price behavior has been investigated very frequently, but not margin behavior.[3]

From *Quarterly Review of Economics and Business*, Vol. 3, No. 3 (Autumn, 1963), pp. 25-33.

* Professor Orin E. Burley of the University of Pennsylvania kindly offered several helpful comments on an earlier draft of this paper.

[1] E.g., Joseph F. Klamon: "Manufacturers have been faced with a demand for a maintained resale price and margin. Then the demand takes the form of a request for wider margins . . ." U.S. Senate, Committee on Interstate and Foreign Commerce, *Resale Price Fixing*, Hearings on H.R. 5767, 82nd Cong., 2nd Sess., 1952, p. 393.

B. S. Yamey: ". . . [The agrument for resale price maintenance] also neglects the fact that competing manufacturers may compete for the retailers' favours by offering higher gross margins." "Resale Price Maintenance: Issues and Policies," *The Three Banks Review*, December, 1960, p. 8.

[2] John Chapman, at an authors' meeting chaired by Charles Dickens, London, May 4, 1852, quoted in Paul Hollister, *The Authors' Wallet* (New York: R. H. Macy and Company, 1954), pp. 53-54.

[3] For an analysis of many of the price studies, see Marvin Frankel, "The Effects of Fair Trade: Fact and Fiction in the Statistical Findings,"

The Federal Trade Commission's 1945 study of resale price maintenance provides surprisingly little information on retail margins. The commission reported that when interstate price maintenance was legalized, many manufacturers of drugstore products set their retail margins at considerably lower rates than the 33⅓ percent of retail that the National Association of Retail Druggists had hoped would become the minimum markup for the trade.[4]

Oxenfeldt has noted a long-run decline in retail margins for whisky, a product subject to resale price maintenance in most states. He found that the dealers were allowed only about 33⅓ percent after World War II, instead of the usual prewar 40 percent. Both prewar and postwar margins were sometimes adjusted to meet local conditions or to serve individual distillers' promotional objectives. The retailers frequently also received small special concessions and allowances, but these came mainly from wholesalers rather than from distillers.[5]

An earlier detailed discussion of fair trade margins appeared in E. T. Grether's classic *Price Control Under Fair Trade Legislation*.[6] Grether compared long-run margin behavior in Great Britain with the changes experienced during the first years of the California law. The California average margin on 718 drugstore products increased between 1934 and 1936, but there were numerous exceptions and divergences from the average. In contrast, two British investigating committees reported little evidence of margin increases under resale price maintenance. Average margins for a small sample of 21 products actually declined markedly between 1895 and 1933. Grether concluded that markups allowed under resale price maintenance would vary from time to time and from item to item. The variations would depend in great part on differences in the strategies, bargaining positions, and market appraisals of different suppliers and dealers, but manufacturers would usually hold the whip hand.

Contrarily, the so-called Lloyd Jacob committee concluded that "distributive margins on price maintained goods are principally determined not by reference to costs, but by a process of bargaining and by conformity to the demands of organized distributors."[7]

In addition to the foregoing, some more recent data are available concerning the margins that American producers have set for at least two groups of fair-traded products: books and drugstore merchandise. These data do not tell us nearly as much as we might like to know about what may happen under resale price maintenance. Nevertheless, they are suggestive and they do shed some light on several aspects of pricing practices.

LIMITATIONS OF THE DATA

The information cited here, both for books and for drug products, comes from trade directories. Such sources provide little or no information about secret allowances and concessions to favored customers. This defect in the data is probably not very important, however, since resale price maintenance is supposedly used to protect the smaller retailers who would not be likely to receive substantial covert con-

Journal of Business, Vol. 28, No. 3 (July, 1955), pp. 182-94.

[4] Report of the Federal Trade Commission on *Resale Price Maintenance* (Washington: U.S. Government Printing Office, 1945), pp. lvii and 213. See also H. C. Nolen and H. H. Maynard, *Drug Store Management* (New York: McGraw-Hill, 1941), pp. 147-49, for comments that contemporary fair trade margins were considered unreasonably low.

[5] Alfred Oxenfeldt, *Industrial Pricing and Market Practice* (New York: Prentice-Hall, 1955), pp. 445-88, especially pp. 468-72.

[6] New York: Oxford University Press, 1939, pp. 277-83 and 307-16.

[7] Great Britain, Board of Trade, *Report of the Committee on Resale Price Maintenance* (London: His Majesty's Stationery Office, 1949), p. 15.

cessions. The absence of information on the portions of total volume moving at each of the different margins quoted is more serious. Properly weighted average margins cannot be computed from the sources used here. Finally, the period for which the data are available is unsatisfactory at both ends. The book and drug product reports start with 1947 and 1949 respectively, although interstate resale price maintenance was legalized in 1937. Both series continue through 1961, but during the last six or seven years the legal status and the practical effects of fair trade have gradually been weakened by adverse court decisions and by increases in the extent of discount and other price-cutting retailing. Consequently the data tend to describe situations in which price is only weakly, rather than rigidly, controlled. Nevertheless, we do have information covering a span of approximately 15 years in which price controls have been used with at least some effectiveness in both commodity groups.

THE BOOK TRADE

The American book business is handled through relatively few outlets, in contrast to the drug products trade. The R. K. Bowker Company includes approximately 850 bookstores and 650 department stores in its "selected" mailing list of retail book outlets. Publishers generally consider only about 400 or 500 of these important enough to warrant salesmen's visits.[8] Considerable debate exists concerning the influence that this concentrated group of retailers exercises over the sales of individual titles and, hence, over the output of individual publishers. Each book published is a (more or less) highly differentiated product, and consequently such factors as intrinsic qualities, author's reputation, newspaper

reviews, and publisher's advertising may be much more influential than retailers' attitudes in creating sales. But some retail customers do ask booksellers for expert advice, and most publishers do seem interested in obtaining good retail display and sales promotion. Consequently bookseller goodwill will seem to be important to book producers.

Some rather indirect evidence suggests that until recently, retail price controls were fairly effective in the book trade. In 1959 the executive director of the American Booksellers Association declared: "Price cutting is no longer confined to the New York metropolitan area; it is now coming to the fore in other parts of the country as well."[9] The implication, that publishers' list prices had been reasonably well maintained outside New York City, is fairly clear.

MARGINS ON BOOKS

Publishers usually quote prices to bookstores at list (retail) minus trade discounts that generally vary with the quantity of books purchased. These discounts are the basic components of the retailers' margins. Most publishers also allow a cash discount of 1 or 2 percent for payment within a stated period, usually 10 or 15 days, from invoice date. Since 1947, the American Booksellers Association has issued an annual directory, *The Bookbuyer's Handbook,* that collates the individual publishers' varied discount schedules, ordering and billing arrangements, and plans for accepting returns of unsold merchandise. This handbook thus tells us what margins publishers have established for purchases of different quantities, although it does not reveal very much about the retailers' average realizations.

The handbooks contain the discount schedules of 28 publishers of trade

---

[8] Chandler B. Grannis, "Structure of a Diverse Industry," in Chandler B. Grannis, ed., *What Happens in Book Publishing* (New York: Columbia University Press, 1957), p. 9.

[9] U.S. Senate, Committee on Interstate and Foreign Commerce, Special Subcommittee on Fair Trade, *National Fair Trade Legislation, 1959,* statement of Joseph A. Duffy, 86th Cong., 1st Sess., 1959, p. 352.

TABLE 1

NUMBER OF PUBLISHERS (OUT OF 28) MAKING INDICATED CHANGES IN PERCENTAGE POINTS OF DISCOUNT OFF LIST OFFERED DEALERS ON PURCHASES OF INDICATED QUANTITIES, 1947-48 TO 1961-62

Quantity	\-3.0 \-3.9	\-2.0 \-2.9	\-1.0 \-1.9	\-0.1 \-0.9	0	+0.1 +0.9	+1.0 +1.9	+2.0 +2.9	+3.0 +3.9	+4.0 +4.9	+5.0 +5.9
5 copies single title			2	7	18		1				
25 copies single title		1	5	4	10	2	6				
50 copies single title	1 •	1	5	2	5	5	7	2			
50 copies assorted titles			2	6	9	2	6	3			
100 copies assorted titles			1	2	8	5	3	8	1		
500 copies assorted titles			2	1	8		2	2	8	1	4

Source: *The Bookbuyer's Handbook.*

books (general adult fiction and nonfiction) who have operated under the same, or substantially the same, name from 1947 through 1961.[10]

Table 1 summarizes the net changes these publishers have announced in their discounts for purchases of 5, 25, and 50 copies of the same title, and for 50, 100, and 500 copies of assorted titles. The available discounts are slightly overstated in that table, since a few of the listed publishers offer some of their discounts only on purchases of books already in print. Also, only the adult rates were used for those publishers who offered different discounts on adult and juvenile books. However, the net distortion does not seem serious. The absence of any information on advertising and special allowances is a greater flaw.

MARGIN BEHAVIOR

Table 1 indicates both the pervasiveness of change in publishers' discount schedules from 1947 to 1961 and the highly individualized nature of those changes. It tends to confirm trade comments on the lack of standardization in publishers' dealer policies.[11] Although we cannot tell what has happened to average discounts, we can readily see that many publishers have altered their schedules. The most pronounced tendency is a reduction of discounts on small orders and an increase on large ones. Only one relatively small increase occurred in the 5-copy and only 8 in the 25-copy brackets, as against 9 and 10 decreases respectively. But 17 increases occurred at the 500-copy level, against only 3 reductions. Examination of year-to-year changes in the schedules suggests that the alterations occurred sporadically throughout the period surveyed, rather than as a sudden response to the alleged recent increases in retail price cutting.

THE DRUG PRODUCTS TRADE

Although the book trade has experienced change, largely through the rise of book clubs and some discount outlets, the drug products trade has probably undergone even more alteration in

---

[10] A. S. Barnes, Inc., Bobbs Merrill Company, Thomas Y. Crowell Company, Crown Publishers, Devin-Adair Company, Dial Press, Dodd Mead Company, Doubleday and Company, E. P. Dutton and Company, Farrar, Strauss and Company (now Farrar, Strauss and Cudahy), Frederick Fell, Funk and Wagnalls, Harcourt, Brace and Company (now Harcourt, Brace and World), Harper and Brothers (now Harper and Row), Houghton Mifflin Company, J. B. Lippincott, Little, Brown and Company, Longmans, Green and Company, David McKay, Macmillan Company, W. W. Norton Company, G. P. Putnam and Son, Random House, Charles Scribner's Sons, Simon and Schuster, Vanguard Press, Van Nostrand Company, and Viking Press.

[11] Hardwick Mosely, "The Role of the Sales Department," in C. B. Grannis, ed., *op. cit.*, pp. 135-36; and Leonard Shatzkin, "We, the Publishers, Have Got to Make Retailing More Profitable," *Publishers' Weekly,* Vol. 173, No. 23 (June 9, 1958), p. 26.

recent years. The most noticeable phenomenon has been the growth of grocery store sales of health and beauty aids. Both toothpaste and headache remedies are commonly sold now in supermarkets and other non-drugstore outlets.[12] The successful entry of the grocers into this trade had at least two effects. On one hand, it increased competition; on the other, it weakened the very considerable collective power druggists once enjoyed vis-à-vis their suppliers. Both probably weakened the influence of resale price maintenance and reduced the pressure for increased margins.[13]

Yet at least as late as 1955, resale price maintenance minima were being well observed in at least one major market, according to the most careful study of fair trade compliance reported to date. Little evidence of purposive price cutting appeared in a painstaking analysis of over 13,000 reports members of a Chicago consumer panel supplied on the prices they paid for headache remedies, toothpaste, and sanitary napkins:

> The evidence indicates that deliberate undercutting of established fair trade prices is rare, even among cut-rate retailers and among retailers who like to offer leader items priced far below usual to draw people into their establishments.
>
> It may be concluded that fair-trade prices for headache remedies, sanitary napkins and toothpaste were well complied with by all important types of outlets in the Chicago retail trading zone during the prosperous years 1953-55.[14]

MARGINS ON DRUG PRODUCTS

Information about toothpaste and headache remedy prices came from two series of annual trade directories: *Drug Topics Red Book* and *American Druggist Blue Book*.[15] Since 1949, both of these directories have attempted to list the cost and fair trade minimum prices of all the items a druggist is likely to sell. Again, the data have their limitations. Some price changes go unreported for considerable periods of time because of the annual nature of the publications.[16] Consequently, we can use these directories only for the study of long-run, rather than year-to-year, price and margin movements. We have no information on long-run changes in quantity and cash discounts, but we do have records of deals and short-run discounts offered on both the toothpaste and the headache remedies.

Cost and minimum retail prices were obtained for 11 brands of fair-traded toothpaste and 14 brands of headache remedies. The difference between cost and retail price was noted for each item in each brand line commonly sold through drugstores, subject to a few

---

[12] The sale of aspirin-based compounds, such as Anacin, is restricted to drugstores in only 2 states—New Jersey and New York—and aspirin itself is confined to pharmacies in only 13 states. *Retailers' Manual of Regulations* (15th ed.; New York: Institute of Distribution, 1960), pp. 409-38.

[13] See Klamon, *loc. cit.*

[14] Ralph H. Oakes, "Resale Price Maintenance in Chicago, 1953-55," *Journal of Business*, Vol. 30, No. 2 (April, 1957), p. 130. Oakes's study was conducted partly as an analysis of an earlier one (Ward S. Bowman, Jr., "The Prerequisites and Ef-

fects of Resale Price Maintenance," *University of Chicago Law Review*, Vol. 22, No. 4 [Summer, 1955], pp. 825-73) that reported considerable non-compliance in some other communities. Oakes concluded that the differences in the findings were partly due to differences in the extent to which the consumer reports had been checked and rechecked and partly to differences in the dates of the two studies. Compliance seemed to increase with the passage of time after the 1952 McGuire Act ended a one-year hiatus in resale price maintenance.

[15] New York: Topics Publishing Company, every September preceding volume date, and New York: *American Druggist*, February of volume year, respectively. Back numbers of these directories are not widely available, and only one or the other of the two books was used for some of the years 1949-61. However, both were examined for most of the years included in the analysis.

[16] Also Oakes mentioned finding some inaccurate listings when he used these directories in his Chicago study (*op. cit.*, p. 111). However, trade authorities feel that both of these publications maintain remarkable standards of accuracy in spite of the magnitude of their reporting task.

TABLE 2
AVERAGE FAIR TRADE PERCENTAGE RETAIL MARGINS FOR TOOTHPASTE[a]
AND HEADACHE REMEDIES BY BRANDS
1949, 1950, AND 1961

Brands	1949	1950	1961	Direction of change 1949 to 1961	Direction of change 1950 to 1961
Toothpastes					
Ammident	NA[b]	30.5%	23.1%		Decrease
Colgate	36.6%	33.3	33.3	Decrease	No change[c]
Craig-Martin	NA	32.9	32.6		No change
Forhans	13.4	23.2	23.4	Increase	No change
Iodent	NA	22.9	24.3		Increase
Ipana	24.4	23.9	24.3	No change	No change
Kolynos	20.0	21.7	23.4	Increase	Increase
Listerine	26.1	26.0	29.7	Increase	Increase
Pepsodent	23.8	29.4	21.6	Decrease	Decrease
Phillips	13.4	14.0	23.0	Increase	Increase
Squibb	33.9	30.5	30.3	Decrease	No change
Headache remedies					
Bayer aspirin	14.8	14.8	22.2	Increase	Increase
Norwich aspirin	50.9	46.0	35.4	Decrease	Decrease
Parke-Davis aspirin	NA	33.3	33.6		No change
St. Joseph aspirin	NA	33.3	33.3		No change
Squibb aspirin	35.8	35.4	34.7	Decrease	Decrease
Anacin	19.4	19.4	21.6	Increase	Increase
B. C. Headache Remedy	15.5	17.1	31.6	Increase	Increase
Bufferin	NA	26.3	26.0		No change
Empirin	NA	33.3	33.3		No change
Midol	16.7	16.7	27.6	Increase	Increase
Salfayne	20.3	NA	29.3	Increase	
Tabcin	NA	31.7	31.0		Decrease
Alka-Seltzer	17.8	17.8	19.7	Increase	Increase
Bromo-Seltzer	23.5	23.5	30.8	Increase	Increase

[a] Very small and guest-size toothpaste tubes omitted.
[b] NA = no fair trade margin reported.
[c] "No change" is used to indicate no substantial change.
Source: *American Druggist Blue Book and Drug Topics Red Book, passim.*

exceptions noted below.[17] This difference was converted to a percentage margin, based on retail, and then an arithmetic average of the margins in each manufacturer's line was computed to give the figures shown in Table 2. The use of averages that were not weighted according to relative margins

probably did not warp the results very much. Particularly in the case of toothpastes there was little dispersion among the margins established at any one time in the directories; toothpowders and aerosol container toothpaste packs; and children's headache remedies and dispenser packs intended for prescription use or for on-premise consumption at the soda fountain. Aspirin margins were computed only for consumer packages containing unflavored five-grain tablets, since that is the standard adult dosage, but all adult packages were included for the proprietary products.

[17] Items excluded were trial or guest-size toothpaste tubes, designed for sale mainly in variety stores at a 10 or 15 cent retail price and a high percentage markup, and only sporadically listed

for the different standard items within each brand line. Moreover, the producers who introduced additional brands during the period studied, e.g., Colgate's Brisk and Pepsodent's Stripe, priced the new lines with margins similar to their established brands.

In spite of the limitations, the data display some interesting characteristics. There is no clear-cut upward trend. Out of 11 brands of toothpaste, 2 show decreases, 4 increases, and 5 substantially unchanged margins from 1950 to 1961. In headache remedies there are 2 decreases, 5 relatively slight changes, and 7 increases in margins. One of these increases resulted from the introduction of a high-margin 10-cent size, so that analysis of only the large-sized packages (the procedure used for toothpastes) would change the headache remedy results to 2 decreases, 6 no changes, and 6 increases.

DEALS

Many commentators complain that consumers are confused by the bewildering variety of ways in which retail prices are quoted. The assortment of "specials," "premiums," "two for one cent extra," "stamp and double stamp," and similar deals advertised in the typical weekend newspaper suggests some of the problems that consumers have in evaluating price offers. In the book trade these complicated pricing practices are more frequently found among the prices quoted to retailers than in the prices quoted by them. In drugs, deals and specials appear fairly frequently at both levels. If the use of complicated price quotations is an indication of belief in consumer irrationality, as some writers argue, we may suspect that many manufacturers and publishers feel that merchants are just as irrational as the ultimate consumers.

One executive in the publishing trade has described the variety of deals offered there in the following colorful, if somewhat exaggerated, terms:

> . . . the advertising appropriation, the special offer of 1 in 10, or 1 in 9, or 1 in 8, or 1 in 7 [free], — the pre-publication offer which is never the same on two succeeding books, the test mailer, the special wrapper band, the qualifying discount, the rack which comes half-free with a certain number of copies at a different discount which is already different from the other discount — but which carries a rebate.[18]

Deals and specials of this type are not reported in *The Bookbuyer's Handbook* and no information was obtained concerning possible changes in such practices in the book trade during the period studied. However, the little information that could be gathered concerning deals offered to druggists suggests that concessions of this sort are likely to be offered in highly individualistic, rather than uniform, fashion.

As noted, retail druggists are offered a bewildering variety of deals and specials, including free goods promotions, temporary discounts and allowances, and special premiums from time to time; 1,069 separate deals, including some that affected only consumer prices, were reported in *The American Druggist* in 1954.[19] That publication attempts to report the details and duration of all deals offered to the retailers, but a few additional specials seem to be included only in a somewhat similar, more restricted list published regularly in *Drug Topics*. Deals listed in both periodicals are analyzed in Table 3.[20]

This table summarizes the frequency with which 11 brands of toothpaste and 10 brands of headache remedies were offered for sale subject to one or more special retailer deals from 1953 through 1959. As before, only toothpaste in

[18] Leonard Shatzkin, *loc. cit.*, p. 26.
[19] House advertisement in its issue of January 31, 1955, p. 95.
[20] Holley S. Jernigan helped in the collection of these data.

TABLE 3

FREQUENCY WITH WHICH INDICATED BRANDS WERE SOLD SUBJECT TO RETAILER DEALS BY QUARTER YEARS, 1953-59 [X = ONE OR MORE DEALS]

Brands	1953				1954				1955				1956				1957				1958				1959			
	1	2	3	4	1	2	3	4	1	2	3	4	1	2	3	4	1	2	3	4	1	2	3	4	1	2	3	4
Toothpastes																												
Ammident		x	x							x	x		x	x														
Colgate		x																x										x
Craig-Martin					x																							
Forhans		x	x																									
Iodent																									x			
Ipana	x	x	x											x		x										x	x	x
Kolynos																			x							x	x	x
Listerine	x	x	x	x	x	x	x	x	x	x	x	x	x		x		x	x	x	x							x	x
Pepsodent	x	x	x	x		x				x	x	x	x	x	x		x	x	x	x	x	x		x	x	x	x	x
Phillips										x	x																	
Squibb						x				x	x								x									
Headache remedies[a]																												
Bayer aspirin															x		x	x	x	x								
Norwich aspirin						x		x										x										
St. Joseph aspirin	x	x	x	x	x	x	x	x	x	x	x	x	x	x			x	x	x	x		x					x	x
Squibb aspirin	x	x	x	x	x	x	x		x		x	x					x	x	x	x	x	x	x		x		x	
Anacin													x	x			x											
Bufferin						x				x					x	x	x	x									x	x
Empirin																						x	x					
Midol																			x	x	x	x						
Tabcin		x	x			x	x			x	x																	
Bromo-Seltzer	x		x														x	x	x									

[a] No deals advertised for Parke-Davis aspirin, B. C. Headache Remedy, Stanback, or Alka-Seltzer.
Source: *American Druggist Drug Topics, passim.*

tubes and aspirin packed in five-grain unflavored tablets are included in the analysis. Consumer deals, such as a free toothbrush with every tube of paste, and retailer deals that offered only inexpensive display signs are excluded. Each brand is treated in these tables as being subject to deals in each quarter in which one or more special offers were available for any number of weeks and on any item in the line. The only exception to this rule is that deals first announced during the last week of any one quarter are attributed to the next quarter. Since many deals last only four or five weeks and affect only one size within the line, Table 3 tends to overstate the availability of deals. But again the net impression is one of vendors who pursue highly individualistic and highly differentiated promotional and pricing policies.

CONCLUSIONS

All of this experience, including Oxenfeldt's and Grether's studies and the data examined here, suggests that resale price maintenance is simply one of the factors that manufacturers consider in formulating their marketing strategies. There have been more increases than decreases among the margins noted here, but there has been no uniformity. The decreases seem most apparent in toothpaste, where vigorous low-margin grocery outlets have become increasingly important, and in small purchases of books, where the dealers probably are unble to exert much bargaining pressure. Without resale price maintenance the decreases might, or might not, have been greater and the increases smaller than they actually were. The data shed no light on that question.

They do indicate that maintained margins can be and have been reduced when manufacturers find that other considerations overrule the dealers' desires for increased markups. They also indicate that individual manufacturers, who operate from different strategic positions, will evaluate both the dealers' wishes and the other considerations differently.

D. CRITICAL ANALYSIS

56. Overview and Appraisal

NATIONAL COMMISSION ON FOOD MARKETING

This chapter begins by identifying important factors influencing the behavior and structure of the food industry, for these are basic to explaining changes in the industry and its economic performance. The chapter then takes up topics particularly relevant to the Commission's assignment. It ends by appraising the industry's efficiency and progressiveness, farm-retail price spreads, the positions of farmers and consumers, and regulatory policies.

THE MARKET ORIENTATION OF THE FOOD INDUSTRY

The food industry and the agriculture that supplies it form a highly productive system in which obtaining raw materials or processing and distributing them ordinarily are not major difficulties. Efficiency in performing these functions is essential to business success, but increasingly the ability to develop and hold markets determines growth and profits of individual firms.

This shift of emphasis from production to selling is accentuated by the changing nature of the consumer market. As family incomes rise, consumers are less influenced by price and are better able to indulge their individual tastes, liking for variety, and desire for

From *Food from Farmer to Consumer*, Report of the National Commission on Food Marketing (Washington, D.C.; Government Printing Office, June, 1966), Chapter 12, pp. 91-103.

services. Changes in the role of women and in family living accentuate the importance of convenience in food preparation. The appeals that can be made to consumers in such a market are much more complex than offering basic foods at minimum prices. Skill in making successful appeals and in shaping consumer preferences is an important determinant of business success in several branches of the food industry.

Although other characteristics often are more important in determining conduct and performance in the food industry, the influence of the industry's market orientation is nevertheless extensive. It helps to explain why farm-retail price spreads for numerous foods are wide and increasing; why firms grow, often by merger and acquisition, beyond the size necessary to produce efficiently; the relative market power of various groups in the industry; the high rate of product innovation; and the survival of distribution methods that use labor and equipment wastefully.

PRODUCT DIFFERENTIATION

Product differentiation is a leading means of gaining and holding a preferred market position. To the extent that a seller can convince consumers that his product is distinct from and in some respects superior to others, he has an element of monopoly in its sale. Successful product differentiation eases the necessity of competing strictly on a price and quality basis with competitors of approximately equal production efficiency.

Among manufacturers, brands backed by extensive advertising and sales promotion are the most common means of gaining access to consumers. New products are an effective form of differentiation, especially if they are genuinely original, useful, and not easily duplicated by competitors. But really new products are not easily created, and much product differentiation consists of minor variations in ingredients, shape, color, or the like.

Food retailers strive to differentiate their services from competitors' by advertising, giving trading stamps, offering prizes, or conducting games. Special sales at featured low prices are essentially promotions that tell little about the prices a consumer will pay for a week's food supply. Parking space, air conditioning, and attractive stores are examples of differentiating devices that, when widely adopted, provide useful services to the public. Retailers' brands succeed primarily because of their price appeal, but many retailers also regard private label as a means of differentiating their stores.

ADVERTISING AND SALES PROMOTION

Advertising and sales promotion are a significant reason for the substantial spread between farm and retail prices. In 1964, food corporations spent $2,172 million for advertising ($1,400 million on domestically produced farm products), and retailers spent $680 million for trading stamps. For the industry as a whole if not for each firm in it, these amounts were added to processing distribution costs and became part of the food bill.

Amounts so added to the food bill were not entirely wasted. Consumers received premiums and other things of value for trading stamps and some other forms of sales promotion. Advertising helped to pay for television, newspapers, and magazines—and made publications costlier to produce. Whether this way of supporting the communications industry is good economic and social policy is outside the scope of a study of the food industry; but the costs added to the food bill are a reason for the size of the bill.

An unknown but substantial portion of advertising and sales promotion serves only to urge consumers to patronize firm A instead of B, or to buy brand C instead of D. It is highly unlikely that costs thus incurred add value to goods purchased by consumers. From the standpoint of the individual firm, however, the expenditures are warranted to hold or expand sales against competitors' similar efforts.

One function of advertising is an appropriate charge to the food bill—dissemination of information about products and prices. Consumers benefit from knowing what products are available, where they are for sale, and at what prices. A particularly significant case is the introduction of new products, discussed in the following section.

Two restraining influences on high selling costs tend to be generated within the food industry. One is the sale of retailers' label products, which are merchandised within the store rather than by extensive advertising. Retailers frequently are able to offer comparable quality under their own brands at lower prices and with more margin for themselves. Competition thus given to advertised brands is keen for staple, fairly homogeneous products, but has not been effective for a number of highly processed products.

The second restraining influence is the discount food store, which commonly gives no trading stamps and eliminates some services and amenities usually offered by supermarkets. Discount stores, operated both by chains and independents, are important in some local markets but have little influence in others.

Consumer grades, and to some extent standards of identity, are another restraining influence, although not one arising within the industry. The widespread use of Government grades in the retail sale of beef has been an important reason for the small amount of product differentiation. Consumer grading of foods is much less extensive than would be feasible.

NEW PRODUCTS

The food industry has developed and successfully introduced many new products of undisputed value to consumers. The costs going into market testing and initial promotion for some new products have been high, as Chapter 9 makes clear. Gaining rapid acceptance of a useful new product is beneficial to consumers and hastens the development of sufficient volume for low production costs.

There is a tendency for some new products to pass from an early stage in which prices and promotion are high to a later stage in which promotion are high to a later stage in which promotion and prices are lower. The second stage is reached when similar products are put on the market by other manufacturers and by retailers under their own brands. Then the product becomes a staple food, and consumer grading often would be feasible.

If price competition fully asserted itself at the second stage, the overall performance would be good. But some products show little tendency to pass from the first stage to the second. Even for products long on the market, prices of advertised brands often remain well above private label prices. In a Commission study of 10 such well-established foods as canned peas and frozen orange juice concentrate, retail prices of advertised brands averaged 21 percent higher than retail prices of retailer brands of generally comparable quality. Means of heightening price competition at the second stage, as by consumer grading, are desirable.

The proliferation of new products indicates that ample incentives exist for product innovation. The opportunity to differentiate products and to participate in a rapidly growing branch of the food industry has been a powerful magnet inducing firms in staple food fields — dairy products, flour milling — to diversify into convenience foods of all kinds.

The changing nature of the consumer market both invites and makes possible a gradual shifting from staple, fairly homogeneous foods to highly differentiated foods. Emphasis on advertising and sales promotion and on new products will continue to increase. Retailers may use their own brands less exclusively for price competition and begin to adopt some of the brand promotion devices of the leading food manufacturers. Total selling costs will be a rising part of the food bill.

CONCENTRATION

Preceding chapters reveal high concentration in some segments of the food industry, especially in the various subdivisions of dry grocery manufacturing, and growing concentration in much of it. (High concentration is used to describe a situation in which the four largest firms in a field have more than 50 percent of the business.) Concentration would have increased more than it did in the past two decades if antimerger action had not been taken by the regulatory agencies. This is one reason why the increase in concentration has been greater when measured by the market shares of the top 20 firms than when measured by 4-firm shares.

EXCEPTIONS TO THE RULE

Growing concentration appears to be a dominant trend under ordinary circumstances, at least until the market share of the four or five largest firms becomes very large. The trend can be reversed for a time by major developments that shake up a branch of the industry or otherwise create unusual conditions. The meat packing industry provides an example. Plant location in the 1930's was uneconomic in light of truck transportation and the changing sources of livestock. Technology permitted new medium-sized plants to be more efficient than old, large ones. This opened opportunities for new entrants, who built plants in the livestock supply area, outcompeted some of the established giants (as meat packers' profit data show), and reduced the former high concentration in the industry. But once the industry has adjusted to this major upset, increasing concentration can be expected.

Concentration in poultry slaughtering apparently diminished in the 1950's as the poultry industry was reorganized and relocated by changes springing from new supply possibilities. But in the 1960's, concentration increased, and further concentration is likely in the future. Concentration in the freezing of fruits and vegetables declined while this industry was growing rapidly in the 1950's. In contrast, fruit and vegetable canning, a long-established industry, became slightly more concentrated during the same period.

Declining concentration in butter manufacture in the 1950's apparently had related, but somewhat different, explanations. Farmers' cooperatives are important in butter and have aimed at low margins; demand for butter has suffered from competition from vegetable fats; and the large dairy companies have shifted their investments to greener pastures. Even so, concentration increased slightly between 1958 and 1963.

In food retailing, the adoption of the supermarket has been substantially completed. The unaffiliated, one-store operators who were a source of new entrants into supermarket merchandising have greatly diminished in numbers. Although internal growth of the largest chains may not increase their market shares, incentives to grow by merger and acquisition are likely to lead to higher concentration in selling. Concentration of purchasing by retailers and wholesalers seems certain to rise.

ECONOMIES OF SIZE

The smallest firms in most branches of the food industry, as in farming, are severely handicapped by inefficient size of operation. Continued decline in their numbers will contribute to higher concentration among remaining firms. But medium-sized firms commonly are, or can be, about as efficient in processing or physical distribution as the largest firms. They usually are entitled to cost-justified discounts for large-volume purchases. Little social gain in these respects is realized by replacing such firms by larger ones.

Advantages in selling—advertising, sales promotion, a sales force—frequently are gained by very large firms. National advertising is extremely expensive, and substantial discounts to large advertisers increase the difficulties faced by smaller competitors. Such advantages of large size do not have corresponding value to the public at large and are not persuasive reasons for accepting high concentration in the food industry.

INTERNAL GROWTH VERSUS MERGER

Growth through internal expansion and growth through merger or acquisition may have entirely different meanings for society. A firm that grows through superior efficiency, service to customers, or innovation, and which does not engage in predatory practices, has demonstrated a public benefit even though the benefit may not outweigh all other considerations. Mergers and acquisitions, however, do not necessarily demonstrate merit in the same sense. Important efficiencies may be gained, especially if both merging firms were inadequate in some way as originally constituted. But the merger or acquisition may represent the joining of two viable firms for reasons of little or no public benefit. Significantly, many of the small retailers taken over by the largest chains in the past 20 years were growing rapidly when acquired.

EFFECTS OF HIGH CONCENTRATION

High concentration in the food industry is undesirable because it weakens competition as a self-regulating device by which the activities of business firms are directed toward the welfare of the public at large. When a few large firms dominate a field, they frequently forbear from competing actively by price; competition by advertising, sales promotion, and other selling efforts almost always increases; and the market power inescapably at the disposal of such firms may be used to impose onerous terms upon suppliers or customers. The breakfast cereal field provides one of the clearest examples in the food industry: Four firms have 85 percent of the business; advertising and sales promotion amount to 19 percent of manufacturers' sales; retail prices of cereals rose more than other retail food prices between 1954 and 1964;[1] profits are nearly double the average for all food manufacturing; and entry of a new competitor would be extremely difficult.

Rising concentration of purchases by chain retailers, wholesalers, and buying groups of retailers limits the alternatives available to suppliers, induces suppliers to make inequitable concessions in order to get business, and makes competition among independent firms a less satisfactory way of organizing the supply industries.

Concentration among buyers tends to beget concentration among sellers. In fluid milk marketing, where the local nature of the market accentuates problems of concentration, dairy firms believe they must expand to bid for the business of large buyers — and then become bigger still, and more diversified, to bear the risk of losing a large customer.

HIGH CONCENTRATION NOT ESSENTIAL

The food industry can have both high efficiency and reasonably low levels of concentration in national and regional markets. High concentration probably cannot be avoided in some local market situations. Even there, results can be generally satisfactory if other sellers or buyers can move in from adjacent markets to correct monopolizing tendencies.

Mergers among small firms, or by small with medium-sized ones, will often be necessary for efficiency and to maintain viable competitors. But if competition is to be an effective regulator of the food economy, high concentration must be prevented even in instances where specific, immediate restraint of trade cannot be identified. The most essential requirement for competition throughout the industry is to assure that a large number of substantial retailers compete in national markets for suppliers' products. Preventing horizontal mergers and acquisitions by the largest firms in each concentrated branch of the food industry is a minimal policy to assure that competition will produce results in the public interest.

VERTICAL INTEGRATION AND DIVERSIFICATION

Much of the vertical integration in the food industry has had some basis in economies achieved by the new arrangement. This was true years ago when chains integrated retailing and wholesaling. Retailer integration into baking and fluid milk processing apparently has reduced costs of distributing these products from plants to retailers' shelves. Feed companies and processors that integrated into broiler production made savings by coordinating formerly independent operations and by rapidly exploiting new production methods. Feeding some cattle has helped packers to even out daily slaughter schedules, and savings in procurement costs may be significant.

In some instances, retailers have inte-

---

[1] Retail prices per pound increased 45 percent (A.C. Nielsen Co.), while the Bureau of Labor Statistics index of retail food prices rose 12 percent.

grated into processing—or threatened to do so—to pressure other groups with substantial power into meeting retailers' demands for changes in distribution methods or for private label products. Integration by suppliers into retailing has been attractive only in special circumstances, partly because a supermarket must handle a much wider range of products than any one supplier manufactures.

Farmers' marketing cooperatives, a form of forward integration by producers, are especially important in fruit, vegetable, and dairy marketing. Farmers also have taken on marketing functions as individuals: Some fruit and vegetable growers have become shippers, some dairymen have gone into fluid milk distribution, and a few cattle feeders are full or part owners of packing plants.

Integration by marketing firms into farm production has been a factor—but not the most important factor—in shifting agriculture away from the family farm. Most fruit and vegetable production has moved out of the family farm class, but the ownership of some production by canners and shippers has had only an incidental part in the transition. The principal threat to the family farmer who feeds cattle is the large commercial feedlot, whether or not operated by a packer. The poultry industry has been the most dramatic example of a change in agriculture induced by vertical integration; but poultry production as it was before World War II would have been drastically altered in one way or another by the technology developed in postwar years.

CONGLOMERATE FIRMS

Growth through diversification has been an outstanding trend in foods. Manufacturers have sought to get into the most rapidly growing parts of the industry by branching out into frozen foods, prepared foods, and convenience products in general. Manufacturers in the dry grocery field have developed highly sophisticated selling techniques and have sought to apply them to a widening range of products. The fact that unrelated foods—as well as soft drinks, detergents, etc.—were all sold through grocery stores and often could be handled by the same sales force or distribution facilities meant that some advantages could be gained by combining them in one firm.

Much of the diversification has been achieved by merger or acquisition, frequently of firms capable of competing on their own. Firms in such established fields as dairy manufacturing, meat packing, and bread baking have diversified into other lines more frequently than firms from other fields have diversified into theirs.

Table 1 shows the sharp rise in conglomerate-type acquisitions by large food manufacturers in the past two decades. Both food and nonfood firms were acquired. Acquisitions of firms engaged in later stages of processing or in distribution also increased; the relative importance of horizontal acquisitions declined. The data are especially influenced by the merger activities of dairy firms.

The size and diversity of the large food conglomerate give it great ability to survive its own mistakes or intense competitive struggles in particular product fields. It can engage in reciprocal trading arrangements not available to conventional firms. Food conglomerates are likely to grow, to reduce the number of independent competitors in the industry as a whole, and to lace the various segments of the industry more nearly into a single system characterized by the kind of nonprice competition in which they excel.

The highly diversified firm is often suspected of drawing upon earnings in one field to sustain losses in another until weaker competitors there are displaced. The fact that firms are not required to report financial data by fields of operation gives conglomerates some

TABLE 1

NUMBER OF ACQUISITIONS BY TYPE, 50 LARGEST FOOD MANUFACTURERS, 1948-65[1]

Period	Total number of acquisitions	Horizontal	Vertical backward	Vertical forward	Conglomerate food	Conglomerate nonfood	Nonclassifiable
Number of acquisitions:							
1948-53	250	191	11	12	17	8	11
1954-59	434	254	13	36	77	39	15
1960-65	301	103	12	36	92	51	7
Total	985	548	36	84	186	98	33
Percent:							
1948-53	100.0	76.4	4.4	4.8	6.8	3.2	4.4
1954-59	100.0	58.5	3.0	8.3	17.7	9.0	3.5
1960-65	100.0	34.2	4.0	12.0	30.6	16.9	2.3
Total	100.0	55.6	3.7	8.5	18.9	9.9	3.4

[1] All acquisitions of firms in the same 3-digit SIC grouping as the acquiring firms were classed "horizontal." Probably this overstated the frequency of horizontal acquisitions.
Source: Records of the Federal Trade Commission.

advantage over their specialized competitors, and questions about playing one field against another go unanswered.

MARKET POWER

Market power is the ability to influence prices or other terms of trade in a way favorable to the business firm. It may be gained through a firm's own strong position or conferred upon the firm by the weakness of those with which it deals. Two groups in the food industry appear to have substantial market power: retailers, including many of the small chains; and large manufacturers, usually diversified, with strong national brands.

RETAILERS

The most important source of retailers' market power is their direct contact with consumers. The retailer controls the shelves from which consumers make selections; when he acts as buyer, he is, in a sense, the purchasing agent for a large number of consumers. Because of the high productivity of agriculture and the food processing industries, eager suppliers press an abundance of products upon the retailer, and he is in a strong bargaining position.

The retailer's position is further enhanced by the great diversity of the items he handles. He must make a good impression with consumers on fast-moving, price-comparison foods, but he has some freedom to play down or do without items which he cannot buy on terms he considers satisfactory. Moreover, his inventory commitment is low relative to most suppliers'; only temporarily and selectively is he likely to have to cut prices to correct an overstocked position. Some suppliers, in contrast, carry large inventories and are weak bargainers when stocks prove excessive.

Large chain retailers gain strength from the number of stores they operate and the diversification of their business over many local markets. A difficulty in one store or one market will not be serious to the firm as a whole; price wars in single markets will be survived easily.

High concentration in a local market does not by itself give a retailer market power when he buys a product in the national market. But competitors in a concentrated local market are likely to adjust their respective selling prices so that costs they have in common are recovered in their gross margins. This is an important reason why retailers seldom absorb for long any large part of the nationwide price increases or decreases for the products they handle.

The high concentration of purchases in national markets for retail sale is an important source of market power for chain retailers and group wholesalers. As the number of buyers is reduced, suppliers are under greater pressure to avoid losing the favor of their customers. But national concentration alone is not necessarily decisive in determining the relative bargaining power of buyers and sellers. For example, concentration among meat packers is higher than concentration among buyers of meat; yet retailers often seem to have more bargaining power than packers in transactions between them. The retailer's direct contact with consumers and his other advantages outweigh the difference in concentration.

MANUFACTURERS WITH STRONG BRANDS

The substantial market power of large diversified manufacturers also stems in considerable part from their access to consumers. These manufacturers have gained their position by establishing strong consumer preferences for their brands by effective advertising and sales promotion. Consumer demand so generated often requires retailers to carry the manufacturers' products.

The size and diversity of many of these manufacturers give them the strength derived from large resources and the advantages of conglomerates in general. They have the ability to exploit developing market opportunities in a wide range of fields, can risk costly product innovation, and often can acquire small firms that seem in a good position to grow rapidly.

OTHER MARKET POWER

Large size creates power for any food firm, at least power against exploitation by others. Firms that normally have no special bargaining power will acquire such strength if suppliers have excess capacity and are struggling for sales outlets at any price exceeding their direct costs. Small retailers frequently get free loans and similar concessions from fluid milk processors caught up in intense competition in local markets.

Unorganized farmers have no positive market power at all and depend upon competition among buyers to obtain the full value that market conditions justify for their products. Especially when products must be sold to buyers in a local market and the local buyers are few, competition may not be fully effective in achieving this result.

TRADE PRACTICES

A number of trade practices in the food industry are sources of conflict between buyers and sellers and sometimes become means of exploitation of one by the other. Price discrimination by sellers among customers is a persistent problem. Discriminations induced by buyers apparently are numerous, but are difficult to detect and to prove against the buyer. Discrimination among market areas is especially troublesome in the dairy and bakery fields. The dairy field is notorious for the frequency with which companies use loans, equipment, and less defensible inducements to obtain retailers' business; such practices are by no means confined to markets in which resale price fixing under State marketing orders prevents price competition.

Unwarranted rejections by buyers of fresh meat, fruits, and vegetables are frequently alleged. Rejections without cause do not seem to be widespread in meats, but the situation in fresh fruits and vegetables warrants concern. Rejection as a means of price renegotiation appears to be common.

In some producing areas, grower-shippers of fruits and vegetables handle other growers' produce under agency arrangements that are shot through with conflict of interest. Trading agreements are informal, and records are frequently poor. Situations may be complicated further by indebtedness by the grower to the shipper. Close supervision of trading practices is needed more in this segment of the food industry than in any other.

There is some evidence of abuses of buying power by distributors in procurement of private label merchandise. Small processors frequently are the principal private label suppliers and depend heavily on private label sales. Buyers have succeeded in transferring costs and risks of carrying inventories to some processors without firm commitments to purchase. Costs of labels and special packs may also be absorbed by the processor. The low profits of the smaller fruit and vegetable canners partly reflect such pressures.

Kickbacks, special favors to buyers, and other forms of commercial bribery occur, although there is no way to measure their frequency. The Commission has had one glimpse of labor racketeering in the food industry.

Instances of deceptive advertising unfortunately offset some of the real information value to consumers that advertising should have. Packages, together with the pictorial and descriptive material on them, are sometimes misleading about the contents. Odd weights make price comparisons difficult more frequently than technical reasons justify. Reduction of package size is a common means of increasing price.

Except in sales to consumers, questionable trade practices almost always reflect the greater strength of buyers over sellers. This is one objective indication of the existence of market power and the direction in which it runs.

CHANGES IN MARKETING CHANNELS

Direct movement of products through marketing channels has reduced the use of—and in some cases eliminated—terminal wholesale markets for fruits and vegetables and for livestock. Economies achieved by direct marketing have been the principal incentive for the change; further shifts toward direct sales are likely.

In livestock marketing, the system replacing terminal market selling itself seems to need revision. The number of local buying and selling establishments in the midwest is unnecessarily large and expensive to maintain; trading practices are difficult to regulate. Avoiding the cost of maintaining packer buyers may be one reason for more cattle feeding by packers in the future.

Terminal markets for livestock now have much more competition from other marketing methods than they did when present regulation under the Packers and Stockyards Act was developed. Some aspects of current regulation appear to be impeding their ability to compete. Changes in the act probably are needed to permit more flexibility in its administration.

THE PRICING SYSTEM

The classic function of price is to coordinate the activities of independent firms so that resources are used to satisfy the demands of consumers as expressed in the market place. While this role is still important, it is being modified in many significant ways; and the problem of getting adequate information about market prices is increasing.

In food retailing, the practice of offering items at special prices confuses consumers about what prevailing prices are, and some of the costs of retailing are shifted from frequently specialed foods to others. One-stop shopping by consumers reduces their sensitivity to prices of individual foods (unless featured), and weakens the pressure on retailers to keep every retail price aligned with the corresponding wholesale price. Higher incomes make consumers less willing to vary purchases in response to moderate price changes.

In the sale of meats, poultry products, and some other foods within the marketing system, buyers and sellers have gone increasingly to the use of formula pricing. The greater the volume sold under formula pricing, the less volume there is on which to establish genuine market prices. Vertical integration also draws volume out of price-making channels. Prices of products purchased on buyers' specifications sometimes are not quotable. The problem of "no price to quote" has reached a critical stage in broilers and eggs and is increasing in turkeys and dressed meat.

Prices of some manufactured foods, especially dry groceries, are strongly administered by sellers and play a minor role, as compared with that of advertising and sales promotion, in determining the volume of sales.

The decline of terminal markets has seriously detracted from their usefulness as sources of price information for fresh fruits and vegetables and for livestock. Livestock traders are paying increasing attention to dressed meat prices, but these markets, also, may become too thin to be reliable.

The widening price spread between farmers and consumers means that a given change in the farm price of a product has a smaller proportionate effect than formerly on the retail price. And consumers are becoming less responsive to changes in retail prices. Thus, a small oversupply at the farm must drive the farm price down sharply before consumers are induced to use the greater supply. Conversely, an undersupply at the farm, as for pork in 1965, will force farm prices to high levels.

As a result of closer trading relationships between producers and processors, together with unsatisfactory price information, some prices are being established well in advance of delivery in poultry and egg marketing. The use of forward pricing and production-period contracts may develop rapidly.

The shift from terminal markets to other distribution channels increases the difficulty of obtaining adequate price information for the Market News Service operated by the U.S. Department of Agriculture. More complete and reliable data could be obtained in some instances, and at lower cost, if buyers and sellers of substantial volume routinely reported prices and quantities to a Market News Office for prompt collation and publication.

EFFICIENCY, PROGRESSIVENESS

The food industry has been, and remains, progressive in most respects. Many new and useful products have been developed; processing methods have been improved in most branches of the industry. Physical distribution and warehousing of many foods have capitalized upon innovations in these fields. Management has been generally progressive in adopting new methods of inventory control, accounting, and the like. Retail stores are attractive, convenient, and afford a wide range of choice to consumers.

Change has left in its wake a number of firms that no longer have a place in food processing and distribution. They are too small for efficient operation, their plants and equipment are obsolete or poorly located, or changes in marketing channels have left them stranded. Some retail markets have more store space than the local volume of business justifies. As a broad generalization, however, the food industry does not appear to have more difficulties of this kind than might reasonably be expected in an industry serving a changing market, achieving progress, and thus undergoing constant reorganization.

Of the specific inefficiencies in the manufacture and handling of goods, several involve the distribution of products from the production plant to retail store shelves. Distribution of bread seems to be inordinately costly. A more efficient distribution system is resisted by most bakers and their driver-salesmen, which has been one reason for vertical integration into baking by large retailers. A somewhat similar situation exists in some fluid milk markets and for much the same reasons; resale pricing of milk under State marketing orders may also retard adjustments. Rack service for foods such as crackers and cookies is an expensive form of distribution. Involved in all of these is the desire of the supplier to manage the display of his product in the retail store to increase sales of his product.

A great deal of bone, fat, and waste meat is still shipped from packing plants to distributors' warehouses at unnecessary cost. Meat cutting in the backrooms of retail stores is more expensive than centralized cutting would be. If full economies were to be gained in this area, consumers would have to accept frozen meat, and some minor technological difficulties would have to be worked out. Field or central prepackaging of fresh fruits and vegetables can be regarded as a similar potential improvement.

The substantial costs built into the price of food as a result of various forms of selling effort—advertising, sales promotion, expensive packaging, salesmen—are an important form of inefficiency in the food industry. Some of the costs are warranted for the introduction of new products and for providing consumers with information about conventional ones. But the only value received by consumers for most of these costs is the indirect benefit of premiums for trading stamps, free television programs, and the like. The power of such selling efforts reduces the role of price competition and thus moderates pressures on the industry to cut costs of other functions.

The industry is expected to be in-novative in the future, as in the past. Inefficient distribution methods probably will give way irregularly to less costly ways of handling and delivering goods between the processing plant and store shelf. Numerous painful adjustments lie ahead as inefficient or by-passed firms, many of them small, leave the field. While efficiency in performing physical functions increases, however, increased emphasis on most forms of selling effort will offset some of the effects of more efficient distribution on costs and prices.

PROFITS

Profits in the food industry were approximately in line with average profits in the economy at large in 1964. Corporate profits after taxes averaged 11.4 percent of stockholders' equity in all of private manufacturing, 11.3 percent in nondurable goods manufacturing, and 9.8 percent in the manufacture of food and kindred products. The First National City Bank tabulations for 1964, based on the larger corporations in industry, show profit rates of 12.1 percent for total trade, 12.5 percent for retail food chains, 12.7 percent for total manufacturing, and 10.7 percent for public utilities. Profits in food manufacturing rose between 1960 and 1964 but declined slightly in retailing.

Profit rates in 1964 in some branches of the food industry, especially in certain dry grocery lines, were well above average—large enough to indicate high barriers to entry and substantial ability to administer prices. The rate of return obtained by the 50 largest retailers was excellent for a low-risk field. It is a fact that the large food retailers almost never lose money.

Profits before taxes, as a percentage of sales, were about 4.7 percent in food manufacturing and about 2.3 percent in food retailing in 1964. Profits were not a large component of sales prices to consumers but were good in relation to stockholders' equity.

FARM-RETAIL PRICE SPREADS

Three questions raised in Chapter 3 [of this Report] were: Are the functions for which marketing costs are incurred necessary? Are the functions efficiently performed? Are profits reasonable? The foregoing discussions of efficiency and profits deal with these questions.

Unnecessary functions in the physical processing and distribution of foods are rarely performed. The major steps in moving products from farmer to consumer must be done, whether by a series independent firms or one integrated firm. Usually the functions require labor, equipment, and other resources that can be obtained only by substantial cost outlays.

While some of the selling function —advertising, sales promotion, salesmen—is socially productive, most of the costs incurred to sway consumers toward one seller or product rather than another add little of value to the food consumers buy. The selling function could not be eliminated in most instances, but in principle, it might be substantially reduced without impairing the value of final products to consumers. This is the chief respect in which the necessity for an important function can be questioned.

Most functions are efficiently performed, if realistic standards are used as criteria. The inefficiencies of too-small operations usually reduce the earnings of the owners rather than adding to the farm-retail price spread. The chief example of functions inefficiently performed include the distribution of bread and, in less degree, milk; rack service for several grocery items; and the lack of centralized cutting of meat.

Profits are higher in some branches of the food industry than necessary to obtain capital. If the average rate of profit on net worth had been the same for the larger food corporations as for public utilities in 1964, however, the difference would have amounted to somewhat less than 1 percent of the retail value of total food.

Lower farm-retail price spreads would be possible (though means of doing this might be very difficult) without reducing services to consumers or unreasonably lowering earnings of the food industry. This is particularly true of a few products for which specific inefficiencies or unusually high selling costs have been noted. But farm-retail price spreads would remain high because processing and distribution are costly even when efficiently performed.

The manner in which a reduced farm-retail price spread might affect producers and consumers varies by product. When farm prices rest on price supports, as is currently true of grains used for bakery and cereal products, benefits would go largely to consumers. For products not price-supported, such as beef, eggs, or lettuce, benefits would be shared by producers and consumers.

OTHER TOPICS IN BRIEF

The adjustment between domestic production and imports of food is constantly in flux, and the effects of imports are sometimes upsetting to the domestic industry. The most notable recent example was the increase of beef imports in the early 1960's, which reached a peak in 1963 when domestic production was rising sharply. Other examples are provided by the fruit and vegetable industry—mushrooms from Taiwan and early season vegetables and strawberries from Mexico. Investment of American capital in Mexican production has played an important role in the latter example. Except for such special situations, however, food imports have recently made a substantial contribution to the American food supply while creating only moderate and short-lived disturbances in the domestic market.

The effects of the termination of the bracero labor program at the end of 1964 were studied briefly but inconclusively. Data from published reports and Commission sources suggest that: (1) Labor difficulties and higher labor costs were encountered by numerous producers of the eight crops formerly most dependent on bracero labor; (2) farm marketings in principal States affected were lower and prices higher in 1965 than in 1964 for six of these eight crops; (3) the total farm value of the eight crops in these States declined 7 percent; (4) producers collectively received somewhat lower net income; (5) employment and earnings of domestic harvest workers rose; (6) secondary effects on processors and shippers occurred where volume or quality of production was materially reduced; and (7) the price, production, and income effects varied widely among crops, areas, and producers. Social effects were important but were not studied. Viewed in a long run context, the termination of the program is hastening trends already under way—less use of foreign agricultural labor, mechanization of the fruit and vegetable harvest, and development of agricultural resources in Mexico. An industrial, high-income economy can best assure itself of remaining competitive in agriculture in the long run by emphasizing what it does most effectively—the mechanization of production.

Demands for individual foods have been increasingly affected by public opinion concerning the healthfulness of particular ingredients and about insecticides, radioactive fallout, and similar matters. As the residual claimant to the consumer's food dollars, the producer is much affected by any changes in demand. Accurate information about the significance of food to health, and responsible dissemination of such information, is in the best interests of all.

POSITION OF CONSUMER

Much of what has been said about efficiency, progressiveness, and profits in the food industry applies to the position of the consumer. The principal criticism of the efficiency of the industry, in the broad sense of the term, is the cost devoted to selling efforts that yield little value to consumers. This point is closely related to the other principal criticism of the food industry from the standpoint of consumers: the difficulty they encounter in trying to buy so as to get the most for their money.

The difficulty takes numerous forms. Some advertising is misleading or downright deceptive; some package sizes and designs exaggerate the contents; essential information that should be contained in labels is often hard to find, illegible, or even missing; package contents may be in odd or nonstandard amounts for no technical reason, making price comparisons difficult; per-pound prices of the "large economy size" occasionally are higher than per-pound prices of smaller sizes; "cents-off" labels proclaim price reductions that may not be genuine; special prices create confusion as to what the going price is; not all products advertised as weekend features are sold at special prices; consumer grades are confined to a few products and are by no means uniformly used even for those; and standards of identity are lacking for many products. At little or no extra cost, consumers could be given more information; and the more skillful shopping this would make possible would more than offset any costs of providing additional information.

But consumers, themselves, must accept a measure of responsibility for the prices they pay and for the objectionable practices observed in the sale of food. Consumers are powerfully influenced by advertising and persistently pay premium prices for much-advertised brands when products of similar quality—sometimes the identical product—are available at lower prices. Impulse buying is common. For some, novelty is an end in itself. Children make a number of purchasing decisions.

Consumer education may modify buying behavior and deserves support. If consumers became highly skilled buyers, many of the objectionable sales practices would lose their effectiveness and disappear. Renewed emphasis on price competition would bring about further economies. The consumer is, indeed, a sovereign; but she is not, as she is so often told she is, an all-knowing, all-powerful, and fully-served sovereign.

POSITION OF PRODUCER

Agriculture is in the midst of sweeping changes that exceed those occurring in food processing and distribution. Most of the changes originate within agriculture itself or arise from sources other than the food marketing system. Prominent among these is the technological revolution that is replacing manpower with machinery and equipment, raising crop yields per acre, and developing more productive livestock. Such changes are reducing the number of workers required in agriculture, increasing the efficient size for a farm, and transforming the farm into a business requiring skillful management, high technical competence, and large investment. The bulk of agricultural production still comes from family farms (in the sense that they employ no more hired than family labor), but some types of production, especially fruit and vegetable production, have moved, to a large extent, out of the family farm class. Probably a selective shift will continue, with the types of farming predominating in the midwest, east, and parts of the south being among the last to make the shift.

IMPACT OF MARKETING CHANGES

Procurement methods growing out of mass merchandising and substantial concentration of distributors' purchases have brought increasing demands to tailor farm production to particular standards, to produce in large volume, and to maintain a steady flow of products. These demands have added to forces already at work to increase the size of farms. In addition, they have brought many farmers into contractual or less formal arrangements with buyers who seek production to meet their specifications. Some farm production has been brought under the ownership of food industry firms partly for this reason—for example, some cattle feeding and egg production.

Integration into farm production by feed manufacturers, meat packers, fruit and vegetable processors, and other nonfarm firms has injected new capital into farming and hence has served to maintain or increase production. The effect has been to reduce or hold down prices and to intensify competition in agriculture. In some instances, the bargaining power of farmers may have been reduced by buyers' access to captive production.

FARMER BARGAINING POWER

Unorganized and unsupported farmers have had to depend upon the competitive bidding of buyers to receive the full market value for their products. If costs rose in the marketing system, the farm price usually was depressed until reduced production in relation to demand lifted prices at all levels of distribution.

Food industry developments pose more clearly than ever before the question of how farmers can obtain sufficient bargaining strength to defend their prices and other terms of sale. Group action is needed if any substantial changes in sales arrangements are to be made. But the scope and effectiveness of group action will be limited unless the groups have the means of planning production in advance, controlling the rate of their own marketing, and negotiating about price.

Farmers' cooperatives are already

extensively engaged in marketing farmers' products. But, with some exceptions, cooperatives are not likely soon to be strong enough to make effective pricing and production decisions. Some form of governmental sanction for collective action will be needed, at least for a substantial period of time. Federal and State marketing orders and agreements are long-standing examples of instruments of this kind, although as conceived and administered they often have been weak or subject to serious shortcomings. But they provide a beginning for a more adequate means of firming up the market structure of agriculture where and while it is needed. One might regard such a device as a bridge on which portions of agriculture can cross from a state of disorganized production to a sufficiently firm structure that no further support is necessary.

Possibilities for effective group effort under the most favorable of circumstances appear to be restricted to the more specialized products — or, like fluid milk, ones sold in local markets. The widely grown basic crops, such as wheat and soybeans, are produced over so large an area by so many farmers that effective group action will be difficult to achieve.

REGULATORY PRACTICE AND POLICY

Controlling concentration in the various branches of the food industry is essential to maintaining a competitive environment favoring an acceptable distribution of market power and a socially useful employment of resources. A horizontal merger or acquisition by a large firm in an already concentrated field tends to break down conditions necessary for effective competition — perhaps in purchasing as well as in selling — even when specific restraint of trade cannot be demonstrated. An effective policy to limit concentration requires acceptance of the view that such general

impairment of competition is a sufficient reason for vigorous antimerger action.

Future developments in the food industry are likely to strengthen further the position of retailers. Maintaining numerous competitive alternatives throughout the marketing system crucially depends on having a large number of significant buyers in national markets for farm and processed products. Thus, it is especially important to prevent further concentration of purchases by chain retailers, retailer buying groups, or wholesalers.

A second broad regulatory need is in the field of discriminatory practices. The availability of the "meeting competition" defense sometimes permits discrimination by sellers to continue even when serious injury is being done to the competitive position of one customer vis-à-vis another. Price discrimination often seems to be induced by buyers, but effective means of dealing with the problem remain to be developed. Discrimination through services given to customers is another area in which enforcement is difficult.

Trading in perishable farm foods, especially at early stages of marketing, needs special supervision because of the speed necessary in transactions, deterioration of products, and the frequent great disparity of bargaining power between buyer and seller. The U.S. Department of Agriculture is a reasonable place to locate responsibility for regulation of trade in these products, but administration of regulatory activities should be separate from the other activities of the Department. Most market structure and trade practice problems arising in markets for meats and dressed poultry, however, are of the type that the Federal Trade Commission and Department of Justice are best prepared to handle.

Regulatory agencies labor under handicaps of timing in dealing with mergers and trade practices. Firms need not give notice of forthcoming mergers or acquisitions. Temporary cease and desist orders cannot be issued to hold in abeyance proposed mergers or unfair trade practices. Both deficiencies should be overcome.

The various statutes—both general and specific—dealing with market power in the food industry collectively seek an equitable and workable distribution of power by restraining concentrations of great strength and by lending support to the weak. Antitrust laws are in the first category; the Capper-Volstead Act and the Federal marketing order program are in the second. Extension of policy in both respects appears desirable; but the policy should be conceived as an impartial effort to achieve an appropriate distribution of power rather than as a commitment for or against any group.

A NOTE ON THE FUTURE

Prospective trends and developments are discussed at several points in this report. The implicit assumption in all cases is that food and agriculture in the future will operate in an economic setting developing naturally out of the recent past. But in mid-1966, two other possibilities cannot be ignored.

The first is that much expanded food aid to underdeveloped nations will place considerably heavier demands on the food production capacity of the United States. Carried far enough, this could relieve the chronic oversupply situation for agriculture, increase farm prices, and reduce the need for helping farmers to gain bargaining power. The impact presumably would be greatest on foods most needed for export. Vertical integration into agriculture might increase as food firms tried to assure themselves of supplies.

The second possibility is inflation arising out of high domestic demands on the economy plus demands growing out of the troubled foreign situation. In this case, costs of processing and distributing food would be caught up in the general advance of labor and materials costs. Probably farm food prices would advance as well. Consumers' concern about the food industry would focus even more sharply upon rising prices.

Neither development would substantially modify the need for the changes in policies, statutes, and services discussed in the following chapter, but the priorities to be given to them might change greatly.

57. Statement of William M. Batten, Roman L. Hruska, and Thruston B. Morton

NATIONAL COMMISSION ON FOOD MARKETING

INTRODUCTION

The report of the National Commission on Food Marketing could have been — and, we feel, should have been — a unanimous one.

The beginnings were promising. A professionally competent staff was engaged. They assembled voluminous data of immense value. For this able research the Commission, the staff, government agencies, and a cooperating business community deserve the praise of Congress and the American people.

Why, then, these separate views? They are forced by unwise and untenable majority "conclusions."

We regretfully report that:

Overriding minority protests, the majority refused to respect Congressional restraints on the Commission.

In critical areas they ignored or misread the evidence.

They ranged into highly controversial areas, many in the realm of economic and legal theory, far beyond the Commission's competence.

Some "conclusions" are unsupported by a single word in Commission records.

Others are anachronisms, disregarded, poorly regarded, or rejected by Congress for decades.

From *Food from Farmer to Consumer*, Report of the National Commission on Food Marketing (Washington, D.C.: Government Printing Office, June, 1966), pp. 125-34.

In the main, the majority's "conclusions" are predilections, political and economic, antedating the Commission's work. The major ones — on concentration (see our sec. II), competition (see our sec. III), and farm marketing (see our sec. IV) — are largely subjective and, in their major premises, in error. Adopted as public policy they would do lasting harm to the consumer and the Nation's economy.

VERDICT FIRST — THEN EVIDENCE

A strangely inverted procedure was imposed by the majority to develop the "conclusions" and report. First, recommendations, later renamed "conclusions," were voted.[1] Next the report was contrived to give the "conclusions" credibility. Thereafter — weeks later — staff documents were completed from which the "conclusions" and the report purport to have been drawn.

---

[1] As explained later in these views, the minority entered a formal protest against the formulation of recommendations by the Commission. At the Apr. 1, 1966, meeting of the Commission, the majority undertook to rewrite the recommendations chapter to delete all recommendations. On Apr. 11, 1966, copies of the revised chapter were distributed to the Commission members. The revision did not remove the recommendations but merely relabeled them as "conclusions." This action was clearly acknowledged in the letter transmitting the revision. It stated: "The structure of the chapter has not been substantially changed."

The "conclusions," therefore, could as well have been formulated before the Commission met.

So let the nation applaud the impressive evidence gathered by the Commission.

Let much of the analytical material in the majority report be read with respect.

But beware the "conclusions."

And may Congress mark well the flouting of its charter.

PUBLIC INTEREST ENDANGERED

The fact that valuable research has been compromised is unfortunate. But the potential injury here, for the American people, is far more serious.

If the majority "conclusions" were by some mischance to become public policy, every citizen would in some measure suffer injury. The ability of the Nation's largest single industry and our most vital enterprise — the food industry — to adjust rapidly to myriad, everchanging consumer demands would be impaired. The Nation around, farmers and processors, distributors and retailers, and finally, the housewives in thousands of stores and at countless checkout counters would rue the day that this Commission was formed.

WHAT THE COMMISSION
SHOULD HAVE FOUND

The huge food marketing complex, like the government itself, is not flawless or infallible. It can never be. We are as determined as any other individuals or groups to help ensure that the industry constantly improves and, indeed, to compel improvements where necessary to safeguard the public health, safety, or interest. But had the majority not indulged their nostrums and notions — had they sought objectively after the truth in food marketing — these would have been the Commission's unanimous findings:

1. Today the food marketing industry provides the men, women, and children of America with the highest quality of food, at the lowest real cost, in the greatest variety and abundance, at the most advance stages of preparation, and with the most useful and attractive packaging conveniences ever known.

2. As demonstrated by the Commission's own data and studies, this industry is intensely competitive and likely to remain so; it is highly innovative; it is unhampered by excessive concentration; it is characterized by profit levels approximating or below those of other American industries.

3. Unless repressive governmental policies and programs are visited upon this industry, it may be counted upon to continue to serve responsibly and efficiently far into the future.

4. A number of economic trends and practices in this industry — as, indeed, in all others — require a continuing watchfulness by the government, the public, and the industry itself, but intemperate proposals (as now put forth by the majority) are unwarranted and would be exceedingly ill advised at this time.

Every fairminded person who will thoughtfully review the evidence before the National Commission on Food Marketing will reach these same conclusions.

In the pages that follow we offer our reasoning in support of these views.

SUMMARY

Our service on this Commission has brought us pleasure — but also regret.

As America has become increasingly urbanized, public demands on the food marketing system have skyrocketed in volume and complexity. Inevitably interest has grown in the performance of the system.

We feel, therefore, that this study was at once desirable and timely. It was needed, and needed now, to afford the Congress, the regulatory agencies, and consumers better understanding of the problems and policies of the food industry and the caliber of its services.

The Commission has developed imposing data, studies, and analyses. These comprise the most authoritative and encyclopedic information ever assembled for those who would appraise this industry. For years to come they will usefully serve in the formulation of public policies.

And yet, we must regret the end result.

We of the minority respected the Congressional charge to the Commission. We were impressed by, and carefully examined, the voluminous data. We were prepared to share in an objective, thoughtful analysis. Much of the majority report is such an analysis. But we must deplore their "overview and appraisal" and their "conclusions."

It was cavalier of the majority to disregard the Congressional mandate and the evidence.

It was a disservice to subscribe to unsupported and unsupportable recommendations, many unacceptable to Congress.

PROCEDURAL INVERSION

These disappointing results flowed from unusual procedures vigorously resisted by the minority. The first paper presented to Commission members for action proposed specific recommendations unsupported by evidence. Many ranged far beyond the scope of the Commission's inquiry.[2]

After the recommendations have been adopted by the majority came successive and varying versions of the majority report. Much of the final document is excellent analytical work. But this is cheapened throughout by specious reasoning contrived to validate the "conclusions."

[2] The Commission staff had previously submitted briefing papers to Commission members, but none of them provided a basis for belief that such recommendations as those proposed would be forthcoming.

This result is understandable, however regrettable. For once the decisions were reached, they had somehow to be justified.

Not until well after the report was written were the documents completed from which the majority purportedly derived their judgments.[3]

DEFIANCE OF CONGRESSIONAL MANDATE

In any case, the "conclusions" are presumptuous because they are extralegal. The Commission had been directed by Congress not to "translate (its) findings and conclusions into specific recommendations for (government or private) action." Its assigned task was to study and appraise the industry. It was to assemble and report facts, objectively evaluated, for the Congress to judge.

The legislative history of the Commission's basic charter reveals Congressional misgivings in initiating this study. There was a concern lest a mandate authorizing legislative recommendations might embroil the Commission in interminable and fruitless political and economic controversies. There was an apprehension, also, that the Commission might trespass into areas other than food.

Given the fleeting life of this group, Congress reasoned, its time should be

[3] At one point it was proposed to delay issuance of the technical studies until after the Commission went out of existence. The effect of this proposal, as minority members pointed out, would be to deny the Commission members access to data required for preparing the report. Even at this writing, portions of the technical studies are missing, and we are unable to judge their validity. At that, the Commission voted on recommendations during its March 1966, meeting, nearly a month before the first technical study was issued by the staff to the Commission. (It is also of interest that, incredibly, it was requested that dissenting views be submitted before the majority report had been completed. We know of no previous proposal, in any Congressional committee or Presidential commission, that a dissent precede a finding. A letter of protest induced the dropping of this scheme.)

spent in thoughtful analysis. Issues transcending the food industry were firmly declared off limits.

This Congressional intent was spelled out by Representative Poage, floor manager of the bill, in the debate on the enabling legislation:

> "The resolution undertakes to set up a Commission to study those relationships (among industry segments) to give us some definite answers, to give us something on which we can make plans with the assurance that we know the facts.

* * *

> "It is quite clear that the basic purpose of this study is to get a clear understanding of how our food distribution system works.

* * *

> "In fact, we should give the greater study to and have a clearer understanding of the relationship which exists between the producer and the consumer of food than exists in any other business institution in the United States, because it affects more people and involves more money. *So the purpose of this resolution is to try to get this out where there will be an intensive and exhaustive study made, where we will have, as soon as the report can be made, real information on which we can act with assurance rather than on the guesswork which has formed the basis of so many of our conclusions in the past.*" [Emphasis supplied.][4]

Congressman Poage was expressing more than one man's opinion.

The report of the House Committee on Agriculture is explicit:

> "Subsection (b), which has been stricken by the committee, imposed upon the Commission the duty of recommending 'such actions by government or by private enterprise and individuals as it deems appropriate'. It seems to the committee that the most appropriate function of the Commission to be established by this legislation is to study the subject to which it has been assigned as thoroughly as possible and to draw therefrom *the soundest possible findings and conclusion, rather than to recommend a course of action for either the Government or private industry.* The Commission's findings and conclusions can be based upon its research and the facts and opinions developed during its studies. *The translation of its findings and conclusions into action, however, requires consideration of all other factors with which the Government and private industry deal. Some of these factors are completely unrelated to the subject matter of this study. It seems to the committee, therefore, that the time and energy of the Commission will be conserved and its effectiveness probably increased if it is able to concentrate on the single broad subject to which it has been assigned, rather than being required also to relate its findings in this field to all of the other aspects of our national and economic life and translate these findings and conclusions into specific recommendations for action.*" [Emphasis supplied.][5]

In the Commission's sessions the minority repeatedly cited the Congressional limitations once we discerned the majority disposition to ignore them. The majority response was to restyle the unauthorized "recommendations" as "conclusions." The object, it seems, was to mislabel the product.[6] Minority protests were voted down.

---

[4] 110 Congressional Record 12314–12315 (daily edition, June 4, 1964).

[5] H. Rept. 1401, 88th Cong., 2d Sess., p. 4 (May 13, 1964).

[6] See app. A in the separate views of Commission members Purcell, May, and Mitchell for the history of the Act creating the Commission. This document was supplied by Congressman Purcell to each Commission member and discussed in detail at the Apr. 1, 1966, meeting of the Commission, in protest against the inclusion of the majority's chapter 13. His protest reasserted and formalized objections voiced previously at the

The consequences of these transgressions confirm the wisdom of Congress in attempting to curb the Commission. By failing to respect the charter the majority haplessly drifted into major legislative and economic errors. In the end they endorsed a host of ill-conceived schemes. Many inescapably range far beyond the food industry. Not a few have been repeatedly rejected by Congress.

MAJORITY NOSTALGIA

Time and time again the majority unaccountably gave way to an atavistic impulse to subject the dynamics of the modern food industry to concepts and panaceas of yesteryear. Note, for example, the following parallel:

A 1921 Attitude:

"Consumers can cooperate to reduce the cost of distribution by assuming a greater responsibility in securing the commodities they require, instead of depending upon retailers to display a great variety of goods with superlative convenience, and spacious display rooms with extravagant furnishings, fixtures and facilities. Such environment is created in response to consumer demand and must be paid for out of the purchase price of the merchandise the consumers buy."[7]

The Majority's Attitude (in 1966):

"The principal criticism of the efficiency of the industry, in the broad sense of the term, is the cost devoted to selling efforts that yield little value to consumers. This point is closely related to the other principal criticism of the food industry from the standpoint of consumers: The difficulty they encounter in trying to buy so as to get the most for their money. . . . But consumers themselves must accept a measure of responsibility for

the prices they pay and for the objectionable practices observed in the sale of food. Consumers are powerfully influenced by advertising and persistently pay premium prices for much-advertised brands when products of similar quality—sometimes the identical product—are available at lower prices."[8]

This reversionary bent led the majority to devote much time and effort to the collection of legislative period pieces conceived a generation or more ago and since repudiated time and again. Their attachment to grade labeling is one example. This proposal has languished in Congress for decades. It was specifically rejected as long ago as 1943. It was attempted almost a decade earlier, but died with the rest of the National Recovery Administration. Now nostalgically, the majority resurrects it in 1966!

Over the years Congressional committees have conducted thorough hearings on premerger notification, temporary cease and desist authority for the FTC, and the Robinson-Patman "good faith" defense. There have been thousands of pages of opposing testimony from market economists, spokesmen for many nonfood industries, and lawyers representing bar associations. The proponents have no less vigorously advanced their supporting views. Armed with such extensive evidence, the Congressional committees have examined these complex issues with great care. And not one of the bills has been approved by Congress.

Now come the majority, embracing them all!

In this exuberant spirit sundry antitrust and other nostrums, interred long ago, have been exhumed. But there has been no examination of their likely impact on the food marketing industry. There has been no attempt to relate them to any other business complex. The staff did not even present to the Commission the pros and cons of these

---

February and March, 1966, meetings of the Commission.
[7] Report of the Joint Commission of Agricultural Inquiry, H. Rept. 908, 67th Cong., 1st sess., p. 12 (Oct. 15, 1921).

[8] Majority Report, chapter 12.

proposals, as extensively developed in the hearings and reports of Congress.

To all of this the minority protested again. We maintained that a preoccupation with issues beyond the charge and competence of the Commission, together with cursory examinations of proposals of vast import to all American enterprise, would weaken the credibility of the Commission's entire effort. We insisted—futilely—that the Commission should labor within the perimeters Congress had defined.

CONCENTRATION DATA
MISINTERPRETED AND MISAPPLIED

In the abstruse area of concentration the majority were unable to anchor their prejudgments to the evidence at hand. They resorted, therefore, to strained deductions. These were derived from "concentration ratio" statistics applied to various parts of the food industry. Later (in our section II) we explain the inadequacy of these ratios and the shortcomings of "concentration" (or "structure") theories as antitrust enforcement tools. Here, however, we note that the majority judgments (chapter 12 and the first "conclusion" of chapter 13) are incompatible with virtually every item of evidence in their earlier product chapters.

In chapters 12 and 13 the majority assert that more rigid antitrust enforcement is needed to restrain "high" concentration. They further state: "High concentration is used to describe a situation in which the four largest firms in a field have more than 50 percent of the business."

Well now, examine the table. Its figures are drawn from the majority's own product chapters. They purport to depict degrees of concentration in various segments of the food industry studied by the Commission. Note that only two groupings—neither properly termed an "industry" for purposes of economic analysis—meet the majority's own very questionable definition of a "highly" concentrated industry.

Considered with our section II discussion, the above data decisively demonstrate that concentration in the food industry presents no serious problems beyond those already adequately policed by antitrust enforcement agencies. Indeed, we find that concentration in food manufacturing and food retailing is generally low, lower in fact than in numerous other industries.

Actually, on closer analysis, one aspect of the majority position becomes wryly amusing. When they are considered together—the above table on concentration and the majority definition of a "highly" concentrated industry—one is forced to conclude that the majority have themselves succumbed to overconcentration. In effect, they are "concentrating" only on the manufacturers of crackers and cookies, and breakfast cereals. But in our section II we point out that the ratio for crackers and cookies has declined since 1954. The remaining concern, then, is breakfast cereals. Here we find (our sec. II) that there is considerable competition for market position, that breakfast cereals compete with many other food products, and (our sec. III) that the type of competition which the majority seem to deplore in that "industry" is real competition in today's consumer oriented economy.

So the majority edifice collapses, lacking a factual base.

COMMENTS ON OTHER "CONCLUSIONS"

Other "conclusions" are similarly puzzling, inconsistent, or unsupported. Several, like those previously cited, are simply grave-robbing in the legislative cemetery. Others are immaterial. A few have merit. In telescoped form, our views on the principal ones are as follows:

Premerger Notification. Every 2 years, as Congress adjourns, compulsory premerger notification again wearily traverses the Congressional bridge of sighs. It has never survived a Congress. This renewed proposal is fated like its predecessors. Its merit is no greater, its defects the same. It would still limit the flexibility essential for business to consummate important transactions. It would still strait-jacket even the government agencies. For, should they fail immediately to file suit when the required data is received, a later suit found justified by careful study could be barred. Thus the flexibility required for effective enforcement could also be lost. The majority ignored not only these defects but also the prospective costs, even though it is clear that the scheme would heavily burden the enforcement agencies.

Temporary Cease and Desist Orders. We have here another Congressional loiterer. It has long had the vehement opposition of bar association and other expert witnesses. It has never emerged from any committee. There is excellent reason. The proposal would make the agencies both prosecutor and judge. To most Americans – and most emphatically to us – this is an odious concept. Again, the Commission did not probe into the far-reaching effects of its "conclusion." It acted irresponsibly, therefore, in endorsing this discredited measure.

Reporting Data to SEC on Sales of Various Divisions of Conglomerate Firms. Another hoary proposal. Long before Congress, it too has had spirited and respected opposition. Even the SEC itself has rejected it. The reliability and usefulness of information gathered as proposed are questionable, for accounting procedures vary greatly from firm to firm, especially on such information as is sought here. And once again the majority disregarded the impact on other industries. Again they ignored the cost. The collection and analysis of the vast volume of data generated by such a law would surely be expensive to government, industry, and ultimately to the consumer.

Continuing Special Surveillance of Food Marketing Firms by the FTC. The Commission has no evidence that the food industry has lacked proper scrutiny by regulatory agencies. As recently as 1959 the FTC thoroughly probed into the industry's structure. The evidence assembled by this Commission strongly indicates that the industry has performed adequately without continual Federal harassment. A "continuing special surveillance" would likely reaffirm the adequacy of performance, but unquestionably would also bring on harassment. We can find no justification for directing the FTC to oversee the food industry as if it were a public utility, a result inherent in the proposal.

Review of the Robinson-Patman Act and Its Administration. We are pleased to agree. The Robinson-Patman Act and other antitrust laws do need early "study and reappraisal" to determine their responsiveness to national needs. Here, however, we are surprised by related majority insinuations that section 2(f) of the act should be modified and that the "meeting competition" defense (the so-called "good faith" defense) is "troublesome" and in some fashion, therefore, needs to be adjusted. The Commission voted overwhelmingly to delete such proposals from its recommendations. We know of no official reversal of that decision.

Mandatory Consumer-grade Labeling. There is no evidence before the Commission that this scheme was sensible, or workable, or rewarding to the consumer even when first advocated in the 1920's and 1930's. It is unthinkable today, as we explain more thoroughly in our section III. One reason – administrative rigidity – was shared with the Commission by Max E. Brunk, Professor of Marketing at Cornell University. He cited a study he made for the Government of consumer reactions to

PERCENTAGE OF BUSINESS ACCOUNTED FOR BY THE FOUR
LARGEST FIRMS

Branch of industry	Year	Percentage
Commercial meat production	1964	29
Young chicken slaughter (federally inspected)	1964	18
Turkey slaughter (federally inspected)	1964	24
Fluid milk	1963	23
Ice cream and ices	1963	37
Fruit and vegetable canning	1963	24
Fruit and vegetable freezing	1963	24
Flour milling	1965	24
Baking	1963	23
Breakfast cereals	1964	85
Crackers and cookies	1964	62
Food retailing (food stores)	1963	18

Government-graded applesauce. The vast majority of consumers participating in the test preferred applesauce graded "C" or "substandard" over applesauce graded "A" or "B." Despite this finding, the consumer views were spurned, the standards were retained, and governmental preference prevailed. Quality judgments, we believe, are highly personal. They are not a special gift of people in the public employ. The simple truth is that individual, sectional, and regional preferences of 200 million Americans can never be captured, cataloged, and compressed into meaningful and workable Federal standards. We believe these personal value judgments are best left with the consumer. This should also be noted—the majority's chapter 12 indicates that consumer grades would involve "little or no extra cost." But here—once again— we have supposition, not fact. No study was made of what grade labeling and its attendant bureaucracy would cost the food industry, consumers through increased prices, and the tax-paying public.

Standards of Identity for All Foods Where "Practicable". The Food and Drug Administration has complete and comprehensive power to establish standards of identity. Rather than utilizing this authority wherever "practicable,"

as the majority proposes, we believe that such standards should be established only where necessary to advance the public interest. But since the matter was not analyzed by the Commission, no "conclusion" should be reached by the Commission in this area.

Packaging and Labeling. Of course packaging and labeling should be informative and honest. The FDA and FTC have ample authority to assure that they are. Current legislative proposals in this area, however, are directed not against fraud and deceit but toward the subjection of packaging to Federal control. The results of such proposals would be higher consumer costs, blighted innovation, impairment of competition, and a transfer of consumer decisions to the Federal apparatus. The majority recommendation, it should be noted, endorses this legislation only "if needed." It isn't.

Establishment of a Department of Consumers. No testimony having been heard by the Commission on this proposal on either side, it is fairly regarded as a fancy, not a finding. We fail to see how "consumers"—a term embracing everyone from infancy to senility—will fare better under yet another layer of bureaucracy. No consumer cataclysm demands the erection of another executive department to give home-to-market care to 200 million Americans atop the countless Federal, State, municipal, and industry protections already provided. Operating from a record barren on the subject, the majority is quite unable to document any such need.

Endorsement of Federal Marketing Agreements and Orders. While the Commission heard some testimony about these devices, there was no study of performance under existing or past marketing agreements or orders, State or Federal, or how growers under such regulation have fared in comparison with growers of unregulated commodities. Neither does the majority report contain any economic or legal analysis of marketing agreements or orders. No consideration was given to how production and marketing limitations would affect (1) the entry of new growers, (2) the price of the product in relation to other products, or (3) consumer demand. We believe that tampering with these programs is unwise, without careful examination of the great complexities involved.

Creation of Agricultural Marketing Boards. Most legislative ventures to benefit agriculture are devised to help farmers help themselves. Not this one. It could be used to force farm producers to their knees before the Secretary of Agriculture. Commodity Boards would be established under the supervision of an Administrator whom the Secretary would appoint. The Boards could control production and marketings. They could negotiate prices. The prices would necessarily be binding upon all producers and processors of individual products and would sharply influence consumer prices as well. And, all the while, the Board's actions would be subject to the approval of the Secretary. We repudiate the whole appalling scheme. The Nation's food production and distribution system must not be turned over to any one person, especially a political appointee, in any administration. Nor can we afford a policy fostering monopolistic ineffi-

ciency and waste. In this proposal is seen the basic flaw in the majority's approach to agriculture, as discussed more fully in our section IV. The majority assume that an oversupply of raw products will plague America in perpetuity. Recent world events make this assumption not only questionable but perilous. New planned scarcity proposals should be shelved at least until we have far better measurements of future food needs in the United States and abroad. The President's new National Advisory Commission on Food and Fiber is charged specifically with this problem. This Commission does not have the basis for an informed judgment.

More and Better Market Information for Producers. Better market information is needed in some segments of agriculture for better producer decisions. But several aspects of the majority's "conclusions" in this area need further study by Congress. An example is the proposal to "require submission of prices, quantities bought or sold, grades, and similar information" from all food industry firms. The burdens and expenses imposed upon both government and industry by so elaborate a reporting system need careful evaluation.

Improving BLS and USDA Reporting Systems. During 1963 and part of 1964 the BLS and USDA data collection and analysis techniques resulted in an overstatement of consumer beef prices by approximately 7 cents per pound. This one erroneous figure and the ensuing profiteering charges contributed greatly to the creation of this Commission. Public confidence in the food marketing system is critically important. It must not be left on so uncertain a footing. The Commission's work in this area should help in developing improvements assuring that such misstatements do not, and cannot, recur.

We see no useful purpose in commenting on the remaining majority "conclusions." Most of them would require the approval of Congress. In its own good time, Congress may wish to determine the need for them.

THE FOOD INDUSTRY IN PERSPECTIVE

More important, considering the mission of this Commission, is a realistic assessment of the food industry. We attempt to do so here, beginning with an effort to place the problems of the industry in historical perspective.

In recent decades there have been massive changes in our economy and society. In part they have been caused by the food industry and in turn have powerfully influenced it. The development of a remarkably advanced farm technology was the first dramatic change. Its result was a huge increase in farm productivity, which then freed most of the population from the land. By the millions they turned to city and factory. There they have contributed to the growth of our huge industrial system with its own vastly expanding productive capacity.

Away from the land, no longer able to produce their own food, the urbanized citizenry needed a marketing system that could feed them efficiently and well. This developing necessity was recognized long ago.[9]

There was an eager response to this demand and opportunity. Packaging and processing methods were refined. They made a wide variety of foods available regardless of season, and greatly reduced the problems of food perishability. Geographic markets for farm products widened. As chain food retailers integrated the wholesale and retail functions, the coordination and distribution of food supplies for retail outlets become more efficient.

Many new developments, including the supermarket, were pioneered in the depression years. But consumer purchasing power was so depressed there was little incentive for the investment to make them flourish. Similarly, the demands on the Nation's resources inhibited the growth and general use of new processing techniques during World War II.

During the war American farmers prospered from high productivity and the wartime demand for raw ingredients. When peace returned, there were revolutionary changes. Farmers eagerly applied new techniques which produced more abundant harvests even as wartime markets declined.

---

[9] The "Osborn Committee" of the New York Legislature in 1912 called for the creation of a highly coordinated, efficiently functioning marketing system to feed the increasingly urbanized society. The FTC made a similar recommendation in 1921. Among other things, the "Osborn Committee" reported as follows:

"The great problem of marketing is to secure a continuous and even flow of food supplies from the producer to the consumer, with a minimum of stoppage on the way and a minimum of handling intermediate between the two. The present method of distribution provides roughly for wholesale and retail stores, and the questions to which our inquiry has been addressed are how far the wholesale stores are necessary and what type of retail store . . . is most economically efficient and most suited to the needs and customs of our people . . .

"The most impressive feature of the retail business (is) the smallness of the average unit, leading to excessive retail cost. . . . The cost of wholesaling is probably about 10 percent. The cost of retailing is about 33 percent, added in both cases to the first cost . . .

"As a plan for general adoption for the distribution of food products on the most economical basis, private retail markets in large units, under centralized management, is the solution. The managers of such a market system should buy, whenever possible, direct from producers . . . deliveries should be direct to the store, and customers should carry away their orders. . . .

"Testimony before this Committee shows that markets of the food department store type could be operated with an addition to cost of products of 20 percent, as against an addition to cost by the wholesaler, jobber, and retailer combined of approximately 40 to 45 percent. . . ."

The Committee report ends with a recommendation, "That the large retail unit, or food department store, buying direct, receiving direct and selling direct, be accepted as the best economic type, and that retailers, wholesalers, and private organizations move toward the development of such stores."

The nature of the demand for farm products also changed, shifting from raw ingredients to convenience and variety The pressure of the growing abundance, plus a growing consumer prosperity, forced many additional changes. Commodity marketing trended toward product marketing. Increasing supplies of every farm product pressed forward on the marketing parts of the food industry. Innovation became imperative to move this abundance efficiently and economically to the consumer.

During the 1950's the supermarket became the everyday reality to American consumers. It was a symbol of change. Indeed, the change continues. Some stores in the 1960's have become bigger and others smaller. The super-supermarket, with emphasis on high-traffic, nonfood departments, has come into being. At the same time, around the corner and out on the highway, we now find the "convenience store," a miniature, modern food store which opens early and closes late. Discount food stores, with a minimum of service and amenities, are springing up in a number of places.

There are many other changes that are not visible to the consumer—changes in technique, in organization, in equipment. They have crisscrossed the food industry in increasing tempo during these postwar years. Some—like the computer—came from outside and were adapted to many uses within the food industry. Others, as in materials handling and merchandising, generated within the industry. All such innovations spread swiftly throughout the industry.

The rapid advances in food production, processing, and preservation have powerfully affected and benefited the consumer. Changes in technology have made it possible to can, freeze, or otherwise process more and more foods. Thereby they have increased the range of consumer choice over a longer time span. New techniques of preparation and packaging have lengthened the shelf life of a variety of products.

Related closely to the technological improvements of recent decades is the affluence of the American economy. It has had many implications for the consumer and hence for the food marketing industry. The enlarged quantity and variety of goods are themselves responses to this development.

Today our national wealth is such that food must compete with nonfood products for a share of expending demand capacity. This growing capacity now enables the consumer to maintain a family diet well above the level of adequacy, even while saving for such major purchases as an automatic dishwasher or television set. Or, she can choose greater leisure time; she can expend a greater share of her affluence for foods at higher stages of preparation.

This consumer mobility of choice has combined with physical mobility, brought about by widespread automobile ownership, to force food into competition with wholly unrelated products. In this level of competition, as well as in intra-industry competition, the food industry faces unique problems.

For not only is there high consumer mobility, not only an ability to change from one processor or one retailer to another, there is also a higher degree of repeat buying in the food industry than in any other industry. Processors, retailers, or manufacturers may induce an initial purchase, but they depend very heavily on constant repeat buying. Promotional efforts are deplored by the majority, but such efforts lie at the very heart of our competitive system. They are often aimed at getting the housewife to try something new. If she is then disappointed, no amount of promotion can get her to try it again. Promotion's relatively low cost per item of food and the absolute necessity of high repeat buying provide the food industry with an unusual selling situation. It is worthy of a higher order of understanding than the majority has deigned to give it.

Change in this industry is neither constant nor all in one direction. The degree of vertical integration by retailers into some areas of processing and manufacturing has increased; in others it has declined. The use by a retailer of private labels fluctuates with his management evaluation of manufacturer-branded products. Product differentiation has been established for some products; for others, efforts to differentiate have had little success.

This continuing, restless change has served the public well. More varieties of food are now available to the consumer at more advanced stages of preparation than ever before. Yet the proportion of disposable personal income spent on food products has declined. Of course, in the food industry as elsewhere changes bring discomfort and dislocation. Some decry, for example, the erosion of traditional functional lines as growers integrate into packing and shipping, milk producers into processing, retailers into wholesaling or manufacturing. In the wake of each change there is inevitably dissatisfaction, usually voiced by those unwilling or unable to adjust.

Because they have focused on such dislocations, the majority find merit in "conclusions" which would poorly serve the public. We doubt most seriously that the food marketing industry could adequately serve the consumer today had these "conclusions" been in effect 20 years ago. It would be calamitous for our country to inhibit further change. We deeply believe that many of the majority's "conclusions" would have that result.

We find that in most significant respects, the food marketing system has commendably kept pace with the demands of rapidly changing America. There is much in the majority report to corroborate this. We know that as change continues, so will adjustments. The government and the public will rightly maintain—and, especially, we of the minority will maintain—an active interest in how well those adjustments are made and how well the industry performs.

Index